MAGNA CARTA

SECOND EDITION

This is a fully revised and extended edition of J. C. Holt's study of Magna Carta, the Great Charter, which sets the events of 1215 and the Charter itself in the context of the law, politics and administration of England and Europe in the twelfth and thirteenth centuries.

The author has added to the first edition (1965) further comment on the development of local liberties, the significance of the famous provision *nullus liber homo*, the political manoeuvres of 1215, and the later history of the Charter, and many other matters. The book is broadened by the addition of an extensive chapter on justice and jurisdiction which embodies an entirely new approach to some of the most crucial and longest-lasting provisions of the Charter. New appendices have been added. Some of these are concerned with the political crisis of 1213-15, for example the alleged meeting at Bury St Edmunds; others examine the Anglo-Norman translations of the Charter and related documents, or the development of perpetual liberties. References are brought up to date throughout and there is an entirely new index.

D0725798

MAGNA CARTA

SECOND EDITION

J. C. HOLT

Emeritus Professor of Medieval History,
University of Cambridge

CAMBRIDGE
UNIVERSITY PRESS

CAMBRIDGE UNIVERSITY PRESS
Cambridge, New York, Melbourne, Madrid, Cape Town, Singapore, São Paulo

Cambridge University Press
The Edinburgh Building, Cambridge CB2 2RU, UK

Published in the United States of America by Cambridge University Press, New York

www.cambridge.org
Information on this title: www.cambridge.org/9780521259705

First published 1992
Reprinted 1994, 1995, 1997, 2001, 2003

A catalogue record for this publication is available from the British Library

Library of Congress Cataloguing in Publication data
Holt, James Clarke.
Magna Carta/J. C. Holt. – 2nd ed.
p. cm.
Includes bibliographical references (p. and index.
ISBN 0 521 25970 3 (hardcover). – ISBN 0 521 27778 7 (paper)
1. Magna Carta. I. Title.
JN147.H64 1991
342.42'029 – dc20
[344.20229] 91–19456 CIP

ISBN-13 978-0-521-27778-5 paperback
ISBN-10 0-521-27778-7 paperback

Transferred to digital printing 2006

To Su

CONTENTS

CONTENTS

PLATES

PREFACE

The seven hundred and fiftieth anniversary of Magna Carta is not the sole reason for the publication of this book. The last comprehensive study of the Charter was McKechnie's, published in 1905 and revised in 1914. Since McKechnie wrote, much work has been done, both in studying the Charter and in publishing the records of the Exchequer and the Curia Regis which are essential to its proper comprehension. One object of this present book, therefore, is to provide an up-to-date study of the subject. But it does not follow the pattern of the previous work. The commentary to which McKechnie devoted nearly three hundred pages is no longer practicable. Furthermore, it embodied the approach of the lawyer concerned with pursuing the provisions of the Charter through subsequent legal developments. The result was a learned work of scholarship, but it was not always closely related to the circumstances in which the Charter was produced. For example, McKechnie allotted more space to cap. 36 of the Charter which concerned the relatively trivial matter of the writ of life and limb, than to caps. 52, 53 and 55 which provided for the restoration of property to those disseised by the Crown. These last clauses were among the most crucial issues between King John and his baronial opponents. Their execution led England into civil war.

The approach of the present work is different from McKechnie's, for it is the work of a historian not a lawyer. Its object is to present the Charter in a context of the politics, administration and political thought of England and Europe in the twelfth and thirteenth centuries. I have discussed some

xi

aspects of the Charter's later history in the first and last chapters, but the book is mainly about the Charter of 1215 and its immediate re-issues, for its later history cannot be understood without a proper grasp of its origins and contemporary significance.

Such a project cannot be an individual effort. It has depended on the work of many scholars, in particular of Lady Stenton, Professor C. R. Cheney, the late Professor Sidney Painter, Mr H. G. Richardson and all those who have edited the relevant volumes of the Pipe Roll Society, the Selden Society and the state papers. I was encouraged to write this book in the first place by Professor V. H. Galbraith. He and Lady Stenton have read the work in typescript and I am indebted to both of them for their comments, suggestions and corrections. Over many years I have enjoyed and benefited from discussions with Professor J. S. Roskell. I have also been helped on particular points by Dr Patricia Barnes, who supplied me with some valuable references to documents in the Public Record Office, Dr R. A. Brown, Professor C. R. Cheney, Mr W. R. Fryer, Mr B. E. Harris, Dr W. D. McIntyre and Miss Anne Pallister.

Dr R. L. Storey read the work in proof and Mr B. E. Harris has helped in correcting proofs.

I owe thanks to the staff of the University Library, Nottingham, for their helpful attention, to Miss Rosemary Hunt, who typed the manuscript and to Mr P. G. Hunter, who compiled the index.

My final debt is to my wife, who has helped in preparing and correcting the final typescript. Without her encouragement this book might have been begun, but it would certainly never have reached completion.

J. C. H.

NOTTINGHAM
August 1964

PREFACE TO SECOND EDITION

This new edition differs from the first in various respects. First, a new chapter entitled Justice and Jurisdiction has been added. This fills a gap in the first edition, for in 1965 I felt that on this topic there was little to be added to what others had done. I hope also that it will fill a gap in much that has been written in the last twenty years or so about the legal history of England in the late twelfth and early thirteenth centuries, for it is concerned with barons as litigants, not as holders of courts. Secondly, I have added some new appendices. Some of these deal with completely new evidence or with problems which have emerged since 1965; some are concerned with difficult and debatable matters best discussed outside the main body of the book. I have not tried to discuss all current debates in this way. On the 'price revolution', 'heritability', and a few similar matters I have simply directed the reader to a reasonable sample of the work of the participants and referred to Holt (1991a) where I discuss them briefly, but more directly. Thirdly, I have revised the text throughout, adjusting it here and there to recent work and adding a few short sections which reflect my own fresh thinking or research. The references in the footnotes have been brought up to date; I hope that I have included all the relevant work which has been done in the last quarter of a century. Finally, the book is provided with a completely new and more comprehensive index.

At the same time I have tried to reduce changes to the minimum, for this, like any other book, is a product of time and place. At one stage I intended to include a clause-by-clause commentary, but it soon became apparent that this would require almost encyclopaedic bulk. Too much work has now been done on the later history of the Charter, on the Crown's feudal incidents, for example, to incorporate anything more than a passing reference. Even more still needs to be done. Much that has been written on a theme as central as the later history of *nullus liber homo*, for example, now needs serious revision; I touch on this in a short addition in chapter 1. In any case such a commentary would have involved so much repetition of material in chapters 8 and 9 that it would have distorted the original shape of the book. It would, in short, have become a different book. So it remains thematic in structure, as it was first designed.

Over twenty-five years many have helped. Thanks to some can now only be a matter of record: Helen Cam, whose postcards always brought fresh ideas or information: Professor C. R. Cheney and Professor V. H. Galbraith, both of whom shared my zest for the subject and on whose contributions I call at several crucial points; and Professor S. B. Chrimes whose down-to-earth questions led me to think a little further, and I hope a little deeper, about events at Runnymede. I am grateful to Professor J. A. Guy for mentioning the preliminaries to the Act of Heresy of 1534, and to Mr D. E. C. Yale for drawing my attention to an original of the charter of 1215 which was still extant in the seventeenth century. Dr Martin Brett was particularly generous in presenting me with the problem of the collection of royal charters in B. L. Harleian MS 458. On the script of this enigmatic document, which came to be known affectionately among us as 'the thing', I benefited from the advice of the late Mr N. R. Ker and of Dr Pierre Chaplais and Dr Malcolm Parkes. On the more general linguistic problems which arise from it and from the Anglo-Norman text of Magna Carta, Professor William Rothwell gave generous and valuable guidance. Dr D. A. Carpenter helped me to correct some errors which were still buried deep in the first edition, and Dr David Crook answered appeals for urgent assistance from time to time. Finally I am particularly indebted to Dr Paul Brand. He read a draft of chapter 5 and suggested several improvements in detail and enabled me to correct a number of errors. He is to be excused of any responsibility for the argument I develop. To all these I express warm thanks.

My wife, to whom this book is dedicated, has helped in correcting the proofs and compiling the new index. She has meticulously and rigorously eliminated that happy variation in the rendering of names which results from work done at long intervals. She has also contributed in many other ways beyond record, as it was when the first edition was completed in 1965.

J. C. H.

Fitzwilliam College
CAMBRIDGE
January 1991

ACKNOWLEDGEMENTS

The author is indebted to the Editor of the *English Historical Review* for permission to draw on material which he first published in article form in that periodical in 1955 and 1957. The document in Appendix 3 is published by permission of the Directeur des Services, Archives de l'Orne, Alençon.

ABBREVIATIONS

Annales Monastici   *Annales monastici*, ed. H. R. Luard, 5
    vols. (Rolls Series, 1864–9)
B.J.R.L.   *Bulletin of the John Rylands Library*
B.L.   British Library
B.N.   Bibliothèque Nationale
Book of Fees   *Liber Feodorum. The book of fees commonly
    called Testa de Nevill*, 3 vols. (Public Record Office,
    1920–31)
Bracton   *Bracton on the Laws and Customs of England*, ed.
    G. E. Woodbine, trans. and rev. Samuel E. Thorne, 4
    vols. (Cambridge, Mass., 1968–77)
Bracton's Note Book   *Bracton's Note Book*, ed. F. W.
    Maitland, 3 vols. (London, 1887)
Brevia Placitata   *Brevia Placitata*, ed. G. J. Turner and
    T. F. T. Plucknett (Selden Society, 76, 1951)
Cal. Charter Rolls   *Calendar of the Charter Rolls*, 6 vols.
    (Public Record Office, 1903–27)
Cal. Docs. France   *Calendar of Documents preserved in
    France illustrative of the history of Great Britain and
    Ireland, 1, 918–1206*, ed. J. H. Round (London,
    H.M.S.O.), 1899
Cal. Inq. P.M.   *Calendar of inquisitions post mortem and
    other analogous documents preserved in the Public Record
    Office, i, Henry III* (H.M.S.O., 1904)
Chron. Battle   *The Chronicle of Battle Abbey*, ed. Eleanor
    Searle (Oxford, 1980)
Chronicles of Stephen, Henry II and Richard I   *Chronicles
    of the reigns of Stephen, Henry II and Richard I*, ed. R.
    Howlett, 4 vols. (Rolls Series, 1884–9)

Chron. Maj.   *Matthaei Parisiensis, monachi sancti Albani, chronica majora*, ed. H. R. Luard, 7 vols. (Rolls Series, 1872–83)

Chron. Melrose   *The Chronicle of Melrose*, facsimile edn, ed. A. O. Anderson, Marjorie O. Anderson and W. C. Dickinson (Studies in Economics and Political Science, London, 1936)

Coggeshall   *Radulphi de Coggeshall chronicon Anglicanum*, ed. J. Stevenson (Rolls Series, 1875)

Curia Regis Rolls   *Curia Rolls, Richard I–Henry III*, 16 vols. (H.M.S.O., 1922–)

Dialogus   *Dialogus de Scaccario*, ed. C. Johnson (London, 1950)

Diplomatic Documents   *Diplomatic Documents preserved in the Public Record Office*, 1, 1101–1272, ed. P. Chaplais (H.M.S.O., 1964)

Early Registers of Writs   *Early Registers of Writs*, ed. Elsa de Haas and G. D. G. Hall (Selden Society, 87, 1970)

Early Yorkshire Charters   *Early Yorkshire Charters*, vols. 1–3, ed. William Farrer (Edinburgh, 1914–16), vols. 4–12, ed. C. T. Clay (Yorkshire Archaeological Society, Record Ser., extra ser., vols. 1–10, 1935–65)

Econ. H.R.   *Economic History Review*

E.H.R.   *English Historical Review*

Electio Hugonis   *The chronicle of the election of Hugh, abbot of Bury St Edmunds and later bishop of Ely*, ed. R. M. Thomson (Oxford, 1974)

Epp. Cant.   *Epistolae Cantuarienses, 1187–99*, ed. W. Stubbs (Rolls Series, 1865)

Excerpta e Rot. Fin.   *Excerpta e rotulis finium in turri Londinensi asservatis, A.D. 1216–72*, ed. C. Roberts 2 vols. (Record Commission, 1835–6)

Foedera   *Foedera, conventiones, litterae et cujuscunque generis acta publica*, ed. T. Rymer, new edn, vol. 1, part 1, ed. A. Clarke and F. Holbrooke (Record Commission, 1816)

Gerv. Cant   *The historical works of Gervase of Canterbury*, ed. W. Stubbs, 2 vols. (Rolls Series, 1879–80)

Gesetze   F. Liebermann, *Die Gesetze der Angelsachsen*, 3 vols. (Halle, 1898–1916)

Gesta Henrici   *Gesta Regis Henrici secundi Benedicti abbatis*, ed. W. Stubbs, 2 vols. (Rolls Series, 1867)

Gesta Stephani   *Gesta Stephani*, ed. K. R. Potter, rev. R. H. C. Davis (London, 1955, 1976)

Glanvill   *The treatise on the laws and customs of the realm of England commonly called Glanvill*, ed. G. D. G. Hall (London, 1965)

Herrschaftsverträge   *Herrschaftsverträge des Spätmittelalters* (*Quellen zur Neueren Geschichte*, XVII, Berne, 1951)

Histoire de Guillaume le Maréchal   *Histoire de Guillaume le Maréchal*, ed. P. Meyer, 3 vols. (Société de l'histoire de France, 1891–1901)

Histoire des ducs de Normandie   *Histoire des ducs de Normandie et des rois d'Angleterre*, ed. F. Michel (Société de l'histoire de France, 1840)

H.M.C.   *Reports and Calendars issued by the Royal Commission on Historical Manuscripts*

H.M.S.O.   Her Majesty's Stationery Office

Honors and Knights' Fees   William Farrer, *Honors and Knights' Fees* (London, Manchester, 1923–5)

Hoveden   *Chronica Rogeri de Hovedene*, ed. W. Stubbs, 4 vols. (Rolls Series, 1868–71)

Letters of Innocent III   *The Letters of Pope Innocent III (1198–1216) concerning England and Wales*, ed. C. R. Cheney and Mary G. Cheney (Oxford, 1967)

Lincolnshire Assize Rolls 1202–9   *The earliest Lincolnshire Assize Rolls A.D. 1202–1209*, ed. Doris M. Stenton (Lincoln Record Society, XXII, 1926)

M.C.C.E.   *Magna Carta Commemoration Essays*, ed. H. E. Malden (London, 1917)

Memorials of St Edmund   *Memorials of St Edmund's Abbey*, ed. T. Arnold, 3 vols. (Rolls Series, 1890–6)

M.G.H., Const.   *Monumenta Germaniae Historica, Constitutiones et Acta Publica Imperatorum et Regum*, ed. L. Weiland, 2 vols. (Hanover, 1893, 6)

Ordonnances   *Ordonnances des Rois de France de la Troisième Race*, vol. 1 (Paris, 1723)

Pedes Finium   *Fines sive Pedes Finium sive Finales Concordiae in curia domini regis*, ed. Joseph Hunter, 2 vols. (Record Commission, 1835, 1844)

Pleas before the King or his Justices   *Pleas before the King or his Justices 1198–1212*, ed. Doris M. Stenton, 4 vols. (Selden Society, 67, 68, 83, 84, 1948–67)

P.R.O.   Public Record Office

Recueil   *Recueil des historiens des croisades, Lois*, 2 vols. (Paris, 1841–3)

Reg. Urban IV   *Registres de Urbain IV*, ed. J. Guiraud (Bibliothèque des écoles françaises d'Athènes et de Rome, 1901–6)

Richard of Devizes   *The Chronicle of Richard of Devizes*, ed. J. T. Appleby (London, 1963)

Rolls of the Justices in Eyre for Gloucestershire, Warwickshire and Staffordshire 1221–2   *Rolls of the Justices in Eyre for Gloucestershire, Warwickshire and Staffordshire 1221–2*, ed. Doris M. Stenton (Selden Society, 59, 1946)

Rolls of the Justices in Eyre for Lincolnshire 1218–19 and Worcestershire 1221   *Rolls of the Justices in Eyre for Lincolnshire 1218–19 and Worcestershire 1221*, ed. Doris M. Stenton (Selden Society, 53, 1934)

Rolls of the Justices in Eyre for Yorkshire 1218–19   *Rolls of the Justices in Eyre for Yorkshire 1218–19*, ed. Doris M. Stenton (Selden Society, 56, 1937)

Rot. Chartarum   *Rotuli chartarum in turri Londinensi asservati*, ed. T. Duffus Hardy, vol. 1 (Record Commission, 1837)

Rot. Curiae Regis   *Rotuli curiae regis*, ed. Sir Francis Palgrave, 2 vols. (Record Commission, 1835)

Rot. de Dominabus   *Rotuli de Dominabus et Pueris et*

Puellis de XII Comitatibus, ed. J. H. Round (Pipe Roll Society, xxxv, 1913)

Rot. de Ob. et Fin. *Rotuli de oblatis et finibus in turri Londinensi asservati*, ed. T. Duffus Hardy (Record Commission, 1835)

Rot. Lib. *Rotuli de liberate ac de misis et praestitis*, ed. T. Duffus Hardy (Record Commission, 1844)

Rot. Litt. Claus. *Rotuli litterarum clausarum in turri Londinensi asservati*, ed. T. Duffus Hardy, 2 vols. (Record Commission, 1833–4)

Rott. Litt. Pat. *Rotuli litterarum patentium in turri Londinensi asservati*, ed. T. Duffus Hardy, vol. 1 (Record Commission, 1835)

Rot. Norm. *Rotuli Normanniae in turri Londinensi asservati*, ed. T. Duffus Hardy, vol. 1 (Record Commission, 1835)

Royal Letters *Royal and other historical letters illustrative of the reign of Henry III*, ed. W. W. Shirley, 2 vols. (Rolls Series, 1862–8)

Royal Writs *Royal Writs in England from the Conquest to Glanvill*, ed. R. C. Van Caenegem (Selden Society, 77, 1959)

Select Cases in the Court of King's Bench *Select Cases in the Court of King's Bench under Edward I*, ed. G. O. Sayles, 3 vols. (Selden Society, 55, 57, 58, 1936–9)

Select Cases of Procedure without Writ *Select Cases of Procedure without Writ*, ed. H. G. Richardson and G. O. Sayles (Selden Society, 60, 1941)

Selected Letters of Innocent III *Selected Letters of Pope Innocent III*, ed. C. R. Cheney and W. H. Semple (London, 1953)

Stubbs's Charters *Select Charters and other illustrations of English constitutional history from the earliest times to the reign of Edward the First*, ed. William Stubbs, 9th edn, rev. H. W. C. Davis (Oxford, 1921)

T.R.H.S.   *Transactions of the Royal Historical Society*
V.C.H.   *Victoria County History*
Walt. Cov.   *Memoriale fratris Walteri de Coventria*, ed.
    W. Stubbs, 2 vols. (Rolls Series, 1872–3)

CHAPTER I

THE CHARTER AND ITS HISTORY

In 1215 Magna Carta was a failure. It was intended as a peace and it provoked war. It pretended to state customary law and it promoted disagreement and contention. It was legally valid for no more than three months, and even within that period its terms were never properly executed. Yet it was revived in the re-issues of 1216, 1217 and 1225. The last version became law, to be confirmed and interpreted in Parliament and enforced in the courts of law. Three of its chapters still stand on the English Statute Book.[1] These embody, with some slight and occasional amendments, four of the original provisions of 1215.[2] No other English legal enactment has enjoyed such long life. Some of these measures survived because they seemed to have a specific value. Until 1970, for example, the prohibition of fish-weirs in cap. 23 still sought to preserve navigation on the Thames and other rivers.[3] Some survived because they were harmless confirmations of rights and privileges conveyed by other instruments. Hence the Charter still declares that the English

---

[1] Caps. 1, 9, 29. The savings clause of cap. 37 also remains. Since the first edition of this book of 1965, when nine chapters survived, cap. 14 was repealed by the Criminal Law Act 1967 c.58, and caps. 8, 15, 16, 23 and 30 by the Statute Law (Repeals Act) 1969 c.52, which came into effect 1 January 1970. The residual chapters of the Charter of the Forest were repealed in 1971. In both cases repeal originated in the proposals of the Law Commission established in 1965. See Pallister (1971), pp. 98–101. For the survival of parliamentary interpretations of cap. 29 of the Charter of 1225 see Pallister (1971), pp. 100–1.

[2] The relation of the chapters is as follows:

1225	1215
cap. 1 (amended)	cap. 1
cap. 9 (amended)	cap. 13
cap. 29 (amended)	caps. 39, 40

[3] 1225, cap. 23; 1215, cap. 33.

church shall be free[4] and still confirms, but does not define, the privileges of the city of London and other towns and boroughs.[5] But the other surviving clause states deeper principles and less restricted privileges. At the other extreme from the fish-weirs of cap. 23 there stands cap. 29, which lays down that no free man is to be imprisoned, dispossessed, outlawed, exiled or damaged without lawful judgement of his peers or by the law of the land.[6] Cap. 29 owes its continued existence to the *pietas* of legislators and lawyers, for it is not now essential or often even relevant to the liberty of the individual. But this *pietas* is in turn a product of the long struggles in which men appealed to this principle against authority. Individual freedom can be justified by many methods. There is no logical reason for including Magna Carta among them. That something survives from 1215 is a reflexion of the continuous development of English law and administration. Magna Carta has been preserved not as a museum piece, but as part of the common law of England, to be defended, maintained or repealed as the needs and functions of the law required. That so much of what survives is now concerned with individual liberty is a reflexion of the quality of the original act of 1215. It was adaptable. This was its greatest and most important characteristic.

Lawyers have been responsible for much of this survival and for the residual veneration of the Charter. Led by Sir Edward Coke they re-instated it as a document of political importance in the seventeenth century. Since then they have produced the two great commentaries, Blackstone's of 1759 and McKechnie's of 1905. The memorial at Runnymede is the work of the American Bar Association and lawyers on both sides of the Atlantic are largely responsible for the annual gatherings of the Magna Carta Society. But the legal profession has not been wholly at one in this. One of the

---

[4] 1225 and 1215, cap. 1.   [5] 1225, cap. 9; 1215, cap. 13.   [6] 1215, cap. 39.

most vigorous criticisms of the Charter's claim to any kind of permanent legal stature was the work of a lawyer, Edward Jenks.[7] Moreover, it is now possible and indeed justifiable for a lawyer to compose a general survey of the freedom of the individual in England with little reference to Magna Carta.[8] Lawyers have not always acted with a single-minded concern for preservation. In 1895 Maitland wrote that 'this document becomes and rightly becomes a sacred text, the nearest approach to an irrepealable "fundamental statute" that England has ever had'.[9] Yet since the Statute Law Revision Act of 1863 Parliament, under the direction of its legal members, had repealed clause after clause of Magna Carta along with other outdated sections of the legal code. This ambivalence was not new in the nineteenth century. In his *Second Institute* Coke did well to select cap. 29 as worthy of especial praise. 'As the gold-finer', he wrote, 'will not out of the dust, threds or shreds of gold, let passe the least crum, in respect of the excellency of the metall: so ought not the learned reader to let passe any syllable of this Law, in respect of the excellency of the matter.'[10] No one reading the *Second Institute* would guess that common lawyers since the fourteenth century had spent a great deal of time and thought on evading the payment of feudal incidents, which Magna Carta regulated and confirmed, by inventing and developing the use and other legal devices.[11] The lawyers of the fourteenth century were not the first to evade or adjust the Charter's terms. In the generation after 1215, lawyers and administrators failed to apply the strictures of cap. 24[12] against the use of the writ *praecipe* to the rapidly proliferating writs of entry which, like

---

[7] Jenks (1904), 260–73.
[8] Harry Street, *Freedom, the Individual and the Law* (Penguin Books, 1963), p. 271.
[9] Pollock & Maitland (1898), I, 173. (Where full details are not given in the footnote, these will be found in the References.)
[10] *Second Institute* (1662 ed.), p. 57.
[11] Plucknett (1948), pp. 544–55. See also Sanders (1956), pp. 105–7.
[12] 1215, cap. 34.

the *praecipe*, had the effect of evading the jurisdiction of private courts.[13] Bracton himself glossed the provision on amercement by peers in cap. 14 in a manner which was almost certainly the exact opposite of what the king's opponents intended in 1215.[14]

Coke and his colleagues did not fight for the whole Charter, but for their own selection from it, and for their own interpretation of that selection. To Coke 'the Charter was for the most part declaratory of the principal grounds of the fundamental laws of England, and for the residue it is additional to supply some defects of the Common Law'. Its provisions had been 'confirmed by the wise providence of so many acts of Parliament',[15] and it embodied fundamental incontrovertible law, which itself went back beyond the Charter to the days before the Norman Conquest. He made the double assumption that a grant of feudal privileges which was more than four hundred years old was relevant to his own society, and that this grant of privileges was not an *ad hoc* statement but a declaration of existing law which was already ancient in 1225 and 1215.[16] In pursuit of this assumption he over-rode even the best authority. 'In the reign of Henry II', he wrote, 'the king exacted an uncertain relief, for so Glanvill saith who wrote in this time. . .and therefore how necessary it was that the ancient relief should be restored is evident.'[17] Coke accepted the Charter against the foremost legal authority of the twelfth century. For him, Magna Carta, not Glanvill, was the better evidence of ancient law.

Coke was seeking the continuous thread in English law. He was concerned with precedent, with principles and judicial decisions which in his view indissolubly linked his world with the past. The modern historian seeks the opposite. For Coke, Magna Carta was an affirmation of fundamental law and the liberty of the subject. For the

[13] See below, pp. 325–6.   [14] 1215, cap. 21 (see below, p. 334).
[15] *Second Institute*, 'Proeme'.   [16] Pocock (1957), pp. 45–7.   [17] *Second Institute*, p. 7.

modern historian it is a statement of liberties rather than an assertion of liberty; a privilege which was devised mainly in the interests of the aristocracy, and which was applicable at its widest to the 'free man'—to a class which formed a small proportion of the population of thirteenth-century England. Before all else the historian seeks the precise contemporary meaning of the Charter, its intent, its vocabulary, its effects. All else is a distortion, an imposition on its 'real' content of anachronistic and perhaps politically motivated misinterpretations. This is not entirely the work of the twentieth century. In the seventeenth century Robert Brady had already asserted against the school of Coke that

the far greatest part of Magna Carta, concerned Tenents in military Service only, and the Liberties, which our Ancient Historians tell were so mightily contended for, if seriously considered, were mainly the Liberties of Holy Church, by which, in most things, she pretended to be free from Subjection to a Temporal Prince; and the relaxation of the original rigor upon which Knights, or Military Fees were first given by the Lords, and accepted by the Tenents.[18]

Brady fully appreciated the double distortion for which modern historians have held Coke responsible. He wrote,

Sir Edward Coke doth not care to hear of the Feudal Law as it was in use at this time, and hath a fine fetch to play off the Great Charter and interpret it by his Modern-Law, that was not then known or heard of, and it hath been and ever was, an Art of some men to interpret and confound New Laws by Old Practise and Usage; and Old Laws by late Usage and Modern Practice; when perhaps if they would endeavour to find out the History of those Laws, the Grounds and Reasons upon which they were made, there would be found no congruity between them.[19]

Much of this criticism of Coke is clearly valid. He treated law, as Brady put it, as though it 'had grown up with the Trees, Herbs and Grass'.[20] Yet it is not quite so secure as either Brady or the modern critics would suggest. It assumes that the exact contemporary sense of Magna Carta can be

[18] *Introduction to the Old English History* (London, 1684), p. 76, quoted Pocock (1957), p. 207.
[19] Quoted by Butterfield (1946), p. 76.   [20] *Ibid.* p. 76 n.

established as a canon whereby Coke and all other 'false' interpreters can be judged. But to seek this is to pursue a will-o'-the-wisp. The essays which commemorated the seven hundredth anniversary of Magna Carta included two by eminent scholars which expressed a notable difference of opinion on the meaning and intent of cap. 39 of the Charter of 1215[21] – the very clause on which Coke concentrated his interpretative talents. Vinogradoff and Powicke represent but two of the many modern interpretations of this clause.[22] Hence to argue that Coke distorted or falsified the 'meaning' of Magna Carta is to convey a false impression. Many of its provisions had no precise meaning. It was not an exact statement of law, either of Coke's law or of what the modern expert knows of thirteenth-century law, but a political document produced in a crisis. It was a product of intermittent negotiations which lasted for at least six months. It was the culmination of hard bargaining and skilful manœuvring. Perhaps it registered too the weariness of the negotiators in the face of the intractable character of the king, the intransigence of some of his opponents and the hard facts of English administration.

There are several important implications in this. First, there is little point in discussing the detailed wording and legal connotation of the Charter without examining the political circumstances which produced it. Far too little recognition has been given, for example, to the fact that the famous words of cap. 39 were derived in 1215, not from the barons but from the king and behind him from Pope Innocent III. In its final form it excluded arbitrary extra-legal action, but it also confirmed rather than weakened the traditional rights of the Crown within the law.[23] Secondly, there is often no hope of establishing a precise contemporary

[21] P. Vinogradoff (1917), M.C.C.E. pp. 78–95; Powicke (1917), M.C.C.E. pp. 96–121.
[22] For another variant see Ullmann (1961), pp.164 ff. (on this, see below, p. 328, n. 154) and for further discussion of cap. 39, below, pp. 327–31.
[23] See below, pp. 329–30.

meaning of particular phrases or clauses. To attempt to do so is in itself to distort. When cap. 16 of the 1215 Charter laid down that no one was to be compelled to do greater service for his fee or free tenement than he ought, clearly the whole content of the clause was concentrated on that single indefinable 'ought'. Here the Crown could impose one interpretation, the barons yet another. Such vagueness affected a great deal of the Charter's purpose. It affected the application of cap. 48 concerning local and forest administration where local juries were required to define 'evil' customs,[24] and it affected all those clauses dealing with the restoration of rights where 'unjust' disseisins or fines had also to be defined.[25] The Charter failed to produce a lasting peace in 1215 just because this looseness of phrasing hid a real and irreconcilable difference of interpretation. Not all its vagueness was of this deliberate kind. Sometimes, as when it conveyed privileges to 'free men', it simply gave allusive recognition to the facts of English society in the thirteenth century.[26] Sometimes it was vague because of the perplexed reaction of men who were trying to grapple with a complex administrative system which was still very much the private perquisite of the king. Hence, for example, the provision that amercements should be proportionate to the nature of the offence and that barons should be amerced by their peers.[27] Who was to establish the exact proportion and who were the barons' peers? The meaning of the Charter leads not so much to precise definitions as to a contemporary range of opinion derived either from a conflict of interpretations or from general imprecision and vagueness of usage. This weakens the case against Coke. If contemporaries themselves were not always agreed then he cannot be written off quite so easily as a 'distorter'. It is a matter not of

---

[24] Caps. 52, 53, 55, 56, 57, 59.   [25] See below, pp. 340–2.
[26] See below, pp. 291–5.   [27] 1225, cap. 14; 1215, caps. 20, 21, 22.

distortion or falsification, but of whether he is to be included or not within the admissible range of opinion.

It is unfortunate that recent criticism has presented the 'common-law interpretation of history', which Coke represented, as the 'predecessor and to a large extent the parent of the more famous Whig interpretation'.[28] The ideas of Coke and his fellows later provided material for the Whig interpretation of history. But Coke was neither a Whig nor a Whig historian. Butterfield wrote,

> We must not forget what is the Whig interpretation of history *par excellence*—the interpretation of the constitutional conflict of the seventeenth century itself. And in this connexion we must note that the older writers [e.g. Coke] confront us with an inversion of the particular structure which we to-day would perhaps expect that interpretation to have. They do not give us an organization of English history for the purpose of expounding the growth of freedom, the evolution of the constitution, the widening of those rights of Englishmen that grow from precedent to precedent. At least if they do this, it is only one aspect of their work. Their history is based on the assumption that English liberty existed from the earliest times.[29]

The contrast between Coke and the Whigs could be carried much further, for Coke did not and could not partake of the powerful element of natural law in the Whig interpretation which underpinned their emphasis on individual liberty. Natural law, an essential component of the Whig interpretation, was, as we shall see, lethal to the survival in England of the common-law attitudes typified by Coke. Moreover, Coke and the Whigs differed in their methods. The essence of Whig history was to read the present back into the past and to interpret the past in the light of selected themes: the growth of liberty, the development of Parliament and, within Parliament, of the House of Commons, the growth of 'nationhood', and so on. The Whigs turned to history not

---

[28] Pocock (1957), p. 46. Compare Hill (1962), pp. 87–8.
[29] Butterfield (1944), pp. 69–70. Butterfield nevertheless continued to apply the term Whig to Coke, *ibid.* pp. 71, 72.

to justify the present; Locke's *Second Treatise* did that for them; but to explain how the present had evolved. Coke's object was quite different. He was not primarily concerned with writing history or interpreting the past. His aim was to call in the past in order to support his arguments about the present. Any judgement he made about medieval society was entirely subsidiary to this. Thus he was on the same track as the later Whig historians but was moving in the opposite direction. There was some occasional confusion since Coke had to assume that the past was like the present. He, like the Whigs, was therefore a disciple of historical continuity. But for him this was derived from the continuous unchanging element of fundamental law. For the Whig historians it was to be found in the progress of English society towards that of their own day. The object of Coke's antiquarianism was permanent, that of the Whigs was evolutionary. Coke was far closer to Bracton and Fortescue than he was to Locke, Macaulay or even Blackstone. He was less the first Whig than the last great medieval commentator on the common law of England. The antiquarianism of the late sixteenth and seventeenth centuries was no new phenomenon. It was the culmination of the medieval search and love for precedent.

The 'myth' of Magna Carta, that interpretation of it which gives it qualities which the men of 1215 did not intend, was part of the document's potential. Some of these myths were late creations, some arose within a generation of 1215. The decisive period in these developments was not Coke's day, but the fourteenth century, when many of the features of Coke's interpretation of the Charter were embodied in parliamentary statute.[30] In the fourteenth as in the seventeenth century the crucial clause was cap. 29.[31]

[30] For what follows and on the whole problem of the history of Magna Carta from the fourteenth century to the time of Coke, see Faith Thompson (1948).
[31] 1215, cap. 39.

Between 1331 and 1368, in six acts, Parliament passed statutory interpretations of this clause which went far beyond any of the detailed intention and sense of the original Charter. First, it interpreted the phrase 'lawful judgement of peers' to include trial by peers and therefore trial by jury, a process which existed only in embryo in 1215.[32] Secondly, the 'law of the land' was defined in terms of yet another potent and durable phrase—'due process of law', which meant procedure by original writ or by an indicting jury. It was construed to exclude procedure before the Council or by special commissions and to limit intrusions into the sphere of action of the common-law courts; it was even applied against trial for trespass in the Exchequer.[33] Thirdly, the words 'no free man' were so altered that the Charter's formal terms became socially inclusive. In the earlier statutes of Edward III of 1331 and 1352 they became simply 'no man',[34] but in 1354 in the statute which refers for the first time to 'due process of law', 'no free man' became 'no man of whatever estate or condition he may be'.[35]

Parliament pressed these new definitions against developing chancery and conciliar jurisdictions. The reassertion of the law of the land in the form of due process was accompanied by the establishment of processes associated with the trial of peers by peers in Parliament. Despite the long interval, the six acts of Edward III's reign were as essential to the lawyers of the seventeenth century as Magna Carta itself. They were adduced in evidence by defending counsel in the Five Knights' Case. Referring to the last of them, 42 Edward III, cap. 3, Selden said that 'the statute is not to be taken to be an explanation of that of Magna

---

[32] Trial by jury was imposed from above, not sought from below, in the later thirteenth and fourteenth centuries (see Plucknett (1948), pp. 114–25).

[33] Thompson (1948), p. 89.

[34] 5 Edward III, cap. 9; 25 Edward III, cap. 4 (*Statutes of the Realm*, I, 267, 321); Thompson (1948), pp. 90, 92.

[35] 28 Edward III, cap. 3 (*Statutes of the Realm*, I, 345); Thompson (1948), p. 92.

Charta, but the very words of the statute of Magna Charta'.[36] They appeared along with the Charter in the debate leading to the Petition of Right. Sir Benjamin Rudyerd declared,

I shall be very glad to see that old, decrepit Law Magna Charta which hath been kept so long, and lien bed-rid, as it were, I shall be glad to see it walk abroad again with new vigour and lustre, attended and followed with the other six statutes; questionless it will be a great heartening to all the people.[37]

In 1641 the act which abolished the Star Chamber and other prerogative courts quoted from the Six Statutes along with cap. 29.[38] Coke and his disciples were following a well-worn track.

The developments between the fourteenth and the seventeenth centuries are not yet fully understood. The view that men lost interest in Magna Carta in the later middle ages and under the Tudors depends heavily on the evidence of parliamentary confirmations. As is well known, these show a sharp decline in the fifteenth century.[39] But this is an unreliable guide to the Charter's continuing importance. For example, in the preliminaries to the Heresy Act of 1534 the Commons expressed concern over the extension of ecclesiastical jurisdiction and the use of the *ex officio* oath. They relied on cap. 29 of Magna Carta, which the clerk transcribed in full in English; even more significantly, among seven statutes which they adduced in support, they included four of the Six Statutes of Edward III, some in summary, some with sections or fragments given *verbatim*. In 1534, therefore, as in 1629, precedents were searched and the linkages properly understood. The whole memorandum is

---

[36] Thompson (1948), p. 332.   [37] *Ibid.* p. 86.   [38] *Ibid.* p. 370.
[39] The practice of counting confirmations originated with Coke, who noted 32 in all (*Second Institute*, proeme). Bémont counted 15 under Edward III, 8 under Richard II, 6 under Henry IV, and one only under Henry V (1892, pp. xlix–l). Faith Thompson totalled 37 conciliar or parliamentary confirmations between 1327 and 1422 of which only 8 belong to the fifteenth century (1948, p. 10 n.).

headed *Magna Carta cap. xxix*.[40] Now the Heresy Act in its
final form says nothing of this and gives no hint that Magna
Carta had stalked through its origination.[41] The statute
evidence, in short, is misleading. There are other indications
that Magna Carta was alive and well. Readings at the Inns of
Court of 1450 to 1550 reveal considerable interest in cap. 11,
dealing with the location of the common pleas, and in due-
process interpretations of cap. 29. It is significant that these
were turned against non-common law jurisdictions of various kinds.[42] That, too, foreshadowed the seventeenth
century.

The seventeenth-century interpretation which Coke typified produced some additions to the fourteenth-century
glosses, but they were in the main minor extensions to, or
clarifications of, an already widely extended range of interpretation. First, Coke openly asserted, what the Six Statutes
had implied, that cap. 29 applied to villeins.[43] Secondly, he
expanded the word 'liberties' so that it became tantamount
to individual liberty. One of his purposes here was to attack
Stuart grants of monopoly, not only those where the
recipients enjoyed some process of restraint against infringers, which evaded due process, but against monopolies
as such. 'Generally', he wrote, 'all monopolies are against
this great Charter, because they are against the liberty and
freedome of the Subject, and against the Law of the land.'[44]
Thirdly, in the debate on the Petition of Right, lawyers

---

[40] *The Complete Works of St. Thomas More*, x, ed. John Guy, Ralph Keen, Clarence H.
Miller and Ruth McGugan (New Haven, 1987), pp. lxii–lxvi. The document in
question is P.R.O., SP 1/82. Magna Carta cap. 29 and the associated statutes are at fos.
57bv–58. All are in English. The translation of cap. 29 (*ibid.* p. lxiv, n. 5) is not drawn
from Rastell's *Great Abridgement* of 1527, for which see Thompson (1948), p. 150.

[41] *Statutes of the Realm*, III, 454–5.

[42] *Spelman's Reports*, ed. J. H. Baker (Selden Society, XCIII, XCIV, 1976–7), II, 57–9, 71–2.
For another law reading of cap. 29 see G. O. Sayles, 'A Fifteenth-Century Law Reading
in English', *Law Quarterly Review*, XCVI (1980), 569–80.

[43] 'This extends to villains, saving against their Lord, for they are free against all men saving
against their Lord' (*Second Institute*, p. 45). This formulation was ultimately derived from
Bracton.

[44] *Ibid.* p. 47. On this see Thompson (1948), pp. 302–4, and D. O. Wagner, 'Coke and the
Rise of Economic Liberalism', *Economic History Review*, VI (1935), 30–44.

argued that Magna Carta established grounds for the writ of Habeas Corpus although this did in fact originate as an administrative order issued by the king's courts.[45] The Petition of Right itself put the final touch to these developments. From the insistence of 1215 that some kind of lawful judgement should precede execution to the principle of 'no arrest without cause shown' of 1628 appears a big jump. The Petition of Right was not so much this as the last of a series of short strides.

Similar developments occurred in the history of other chapters. Over the years cap. 30[46] suffered an even more violent change of character. Initially it was mainly aimed against restrictions on the movement of alien merchants. It was regarded with some ambivalence since it could be used to protect the interests of foreign merchants against the native trader. It was therefore potentially inconsistent with cap. 9 which confirmed the privileges of London and other towns. Hence one of the most striking early appeals to it came from the representatives of the Italian company of the Bardi in 1320 who claimed exemption from the wool staple on the grounds 'that it is contained in Magna Carta that all merchants may come into the realm, stay therein and return thence safely and securely with their goods upon paying the due and accustomed customs'.[47] But within a few years from this the clause was extended to cover denizens as well as aliens. An act of 1328 temporarily abolished the wool staple 'so that all merchants strangers and privy, may go and come with their merchandises into England, after the tenor of the Great Charter'.[48] This act, and others subsequent which likewise extended the sense of the clause, arose from the quarrels between alien and native merchants and the

---

[45] Thompson (1948), p. 325. The Petition of Right itself did not take this line, but nevertheless associated arrest without cause shown and *habeas corpus* in the same clause. For the history of Habeas Corpus see Edward Jenks, 'The story of Habeas Corpus', *Law Quarterly Review*, XVIII (1902), 64–77, and Holdsworth, *History of English Law*, IX, 104–25.

[46] 1215, cap. 41.   [47] Thompson (1948), p. 111.

[48] 2 Edward III, cap. 9 (*Statutes of the Realm*, I, 259); Thompson (1948), p. 112.

arguments engendered by government policy towards the wool staple. They were not intended to provide general protection against prerogative taxation of trade. Nevertheless, they could be exploited in this way. Cap. 30 became the first chapter of Magna Carta to figure as a precedent in the contentions of the seventeenth century, first in Bate's case of 1608 and then in the debates on the Crown's new impositions on trade in the Parliament of 1610. Here, as in the later debates on cap. 29, William Hakewill relied on the fourteenth-century interpretations of this clause.[49] Twenty years or so later Coke simply treated the decision against Bate as illegal. 'A decision was given in the Exchequer', he wrote, 'for an imposition set upon currants, but the common opinion was, that the judgement was against law, and divers express acts of Parliament; and so by that which hath been said it doth manifestly appear'.[50] Moreover he applied this chapter, like cap. 29, against monopolies: 'All monopolies concerning trade and traffique are against the liberty and freedome declared and granted by this great Charter, and against divers other Acts of Parliament, which are good commentaries upon this Chapter.'[51] Much rich juice was ultimately squeezed from the unripened fruit of 1215.

This extension of the range of interpretation followed two main lines. First the Charter was used as a yardstick of legality against which new measures could be assessed, and accepted or rejected. Secondly, the sense of the Charter was repeatedly re-interpreted to ensure that it conformed to new social and political conditions. Both lines derived from the assumption that the Charter was fundamental law. This was not a fiction of the seventeenth century or even of the fourteenth. It was implicit in the original purpose of the Charter, for such a grant of liberties in perpetuity could not be made effective except by treating it as fundamental law. The drafters of the Charter did not themselves envisage this

[49] Thompson (1948), pp. 249–55.   [50] *Second Institute*, p. 63.   [51] *Ibid.*

continuous process of re-interpretation. There is no evidence at all that their remedies were broadly conceived because they saw the need to cater for future generations. Nevertheless they insisted that their demands should be met in as permanent a form as was possible. Furthermore, they exploited the weaknesses of Henry III to ensure that the Charter was confirmed in perpetuity by the first of John's successors. Thereby they made the first English statute.[52]

The first official interpretation of the Charter came in 1234 when king and magnates elucidated the intentions of cap. 35 concerning sheriff's tourns and the sessions of the courts of hundred and wapentake.[53] It was first expanded to cover major extensions of royal policy which had circumvented its original provisions, in the Confirmation of the Charters of 1297. This and the Petition of Right were in the same line of descent. They were both intended as glosses on a sacred legal text. Over four centuries there were gradual shifts in emphasis. In 1441 Chief Baron Frey made a famous statement of the relationship between the king and law. 'The law', he asserted, 'is the highest inheritance that the king has, for by the law he himself and all his subjects are ruled. And if the law were not, there would be no king and no inheritance.'[54] This derived from the traditional distinction between kingship and tyranny, which assumed that king and law ruled together. It was rather different from Coke's bald assertion that Magna Carta was 'such a fellow that he will have no sovereign', and different again from his argument 'that the common law hath so admeasured the prerogatives of the king, that they should not take away nor prejudice the inheritance of any; and the best inheritance that the subject

[52] Holt (1972); Holt (1985), pp. 18–19. For further discussion of grants in perpetuum see below, pp. 518–22.
[53] Powicke (1947). 1. 147–8 (see below, pp. 394–6).
[54] S. B. Chrimes, *English Constitutional Ideas in the Fifteenth Century* (Cambridge, 1936), p. 74; T. F. T. Plucknett, 'The Lancastrian Constitution', *Tudor Studies*, ed. R. W. Seton Watson (London, 1924), pp. 164 ff.

hath is the Law of the Realm'.[55] This was a development of the old principle of Bracton's *Addicio* that the king was beneath the law. Ultimately it helped to bring a king to the axe, but it would require extraordinary hindsight to discover that consequence in Coke.

The legal antiquarianism of Coke and his fellows marked the final fruition of medieval concepts of law and medieval forms of political argument. By the end of the seventeenth century Brady and others had attacked its historical inaccuracies and were breaking through to the realities of medieval law and administration which lay behind the assumptions of Coke and his fellows.[56] Historical criticism of this kind, however, was only one and that a minor reason for the sudden disappearance of the ancient fundamental law which Coke had expounded. Much more important was the spread of concepts of natural law and natural rights. Hobbes and Locke were the real enemies of legal precedent, for once positive law was based on natural law and that on natural right and reason, the need for precedent vanished. Hence there was no room for ancient law in the monolithic structure of the *Leviathan* or in the *Second Treatise of Civil Government*. Coke and his work were outmoded, irrelevant, and of antiquarian rather than political interest, a mere aberration which Hobbes dismissed in a few brief sections of the *Leviathan*.[57]

However, the advent of natural law marked not the end but yet another stage in the history of Magna Carta. Henceforth in England it became the political property of the radicals. Hitherto the Charter had been closely tied to the common law and the common-law courts. As a result of repeated parliamentary confirmations it had also been linked to the survival and expansion of the powers of Parliament. Now radical thinkers turned it against both. For them the

---

[55] *Second Institute*, p. 63.
[56] Pocock (1957), pp. 182 ff.; D. C. Douglas, *English Scholars* (London, 1951), pp. 119–38.
[57] Hobbes did discuss the Charter in the *Behemoth* (see Pocock, 1957, pp. 166–9).

liberties conveyed in the Charter were the birthright of free-born Englishmen, to be asserted against a parliament which could be just as arbitrary as the king had been, and against a system of common law which enabled the legal profession to batten on the litigating public and to join hands with parliaments in imposing an intolerable tyranny on the land. The real successors of Coke were not the Whigs, but the Levellers in the seventeenth century,[58] John Wilkes in the eighteenth century, and their successors among the Radicals of the early nineteenth century. It was only with the spread of Utilitarianism that the Charter finally came to the end of its long and varied political career in England.[59]

It also survived in America. There too the fight was not in defence of law and Parliament against the king, but for the rights of the colonists against both king and Parliament. Both for the radicals in England and for the Americans the chief value of the Charter lay in the fact that it was a concession, which had been granted or confirmed in the past; it was, as it had always been, a fault in the armour of authority. And just as the Charter was claimed by the English Radicals as a natural birthright, so in America some of its principles came to be established as individual rights enforceable against authority in all its forms, whether legislative, executive or judicial, whether represented by Crown, governor or council, or later by state and federal government. This embodied two streams of thought. On the one hand it was drawn from English law which came to be embodied in the legal structure of the early colonies.[60] Cap. 1 of the Massachusetts Body of Liberties of 1641, for example, did not quote, but

---

[58] Some of the Levellers, however, rejected the Charter in favour of natural law (see Hill, 1962, pp. 75–82). But they were not consistent. Overton, who described the Charter as 'but a beggarly thing', also went to Newgate prison clasping Coke's *Second Institute* to his bosom (Haller, *Tracts on Liberty*, III, 385–7). I owe this reference to the kindness of Anne Pallister.

[59] For the history of the Charter since the seventeenth century see Pallister (1971) and R. J. Smith, *England's Gothic Bequest* (Cambridge, 1987).

[60] H. D. Hazeltine, 'The Influence of Magna Carta on American Constitutional Development', *M.C.C.E.* pp. 184–97.

seems to have been based on cap. 29 of the Charter.[61] On the other hand it incorporated natural law. In England the two had been inimical. In America they worked hand in hand. Hence the Virginia Bill of Rights of 1776 called on Locke to assert in cap. 1 that 'all men are by nature equally free and independent, and have certain inherent rights ... namely, the enjoyment of life and liberty, with the means of acquiring and possessing property, and pursuing and obtaining happiness and safety', and on Magna Carta in cap. 8 to lay down that no man was to be deprived of his liberty, 'except by the law of the land or the judgement of his peers'. Indeed the due process of law of cap. 29 came to be embodied in the Bill of Rights of state after state and was carried on from the eighteenth to the twentieth century. It was no longer so much a law as a statement of political principle. The Charter only survived alongside natural law by being raised to the same universal terms. Cap. 29 had become a convenient formulation of a natural right. This was as far removed from Coke's thoughts as Coke had been from the Great Charter itself.[62]

The history of Magna Carta is the history not only of a document but also of an argument. The history of the document is a history of repeated re-interpretation. But the history of the argument is a history of a continuous element of political thinking. In this light there is no inherent reason why an assertion of law originally conceived in aristocratic interests should not be applied on a wider scale. If we can seek truth in Aristotle, we can seek it also in Magna Carta. The class and political interests involved in each stage of the Charter's history are one aspect of it; the principles it asserted, implied or assumed are another. Approached as

---

[61] *Ibid.* p. 193; W. Macdonald, *Select Charters illustrative of American History 1606–1775*, pp. 73–4.

[62] A. E. Dick Howard, *The Road from Runnymede, Magna Carta and Constitutionalism in America* (Charlottesville, 1968); Philip B. Kurland, 'Magna Carta and Constitutionalism in the United States: "The Noble Lie"', in Thorne, Dunham, Kurland and Jennings (1965), pp. 48–74.

political theory it sought to establish the rights of subjects against authority and maintained the principle that authority was subject to law. If the matter is left in broad terms of sovereign authority on the one hand and the subject's rights on the other, this was the legal issue at stake in the fight against John, against Charles I and in the resistance of the American colonists to George III.

The principles of the argument were not the only common element. One of the issues which led to the War of Independence was the Crown's refusal to abandon in America those prerogatives which had already been destroyed in England. Among the issues between Charles I and his subjects were the Crown's powers of arrest and imprisonment, its exploitation of feudal revenues and feudal incidents which the Stuarts had revived, its antiquarian search into prerogative forms of taxation and its revival of the forest law. Charles himself was conscious enough of the link with the past. His answer to the Petition of Right was that he would agree to confirm the Charter but 'would not have his prerogative straitened by any new explanation of Magna Carta'.[63] To confirm Magna Carta was a traditional palliative of medieval kings. Charles was later to call on the Charter as an argument for retaining episcopacy.[64] Indeed it was he, not his opponents, who claimed to stand for the ancient Constitution.

The history of the documents themselves carried problems from one period to another. The debate was sometimes confused by the difficulties of the text. In the thirteenth century men still appealed to the 1215 Charter even though it was no longer valid in law.[65] Within two generations of

---

[63] Butterfield (1944), p. 68.
[64] 'As a King at his coronation, he hath not only taken a solemn oath to maintain this order, but His Majesty and his predecessors in their confirmation of the Great Charter, have inseparably woven the right of the Church into the liberty of the subjects.' Gardiner, *Constitutional Documents*, p. 328. Charles's appeal to the coronation oath also had many medieval precedents.
[65] See below, pp. 397–400.

Runnymede the chroniclers of St Albans confused the texts of 1215 and 1225 in complete uncertainty as to what was valid and what was not.[66] In the seventeenth century Coke never used the Charter of 1215. His commentary, like most of the early seventeenth-century debates, was based on the re-issue of 1225. He only seems to have known of the 1215 Charter from the chronicle of Matthew Paris.[67] Others printed the St Albans version with little or no attempt to collate it with the authentic texts, and it was not until Blackstone's Commentary of 1759 that the two versions of 1215 and 1225, and the confused nature of the St Albans text, were properly and finally distinguished.[68]

But if textual confusion facilitated 'distortion' it was not itself the cause of it. 'Distortion' indeed was inherent in the Charter itself and in the whole debate. When Coke asserted that the Charter simply re-established ancient rates of relief, he not only misled his public; he was himself misled by the Charter. Just as Coke used Magna Carta as a defence of 'ancient liberties' against the Stuarts, so the barons of the Charter called on the Laws of Edward the Confessor and Henry I to maintain what they alleged was ancient custom against the government of King John. They distorted just as much as, if not more than, Coke.[69] Indeed, in the decade or so before the final crisis of 1215, the Laws of Edward and Henry were suitably doctored in order to strengthen the case against kings who acted unjustly and without the due forms of consent.[70] Hence it is quite invalid to treat Magna Carta as a kind of datum from which all subsequent departure was unjustified. Magna Carta was simply a stage in an argu-

[66] Holt (1964), 67–88.
[67] *Second Institute*, 'Proeme'. Coke here reveals no knowledge of the two originals of 1215 which came into the hands of Sir Robert Cotton, 1629–31. Nor did he try to collate the authentic text on which he commented in the *Second Institute* with the St Albans version which embodied both the 1215 and 1225 texts.
[68] See Butterfield (1944), pp. 25–30. [69] See below, pp. 300–2.
[70] See below, pp. 93–5.

ment and bore all the characteristic features of the argument – the erection of interests into law, the selection and interpretation of convenient precedent, the readiness to assert agreed custom where none existed. It was not only law: it was also propaganda. Hence to accuse Coke or anyone else of 'distortion' is scarcely illuminating, for to distort a distortion is little more than venial. To describe him as a Whig is scarcely justified unless the same label is to be applied to Magna Carta itself, for both equally 'distorted' the past in the interests of the present. Indeed to do that would be to admit Coke's case. It would be tantamount to accepting that the facts themselves are 'Whig'.

The problem posed by the history of the Charter is not why and how it came to be 'distorted', but why it rather than any other document came to play the rôle it did. Initially it was called great not because of the greatness of its quality, not because, as Coke put it, it was *magnum in parvo*,[71] but because of its large size and to distinguish it from the companion Charter of the Forest.[72] Immediate contemporaries made no great claim for it. Yet it was a royal grant which survived as a basis for liberties rather than any claim which might have been based, for example, on the reign of Stephen, and it was this particular royal grant which survived rather than the earlier Charter of Liberties of Henry I.[73] Moreover, it not only survived but it became a sacred text, glossed, interpreted and extended, but in medieval times rarely questioned. The explanation of this is to be found not only in the years which followed 1215, but in the political crisis which produced the Charter and in the years before, during which the demands it expressed were slowly taking shape. The subsequent history of the Charter derived from the Charter itself. It re-

---

[71] *Second Institute*, 'Proeme'.   [72] White (1915), 472–5; (1917), 554–5.
[73] See below, pp. 36–8; 475–6.

flected in its quality the character of the men who achieved it and the nature of the society in which it came about. It is to these themes that the remainder of this work is devoted.

CHAPTER 2

GOVERNMENT AND SOCIETY IN THE TWELFTH CENTURY

Twelfth-century England had no constitution. There was no general system of government in which powers were balanced, functions allotted and defined, rights protected, and principles stated or acknowledged. Instead there were the materials from which a constitution of some kind might ultimately and indirectly be compounded. Government was evolving routine procedures, methods which it found convenient to use in most, but not necessarily all, circumstances. It operated in a society in which privilege seemed to be part of the natural order of things: privilege attached to this or that particular status, or privilege which individuals held as a result of royal favour, or privilege which great corporate institutions held as necessary conditions of their function. From these primitive elements to a settled constitution was a long, tortuous and often bloody journey in which the grant of charters of liberties was but one, and that an early, step. It was nevertheless a hazardous step, one which required determination and organization on the part of those who demanded and received such grants, and one which was necessitated by the power and complexity of the administrative machine under the control of those who granted them. It was a step which required considerable sophistication on the part of both, for it involved a fusion of the government's routine on the one hand with the privileges of the subject on the other. On the one side, routine procedures which the government had hitherto developed as administrative and political convenience dictated were now being conferred as rights to which the subject was entitled. On the other side, the privileges which the subject had hitherto enjoyed because of status, grant or prescription were now being extended to cover administrative procedures which were often of recent origin, which were never the exclusive concern of one particular subject, which might not be the concern even of one particular grade within the feudal hierarchy, and which could only be held by the recipients in common, in some kind of corporate capacity. All this required a refined political theory, subtler and more searching than that provided by the simple concepts of feudal allegiance; and the need was all the greater since the recipients of these grants of liberties never brought themselves to think outside the terms of reference prescribed by the society in which they lived, in which monarchical government, more or less immediate, was the basic component of any polity. Hence, in seeking liberties they required their kings to promulgate acts of self-limitation in which they agreed to restrict their own freedom and initiative, apparently of their own free will. This not only led the seekers and grantors of liberties into vigorous and prolonged argument. It also meant that a grant of liberties was never so secure that it ceased to be a matter of debate and political friction. Liberties forgotten were liberties dead.

Magna Carta was intimately connected in this way with developing political theories of the twelfth century. It was also a direct product of war. It was occasioned directly by failure in war, by the loss of Normandy in 1204 and by the defeat of John's ambitious campaign in Flanders and France in 1214. If the Charter had any single predominant source, it is to be found in the manner in which the Angevin kings of England exploited their realm in an attempt to expand and defend the continental empire of which England became a part with the accession of Henry of Anjou in 1154. Indeed, war, the emergence of international systems of alliance, the development of war economies, of advanced methods of taxation and other forms of fiscal exploitation, were just as characteristic of the twelfth century as were the political ideas stemming from the cathedral schools, the newly emerging universities and the everyday practice of the courts. War was the compulsive urgency behind administrative experiment and in the hundred and fifty years before the Charter England had had a full measure of this compulsion. But England was no exception in twelfth- and thirteenth-century Europe, and Magna Carta was far from unique, either in content or in form. In 1183, as part of the Treaty of Constance, the Emperor Frederick Barbarossa ended an unavailing war in northern Italy by granting the towns of the Lombard League a series of liberties which gave them practical independence of imperial rule.[1] In 1188 King Alfonso IX of León, in the midst of a long feud with Castille, promulgated ordinances in the *cortes* of León which conferred important feudal privileges on his vassals.[2] In 1205 King Peter II of Aragon, after costly foreign adventures, drafted, but did not promulgate, important concessions for his subjects of Catalonia.[3] In 1220 the young Emperor Frederick II bought support for his bid to unite the Empire and the Sicilian kingdom by granting special privileges to the ecclesiastical princes of the Empire.[4] In 1222 King Andrew II of Hungary ended a period of expensive adventures abroad by granting the Golden Bull to his vassals.[5] Nine years later Frederick II's son, Henry VII, found it necessary to quieten opposition in Germany by expanding and adding to his father's concessions of 1220 and extending them to the secular princes of the Empire;[6] his father, increasingly embroiled in the affairs of Lombardy and Italy, confirmed the grant within a year. In 1282–3 the War of the Sicilian Vespers compelled Charles of Anjou and Charles of Salerno, on the one hand, to issue reforming ordinances in a bid to

[1] *M.G.H., Const.* I, 411 ff. [2] Muñoz y Romero (1847), pp. 102–6.
[3] T. N. Bisson, 'An "Unknown Charter" for Catalonia (A.D. 1205)' in *Album Mályusz* (1976), 61–76.
[4] *M.G.H., Const.* II, 86 ff. [5] Marczali (1901), pp. 134–43.
[6] *M.G.H., Const.* II, 418–20.

recover Sicily and stave off rebellion in southern Italy,[7] and on the other forced the invader of Sicily, Peter III of Aragon, to buy support for an expensive foreign policy by conceding the *Privilegio General* to his subjects.[8] There was only one striking exception in thirteenth-century Europe to this regularly repeated association of war with the concession of liberties, and that was the Capetian monarchy of France. In this case continued success staved off the inevitable retribution for foreign adventure until the next century when the exhaustion of French resources in the Aragonese crusade and the campaigns in Flanders eventually showed that France was no exception. Philip IV's great reforming ordinance of 1303 was here but a preface to the various provincial charters which his successor, Louis X, was forced to concede in 1315.[9]

This reiteration of the same story throughout western Europe carries obvious implications. There was nothing particularly striking or extraordinary in the fact that King John had to end a period of disastrous wars in 1215 with the grant of a charter of liberties to his subjects. Magna Carta reflected English conditions, just as the *Privilegio General* did those of Aragon or the Golden Bull those of Hungary, but it did not spring from any insular genius, nor was it more searching or more radical than its continental parallels. A dispassionate observer in the thirteenth century would have attached no greater significance to the Great Charter than to the Golden Bull or the *Privilegio General*, nor would he have predicted that the English grant would in the long run have the greater influence. In the early years of the fourteenth century, indeed, such an observer would probably have shown no great surprise that many rulers throughout western Europe had at some time found it necessary to make such grants. To him grants of liberties would have seemed to

---

[7] Trifone (1921), pp. 93–105.   [8] *Herrschaftsverträge*, pp. 17–43.

[9] *Ordonnances*, I, 354–68, 551 ff.

embody the natural reaction of feudal societies to monarchical importunity. If he were a royal servant of a cynical bent he might have reflected that they were one of the probable costs of administrative inventiveness and efficiency. And indeed this paradox epitomizes the long and tangled conflicts which produced these liberties, for those same actions whereby kings overhauled and improved the government of their realms were often regarded by their subjects as tyrannous invasions of ancient right and custom.[10]

In England the Norman and Angevin kings followed three such broad lines of policy. First, they exploited many of the functions traditionally attached to feudal lordship as financial resources for their wars and as instruments of political discipline to compel support, and to stave off and defeat rebellion. Secondly, they vigorously developed new methods of administration which lay quite outside the relatively primitive systems of government which elementary feudal relationships subsumed. Finally, to execute their policies, they created an establishment of *curiales* who owed power and position to efficient service of the Crown. These were policies typical of the west European monarchies at this time, but in England they were particularly telling. England was wealthy enough to be worth exploiting, small enough to be exploited efficiently, and was controlled by kings whose powers were in part derived from conquest. Elsewhere in Europe such conditions existed only in Sicily, and the parallel between the two was emphasized for contemporaries by the fact that the conquerors of both came from Normandy;[11] both realms played vital rôles in international politics, the one in northern, the other in southern Europe; both were the centres of empires and of imperial dreams and

---

[10] For a general comment on charters of liberties, written from a different standpoint, see R. Van Caenegem, 'Le Problème des Chartes de Libertés', in *Album Mályusz* (1976), 3–15.

[11] C. H. Haskins, 'England and Sicily in the Twelfth Century', *E.H.R.*, xxvi (1911), 433–47, 641–65; Evelyn Jamison, 'The Sicilian Norman Kingdom in the Mind of Anglo-Norman Contemporaries', *Proceedings of the British Academy*, xxiv (1938), 237–85.

ambitions. Yet the kings of England had advantages even compared with their Norman counterparts in Sicily, for the circumstances of the Norman conquest ensured that their settlement of England bore the tenurial imprint of their English and Scandinavian predecessors. The resulting rarity of compact and distinct territorial baronies deprived the Anglo-Norman aristocracy of one of the most important conditions for the maintenance of honorial justice and administrative and political resistance to the pretensions of the Crown. Moreover, the scattering of the lands of the king through almost every shire in the land meant that royal influence was ever-present. Everywhere in western Europe the royal demesne and the exercise of royal justice marched hand in hand; the second was rarely exercised effectively far from the bases which the first provided. Hence the tenurial structure of Anglo-Norman England ensured the supremacy of the royal sheriff over the aristocratic bailiff; it facilitated the rapid penetration of civil jurisdiction by royal justices and royal procedures, so that within a century of the Conquest the baronial courts were already surrendering to the advantages of a centralized and efficient exercise of jurisdiction; and it enabled the Crown to enforce its demands for aid and service throughout the land. It also meant that rebellion in defence of aristocratic privilege and alleged or actual baronial prerogative was from the start deprived of that secure *point d'appui* which compact baronies provided; even at an early date English rebels aimed not at excluding the king's government but at controlling it. When, under Stephen, Geoffrey de Mandeville and his like sought hereditary shrievalties and justiciarships they were giving implicit recognition to this inherent strength in the position of the Crown; outside marcher territory the cause of aristocratic independence, pure and simple, was not even stillborn; it was inconceivable. Hence while the demand for liberties on the continent was aimed at municipal independence, as in Lombardy in 1183, or at aristocratic immunity, as in the

German concessions of 1220 and 1231 or the French charters of 1315, in England it was aimed at the control and subjection of the administrative functions of the Crown. These came to be regarded, not as competitive intrusions into local affairs, but as necessary machinery, in the direction and exercise of which the community must participate. The community of the realm of the thirteenth century had its roots deep in the social and tenurial structure of Anglo-Norman England.

Yet the organization of such opposition to the pretensions of the Crown required thought and time: thought because it depended on a political theory of monarchical responsibility and communal participation in government, time because it could only spring from generations of experience of a royal government developing both in function and efficiency. Meanwhile circumstances told in favour of the Crown. Its policies were so related to existing conventions and political assumptions that it was usually able to present or fabricate some legal justification for its policies, if any were required. King John demanded reliefs which sometimes amounted to thousands of pounds, but there was nothing to determine the size of such payments and the amounts were therefore negotiable. Kings sold the marriage of heiresses for high prices on a marriage market, but there was no one to deny their right to dispose of heiresses and there were always eager buyers. No one could find grounds for preventing the Crown from controlling the estates of royal wards, or from improving the administration of its own estates. No one would deny its rights to pecuniary aids or to military service. All were agreed that the king, even if only considered as a feudal lord, had responsibilities in exercising justice among his vassals. All this was accepted because the Crown's tenants-in-chief, those namely who could oppose them most effectively, depended on these same rights for the maintenance and effective exploitation of their own estates. The great men of the land and the king derived their power from the same sources. Nothing was so ingrained in their minds as title to property.

Yet the majesty of the Crown, the territorial power of the monarchy and the increase in administrative skills enabled the Norman and Angevin kings to make far more of these rights than they had ever been intended to contain. From the English Danegeld sprang attempts to assess and re-assess effective taxation on land. From the king's right to pecuniary aid sprang the effective taxation of revenues and chattels. From the king's right to improve the administration of his own demesne lands sprang improved methods of administering both secular and ecclesiastical lands in royal custody and attempts to raise the profits of the administration of the shires above the established levels of the ancient farms. From the king's responsibilities in exercising justice sprang a jurisdictional system which eroded the feudal courts and became a major source of profit to the Crown. From the king's hunting rights emerged a concept of the royal forest and a special legal system for its administration which was used as a means of preventing or exploiting the effective economic development of private land within the royal forest. From the king's right to feudal military service there developed a system, part military, part financial, whereby kings expected their vassals to contribute either in men or in money to armies which served for long periods on the continent and marched to the furthest limits of the Angevin Empire. In almost every field the vassals of the Crown were faced with a system of government which was increasingly burdensome and detestable, but which was nevertheless securely grounded in the traditional rights compounded in the Anglo-Norman monarchy of the Conqueror.[12]

This could not be done without men to work the system. It required the creation of a class of administrators, many of them ordained clergy, who operated the central machinery

---

[12] For a discussion of some of these problems, see J. O. Prestwich (1954), 19–43.

of government, acted as itinerant justices, ambassadors or financial agents, and ultimately found reward, if not always rest, in preferment to a bishopric. These were the men who, as Peter of Blois remarked, 'covered the land like locusts'.[13] But they were not alone. The king also called on laymen: great lords who supported him in war and gave him counsel and advice; men of proved administrative ability who acted as sheriffs, barons of the Exchequer and justices; military commanders and castellans who directed the king's campaigns abroad and were his first line of defence against rebellion at home. These men could only be maintained by reward, by the skilful exercise of royal patronage in which land, privilege, the marriage of an heiress or the custody of a royal ward, were used to rivet them securely to the interests of the king. The Crown's exploitation of its feudal prerogatives and its exercise of patronage therefore went hand in hand in 'raising men from the dust' as in the reign of Henry I,[14] or in giving Tourangeau, Poitevin and Flemish soldiers a stake in the country as in the reign of King John. The royal favour was streamed towards those who were useful or too powerful to be ignored; it was diverted from those who could be crushed or were too dangerous to be encouraged. The effect was to intrude new men into a social hierarchy which was rigid enough to react with violent prejudice against the newcomer and the foreigner, but was not yet so rigid that it attempted to exclude the *nouveau riche*, the soldier or the administrator by laying down strict qualifications of blood and birth as conditions of entry. The Anglo-Norman baronage was not a *noblesse*. Moreover it was fed on ideals and literary conventions in which lords alternately

---

[13] *Epistolae Petri Blesensis*, in Migne, *Patrologia Latina*, CCVII, p. 298.
[14] For a later re-assessment of Henry I which concentrates on this theme, see Southern (1962), 127–69. See also Barbara M. Walker, 'Henry I's "Old Men"', *Journal of British Studies*, VIII (1968), 1–21; C. Warren Hollister, 'Magnates and curiales in early Norman England', *Viator*, VIII (1977), 63–81, 'Henry I and the Anglo-Norman Magnates', *Anglo-Norman Studies*, II (1979), 93–107; Green (1986), pp. 134–214; Charlotte A. Newman, *The Anglo-Norman Nobility in the Reign of Henry I* (Philadelphia, 1988), pp. 91–162.

rewarded faithful and valuable service in this way, or punished the treacherous or the disobedient by exclusion from favour, the manifestation of ill-will or some open act of disciplinary violence. Thus the king's exercise of patronage and disposal of his favour was no easier to attack than his exploitation and expansion of his feudal prerogatives.

These developments in government occurred in a society which was rapidly becoming richer, more varied and more settled, a society which revolved around land, its inheritance, division, sale, conveyance and exploitation. All this necessitated a more effective and more complicated legal system which would provide not only for the interests of individual landowners but for the needs of great corporations, both chartered towns and ecclesiastical foundations. Meanwhile the rarity of concentrated baronies, the creation of marriage portions, the processes of subenfeoffment whereby tenants-in-chief also came to hold property as mesne lords, ensured that no effective distinction could be drawn between a class of undertenants and the smaller body of men who held directly of the Crown. The new legal structure therefore had to provide security throughout the whole social range of free tenants; there could be no caste distinction. And this was emphasized by the concentration of legal processes not in the feudal courts, but primarily in the courts of the local communities of shire, hundred and town, in which territorial power created social and political influence rather than legal privilege. By John's reign the 'county' had come to be the great administrative and social force in medieval England, at once an administrative circumscription, a local court, and a focus for local loyalties and local society. Administratively and geographically it was the shire, the *comitatus*; socially and emotionally it was the native homeland, the *patria*. It could be represented, it could negotiate with the king, it could suffer penalties and it could hold privileges. It was the bedrock of English society and government.

Kings governed this society in a manner which was essentially contradictory. Much of their administration was concerned with meeting social needs, with providing the order and the routine systems of administration which such a society increasingly required. Much again was concerned with exploiting economic development by improving the yield of royal estates, or tightening up the forest law, or devising new methods of taxation which would keep abreast with the increasing wealth of the country. Here the Crown was simply doing in its own way what other landowners were also doing in their appropriate fashion; Domesday Book had its 'satellite' private surveys, just as the Exchequer Pipe rolls were mirrored in the Pipe rolls of the bishopric of Winchester. Both Crown and private landowner were competing to exploit the new wealth; just as the monks of Bury could assert that the 'revenues and issues of all good vills and boroughs of England are growing and increasing to the good of their possessors and the profit of their lords',[15] so King Richard's ministers could lay down that land was to be taxed 'according to whether the land is good or bad and whether the price is rising or falling'.[16] Sometimes in this process the Crown enjoyed economic windfalls which were quickly exploited by administrative genius. By the third quarter of the twelfth century the need for financial credit had attracted a large enough body of wealthy Jews to England for them to become one of the major fiscal resources of the monarchy, all the more easily exploited because the Jews had few defences in times of crisis when the Crown's needs were urgent, and because their debtors had no defences at all once the Jew was dead and his loans had reverted to the Crown, which was only too ready to execute the doctrine of the Church that the usurer should not be allowed to pass on the profits of his trade to his heirs. The England of King Richard and King John presented numer-

---

[15] *Chronicle of Jocelin of Brakelond*, ed. E. H. Butler, p. 77.   [16] *Hoveden*, I, 265.

ous rewarding possibilities of this kind which had not been available to the Conqueror: new possibilities of taxing trade, of establishing and exploiting regalian mining rights, of controlling weights, measures and currency. None of these were open to similar exploitation by the king's tenants-in-chief, although they too were quick enough to use the new facilities for credit and to embark on trading and industrial ventures of their own. Hence the Crown enjoyed advantages in a world of economic opportunity in which all were driven on to success or down to disaster by rapidly rising prices and increasing costs which, if measured in the wages normally paid to knights, trebled in the forty years between the accession of Henry II and the early years of John. It was a world of great possibilities, but no place for the economically naïve, a fact of which some aristocratic families were made only too aware before Henry and his sons were dead.[17]

Even this, however, was not in itself sufficient to provoke a crisis of the dimensions of that which occurred in 1215. Competition for the rewards which economic development made possible could be, and was often, settled by compromise. If orders went out for the re-assessment of taxation on land to adjust it to the real value of estates, the Exchequer was ready to accept down payments which were much lower than the tax would properly have yielded, but which released it from the burdensome task of assessment.[18] If the government laid down strict regulations prescribing weights and measures, it was equally ready to sell exemptions to the cloth towns which presumably found it easier to buy this privilege than remake their looms to the newly prescribed

---

[17] For the effects of price inflation see Harvey (1973) and Palmer (1985), and for further comment and some reservations see Holt (1985a), pp. 20–1; (1991a), 17–18. In considering its effects we should remember that the law of inheritance was related in the first place, not to price movements, but to family structure, although both may respond to economic circumstances; and that, at the maximum estimate of a three-fold increase in prices between 1180 and 1220, the average annual rate of inflation was 2·78 per cent.

[18] See the arrangements made for the collection of the carucage of 1198 (*Hoveden*, IV, 46; *Pipe Roll 1 John*, pp. xix–xx; S. K. Mitchell, 1914, pp. 7–9).

national standard.[19] If the king and his officials were eager to enforce the forest regulations against the extension of the cultivated area within the royal forest, it was often only in order to levy fines and regular annual rents for such 'assarted' lands. If properly paid the Crown barked rather than bit. Yet this ever-present possibility of relaxation, politically enervating though it was, points to the essential cause of the crisis of 1215, for it marks the ultimate unwillingness of the Crown to submit itself to conventional or enacted rules similar to those it was imposing on others. In a society which increasingly required settled forms of legal procedure, accepted rules of inheritance and succession, and methods of administration which acknowledged rights of ownership, there was less and less room for a Crown which provided all this and yet reserved to itself the right to break, ignore, withhold, or suspend these very rules at its own convenience, or bent and twisted them to suit its immediate interest. It did not matter that the Crown was the most active experimental force in twelfth-century administration, for this was its crime as well as its justification. It mattered little that it ignored or suspended legal process less because of the whim of the king than because of the need to enforce policy ruthlessly in a society which, for all its increasing maturity, was often still on the verge of civil war. Retribution came simply because the Crown's unharnessed energy became steadily less convenient in an increasingly hidebound world. 1215 marked the decision to demand from the Crown that regularity of procedure and treatment which barons, knights and townsfolk had come to expect and had been led to accept in their dealings with each other. The pupils were now teaching the master the lesson he had taught them.

It was a lesson instilled over generations, and it is far from easy to determine the process of its growth, for it and the

---

[19] See Lady Stenton's comments on the enforcement of the Assize of Weights and Measures of 1196 in *Pipe Roll 4 John*, pp. xx–xxi.

evidence grew together. The trend towards orderly government, the multiplication of records, and their increasingly
secure preservation were all part of the same process. It is no
accident that Magna Carta occurred in the reign of John for
it was only then that the activity of the government was first
fully recorded, and this in itself has ensured that more of the
record has survived. To proceed back from John's reign is to
enter a much darker period, illuminated in the reign of
Henry II by the annual Exchequer accounts enrolled in the
Pipe rolls, and in earlier reigns still by the Pipe roll of 1130,
the early twelfth-century legal collections, the sparse survival of writs and charters, and the solitary monumental
achievement embodied in Domesday Book. Hence it is
frequently impossible to distinguish between new policies
and new evidence, and there is little doubt that this has
contributed to those interpretations which have laid the
blame for the events of 1215 on the personality and failings
of King John. Origins are never easy to trace, least of all the
origins of political discontent, and the origins of the rebellion
of 1215 were much older than John's reign and lay much
deeper than the shallows of his character.

Despite the sparsity of the early evidence it is quite certain
that some of the issues of 1215 were under review at a very
early stage in the development of Anglo-Norman government. The Charter of Liberties of Henry I puts this beyond
any doubt.[20] In some ways this charter is a readily comprehended piece of evidence. It moved easily through concessions on a wide range of feudal matters: tenants-in-chief
were to pay reasonable reliefs; the king's control of marriages was to be strictly limited; widows were to have their

[20] The text of one version is given below, appendix 4, p. 412. It is also available in *Stubbs's
Charters*, 9th ed., pp. 117–19. For the many MSS of the text see Liebermann (1894) and
Regesta Regum Anglo-Normannorum, II, ed. Charles Johnson and H. A. Cronne (Oxford,
1956), no. 488. See also D. Whitelock, M. Brett, and C. N. L. Brooke, *Councils and
Synods*, I, pt. II (Oxford, 1981), no. 108. There is no surviving original, but the MS
tradition is too consistent to permit the amendment to cap. 6 proposed by S. E. Thorne
(*E.H.R.*, XCIII, 1978, 794).

dower and marriage-portion and were not to be distrained to marry; and barons were to have free testamentary powers. But it did not penetrate far beyond the rough-and-ready exploitation of the feudal prerogatives of the Crown which marked a comparatively primitive state in the development of royal administration. On wider topics it forbade excessive pecuniary penalties and acknowledged the principle that they should fit the crime. It touched on another vitally important matter in laying down that the bounds of the royal forest were to be restricted to the limits established at the death of William I, and it also acquitted the demesnes of knights from paying geld.[21] But it had nothing to say of the attempts made by William Rufus's minister, Ranulf Flambard, to extend taxation on land,[22] or of the recurrent demands for military service which the stormy history of the early Norman kingdom necessitated, or of the financial exploitation of shire administration. Moreover, it is not easy to relate it to contemporary practice even where it dealt with comparatively simple feudal matters. It repeatedly assumed or stated that the government of William Rufus had overstepped the mark: in assessing reliefs, in accepting proffers for land and in extending the royal forests.[23] It also implied that both William II and William I had been guilty of excess in the monetary penalties which they had exacted.[24] But Henry's charter was the work of a transitory crisis; it was almost an election address in which he was concerned to buy support by denouncing the less popular actions of his predecessors. Hence it conveys an exaggerated impression of the clarity of feudal custom and of the sharpness of the contrast between it and the exactions of William Rufus. Indeed on many points its provisions are the first surviving indication of what custom was, or was

---

[21] For a discussion of the significance of this concession, see Hoyt (1950), pp. 52–8.
[22] See R. W. Southern, 'Ranulf Flambard and Early Anglo-Norman Administration', *T.R.H.S.* 4th ser., XVI (1933), 106–9.
[23] Caps. 2, 6, 10.   [24] Cap. 8.

thought to be, and even then they were frequently vague. For example, Rufus's demands for large sums from tenants succeeding to estates[25] were now to be replaced by 'just and lawful' reliefs, whatever that might mean;[26] use was also made of the time before the accession of the Conqueror[27] or the law of King Edward[28] as conveniently vague terms of reference. Good and evil customs were not so easily separated as the opening words of the charter suggested. Indeed the charter seems to have defined custom as much as it was defined by it. But it was custom as an ideal rather than a fact, for once he was past the point of crisis Henry I conveniently forgot it. The financial burdens and political control revealed in the Pipe roll of 1130 are a far surer guide to the nature and quality of his rule than the hasty promises of 1100. The charter remained a dead letter, even for those who might have profited from it most. Despite the many apparent opportunities, it never became an objective or rallying point of rebellion until, almost a hundred years old, it came to be involved in the genesis of Magna Carta. It was to the struggle for the greater and later concession that it owed its fame.

This sharp contrast stands as a warning against any easy assumption that development was even and continuous. The 'anarchy' of Stephen's reign provides yet another, for like the temporary crisis which affected Henry's fortunes in 1100, it forced the Crown to make concessions. This time, however, the crisis was severe and prolonged. Some measure

---

[25] Cap. 2. The sense of *redimet* seems to be that the tenant was required to pay an amount comparable to the purchase price of the land, thus confusing the relief with a proffer for land to which a petitioner had no claim.

[26] One contemporary indication is to be found in the Leis Willelme, cap. 20, 24, which states that a vavassor was expected to pay a relief of 100s. This conforms to later payments of 100s. per fee demanded from tenants in knight service, but the Leis confuses this payment with the English heriot, and the payment is not stated to be per fee (*Gesetze*, I, 507).

Some twelfth-century charters suggest that reliefs might be lower than 100s. per fee (F. M. Stenton, 1961, pp. 163–4).

[27] Cap. 8.   [28] Caps. 9, 13.

of its depth is to be found in the Pipe rolls of the early years of Henry II, which record levels of revenue far lower than those he obtained in the middle years of the reign and far lower than the astonishing figure of royal revenues indicated by Henry I's Pipe roll of 1130. If this is to be taken at its face value Henry's revenues in this year amounted to nearly £24,700. Against this, Henry II's revenues, as recorded in the Pipe rolls, only exceeded £15,000 once in the first decade of his reign, only exceeded £20,000 four times in the first twenty years, and only surpassed the figure for 1130 on three occasions during the whole reign.[29] This striking contrast is only partially explicable in terms of the increasing use of the Chamber and special Exchequers as alternative machinery of account which left little if any record on the Pipe rolls.[30] It also represents a real and serious setback in the advance of the administrative and financial powers of the Crown. This was manifested in many ways: in the large number of individual exemptions from Danegeld and shire aids which were recorded in the early rolls of Henry II, and

[29] I have used the figures provided by Ramsay (1925), I, 53–191. I have not accepted his addition to the revenues of 1130 of an estimated £2000 for missing counties.

Ramsay's figures are for the revenues paid or accounted for, not revenues assessed. Figures for the latter are given by Stubbs (*Gesta Regis Henrici Secundi*, Rolls Series, II, xciv, xcix) and have been used by some later writers (J. O. Prestwich, 1954, 23); they present an even more dramatic contrast but are less indicative of real income or of the Exchequer's capacity to enforce collection. Neither set of figures distinguishes between revenue assessed in the current year and revenue assessed previously. This matter is of special importance in the case of the isolated roll of 1130, which deserves re-examination aimed at establishing the probable dates of the original assessments, and estimating the amount of backlog. Whether this roll represents an exceptional or normal year for Henry I will be more difficult to determine. It would, however, be surprising if further investigation were to confirm Ramsay's view that 'the year cannot be considered a typical one, but rather one of moderation, and relaxation of taxation' (Ramsay, 1925, I, 53). Compare Doris M. Stenton (1964), pp. 62–5.

In an exhaustive recalculation of the roll of 1130 Green (1982) has amended Ramsay's figure to £26,480. For recalculation of some of his figures for later years and for comment on his method see Holt (1984), 95–7.

[30] See J. E. A. Jolliffe, 'The Chamber and the Castle Treasures under King John', *Studies in Medieval History presented to F. M. Powicke* (Oxford, 1948), pp. 117–42; 'The Camera Regis under Henry II', *E.H.R.* LXVIII (1953), 1–21, 337–62; H. G. Richardson, 'The Chamber under Henry II', *E.H.R.* LXIX (1954), 596–611; R. A. Brown, 'The Treasury of the Later Twelfth Century', *Studies presented to Sir Hilary Jenkinson* (Oxford, 1957), pp. 35–49; Richardson & Sayles (1963), pp. 229–39.

perhaps even more in what the rolls do not contain. It is not until 1163 and 1165 that they record judicial activity comparable to that in the roll of 1130. In 1130 eleven counties in the custody of Aubrey de Vere and Richard Basset had yielded a surplus revenue of 1000 m.[31] No such increase was demanded by Henry II until the last few years of his reign, and the leeway was not finally made up until the reign of John.[32] These are symptoms of the malady which had afflicted the Crown under Stephen. It had been serious – hence Henry's vigorous repudiation of claims based on title and precedent established under his predecessor. It was also important, for it interposed a long period of relaxation between the organized and oppressive administrations of Henry I and Henry II. It therefore threw Henry II's work into relief, exaggerated its novelty and added to its apparent burdens. Try as he might, Henry II could not escape from Stephen.

Henry II's reign was the turning point. The Charter of Liberties of Henry I was concerned with a relatively primitive administrative machine which was still exploiting the perquisites of the Anglo-Saxon monarchy. The Great Charter of 1215 probed into a vastly more complicated system of government. The difference between the two is the measure of Henry II's achievement, for Stephen's reign deprived him of immediate and easy access to the administrative processes of his grandfather's government, and by the end of his reign he had created a pattern of government which Hubert Walter, minister first of Richard and then of John, and John himself, for all their inventiveness, did little more than develop and amend in detail. Henry II was the architect both of the fortunes and failings of his house; he, perhaps even as much as John, was the real object of attack in Magna Carta. Yet this was not explicit in the Charter, for blame is usually attached to those who consummate rather

[31] *Pipe Roll 31 Henry I*, p. 63.   [32] Mills (1925), 158–61.

than originate disasters. John consummated what Henry II had begun. Even the loss of Normandy was foreshadowed by the progressive abandonment of Henry's ambitious projects in southern France which was marked by the Treaty of Montmirail, the rebellion of 1173 and his final humiliation at the hands of Philip Augustus and his own sons at Gisors at the end of his life. This ominous recurrence of failure could not be halted. And as the Angevins moved from Henry's grandiose schemes, through their far-flung systems of alliance, their defensive campaigns and their family squabbles to the final disaster, so they increased their demands on England. In so doing they forced the realm into a mould the shape of which it has borne throughout its history. For all their failures and failings, Henry and his sons were great kings.

This new administrative drive gathered increasing momentum as Henry's reign progressed. In his assizes he brought together procedures and instruments, used voluntarily and intermittently hitherto, into a national system of criminal and civil justice.[33] Beginning in 1158 he and his sons adjusted the system of military service so that it could provide the small, expert, long-term force which their continental campaigns required; they re-assessed scutage, replaced or supplemented it by fines, and experimented with several methods of converting a feudal levy into a professional army.[34] By the later years of his reign Henry was administering escheats and wardships through custodians who were expected to account for the total yield rather than a fixed farm. This method, best illustrated in the *Rotuli de Dominabus* of 1185, was developed by Hubert Walter, who also demanded increments on the farm of royal demesnes

---

[33] For assessments of the antecedents to Henry's measures see Naomi Hurnard (1941), 374–410; R. C. Van Caenegem, in *Royal Writs* (1959); Doris M. Stenton (1964), 22–53; R. C. Van Caenegem (1973).
[34] Powicke (1961), ch. VIII, is still essential reading. For later evidence see *Pipe Roll 17 John*, pp. 71–84; and for an important revision of the effects of these developments see Keefe (1983).

and shires, and by John who used custodians to administer the ecclesiastical estates in his hands during the Interdict and even attempted to extend the system to the shires by appointing custodian sheriffs who were expected to account for their total receipts.[35] Henry extended the royal forests to the widest bounds they ever reached and vigorously exploited them through punitive investigations; his sons continued the work in the eyres of 1198, 1207 and 1212.[36] The Jews, the one major source of credit in England at this time, were brought under similar close scrutiny with the establishment of the special Exchequer for the collection of the debts of Aaron of Lincoln in 1186 and of an Exchequer of the Jews and a secure system for the enrolment of debts in 1194; these methods both gave the Crown an accurate basis for assessing taxation on the Jews and facilitated the collection of their debts when their death brought their outstanding assets into the hands of the Crown.[37] Henry, his sons, and their ministers took all this in their stride and more. They experimented with new systems of taxation: in 1194, 1198 and 1200 with attempts to re-assess taxation on land; in 1188, 1194, 1203 and 1207 with methods of taxing revenues and chattels;[38] in 1202–5 with a highly organized customs system;[39] in 1211 with duties on imported dyestuffs;[40] in 1198 and throughout John's reign with a levy on the Cornish tin industry.[41] Meanwhile they exploited the Crown's

[35] On the demesne see Hoyt (1950), pp. 92 ff., and Harvey (1974), 345–59; on the increments and profits on shires see Mills (1925), 151 ff.; Painter (1949), pp. 122–3; Holt (1961), pp. 152–7; Harris (1964); and Carpenter (1976); on the Interdict see Cheney (1949), 129 ff.

[36] See the introductions to the Pipe rolls of the relevant years, and Young (1979), pp. 18–73.

[37] Alice C. Cramer, 'The Origins and Functions of the Jewish Exchequer', *Speculum*, XVI (1941), 226–9; H. G. Richardson, *The English Jewry under the Angevin Kings* (London, 1960), pp. 135 ff.

[38] Mitchell (1914); idem, *Studies in Medieval Taxation*, ed. S. Painter (New Haven, 1951). See also the Pipe rolls of the relevant years.

[39] *Pipe Roll 6 John*, pp. xliii–xlv; N. B. Gras, *The English Customs System* (Cambridge, Mass., 1918), pp. 48–53, 217–22.

[40] *Pipe Roll 13 John*, pp. 186–7.

[41] G. R. Lewis, *The Stannaries* (Cambridge, Mass., 1924), pp. 35–7, 133–6.

feudal prerogatives as never before. The Pipe rolls of the later years of Henry II are the first to record with any frequency those heavy reliefs, amercements, fines and offerings which were to become an object of attack in Magna Carta.[42]

Within this massive expansion three periods seem to have been especially important: first, the years of re-organization following the rebellion of 1173 in which Henry began to impose punitive monetary penalties more and more frequently and set on foot that recovery of royal rights and re-imposition of discipline which culminated in the Assize of Northampton of 1176; secondly, the years after 1194 when Hubert Walter re-organized English administration in order to pay King Richard's ransom and finance the defence of Normandy;[43] and finally the period after the loss of Normandy in 1204, when the means of government, now for the first time under the continuous personal supervision of the king, were directed increasingly towards a war of reconquest. England had become the remnant and the basic substance of the Angevin empire, the sole remaining source of an army capable of fighting the French and of the subsidies vital for maintaining alliances on the continent. Yet when rebellion came there is little indication that it was caused by financial exhaustion. It sprang rather from a refusal to suffer it.

To describe any medieval government as a system or pattern, still more one which helped to mould a country's history, is to claim much. In this case the claim is easily justified. Henry's legal measures pieced together the framework of English justice. He and his sons established methods of taxation from which the classic subsidy of medieval and

---

[42] See Round's introductions to *Pipe Roll 22 Henry II*, pp. xxii ff.; *Pipe Roll 23 Henry II*, pp. xxiii, xxv–xxvi; *Pipe Roll 28 Henry II*, pp. xxii ff. He emphasized the point again in *M.C.C.E.* p. 62.

[43] See, for example, Lady Stenton's comment on the rolls on the middle years of Richard's reign, that 'they give the impression of a country taxed to the limit' (*Pipe Roll 9 Richard I*, p. xiii).

Tudor England was derived. They established many of the administrative concepts of medieval England, from the ancient demesne of the Crown[44] to the private franchises of the great palatinates.[45] Their methods of military administration foreshadowed those on which were raised the armies of the Hundred Years War. And they ensured that every branch of the administration was subjected to central supervision through the transfer of information on interlocking records and enrolments which ensured central control by the Exchequer and the king's itinerant household offices of Chamber and Wardrobe. Here too, in seeking mobility, speed and simplicity, they set the pattern for the future in devising methods of household account and in using a small seal as a method of authorizing royal orders.[46] They created a system capable of functioning in the absence of the king; indeed, it reached one of its peaks of efficiency during Richard's wars in Normandy when it was under the able direction of Hubert Walter. It was even capable of functioning effectively during the long minority of Henry III, after a civil war and a foreign invasion. And they imposed it throughout the whole realm. Henry, and John more emphatically still, were the first kings to bring the northern counties under secure control and submit them to a burden of government comparable to that on the rest of the country.[47] Angevin government was not only systematic, but national, even on occasion imperial.[48]

---

[44] Hoyt (1950), pp. 171 ff.   [45] Helen M. Cam (1957), 427–42.

[46] On the financial aspects of this see above, p. 39, n. 30. On the administrative aspects see T. F. Tout, *Chapters in Administrative History*, I, 151–69; V. H. Galbraith (1948), ch. 5; and H. G. Richardson's introduction to *Memoranda Roll 1 John* (Pipe Roll Soc., new series, XXI).

[47] Holt (1963), pp. 13–14; Holt (1961), pp. 194–216.

[48] For a comprehensive examination of Henry's continental administration see J. Boussard, *Le Gouvernement d'Henri II Plantagenet* (Paris, 1956). Boussard is enthusiastic – 'Pour une grande part, la France de saint Louis et l'Angleterre d'Édouard Ier sont le prolongement de l'œuvre d'Henry II' (p. 582). Compare my later doubts expressed in Holt (1985a), 42–4. These reservations were not shared by the late John Le Patourel whose intended work on the Angevin Empire was incomplete at his death. Something of its flavour is indicated in Le Patourel (1964, 1984). See also Gillingham (1984).

The rebellion of 1215 was directed against this system. It was aimed at limiting it, controlling it or destroying it. It was not concerned simply with the particular features of 'abuses' for which King John was personally responsible. It was concerned with the system as a whole. It placed Henry II, Richard I, John, their ministers and all their work, under examination and where necessary criticism. This was recognized long ago by Charles Bémont[49] and by Round.[50] It is an essential truth from which historians have been diverted far too readily by the absenteeism of King Richard, the colourful and vicious personality of King John, and the almost unquestioning acceptance in the Great Charter of the legal work of Henry II. It is quite unrealistic to maintain, with McKechnie, that 'powers used moderately and on the whole for national ends by Henry, were abused for selfish ends by both his sons'.[51] The Angevins stood or fell together. King John knew this. His opponents acknowledged it. The arguments between the two centred on it.[52] The system was attacked, not because it was abused, but because of what it was, and not simply because it aroused antagonism, but also because, as time passed, it revealed weaknesses and even invited criticism and opposition. It was not designed to fend off a rebellion the like of which no one foresaw.

The most obvious of these weaknesses arose from the Crown's need to underwrite the position of its supporters and officials with landed endowment. Such reward for service could scarcely be avoided given the social conventions of the time; it was an essential means both of emphasizing the value of the king's friendship and of bolstering the power and influence of his men. It could be met to some extent by rewarding the faithful with the grant of a well-endowed heiress or an escheat, but in the long run it

---

[49] Bémont (1892), pp. xv, xxii. [50] M.C.C.E. p. 62.
[51] McKechnie (1914), p. 20. [52] See below, pp. 115–17, 234.

involved the depletion of Crown lands. At the end of the twelfth century Gerald of Wales looked back on Stephen and Henry II as the great wasters of the royal demesne.[53] Under Henry I these alienated lands were valued in the Pipe roll of 1130 at £41. 6s. 8d. By 1154 the total had risen to £2450. 17s., and it continued to increase thereafter.[54] The resulting loss of revenue was not of major importance, for it was more than counter-balanced by increased efficiency in administering the remaining estates and the escheats and wardships which supplemented them. More serious was the fact that this exercise of royal patronage was a very uncertain political instrument. To endow a trusted supporter or official was one thing; to obtain similar support and service from his descendants was another. Indeed, as Stubbs indicated in a few perceptive paragraphs, the rebels of 1215 included many whose ancestors had been 'new men' in the reigns of Henry I or Henry II and had owed power and position to their service to the Crown.[55] Patronage controlled the first generation; thereafter, to be effective, it had to be renewed. Moreover, as time passed, it became less easy to exercise. The Conqueror had very nearly a free hand and the *tabula rasa* of a conquered country in planning the distribution of rewards.[56] The many rebellions between 1088 and 1106 gave Rufus and Henry I the opportunity to reward their supporters with forfeited estates.[57] But each successive wave of endowment left families high and dry in relative tenurial security. Moreover the opportunities for the replacement of the politically unreliable became less

---

[53] *Opera* (Rolls Series), VIII, 316.
[54] Ramsay (1925), I, 65, 185. See also Southern (1962), 157–69, and Green (1979, 1982) and (1986), 55–66. As she points out, the figure for *terrae datae* for Henry I is surprisingly low and may reflect a recent reassessment of the county farms which embodied earlier alienations; these, as she demonstrates, were very considerable. However, the extent of earlier alienation is not immediately relevant to my argument at this point.
[55] Stubbs (1896), I, 580–1 (see also Holt, 1961, p. 232).
[56] He had of course to pay attention to contributions which had been made to the expedition of 1066, to the status of his followers and to the existing pattern of English tenure.
[57] Southern (1962), 134, 160 ff.

frequent and less easy to grasp. The conflict between Stephen and Henry II was the last great occasion of this kind prior to 1215 and, since it was settled by compromise in 1153, it produced not so much a clean sweep as a mass of conflicting claims which bedevilled the business of the courts during the next generation. Henry and his sons ruled a much more settled realm in which their own legal measures reinforced inheritance and rights of tenure and in which local society had greater permanence and cohesion. To 'raise men from the dust' as Henry I had done was no longer so easy; the 'new men' were now regarded as upstarts and newcomers. The Conqueror's men had come not only from his own duchy, but also from Flanders, Brittany and Poitou. Under John, Poitevins, Tourangeaux and Flemings were coming to be denounced as aliens; one of the most potent and tiresomely reiterated complaints against him was that he had ignored his native subjects and relied on foreigners.[58]

However, Angevin government was not so narrowly based as this complaint would immediately suggest. The great offices of state, the positions in the household, the shrievalties and castellanships, were necessarily restricted in number and normally remained within the grasp of a small favoured group. But the whole system of administration depended on the co-operation and participation of barons, knights and free men throughout the land. They were required to play their part in war; they were used to assess taxes both on themselves and on others; they served as jurors, coroners, deputy-sheriffs, foresters, regarders and verderers, sometimes as justices or ambassadors. The local courts depended on them for their proper functioning; without them the new judicial procedures could not have worked; and as the king moved about the country so the greater among them came to his court to witness his acts, to give counsel or provide information, to present petitions or

[58] Holt (1963), pp. 24–6.

to receive instructions. One of the main effects of the measures of Henry II and his sons was to educate their subjects in government. As Stubbs remarked, the Great Charter was 'the consummation of the work for which unconsciously kings, prelates and lawyers' had 'been labouring for a century'.[59]

This paradox comes close to the heart of the matter. In the last resort the governed were also the governors. Indeed so far removed were the king's officials from the standards of efficiency and honesty of a modern civil service that their operations had to be submitted to periodic scrutiny. Angevin government owed much of its effectiveness to organized inquiry: to special and general commissions in which justices investigated royal rights, the efficiency of local administration and the behaviour of the king's officials.[60] In doing this they sought their information from local landowners in the local courts; in 1170 it was the 'barons, knights and free men of the shire' who answered the articles of the Inquest of Sheriffs which led to the dismissal of many of Henry II's local agents.[61] Such inquiries were designed primarily to protect the king's interests, but they could be used equally well to protect his subjects against the predatory official. In 1213 King John turned to investigations of this kind as a means of quietening discontent,[62] and in 1215 the barons appropriated these procedures to investigate the 'evil customs' of sheriffs and foresters through juries of twelve knights in each county. Here they drew directly on Angevin methods of government, simply changing emphasis and aim. Their measures had exact, even more detailed, precursors in caps. 1 and 8 of the inquest of 1170.

Court and country, therefore, were interdependent, not sharply divided. In contemporary thought the king and his

[59] Stubbs (1896), I, 571.
[60] For the development of the special and the general eyre in the Angevin period see Helen M. Cam, *Studies in the Hundred Rolls* (Oxford Social and Legal Studies, VI), pp. 10–20.
[61] *Stubbs's Charters*, p. 176.   [62] See below, pp. 212–13.

'native men' ruled the land together. In practice they worked in a necessary but uneasy relationship like that between a domineering conductor and a long-established orchestra. This interplay of function and interest marked every part of English society, for the local landowner was called to administer not just at the behest of the Crown, but because he held feudal property with judicial and administrative perquisites, and because he could make wider and wider claims to liberties based on prescriptive title or royal grant. Nowhere is the trend towards the Great Charter better or more subtly illustrated than in the proliferation and ramification of liberties and privileges. The Angevins not only taught their vassals to participate in government. They unwittingly led them to believe that they could get the kind of government they wanted.

CHAPTER 3

PRIVILEGE AND LIBERTIES

The exercise of royal patronage was both a personal and a social function. Kings could not restrict it to their immediate followers. All their tenants-in-chief were their immediate vassals with a claim upon the royal favour and an expectation of reward. Moreover most kings were in need of money. They might grant privilege for both financial and political gain, and at a crisis in royal fortunes, as under Stephen, the stream of privileges quickly expanded into a torrent. There were two aspects to the sale of privileges, the seller's and the buyer's. On the one hand it reflected the policies and difficulties of the king. On the other it represented what his subjects wanted to buy. Their proffers, recorded from the earliest Pipe roll onwards under the heading of 'new agreements' or 'new offerings', are one of the surest guides to their social and political aspirations.

These records reveal significant changes in the dispensation of privilege in the course of the twelfth century. The Pipe roll of 1130 and the rolls of the early years of Henry II suggest that the king's grants were making few permanent intrusions into the powers of the Crown. The most obvious of these is to be found in the numerous pardons of Danegeld, but, that apart, there is little evidence of irrecoverable wastage.[1] The rolls of John's reign present a very different picture. By his time the sale of privileges had come to involve the permanent and final alienation of the rights of

---

[1] For a discussion of Danegeld under Henry II see Painter (1943), pp. 74–9, and Judith A. Green, 'The last century of Danegeld', *E.H.R.*, XCVI (1981), 241–58. As Dr Green pointed out elsewhere (1979), there was severe erosion of the Domesday *terra regis* under William Rufus and Henry I.

the Crown. It is not easy to pin this change down within narrower limits, partly because the offerings recorded in the Pipe rolls are only a proportion of the total, but the crucial period seems to have come with the accession of Richard I. He, more than any other, wasted his inheritance in the massive sale of office and privilege in which he engaged before his departure on the Crusade. From this there was no recovery. Driven on by financial need and political difficulties, Richard engaged in further alienations after his return to Europe in 1194. Similar policies were followed by John, on his accession, again during the final crisis of the Norman wars in 1203–4, and finally during the political crisis of 1212–15. The contrast between Henry II and his sons lies not so much in any abuse by them of his system of government, as in the fact that they proceeded to sell what he had accumulated.

The motive in this was to raise money, to sacrifice the slow but sure returns which might be obtained from the maintenance of a royal forest, for example, for the quicker yield expected from a proffer for a charter of disafforestation. How far this contributed to a significant depletion in royal resources cannot be determined. However, its most important results were not financial but political. In the long run the sale of privilege whetted and even created an appetite for liberties. Men came to think that what they obtained by purchase should be theirs by right, and that what some could buy should be equally available to all. In 1215 those who hitherto had bought or tried to buy liberties now combined to fight for them.

However, this was the culmination of a long educative process in which social change, administrative development and the financial needs of the Crown all combined. It can best be illustrated by the emergence of certain types of proffer which the king came to accept and his vassals to make with increasing frequency. For example, by John's reign it had become quite common for men to buy the privilege of freedom from suit at the courts of shire and hundred and quittance from sheriff's aid. This privilege usually extended to the purchaser's free tenants; sometimes it included freedom from service on assizes and juries of recognition. Such a privilege might cost 50 m. or 100 m. Although the Pipe roll of Henry I contains earlier precedents,[2] it owed its form and popularity to the vast extension of the operations of royal justice under Henry II and his sons. It also owed something to the increasingly urgent demands for personal service overseas, for both Richard and John seem to have been ready to grant this privilege temporarily to those who gave such service. But if in this direction it was closely related to the administrative developments of the twelfth century, in another it was also connected with the crisis of 1215, for it was a precursor to the demand expressed in the Articles of the Barons that only the jurors and the two parties should be summoned to assizes.[3]

This link between the demands and arrangements of 1215–17 and the earlier purchase of privilege can be traced over a wide field. The extensive disafforestation initiated by the Charter of the Forest of 1217 was prefaced by numerous licences to cultivate land within the bounds and by the purchase of complete disafforestation. Men also tried to ensure that they should not be brought into court as either parties or jurors outside the counties in which they lived,[4] just as in 1215 they laid down that assizes were to be held in the county in which they originated.[5] Long before 1215 a man might make a proffer to be allowed to pay a 'reasonable' relief of £100 for a barony, the very sum laid down in Magna Carta.[6] Perhaps most strikingly of all, the Crown

---

[2] See the offer of £100 from the judges and jurors of Yorkshire that they might be released from further service (*Pipe Roll 31 Henry I*, p. 34).

[3] Articles of the Barons, cap. 8. See also Doris M. Stenton (1962), pp. 91–4.

[4] See the offer of Henry Batail in 1204 (*Pipe Roll 6 John*, p. 44; *Rot. Litt. Pat.* p. 38*b*).

[5] Magna Carta, cap. 18.

[6] *Pipe Roll 10 Richard I*, p. 222. It should be remembered that this is the only known definition of a 'reasonable' baronial relief prior to 1215. For reliefs see below, pp. 304–6.

was coming to accept so many proffers concerned with the marriage of heiresses and the remarriage of widows, that the principles laid down in 1215 did little more than confirm existing trends and ideas.[7] The Pipe roll of 1130 and the early rolls of Henry II reveal the existence of a vigorous marriage market under the direction of the Crown. The proffers of these years usually took the form of a straightforward bid for the hand of an heiress or widow. Some of these came from relatives who were trying to keep control of the marriage within the family; this motive certainly lay behind many similar offers made in the reign of King John. By his time, however, such offers had been supplemented by others in which this implied attempt to exclude royal influence was now stated explicitly. One of the first great stages in the emancipation of women is to be traced in the emergence of the proffer that they should not be distrained to marry for a second time without their consent. Such offers might come from a relative of a widow, perhaps from her father; many, however, came from the widow herself. They not only gave her freedom from a forced marriage but also frequently ensured that she received her proper dower and inheritance. Some widows even fined not only for their own freedom but also for the custody and marriage of their children.

The process is typically illustrated by the instances in the Fine roll of 1199. Nichola of Hemingford, widow of William le Rous, offered £100 so that she should not be forced to marry; it was accepted on condition that if she decided to marry again she should do it at the king's advice.[8] The widow of Ralph of Cornhill offered 200 m. and three palfreys that she should not be married to Godfrey of Louvain, that she could marry whomsoever she wished and have seisin of her lands; it was noted that she had married at her own choice and that the money was to be

---

[7] On the following compare Doris M. Stenton (1957), p. 51.
[8] *Rot. de Ob. et Fin.* p. 29.

paid.[9] Sibyl of Tingrith offered 200 m. for having her lands
in Martock and Wendover and for licence to marry whomsoever she wished of the king's faithful men.[10] Gundreda,
widow of Geoffrey de la Huse, offered 200 m. for the
custody of Geoffrey, her son and heir, and that she might
arrange his marriage when of age with the advice of friends
and relatives.[11] Such offers were not always successful;
Gundreda de la Huse's was cancelled and it was noted on the
roll that the custody of her son had been given to Robert de
Tregoz.[12] Nor were they directed exclusively against the
Crown's free exercise of its rights of marriage. On this same
roll Robert of Tattershall offered 15 m. that the mother of
William de Scalers should not be married except on the
king's instruction.[13] Nichola, daughter of Roland de Verdun, also produced 2 m. for an inquiry whether she had
been disseised of her land in Offerton and Aston on the
occasion when the earl of Chester had married her off to
Ansketil de Briquessart, whether she had held that land in
chief of the king, and whether accordingly she should have
been in the gift of the king and not of the earl of Chester.[14]
Yet the main effect of such proffers was to limit the Crown's
freedom of action. They form a link between the reforms
promised in the Charter of Henry I and the restrictions
imposed in caps. 7 and 8 of Magna Carta.

The Fine roll of 1199 is not in any way atypical. By the
last few years of his reign John was accepting such proffers
very frequently; they were recorded in phrases which
approach common form and approximate to the wording of
the Charter.[15] On these points John's concessions of 1215
can scarcely have contained any novelties to the men who
had drafted them. They were simply conveying in general
what the king had hitherto sold in particular. The same was
true of the provision that heirs should not be 'disparaged' by

9 *Ibid.* p. 37.   10 *Ibid.* p. 2.   11 *Ibid.* p. 8.   12 *Ibid.*
13 *Ibid.* p. 29.   14 *Ibid.* p. 47.   15 See below, pp. 197–9.

marriage to someone of lower social status.[16] This simply restated a principle which King John had often imposed when he granted custody of heirs with their marriage. He might insist on it even when the recipient was one of his favoured agents. The Fine roll of 1199 records that William Briwerre, one of the barons of the Exchequer, offered 210 m. for the custody of the lands of Ralf Murdac and Walter de Glanville and the marriage of their daughters, on the condition that they should not be disparaged.[17] One could choose any Fine roll of John's reign and find a scattering of such entries.[18] 'No disparagement' was becoming one of the stock phrases of government. In 1215 the Crown had to honour it.[19]

In many ways therefore the Charter simply confirmed what men had come to expect from government and had often bought as a royal boon. There is, nevertheless, a big difference between the individual purchase of a privilege and the acquisition of that privilege by a community. The shift from individual to communal or corporate privilege was indeed one of the decisive achievements of 1215. Yet even here there were strong, determining precedents. Magna Carta was not a sudden jump into the darkness of corporate liberties but rather the last strides of a long journey which had started far back in the history of the English kingdom, and which had been illuminated in the twelfth century by the increasing confidence with which men sought and granted such liberties. In the forefront of this march had been the towns. In 1215 Magna Carta owed much to the precedent of municipal privilege.

In some respects this debt is obvious. The barons' victory was secured by the capture of London and the support of what must have been an influential section of the city. The

---

[16] Magna Carta, cap. 6.   [17] Rot. de Ob. et Fin. p. 10.
[18] For a discussion of similar arrangements later in the reign see below, pp. 190–1, 197–9.
[19] For further discussion of 'no disparagement' see Holt (1985b), especially pp. 24–8 where further evidence is produced that the proviso originated with the Crown.

Charter itself confirmed and extended the privileges of London and other towns.[20] One of the baronial leaders, Robert fitz Walter, was lord of Baynard Castle and hence Procurator and banneret of London and commander of the city host.[21] The Mayor of London, Serlo the mercer, was one of the Twenty-Five barons set up by the security clause of the Charter, and indeed the Twenty-Five may have owed something of their constitution to the capital, for the only obvious precedent for such a number is in the London council of twenty-five mentioned by the city chronicler, fitz Thedmar, under 1200–1.[22] Besides these superficial connexions there were deeper, more obscure ties. One of the clearest expressions of the constitutional views which lay behind the Charter comes from the well-known London version of the laws of Edward the Confessor.[23] Moreover, the whole baronial movement seems to have been infected by doctrines which stemmed ultimately from the communal movements of the continent and perhaps more immediately from the commune established at London in 1191.[24] Just as communal liberties had been won by a sworn association whereby citizens pledged themselves to fight for their liberties, so the barons pledged themselves to fight for the liberties of the realm. Contemporaries described their oath, like other communal oaths, as a 'conjuration'. Just as the Londoners had required Stephen in 1135 and John and the magnates in 1191 to pledge support of their liberties,[25] so the barons in 1215 required John and his supporters to

[20] See below, pp. 241, 320–1.
[21] Williams (1963), pp. 26–7. For further links between fitz Walter and the ruling city families see ibid. p. 51 and Brooke (1975), pp. 53, 216. Fitz Walter's title was of some formal importance. In 1216 he preceded the Mayor in performing homage to Prince Louis of France (Annals of Southwark and Merton, p. 50).
[22] Liber de Antiquis Legibus, p. 2.
[23] See below, pp. 93–5.
[24] For the London commune see Round (1899), pp. 219–60; James Tait, The Medieval English Borough, pp. 177–83; Williams (1963), pp. 9 ff. and Brooke (1975), pp. 45–7. There are less obvious precedents in the Norman communes founded by Richard and John (see Powicke, 1961, pp. 211–12).
[25] Gesta Stephani, p. 4; Richard of Devizes, pp. 48–9; Hoveden, III, 141.

pledge their acceptance of the Charter. Indeed, in demanding a general oath in which all pledged support to the Twenty-Five baronial guarantors, the barons seem to have envisaged the establishment of one great 'commune of all the land'.[26] They were not alone in borrowing in this way. King John had already adapted the communal oath and organization in preparing the national militia in the face of a threatened French invasion in 1205.[27] The barons were now turning his own methods against him.

Besides this general debt to the doctrines underlying municipal privilege the men of 1215 could acknowledge many detailed precedents to their demands in the borough charters of the twelfth and thirteenth centuries. On mercantile questions this was obvious. Cap. 41 of the Charter was an amplification of the very common provisions in municipal charters concerning freedom to trade and free access to markets.[28] Cap. 33, which provided for the destruction of fish-weirs on the Thames, Medway and elsewhere, was an immediate repetition of a privilege included in the London charters of 1196 and 1199.[29] Moreover many towns had already obtained limitations on feudal rights of lordship which were closely similar to those the Charter eventually contained in 1215. By 1200 Tewkesbury, Haverfordwest, Pembroke, Cardiff and Bideford had all acquired freedom from relief or heriot or a fixed limitation on these charges.[30] The burgesses of Okehampton had largely excluded the lord's rights of marriage over heiresses and widows.[31] At Pembroke the wardship of heirs and their inheritance lay with those to whom the deceased had committed it, or, if

---

[26] 'communa totius terrae', Magna Carta, cap. 61.

[27] Gerv. Cant. II, 96–7. This document deals with the organization of the 'communes' of shires, towns and vills under local constables who were to be responsible for the mustering of their local forces. All over twelve were to swear to obey their orders (see also Stubbs's Charters, pp. 276–7).

[28] Ballard (1913), pp. 197–9, 214–16.

[29] Ibid. p. 200. The Medway was not included until 1199. Magna Carta added the phrase 'and throughout all England'.

[30] Ibid. pp. 75–6.   [31] Ballard (1913), pp. 76–7.

intestate, with his friends.[32] At Egremont the burgesses gave their lord an aid for the ransoming of his body, the knighting of one of his sons, the marriage of one of his daughters, or, under the view of twelve burgesses, when the knights of the fee gave an aid.[33] The burgesses of Swansea were already used to a limitation on their lord's demands for military service: if they could return from an expedition the same night, then they went at their own expense, if not then their lord paid.[34] At Corbridge the lord's bailiff was forbidden to take prises for his own use except by the will of the burgesses, provided that they did not refuse to sell their goods to him if necessary.[35] In many of the major towns there was some regulation restricting the size of amercements, either by imposing a fixed limit, as at London in 1131 or at Bristol in 1188,[36] or by insisting that amercements should be imposed according to customary local procedures, as at Winchester in 1190,[37] or by providing for the assessment of forfeitures by a jury, as at Pontefract in 1194.[38] Throughout the land, in fact, townsmen already enjoyed many of the privileges which the barons sought from the king in 1215.

This accumulation of privilege must have had its effects outside the limits of the boroughs. The city walls were no constitutional *cordon sanitaire*, if only because these privileges involved the grantors as well as the recipients, king and magnates as well as burgesses. Swansea owed its privileges to William, earl of Warwick, Tewkesbury its to the earls of Gloucester. The author of the privileges of Egremont was Richard de Lucy, who died in 1212; his widow married Thomas of Moulton, one of the leading opponents of King John in Lincolnshire, and his daughters married Thomas's sons.[39] Pontefract owed its privileges to Roger de Lacy,

---

[32] *Ibid.* p. 78.　　[33] *Ibid.* p. 91.　　[34] *Ibid.* p. 89.　　[35] *Ibid.* p. 235.
[36] *Ibid.* pp. 151–2.　　[37] *Ibid.* p. 152.　　[38] *Ibid.* p. 154.
[39] For further comment on Thomas see below, pp. 61–3, 110, and Holt (1961), pp. 57–9, 155–6.

constable of Chester, whose son, John, was one of the Twenty-Five barons of the Charter in 1215.[40] Another of the Twenty-Five, John fitz Robert, was the author of the charter which gave the burgesses of Corbridge their freedom from arbitrary prises, and William Marshal, earl of Pembroke, under whose seal the Great Charters of 1216 and 1217 were issued, was responsible for the limitation of reliefs at Haverfordwest and of rights of marriage at Kilkenny. But before all these there was King John himself who was one of the chief authors of municipal privilege throughout the land and was intimately connected with the development of the liberties of London, from his alliance with the Commune in 1191 to his attempt to retain the allegiance of the capital in 1215 by the grant of an elective mayoralty.[41] John's borough charters cannot be explained away entirely as political or financial expedients to which he resorted in times of crisis. One of the most remarkable grants of the twelfth century was made to Bristol in 1189–91. This laid down that no one was to be fined 'except according to the law of the hundred'[42] up to a maximum penalty of £2. No burgess was to be distrained for a debt unless he were the principal or a guarantor. Burgesses and widows of burgesses could marry themselves, their sons and their daughters without the licence of their lords. No lord was to have custody or gift of heirs, heiresses or widows because of some extra-burghal tenure held of him, but only of the estate which pertained to his fee for as long as the heir was a minor. This grant anticipated many of the demands of 1215: on pecuniary penalties, on distraint for debts, and on rights of marriage and wardship. Its author was John, count of Mortain, the future king.[43]

[40] The burgesses paid Roger £200 for their charter. For the original see *H.M.C.* 8th Report, 1, 269b–70.
[41] *Rot. Chartarum*, p. 207.
[42] Bristol was a hundredal borough.
[43] Ballard (1913), pp. 77, 78, 152, 165. The charter is illustrated in *The Little Red Book of Bristol*, ed. F. B. Bickley (Bristol, 1900), 1, 22.

This precocious development of borough privilege was derived from the concentration of municipal population and the distinctive social and economic rôle which the towns played. They were readily comprehended entities. Other communities, like shires, were less concentrated, less specialized and less close-knit. Nevertheless, by the end of the twelfth century, they too were beginning to obtain communal liberties, and under John more and more were able to exploit the financial distress of the Crown by buying a privilege. Their main ambitions were disafforestation and some measure of control over the office of sheriff.

In the case of the royal forests numerous local communities had already by 1215 obtained partial or complete exemption from the forest regulations. Indeed the forest had been so reduced in extent that the Charters of 1215 and 1217 did little more than set the seal on the existing state of affairs. Here Richard and John were entirely responsible, for their father had carried the bounds to the widest extent they ever reached. They simply sold off much of what he had won and more. As early as 1190 Richard accepted 200 m. from the men of Surrey for the partial disafforestation of their county, and £100 from the men of Ainsty wapentake, Yorkshire, for the total disafforestation of their wapentake.[44] He also began the disafforestation of the Lincolnshire Fen between the Welland and the Witham.[45] At about the same time Count John, who was lord of the honour of Lancaster, accepted £500 from the men of Lancashire in return for a charter which released them from offences against the vert and gave them rights of chace within the forest of Lancashire.[46] John confirmed these arrangements when he came to the throne, and, as his financial difficulties

[44] *Pipe Roll 2 Richard I*, pp. 67, 155.
[45] W. Fulman, *Rerum Anglicarum Scriptorum Veterum* (Oxford, 1684), 1, 456.
[46] W. Farrer, *Lancashire Pipe Rolls and Early Charters* (Liverpool, 1902), pp. 418–19. The right of chace here excluded the hart, hind, wild boar and goat.

increased, he turned increasingly to the sale of forest and other privileges as a means of escape. In July 1203, at the height of the crisis in Normandy, he instructed the chief forester, Hugh de Neville, to sell forest privileges 'to make our profit by selling woods and demising assarts'.[47] By the end of 1204 the men of Devon, Cornwall, Essex, Shropshire, and Staffordshire had all obtained charters of partial or total disafforestation; similar privileges had been obtained by the men of Ryedale, Wharfedale and Hertfordlythe in Yorkshire and by the marshland vills of Surfleet, Gosberton, Quadring and Donington in Lincolnshire.[48] By 1209 the men of Somerset had also bought forest privileges of some kind,[49] and in April 1215 the men of Cornwall made a bid to extend the disafforested area in their county even further.[50] All this was additional to a large number of individual licences to assart which the king or Hugh de Neville granted at this time. Here, if anywhere, the Crown was squandering its resources. Most of the disafforestations acquired by local communities were granted *in perpetuum*.

The alienation of control over local government was more gradual and less sharply defined. The earliest surviving Pipe roll, of 1130, records an offer of 200 m. from Hugh de Warelvill for having the counties of Northamptonshire and Leicestershire.[51] It is possible that this individual proffer, like some made later, was in effect a communal one in which a principal was backed by other local men. Such seems to

---

[47] *Rot. Litt. Pat.* p. 31b.
[48] See *Foedera*, I, part I, 89 for the Devon charter. The rest are in *Rot. Chartarum*, pp. 121, 122, 122b, 123, 128, 132–3. See also *Cartae Antiquae Rolls* (Pipe Roll Soc., new series XVII), no. 295.
[49] In 1214 they were called to send twelve discreet knights of the shire to the king to discuss a proffer they had made to Hugh de Neville during the last forest eyre, for the preservation of their liberties. Similar letters were sent to Devon and Cornwall (*Rot. Litt. Claus.* I, 181).
[50] *Rot. Litt. Claus.* I, 197.
[51] *Pipe Roll 31 Henry I*, p. 85.

have been the case when Thomas of Moulton offered 500 m. and five palfreys for the shrievalty of Lincolnshire in 1205, for his offer was backed by a group of local men, many of whom joined him in rebellion in 1215.[52] But by this time the rolls had begun to record similar proffers which were clearly communal in origin. The men of Lancashire offered 100 m. in 1199 and the same in 1204 in order that Richard de Vernon might be their sheriff.[53] In 1204 the forest charter obtained by the men of Devon also included several important administrative liberties. The sheriff was to hold his tourn once a year and was not to use it as a pretext against anyone; he might make other circuits for attaching the pleas of the Crown along with the coroners and for keeping the peace, but he was not to take anything for his own use; the shire court was empowered to give bail for men arrested by the sheriff so that none should remain in prison because of his malice; if a sheriff misbehaved then he would be in the king's mercy and would be replaced by someone more suitable.[54] In 1208 the men of Cornwall sought and obtained the king's agreement that their sheriff should be chosen from the men of the county,[55] and in 1210 the men of Dorset and Somerset purchased a similar privilege which specifically excluded William Briwerre and his men, for William was both a local landowner and a baron of the Exchequer, an experienced sheriff who would scarcely have provided the men of these counties with the benevolent local administration they were trying to obtain.[56]

These arrangements, and the parallel and often closely associated bids for disafforestation, are true forerunners of

---

[52] *Rot. de Ob. et Fin.* pp. 369–70 (see also Holt, 1961, p. 74).
[53] *Rot. de Ob. et Fin.* p. 38; *Pipe Roll 6 John*, p. 6.
[54] *Foedera*, I, part I, 89.
[55] *Pipe Roll 10 John*, p. 183.
[56] *Pipe Roll 12 John*, p. 75. The grant also pardoned 100 m. increment on the farm of the two counties (*Cal. Charter Rolls*, I, 281–2). On William Briwerre see Turner (1988), pp. 71–90 and below, pp. 130, 202–3, 378.

the Great Charter. In 1215 the king's opponents made no attempt to enforce rigid control over the king's choice of officials apart from their insistence that he should dismiss his Tourangeau agents.[57] But they did include the provision in the Charter that officials should know the law of the land,[58] and since the law of the land was still subject to innumerable local variants[59] this was at least a demand for administrators who would be locally congenial. By 1215 the privileges purchased earlier had proved difficult to maintain. In Lancashire Richard de Vernon was finally dismissed in 1205, apparently for contempt of the king's instructions.[60] In Lincolnshire Thomas of Moulton was unable or unwilling to exploit his office sufficiently to avoid increasing indebtedness to the Crown which ended in loss of office and imprisonment in 1208.[61] In Dorset and Somerset, on the other hand, the men of the county were still trying to maintain the concession they had won as late as 1245 when they obtained a confirmation of John's charter from Henry III;[62] their privilege had still been in force in 1234 when they presented three candidates for the shrieval office from whom the king chose one.[63] But if in many cases the practical results of these moves were only temporary they are nevertheless of great significance in revealing men's feelings about local government. The price of these privileges was high. The men of Devon offered 5000 m. for their charter of 1204, while the administrative privileges of the men of Cornwall cost 1300 m. and those of the men of Dorset and Somerset 1200 m.[64] There are only occasional indications that any one individual predominated in making these payments. Thomas of Moulton clearly did in Lincolnshire, and the Abbot of St Mary's, York, was prominent in maintaining the disafforestation acquired for the wapentake

[57] Cap. 50.   [58] Cap. 45.   [59] See below, pp. 111–12.
[60] Pipe Roll 7 John, p. 180.   [61] Pipe Roll 10 John, p. xviii; Holt (1961), pp. 155–6.
[62] Cal. Charter Rolls, 1, 281–2.   [63] Patent Rolls 1232–47, p. 50.
[64] Pipe Roll 6 John, p. 85; Pipe Roll 10 John, p. 183; Pipe Roll 12 John, p. 75.

of Ainsty.[65] On the other hand the proffer from Devon specifically excluded the Earl and the Bishop of Exeter; since a special commission was used to collect the money it seems likely that a large number of men contributed.[66] Probably the decision to acquire grants of this kind was made initially by the relatively small group of knights which tended to dominate the shire court: the men with administrative experience, the wealthier landowners, the stewards of the great lords.[67] But the rest of the more important landowners of the shire then had to be convinced. The purchases must have been preceded by extended discussion. Agreement was necessary on the exact privileges to be obtained, and the amount to be offered to the king. Those in charge of negotiations might find that he tried to force up the bidding, as he did with the men of Lancashire in 1200.[68] There was time and opportunity enough for men to air their grievances and voice or exchange their views on the conduct of local administration and the king's financial needs. The bid for privilege must, in fact, have been prefaced by discussions and arguments similar in many ways to those which preceded the final revolt. The objective was the same in each case; the difference lay simply in intensity and method.

That the political community of the shire was ready to incur the cost and trouble which all this involved suggests that men felt deeply and thought carefully about the conduct of local government. In one case, that of Somerset, some of the undercurrents which led to the proffer made in 1210 are casually revealed by the record of an action reported by a jury of twelve knights in the Trinity term of 1204.[69] A certain William le Denys had produced in the

[65] *Rot. de Ob. et Fin.* p. 54.   [66] *Pipe Roll 6 John*, p. 85; *Rot. Litt. Claus.* I, 10b.
[67] See Doris M. Stenton (1962), pp. 109–10.
[68] The Justiciar, Geoffrey fitz Peter, was instructed to increase the offer from 100 m. to £100, if he could (*Rot. de Ob. et Fin.* p. 38).
[69] *Curia Regis Rolls*, III, 129–30.

shire court a writ ordering Alan the sheriff[70] to see that he received 60 m. damages which he had suffered as a result of disseisin by Richard Revel. Richard Revel the younger was in court and, on hearing this, he asked the sheriff to deal justly with his father, his brother and himself, for they were native born and local gentry.[71] The sheriff replied that he was well aware of this but that he was bound to execute the writ. Richard repeated his statement and received the same reply. Richard again asserted that he and his family were native born and local gentry and added that the sheriff was a newcomer. The sheriff admitted that he came from other parts where perhaps, he added, he also might be considered as local gentry. Tempers must now have been roused for the rest of the story runs as follows: One of the sheriff's sergeants tried to execute a royal writ for the arrest of a clerk who was present in court. Richard prevented him, saying that the clerk ought not to be imprisoned without judgement,[72] and the sheriff himself had to arrest the clerk. William Revel here intervened to pacify his brother and to ask that the clerk should be released on pledges. The sheriff, for good measure, now tried to arrest both Richard and William. William retorted that he saw no royal order for his arrest and asked the court whether he ought to be imprisoned without such an order. He added that he had been in prison before for the king's sake and would stand to answer before the king wherever he desired. The interest of this case lies not only in its illustration of the deep-rooted prejudices of the local knight against the outsider, prejudices of special significance when related to the demands of 1215, but also in the skill with which Richard Revel and his brother played their hand, first whipping up the emotions of their audience,

---

[70] Alan of Wighton, the under-sheriff to Hubert de Burgh in 1204 (*Pipe Roll 6 John*, p. 175).
[71] The phrase is 'naturales homines et gentiles de patria'.
[72] 'Nisi per judicium': the roll is defective here. One copy adds the words 'quod cor eorum desiderat' (*Curia Regis Rolls*, III, 130).

then stating that imprisonment should only follow a judgement and denying the sheriff's right to arrest without a royal
writ, then appealing to the opinion of their fellows in the
court and finally volunteering to appear before the king
himself.

Once obtained, these liberties were defended with equal
vigour and skill. Ten years after the men of Devon had
obtained their charter of 1204 they were forced into its
defence by the sheriff, Eudo de Beauchamp. Six knights of
the country and the prior of Kerswell were summoned
before the justices of the Bench to answer allegations by the
sheriff that they had refused to give judgement in the court
of four Devon hundreds on those who had defaulted in
answer to the sheriff's summons.[73] The knights had argued
in the local court that the sheriff was seeking to use the
defaults as a pretext[74] and that they would not give
judgement since to do so would be contrary to the liberty of
the charter which the king had given them. They had also
successfully withstood the sheriff's efforts to bring pressure
to bear. When he asked who were these men who refused to
do judgement and complete the king's business, they readily
agreed that their names should be enrolled. When he
distrained their stock in order to compel them to answer for
their behaviour in the shire court they came to the shire
court and sought recovery as a matter of right on grounds of
unjust distraint. When the sheriff asked whether they wished
to carry their case further they again allowed their names to
be enrolled and, once before the king's justices, they produced the charter of 1204, denied any default or offence
against the Crown and alleged that the sheriff had been using
his tourn to levy monetary charges on the hundreds as in the
bad old days before they had acquired their charter. They
showed no sign of flinching or withdrawing from their
position. Indeed they expressed surprise that the matter had

---

[73] *Curia Regis Rolls*, VII, 158–9.   [74] 'quasi quaedam occasio'.

not ended in the shire court when the sheriff returned their stock to them. It might well have done so if the sheriff had not reported it to the Justiciar, Peter des Roches, who brusquely informed him that to remain silent would be against the interests of the Crown and would put him in mercy in both life and chattels. The justices of the Bench postponed judgement and the roll records no conclusion to the case; the impression is that the knights of Devon had at least won the first round, despite the intervention of des Roches.

The vigorous search for and defence of administrative liberties is typical of local English society at this time. The evidence of it crops up in unexpected places. In 1207 Peter de Brus, lord of Danby and Skelton, bought the wapentake of Langbargh in Cleveland for 400 m., promising the annual render of the ancient farm and an increment of £20.[75] The proffer appears on the rolls as a straightforward offer for an individual privilege, no different from hundreds of others. But the survival of the following charter, issued by Peter de Brus between 1207 and Michaelmas 1209, gives it much greater significance:[76]

Know that I have granted and confirmed by this my present charter to the knights and free-tenants of Cleveland and their men that none of them shall be summoned or impleaded in the Wapentake of Langbargh except by consideration of the Wapentake or through a reasonable 'sacrabar',[77] nor shall they be troubled by pretence of a plea; and if any

---

[75] *Pipe Roll 9 John*, p. 70.
[76] *The Chartulary of Guisborough*, ed. W. Brown (Surtees Soc., LXXXVI, 1889), I, 92–4. The charter can scarcely antedate Peter's offer to the king. Robert Walensis, who witnessed the charter as sheriff, ceased to hold office at Michaelmas 1209.
[77] In 1965 I followed F. M. Stenton, *The Danes in England*, pp. 35–6 and Doris M. Stenton (1964), pp. 55–6, 124–37 in interpreting 'sacrabar' as a public prosecutor peculiar to the Danelaw. This has now been shown to be incorrect. The primary sense, which appears in Bracton, is of a private suitor prosecuting a manifest thief, whence it was applied to the suit of such a person and to jurisdiction over such suits. In the present context it means no more than 'suit', the intention simply being that the men of the wapentake should not be subjected to unreasonable or irregular impleading. See J. M. Kaye, 'The Sacrabar', *E.H.R.*, LXXXIII (1968), 744–58. It remains probable, however, that the word was of Scandinavian origin.

of them incurs a forfeiture it shall be assessed according to his chattels and according to the offence for which he incurred it. I also grant to them that my sergeants in the Wapentake shall swear to observe and maintain these liberties faithfully according to the tenor of my charter; and if any of them is condemned for this, he shall be removed by me or my heirs and be replaced by another. I also concede to them that the chief sergeant of the Wapentake shall have no more than three horses and three mounted sergeants under him, namely two in Cleveland and one in Whitbystrand. And in return for these liberties the same knights and free-tenants have conceded that if the sergeant of the Wapentake of Langbargh can show by a reasonable account that he cannot make up the farm of the lord king, namely 40 m., and his reasonable expenses from the issues of the Wapentake, then the same knights and free-tenants will pay the residue of the due farm of 40 m., allowing for the reasonable expenses of the chief sergeant as testified by me and my stewards. I concede all the aforesaid liberties to the knights and free-tenants of Cleveland and their heirs to be held of me and my heirs in perpetuity. Witness Roger, constable of Chester, Robert de Ros, Eustace de Vescy, Robert Walensis, then sheriff of Yorkshire, Walter de Fauconberg, Ruald, constable of Richmond, Brian fitz Alan, John of Birkin, William fitz Ralph, Walter of Boynton and many others.

Peter de Brus was a leading figure in the rebellion in the northern counties at the end of John's reign. Among the witnesses who were still alive, Ruald, constable of Richmond, Brian fitz Alan and John of Birkin were all rebels; Robert de Ros and Eustace de Vescy were among the most important figures in the rebellion; both were members of the court of Twenty-Five. In short, men who were closely concerned with the liberties of 1215 are here shown applying closely related liberties in northern Yorkshire at least six years earlier. Here, as at Runnymede, the agreement was embodied in a charter. While the Great Charter was a grant in favour of all free men of the realm, Peter's was in favour of the knights, free-tenants and their men of Cleveland. While the Great Charter forbade that men should have to answer allegations based on the unsupported complaint of a bailiff, Peter promised that men should only be 'impleaded by the consideration of the Wapentake or through reasonable sacrabar'. Peter's officers, like John's men in 1215, had to swear to observe the agreement, and both documents show the same desire to avoid burdensome government by local officials. The Cleveland charter, like the Great Charter, laid down that monetary penalties were to be assessed with reference to the nature of the offence and the wealth of the offender. The first of these limitations also appears in the charter of Henry I. Indeed Peter's charter differs from the two royal charters at this point no more than they differ from each other.[78] Finally, like Magna Carta, the liberties of Langbargh were granted *in perpetuum*.

These are liberties displayed on the surface of local politics. The witness-list, containing as it does the sheriff of Yorkshire, Roger de Lacy constable of Chester, and his deputy, Robert Walensis, two great barons of the county, Robert de Ros and Eustace de Vescy, major tenants of the honour of Richmond, and, in Walter of Boynton, the treasurer of the abbey of St Mary's, York, indicates that it was promulgated in the county court. That the charter survives in the cartulary of the priory of Guisborough, a Brus foundation, suggests that the knights and freemen of Langbargh deposited their charter in the local monastery. Where better to find a treasury for their wapentake?[79] The negotiations which came to fruition in the charter can hardly have been driven by grievances against Peter de Brus because he had only recently acquired control of the wapentake. One important item of information is missing. We do not know what the knights and free tenants paid to Peter for

---

[78] 'Si quis baronum sive hominum meorum forisfecerit, non dabit vadium in misericordia pecunie sue, sicut faciebat tempore patris mei vel fratris mei, sed secundum modum forisfacti ita emendabit sicut emendasset retro a tempore patris mei . . .' (Henry I, cap. 8). 'Si aliquis eorum in forisfacturam ceciderit, amensurabitur secundum catella sua et secundum delictum per quod ceciderit' (Cleveland). 'Liber homo non amercietur pro parvo delicto, nisi secundum modum delicti; et pro magno delicto amercietur secundum magnitudinem delicti, salvo contenemento suo' (Magna Carta, cap. 20).

[79] Guisborough lay roughly in the centre of the more fertile part of the wapentake extending down the northern slope of the Cleveland Hills to the Tees and the coast. The alternative, Whitby, lay at the eastern extremity of the wapentake and was a refoundation of the Percys.

their privileges. If we did, it might well seem that Peter's proffer to the king was bolstered by a proffer from the local knights to him; that Peter and his tenants, in short, had set out to get control of local government on terms agreed amongst themselves which the charter carefully specified. Henceforth only the pleas of the Crown, with attachment by the sheriff and coroners, and the pleas of the sheriff remained outside their immediate control (and no doubt they would provide the coroners). That there was some such arrangement is inherently probable, and two features of the transaction make it very likely. Peter acquired the wapentake for himself and his heirs; his charter conveyed the liberties in perpetuity. The charter specified a farm of 40 m.; this amounted to the ancient farm and the new increment agreed by Peter with the king.[80]

That is as far as reasonable reconstruction can go. All the local associations which led the knights and free-tenants of Langbargh to combine with Peter de Brus lie hidden. Communities of this kind were not created, but rather reinforced by the purchase and possession of such liberties. Their interests were expressed in many ways and common action took many forms, in response to king or lord, or simply to order their day-to-day existence. Custom lay at the heart of this, whether expressed in charters or not.[81] Langbargh is extraordinary in that its customs were embodied in a charter, and one which still survives. Elsewhere the evidence is less tidy. To choose a location quite different

---

[80] *Pipe Roll 10 John*, p. 140. The equation is not exact since the ancient farm of 10 m. was accounted *blanche*.

[81] See Helen M. Cam, 'The Community of the Vill' in her *Law-finders and Law-makers in Medieval England* (London, 1962), pp. 71–84; and 'The Theory and Practice of Representation of Medieval England' *ibid.*, pp. 159–75; also Susan Reynolds, 'Law and Communities in Western Christendom', *American Journal of Legal History*, xxv (1981), 205–24. The whole problem is now illuminated by Reynolds (1984a), especially pp. 101–54, 219–49. The modern trend of thinking places weight on the autonomous sense of community engendered by the community's own political economy. In this light Robert Boutruche, *Seigneurie et Féodalité* (Paris, 1970), pp. 141–7, and especially F. W. Maitland, *Domesday Book and Beyond* (Cambridge, 1897), pp. 340–56, still deserve close attention.

from Langbargh, a journey along the northern coast of Kent might begin in Thanet where, in 1198, the local community fought a notable action against the abbot of St Augustine, Canterbury. He required them in their pleas to follow his court: they claimed the right to plead solely at Minster in Thanet – an exact analogy to the complaint met by cap. 17 of Magna Carta that common pleas 'should not follow our court but shall be held in some certain place'.[82] Moving westwards we would come to the great royal hundredal manor of Milton Regis. Milton possessed a charter which confirmed privileges going back to the reign of Henry I. We do not know the detailed terms; indeed we only know of its existence because in the spring of 1205 the men of the hundred carried away King John's confirmation before it could be entered on the charter roll.[83] But it was a prize of great value: it had cost them 200 m.[84] Moving yet further west we might end our journey at Swanscombe Down, the site of a legendary encounter between William the Conqueror and the men of Kent. There, so the tale went, King William agreed to a treaty which confirmed all their ancient laws and customs, thereby preserving in Kent alone the ancient liberty of the English. The story was first recorded at St Augustine's, Canterbury c. 1220.[85] Kent, as much as Langbargh, would provide ready listeners to Magna Carta.

The establishment of local liberties was not the work of a momentary whim but of an ingrained attitude of mind. These privileges could only be maintained by persistent vigilance and repeated renewal of the original instruments. The men of Ainsty wapentake, which was disafforested in

---

[82] *Curia Regis Rolls*, VII, 343. See also below, p. 185.
[83] *Rot. Chartarum*, p. 150. For the manor, which had a TRE value of £200 in 1086, see *V.C.H. Kent*, III, 180, 187. As a manor of the ancient demesne it lay outside shrieval jurisdiction. See E. Hasted, *The History and Topographical Survey of the County of Kent* (Canterbury, 1797–1801), VI, 2–3, 172–3, where there is information on the later liberties of the manor.
[84] *Rot. de Ob. et Fin.* p. 269.   [85] See Holt (1985), pp. 9–13.

1190, had to pay for confirmations in 1200 and again in
1208.[86] The Londoners, far from resting content with the
inclusion in the Great Charter of the prohibition on fish-
weirs which they had obtained in 1196 and 1199, returned
yet again to obtain a separate confirmation of this particular
concession from Henry III in 1227.[87] Indeed many local
communities, once they had tasted the benefits of these
liberties, seemed ready enough to return for more. The
Cornishmen who obtained partial disafforestation in 1204
returned to buy the right to a local sheriff in 1208 and yet
again to buy the disafforestation of the rest of their county in
March 1215.

Such men were stubborn, persistent and organized. They
even dreamed of reform. One of the stories which Gerald of
Wales picked up on one of his journeys to Lincolnshire
concerned a penurious local knight, one Roger of Asterby,
who encountered visions of St Peter and the archangel
Gabriel while walking through his fields.[88] Roger was a
cautious man: he established the *bona fides* of his visitors by
requiring them to recover his coat of mail which he had
pledged to Aaron the Jew of Lincoln in return for a loan.
When they had completed this task and performed other
miracles, Roger agreed to do their bidding, which was to lay
seven divine commands before King Henry II. These commands were that the king should maintain his coronation
oath and the just laws of the realm; that nobody should
suffer the death penalty without judgement, even though
guilty; that inheritances should be restored to their rightful
owners and that right should be done; that justice should be
given freely and without charge; that the *servitia* of his
ministers should be restored; and, finally, that the Jews

---

[86] *Rot. de Ob. et Fin.* pp. 54, 434. It was only on the last occasion that the disafforestation of
Ainsty was granted *in perpetuum*. Compare *Rot. Chartarum*, pp. 40b, 176b. See also *Rot. de
Ob. et Fin.* p. 157, for a renewal of the forest privileges of the men of Surrey at the cost of
300 m.
[87] *Cal. Charter Rolls*, I, 23.
[88] *Opera*, VIII, 183–6.

should be expelled without their bonds and pledges which should be returned to the debtors who had surrendered them. Roger carried these commands to Henry and promised him seven fruitful years of life if he executed them and took the Cross. Henry did so only for a single night; in the cold light of the next day he delayed matters and nothing further happened.

This story presents Roger of Asterby as a country visionary prophesying doom, and is used by Gerald of Wales simply to add point to his general picture of Henry II's progressive moral decline. However, there was undoubtedly a Roger of Asterby living in Lincolnshire in the last years of the twelfth century when Gerald visited the county.[89] Moreover, Roger's commands catered for knightly rather than clerical interest. Retailed though it is by a clerk, the proper audience for this story was the knights of the shire who bore the brunt of Angevin government. This was the kind of myth from which the bid for liberties, both local and national, derived its potency. Whether as a stimulant or a sedative such tales must have stirred the deepest wells of political consciousness in the most backward of backwoodsmen. Many must have dreamed the dreams of Roger of Asterby before they combined to purchase liberties or to wring them from the Crown by force in 1215.

Between the myth and the practical there was still a large gap. At the time when Gerald of Wales heard the tale of Roger of Asterby men had not yet moved far beyond the comparatively sure ground where liberties were the perquisite of local communities. A borough was a distinct and easily comprehended entity; there was no difficulty in accepting that it held corporate privilege. A shire was not so easy to imagine in this rôle, but even in this case there was a shire court which answered to the Crown for the exercise of its functions and through which the purchase of liberties was

⁸⁹ See *E.H.R.* LXIX (1955), 10 n. For further comment on Roger's dream, see Robert Bartlett, *Gerald of Wales* (Oxford, 1982), pp. 66–7.

most probably arranged. But Roger of Asterby was laying down commands which applied to the realm as a whole, and this was easier to achieve in myth than in reality. To realize this myth men had to do more than combine to purchase liberties or organize rebellion. They had to create and act upon a theory that the community of the realm was capable of the corporate possession of liberties. This was at once the underlying assumption, the essential achievement and the justification of the rebellion of 1215.

CHAPTER 4

CUSTOM AND LAW

Resistance to the abuse of monarchical power in the twelfth and thirteenth centuries was based on assumptions which permeated the society of western Europe. Magna Carta was more than a simple reaction against Angevin government, and more than a statement of the privileges which the Angevins had made available; it was also a statement of principles about the organization of a feudal state. As such it drew on a common body of experience and custom which, with local variants, was shared throughout western Europe and the Latin states in the east. Hence the Norman and Angevin kings had to contend with men who shared strong views on the constitution of society, on title to feudal property, on the right to judgement and on the proper conduct of lords and kings. The Angevins gave their men the grievances and the education in government which were woven into the tapestry of Magna Carta. But the warp and weft were derived from the structure of society itself.

This common experience was embodied in custumals and law-books, it was formulated in statutes, it was sharpened by the conflict between Church and State, it was laid down as assizes when new states were founded, and it was stated in charters of liberties when the interaction of royal policy and aristocratic interests exploded into political crises. Together these scattered and widely different sources reveal legal and political principles of remarkable permanence and pervasiveness. For example, the insistence on judgement by peers in cap. 39 of Magna Carta was simply an assertion of a generally recognized axiom. It received its first clear statement in the edict of the Emperor Conrad II of 1037 which laid down that military tenants were not to be deprived of their fiefs 'except by the laws of our ancestors and the judgement of their peers'.[1] In Italy it was repeated in the Treaty of Constance of 1183[2] and the concessions of Charles of Salerno of 1283.[3] It was accepted procedure in actions between king and barons in the kingdom of Jerusalem.[4] In France it cropped up in a wide variety of sources, in custumals and reports of actions in royal and honorial courts.[5] In Normandy, it was bluntly stated in the Ancient Custumal of *c.* 1200 in the form—'peer ought to be judged by peer'.[6] In England the same principle was asserted in the Laws of Henry I in the form—'each man is to be judged by his peers of the same neighbourhood'.[7] It was assumed in the organization of the great honours in the early twelfth century[8] and a man might still call upon his peers to substantiate his case in the royal courts at the end of the century.[9]

This principle or method of judicial procedure owed its pervasiveness to the general assumption in feudal societies that a lord was bound to do justice to his men and that

---

[1] 'nullus miles . . .sine certa et convicta culpa suum beneficium perdat nisi secundum constitucionem antecessorum nostrorum et judicium parium suorum' (*M.G.H., Const.*, I, 90).

[2] 'Et si qua controversia de feudo orta fuerit inter nos et alium qui sit de Societate, per pares illius civitatis vel episcopatus, in quo discordia agitur, secundum illius civitatis consuetudinem in eodem episcopatu terminetur, nisi nos in Lombardia fuerimus; tunc enim in audientia nostra, si nobis placuerit, causa agitabitur' (*M.G.H., Const.* I, 415).

[3] 'Si comites, barones et feuda tenentes in regia curia personaliter seu realiter litigabunt, vel conveniant et accusent alios, sive conveniantur aut accusentur ab aliis, per compares absolvi debeant aut etiam condemnari, et ipsorum cause qualescumque fuerint, prout melius et citius poterunt, terminentur' (Trifone, 1921, p. 100).

[4] 'Et cegont se que ses pers l'averont jugé d'aver, si peut bien commander li roys ou la royne que tant tost en soit faite la justise, se il veut.' 'Et por ce ne peut (le roi) mie metre jà main sur son home lige, sans esgart de ses pers' (Le Livre au Roi, cap. xxv, *Recueil*, I, 623–4).

[5] B. C. Keeney (1952), pp. 12–31.

[6] 'Par per parem iudicari debet' (Le Très Ancien Coutumier de Normandie, *Coutumiers de Normandie*, ed. E. J. Tardif, Rouen, 1881, I, cap. xxvi).

[7] 'Unusquisque per pares suos judicandus est, et eiusdem provinciae' (Leges Henrici Primi, cap. 31.7; *Gesetze*, I, 564. Cp. Leis Willelme, cap. 23; *ibid.* I, 511).

[8] F. M. Stenton (1961), pp. 60–1.

[9] *Rot. Curiae Regis*, II, 90.

vassals were bound to attend and constitute their lord's court. It also survived simply because it was a principle, a generalization open to interpretation, special construction and evasion. Yet it is only one example of many common principles, some of which were much more precise and categorical. For example, the feudal aristocracy reacted with astonishing single-mindedness throughout western Europe against demands for military service outside the realm. In England, Magna Carta contained no provision specifically on this point, but the burden of such service had contributed largely to the outbreak of rebellion and a demand for its limitation was initially included in the baronial programme.[10] On the continent there was a widespread demand for the limitation or control of such service. In his statutes of 1188 Alfonso of León agreed that he would not make war or peace except by the advice of the bishops and nobles of the realm.[11] In Aragon in 1283 Peter III agreed that he would only make war by the advice of nobles, knights and townsfolk and that the nobles were not bound by the conditions of their feudal tenures to serve overseas.[12] In the Latin kingdom in the east it was recognized that the king could only ask for service outside its frontiers if it was to the general profit of the realm and even then the service was to be at the king's expense.[13] In Hungary the Golden

[10] See below, pp. 218–21, 239–40. See also the Cheshire Magna Carta, cap. 14, below, pp. 379–80. Note, however, that the 'realm' included Normandy. See Holt (1987), pp. 63–4. The 'unknown' charter would add Brittany (cap. 7, see below, p. 239).

[11] 'Promissi etiam, quod non faciam guerram vel pacem vel placitum nisi cum concilio episcoporum, nobilium et bonorum hominum, per quorum consilium debeo regi' (Muñoz y Romero, 1847, p. 103). For the meaning of *placitum* see Evelyn S. Procter, 'The interpretation of clause 3 of the decrees of León (1188)', *E.H.R.*, LXXXV (1970), 45–53.

[12] 'Item quel senyor rey, en sus guerras e en sus feitos que tocan a las communidades, que los ricos homes, mesnaderos, cavalleros e los hondrados ciudadanos e omes buenos de las villas sean en su consello e tornan en lur hondra assi como solian en tiempo de su padre' (cap. 5); 'Item que los ricos homes Daragon no sian tenidos por las honores ni por las tierras que tienen del senyor rey de servirlo por aquellas fuaras de su senyorio ni passar mar' (cap. 24) (*Herrschaftsverträge*, pp. 19, 22).

[13] Le Livre au Roi, cap. XXIX, *Recueil*, I, 626. For the well-known debate on overseas service in the court of the kingdom of Cyprus in 1271 see *ibid.* II, 427–34, and for a general discussion of the evidence, La Monte (1932), pp. 155–7.

Bull of 1222 included the provisions that only the counts, and knights who were serving for pay, were bound to give service outside the realm.[14] In France, the Statute of Pamiers of 1212, which established the customs of the new crusading state created by Simon de Montfort and his associates in Toulouse and Narbonne, laid down that the count was not entitled to service except by grace and at his own pay if he wilfully intervened in wars which were irrelevant to the safety of himself or his country.[15]

Such views died hard. More than a century later the nobles and knights of Champagne asserted that any summons to military service should be made within the county and that they should not be required to serve outside the bounds of the county except at the king's own expense.[16] In both these French examples the argument that military service should be local was closely similar to that which the northern opponents of King John advanced in 1213–15.[17]

Military service created widespread and perennial acrimony. The problem of enforcing some real control over capricious kings was less enduring, yet even here the radical provisions of cap. 61 of Magna Carta had parallels elsewhere. In the kingdom of Jerusalem it was recognized that the king's vassals might resort to the renunciation of fealty

---

[14] 'Si autem Rex extra regnum exercitum ducere voluerit, servientes cum ipso ire non teneantur, nisi pro pecunia ipsius et post reversionem iudicium exercitus super eos non recipiet...Item si extra regnum cum exercitu iverimus, omnes qui comitatus habent, vel pecuniam nostram, nobiscum ire teneantur' (Marczali, 1901, pp. 136–7).

[15] 'Verum si comes non necessitate sua aut terre sue, set pro voluntate propria vellet juvare aliquem vel aliquos in guerra sive vicinos sive remotos, milites sui supradicti non tenentur eum sequi in hoc aut eidem servire per se vel per alios, nisi hoc facerent ex amore et beneplacito suo', Statute of Pamiers, cap. 17 (Vic & Vaissette, 1872–1904, VIII, col. 629).

[16] 'Sur ce que il disoient que par la Coustume de Champagne, quand nous semonions les dis nobles, pour ost, ou pour chevauchiée, la semonce doit estre faite dedans les termes de Champagne, et de qui nous les poons mener a certains gages parmi la Comté, mais ailleurs ne les poons-nous mener, ne sievre ne nous doivent, se n'est a tous frais et a tous cousts' (*Ordonnances*, I, 576).

[17] See below, pp. 218, 220, and Holt (1961), pp. 88–92.

and rebellion in certain specified circumstances, as, for example, when the king imprisoned or deprived a vassal without judgement or persistently denied justice to his men.[18] In Hungary King Andrew II agreed in the Bull of 1222 that 'if we or any of our successors ever wish to revoke this concession in any way, bishops, lords and nobles, each and every one, both now and in the future have our authority to resist and contradict us and our successors without taint of any infidelity'.[19] In Aragon, in the *Privilegio de la Union* of 1287, King Alfonso III pledged the good behaviour of the Crown by the surrender of sixteen castles and the acknowledgement that his vassals could choose another king if he contravened their privileges;[20] in surrendering castles he provided a guarantee which had also been considered in England in 1215 in an unofficial version of Magna Carta which survived at St Albans.[21] Even the papacy was affected by this kind of constitutional thinking. When Urban IV arranged to transfer the kingdom of Sicily to Charles of Anjou in 1263 he laid down that Charles was to force his new subjects to swear that they would transfer their fealty to the pope if he or his successors departed in any way from the conditions under which the pope was investing him with the kingdom. Urban optimistically ordered that the oath should be renewed every ten years in per-

---

[18] La Monte (1932), p. 103.
[19] 'Statuimus eciam, quod si nos, vel aliquis successorum nostrorum aliquo unquam tempore huic disposicioni contraire voluerit, liberam habeant harum auctoritate, sine nota alicuius infidelitatis, tam Episcopi, quam alii Iobagiones et Nobiles Regni nostri, universi et singuli, presentes et posteri, resistendi et contradicendi nobis et nostris successoribus in perpetuum facultatem' (cap. 31, Marczali, 1901, pp. 141–2). This clause was abandoned in the 1231 re-issue and replaced by the penalty of excommunication (*ibid.*).
[20] *Herrschaftsverträge*, pp. 34–5 (cp. *ibid.* pp. 39–40). For further comment and a study of the legendary privileges of Aragon in part derived from the *Privilegio* see Ralph E. Giesey, *If Not, Not: the Oath of the Aragonese and the Legendary Laws of Sobrarbe* (Princeton, 1968), especially pp. 87–101; and José-Luis Martin, 'Privilegios y Cartas de Libertad en la Corona de Aragon (1283–1289)' in *Album Mályusz* (1976), pp. 123–70.
[21] See below, p. 345, and Holt (1961), pp. 116–18.

petuity.[22] In the light of this it would perhaps be hasty to condemn the security clause of Magna Carta as unrealistic. Liberties throughout western Europe embodied constantly recurring privileges. They asserted the property rights of the king's vassals and the limitation of the Crown's feudal prerogative; they insisted on lawful process against arbitrary action by the king or his ministers, and maintained that judges and administrators should be native born or local men; they insisted on the maintenance of ancient right and custom and the repeal of new impositions whether fiscal, administrative or jurisdictional. They relied on the same forms of security. Just as King John swore to observe the terms of the Great Charter in 1215, so Simon de Montfort swore to observe and maintain the Statute of Pamiers in 1212,[23] Andrew II of Hungary the Golden Bull in 1231[24] and Alfonso III of Aragon the *Privilegio de la Union* of 1287.[25] These liberties were cognate. There is no need to explain the many similarities between them as derivatives from some basic grant or legal code. There is no sound reason, for example, for believing that the Golden Bull owed anything to Magna Carta or that either of them owed anything directly to the assizes of the kingdom of Jerusalem or the Statute of Pamiers.[26] Nowhere is there the exact

[22] 'Item dictus comes. . .jurare faciet omnes eorumdem regni et terre comites, barones et nobiles ac milites, cives et burgenses ceterosque alios, quod toto posse facient et curabunt quod dictus comes et ejus heredes omnes et singulas hujusmodi condiciones ac universa et singula premissa inviolabiliter observabunt, nec ullo umquam tempore venient contra illa; et si eum vel heredes suos a predictis regno et terra in quibuscumque casibus juxta tenorem conditionum et penarum cadere contigerit, vel ipsos juxta eundem tenorem illis privari, seu concessionem factam eis de ipsis evacuari et irritari per Romanum pontificem, nullatenus eis, sed Romano tantum pontifici obedient et intendent, tamquam regi Sicilie et ipsorum domino temporali. Hoc etiam juramentum de decennio in decennium renovabitur, et tam idem comes quam singuli heredes sui, qui in eisdem regno et terra succedent, illud perpetuo singulis continuis decenniis renovari facient et prestari' (*Reg. Urban IV*, II, 123).
[23] Vic & Vaissette (1872–1904), VIII, col. 634.
[24] Marczali (1901), p. 142.
[25] *Herrschaftsverträge*, pp. 35, 40.
[26] For the most explicit exposition of this thesis of direct transference see C. d'Eszlary, 'L'influence des Assises de Jérusalem sur la Bulle d'Or hongroise', *Le Moyen Age*, 4th ser., IX (1954), 335–78, where earlier views are collected. See also the same writer's

verbal identity to establish such a link. Nowhere was there an exact identity of situation. Men from many different countries met and talked on pilgrimages, diplomatic missions and on the crusade. But they had no need to borrow constitutional solutions and legal principles from each other. In their home-lands they faced similar developments in monarchical power. They called on similar deep-rooted and unquestioned assumptions about feudal rights and legal process. They turned to the same system of securities which depended on oaths, pledges, guarantees and guarantors, and they naturally provided similar political and legal solutions to keep royal power in check. The liberties of the twelfth and thirteenth centuries were no infection spreading from one country to another; they were part of the very atmosphere.

Yet the assumptions and conventions on which these liberties were based did not pass unchallenged. Royal power always tended to circumvent or erode them. Moreover there were rival concepts derived from a theocratic view of kingship and from the simple fact that there could be no lordship without authority, which always stood in unresolved competition or even open conflict with them. Despite feudal custom, kings behaved on occasion in as arbitrary a manner as convention and immediate political circumstances would allow. The English records of the twelfth century bear frequent witness to the operations of the king's will, to actions stemming from his wrath which were executed by force and violence.[27] To be in the king's mercy, to have to purchase his good will, was one of the more likely fates which might befall an active, ambitious vassal. All this stemmed from the fact that for all its increasing refinement, government was still very personal. A

paper read to the Académie des Inscriptions et Belles Lettres in 1953, 'La Magna Carta et son origine française' (privately printed, Munich, 1956). For earlier essays in comparison see R. Altamira, 'Magna Carta and Spanish Medieval Jurisprudence', *M.C.C.E.* pp. 227–43, and Hantos (1904).

[27] For a full discussion of this see Jolliffe (1963), pp. 50–136.

king's first responsibility was still to manage his vassals, to reward the faithful, to promote the efficient, to suppress the dangerous, and to harry the ineffectual. In the process kings overrode, ignored and exploited such law as there was to their own convenience. They disseised and dispossessed their men on a multiplicity of grounds, sometimes with little regard for legal process. Henry I deprived men for offences against the forest law;[28] Henry II disseised one who had refused dinner to one of his huntsmen,[29] and another who gave support to his arch-enemy, Becket;[30] Richard I was alleged to have seized the land of a minor in royal custody;[31] and John disseised men by royal precept,[32] or seized property and destroyed buildings to make way for the improvement of a castle.[33] Bracton still recorded these activities of the Angevins in the reign of Henry III.[34] These kings were equally ready to demand pledges of good behaviour from their subjects in the form of hostages.[35] King John sometimes demanded special charters of fealty and the surrender of castles.[36] All used the threat or fact of imprisonment as a potent deterrent. For some these procedures

---

[28] *H.M.C.* 7th Report, p. 587. That such punishment was general is implied by the Assize of the Forest, cap. 1 (*Stubbs's Charters*, 9th ed., p. 180).

[29] *Bracton's Note Book*, case no. 769.   [30] *Pipe Roll 5 John*, p. 103.

[31] *Pipe Roll 13 John*, p. 34.   [32] *Rot. de Ob. et Fin.* p. 332.

[33] *Cal. Charter Rolls*, I, 209.

[34] *Bracton's Note Book*, cases no. 49, 769, 994, 1593.

[35] There are many references to hostages in the Pipe rolls of Henry II's reign. Some of these were probably taken from the Irish or Welsh. For a hostage taken on the order of Hubert Walter in 1194, see *Three Rolls of the King's Court*, ed. F. W. Maitland (Pipe Roll Soc.), p. 9.

Under John, see the cases of Roger de Lacy (*Hoveden*, IV, 91–2, *Rot. Chartarum*, p. 102*b*), William d'Aubigné of Belvoir (*Hoveden*, IV, 161), John de Courcy (*Rot. Litt. Pat.* p. 45*b*), Robert de Ros (*ibid.* p. 59*b*, *Rot. Litt. Claus.* I, 99), Roger de Montbegon (*Rot. de Ob. et Fin.* p. 275), Robert de Vieuxpont (*Rot. Litt. Pat.* p. 89*b*), William Marshal (*Histoire de Guillaume le Maréchal*, ll. 13257–78, 13355–419, 14319–428, and *Rot. Litt. Pat.* p. 94*b*), and Robert de Vaux (*Pipe Roll 13 John*, p. xxxi; *Rot. Litt. Pat.* pp. 95, 96).

Wendover's muddled account of a general demand for hostages following the Interdict finds little supporting evidence. However, a considerable number were taken from those suspected of complicity in the plot against the king in 1212 (see Holt, 1961, p. 83).

[36] See below, pp. 193–5.

were disastrous. Matilda de Briouze and her son died in a royal prison. Besides this dramatic instance there were many others which, if less obviously violent, were nevertheless injurious to those who suffered in them. In 1219, for example, Richard Noel appeared before the justices to claim land in Davington and Hockering in Kent from Reginald of Cornhill. His case was that he had inherited the land from his brother to whom King Richard had given it, but that it had pleased King John to put him in prison and seize his land. He had offered the king 50 m. for his release and the recovery of the estates but had defaulted on the terms of payment after he had paid 18 m. and 40d. and thereupon Reginald's father, who was then sheriff, had seized it into his hand.[37] At about the same time William, son of Baldwin, surrendered property in Nottingham to Alexander de Vilers at a rent of 2s. in return for 40 m. which Alexander had given him to procure his release from the king's prison.[38] These men, if they did not suffer in life and health, suffered in their property. For all the protection given to seisin by the legal measures of Henry II, this was still their most vulnerable spot. Many others suffered similarly. Some were disseised by the king's will, some lost estates during a minority, some had to sell land to pay the costs of litigation in the king's court, some to meet a ransom, some to meet the burden of debt to the Crown incurred by excessive speculation in the marriage market or by the imposition of some pecuniary penalty. Disaster came in many forms but usually had but one result.

By the side of these powers the king enjoyed an ill-defined capacity to direct, suspend or withhold justice. Behind the keen interest of Henry II and John in the operations of the courts of justice there lay a ready instinct to ensure that judgement inclined favourably towards the king's friends and ministers and away from those who were out of favour

---

[37] *Bracton's Note Book*, case no. 17.　　[38] *H.M.C. Hastings MSS*, i, 117.

or distrusted.[39] On occasion John's writs assumed that customary procedure should give way, if necessary, to royal prohibition.[40] He exercised a wide suspending power in favour of those who were engaged on his service; by 1206 all those who joined his armies seem to have enjoyed a stay in legal action during the period of their service.[41] Like Richard before him he used the occasion of his accession to enforce payment for the confirmation of privilege; he even instructed his justices not to accept individual pleas based on charters or letters patent of his ancestors which he himself had not confirmed.[42] Indeed his accession itself had an immediate effect on one important legal issue for it established the succession of an uncle against a nephew representative of an elder line. For a time this settled what was then a debatable issue. It led to immediate stays in private cases where similar inheritance was involved; these were now referred to the king's decision;[43] and the 'king's case' continued to affect the course of English law until the death of Eleanor of Britanny, the surviving descendant of John's elder brother, Geoffrey, in 1241.[44] This was despite the fact that legal opinion, including Bracton, came down with less and less hesitation on the side of the nephew.[45]

In the seventeenth century such royal intrusions into the sphere of law might well have engendered furious debate about the royal prerogative and the status of statute law and judicial decision. In the twelfth century those who discussed

---

[39] See below, pp. 106–11, 206–11; Holt (1961), pp. 172, 236–7; Painter (1949), pp. 262–3.
[40] *Curia Regis Rolls*, III, 215.
[41] Flower (1943), pp. 337, 345. For examples see *Rot. Curiae Regis*, II, 3; *Curia Regis Rolls*, II, 157, 172, 216; III, 339; IV, 182, 234; V, 162, 200, 208, 328.
[42] See his letters of Michaelmas 1200: 'Dominus rex mandavit per breve suum justiciariis in banco quod nichil (faciant) alicui propter cartas vel litteras patentes quas habent de antecessoribus (suis) nisi viderint confirmacionem suam de aliqua re que coram ipsis tractetur' (*Curia Regis Rolls*, I, 331). For further discussion see below, pp. 161–2.
[43] *Pleas before the King or his Justices, 1198–1202*, ed. Doris M. Stenton (Selden Soc., LXVII, nos. 484, 528).
[44] Plucknett (1948), pp. 678–80.
[45] Pollock & Maitland (1898), II, 285. For more on the *casus regis* see Holt (1991b).

such matters seemed quite ready to accept that law and will each had its place in the constitution of the state. This is obvious in Richard fitz Neal's *Dialogue of the Exchequer* and, to a less extent, in Glanvill. Both accepted that the size of the relief of a knight was fixed by custom at £5 per fee, yet both were equally convinced that the king's barons had to seek what terms they could from the king in determining their reliefs.[46] Fitz Neal also seems to have accepted without question that the king 'decreed' the amount to be paid per fee when scutage was levied on the land.[47] Finally, in discussing the contrast between forest laws and common law he enunciated the separation of royal will and law in a passage which deserves to be a *locus classicus* of dualistic constitutional doctrine:

The whole organization of the forests, the punishment, pecuniary or corporal, of forest offences, is outside the jurisdiction of the other courts, and solely dependent on the decision of the King, or of some officer specially appointed by him. The forest has its own laws, based, it is said, not on the Common Law of the realm, but on the arbitrary decree of the King; so that what is done in accordance with the forest law is not called 'just' absolutely, but 'just' according to the forest law.[48]

These views are all the more important in that they come from a great administrator who was concerned with stating practice probably even more than theory. They seem to represent a generally accepted attitude. In other spheres of administration the king's will was not recognized as so potent and overwhelming. Yet it might intrude almost anywhere. Among the many experiments aimed at devising effective warranty in private deeds in the thirteenth century there was one which appears fleetingly in a charter of Henry of Thrumpton of *c.* 1250. In this Henry conveyed to Roger fitz Ralph of Beeston, John, son of Robert of Beeston, and all his family and chattels free and quit of all serfdom in

---

[46] Glanvill, IX, 4, ed. Hall, p. 108; *Dialogus*, p. 96.   [47] *Dialogus*, p. 52.
[48] *Ibid.* pp. 59–60. Here, and in other passages taken from the *Dialogus*, I have largely followed the editor's translation.

perpetuity so that Henry and his heirs should have no further claim over him 'notwithstanding remedy by law or king'.[49] There could be few clearer or more casual attestations of the pervasive power of the Crown.

Few men engaged in public affairs tried to resolve this potential and actual conflict between royal will and law. Perhaps of all of them Richard fitz Neal came nearest to doing so:

Although the wealth of kings is not invariably theirs by strict process of law, but proceeds sometimes from the laws of their countries, sometimes from the secret devices of their own hearts and sometimes even from their mere arbitrary will, their subjects have no right to question or condemn their actions. For those whose hearts are in the hand of God, and to whom God himself has committed the sole care of their subjects, stand or fall by God's judgement and not man's.[50]

Yet even fitz Neal's views were not as clear-cut as this passage and modern interpretations of it would suggest.[51] It is part of his prefatory address to King Henry, and even here the Law of the Exchequer crept in before the end: 'The Exchequer has its own rules. They are not arbitrary, but rest on the decisions of great men; and if they are observed scrupulously, individuals will get their rights, and your majesty will receive in full the revenue due to the Treasury.'[52] Elsewhere in his work similar limitations on royal power were expressed even more clearly. In defining the function of the officers of the Exchequer he laid down that they were 'to look after the king's interests yet without inequity, according to the established laws of the Exchequer'.[53] Fitz Neal was no absolutist. Still less was Glanvill, who, like Bracton later, could at one and the same time quote one of the most celebrated absolutist tags from the Institutes of Justinian—'what pleases the prince has the force of law' – and state that law is promulgated by the

[49] 'Non obstante legis vel regis remedio', *H.M.C. Middleton MSS*, p. 64.
[50] *Dialogus*, p. 1.   [51] Cp. Richardson & Sayles (1963), p. 143.
[52] *Dialogus*, p. 3.   [53] *Ibid.* p. 13.

counsel of the nobles and the authority of the king, on dubious points which are to be defined in council.[54] No doubt the steady expansion of the study of Roman law created possibilities for the formulation of absolutist political doctrine. But it is easy to exaggerate them. Even in the Empire, where rulers were prone to windy expositions of their sovereignty, authority was matched by responsibility, royal power by the concept of the interests of the realm and the safety of its inhabitants.[55] When Barbarossa reviewed his authority in pompous phrases in the preamble to the Treaty of Constance, it simply prepared for the massive alienations of real power which followed in the body of the text.[56] He was doing little more than whistle in the dark. The enunciation of Roman law might indicate a strongly authoritarian rule or cloak real loss of power under the fiction of delegated public authority. In the Empire it did both. In England it had deep but less well defined effects: on the arrangement of Glanvill's law-book,[57] for example, and on the logic of legal thinking. Under John, Roman law was taught at Oxford,[58] and Englishmen abroad made reputations as canonists and civilians. But this left no coherent theory of sovereignty. Occasionally the records betray an

---

[54] Glanvill, Prologue, ed. Hall, p. 2.

[55] See the Roncaglia decrees of 1158: 'Imperialem decet sollertiam ita rei publicae curam gerere et subiectorum commoda investigare, ut regni utilitas incorrupta persistat et singulorum status iugiter servetur illesus' (*M.G.H., Const.*, I, 247).

[56] *M.G.H., Const.* I, 411–12.

[57] T. F. T. Plucknett, *Early English Legal Literature* (Cambridge, 1958), pp. 19–41.

[58] H. G. Richardson, 'The Oxford Law School under John', *Law Quarterly Review*, LVII (1941), 319–38. See also C. R. Cheney, 'Hubert Walter and Bologna', *Bulletin of Medieval Canon Law*, n.s. II (1972), 81–4; C. E. Lewis, 'Canonists and Law Clerks in the Household of Archbishop Hubert Walter' in *Seven Studies in Medieval English History and other Historical Essays presented to Harold S. Snellgrove*, ed. R. H. Bowers (Jackson, 1984), pp. 57–63, reprinted from *Colloquia Germanica*, II (1970); R. V. Turner, 'Roman Law in England before the Time of Bracton', *The Journal of British Studies*, 1975, 1–25; P. Stein, 'Vacarius and the Civil Law', in *Church and Government in the Middle Ages, Essays presented to C. R. Cheney*, ed. C. N. L. Brooke, D. E. Luscombe, G. H. Martin and Dorothy Owen (Cambridge, 1976), pp. 119–37; R. W. Southern, 'Master Vacarius and the Beginning of the English Academic Tradition' in *Medieval Learning and Literature, Essays presented to R. W. Hunt*, ed. J. J. G. Alexander and M. T. Gibson (Oxford, 1976), pp. 257–86.

authoritarian tone. In 1194, for example, the royal justices condemned the sentence of excommunication which Archbishop Geoffrey of York had pronounced against William de Stuteville, sheriff of Yorkshire, with the phrase: 'this excommunication is considered to have been made contrary to the royal dignity and excellency'.[59] There is another case of the same year where a novel disseisin is apparently said to have been made 'to the damage of the crown of the lord King Richard'[60] and yet another in which Gerard de Camville was charged with lèse-majesté.[61] But this was the year of Richard's return from Germany, when men may well have been unusually sensitive about the king's majesty after his capture and enforced submission to the emperor. Such phrases remained rare, most useful perhaps when the Crown was engaged in defending its preserve against the claims of the Church, but far from indispensable even for that. King John made no great play with them. He relied rather on his interpretation of the traditional rights of the English monarchy. St Wulfstan was his defence against Pope Innocent, not Justinian. On the one occasion when he expressed views on the relationship between the prince and law it was simply to say that he had never heard that a new assize could be introduced into the land of anyone without the assent of its prince.[62] This was a long way from Justinian. So also, but in a different direction, was Alexander the Mason who apparently upheld the king's power during the Interdict by arguing that he was the 'rod of the wrath of the Lord, ruling his people like a rod of iron and dashing them in pieces like a potter's vessel'.[63] Justinian would have

---

[59] 'Consideratum est excommunicatio illa facta est contra regalem dignitatem et excellenciam' (*Three Rolls of the King's Court*, Pipe Roll Soc., p. 50).
[60] 'In lesionem coronae domini Regis Ricardi' (*Rot. Curiae Regis*, I, 31).
[61] 'Praeterea appellaverunt eum de laesione regiae majestatis', *Hoveden*, III, 242.
[62] 'Est inauditum tempore antecessorum nostrorum et nostro scilicet quod assisa nova statuatur in terra alicujus sine assensu principis terre illius' (*Rot. Litt. Pat.* p. 72).
[63] *Chron. Maj.* II, 527. See also F. M. Powicke, 'Alexander of St Albans: a literary muddle', *Essays in History presented to R. L. Poole*, pp. 246 ff.

had little need for this fire and brimstone. There is no sign that King John had any either.

Authoritarian impulses ran deep in twelfth-century administration. In contrast, these rationalizations of them were ill formed, unusual and, except for Alexander the Mason's, less than half-hearted. Against them there was a much more potent stream of thought which emphasized the responsibilities of the prince and his subordination to law. The basic element in this lay in the traditional distinction between kingship and tyranny, between government according to law and government by will, which ran back in medieval thinking to St Augustine, Isidore and other sources. In the twelfth century this distinction was fully and skilfully developed – most obviously in the *Policraticus* of John of Salisbury[64] – and it became axiomatic in scholarly discussion and literary thinking. Gerald of Wales devoted several pages of his 'Education of a Prince' to it. He wrote,

A king, who gets his name from ruling, is held to rule first himself and then the people under him. But it is in the nature of the tyrant, who gets his name either from the city of Tyre, the nursery of tyrants, or more likely from the poisonous serpent Tyrus, to oppress the people with his furious sway.[65]

This distinction between will and law was accepted by both Glanvill and fitz Neal despite the latter's more authoritarian tendencies.[66] Chronicler after chronicler used it or showed knowledge of it. It pointed their criticisms. To William of Newburgh, King Richard's chancellor William de Longchamps was 'Caesar and more than Caesar', 'an insuppor-

---

[64] J. Dickinson, 'The Medieval Conception of Kingship and some of its Limitations as developed in the Policraticus of John of Salisbury', *Speculum*, I (1926), 325 ff.

[65] 'Rex autem, qui a regendo dicitur, primo se ipsum, deinde subditum sibi populum, regere tenetur; tyranno vero, qui vel ab urbe Tyro, quae tyrannos educare solet, vel potius a Tyro serpente venenosissimo nomen trahere potuit, proprium est violento dominatu populum opprimere', *De Principis Instructione*, cap. XVI. *Opera* (Rolls Series), VIII, 54.

[66] See above, pp. 84–7.

table tyrant'.[67] Many agreed with him at the time, just as many later argued that John's rule was tyrannous or that he had evil advisers who pandered to his will;[68] 'a tyrannous whelp', wrote Gerald of Wales, 'who issued from the most bloody tyrants and was the most tyrannous of them all'.[69]

This was knock-about criticism which need raise little surprise. What is both more surprising and more significant is that the distinction between law and will represented a stream of thought which ran deep in the everyday thinking and arguments of articulate laymen. They applied it practically and expressed it vigorously in their legal actions, so much so that the records of the king's court are one of the major sources for the political thought of his subjects. In extreme instances these arguments were turned directly against the Crown. Hence an attorney of Gilbert de Gant, one of the leaders of the Lincolnshire rebellion in 1215, argued that Henry II 'had done his will and not what he ought' in confirming a charter made by a grantor on his death-bed.[70] Another important landowner, Peter fitz Herbert, boldly stated that his father had held land in Parham which he was now claiming against the abbot of Westminster, 'as of right and fee in the time of King Henry II', and that he had been disseised by the will of that king. This was a claim which he repeated at least twice. It was accepted by the court which ordered an inquiry into whether Herbert was in seisin prior to Henry II's arbitrary action. Ultimately the jurors confirmed his case and recorded that the grounds for the disseisin were uncertain, but that they thought it had been done by the will of Henry II.[71] The same tones were

---

[67] 'Caesar et plus quam Caesare.' 'Denique ipsum illo tempore in Anglia et plusquam regem experti sunt laici, et plusquam summum pontificem clerici; utrique vero tyrannum importabilem' (*Chronicles of Stephen, Henry II and Richard I*, 1, 333).

[68] *Chron. Maj.* II, 533.

[69] 'Catulum tyrannicum, cruentissimis a tyrannis parentaliter exortum ipsumque tyrannorum omnium tyrann[ic]issimum.' This is Gerald's valedictory and final judgement (*Opera*, VIII, 328).

[70] 'Libitum suum fecit et non quod debuit' (*Curia Regis Rolls*, IV, 43).

[71] *Curia Regis Rolls*, VI, 177, 287, 296. For further discussion and some qualification see below, pp. 135-6.

sounded even more vigorously by Ruald fitz Alan, constable of Richmond, a hard-bitten opponent of King John who was among the witnesses of Peter de Brus's Langbargh charter. In 1208 he alleged that Henry II had deprived his grandfather without judgement of four manors and six and a half fees which were his right as half the fee of the constable of Richmond. Here the jurors were firm and stated that Henry had so disseised him 'by his will and without judgement'.[72]

Some of the significance of such cases lies in the very casualness with which these phrases were advanced by plaintiffs and accepted by the court. They were not the monopoly of a revolutionary party. In 1219, in an action of darrein presentment against Nicholas de Stuteville, the abbot of Valmont made the same allegations against King John as Ruald fitz Alan had made against Henry II, namely that in presenting to a benefice he had acted 'unjustly and by his will'.[73] Such charges were not always directed against the king. In 1194 the allegation of arbitrary action was used by a plaintiff, Hamo Piron, who disapproved of his father's second marriage and alleged that his father, Henry, had married his stepmother 'by his will, not by the gift of the King or by the counsel of Hamo [Henry's father]'. Hamo, it should be noted, was still a minor, for the roll records that he pleaded as a boy.[74] Indeed John himself used and accepted these phrases. When he intervened in litigation about Crowland and Spalding marshes in 1191 he alleged that a charter of confirmation of Richard I had been made by the will of the Chancellor, William de Longchamps, the abbot of Crowland's brother. He was discomfited when the original grant of Henry II was produced for his inspection.[75] Later, as king, he was quite ready to accept and investigate allegations that he or his predecessors had

---

[72] Ibid. v, 148, and below, pp. 147, 157.
[74] Three Rolls of the King's Court, p. 9.
[73] Bracton's Note Book, case no. 39.
[75] Doris M. Stenton (1964), p. 169.

disseised men by will and without judgement.[76] There was no escape from contemporary assumptions, even for the king.

The effect of this was to contrast arbitrary action by the Crown with a concept of law and legal process. To do something by will was to act without the judgement of a court, to ignore title to property which legal process might establish. Where legal process could not reach, the same effect could be achieved by contrasting will with the even vaguer standard of the 'reasonable'. Men wanted the law to be enforced 'reasonably' or wanted reliefs or aids to be 'reasonable', or, as in Peter de Brus's Langbargh charter, casually assumed that officials would account 'reasonably'. Thus reason and justice were equated and marched hand in hand. Nothing is so striking in the legal records of John's reign as the subject's assumption of a right to justice, to a reasonable application of legal process to his own particular case. They appealed to it frequently and pointedly. Robert de Courtenay and Alice his wife, for example, offered money to be treated 'according to the custom and assize of the kingdom' in their claims to the vill of Caldbeck.[77] William de Mowbray did the same to be treated 'justly according to the custom of England' in the case arising from the claims of William de Stuteville to his barony.[78] Robert Bardolf asked the king to maintain and defend him 'according to the custom of England' against his other lords.[79] Others asked for cases to proceed according to the custom of the realm,[80] or complained of actions contrary to the

---

[76] See Turner (1968), pp. 201–67. For both political and procedural reasons it was easier to allege disseisin against the king's predecessors than against the reigning monarch. In John's case the seizure of *terra Normannorum* led to some disseisins which he was ready to investigate and correct. However, the clearest example of John investigating his own actions of disseisin is provided by the long running dispute over the Lucy inheritance (below, pp. 164–5, 202–3, Painter (1949), pp. 75–6, Turner (1989), pp. 163–6). See his letters of 22 June 1213 to Geoffrey fitz Peter, also directed separately to the barons of the Exchequer (*Rot. Litt. Claus.* I, 136*b*).

[77] *Pipe Roll 8 John*, p. 45.   [78] *Pipe Roll 3 John*, p. 157.

[79] *Pipe Roll 5 John*, p. 103.   [80] *Curia Regis Rolls*, VI, 279.

custom of the realm,[81] or made special provision that they should not be disseised without the judgement of the king's court.[82] These were not empty phrases. On the contrary they expressed a pervasive confidence in litigation. Men were ready to attempt to use the processes of assize against the Crown itself.[83] The king's justices themselves were ready to contrast the principles of laws with the actualities of royal behaviour. Under Henry II Ranulf Glanville had sustained the privileges of the monastery of Abingdon with the words: 'the lord king neither wished nor dared to attack or alter such ancient and just customs'.[84] Under John the royal justices reacted to an action between uncle and nephew into which the 'king's case' had decisively intruded by entering on the roll: 'Let it be noted that that inquest was made by the order of the lord king and not by the consideration of the court or according to the custom of the realm.'[85]

By this time the characteristic theories of the opposition to the Crown had been brought together in a recension of the Laws of Henry I and Edward the Confessor in which they were embodied in a number of extended interpolations.[86] These traversed familiar ground: 'Right and justice ought to rule in the realm rather than the perversities of will; law is always made by right, but will and violence and force are not right.'[87] This was incorporated in a loose version of the coronation oath which laid down that the king was to do all things rightly in his realm by the judgement of

---

[81] *Ibid.* I, 334, 376.   [82] *Rot. de Ob. et Fin.* p. 289.
[83] *Curia Regis Rolls,* III, 113; V, 43, 67, 165 (see Flower, 1943, p. 141); all cases of presentment to benefices.
[84] *Chron. Monasterii de Abingdon* (Rolls Series), II, 298.
[85] *Rot. Curiae Regis,* II, 189.
[86] The significance of these interpolations was recognized and clearly indicated for the first time by Powicke (1928), p. 114.
[87] 'Debet enim ius et iustitia magis regnare in regno quam voluntas prava; lex est semper quod ius facit; voluntas vero et violentia et vis non est ius' (Leges Edwardi, 11, 1, A 6, Gesetze, I, 635).

the magnates of the realm, that he was to fear God and
protect the Church, that he was to maintain good laws
and customs and destroy evil practices, that he was to
perform just judgements by the advice of the magnates,
and finally, a point included in the oath for the first time
here, that he was to maintain the rights of the Crown.[88]
Other significant claims were scattered throughout the
work. In the midst of a discussion of the hundred court
the writer interpolated the principle that 'nothing ought
to be demanded or taken except of right and reason, by
the law of the land, by justice and the judgement of a
court, without guile', as had been laid down by magnates,
bishops and the wise men of the land.[89] Similarly, in
discussing the duties of the ancient office of alderman he
inserted the duty of maintaining the laws, liberties, rights,
and just and ancient constitutions of the realm.[90] Indeed
he envisaged the magnates assembling in regular moots
in which they were to swear fealty to the king, elect
sheriffs and constables every year, and deal with local and
national emergencies as they arose.[91] All this stated the
principles which underlay Magna Carta; indeed on one
practical question, the election of local officials, it looked
beyond the Charter to the constitutional demands of the
later thirteenth century. The author of these views is
unknown, but the interpolations first survive in a collection
of laws, including the Laws of Edward the Confessor, which
was put together in London in the first decade of the
thirteenth century.[92] There is no other known source.
These were the notions on which the mayor and commune

---

[88] Leges Edwardi, 11, 1, A 6–9, Gesetze, I, 635–6. For further discussion of the last point see
below, pp. 118–19.
[89] Leges Henrici Primi, 8, 1 b, Gesetze, I, 554.
[90] Leges Edwardi, 32, A 2, Gesetze, I, 655.
[91] Leges Edwardi, 32, A 3, 4, B, B 1, B 8, Gesetze, I, 655–7.
[92] Liebermann, Über die Leges Anglorum saeculo xiii ineunte Londiniis collectae (Halle, 1894),
pp. 38–64, 91–100, Gesetze, I, 732–45; III, 340; idem (1913), 732–45.

and members of the chapter of St Paul's, and perhaps others too, could draw in 1215.[93]

It is important not to attribute too much significance to this statement of responsible government by counsel. It is set against an antiquarian background and is concocted of scattered interpolations which assert principles and state assumptions rather than attempt a logically coherent argument. However, these views stood in sharp contrast to the occasional assertions of authoritarian principles which emanated from the opposite side. Some authorities have gone so far as to see this as a clash of basic principle, in which the Angevins were moving towards a new authoritarian monarchy,[94] or one in which 'ascending' and 'descending' concepts of law were meeting in inevitable and head-on collision.[95] In fact it was not like this. Contemporaries did not see it in this way. The records permit such interpretations only at the cost of excluding a great deal of the evidence. The period permits this analysis only at the cost of ignoring the muddle and confusion which made up the greater part of human endeavour. For the essential kernel of truth was that the issues between the Angevins and their opponents were not clear-cut. Their arguments turned not so much on establishing one set of principles against another as on enforcing opposing interpretations of principles which were the common inheritance of both parties. This was the main reason for the inadequacy, obscurity and ambiguity of some of the provisions of the Great Charter.

[93] For general comment on the role of London see Holt (1985), pp. 13–17. I am not persuaded by the argument of Richardson (1948, p. 75 n; 1949, pp. 60–1; 1960, pp. 66–7) and Richardson and Sayles (1966, pp. 57–9) that the third recension of the coronation oath can be separated from the work of the London interpolator and given an earlier date of c. 1154, or that the whole interpolation should be so dated. While it is clear that 'Bracton' knew of the interpolation, there is no evidence that his information was derived from a source other than the London MSS. The MSS evidence, therefore, provides no good ground for abandoning the date advanced by Liebermann and Bateson (1902, p. 482). Compare Cheney (1968), pp. 286–8.

[94] Jolliffe (1955), esp. pp. 131–6.

[95] Ullmann (1961), pp. 117–211; idem, 'Law and the Medieval Historian', Reports of the 11th International Historical Congress (Stockholm, 1960), III, 34–74.

Neither party in the struggle fitted the neat doctrinal divisions in contemporary thinking. King John was as likely, indeed likelier, to appeal to custom as to the authoritarian principles which occasionally informed his government. Royal writs casually laid down that deputies were to be named and a duel was to proceed 'according to the custom of England',[96] or that an assize of darrein presentment was to go forward 'justly according to the custom of England',[97] or that a plea of service was to go forward 'according to the law and custom of England',[98] or that an inquiry was to be held into the blood relationship of two men to decide whether one could defend the other in a murder trial 'justly and according to the custom of England'.[99] These were not idle words. They recur again and again. Where custom and royal orders conflicted, custom often had the last word. Writs sometimes provided that a grand assize was to proceed 'unless reason or the custom of the realm opposed it',[100] or that a case of advowson was to go forward and 'was not to be stayed because of any prohibition ordered in our other letters'.[101] John even ordered the Justiciar not to do anything 'contrary to the custom of the realm' on account of any letters which the king had issued on behalf of one of the participants in a civil dispute.[102] He was ready to agree that the Crown's financial demands might create precedents to his subjects' disadvantages. In seeking aid from the knights of Lancashire for the reconstruction of Lancaster castle in 1208, he stated that he was asking for help 'not as of custom, but as of grace and on this occasion only'.[103] On many occasions he was ready to take advice in the traditional manner from the magnates of

[96] *Curia Regis Rolls*, II, 227.   [97] *Ibid.* III, 215.   [98] *Ibid.* V, 33.
[99] *Ibid.* I, 428.   [100] *Ibid.* II, 223.   [101] *Ibid.* III, 57.   [102] *Ibid.* III, 27–8.
[103] *Rot. Litt. Pat.* p. 87. Compare the letters of Hubert de Burgh to the monks of Canterbury (*H.M.C.* 5th Report, p. 433), and for a similar proviso in private charters see William de Roumare's enclosure of the wood of Bolingbroke, *c.* 1135 (*Documents illustrative of the social and economic history of the Danelaw*, ed. F. M. Stenton, British Academy, *Records of Social and Economic History*, V, 1920, no. 499).

the land. Important cases were postponed 'because the lord king wished to do to each as he ought according to the counsel of his barons'[104] or 'until the archbishop and other great and wise men of the land could be present'.[105] And many of the legislative and financial measures of the reign were stated to have been made 'with the counsel of our barons'.[106] In 1205 the Assize of Money was made 'by the common counsel of our realm',[107] and the arrangements for the muster of forces for the defence of the realm against a threatened French invasion in the same year were made with 'the assent of archbishops, bishops, earls, barons and all our faithful men'.[108] Even the Thirteenth of 1207, the most severe and effective tax of the reign, was arranged by 'common counsel and the assent of our council at Oxford'.[109] It is now impossible to define the reality which lay behind these phrases. No doubt 'counsel' was frequently selected and severely slanted in favour of the king. But in some ways the reality mattered less than the form. Every time a royal writ made a statement of this kind it represented a public acknowledgement of ideas which ran clean counter to any schemes for arbitrary rule.

This doctrinal eclecticism was evenly matched on the other side. Baronial plaintiffs were as ready to acknowledge or appeal to the royal will and majesty as the king was to assert the predominance of custom.[110] Hence Robert de Ferrers called in the 'dignity of the king' to support a preposterous claim that inheritance lay not between coheiresses but with the unmarried daughter in the king's gift, by asserting that King John died seised of this prerogative and that, if the case proceeded, 'the lord king would lose his dignity'.[111] Others readily bowed to the king's decision

---

[104] *Curia Regis Rolls*, I, 392.   [105] *Ibid.* III, 124.   [106] *Rot. Litt. Pat.* p. 41.
[107] *Ibid.* p. 54b.   [108] *Ibid.* p. 55.   [109] *Ibid.* p. 72b.
[110] See Van Caenegem (1973), pp. 34–5 on 'the irrepressible urge of plaintiffs to rush to the king instead of trying the local courts' a century or so earlier.
[111] *Bracton's Note Book*, case no. 12.

even when their own interests were directly involved. In 1205 Pentecost of Wandsworth ended a claim against the king by stating that he sought nothing 'except at the will of the lord king'.[112] Others turned to the king for help. In 1208, for example, Maurice de Gant offered the large sum of 100 m. for the purchase of several writs *praecipe*, for the king to help him in the claims which they involved and to do right to him in the matter of his properties in the Crown's hands 'as was just according to the will of the King'.[113] Others abandoned the struggle. Alexander of Caldbeck, who was faced by opponents who had already purchased the king's support in a dispute over the vill of Caldbeck, withdrew from his case 'because the lord king did not wish him to have it'.[114] Others used the king as a kind of legal protection. Peter de Brus offered 200 m. and two palfreys for the seisin of the manors of Carlton and Camblesforth with the proviso that he was not to be disseised except by order of the king if anyone attacked his claim.[115] Sometimes parties placed themselves on the king's arbitration by mutual agreement.[116] Sometimes a party sought the king's will as a matter of unilateral choice. Hence when Helen, daughter of Richard de Moreville, sought land in Whissendine of which the jurors agreed that she had been disseised during the Scottish war of 1173-4, her opponents, headed by Earl David of Huntingdon, stated that they would not accept the verdict of a jury; they said instead that 'the king could do his will'.[117] Even the king's justices, confident though they might be on occasion in asserting law and custom, nevertheless bowed to the king on certain matters.

---

[112] *Curia Regis Rolls*, III, 309.
[113] *Rot. de Ob. et Fin.* p. 427; *Pipe Roll 10 John*, p. 89.
[114] *Curia Regis Rolls*, IV, 99. His opponents were Robert de Courtenay and his wife who had already made an offer to be treated 'justly according to the custom and assize of the kingdom' in their claim to Caldbeck. See above, p. 92.
[115] *Pipe Roll 6 John*, p. 188.
[116] See an action between John Marshall and the Master of the Temple (*Curia Regis Rolls*, I, 374). See also *Pipe Roll 6 John*, pp. xxii ff.
[117] *Curia Regis Rolls*, VI, 273-4.

Hence the justices of the Bench in 1194 postponed judgement, on the king's order, in a case which turned ultimately on a grant by Henry II.[118] Similarly the justices on eyre in Lincolnshire in 1202–3 postponed a case which involved a royal charter because they were unwilling to adjudicate on the matter by themselves.[119] Who were the justices to debate a royal grant?

Hence the parties and the arguments in the debate did not coincide. Yet this is only an elementary complication. Behind the arbitrary actions of the government, the appeals to law and custom, or the acceptance of a royal decision, there lay social standards which are now difficult to understand or grasp. They were set by a society in which men had to accept far more violence, far more 'injustice' than is readily comprehensible. The law itself was violent. It relied on violence for its execution. The king's officers were liable in their bodies for the conduct of their offices. Imprisonment was an ever-present threat, against mismanagement, disobedience or the acceptance of bribes.[120] Likewise the ordinary landowner was responsible in his chattels and thereafter in his lands for the proper performance of his services. Seizure of chattels and land, the usual process of distraint, was the universal panacea to which all turned to ensure compulsion. Violence or the threat of it broke through recurrently. When in 1203 the king instructed the men of Holderness to pay their accustomed corn renders to the church of Beverley he pointed out that he had instructed the sheriff of Yorkshire to seize the bodies and chattels of those whom the Provost and Chapter of Beverley excommunicated on this account; the sheriff was to hold them in prison 'according to the custom of England and the liberty of the church of Beverley' until they had made full satisfac-

[118] Three Rolls of the King's Court (Pipe Roll Soc.), p. 3.
[119] Lincolnshire Assize Rolls, 1209–9, case 1265.
[120] See the case of Geoffrey de Meaux (Curia Regis Rolls, VI, 235, 289).

tion.[121] Such threats were not out of place in a society in which administration might develop into a running battle between the king's officers and the men they ruled. One of the great men of Holderness was Robert de Ros, famous as one of the Twenty-Five barons of the Charter. But he was also a vigorous and persistent disseisor whose men attacked the bailiffs of the sheriff of Yorkshire in 1220 with bows and arrows, putting them to flight and wounding some.[122] Yet Robert was mild by the side of Warin of Walcote, an 'honest itinerant knight' of Stephen's reign who took Isabel of Shuckburgh to wife by force and who fell into poverty after King Henry's peace had been proclaimed because he was no longer able to rob in the manner to which Stephen's anarchy had accustomed him. Ultimately he was ambushed and taken on King Henry's order. He was led before the king at Northampton, 'and King Henry, that he might set an example to others to keep his peace, by the counsel of his barons ordered him to be put into the pillory and there he was put and there he died'.[123] This was no isolated example of social maladjustment. As late as 1267 men still recalled the case of Richard of Haselbury who had followed in Warin's footsteps in John's reign. He was taken as a plunderer, beheaded and then hanged by the feet.[124]

A society in which these things happened was prepared for royal violence. When King John demanded the surrender of castles, or imposed monetary penalties, or exacted charters of fealty, as guarantees of his vassals' good behaviour, he was adding little to sound and accepted contemporary practice. Philip Augustus did exactly the same in France.[125] In England many of the rebels who made their

[121] *Rot. Litt. Pat.* p. 35*b*.   [122] *Curia Regis Rolls*, VIII, 198.

[123] *Rolls of the Justices for Gloucestershire, Warwickshire and Staffordshire, 1221*, ed. Doris M. Stenton (Selden Soc. LIX), case 390. See also Doris M. Stenton (1962), pp. 34–5.

[124] *Cal. Patent Rolls, 1266–72*, p. 66.

[125] See *Layettes du Trésor des Chartres*, ed. A. Teulet (Paris, 1863), vol. I, nos. 478, 773, 799, 805, 870–1, 881–7, 892–6, 932, 954–5, 988–94, 996–1001, 1026, 1040. There are many other examples both in this work, in the *Catalogue des Actes de Philippe Auguste*, ed. L.

peace with William Marshal and his associates in 1217 had to make out charters of fealty in which they pledged all their land and agreed that it would revert to King Henry if they ever left his service.[126] Indeed the pledge of land was soon adapted as a special form of warranty in private deeds.[127] Even the exaction of hostages does not seem to have been an excessive disciplinary measure. The rolls of 1194 refer to a hostage taken on the orders of Hubert Walter, archbishop of Canterbury.[128] After the civil war of 1215–17 the government ordered the release (against the surrender of hostages) of Gilbert de Gant, who had been captured at the battle of Lincoln.[129] In 1220 the government accepted hostages from William d'Aubigné of Belvoir prior to his providing sureties of good behaviour,[130] and from Roger Bertram of Mitford as guarantees of his faithful service, in return for his recovery of Mitford Castle, and for other reasons specified in a charter.[131] Indeed as late as 1223, when the civil war was long past, the Londoners had to promise to surrender on demand thirty hostages, mostly sons of the leading London families, as guarantees of the city's peace and faithful service to the king.[132]

Delisle (Paris, 1856), and in a register of Philip Augustus preserved in the Vatican Library (MS Ottobon, 2796) and described in *Archives des missions scientifiques et littéraires*, 3rd ser. vol. VI (1880). See also J. W. Baldwin, *The Government of Philip Augustus* (Berkeley, 1986), pp. 266–9.

[126] The Chancery Miscellanea (34/8, nos. 1–23) still include a set of some twenty charters of fealty made out in this form by the *reversi* at the end of the civil war. They were probably drawn up to a Chancery proforma and in one (no. 10) the name of the grantor, Alice Cokerel, looks like an insertion in a space left blank for the purpose. The witness lists usually include the names of William Marshal, Ranulf, Earl of Chester, the Earls of Arundel and Warenne and Hubert de Burgh. A further group of five similar charters was discovered in the unsorted Chancery Miscellanea in 1962. For this last information I am indebted to Dr Patricia M. Barnes.

[127] An early thirteenth-century grant of land in Arley by Oliver de Verigny to John de Hommet contains the following: 'Et si ego Oliverus vel heredes mei aliqua occasione huic carte contrarie voluerimus, concedo quod prefatus Johannes et heredes sui totam terram de Escremeuvile absque contradictione habeant' (University of Nottingham, Middleton Deeds, MiD, 4825, 4826).

[128] *Three Rolls of the King's Court* (Pipe Roll Soc.), p. 9.
[129] *Patent Rolls, 1216–25*, p. 99.   [130] *Ibid.* p. 246.   [131] *Ibid.* pp. 246–7.
[132] *Rot. Litt. Claus.* I, 569.

All this makes it difficult to read this period as though all the right were on one side and all the wrong on the other. Yet that is the view embodied in the Great Charter. It is an *ex parte* view and requires vigilant correction. Moreover it overlooks the fact that others behaved like the Angevins. Against the manner in which Henry and his sons exploited the jurisdictional superiority of the Crown should be set John's charter to the men of Durham of August 1208. This confirmed their privilege to plead according to 'the common and right assize of the realm of England' in the court of the bishop of Durham, if they were impleaded or if any sought right against them. They were not to answer for their free holdings except by the writ of the king or his justiciar, as they had done in the time of Henry II. The bishop might impose monetary penalties according to his own assize, but if he seized and held their stock despite their offer of guarantees, or sureties, then the sheriff of Northumberland was to see that it was restored and that they got just treatment.[133] Angevin justice was sought as well as feared. Against the Crown's exploitation of distraint should be set the complaint of Walter, attorney of Herbert de St Quentin and Agnes his wife, who told the king's justices in 1206 how the count of Aumale had seized his clients' stock and distrained their land of Mappleton on the grounds that they had defaulted in the homage, relief and service which they owed to Peter de Brus, the chief lord of Mappleton. Walter's case was that his clients held of Alice de Stuteville and that it was up to her to acquit them of service to Peter; he estimated their losses at £50 or more.[134] Against the Crown's readiness to imprison should be set a case in which this same Herbert de St Quentin was involved in 1205, in which he and Ranulf of Mappleton were accused of doing damage to the lands of William de Rocheford while the latter was in the king's prison. William, in his turn, had

---

[133] *Rot. Chartarum*, p. 182.   [134] *Curia Regis Rolls*, IV, 220.

imprisoned some of Herbert's men.[135] Against the Crown's exploitation of its rights of wardship should be set the story of the boy Thomas Saucer, of Thornaby in Cleveland, who was given in custody by Adam de Brus, chief lord of the fee, to Henry fitz Hervey of Bilsdale, and was compelled by his custodian to swear that he would renounce his inheritance to him when he came of age. 'And this he did', the record runs, 'so that he might avoid death.'[136] And against the overweening vigour of the Angevin kings should be set the example of Roger de Montbegon who, on failing to obtain lawful seisin of his lands in Wheatley and Clayworth after the civil war of 1215–17, refused to accept the considered judgement of the county court. He withdrew in anger, threatened to resort to self-help, ignored the summons of the court when knights were sent to recall him, and behaved in such a way that the court noted that he would have been arrested if he had not been 'a great man and a baron of the king'.[137] Roger was one of the Twenty-Five barons of 1215. King John was not alone in being capable of irate *hauteur*.

Such behaviour breaks the limits of neat theoretical categories. These in any case often seem unreal when set against the complications of contemporary law and administration. Sometimes even John does not seem to have known where he stood. On two separate occasions for example he sent orders to the Justiciar, Geoffrey fitz Peter, that assizes should proceed justly and according to the custom of England 'unless it has been prohibited by our special mandate'.[138] Here customary justice was being enforced by a special royal order on condition that there had been no previous special order prohibiting it; confusion

[135] *Ibid.* III, 37, 313.
[136] 'Genealogia antiquorum dominorum de Thormoseby in Clyveland', transcript from the Chartulary of Byland Abbey in Bodleian Library, Dodsworth MS 94, fo. 35.
[137] *Royal Letters, Henry III*, ed. W. W. Shirley (Rolls Series), I, 101–4.
[138] *Curia Regis Rolls*, III, 215. *Pleas before the King or his Justices, 1198–1202*, case 759.

could run little deeper. Others were in similar difficulties, like the sheriff who, when faced with contradictory writs from King Richard and Archbishop Hubert Walter, had to turn to the shire court for advice.[139] Indeed contradictory action and contradictory or overlapping spheres of jurisdiction lay behind many of the apparently simple cases in which men appealed in clear-cut terms against disseisin or against arbitrary action by the Crown. Some disseisins, for example, arose from the enforcement of the judgement of a private court in which a lord was pursuing the time-honoured method of distraint to ensure the performance of services.[140] Hence the prior of Luton, summoned to answer for the unlawful disseisin of Reginald son of Hereward and Isolde his wife, stated that he had seized the land 'by the judgement of his court for the default in his services and revenues and that he had his court present which agreed to this'. In the circumstances the king's court simply ordered that he should restore the land on pledges and summon the plaintiffs to his court to answer for the arrears of revenues and services, 'and treat them justly by the just judgement of his court'.[141]

It is clearly very difficult to determine where right lay in such a matter. This is equally so in cases which involved the Crown. For example, in both those actions in which Peter fitz Herbert and Ruald fitz Alan alleged that their ancestors had been unlawfully disseised by the will of Henry II,[142] the real issue seems to have arisen from conflicting rights of tenure originating in the anarchy of Stephen's reign and its resolution in compromise in the Treaty of Westminster of 1153. Peter's claim went back to his grandmother, who had held the estate in dower, and who according to Peter's

---

[139] *Three Rolls of the King's Court* (Pipe Roll Soc.), p. 34.
[140] *Northamptonshire Assize Rolls.* ed. Doris M. Stenton (Northants. Record Soc., v, 1930), cases 782, 816, 821. *Three Yorkshire Assize Rolls*, ed. C. T. Clay (Yorkshire Archaeological Soc., Record Series, XLIV, 1911), p. 2; *Rot. Curiae Regis*, II, 117.
[141] *Three Rolls of the King's Court* (Pipe Roll Soc.), p. 134.
[142] See above, pp. 90–1.

opponent, the abbot of Westminster, had 'thrust herself into the estate in time of war as many others did'.[143] Ruald's case was clearer since his ancestors had held the whole fee of the Constable of Richmond in the reign of Henry I. The estate seems to have become divided because the Empress Matilda granted it to the Rollos family which continued to hold half of it when Henry II came to the throne. It was not until William de Rollos sided with Philip Augustus in 1204 that Ruald's family could attempt successful recovery.[144] But Henry II was not so much in the wrong as Ruald's charge of arbitrary disseisin would suggest; he seems rather to have compromised in resolving conflicting claims by partition. This affected the tenants of the estate besides the principals. When Ruald regained control in 1205 several tenants of the Rollos fee made a proffer to the king that they might recover the land of which Ruald had disseised them, continue to hold it as they had done in William de Rollos's time, and not be disseised except by the judgement of the king's court.[145] Clearly Ruald, the disseised, was now the disseisor.

Descent and tenure were still beset by many problems.[146] They might be affected by the apparently casual omission of formal phrases from a charter. A long-fought action in which William, earl of Salisbury, and Ella his wife, followed

[143] *Curia Regis Rolls*, VI, 296, and below, pp. 135–6.
[144] *Early Yorkshire Charters*, v, 89, 91–2. For a more general discussion of this and similar cases see below, pp. 155–7.
[145] *Rot. de Ob. et Fin.* p. 289.
[146] Apart from an amendment to the first sentence I have let this paragraph stand as in the first edition. It now involves an extensive literature impossible to summarize here. For some of the main arguments see S. E. Thorne (1959), pp. 193–209; R. H. C. Davis, 'What happened in Stephen's Reign', *History*, XLIX (1964), 1–12; J. C. Holt, 'Politics and Property in early medieval England', *Past and Present*, 57 (1972), 3–52; S. F. C. Milsom (1976); J. C. Holt, 'Feudal society and the Family in early medieval England', II, Notions of Patrimony' *T.R.H.S.*, 5th ser., XXXIII (1983), 193–220; P. R. Hyams, 'Warranty and Good Lordship in Twelfth Century England', *Law and History Review*, V (1987), 437–503; Joseph Biancalana, 'For Want of Justice: Legal Reforms of Henry II', *Columbia Law Review*, 88 (1988), 433–536; John Hudson, 'Life-grants of land and the development of inheritance in Anglo-Norman England', *Anglo-Norman Studies*, XII (1989), 67–80; R. H. C. Davis, *King Stephen* (London, 3rd edn, 1990), pp. 150–3.

by their son William, claimed the custody of Sarum castle and the county of Wiltshire in fee, came ultimately to depend on the terms of a grant of them to William of Salisbury by Henry II. The issue turned on whether William had held them as of right or in bail of the king; the charter did not speak of bail or fee, nor did it mention any heritable right, and hence under John and again in 1237–8 the claim to inheritance was rejected.[147] They might be affected again by complexities of descent and family history into which the king's wish might well intrude. Hence at one stage in the history of the Mandeville barony of Marshwood King Henry I decided that a child of a second marriage should take precedence and inherit 'because he was the better knight'.[148] Even those apparently in secure possession of their land might be persuaded into an exchange, sale, or some kind of surrender in which part of their inheritance passed to the Crown;[149] and where descent was uncertain or debatable, possession might be achieved only by the payment of an inordinately high relief.[150] In these circumstances justice and injustice, law and will, were abstract terms, useful in argument but not strictly or immediately applicable to actual situations.

These difficulties were all the greater because the Crown and its opponents occupied the common ground of justice and custom. To dig into these words is not to strike hard, sharp definitions or even clear practices and opposed claims and arguments. There is no sure touchstone of what was lawful, what was unlawful, of where contemporaries might

---

[147] *Bracton's Note Book*, case no. 1235.

[148] *H.M.C. Wells*, I, 527–8; *Pipe Roll 10 John*, p. 113; F. M. Stenton (1961), pp. 37–8.

[149] For the intrusion of Henry II into the Brus fee in Danby see Holt (1961), pp. 179–81. See also the curious collection of charters in the *Black Book of the Exchequer*, I, 371–4, which record exchanges, sales or surrenders by Hamelin, Earl Warenne, Walter Crok, Henry of Clinton and Alice de Belleau.

[150] Hence, for example, Robert de Ros's offer of 1000 m. for the succession to the lands of Walter Espec in 1158 seems to have been aimed at securing the lion's share of Espec's lands, which descended through co-heiresses, against the claims of other representatives (*Pipe Roll 4 Henry II*, pp. 140, 146).

have considered that the Crown overstepped accepted limits. Indeed there was an uncertainty at the very core of the idea of justice, for to contemporaries the dispensation of justice passed almost insensibly into the satisfaction of petitions and the exercise of patronage. Richard fitz Neal wrote:

Offerings are said to be made in hope, or for future advantage, when a man offers a sum to the King to obtain justice about some farm or rent; not, of course, to ensure that justice is done—so you must not lose your temper with us and say the King sells justice—but to have it done without delay. Note also that the King does not accept all such offers, even though you may think him to overstep his limit. To some he does full justice for nothing, in consideration of their past services or out of mere goodness of heart; but to others (and it is only human nature) he will not give way either for love or money; sometimes owing to the deserts of those who hold what is sought, sometimes because the petitioners have done nothing to deserve it, being censured for offending against the realm or the King himself.[151]

Again, the exercise of justice was a kind of property from which the lord derived profit. It was his justice; he was obliged to give it, but the form in which he gave it had emerged from the manner in which he and his predecessors had conducted his court and was to that extent under his control. Hence for Glanvill the procedure of grand assize was 'a royal favour bestowed on the people by the clemency of the prince with advice of the nobles'.[152] If the prince could bestow it, he could also withhold it. Above all he could use it to reinforce his control over his vassals.

Thus the Angevins, even John, were normally able to take action against the recalcitrant by lawful and accepted procedure. The procedure was not always the same; something depended on the circumstances of each case; but they usually made some effort to dress up royal action in the trappings of the law. Hence in 1201 John proceeded 'by the judgement of

---

[151] *Dialogus*, p. 120. I have largely followed the editor's translation.
[152] Glanvill, II, 7, ed. Hall, p. 28.

his court' against Geoffrey, Archbishop of York, who had excommunicated royal officials and refused to pay taxation.[153] He used similar methods in 1204 against John de Courcy, lord of Ulster, who stood in the way of his schemes and the ambitions of the Lacy family in Ireland. He wrote to Meiler fitz Henry, the Justiciar, and Walter de Lacy, de Courcy's chief enemy,

We order you that you shall have John de Courcy summoned to come into our service without delay as he swore he would and for which he gave his hostages, and you shall give him a suitable term for this by the counsel of our barons and faithful men of Ireland. And if he does not come within that term you shall execute the judgement of our court in this matter. And if the judgement of our court deprives him of his lands then you shall ensure that Walter de Lacy and Hugh his brother shall have eight cantreds of that land next to their land of Meath, to be held of us by the service which shall be agreed upon among you.[154]

With this broadly hinted encouragement the judgement of a court was enthusiastically executed; de Courcy was deprived of his lands within a year and Hugh de Lacy was made Earl of Ulster.[155] In his dealings with the rebellious Poitevin barons in 1201 John tried a different tactic. Here he demanded that they should accept trial by battle against expert champions of his own choosing; in return the Poitevins demanded judgement by peers.[156] In his conflict with William Marshal in 1205, in contrast, an offer of trial by battle was made by William; John countered with a demand for judgement 'by his barons' and later turned to his household knights, his 'bachelors', to find someone to stand against William.[157] In 1210, on the other hand, William did not offer battle immediately, but put himself on the judgement of the court, again apparently consisting of the king's

[153] *Rot. Chartarum*, p. 102.   [154] *Rot. Litt. Pat.* p. 45.
[155] Painter (1949), pp. 46–7; Jocelyn Otway-Ruthven, *A History of Medieval Ireland* (2nd edn, London, 1980), pp. 74–5.
[156] *Hovedén*, IV, 176.   [157] *Histoire de Guillaume le Maréchal*, ll. 13,149–256.

barons.[158] In both these instances the judicial processes offered William a measure of protection. This was not the case in 1210 when John took action against William de Briouze and his family. William was quickly driven into exile, and yet seven earls and seven barons put their seals to a document in which John outlined and justified the procedure he had followed, demonstrating that William had been summoned according to the Law of the Exchequer and distrained and finally outlawed for contumacy according to the law of the land.[159] The king used the same measures in 1212 when faced with the plot organized by Robert fitz Walter and Eustace de Vescy. These two were summoned three times in the shire courts and outlawed when they failed to answer the final summons.[160] John once more proceeded by the law of the land. The only precaution he found it necessary to take was to pack the court which outlawed fitz Walter.[161]

By far the most significant of these cases was that of William de Briouze, not only because of its dimension and the ferocity with which John pursued this family but because the king here relied on the law of the Exchequer as well as the law and custom of the realm. In the Exchequer John had a court which was subservient to the king's interests within the broad limits of its own routine,[162] and which could be used to deprive men of their land, even to imprison them, in pursuing the recovery of the king's debts. These powers are not fully revealed in the *Dialogue of the Exchequer*, which fails to pursue the fate of the recalcitrant debtor to its end, and simply leaves it that his case would be discussed at the end of the Exchequer session.[163] Nor was much added in the new Exchequer regulations of 1201, which tightened up procedure in matters of detail and provided for distraint on land where the debt arose from a

---

[158] *Ibid.* ll. 14,311–18.   [159] *Foedera*, I, part I, 107–8.   [160] *Coggeshall*, p. 165.
[161] *Rot. Litt. Claus.* I, 165b–166.   [162] See above, p. 86.
[163] *Dialogus*, pp. 116–18.

fine for land.[164] In fact the Crown was ready to distrain on
land in the pursuit of all kinds of debt.[165] It could compel
debtors to surrender land and hold it at farm from the
Crown.[166] In extreme cases it imprisoned baronial debtors as
a measure which enforced payment and political discipline
at one and the same time. When Thomas of Moulton
bought the shrievalty of Lincolnshire in 1205 one of the
terms was that he should not be deprived of the office unless
he did something 'for which he ought to be disseised by the
judgement of a court'.[167] Within three years he had fallen
behind in the payments due on his proffer, and for this, and
incurring the king's displeasure on other matters, he was
imprisoned in Rochester Castle. The process in this case was
almost certainly a judgement in the Exchequer.[168] There
were other cases where debt, distraint and imprisonment
were closely associated, and it is highly likely that the
Exchequer was the enforcing authority in these, too. In the
Exchequer, in short, men got their judgement, but it was
sometimes one of dire consequences which achieved precisely what their demand for judgement was designed to
avoid. Yet it was the king's court, and its sphere of
jurisdiction could not be challenged directly. When the
barons tried to circumvent it in the Great Charter by laying
down that barons were to be amerced by their peers[169] they
were soon countered by the gloss of the greatest of thirteenth-century judges 'that is by the barons of the Exchequer
or before the King himself'.[170] This put them back where
they had started. The Crown's exploitation of its courts had
made the formulation of a clear baronial policy impossible.
They might demand judgement by peers or by the law of
the land, but neither they nor anyone else could give these

---

[164] *Hoveden*, IV, 152.   [165] For examples see *Rot. Litt. Claus.* I, 72b, 98b.
[166] *Curia Regis Rolls*, II, 259; III, 287.   [167] *Rot. Litt. Pat.* p. 57b.
[168] He was in the custody of the Barons of the Exchequer prior to his imprisonment, *ibid.* p.
85b (see also Holt, 1961, pp. 182–3).
[169] Magna Carta, cap. 21.   [170] Bracton, *De Legibus*, III, fo. 116b, tr. Thorne, II, 330.

well-worn phrases a precise connotation within the framework of the existing legal processes. Here they were in an
impasse, for what mattered was not the outward forms of
legal action but the spirit which directed them. In 1218
Nicholas de Verdun offered 200 m. to be acquitted of £551
of the aid of the knights of the honour of Leicester which
were demanded of him from the time when his father had
been sheriff of Warwickshire and Leicestershire. It was
discovered that the debt could not be traced against the
name of his father in the rolls of Henry II or Richard I, and
it was accepted that it had been placed against Nicholas
through the suggestion of Reginald Basset 'by will and
without judgement' in the time of King John. William
Marshal, Peter des Roches and the Justiciar, Hubert de
Burgh, now decided, with the council of the king, that
Nicholas was to be acquitted. He had got justice, formally
through the judgement of the great men of the land in
council, but in fact because of the political accident of a
minority, for it was this which enabled them to give such a
judgement. Even then the Exchequer required Nicholas to
pay his offer of 200 m. within three years.[171] The barons
who were directing the affairs of the land were not giving
justice away in such a matter.

Justice and judgement then were a matter for argument.
So even more was custom. Men were ready enough to talk
of the custom of the realm or even of local custom, but
where they did so they usually thought of customary
procedure. Hence those who referred to the law of the
shire[172] or of a particular borough[173] were concerned with
routine procedure in the shire court or with the more varied
local procedures of the borough courts.[174] Similarly men

---

[171] *Pipe Roll 2 Henry III*, pp. 42–3. For earlier evidence on this case and further discussion
see *Pipe Roll 11 John*, pp. xxv, 16–17, and Doris M. Stenton (1962), p. 50.
[172] *Pleas before the King or his Justices, 1198–1202*, case 52.
[173] *Three Yorkshire Assize Rolls*, p. 2.
[174] *Bedfordshire Assize Rolls* (Bedford Historical Record Soc., I, 1913), p. 210.

referred to the custom or assize of the realm to establish the age at which minors could plead[175] or the proper procedure for the pronouncement of outlawry.[176] The custom of the realm, or the law or assizes of the realm, cropped up in writ after writ, in action after action; plaintiffs asked that actions should proceed according to the custom and law of the realm, and the king laid down that his justices and officials should follow the law and custom of the realm. The phrases were recited almost as if they were meaningless rhetoric, and it was this which made them dangerous, for they were not so much meaningless as ambiguous, and in this lay the seeds of argument.

Custom and law largely consisted of routine procedure which had been hallowed by long usage. Occasionally it was reinforced by assizes or statutes produced by the king and his counsellors, but as late as 1215 there was still little enough substantive regulation to warrant the name of law. Hence custom was largely produced by the operations of the courts: by the local courts, by the central courts, where the Exchequer, for example, engendered the law of the Exchequer, and by the king acting with advice. Now in the case of the king this process was self-contradictory and likely to provoke debate. On the one hand he was creating custom because the extension of routine procedures was essential to efficient government. On the other, in so doing, he was in the long run restricting his own freedom of action since routine so created was not easily broken, evaded or rejected once its acceptability had given it the accolade of good and lawful custom. Hence when Henry II, for example, laid down that the assize of Northampton was to run as long as it pleased him,[177] he gave no recognition to the possibility that he might be starting something which he could not stop. Yet this happened regularly; on a wider scale, for example,

---

[175] *Curia Regis Rolls*, I, 279, 284.
[176] *Pleas before the King or his Justices, 1198–1202*, case 746.
[177] *Stubbs's Charters*, p. 179.

Magna Carta accepted and took over practically all the judicial procedures of Henry II, whether King John liked it or not. And in such processes several changes occurred. The Crown's routine convenience was converted into the subject's customary right; procedure and routine process were used to manufacture substantive law, a transmutation which quickened once men had begun, as Glanvill had, to compare English custom with the Roman *Leges*;[178] and custom, about which the Crown and its subjects might argue, was converted into statute which brooked no debate. It was just this which Magna Carta achieved.[179]

The first hesitant steps in these directions were pure fiction. Men convinced themselves that their present circumstances could be compared with an ideal past which had been governed by good and ancient laws. They therefore demanded the restoration of the Laws of Edward the Confessor and Henry I as the basic condition of reform, and they dragged out the charter of Henry I from the forgotten recesses of monastic and cathedral repositories and insisted on its confirmation. In some respects this appeal to tradition is readily comprehensible. The history of the Normans in England formed a unity stretching back to 1066 which could easily be grasped. Men were used to claiming title 'from the conquest' even though tenure at the death of Henry I or the coronation of Henry II was all that was required in law.[180] Moreover the coronation charters of the various kings traced custom and law back from 1154 to the reigns of Henry I and William I and so to the old English monarchy. In 1161 the penultimate English king, Edward the Confessor, had been canonized. In the late twelfth century his sanctity was known to include the remission of taxes.[181] Hence Edward's

---

178 Glanvill, Prologue, ed. Hall, p. 2.
179 For an examination of some of these points against a wider background of civil and canon law see F. Cheyette, 'Custom, Case Law, and Medieval Constitutionalism', *Political Science Quarterly*, LXXVIII (1963), 362–90.
180 Flower (1943), pp. 143–4.   181 Gerald of Wales, *Opera*, VIII, 130.

memory was potent reinforcement for those who favoured governmental moderation. Even the papal nuncio, arguing his master's case before King John during the Interdict, could contrast the good customs of the holy Edward with the evil laws introduced by William the Bastard.[182]

However, this appeal to tradition cannot be attributed entirely to the circumstances of the Norman Conquest, for it was also widespread on the continent. In the Golden Bull Andrew II of Hungary confirmed the privileges which his men had held in the time of St Stephen.[183] In France, in 1314, Philip the Fair confirmed the liberties which his subjects had held under St Louis,[184] and a year later Louis X had to acknowledge claims that evil customs had grown up since the time of the blessed Louis. In the kingdom of Sicily, where no member of the ruling family had achieved canonization, men had to make do with the memory of good King William II as a suitable standard to which Pope Urban required the Angevins to conform in 1263, and which they promised to accept when the events of 1282–3 forced reform upon them.[185] Much of this had a clear political purpose. The men of Amiénois dragged St Louis in to cover demands which included private warfare.[186] The nobles of Burgundy also appealed to his reign as if it established a standard of aristocratic privilege.[187] In Sicily the reign of William the Good was used as a basis for reduced taxation.[188] Everywhere these venerable monarchs were being used to resist and restrain the intrusions of their successors into the liberties of their subjects.

In some countries kings helped to bring this retribution upon their own heads, for they too had appealed to tradition to establish or recover royal rights. In Sicily the appeal to

[182] Annals of Burton, *Annales Monastici*, I, 211. For a discussion see *E.H.R.* LXX (1955), 7, n. 3, and the authorities there cited, also Emma Mason, 'St. Wulfstan's staff: a Legend and its Uses', *Medium Aevum*, LIII (1984), 157–79, and Holt (1985a), pp. 7–9.
[183] Marczali (1901), p. 134. [184] Dufayard (1894), 289; *Ordonnances*, I, 551.
[185] *Reg. Urban IV*, II, 122; Trifone (1921), p. 100. [186] *Ordonnances*, I, 562, 4.
[187] *Ibid.* I, 558 ff. [188] Trifone (1921), p. 100.

William the Good was first made by the Emperor Frederick II in an effort to recover rights of the Crown which had been lost during his own stormy minority. Likewise in England Henry II was responsible for the search for precedents in the reign of Henry I, for he deliberately set out to re-establish the Crown as it had been on the day his grandfather died. Hence for example he confirmed to the citizens of Exeter 'all the rightful customs which they had in the time of King Henry my grandfather, revoking all evil customs which have arisen there since his day'.[189] Hence, too, the royal courts steadily rejected claims to property based on possession in the reign of Stephen.[190] Henry II himself had helped to create the tradition which was to be used against his sons.

By 1215 this tradition had been entirely appropriated by King John's opponents. Its great merit, as contemporaries clearly appreciated, was to aim the attack against all the Angevins together, against Henry II as well as John and Richard. 'This year', wrote the Waverley annalist, 'there arose a great quarrel between the king and the barons of England, who sought from him the laws of St Edward and the liberties and free customs of other later kings, which had been corrupted and borne down in the reign of his father and especially in his own time.'[191] Abbot Ralph of Coggeshall put the same point concisely in stating that the barons were demanding the abolition of the 'evil customs which the father and brother of the king had created to the detriment of church and kingdom, along with those abuses which the king himself had added'.[192] The accession of Henry II, in short, was to mark the division between good and evil government, between valid custom and unlawful arbitrary innovation. This was reinforced in various ways. One was to doctor the Laws of Edward the Confessor and Henry I by

---

[189] Ballard (1913), p. 6.
[190] *Curia Regis Rolls*, IV, 217.
[191] *Annals Monastici*, II, 282.
[192] *Coggeshall*, p. 170.

interpolating later doctrines under the guise of old and laudable custom.[193] Another was to associate a tradition of good government with the name of Henry I, who according to the interpolator of the laws was 'the keeper of the beasts and the guardian of the flocks' who 'did right and justice in the land'.[194] Yet another was to vilify the Angevins as a tyrannical incestuous brood, sprung from the devil and doomed to defeat at the hands of the law-abiding kings of France.[195] All this was fiction. The 'good old times' of Henry I were an invention. But they were a telling, relevant invention in view of the tremendous administrative advances which had been made since the accession of Henry II. The division provided in the investigation of feudal tenures in 1166, in which enfeoffment up to 1135 was described as 'old' and enfeoffment since as 'new', could also have been applied to many other branches of the administration: to taxation, to the royal forests, to the administration of the Jews, to the administration of justice. John, perhaps more than anybody, was conscious of the debt he owed to his father. Time and again he turned to his father's reign in establishing royal rights or justifying royal policy, whether it was in reclaiming royal demesne,[196] or instructing the chief forester in the maintenance of the royal forest.[197] In 1215 he tried to stand firm, with the custom of his father's reign as one of his main lines of defence. Kings reacted differently to their subjects' use of fictitious history. In France in 1315 Louis X solemnly agreed to investigate the registers to

[193] See above, pp. 93-5.
[194] Liebermann (1913), 739. Late twelfth-century opinions on Henry II were usually much less glowing. The author of the 'London' Leges, for example, describes him in almost similar terms to those he uses for Henry I and then adds: 'Crimina vero sua fuerunt publica et valde notoria' (*ibid.* p. 742). Henry II's comparative unpopularity must not be attributed solely to the harshness of his administration, although this certainly played a part (see Gerald of Wales, *Opera*, VIII, 160); the murder of Becket rendered any balanced judgement impossible.
[195] Gerald of Wales, *Opera*, VIII, 301-2, 309, 328.
[196] *Curia Regis Rolls*, I, 252, 419, 428; *Rot. Litt. Claus.* I, 55.
[197] *Rot. Litt. Pat.* p. 3b.

discover, so he alleged, whether the rights claimed by his subjects had really existed in the time of St Louis.[198] In Sicily, in 1283 the decision on what exactly were the customs of good King William was referred to Pope Martin IV who replied that it would not be proper for him to give an opinion in such an uncertain matter, especially since it would affect the future state of the realm of Sicily.[199] In England John was cast in a more subtle mould. On the one hand he relied on the fact that his own government had grown out of his father's so closely that no real separation of the two was possible. On the other he proceeded to sow confusion by suggesting that he should abandon the 'evil customs' of his own reign whilst retaining the practices of his father's reign.[200] In short he tried to abandon the husk while retaining the real core of power on which Angevin government was based. He might be condemned as an innovator, but not his father. On this he largely won his case. Magna Carta left much of Henry II's work untouched.

Hence on the question of custom, as on the question of judgement, the Crown came to be engaged in an exhaustive argument. Neither it nor its opponents abandoned the ground chosen for debate. Even in Magna Carta there was no complete resolution of some of the major points at issue.[201] It was a hard slogging match with no dramatic advance or withdrawal. The striking developments in the argument occurred elsewhere, especially in men's attitude to right and law. These concepts could be covered by the single term *ius*. Both just judgement and custom led in the end to right; indeed their major function was to establish right. Now 'right' had a simple traditional meaning; men sought land or castles 'as their right'; rights of this kind were even tangible, and when used in this way the word was not

[198] *Ordonnances*, I, 564, 572.   [199] Trifone (1921), p. 100; Potthast, *Regesta* II, 1780.
[200] See below, pp. 234, 341–2.   [201] See below, pp. 297–302.

117

particularly explosive. But even in its origins in Roman law, it also had a second meaning, that of laws, and by the twelfth century Glanvill, for example, moved easily, almost unconsciously, from one sense of the word to the other. Hence rights and law came to be confused, and right came to be viewed as something more than simple individual title. It now became an impersonal right attached to an institution; it even developed into the rights enjoyed by the realm. In the latter case right and law were equated, for law was now viewed as something to which the community and each one of its members was by right entitled. Magna Carta fulfilled both senses of the word for it was at one and the same time a collection of rights and a statement of law.[202]

This contributed first to the concept of the rights of the Crown, to a doctrine of inalienable sovereignty which continued to subsist apart from the succession of particular kings.[203] By the coronation of Henry III, and possibly even earlier, a promise to preserve the rights of the Crown had been included in the coronation oath.[204] By then the concept was familiar and well worn. King Stephen granted the hundred of Stowe to the abbey of St Edmund 'saving the right of my Crown';[205] he also issued his second coronation charter 'saving my royal and lawful dignity';[206] and John, for example, granted the shire of Westmorland to one of his staunchest supporters, Robert de Vieuxpont, 'saving the pleas which pertain to our Crown and saving the royal dignity'.[207] But it had also come to be confused with parallel but very different ideas. One of the earliest

---

[202] For the above and some of what follows, see Holt (1960), I, 57–69.

[203] For an excellent general treatment of the theme, see Riesenberg (1956), esp. pp. 98 ff.

[204] Richardson (1960), 151–74. Richardson argued for carrying this additional clause in the oath back to the coronation of Henry II. But see above p. 95, n. 93.

[205] *Stubbs's Charters*, p. 122.

[206] 'Haec omnia concedo et confirmo salva regia et justa dignitate mea' (*ibid.* p. 144).

[207] 'Salvis nobis et haeredibus nostris placitis omnibus quae ad Coronam (nostram) pertinent, et salva dignitate regali' (*Cal. Patent Rolls, Richard II, 1396–9*, pp. 344–5).

and most forceful statements of the concept was made by the interpolator of the Laws of Edward, who, in a section headed 'Of the right and perquisites of the Crown of the realm of Britain', laid down that the king 'ought by right to preserve and defend all lands and honours, all dignities, rights and liberties of the crown of this kingdom, in their entirety and integrity, without diminution, and with all his power restore to their due and former state the rights of the realm which have been dispersed, destroyed or lost'.[208] Now the rights of the Crown and the rights of the realm were not necessarily the same thing in the eyes of all men. King John might summon men to a council to consider 'the common utility of our realm',[209] and Pope Innocent could condemn Magna Carta as impairing John's rights and dignity to 'the detriment of the royal right and the shame of the English nation',[210] but on the other hand the barons could equally well demand in 1205 that the king should swear to preserve the *iura* of the realm by their advice,[211] and in 1216 Prince Louis could equally well argue that John should be condemned for failing to preserve the rights and customs of the church and realm of England.[212] The right, interest, or utility of the realm was a weapon which both sides in the argument could use.

In this atmosphere men began to demand the restoration of right, or assert their right to judgement, or demand the confirmation of good and ancient custom, with increasing confidence. They were encouraged by the recurrent crises

---

[208] 'Debet vero de iure rex omnes terras et honores, omnes dignitates et iura et libertates corone regni huius in integrum cum omni integritate et sine diminutione observare et defendere, dispersa et dilapidata et amissa regni iura in pristinum statum et debitum viribus omnibus revocare' (Leges Edwardi, 11, 1 A 2, *Gesetze*, 1, 635). For a full discussion see Richardson (1949), 44 ff.; (1960), 151–74.

[209] *Stubbs's Charters*, p. 277.

[210] *Selected Letters of Innocent III*, pp. 215–16.

[211] *Gerv. Cant.* 11, 97–8. Here Gervase illustrates very clearly the dual sense of *iura*.

[212] Chronicle of William Thorne in Twysden, *Scriptores Decem*, 11, col. 1869.

which compelled the Angevin kings and their ministers to acknowledge the increasing swell of discontent. That the Crown might have been responsible for evil customs was publicly admitted in Henry II's settlement with the Church in 1172, in which Henry promised to do away with the 'evil statute of Clarendon and all bad customs which had been introduced into the Church of God in his day, and to moderate any evil customs which might have come into use before his time, according to the instructions of the lord Pope and the advice of churchmen'.[213] When Henry died further damaging admissions were made. Queen Eleanor, who proclaimed a general amnesty on her son's behalf, ordered that 'all those who had been seized and held by the will of the King or his Justiciar, and were not detained by common right of shire or hundred, or because of an appeal, should go free'. When Richard landed in England he continued her work by restoring all those whom his father had disinherited, to their former rights.[214] The quarrels between Count John and Richard's chancellor, William de Longchamps, gave further encouragement to the demand for justice and to the practice of conciliar government. John himself announced that it had been decided 'by the common deliberation of the faithful men of the lord king' that writs were to run under the king's seal throughout the land[215] and in his agreement with de Longchamps in 1191 he made provisions for the exercise of justice which were a prelude to those of 1215:

It is conceded that bishops, abbots, earls, barons, knights and free tenants shall not be disseised of lands and chattels by the will of the justices or the ministers of the lord king, but that they shall be dealt with by the judgement of the court of the lord king according to the lawful

---

[213] Becket Materials, IV, 415.   [214] Hoveden, III, 4–5.
[215] Epistolae Cantuarienses, 1187–9, ed. Stubbs (Rolls Series), p. 348; Gerv. Cant. I, 509.

customs and assizes of the realm or by the mandate of the lord king.[216]

By John's reign the symptoms of the malaise were less dramatic but more widespread. Men openly sought their rights in the king's court, even against the Crown. They readily alleged that there had been arbitrary procedure, even unjust disseisin, on the part of the king or his predecessors. They were prepared to argue that a sheriff had acted by force,[217] or that a custodian had wilfully wasted a ward's estate,[218] or that they should not be required to pay aids to their lord other than to ransom his body, knight his eldest son, or marry his eldest daughter.[219] As time passed they were readier to exploit the king's difficulties in order to gain their ends. In 1199 John's agents in England obtained his recognition by promising the restoration of rights to a group of discontented lords.[220] In 1201 some of the earls apparently refused to follow John abroad unless their rights were restored.[221] In 1205 a threat of rebellion and invasion led to a royal promise to preserve the 'iura of the realm'.[222] These incidents were described by Howden and Gervase of Canterbury in phrases similar to those which later writers attached to the promises and concessions which the king was

---

[216] 'Sed et concessum est quod episcopi et abbates, comites et barones, vavassores et libere tenentes, non ad voluntatem justitiarum vel ministrorum domini regis de terris vel catallis suis dissaisientur, sed judicio curiae domini regis secundum legitimas consuetudines et assisas regni tractabuntur, vel per mandatum domini regis' (*Hoveden*, III, 136).

[217] *Curia Regis Rolls*, VI, 361.

[218] *Pipe Roll 4 John*, p. 66. Compare *Curia Regis Rolls*, VIII, 75–6.

[219] See the complaints of the tenants of Robert de Mortimer against a demand to give him aid for service in Poitou in 1207: 'Dicunt quod tenent tenementa sua libere et per liberum servicium, et nullum auxilium facere consueverunt antecessores sui nec ipsi aliud auxilium facere debent nisi ad redempcionem domini sui vel ad primogenitam filiam suam maritandam vel ad faciendum primogenitum suum militem; nec aliud auxilium ei facere volunt nisi curia consideravit' (*ibid.* V, 39).

[220] 'Praedictus Johannes Normannorum dux redderet unicuique illorum jus suum, si ipsi illi fidem servaverint et pacem' (*Hoveden*, IV, 88).

[221] 'Mandaverunt regi quod non transfretarent cum illo, nisi ille reddiderit eis jura sua' (*ibid.* IV, 161).

[222] 'Jurare compulsus est quod jura regni Angliae de eorum consilio pro posse suo conservaret illaesa' (*Gerv. Cant.* II, 97–8).

forced to make from 1213 onwards, including the final concession of 1215 itself.[223] Men were not aware of a sudden break in this development either at the beginning of John's reign or anywhere else within the Angevin period. Hence from 1212 onwards they slid into a major crisis all the more readily because they were rehashing old arguments and repeating old demands. They saw the process whole. They could not see when or how it would end.

[223] 'Ibi quoque jura sua baronibus, et aliis de quibus indubitanter constabat quod eis competebant, rex restituit' (*Coggeshall*, p. 172). 'Reddiditque in continenti rex unicuique jus suum' (*Walt. Cov.* II, 221). '. . .venerunt ad regem multi nobiles de regno, exigentes jura sua terrarum et possessionum ...' (*Chron. Maj.* II, 606). Compare the king's letters announcing the settlement at Runnymede to William Longespee, Earl of Salisbury (appendix 11, below, p. 495).

CHAPTER 5

JUSTICE AND JURISDICTION

These matters must now be set in a jurisdictional frame-work; for men wove their political theories from words first spun in legal contexts. It has long been recognized that the cry for justice in 1215 exhibited some very peculiar, apparently contradictory features. On the one hand the Charter demanded that royal justice should be more accessible and better administered.[1] On the other, it forbade unlawful arrests and disseisin, the sale or delay of justice, and it promised restitution for unjust fines and amercements.[2] Apparently men wanted more, but were not altogether pleased with what they had. This contrast is striking and is to be explained by another. The common law of the Angevins gave the undertenant the opportunities and protection of varied routine procedures. But it left the tenant-in-chief still exposed to the vagaries of the king's will. This is the clue to the judicial provisions of the Charter. By and large it approved of what the undertenant had enjoyed and con-demned what the tenant-in-chief had suffered. Hence it sought to give the magnate a legal security like that enjoyed by the freeman. During the minority of Henry III this was largely achieved. The protection of the law moved up, not down, the social scale.

Within a surprisingly short space of time the procedures which took shape under Henry II and his sons became manifestly popular. It was not simply that, within a single life-span, they had come to provide generally accepted and readily accessible procedures. They also attracted a wider

---

[1] Caps. 17–19; also cap. 35 (1225).   [2] Caps. 39, 40, 55.

and wider social spread of litigants. Glanvill's sample writ of *mort d'ancestor* concerned, not a hide of land, but a mere virgate;[3] it initiated what became the commonest of all possessory actions. The first Foot of Fine was filed in the Treasury on the order of the Justiciar, Hubert Walter, and to the benefit of his brother Theobald, on 16 July 1195.[4] Within little more than a decade the surviving Feet of Fines testify that the final concord before the royal justices had become a standard instrument for the transfer of land among the freeholders of Norfolk: small holders conducting small transactions.[5] Many of these men resorting to the courts were concerned with, and may well have held, no more than 10 acres or so. Godwin the Taylor who brought actions of right leading to the grand assize and reached final concord concerning land in Syderstone, 2 acres in 1198 and 6 acres in 1200, would be unknown to us but for his resort to the court. The same is true of the two men, Robert son of Aselac and Humphrey son of Siward, with whom, respectively, Godwin divided these petty holdings.[6] The same story is told by a much neglected little roll which records the names of those who placed themselves on grand assize in the county courts during the reign of Richard I.[7] Of the 136 actions it records most were concerned with small parcels of a few acres, sometimes as low as half an acre or 3 roods, or to services amounting to a few pence *per annum*.[8] Two actions, one for a knight's fee, and one for half a fee, are

---

[3] ed. Hall, p. 150.
[4] *Feet of Fines, Henry II and Richard I* (Pipe Roll Society, XVII, 1894), p. 21. For comment see Cheney (1967), pp. 95–6.
[5] See the illuminating comments of Miss Barbara Dodwell, *Feet of Fines – Norfolk 1198–1202*, Pipe Roll Society, n.s., 27, pp. xxvi–xxxix. For further material see *Feet of Fines – Lincolnshire 1199–1216*, Pipe Roll Society, n.s., 29. Compare also below, p. 125, n. 12.
[6] *Feet of Fines – Norfolk*, nos. 178, 252. The Fines, of course, do not in themselves indicate the size of the litigants' holdings, but they do provide some evidence on the general size of Norfolk tenements. See Miss Dodwell's comments, *ibid.* pp. xxxiii–xxxvi.
[7] *Curia Regis Rolls*, I, 1–14. Since the last membrane is endorsed *tempore regis Johannis*, it probably extends into the early years of John.
[8] *Ibid.* I, 7, 14, and for an action concerning the rent of 8d for a toft in Ancaster, *ibid.* I, 10.

quite exceptional.[9] One action concerned a demand for servile services.[10]

So there was intense downward social pressure in certain functions of the legal system. Increasing governmental resources made procedures more readily available. As the twelfth century advanced more men from a wider social range could afford to resort to the courts more frequently. The assizes, and the final concords agreed before the royal justices, filed as Feet of Fines, provided just that mass-produced, relatively cheap form of security they required.[11] In John's reign they responded eagerly to new opportunities. They put to good use the royal eyres of 1200, 1201 and 1204.[12] They took to the writ *praecipe* when it became generally available during the last of these.[13] It was not all sweetness and light. Procedures were full of traps for the unwary. Penalties and amercements were heavy. Moreover, the popularity of royal justice extended only to civil actions. Local communities, at one and the same time, wanted to gain readier access to the assizes, but also to restrict the criminal procedures of the courts of shire and hundred to the traditional intervals and to limited sessions.[14] But, by and large, for the ordinary litigant, knight or freeman, it was an effective system, probably more so than anything else available in western Christendom. The grievance of 1215 was simple. The last general eyre of John's reign ended in

---

[9] *Ibid.* 1. 5, 9.   [10] *Ibid.* 1, 3.

[11] On the use of the action of *mort d'ancestor* and the grand assize as access to a final concord see C. W. Foster, *Lincolnshire Final Concords*, II (Lincs. Record Soc., XVII, 1920), p. xxxvi, and Margaret Walker in *Feet of Fines – Lincolnshire*, p. xviii.

[12] For 1200 and 1201 see *Pleas before the King or his Justices*, I, 56–86, 93–124. For 1204 see *Curia Regis Rolls*, III, v–vii, and *Pipe Roll 6 John*, pp. xi–xxxiii. This last eyre also yielded a crop of royal charters dealing with small areas acquired by unimportant people (*Rot. Chartarum*, pp. 137b, 140–1).

[13] *Pipe Roll 6 John*, pp. xxiii–xxxiii.

[14] MC (1217), cap. 35. See also above, pp. 62, 66 and below, pp. 390–1. Compare also the penalty of 60 m. imposed on the citizens of Exeter for their offence against the justices in eyre in 1219 (*Curia Regis Rolls*, VIII, 139). For details, which allegedly involved an attack on the justices' sergeant, apparently the work of the local bakers, and to subsequent arrests by Peter de Maulay, castellan of Corfe, see *Devon and Cornwall Notes and Queries*, XX (1936–8), 351–2.

1209. In the same year the Bench was closed. Thereafter justice was largely administered *coram rege*.[15] As a result of these measures the service which the Crown had provided was seriously attenuated. Hence the Charter's promise that common pleas should be held in a 'certain place' and that royal justices would visit the county courts to hold the petty assizes four times a year – an expression of unrealistic reforming zeal which could never be attained in practice.[16] Nevertheless, something like it was achieved in the general eyre begun in 1218 when the justices went out 'seeing to the revival of the laws in their pleas and causing them to be observed according to the aforesaid charter of King John'.[17] There was a real foundation to this contemporary enthusiasm. The work done by these justices was immense, extending from 1218 to 1222.[18] Moreover the demand for justice was real. The Pipe rolls of Henry III's early years contain a surprisingly large number of proffers for writs *pone*, which transferred cases to the eyre or Bench, and for actions of attaint.[19] Normal service was being resumed.

That was all very well for the undertenant. The tenant-in-chief was in a different fix. The king enjoyed a complex, diversified judicial competence. He had an overriding duty as king to maintain right and justice. Then, as lord, he did justice to his immediate tenants, his barons, the tenants-in-chief. Finally, as both king and lord, he supervised lesser

---

[15] M. T. Clanchy (1985), pp. 229–32. For further discussion of the reasons for these measures see below, pp. 186, 324. See also *Pipe Roll 12 John*, pp. xiv–xxii for the special eyres of 1210. The Bench was reactivated in 1214.

[16] Cap. 18. The provision was amended to once a year in 1217 (cap. 12). That, too, was beyond the government's resources. Later the demand was met to a greater degree by special commissions of assize. See Pollock and Maitland (1898), I, 200–1 and Plucknett (1948), pp. 101–2, 156–7.

[17] *Annales Monastici*, II, 291.

[18] D. Crook, *Records of the General Eyre* (H.M.S.O., 1982), pp. 71–8. See also the three volumes of rolls of justices in eyre edited by Lady Stenton, Selden Soc., vols. 53, 56, 59 (1934–40) and *Pipe Rolls 2, 3 and 4, Henry III*.

[19] *Pipe Roll 2 Henry III*, pp. xx–xxi; *Pipe Roll 3 Henry III*, pp. xvii–xviii, xxv–xxvi; *Pipe Roll 4 Henry III*, p. xviii.

jurisdictions, especially at the request or application of a litigant. Much of the procedure of John's reign had originated in this supervisory function of the king's court: certainly the writ of right, most probably the assize of *mort d'ancestor*, and in some degree the assize of *novel disseisin*. It had infiltrated through and around this original function so that a litigant would turn to it in the first instance; access to it through the writs was in most circumstances a matter of course. This was the common law. Yet embedded within it there still remained the king's jurisdiction over his immediate vassals. To call this feudal is to use a word to which there are now fashionable if misdirected objections.[20] It may be too simple a definition, for in such cases the feudal lord was also king, his jurisdiction reinforced by all the authority of the Crown in tribunals from which there was no appeal. Nevertheless, the line between the immediate and supervisory jurisdiction of the king was drawn by tenure. His immediate jurisdiction was less fettered by procedure. Without necessarily implying that it was always red in tooth and claw, it is true to say that it drew its strength, not from the assizes of Henry II, but to a past which stretched back to Domesday Book and the Norman Conquest. It was primitive, and its essence was lordship.

Within this the tenant-in-chief was no longer the lord of a court, the role which he so often plays in our legal histories, but merely a litigant. As such he was by no means isolated from other litigants. Most tenants-in-chief were also undertenants; many of them, on being vouched to warranty, took over and fought their tenants' actions; undertenants, meanwhile, might well be treated as holding immediately of the Crown if the barony of which they held escheated or came

---

[20] It is a pity that Elizabeth Brown's criticism of the 'construct' of feudalism has directed attention away from contemporary evidence (*American Historical Review*, 79 (1974), pp. 1063–88). Quite apart from *feodum*, the words *feodalis* (feudal man), *feodatarius* (both as noun and adjective), and *feodaliter* were all in use. It is a mistake to ignore the contemporary sense and resonance of these words and the notions which engendered them and were nurtured by them. For an example see Appendix 2, below, p. 412.

into royal custody. No jurisdictional zone was totally isolated. The common law bred common knowledge. It must, therefore, have been all the more obvious to the tenant-in-chief that he was in a much less secure and predictable situation than his men. He was faced with the fact that the common law was designed primarily to supervise and circumvent his jurisdiction, not to meet his needs as litigant. Some shortcomings were obvious. He could have no access to the writ of right because that was directed to the lord of a court and the king could not direct it to himself.[21] Similar problems beset the possessory actions. He would find it difficult to use the writ of *mort d'ancestor* because that assumed that the tenant had been put in seisin by a lord;[22] if the lord were the king the writ would be self-contradictory, all the more so if the king, as lord, had intruded to retain the estate in his own hand.[23] The writ of *novel disseisin* might seem more accessible, largely because by John's reign its function had become diverse, but here too there was an element of self-contradiction if it was directed against the agents of the king as lord.[24] It could not be brought against the king, and in fact it was little used. Yet the king's jurisdiction over his tenants-in-chief was not totally unstructured, an unbridled manifestation of will. The writ *praecipe* was available to the magnate as much as to the knight; indeed it became the baron's writ of right. He could obtain recognitions of particular issues, challenge entry and record concords. Indeed baron and king alike drew on the common law even though for them it was inappropriate and incomplete. They were like actors with a defective script. They had to make some of it up as they went along.

In this confined world litigation did not conform to the statistics of common law actions which can be culled from

[21] Glanvill, XII, 2–3, ed. Hall, p. 137.
[22] Milsom (1976), pp. 164–76. The assumption, however, is derived from the probable logic of the action rather than certain documentary proof.
[23] As envisaged by Hall, p. 149n, and indeed by the Assize of Northampton, cap. 4.
[24] Milsom (1976), pp. 8–25.

the Pipe rolls. The assize of *mort d'ancestor*, generally in so great demand, was used only occasionally, sometimes in very unusual circumstances. One or two cases seem relatively straightforward. William of Bamburgh, for example, had been in Scotland when his father, Odo, died. King Richard took the land into his hand and in 1200 William proffered 5 m. for an inquiry into the matter. Within weeks the claim was acknowledged, the proffer was replaced by one of 10 m. which was in effect a relief; in 1212 William son of Odo was securely in possession.[25] Throughout there was no mention of either writ or assize; the intended inquiry was an 'inquisition', as it had to be if it was the king at fault. William was a minor tenant, holding by sergeanty. At the other end of the social scale, in 1201, Richard earl of Clare proffered £100 for a writ of *mort d'ancestor* against Roger de Tosny claiming that his uncle, also Richard, had died seised of Saham, Norfolk. Richard de Clare had held Saham as *terrae datae*, but the king had granted it to Roger de Tosny and his heirs in 1199. The earl, apparently, was hoping to convert his uncle's temporary enjoyment of a royal manor into something more permanent. The bid failed; the matter probably never came to court; the Tosnys remained in possession and ultimately gave their name to Saham.[26] Some cases involved the descent or division of baronies. Each exhibits its own peculiarities. An action between Fulk fitz Warin, husband of Hawise, one of the three daughters of Joscy de Dinant, and Peter fitz Herbert originated in 1191 with proffers for the inheritance of the heiresses.[27] By the summer of 1194 Fulk and the other heirs general and their representatives had brought an action of *mort d'ancestor* against Herbert fitz Herbert over Carlton and Stanton, Wiltshire.[28] The action was postponed, first because Peter

[25] *Rot. de Ob. et Fin.* pp. 86, 114; *Book of Fees*, p. 204.
[26] *Rot. de Ob. et Fin.* p. 178; *Rot. Chartarum*, p. 25b.
[27] *Pipe Roll 3 Richard*, pp. 120, 121.
[28] *Three Rolls of the King's Court* (Pipe Roll Soc., XIV, 1891), p. 3.

fitz Herbert, who had inherited the lands from his brother and was now apparently in seisin, was overseas in the king's service, and then because the lands were found to be in the king's hands pending restoration to the right heir.[29] By 1196 the action was under way again but to no immediate avail for renewed proffers were made in 1199. By then it was proving expensive: 40 m. for the assize in 1194, 60 m. for its renewal in 1199.[30] There seems to be no record of any resolution of the case under John. Peter fitz Herbert was apparently still in control in 1235–6; by 1242–3 a division had taken place but the feudal dependency of at least one tenement was still confused.[31] By contrast a dispute over the barony of Odcombe looks like a short sharp shock. In 1199 Walter Crok proffered 200 m. for a recognition of *mort d'ancestor* for half the barony, which had been held by Walter le Bret. His opponent, John de Montagu, proffered 400 m. to stay the action if an inquiry established that Walter had been seised of the land after the death of his uncle Walter le Bret (which would have barred the assize), for the king's confirmation to him of both halves of the barony, and for inquiries into disseisins committed against his father.[32] Within a year Crok surrendered his half to the powerful courtier, William Briwerre, for the benefit of Briwerre's son. Briwerre acquired the other half by 1202.[33] In 1265 local jurors recalled that these lands had been alienated fron the true heirs through the power of William Briwerre the elder, and there is little doubt that the formal proffers and proceedings recorded in 1199–1200 were closely linked to his machinations.[34] These actions took place between parties who lay just outside the bar which denied

[29] *Ibid.* and *Rot. Curiae Regis,* I, 37.
[30] *Pipe Roll 6 Richard,* p. 200; *Rot. de Ob. et Fin.* p. 38.
[31] *Book of Fees,* pp. 423, 713–14, 729.
[32] *Curia Regis Rolls,* I, 239; *Rot. de Ob. et Fin.* pp. 10, 23.
[33] *Pipe Roll 2 John,* pp. 99–100; *Pipe Roll 4 John,* p. 256.
[34] *Cal. Inq. P.M.,* I, no. 597. Briwerre took over payment of £100 outstanding on the proffer of Walter Crok (*Pipe Roll 2 John,* p. 97); John of Montagu's proffer was compounded in a smaller amercement of 100 m. in 1201 (*Pipe Roll 3 John,* p. 223).

the assize to litigants of the same stock. This was not always so. Alexander and Cecily de Crevequer were cousins. The issue between them was analogous to the *casus regis*.[35] In 1203 Alexander proffered 40 m. for a writ of *mort d'ancestor* against Cecily as tenant of the barony of Redbourne.[36] The pleadings are recorded. Cecily tried, without success, to except the assize on the ground that their fathers were brothers and therefore of too close a stock. Thereafter both parties put themselves to a jury on the question of whether Alexander's father had died seised. The result is not recorded, but it must have been in Cecily's favour, for Alexander agreed to a concord and appears as a tenant of a half fee held of the barony in 1212.[37] This was a marginal case for the assize, but clearly took that course. Another dispute, between Elias Foliot and Wiscard Ledet in 1204 over the barony of Chipping Warden, is even more marginal. Here the parties were uncle and niece. Foliot proffered 200 m. for an inquisition whether his mother, on the day she died, was seised in demesne and fee of West Warden, of which he was the nearest heir. Wiscard Ledet, acting for his wife, Elias's niece, countered with a proffer of 200 m. and two palfreys for the land of Richard Foliot, his father-in-law, of which he was seised on the day he died.[38] No pleadings are recorded, but Elias Foliot either lost or did not proceed; the barony descended through the heirs of Wiscard Ledet.[39] Throughout the record of the case there is no mention of either writ or assize; they are suggested only by the terms of the proffers. Like William son of Odo's proffer, Wiscard Ledet's was a quasi relief.[40]

---

[35] *Lincolnshire Assize Rolls, 1202–9*, pp. lxxx–lxxxii; *Rot. de Dominabus*, pp. xxxiv–vi, 7n.

[36] *Rot. de Ob. et Fin.* p. 113.

[37] *Curia Regis Rolls*, II, 218, 223–4; *Book of Fees*, p. 189.

[38] *Pipe Roll 6 John*, p. 139.

[39] Ledet gradually paid off his debt. Foliot's was still outstanding at his death in 1207 'for he did not have nor could he have that for which he proffered' (*Pipe Roll 9 John*, p. 133).

[40] Compare also Henry son of Hugh de Neville who in 1199 proffered £100 'for having the land of which his father was disseised on the day he died, whose nearest heir he is, and for his relief' (*Rot. de Ob. et Fin.* pp. 11–12).

These cases are few. Nevertheless, they demonstrate that tenants-in-chief could and did use the assize of *mort d'ancestor*. Their proffers mention the writ, or the assize, or seek a recognition which was clearly answering the question which the assize required. Disseisin was a different matter. There were many allegations of disseisin, but there seems to be no example of a straightforward case of *novel disseisin* between one tenant-in-chief and another over a tenancy-in-chief throughout the legal records of the reign of John.[41] The assize did not fit what the tenant-in-chief required. He could not argue that he had been disseised without judgement when the disseisor, a fellow tenant-in-chief, could have no jurisdiction in the matter. By the same token the justification that judgement had occurred was denied to the disseisor. Against the king as disseisor the assize was useless, for he could not direct this or any other writ against himself.[42] It was only in the aftermath of civil war that the tenant-in-chief came to use the assize at all freely.[43] Before that his actions of disseisin were set in a looser framework. Bits and pieces of them were derived from the assize – the twelve recognitors, the mise which almost always required them to answer a question of fact – but they were assembled *ad hoc*. The actions therefore fall into no particular category or pattern except for one group involving writs of entry. Many

---

[41] No doubt exceptions will be found to this hazardous generalization. A possible one is a proffer of 20 m. made in 1199 by Manasser Arsic for a recognition of *novel disseisin* against Theobald Walter in Ireland. Theobald made a counter-offer of 80 m. on the condition that the case would be transferred to the king should he or his brother, the archbishop of Canterbury, so wish (*Rot. de Ob. et Fin.* pp. 27, 30). No further action is recorded. I have been unable to establish whether it concerned a tenancy-in-chief.

[42] Pollock and Maitland (1898), I, 515–17. See also Ehrlich (1921), pp. 12–38, especially pp. 24–5, and Turner (1968), pp. 236, 252–3, 261–3. For the particular matter of disseisin not lying against the Crown see Bracton, fo. 171b, tr. Thorne, III, 43, and for examples see *Lincolnshire Assize Rolls, 1202–9*, no. 1143 and *Curia Regis Rolls*, III, 57.

[43] My argument here, like Ehrlich's, is congruous with Professor Milsom's emphasis on the disciplinary origins of *novel disseisin* (Milsom, 1976, pp. 1–35). If it originated as an action of tenant against lord, and could not be levied against the king, *a fortiori* the tenant-in-chief could not use it. This should be compared with the rapidly expanding use of the assize by undertenants. See Sutherland (1973), pp. 43–76, especially pp. 47–50.

of them, like the writs of entry, concerned both possession and title. In many such cases the disseisin was long past and the allegation was often part of a more complex dispute traversing generations. In 1200, for example, Alexander of Caldbeck alleged that Reginald de Lucy disseised his grandfather while he himself was a minor in wardship.[44] In the same year Robert Buissel maintained that his father had been disseised unjustly and without judgement in the time of John count of Mortain, that is, before 1194.[45] Yet another action brought in 1201 by Aubrey de Vere, later earl of Oxford, went even further back to the claims his father had as a tenant of the abbey of Westminster in Feering in the time of Abbot Gervase, deprived of office c. 1157. In this case the justices were conscious of the standard procedures on disseisin because they recorded that the writ was *extra assisam* and that this was to be discussed with the lord king.[46] All these recognitions sought to establish some of the facts within more general disputes – seisin of an inheritance in the case of Caldbeck, title to an inheritance in the case of Buissel, and probably hereditary title to a farm in the case of Vere. They were special operations and they cost accordingly: for Alexander of Caldbeck 50 m. and a palfrey in 1200, £100 in 1204; for his opponent, Robert of Courtenay, 50 m. and a

[44] *Rot. de Ob. et Fin.* p. 79 and for the renewal of the action in 1204 *Pipe Roll 6 John*, p. 143. For the pleadings, which were not an assize but a sworn recognition (*jurata*), see *Curia Regis Rolls*, III, 117; IV, 99. Alexander and his land were in his grandfather's custody by his father's concession when the grandfather was disseised. I have included this case with considerable hesitation because Caldbeck was, or became, a tenancy of the Lucy barony of Allerdale. However, the pedigrees advanced by Alexander, though confused, hint at some claim to hold in chief. See J. Nicholson and R. Burn, *The History and Antiquities of the Counties of Westmorland and Cumberland* (London, 1777), II, 134–5; *Early Yorkshire Charters*, VII, 17–18 and, for further comment, *Pipe Roll 6 John*, pp. xx–xxi.

[45] *Rot. de Ob. et Fin.* p. 49; *Curia Regis Rolls*, I, 262. For the context see Holt (1961), p. 240.

[46] *Curia Regis Rolls*, I, 464–5. The words *extra assisam* may well simply mean that the disseisin was not novel. If so, the comments of Flower (1943), p. 342 and Turner (1968), p. 112 are inappropriate. The current limitation was Michaelmas 1198 (Flower, 1943, p. 159; Sutherland, 1973, p. 55). The tenure probably originated in a farm. See Barbara Harvey, *Westminster Abbey and its Estates in the Middle Ages* (Oxford, 1977), pp. 79–85. On Gervase see Richardson and Sayles (1963), pp. 413–21 and Harvey, p. 81. Note that the plea was not directed against the Crown although Aubrey refers to disseisin by the will of Henry II. Compare Turner (1968), p. 112.

palfrey in 1200, 300 m. and two palfreys in 1206;[47] for Robert Buissel 100 m. and 20 m. increment in 1200–1, for his opponent, Hugh Buissel, 400 m. in 1202.[48] Exceptionally, no proffer is recorded for Aubrey de Vere. These actions failed. Caldbeck and Courtenay were still in contention in 1206; no conclusion is recorded. De Vere quitclaimed his rights in Feering to the abbey of Westminster.[49] The Buissels suffered worse than failure. In 1205, impoverished by litigation, they surrendered their barony and their debts to Roger de Lacy, constable of Chester.[50]

It is difficult to see why men became involved in such *imbroglios*. But the Buissels were not alone. Another example is provided by Gilbert Hansard, tenant of the bishopric of Durham, whose case came to the king in 1211 when the see was vacant and in the king's hands. Gilbert offered 40 m. for an inquiry by twelve knights whether King Richard received into his custody along with Gilbert 5 carucates of land in Hurworth which Gilbert had not recovered when he came of age and of which he now claimed seisin. The tenant was Brian fitz Alan, husband of Gilbert's sister, Alice, who was summoned to show by what warrant he held the land. The process soon became a mess: the knights presented a confused verdict and were amerced 30 m. for their pains; Alice, who claimed the land as her marriage portion, agreed to warrant it to her husband but maintained that 7 carucates, not 5, were at stake; she sought a grand assize, claiming that the inquisition had never been on oath. This the king refused, and on the basis of the inquisition gave Gilbert seisin. For this Gilbert proffered £100. Then, to cap all, he released the land to Alice and her husband Brian. To all appearances, a year's litigation returned all parties to the starting-point. Perhaps Gilbert's only gain was to establish that Hurworth was held of him; this at the cost of £100 and

[47] *Rot. de Ob. et Fin.* pp. 79, 95; *Pipe Roll 6 John*, p. 143; *Pipe Roll 8 John*, pp. 44–5.
[48] *Rot. de Ob. et Fin.* pp. 49, 188; *Pipe Roll 3 John*, p. 273.
[49] Harvey, *Westminster Abbey*, p. 341.   [50] Holt (1961), p. 240.

40 m. and, inadvertently, 30 m. to the knights of Durham. They had largely themselves to blame.[51]

Probably the most common feature of these varied actions is that in some way or other they challenged past actions of the Crown. It is important not to see political significance in each and every such case. When a plaintiff alleged wrongs before the court, amounting to justice bypassed or denied, falsified or misapplied, some of the mud was bound to stick to the king as lord of the court. Nevertheless, he may well not have been the main target. The matter is well illustrated by a case involving an under-tenancy. In 1211 Peter fitz Herbert brought an action of right against the abbot of Westminster seeking six and a half hides in Parham, Sussex. The circumstances are not entirely clear, but it seems likely that fitz Herbert was exploiting the circumstances of the Interdict in attempting to revive a hereditary claim to land originally held at farm.[52] The abbot's defence rested securely on letters of Henry I adjudicating the manor to Abbot Herbert against fitz Herbert's grandfather and on a further confirmation by Henry II. Peter fitz Herbert argued that his father had been in seisin and had been disseised by the will of King Henry II. Indeed he offered two palfreys and then four Norwegian hawks for an inquiry whether he had been so disseised. What happened is not recorded, but it did him some good, for the abbot obtained his quitclaim in return for £100, which may well have been precisely what he was seeking.[53] However, the striking feature of the case is the allegation of disseisin by will of the king. And it is clear that while in one direction this

---

[51] *Curia Regis Rolls*, VI, 188, 241–2; *Pipe Roll 13 John*, p. 34. The argument equates the land which Alice's father gave her 'ad se maritandum' with the land which her husband, Brian, held 'cum uxore sua'. No account was entered for Gilbert's proffer of 40 m. unless on the lost roll of 1213. The original seizure into King Richard's hands must have taken place during the vacancy of the see in 1195. My reading of this case differs somewhat from Turner's (1968), pp. 186–7.

[52] *Curia Regis Rolls*, VI, 176–7. Compare the action of Aubrey de Vere, above, p. 133.

[53] Harvey, *Westminster Abbey*, p. 359.

leads to the conflict between the notions of will and law, in another, in its precise legal context, it simply means that Henry II had acted without judgement. He had acted administratively, the matter had not come to a court, and therefore Peter was not bound by what the king had done and could now challenge it. Equally important, it was not the main issue; this lay between Peter and the abbot of Westminster and turned on whether Peter's father had been seised; King Henry's wilful act simply explained how he had come to lose his seisin.

Nevertheless these procedures could be used by those nursing grievances consequent on royal actions. Rebellion and civil war were accompanied by sequestration, the consequences of which were long-lasting. In 1201 Earl Patrick of Dunbar proffered 40 m. and four palfreys for a recognition whether his great-uncle, Edgar, was seised in fee of the townships of Bewick, Eglingham and Lilburn at the beginning of the war between King Henry II and his son and whether he was disseised as a result of the war; the prior of Tynemouth and the abbot of St Albans were now the tenants.[54] In a closely similar action Roland of Galloway pursued the claim of his wife to the tenancy which her father, Richard de Moreville, had held of the Scottish earls of Huntingdon and had lost on the same occasion; the bid for this recognition was one of the largest ever offered: 500 m.[55] Count John's rebellion of 1194 produced similar grievances. Roger de Montbegon proffered 10 m. for a recognition whether he had been disseised of Kelsey, Lincs., for his service to the king when he was count of Mortain.

[54] *Rot. de Ob. et Fin.* p. 120; *Curia Regis Rolls*, I, 439. He proffered a further 10 m. for a similar investigation into the service of Thomas son of Liulf in which he was apparently successful (*Pipe Roll 3 John*, p. 248; *Pipe Roll 6 John*, p. 44). The main proffer was pardoned in 1205 (*Pipe Roll 7 John*, p. 16).

[55] *Rot. de Ob. et Fin.* pp. 84–5; *Curia Regis Rolls*, I, 375. The plea was dropped by Roland's widow and the bid raised to 600 m. and six palfreys when she and her son, Alan of Galloway, renewed it in 1211 (*Pipe Roll 13 John*, p. 268). For the context see K. J. Stringer, *Earl David of Huntingdon* (Edinburgh, 1985), p. 114.

The sheriff was to carry out an inquiry and notify the king of the result.[56] Likewise in Dorset Alan of St George and Brian Tollard were in dispute after Brian had been outlawed and disseised in the cause of the count and then restored by the king. Alan proffered 50 m. to support his plea that his wife, who had born him a son, was heir to land now held by Brian. It did him no immediate good. The plea was stayed because Brian was overseas in the king's service and it was finally settled by concord three years later.[57] These cases come from 1201. Those of Roland of Galloway and Patrick of Dunbar are so similar as to suggest a common source of legal advice. All belong to King John's own eyre. It was a good time to air grievances and test the new king's metal. But they did not signal a widespread attack on arbitrary action by the Crown.

They hint rather at procedural uncertainty in unchartered territory. They tended to combine elements of *novel disseisin* and *mort d'ancestor* with a good dash of what was coming to be embodied in the writ of entry *sur disseisin*. They were open to challenge and must have inspired less than total confidence. Faced with the claim from Earl Patrick, the abbot of St Albans and prior of Tynemouth claimed that there ought to be no jury because it was 'against the assize of the realm'; they sought the consideration of the court whether the case ought to proceed. The earl refused to plead on that and asked that the king's order (for a recognition) should be carried out. The attorney of the abbot and prior then diverted the case by claiming that Patrick's ancestor, Edgar, had a son still living. The case was adjourned.[58] An equally ingenious resistance was devised by Earl David of

---

[56] *Rot. de Ob. et Fin.* p. 123. No result is recorded.
[57] *Curia Regis Rolls*, II, 98; III, 103; *Pipe Roll 3 John*, p. 82. The reference to the son indicates that Alan's wife was probably dead. The tenancy was of the honour of Gloucester, then in the king's hand. In 1212 it was noted that Brian held it from the time of King John (*Book of Fees*, p. 93).
[58] *Curia Regis Rolls*, I, 439.

Huntingdon when the Moreville claim was renewed by Helen de Moreville and her son, Alan of Galloway, in 1211–12. This time the recognition was sworn and it pronounced that Richard de Moreville was seised before the war of 1173–4 and had been disseised on account of the war. But David and the men enfeoffed on the Moreville tenancies argued that they had not and would not put themselves on any inquisition – with some justification, because it had taken place before they were summoned. They simply said that 'the lord king can do his will' – *dominus rex potest facere voluntatem suam.*[59] Both parties then vouched the king of Scotland to warrant the terms of the original grant to Earl David.[60] In the political circumstances of 1212 this was unlikely to be easily obtainable. The earl's resistance continued when he was asked to warrant his charter to Alan. He agreed to acknowledge his charter (*congnovit cartam*) but refused to go further: no one had impleaded him, he claimed; when he was impleaded and called to warrant he would do his duty. All in all, a crusty performance from a senior earl. Despite this, he later surrendered and agreed to warrant; and most of the Moreville lands were restored, with the tenants compensated, by 1214. From 1212 onwards the earl was in no political position to risk further resistance.[61] By the same token King John required the support of Alan of Galloway: at least 300 m. of his proffer were pardoned.[62]

In these cases there is very little indication of new procedures: an assize if appropriate, a recognition, a final concord if it could be attained; these were the tools which

---

[59] An inquisition was not an assize, which they would have been compelled to answer.

[60] *Curia Regis Rolls*, VI, 274.

[61] *Ibid.* vi, 274, 280, 362; vii, 189, 213. See also Stringer, *Earl David of Huntingdon*, p. 114 and Holt (1961), pp. 83.

[62] *Pipe Roll 14 John*, 133. By 1214 the debt was reduced to £3 and six palfreys which were quit on payment, but whether the remainder of the total of 600 m. was reduced by pardon or payment it is impossible to say, since no Pipe roll survives for 15 John (*Pipe Roll 16 John*, p. 23). John called on Alan for 1000 men of Galloway for the Welsh expedition of 1212; on 5 May 1215 a prest of 300 m. was authorized for him (*Rot. Litt. Claus.* I, 131b, 198b).

were there to be used or misused, bent and twisted into novel shapes for the job in hand. Very occasionally 'entry' figures in an action. In 1200 William of St Mère Eglise, bishop of London, certainly purchased a recognition of entry as guardian of Maurice de Gant, but to no apparent effect, and when Maurice came of age he claimed in right.[63] William, as a royal justice, would be well acquainted with the most up-to-date procedures. In one action, from 1204, entry was given a sharper political edge. Robert de Vaux proffered 15 m. for an inquiry whether his father Robert had been disseised of 6 virgates in Wilnecote, Warks., by the will and force of William de Longchamps, chancellor of King Richard, and as to what right Robert and his ancestors had in the land, and whether Waleran Bigard, subsequently put in seisin by the chancellor, had any other entry than through the chancellor. In the characteristic fashion of an action of entry Robert sought to determine the issue on the basis of the facts alleged in the pleading. His fine included seisin if the inquiry went his way. The roll simply notes that he was to have his inquisition, a hint that subsequent seisin was another matter.[64] No pleadings or result are recorded. The case was an unimportant one and cleared no new path. For the rest the records seem to be silent. The writ of entry was no panacea. It developed slowly, its use scarcely affected by the decision of August 1204 that henceforth the writ of entry *sur disseisin* should be available *de cursu*.[65] No great new process to satisfy the magnates' needs was invented at any point in the reign of John.

If that holds true of seisin, what of right? For except in

---

[63] *Rot. de Ob. et Fin.* p. 61.   [64] *Ibid.* p. 214.

[65] *Rot. Litt. Claus.* I, 32b. See especially G. D. G. Hall, 'The early history of Entry sur Disseisin', *Tulane Law Review*, XLII (1968), pp. 584–602, and *Early Registers of Writs*, pp. xxvii–xxviii, xlii–iii, cv–cvi, cxxxi, cxxxvi. It should be noted, as indeed Mr Hall points out, that the *de cursu* writ of 1204 is limited to action against the disseisor's heir.

error, the two were clearly distinguished.[66] An action in right was *capitale placitum*.[67] Title was corroborated by the duel or the grand assize of twelve knights. The action was altogether more complicated and more costly. The shrewd litigant or lawyer went first for seisin if he could: let the opponent plunge into the complexities of title.[68] Likewise, the successful litigant or beneficiary of royal favour often protected his position with the proviso that he was not to be assailed except *de recto* or by grand assize.[69] However, the action of right was no better adjusted than the petty assizes to the baronial litigant seeking immediate justice in the king's court. Glanvill's writ of right is directed not to the tenant, but to the tenant's lord; it instructs him to do full right: otherwise the sheriff will intervene.[70] Likewise the rule *nemo tenetur*, that no one need answer for his free tenement unless impleaded by writ of the king or his Chief Justiciar, was set by Glanvill within the framework of private juris- diction; the king's writ expressed a supervisory role.[71] There survives one precious example of an attempt to adapt this writ of right to the Crown's immediate jurisdiction. In 1200 Simon son of John proffered 6 m. for lands in Northumberland and for a writ of right concerning 2 carucates of land in Whittingham. The writ, entered on the

---

[66] See the proffer of the advocate of Béthune seeking seisin of his lands in England and for having right in three named manors. The decision was – *Faciet ei judicium curie sue tam de jure quam de saisina* (*Rot. de Ob. et Fin.* p. 59). But compare the sloppy terminology of the proffer of Sibilla de Plugenet and Hawise de Dinant *pro habendo recto ... per breve de recognitione de morte antecessoris* (*Rot. de Ob. et Fin.* p. 38). There is a more understandable confusion in the proffer of Baldwin Giffard and others (*Rot. de Ob. et Fin.* p. 50).

[67] *Ibid.* pp. 48–9, and compare *Curia Regis Rolls*, I, 227.

[68] See the action between the Crevequers, above p. 131.

[69] See the charter to Henry de Longchamps, 7 March 1205 – *nec ipse nec heredes sui implacitentur de predictis tenementis per breve de morte antecessoris set tantum per breve de recto* (*Rot. Chartarum*, 146*b*). Compare the proffer of Hugh de Gournay for Wendover, 1209 – *non trahatur inde in placitum nisi per breve quod appellatur breve de recto* (*Pipe Roll 11 John*, p. 181). There was a similar proviso in Robert de Mandeville's proffer for the barony of Marshwood (*Pipe Roll 10 John*, p. 113n). In this case his opponent, Henry de Tilly, failed in an action of entry on the ground that Robert had been put in seisin by King John (*Curia Regis Rolls*, viii, 23–4).

[70] Glanvill, XII, 3, ed. Hall, p. 137.

[71] Glanvill, XII, 2, 25, ed. Hall, pp. 137, 148.

dorse of the Fine roll, was addressed to the sheriff; otherwise it conforms exactly to Glanvill's writ of right:

We command you to do full right without delay to Simon son of John in respect of two carucates of land in Whittingham with appurtenances which he claims to hold of us by the service of 40s. a year and the customs and services pertaining to drengage, which Vincent of Burton is withholding from him, lest no further etc.[72]

It was probably unusual. It involved a small, remote estate held by rent and servile services.[73] It is unthinkable that in a parallel action involving great men and many fiefs scattered through the shires, either the parties or the king would be content to commit an issue to the sheriff and the county court, still less to several such. Both king and litigants wanted the action to take place in the king's court. In the absence of an intervening lord, the demandant had to get at the tenant. The tenant was the only person who could answer unless the king, as lord, was himself to do so.

The one instrument which met the bill was the writ *praecipe quod reddat*:

King to the sheriff, greeting. Command N. to render to R. justly and without delay, one hide of land in such-and-such a vill, which the said R. complains that the aforesaid N. is withholding from him. If he does not do so, summon him by good summoners to be before me or my justices on the day after the octave of Easter, to show why he has not done so. And have there the summoners and this writ.[74]

This is the first writ to be described by Glanvill. He presents it as an administrative act – a writ of summons based on the failure of the tenant to carry out a royal order of restoration. It is the immediate instrument available to a complainant whose case 'ought to be, or the lord king is willing it should be, tried in the king's court'. The first category of case to be determined in the king's court is the *placitum de baroniis*;[75] and, as Glanvill's account unrolls, it is

[72] *Rot. de Ob. et Fin.* pp. 54–5, 75.
[73] A tenant in drengage was liable to tallage, heriot and merchet (*Book of Fees*, p. 598).
[74] Glanvill, I, 6, ed. Hall, p. 5.   [75] Glanvill, I, 3, 5, ed. Hall, pp. 4, 5.

clear that in such a plea the writ should lead to trial by battle or the grand assize.[76] Hence the *praecipe* was a preliminary to an action of right, and that in the king's court 'before me or my justice'.[77] Much turned on the accessibility, adequacy and predictability of this procedure.

In baronial actions the *praecipe* appears only very occasionally *eo nomine*.[78] Usually it lies hidden behind an action of right. The transition from the writ to the action is easy to follow. In 1208, for example, Thurstan de Montfort proffered 50 m. for two writs *praecipe*, one against Eustace de Vescy, the other against Nicholas de Stuteville. The subsequent action against de Vescy took the characteristic form of an action of right.[79] More clearly still, in 1205, Maurice de Gant proffered 100 m. for several writs *praecipe* 'and that the king should aid him in having his right which he claims by the said *praecipe*'. Once again the subsequent actions were actions of right, one of which, against William de Coleville, went to the grand assize.[80] Maurice de Gant's proffer is revealing. The *praecipe* was the baron's writ of right, or as near as he could get to it. It is as a writ of right that it is usually described in baronial actions recorded in the Plea rolls of John's reign; and it is very likely that any reference to a *breve de recto* in such actions is in fact to the *praecipe*. The

[76] Glanvill, books I and I. It is in book III that he introduces warranty and tenure of other than the king. The change is marked at the beginning of book III – 'When only the tenant and no one else needs to be present to answer to the case, the order of pleading which is observed in court is that which we have stated above' (ed. Hall, p. 37).

[77] Glanvill, II, 15, ed. Hall, p. 33.

[78] See *Thurstan de Montfort* v *Maurice de Gant*, discussed below, p. 156. See also Milsom (1976), p. 68. Compare the proffer of one palfrey of Annote, daughter of William son of William, for a *praecipe de rationabile parte* of the small barony of Hepple, Northumberland (*Pipe Roll 6 John*, p. 44), and, in an action between barons but not concerning a tenancy-in-chief, Eustace de Vescy's proffer in 1206 of 5 m. for a *praecipe* against Nicholas de Stuteville concerning 1000 acres of land in Cottingham, part of the considerable holdings which Vescy held of Mowbray/Stuteville, not all of which have been identified (*Rot. de Ob. et Fin.* pp. 350; *Early Yorkshire Charters*, IX, 119–20).

[79] *Pipe Roll 10 John*, p. 164; *Curia Regis Rolls*, V, 311. For further discussion of the case see below, p. 156.

[80] *Rot. de Ob. et Fin.* p. 427; *Pipe Roll 10 John*, p. 89; *Curia Regis Rolls*, VI, 96. See also *Early Yorkshire Charters*, VI, 36–7.

matter is put beyond serious doubt by royal grants, which gave beneficiaries protection from legal challenge except by writ of right. Such a proviso cannot have envisaged Glanvill's writ of right. It must therefore refer to the mandatory action initiated by the *praecipe*.[81]

We might expect, therefore, that actions concerning baronies would follow the procedures described in the first two books of Glanvill's treatise: the writ *praecipe* summoning the tenant; the appearance of the parties, subject to essoins; the statement of the claim and proffer of battle by the demandant; the choice of battle or the grand assize by the defendant, leading to a verdict or a final concord. Sometimes, to be sure, that happened, although the action might well be prolonged.[82] More frequently the process was fragmented by royal intervention, by requests for special investigation of particular matters, by postponements of one kind or another at the behest of one of the parties, or of the court, or of the king. Hence the *praecipe* might well launch the baronial litigant on a tortuous and costly course with uncertain hope of success. For him it was not a writ *de cursu* available on demand and at a standard charge in chancery. It required a special proffer and was therefore expensive; 5 m. or a palfrey was a cut price, 50 m. or more not unusual. Once obtained, it was not entirely adequate for the purpose to which it was now put. It was a blunderbuss of a writ. Of the various forms of *praecipe* in Glanvill's treatise the *praecipe quod reddat* for land is the only one which is entirely

---

[81] For an exception see the case of Simon son of John, above, p. 141. A *praecipe* to the sheriff or other agent is more probable than a *praecepimus* to the tenant. In addition to the reasons advanced by Van Caenegem (*Royal Writs*, pp. 234–5), the *praecipe* had the advantage of bringing into play the usual procedures of summons. A *praecepimus* to the tenant was appropriate, of course, where the demandant claimed to hold of him, but then it took the form of Glanvill's writ of right.

[82] For an example beginning with a proffer *pro habendo recto* and proceeding through a standard action of right to the waging of the duel and a final concord see *Vescy* v. *Saususmere* (with Tilly as warrantor)(*Pipe Roll 2 John*, pp. 109, 110; *Curia Regis Rolls*, I, 285–6; II, 188; *Pedes Finium Ebor.*, Surtees Society, XCIV, 1894, pp. 90–1). The action began before John's accession and was concluded 4 May 1204.

unspecific.[83] It contained no statement that the demandant was claiming *sicut ius*; that is no more than implied by the order that the tenant was to restore him *juste* to land of which he claimed to have been deprived. It contained no statement of whom the demandant claimed to hold. In the earliest MSS of Glanvill's text it was rubricated as 'The writ for making the first summons', and indeed the summons was its prime purpose.[84] That apart, it was imprecise.

It was but one route into a jurisdictional structure which was much more fluid than Glanvill's account would suggest. In Hilary term 1201 Roger constable of Chester and Gilbert de l'Aigle were in dispute before the king over the dower of Isabella, Gilbert's wife, relict of Roger's ancestor, Robert de Lacy, who died in 1193.[85] Roger asked for the record of the action which had been conducted in the court at Westminster. Gilbert sought view of the writ by which he was impleaded. The court took the view that there could be no writ because the pleas had begun 'with a certain inquisition concerning which the king had instructed that if it were done according to the custom of England it should hold, if not it should be quashed'. Gilbert maintained that he and his wife had been disseised by the said inquisition contrary to the custom of England and that the king's court had adjudged seisin to them of the lands of which they had been disseised on that ground (*ea occasione*), but that they had not yet recovered seisin of one knight's fee and the wood of Roundhay. The case went on to depend on the dower promised to Isabella on the occasion of her marriage and assigned to her by Roger on his father's death. In this Roger de Lacy offered to put two disputed matters to a jury. This

---

[83] Glanvill included nine *praecipes* in his treatise; eight of them give some indication of the claim, whether to advowson, dower, terms of concord, homage or debt (Glanvill, IV, 2, ed. Hall, p. 45; VI, 15, ed. Hall, p. 66; VIII, 4, ed. Hall, p. 97; IX, 5, ed. Hall, p. 109; X, 2, 4, 7, 9, ed. Hall, pp. 116–17, 118, 122, 125). See also Hall, pp. 179–80.

[84] Its broader function and later history is reflected in the rubric of a later MS – *Breve de recto* (I, 6, ed. Hall, p. 5 n.b.).

[85] The relationship was distant. Robert de Lacy was Roger's first cousin, twice removed. This may have contributed to the dispute. See *Early Yorkshire Charters*, III, 199.

would have been formed from the knights of Yorkshire, and Gilbert rejected it on the ground that the marriage had taken place in Holland, Lincs. The court offered to Gilbert a jury of lawful men of the neighbourhood and of those present at the marriage, allowing him reasonable rejection of jurors he did not want. This, too, he refused, and the court, at a loss, resigned itself to leaving Isabella simply with the dower which the inquisition recognized as hers (*quam ea congnoscit*).[86]

That case began with no writ but with an inquisition subsequently adjudged to have been made contrary to the custom of England. Roger de Lacy wanted, and indeed the court offered, further inquisitions on particular issues. Gilbert de l'Aigle seems to have relied on the judgement that the first recognition had been judged illegal and that seisin should follow. In one aspect the case calls on standard formalities: the effective defence that a demandant could not claim seisin of land of which the tenant was not then seised and that the lands claimed were not in the tenant's hands;[87] the need for both parties to agree to a recognition; the constitution of the jury; the judicial view that the matter could only be resolved by a jury of those who knew how the bride had been dowered. In another sense it is unstructured. There was no original writ. The first recognition, for some reason, had been contrary to custom. Subsequent recognitions were proposed and rejected. The action ground to a halt.

There are varied examples of such fluid procedures. Some men tried to reach concord without going to the action of right. This surfaces in the records because concords concern-

---

[86] *Curia Regis Rolls*, I, 375–6. My reading of this case attaches the king's mandate to the earlier rather than the current proceedings. A literal interpretation might relate it otherwise, but would do little to alter the outline of the case. The tense used in subordinate clauses, as here, is a recurrent difficulty in interpreting the record of scribes reporting direct speech within a sequence of events, especially a sequence of sessions.

[87] Roger de Lacy argued that Gilbert should not be given seisin of the knight's fee because he had never been seised. He also stated that Roundhay was in the hands of the king. Gilbert did not counter.

ing tenancies-in-chief required the king's approval and he could, and sometimes did, reject them.[88] Some made fine, as plaintiffs, for a grand assize, on the face of it a highly unusual procedure which must in effect have been a proffer for a recognition of a jury of knights.[89] Some sought recognitions of knights or lawful men; others refused to accept them; yet others challenged the worth of jurors. And over all these complexities there stood the authority of the king. He could accept or reject a concord.[90] He could deny access to the grand assize and insist that a prior recognition should settle the issue.[91] He could allow a recognition without prejudice to an assize.[92] He might even allow a grand assize to which he himself was party.[93]

Some actions began without any writ at all, as *querelae* or verbal plaints.[94] This seems to have been so in an action between Eustace de Vescy and Richard de Umfraville over the custody of Henry Batail. It began as an *appellatio* which was brought to a concord before the justices which was subsequently quashed by the king. When the case subsequently came before the king it was opened with a plaint by Richard's attorney – *queritur*. No writ was mentioned. The

---

[88] *William de Lanvallei* v. *Hugh de Beauchamp* concerning the barony of Eaton Socon. The formalities of the concord were due for completion in Easter and Trinity terms 1200, when it was noted: *et interim querant inde assensum domini regis: sin autem, Hugo sit tunc responsurus de capitali placito* (*Rot. Curiae Regis*, II, 279; *Curia Regis Rolls*, I, 227). For the subsequent grand assize and recognition, still under way in 1203, see *Curia Regis Rolls*, I, 340; III, 14. For other examples see *Vescy* v. *Umfraville*, below, pp. 185–6, and *Scotigny* v. *Scotigny* concerning the capital messuage of the barony of Stainton le Vale, Lincs. (*Curia Regis Rolls*, IV, 162; *Pipe Roll 7 John*, p. 211).

[89] The choice between duel and the assize lay with the tenant (Glanvill, II, 6, ed. Hall, p. 26). But compare *Richard Herriard, plaintiff* v. *Gilbert de Hauville* concerning land in Southorp (in Herriard, Hants) (*Pipe Roll 7 John*, p. 129). See also the case of Ralph son of Wigan concerning Swerford, Oxon, where Ralph asked for an inquisition of knights, which seems subsequently to have been treated as a grand assize (*Rot. de Ob. et Fin.* p. 21; *Curia Regis Rolls*, I, 176). If so, in this case it was the knights, not the procedure, which defined the 'grand assize'.

[90] See *Lanvallei* v. *Beauchamp* above, n. 88, and *Vescy* v. *Umfraville*, below, pp. 185–6.

[91] *Hansard* v. *fitz Alan*, above p. 134.

[92] *Fitz Herbert* v. *abbot of Westminster*, above p. 135.

[93] See letters in favour of the earl of the Isle (*Rot. Litt. Claus.* I, 17b).

[94] For background see *Select Cases of Procedure without Writ under Henry III*, especially pp. liv–lvi.

JUSTICE AND JURISDICTION

court *coram rege* was able to settle the matter on the spot in
Richard's favour on the ground of seisin. Eustace was
amerced 300 m.[95] The *querela* also seems to have been used in
the important action of 1208 concerning the constable's fee
of the honour of Richmond. In defending his tenure against
the claims of a distant heir of the rival family of Rollos,
Ruald fitz Alan asked the court to note that 'he had not been
cited as for a plea'.[96] He clearly expected a writ of summons.
There was none. In his proffer for the Rollos half of the
constable's fee he had already provided that he should not be
disseised unless by judgement of the king's court.[97] The
judges now referred the matter to the king and Ruald seems
to have settled the affair by a further gift of 40 m. and a
palfrey.[98]

Cases of supreme legal and political importance can reveal
this same procedural vagueness. The claim made by Geoffrey de Say to the Mandeville inheritance in 1214 began
within the routine framework. Geoffrey, with his son
Geoffrey as his attorney, brought a writ – presumably a
praecipe – which was woefully drafted. His opponent,

[95] *Curia Regis Rolls*, v, 36n., 58–9; *Rot. de Ob. et Fin.* p. 421. This argument assumes
that the *appellatio* was concerned with the custody. No other issue is recorded. Either
way, the record of the action *coram rege* stands by itself. It is certain that the *appellatio*
and the concord preceded the case before the king. This was heard in Michaelmas. The
concord was quashed and the responsible justices penalized prior to 15 August (*Rot. de
Ob. et Fin.* pp. 386, 387, 447). Turner (1968), p. 147n. seems to adopt a different
chronology.
[96] *Et preterea Rualdus dixit quod voluit quod curia sciret quod non fuit citatus velut ad placitum*
(*Curia Regis Rolls*, v, 148).
[97] *Rot. de Ob. et Fin.* p. 253.
[98] *Curia Regis Rolls*, v, 234, 249. The record of the action is confused. It refers to Ruald's
proffer of £100 and two palfreys for an inquisition whether his grandfather had been
disseised by the will of Henry II. The literal reading is that the proffer was
contemporaneous with the plea, and it was so read by Sir Charles Clay (*Early Yorkshire
Charters*, v, 92). But this is unlikely to be the case. The proffer of £100 and two palfreys
which Ruald made for these lands is recorded in 1205 (*Rot. de Ob. et Fin.* p. 253), and
it is to that that the pleadings must refer. No other proffer was recorded in 1208
except that of 40 m. and a palfrey noted above. But if this is the case, and it seems
the most likely explanation, a difficulty remains: the proffer of 1205 does not refer to
an inquest, yet according to the plea it was made *pro habenda inquisitione*. Once again,
the tenses of reported actions and speech within the record of a Plea roll create
difficulties.

147

Geoffrey de Mandeville, was able to deny that he was seised of all that Geoffrey claimed, including Sawbridgeworth and Edmonton, which Geoffrey de Say himself held. The case was dismissed. De Say was amerced for a false claim, but was told that he could seek another writ if he so wished.[99] He did not do so. Instead his son went to Poitou and on or before 11 July he proffered 15,000 m. to the king for the lands of Earl William de Mandeville of which his father, now dead, had been disseised by King Richard *voluntarie*. The fortunate chance of the separation of the king from his justices provides a glimpse of what happened next. The king wrote from La Rochelle to Peter des Roches, Chief Justiciar, instructing him to consult John de Gray, bishop of Norwich, and William Briwerre, baron of the Exchequer, 'and do what seems most expedient'.[100] No subsequent action is recorded.[101] The decline from lawful procedure into expedience was something in which the demandant shared. Geoffrey de Say had been allowed to sue out another writ. His son chose another course.

It may well be that the more important a case politically, the more likely it was to take such a free-wheeling, unpredictable course. We know of an action between Ranulf earl of Chester and William of Béthune through a single entry on the Plea rolls which records that the king wished to act by the counsel of his barons.[102] Another famous dispute suggests something similar. The action between William de Stuteville and William de Mowbray over the honour of Mowbray began in March/April 1200 with a proffer from Stuteville 'for having right'.[103] He nominated attorneys in

[99] *Curia Regis Rolls*, VII, 110–11. See also below, pp. 206–8, and Holt (1991*b*), pp. 35–6.
[100] *Rot. Litt. Claus.* I, 168*b*.
[101] That is in 1214–15. The issue was not finally brought to concord until 12 Edward I, 1283–4 (*Feet of Fines for Essex*, ed. R. E. G. Kirk and F. E. Kirk, Essex Archaeological Society, 1899–1949, II, no. 136).
[102] *Curia Regis Rolls*, I, 392; Turner (1968), p. 169. Each sought seisin of land then in the king's hands.
[103] *Rot. de Ob. et Fin.* p. 55; *Rot. Chartarum*, pp. 61*b*–62.

the Easter term of the Bench,[104] but no further action was recorded during the absence of the king in Normandy from May to October 1200. On his return he visited Lincolnshire in November and again in the new year. On the second occasion Mowbray countered Stuteville's bid with a proffer 'to be dealt with justly and according to the custom of England'.[105] The parties came before the king at Louth on 21 January, and reached agreement *consilio regni et voluntate regis*.[106] The terms were recorded on the Plea roll,[107] but the matter had clearly gone to the judgement of king, judges and barons – a great court: no other interpretations of the 'counsel of the realm' seems likely.

We may be tempted to dismiss the 'justice' available to the tenant-in-chief. Yet before analysing its many faults it is worthwhile noting that for some of them it worked adequately enough. Maurice de Gant launched the various writs *praecipe* aimed at recovering his dilapidated inheritance some time before Easter 1208. He and his cousin Gilbert, his main opponent, reached final concord in October 1209.[108] True, Maurice and his guardian had fought a prolonged and fruitless action against Gilbert's predecessors, and Maurice remained embattled in a number of secondary actions on to 1213,[109] but one portion of the action, at least, proceeded with despatch. Other baronial litigants also brought their

---

[104] *Rot. Curiae Regis*, II, 231.
[105] *Rot. de Ob. et Fin.* p. 102. I am inclined to think that Mowbray's proffer coincided with, or immediately preceded, the action before the king. The date of 1200 in the running heads of the printed edition of the Fine roll is plainly wrong. Compare the dates of the related charters.
[106] *Hoveden*, IV, 118. There is every reason for accepting Howden's authority here. His narrative seems to embody the main points of the count. He could well have been an eye witness.
[107] *Curia Regis Rolls*, I, 380. The record on the Plea roll is not the final concord, but the terms which were to be drafted in a final concord. This was to be received by the parties in the Easter term, but at Easter further delay was incurred and new details added (*Curia Regis Rolls*, I, 440).
[108] *Rot. de Ob. et Fin.* p. 427; *Pedes Finium Ebor., regnante Johanne*, ed. W. Brown (Surtees Society, 1897), p. 157.
[109] *Early Yorkshire Charters*, VI, 36.

actions to final concord, some relatively quickly, some, more usually, only after prolonged litigation extended by essoins and stays.[110] Occasionally litigants shared a proffer in a common bid to obtain a legal ruling.[111] Yet this was rare. There was no easy routine passage from *mort d'ancestor* or an action of right to a final concord as there was with the undertenantry. Any litigant at any level had to put up with the law's delay. The baronial litigant was likely to suffer it in an acute form. Some became weary or disenchanted. Some actions ended by default of one of the parties or simply petered out.

Over all such actions there loomed the question of costs. These were never standard, almost always heavy, not infrequently exorbitant, and occasionally immense, involving sums far larger than a litigant could afford or see his way to pay. Geoffrey de Say's proffer of 15,000 m. for right in the Mandeville inheritance made sense only if Geoffrey could devote the net revenues of the Mandeville estates entirely to its repayment for the next five to ten years – either that or recourse to the money-lenders. Perhaps it never made sense. Perhaps it was a rash offer made by a rash young man amidst the Poitevin adventure of 1214. Yet this is only the pinnacle of a scale of rising costs. Some of the charges for assizes and recognitions have already been mentioned.[112] The costs of actions of right were necessarily larger. The higher the court, the more complex the case, the

---

[110] *Windsor* v. *Windsor* concerning the barony of Eton, 1191–8 (*Pipe Roll 3 Richard*, p. 109; *Feet of Fines 9 Richard I*, no. 151). *Vescy* v. *Saususmere/Tilly* concerning Rotherham, pre 1199–1204 (*Pipe Roll 2 John*, p. 109; *Pedes Finium Ebor.*, pp. 90–1). *Briouze* v. *Nonant*, 1199–1205 (*Rot. de Ob. et Fin.* p. 46; *Pedes Finium*, II, 65–6). *Crevequer* v. *Crevequer* 1201–1203 x 1212 (*Rot. de Ob. et Fin.* p. 113; *Curia Regis Rolls*, II, 218, 223–4; *Book of Fees*, p. 189).

[111] See the proffer of Simon of Kyme and Robert the Chamberlain concerning three-quarters of a knight's fee in Merston, Lincs., a proffer which followed an earlier attempt at an action of disseisin by Simon (*Rot. de Ob. et Fin.* pp. 111, 113). The issue was whether the land was held in chief or of the honour of Gloucester and was resolved in Robert's favour (*Curia Regis Rolls*, II, 27, *Book of Fees*, p. 186). The case is noted by Milsom (1976), p. 78, n.5.

[112] See above, pp. 129–30, 133–4.

lengthier the procedure, the greater the expense: that is the natural law of the lawyer's world in which all litigants are entrapped. Under John it had its own peculiar refinements. If a demandant sought special procedures, he would pay heavily for the privilege. In 1204–5 Richard Herriard, seeking as demandant to initiate a grand assize concerning land in Southorp in Herriard, proffered 100 m. and the service of a knight: a large sum for a small estate proffered by a long-established justice of the Bench.[113] If a defendant sought to stay an action the costs would be just as heavy, or even heavier: 100 m. and three palfreys from Nicholas de Stuteville in 1201 for respite against the claims of Maurice de Gant,[114] £1,000 and fifteen palfreys from Gerard de Furneval in 1207 for peace concerning the claims of Nigel de Luvetot.[115] In all kinds of litigation demandant and tenant competed in their bids: in 1200–1, 3000 m. from William de Stuteville (a proffer which embraced other privileges), 2000 m. from his opponent William de Mowbray;[116] in 1199, 200 m. from Walter Crok for an assize, 400 m. from his opponent, John de Montagu, to stay it;[117] 100 m. from Robert Buissel in 1200, 400 m. from his cousin Hugh in 1202, seeking to preserve his tenure;[118] in 1200 50 m. and a palfrey from Alexander in pursuit of his claims in Caldbeck, the same from the tenant, Robert de Courtenay, to stay the action, £100 from Alexander yet again in 1204, countered by 300 m. and two palfreys from Robert de Courtenay in 1206;[119] 50 m. and two palfreys from Thurstan de Montfort for two writs *praecipe* in 1208, 300 m. and five palfreys from one of his opponents, Nicholas de Stuteville,

[113] *Rot. de Ob. et Fin.* p. 287.
[114] *Pipe Roll 3 John*, p. 23. For the case see above, p. 142.
[115] *Pipe Roll 9 John*, p. 74. For the case see below, p. 154.
[116] *Rot. de Ob. et Fin.* pp. 55, 102; *Rot. Chartarum*, p. 61b.
[117] *Rot. de Ob. et Fin.* pp. 10, 23.
[118] *Ibid.* pp. 49, 188. The second payment was also a penalty for default.
[119] *Ibid.* pp. 79, 95; *Pipe Roll 6 John*, p. 143; *Pipe Roll 8 John*, pp. 44–5.

for confirmation of his tenure in 1210.[120] Thus was justice sold.

The costs were inflated in various ways. Payment of these proffers could usually await the outcome of the case.[121] In the *Dialogus de Scaccario* Richard fitz Neal indicated that those who lost their cases might expect lenient treatment.[122] In practice, the losers' debts rarely remained unpaid, although the account for them might drag on over several years. Moreover, fitz Neal's ill-defined principle was soon crystallized into the proffer of a bonus for success. In 1194 Geoffrey de Mandeville pursued his claim to the barony of Marshwood with a proffer of 100 m. 'for the consideration of the court' and a further 400 m. on recovery of his seisin. The same tactic was followed in 1200 by his son, William, seeking the record and reasonable judgement of the king's court; he proffered 100 m. which he agreed to pay if he lost, and 500 m. if he won.[123] In 1199 William de Briouze took the same line in his challenge of the Nonant tenure of Totnes: £100 if he lost, 700 m. if he won.[124] These two cases point to a further complication which added to the costs: in a claim to a barony a proffer for justice might also be a relief for the succession. So in 1203 Christina of Windsor fined 220 m. for a recognition that she was the nearest heir to Walter of Windsor and for seisin of the land he held on the day he died.[125] In the case of Richard de Lucy this confusion of legal proffer and relief appears explicitly. In 1200 he proffered 300 m. for his land in Copeland and elsewhere, for freedom to marry as he

---

[120] *Pipe Roll 10 John*, p. 164; *Curia Regis Rolls*, VI, 40.
[121] They were categorized as offerings made *in spem* concerning which 'the king has ordained that the applicants shall not pay any portion of what they have offered until they have had justice' (*Dialogus*, p. 120). Compare an action of various demandants against William Briwerre, 1199, where the sheriff was ordered not to distrain for their proffer of 50 m. 'antequam inde rectum habuerint' (*Rot. de Ob. et Fin.* p. 50). Many, however, hastened on a favourable judgement by beginning payment while their case was in progress.
[122] *Dialogus*, p. 120.   [123] *Pipe Roll 6 Richard*, p. 190; *Rot. de Ob. et Fin.* p. 44.
[124] *Rot. de Ob. et Fin.* p. 46   [125] *Pipe Roll 5 John*, p. 132.

wished, and for his reasonable share in the land he claimed against his cousin Hawise's husband, Baldwin count of Aumale, for which fine he was quit of his relief.[126] Then there were predators in the field, the men who were in royal favour and served as great officials and counsellors. William de Briouze was rising to this height when he made his claim to Totnes. William de Stuteville was the most powerful and trusted of John's northern officials when he brought William de Mowbray to court. William Briwerre's predations became notorious.[127] Archbishop Hubert Walter supported the bids of his brother Theobald.[128] The *curialis*, whether lord, bishop or ambitious upstart, enjoyed speculative advantages. He would be in favour at court, he knew the judges, he could call on friends in government to back his bids as guarantors, he could risk a higher bid in the expectation that he could use the fruits of office to meet his payments or obtain a remission or reduction through continued service to the king.[129] Others, who enjoyed neither favour nor office, took larger risks. They too speculated. Proffers, as fitz Neal put it, were made *in spem*.[130] Indeed any litigation was speculative.

So if justice was sold it was also bought. Why then did men incur costs which might leave them and their descendants encumbered with debt? Some, certainly, came to court to confirm family settlements or to dispute family arrangements which had gone wrong. Maurice de Gant's actions against Gilbert de Gant and others concerned lands alienated or lost through the marriage of his grandmother to Robert de Gant.[131] The claims of Eustace de Vescy against Nicholas de Stuteville, of Gilbert Hansard against Brian fitz Alan, and of Henry de Bohun and Roland and Alan of Galloway against Earl David of Huntingdon all concerned

---

[126] *Rot. de Ob. et Fin.* p. 45.   [127] See above, p. 130 and Turner (1988), pp. 71–90.
[128] *Rot. de Ob. et Fin.* p. 30, and above p. 132 n.
[129] For some detailed examples and comparisons see Holt (1961), pp. 232–41.
[130] *Dialogus*, p. 120.   [131] *Early Yorkshire Charters*, VI, 36.

marriage portions.[132] Some actions arose from the conflicting claims of collateral branches, between uncles and nephews or nieces, or between cousins. Nigel de Luvetot's claim against Gerard de Furneval; the conflict amongst the Buissels, and amongst the Crevequers, and the Foliots.[133] Apportionment among co-heiresses was another fruitful source of litigation, as with the Scotignys,[134] and with the heirs general of William son of Duncan who divided up vast estates which included Cockermouth, Copeland and Skipton.[135] One action involved the highly unusual partition of a barony, Eton, between male heirs of the Windsor family and the subsequent division of one of the halves between heiresses.[136] With this exception all these cases were prompted by the common occurrences of family history. There must have been many more, settled quietly and amicably, without recourse to the courts. Nevertheless family law included the ruling family. It is no accident that Geoffrey de Say's claim to the honour of Mandeville, which had been interwoven with the *casus regis* since 1186, yielded the highest of all legal proffers – 15,000 m. Politics contaminated law. That is to put it crudely. In dealing with the *casus regis* it does not come amiss.

More generally also the law had to pay attention to past politics, to claim and counter-claim stemming from seizures and conflicting royal grants going back past the rebellion of Count John and the young king's war of 1173–4, through the settlement of the land by Henry II in the years following his

[132] Ibid. IX, 8, 119–20, 177–9; C. T. Flower (1943), pp. 128–9; Stringer, *Earl David of Huntingdon*, pp. 114–15.
[133] For Luvetot v. Furneval see *Early Yorkshire Charters*, III, 3–5 and the correction to the pedigree by C. T. Clay, *ibid.* VI, 209, n.2. For the others see above, pp. 131, 133.
[134] *Curia Regis Rolls*, IV, 162.
[135] *Early Yorkshire Charters*, VII, 13–21.
[136] There is some doubt whether William and Walter of Windsor were brothers or cousins. As Sanders points out (1960, pp. 116–17), the fine of 1198, which is the crucial evidence, implies that they were cousins (*Feet of Fines, Richard I*, Pipe Roll Society, XXIII, no. 151). Nevertheless twinning is the probable explanation of the division. For the later proffers involving the heiresses see *Pipe Roll 5 John*, p. 212; *Rot. de Ob. et Fin.* p. 346; *Pipe Roll 8 John*, p. 41.

accession to the conflicting bids and rewards of the reign of Stephen, back to the deprivations of the supporters of Duke Robert of Normandy and the establishment of the 'new men' of Henry I, back even to the troubles and rebellion of the reign of Rufus, back almost to Domesday Book. A proffer of 1199 made by Ralph son of Wigan, seeking the restoration of an estate held in sergeanty, illustrates this long trail of evidence and argument. He offered 40 m. for an inquiry of lawful knights whether Geoffrey Luvet had forfeited Swerford, Oxon., in the time of King Henry I, whether King Henry held it as his escheat and then granted it in inheritance to Wigan the Marshal, father of Ralph, and whether Matilda d'Oylly, who claimed it as her dower, had recovered it while Ralph was overseas in the service of King Richard. The king was to be informed of the result.[137] The case was hanging fire in Trinity term 1200, when the parties were given a day 'to hear the will of the king whether he wished a grand assize to take place whether the land belonged to the barony of Henry d'Oylly or was a sergeanty held of the king'. The case went to the assize but was adjourned *sine die* in Easter 1201 when Henry d'Oylly was overseas in the king's service; later evidence indicates that he remained in possession.[138] In Hilary 1201 the judges *coram rege* had the case annotated *loquendum cum domino rege*.[139] More was at stake than the title to a sergeanty. Only the king could determine royal grants.

Action after action, including some of the most important and most expensive, was generated in this way. A single act of disseisin could have consequences which spread through the structure of ownership like an inherited disease. In 1106 Robert de Stuteville fought on the side of Duke Robert of Normandy at Tinchebrai, was captured and deprived of his lands. Henry I granted the major part of his estates to Nigel

---

[137] *Rot. de Ob. et Fin.* p. 21.
[138] *Curia Regis Rolls*, I, 176, 376–7, 429; *Book of Fees*, pp. 828, 837.
[139] *Curia Regis Rolls*, I, 377.

d'Aubigny, ancestor of the second house of Mowbray, and other lands to Geoffrey Murdac. Robert de Stuteville's grandson, also Robert, regained favour under Stephen. He was restored by Henry II to all the holdings which had gone to Geoffrey Murdac and, in a concord of 1158, also recovered ten knights' fees from Roger de Mowbray.[140] The action between William de Stuteville and William de Mowbray held at Louth in 1201 was a further attempt to settle the Stuteville claim.[141] Meanwhile, on a different genealogical track, Thurstan de Montfort attempted to recover Geoffrey Murdac's holdings against Nicholas de Stuteville and Eustace de Vescy.[142] The king and his court were presented with tangle after tangle of this kind as claimants presented and tenants fought off such long-nursed claims and grievances. William de Briouze's bid for Totnes went back to the marriage of his great-grandfather to the daughter of Joel of Totnes. Joel had been dispossessed by William Rufus, who had put in Roger de Nonant, ancestor of William's opponent in 1200.[143] Robert de Mandeville's claim to Marshwood arose from the dispossession of his line in favour of the junior branch of the family by Henry I.[144] The dispute over Eaton Socon lay between William de Lanvallei, whose ancestor, a St Clair, was tenant under Henry I, and Hugh de Beauchamp, whose grandfather had been put in by Henry II.[145] The division of the constable of Richmond's fee, which Ruald fitz Alan was able to set to right after 1204, went back to Henry II's confirmation of the opposing family by the Empress Matilda; Ruald's claim was

---

[140] This is the most likely reconstruction of incomplete evidence. See *Early Yorkshire Charters*, IX, 2–5, 99–100, 116–17; *Charters of the Honour of Mowbray 1107–1191*, ed. D. E. Greenway, British Academy, Records of Social and Economic History, n.s. I, 1972, pp. xvii–xxxii.
[141] See above, pp. 148–9. Stuteville was apparently able to reopen the case because the earliest concord of 1158 had not been confirmed in the king's court (*Hoveden*, IV, 118).
[142] See above, p. 142.
[143] Painter (1949), pp. 41–2; Frank Barlow, *William Rufus* (London, 1983), p. 171.
[144] *Pipe Roll 10 John*, p. 113n.
[145] Sanders (1960), pp. 40–1; G. H. Fowler, 'The Beauchamps, Barons of Eaton Socon', *Bedfordshire Historical Record Soc.*, II (1914), 61–91.

founded on tenure of the whole fee in the time of Henry I.[146] In the case of Wendover, a royal manor recorded under the *terrae datae* of Buckinghamshire, the claims went back to opposing dispositions by Stephen and Henry II in favour of Hugh de Gournay and Faramus de Boulogne. In 1209 Hugh de Gournay's son, also Hugh, offered 700 m. in a successful bid to recover the manor.[147]

Most of these cases were sensitive politically. Some of them affected the balance of feudal power. Some were linked to the royal title. All of them raised major legal questions. How was one royal grant to be reconciled with another? What was to be done when a king contradicted a predecessor? What sort of consistency was to be expected of royal action? What sort of warranty could the king's barons expect from their lord? The plain answer was that consistency was impossible. And indeed the litigant did not seek consistency: what he wanted from the king was a favourable response. The king, in his turn, could not achieve consistency. To provide it would impede his political initiative. Morever, too many claims and counterclaims had been implanted. So he responded with evasive action. The litigant sought warranty. This, only too often, the king could not or would not provide.

The dispute over Wendover posed just this problem. Sybil of Tingrith, vouched to warranty in 1212 by the prior of Southwark, based her case on a charter of Henry II, granting the manor to her father, and on a confirmation of Richard I, both of which she produced in court. Her opponent, Hugh de Gournay, based his case on a charter of Henry II confirming the dower of his mother, which specifically confirmed the grant of Wendover by King Stephen to his father. This, too, was produced in court. The jury was in no doubt as to what had happened. Henry II had allowed Hugh's father to retain the manor until after

[146] See above, p. 147.
[147] *V. C. H. Bucks*, III, 23–4; *Pipe Roll 11 John*, p. 181; *Curia Regis Rolls*, VI, 272–3.

the campaign to Toulouse of 1159; on his return he had seized it and bestowed it on Sybilla's father. Henry's charters were in direct conflict. The court reserved judgement. No conclusion is recorded. Hugh de Gournay was in possession and remained so until 1215.[148] For the litigant, then, a royal charter was insuperable evidence in an action in a royal court. Like the attorney of the abbot of Westminster, defending his title to Parham against Peter fitz Herbert in 1211, he could ask whether he should be required to answer 'over and above the witness which King Henry the grandfather had borne by his charter'.[149] Nicholas de Stuteville, likewise, began his defence against the claims of Thurstan de Montfort by asking that the king should enforce the charter of his father and that he should hold in peace according to its terms unless the court considered he ought to answer.[150] A charter was worth quoting even when there was no apparent challenge to a title.[151] Likewise it was a potentially explosive weapon even when suppressed.[152]

The record of the king's court was of almost equal value. The dispute between Ralph Gernon and Richard fitz Hubert and his wife, Isabel, over the soke of Dunham, Essex, which came before the royal eyre in 1204, involved a chirograph made in King Richard's court which was the starting-point of Richard's defence: he would go beyond it

---

[148] *Curia Regis Rolls*, VI, 272–3. During John's reign and the minority of Henry III the issue was determined primarily by the political allegiance of Hugh de Gournay. Sybilla had been in possession in 1200. She was challenged by Hugh in 1201, but was saved by his desertion of King John in May 1203. However, Hugh returned to the king's allegiance in 1205 and received control of Wendover in 1209 – hence the action of 1212 (*V. C. H. Bucks*, III, 24); Powicke (1961), pp. 341–2. The issue was concorded in 1223 (*V. C. H. Bucks*, III, 24).

[149] 'Et attornatus abbatis petit consideracionem curie si ipse debeat respondere super testimonium quod Henricus rex avus facit per cartam suam' (*Curia Regis Rolls*, VI, 177).

[150] *Ibid.* VI, 40. Compare Henry du Puiset's successful defence of his tenure of Market Weighton on the evidence of charters of Henry II, Richard and John (*Curia Regis Rolls*, III, 148).

[151] See the confirmation of William Marshal's marshalsea in 1199, which recited a plea in the court of Henry I, subsequently confirmed by charter, which established his title (*Rot. Chartarum*, p. 46b).

[152] See the case of Henry de Bohun, below, p. 160.

'if it did not suffice'.[153] Henry de Bohun, earl of Hereford, launched his claims to Ryhall by seeking such seisin as was acknowledged in the court of King Henry and again of King Richard.[154] Likewise Roger constable of Chester began his action against Gilbert de l'Aigle by seeking 'his record of his plea'.[155] In 1200 William de Briouze, in pursuing his claim to Totnes, and William de Mandeville, in pursuing his claim to Marshwood, each sought 'record and reasonable judgement'.[156] Men sought a similar firm base for their rights when they included in their proffers the proviso that they were not to be disseised except by judgement of the court or sought treatment according to the custom of England.

Of all this King John was very wary, bringing into play all the resources of his probing legal intelligence. Cases attracted his attention. When the Buissel dispute came before his court in 1199–1200 it was apparent that there might have been faulty procedure and false judgement in his court when count of Mortain. The matter was all the more serious because a royal charter of 10 October 1199 had been issued confirming Hugh Buissel's tenure.[157] On Robert Buissel's application Hugh was now to appear before the king bringing all his charters and muniments. Moreover the sheriff of Lancashire, Richard de Vernon, on whose evidence and statement Hugh had been awarded his charter, was also to appear to show why he had given the king so to understand.[158] Unfortunately the subsequent pleadings are not recorded, and the case went by default. There is other evidence that King John examined charters with very close attention. When in 1200 Geoffrey fitz Peter sought royal

[153] *Pleas before the King or his Justices*, III, no. 913.   [154] *Pipe Roll 6 John*, p. 254.
[155] *Curia Regis Rolls*, I, 375–6.
[156] The 'record' was in the first case of the king and in the second of the king's court (*Rot. de Ob. et Fin.* pp. 44, 46). Usually 'record' meant record of the particular plea as pleaded so far. Mandeville may also have referred to the action begun by his father in 1194 (*Pipe Roll 6 Richard*, p. 190). There is no such immediate precedent for the claim of Briouze.
[157] *Rot. Chartarum*, p. 27b.   [158] *Rot. de Ob. et Fin.* p. 49; *Curia Regis Rolls*, I, 262.

confirmation of charters of Hugh de Courtenay and Henry de Tracy conveying to him the manor of Moreton, it was by special command of the king that the word *rationabiliter* was deleted from the phrase 'as the charter bears witness'.[159] Courtenay and Tracy were competing claimants to the honour of Bradninch: they could not both give; hence the king avoided lending the full weight of his confirmation to either.[160] He was well aware that charters could be dangerous. On 28 April 1200 he granted to Henry de Bohun the title of earl of Hereford along with an allowance of £20 a year from the third penny of the county. In return the new earl submitted a charter guaranteeing that neither he nor his heirs would claim anything in virtue of the charter which Henry II had given to Roger earl of Hereford in 1155 confirming Roger in the massive gains in land, office and title achieved by his father Miles of Gloucester. Henry de Bohun was now to surrender this charter and it was placed in the priory of Winchester. If the king had an heir by his wife, Godfrey de Lucy, bishop of Winchester, was to destroy it. If not, it was to be returned to Henry de Bohun to make the best he could of it.[161] The king was plainly not prepared to allow any disturbance of the complex division of the inheritance of Earl Roger between his three daughters, of whom Henry de Bohun had married one.[162] Furthermore, the provision for the destruction or return of the charter indicates that he had not forgotten the ancient feudal depen-

---

[159] *Rot. Chartarum*, p. 79b.
[160] For further details see Painter (1949), pp. 38–9. My interpretation is diametrically opposed to Painter who argues that: 'Presumably without the "reasonably" the confirmation was valid in all circumstances.' The point is settled by a further example in which similar action was taken in a confirmation of a charter of Hugh de Montfort where both *rationabiliter* and *rationabilem donationem* were deleted because Hugh had no right to give (*Rot. Chartarum*, p. 93). Compare also *Ledet v. Bruiera*, Hilary 1210, where the demandant's attorney argued that a confirmation of Henry II ought not to harm his case because it conceded nothing but the reasonable gifts of the donors (*Curia Regis Rolls*, VI, 19–21).
[161] *Rot. Chartarum*, p. 53.
[162] D. Walker, 'The "Honours" of the Earls of Hereford in the twelfth century', *Trans. Bristol and Gloucestershire Archaeological Society*, LXXIX, pt. II (1960), 174–211.

dence of the earls of Hereford on the earls of Gloucester whose rights now resided in Isabella of Gloucester, his first wife, whom he was in the process of divorcing.[163] So what should the king warrant and what not? What did his warranty mean? Was it anything more than the confirmation of a predecessor's charter? One procedural matter was clear enough: he could not be vouched to warranty in the ordinary way; that would be to substitute him for a litigant and have him directing writs at himself.[164] Occasionally the king might be pleased to provide *escambium*, which was the practical consequence of warranty.[165] But he could also turn his back on a request for warranty and let a case go in consequence to the grand assize.[166] In confirming charters of his predecesssors John laid down firm rules. By Michaelmas 1201 he had instructed the justices of the Bench that 'they were to do nothing for any one concerning any

[163] For details of the feudal dependency of Hereford on Gloucester see R. H. C. Davis, 'The Treaty between William earl of Gloucester and Roger earl of Hereford' in *A Medieval Miscellany for Doris Mary Stenton*, ed. Patricia M. Barnes and C. F. Slade, Pipe Roll Society, n.s. xxxvi (1960), pp. 139–46. Since the process of divorce was either complete or nearing completion at the date of the charter the words 'uxore nobis disponsata' cannot refer to Isabella of Gloucester. In any case, the words had a general rather than a particular sense. See H. G. Richardson, 'The marriage and coronation of Isabella of Angoulême', *E.H.R.*, LXI (1946), 289–314, and *E.H.R.*, LXV (1950), 360–71; corrected by F. A. Cazel and S. Painter, 'The marriage of Isabella of Angoulême', *E.H.R.*, LXIII (1948), 83–9, and *E.H.R.*, LXVII (1952), 233–5. On the descent of the honour of Gloucester at this point see *Earldom of Gloucester Charters*, ed. R. B. Patterson (Oxford, 1973), pp. 5–6.

[164] Bracton, fo. 382b, tr. Thorne, IV, 197. For an earlier statement of 1219 that the king could not be vouched to warranty in an action of disseisin see *Rolls of the Justices in Eyre for Lincolnshire 1218–19 and Worcestershire, 1221*, no. 297 and for further examples see Turner (1968), pp. 265–6. The matter is not discussed by Glanvill although his book III is wholly devoted to warranty (ed. Hall, pp. 37–43).

[165] Bracton, fo. 382b, tr. Thorne, IV, 197; and see the cancelled charter to the count of Perche, 1200, assigning him 1000 l. Ang. in lands of the new feoffment of Henry of Essex, in which the king agrees to warrant existing tenants by *escambium* (*Rot. Chartarum*, pp. 64b, 96).

[166] *Robert fitz Amaury v. Walter de Ribof and his wife* who called Simon of Kyme to warranty concerning a half knight's fee in Bilborough, Notts. Simon relied on a charter of Henry II confirming his grandfather in his tenements, including Bilborough, and proffered 30 m. for King John to warrant. Robert fitz Amaury proffered 20 m. that the plea should proceed according to the custom of the realm. The king took the lower proffer and Simon of Kyme put himself on the grand assize (*Curia Regis Rolls*, VI, 279). See *Honors and Knights' Fees*, I, 182–4; Milsom (1976), p. 63, n.2.

matter brought before them on account of charters or letters patent which they [the litigants] had from his ancestors unless they saw his confirmation'.[167] Where new grants were concerned and title might be in doubt or merely open to question, King John, like Hubert Walter before him, resorted to evasive action. Offers were received or grants made 'saving the rights of all others in the court of the king',[168] or subject to the proviso that the beneficiary 'should do right in, and according to the judgement of, the court of the king if any wished to plead against him therein',[169] or subject to 'standing by the judgement of the king's court if any impleaded him'.[170] This last proviso and the similar proviso of standing to right in the king's court became almost standard formulae under John, to be deployed whenever a grant or confirmation might be challenged. Hence Robert fitz Walter agreed to stand to right when he offered 300 m. for the land of his uncle, Godfrey de Lucy, bishop of Winchester, a most intricate and contested succession involving the honour of Ongar.[171] Peter de Brus, likewise, promised to answer any plea in his bid for Carlton and Camblesforth.[172] Earl Warenne agreed to very special arrangements, that he would stand by the advice of the king, Geoffrey fitz Peter, the earl of Arundel and others concerning the manor of Roding of which he had been given seisin in preference to Doun Bardolf.[173] The proviso cropped up

---

[167] *Curia Regis Rolls*, I, 331. There is a hint in a damaged entry of 1202 that the ruling carried penalties for those who attempted to evade it by continuing to use unconfirmed franchises (*Rot. de Ob. et Fin.* p. 190). For the more general implications of the ruling see Holt (1991a), pp. 12–13. It is likely that the ruling was in force from John's accession. See the confirmations to the abbot of Cirencester and the earl of Leicester (*Memoranda Roll 1 John*, pp. 41, 46).

[168] Henry mayor of London, offering 40 m. for two fees which had belonged to Henry Malesmains (*Pipe Roll 10 Richard*, p. 171).

[169] Osbert de Longchamps, seeking restoration of the custody of the gaol of London and the king's houses in Winchester (*Pipe Roll 10 Richard*, p. 210).

[170] William Briwerre, seeking the manor of Foston. In this case he had indeed to stand to right because his claim was challenged (*Pipe Roll 10 Richard*, pp. 160, 181).

[171] *Pipe Roll 6 John*, p. 34; and below, pp. 164–5.

[172] *Pipe Roll 6 John*, p. 188.

[173] *Rot. Lib.*, p. 92. See *Honors and Knights' Fees*, III, 323.

in legal actions: *Courtenay* v. *Caldbeck, Hansard* v. *fitz Alan*.[174] By John's reign it had become a standard option. An escape route had been opened up. The king could avoid complete commitment. It was all the easier because there were parallels in other exercises of his authority. Grants of land could now be conditional, like grants of markets or of private forests, or pardons for homicide.[175]

This treatment of warranty may or may not have been the straw which broke the camel's back. It is more important that it illustrates the confusion which surrounded the achievement of right and the exercise of justice. In theory the king would exercise the judgement of a Solomon in determining who had the greater right. In practice one case might affect another, one claim might be older and more assiduously nursed than another, one going back to a *tempus guerrae*, another to the good old days of Henry I. In the end, right might have to be pursued through a historical maze, wherein the king gave uneasy direction to an uncertain conclusion. There need be no surprise that the rules of the game were fluid and the charges for entry high: so much to launch a plea, so much to win it, so much to counter or stay the manoeuvres of the opponent using exactly the same *modus operandi*. The tenant-in-chief might well cast an envious eye towards his litigious undertenants happily pursuing their ends along the tramlines of *mort d'ancestor, novel disseisin*, writs of right and final concords. The plain truth was that in 1215 the undertenant had access to a system of justice which was far more predictable than that available to

---

[174] *Rot. de Ob. et Fin.* p. 95; *Curia Regis Rolls*, VI, 188. For these see above, pp. 133, 134.
[175] This is at its most obvious in grants of markets and fairs which, from 1200 onwards, were almost always subject to the proviso that they should not be to the harm of neighbours (R. H. Britnell, 'King John's early grants of markets and fairs', *E.H.R.*, XCIV (1979), 90–6). Similar provisos occur in the much rarer grants of private forests; see the licence to Baldwin count of Aumale for Appletreewick (*Rot. Lib.*, p. 68). Compare also the king's pardon for homicide given with the proviso that the pardoned felon should stand to right against other claims arising from his crime (i.e. from the relatives of the victim). See Naomi D. Hurnard, *The King's Pardon for Homicide before AD 1307* (Oxford, 1969), pp. 194–213.

the great man opposed to his equal in the king's court. With the common law the litigant knew where he stood and how to proceed. The magnate in the king's court was altogether less certain and secure.

Some brought their actions to court only after long delay: some not at all. They proceeded instead by offer and counter-offer for right or seisin. Admittedly, the surviving legal records are incomplete. Part of the story is missing. But, when all allowance is made for that, it seems likely that some cases never came to a formal record of judicial proceedings; they must have been settled instead by informal discussion of whomsoever the king chose to consult, by political considerations, by the king's *voluntas*, his personal decision, at worst his whim. That was how the issue was determined between Geoffrey fitz Peter and Geoffrey de Say in 1189–90. There was no record of legal proceedings before 1212.[176] The division of the Percy estates followed a similar course.[177] Admittedly both these disputes impinged on the *casus regis*: that did not deter undertenants from launching legal actions on the very same issue.[178] Moreover, major disputes arising from other issues followed a similar course. The descendants of William de Tracy, murderer of Thomas Becket, all resorted to the proffer to gain or defend possession; Oliver de Tracy, demandant, 1000 m., giving way to Henry de Tracy, William's son, also 1000 m.; Hugh de Courtenay, the tenant and William's nephew, 2000 m.[179] Although Henry gained possession no pleas are recorded. The contestants at odds over the estates of Richard de Lucy, Henry II's Justiciar, who died in 1179, behaved likewise.

---

[176] See above, pp. 147–8, and below, pp. 206–8.

[177] The division between William and Richard de Percy was put into effect in 1204, William then being a ward of William Briwerre. There was no legal action until Trinity 1214, although a subsidiary action concerning the service of Alan de Arches occurred in 1212 (*Curia Regis Rolls*, VI, 321; VII, 160).

[178] Holt (1991b), pp. 32–4.

[179] *Rot. de Ob. et Fin.* pp. 15–16, 69; *Pipe Roll 1 John*, p. 198; *Rot. Chartarum*, p. 61. For Hugh de Courtenay's relationship and tenure see J. H. Round. *Cal. Docs. France*, pp. 194–5. See also Painter (1949), p. 38.

Proffers came from heirs, from guardians, from heiresses down to grand-daughters, and from husbands of heiresses, but no litigation was recorded until 1219, forty years on.[180] Only one thing softened the harsh reality of bid and counter-bid. Occasionally parties reached agreement out of court.[181] So much for the superiority of royal justice.

In 1215 the gates were unbarred. During the week following the settlement at Runnymede on 19 June King John committed himself to some fifty acts of restoration.[182] We know of these entirely through the resulting executive mandates. These reveal enough to suggest that the king's opponents were now injecting into the king's court the regularity of procedure which it had long lacked. Several actions drew immediately on the language and procedure of the assize of *novel disseisin* – now, under the terms of cap. 52 of the Charter, directed against the king himself. Restoration was ordered to Ralph Cheindeduit of £2 rent in Netley 'if he was disseised unjustly and without judgement of the rent . . . by us or our bailiffs'. Similar letters were issued in favour of Roger de Leonibus and Ranulf fitz Robert. In all cases the letters went close and the sheriff or bailiff was instructed to

---

[180] The main proffers were: 1194, Roese of Dover, grand-daughter and co-heiress, for succession, £700 (*Pipe Roll 6 Richard*, p. 250); 1198, Godfrey, bishop of Winchester, son, for that part of his inheritance for which Roese of Dover had made fine etc., £1000 (*Pipe Roll 10 Richard*, p. 26); 1204, Robert fitz Walter, nephew of Godfrey de Lucy, for the lands of his uncle, 300 m. (*Pipe Roll 6 John*, p. 34); 1204, William Briwerre, for wardship and marriage of the heirs of Roese's first marriage and custody of her dower, £800 (*Rot. de Ob. et Fin.* p. 229); 1207, Roese of Dover, for the renewal and completion of her proffer of 1194, etc. £100 (*Rot. de Ob. et Fin.* p. 414); 1214, Richard de Rivers, for the marriage of Maud, sister of Roese, £500 (*Rot. de Ob. et Fin.* pp. 517–18). For the legal action of 1219, concerning Lessness, Kent, see *Curia Regis Rolls*, viii, 25–6; for a further action of 1223, concerning Newington, Kent, see below, pp. 202–3 and *Curia Regis Rolls*, xi, no. 416. There was later contention in 1225 and 1227, which is essential to an understanding of the complex descent; see *Curia Regis Rolls*, xii, no. 136 and *Bracton's Note Book*, iii, 591–4, no. 1764. J. H. Round established the main facts in 'The heirs of Richard de Lucy', *The Genealogist*, n.s. xv (1898), 129–33. For further comment see Painter (1949), pp. 74–7 and Turner, 'The Mandeville Inheritance, 1189–1236', *Haskins Society Journal*, i (1989), 163–6. Round provided a chart-pedigree (p. 130): cp. Turner (p. 172), which omits a generation between Roese I and Roese II.
[181] Certainly before 1212 and most probably by 1198 Geoffrey fitz Peter surrendered to Geoffrey de Say the two great Mandeville manors of Sawbridgeworth and Edmonton.
[182] For the political context of these actions see below, pp. 359–62.

execute the writ if unjust disseisin had occurred: so presumably some local investigation, formal or informal, settled the matter.[183] Some actions embodied an element of *mort d'ancestor*. Geoffrey de Mandeville's claim in Kingshill was based on tenure as his father had it, and all the lands, liberties and advowsons of the earldom of Gloucester he claimed by right of succession *iure uxoris* to William earl of Gloucester.[184] Some cases were concerned with right. Robert fitz Walter recovered Hertford castle, Richard de Muntfichet gained custody of the forest of Essex, William de Lanvallei obtained the manor of Kingston, Somerset, and Nicholas de Stuteville sought the restoration of Knaresborough, each *tamquam ius suum* or some such phrase.[185] In this last case judgement was given by the Twenty-Five, operating through four of its members, and pronouncing its judgement as *judicium et ius regni*. The impression given by the executive writs is that once the facts were established and judgement given, restoration followed. The king's will had ceased to intervene. Some indication of the king's straits is given by the restoration of Trowbridge to Henry de Bohun earl of Hereford. The case was decided on 19 June, the day of final peace. The king sought respite. The earl would not concede it on the land and only allowed it on the castle up to 28 June.[186] In one illuminating case the establishment of the facts carried the action to a lesser court. On 19 June John wrote to the sheriff of Yorkshire inquiring into an inquisition which had allegedly taken place in the county court into a hereditary claim by William de Mowbray to the custody of York castle and the forest of Yorkshire, and to the tenure of the manor of Pocklington in demesne. De Mowbray must have presented

---

[183] *Rot. Litt. Claus.* I, 216. A different procedure is suggested by a writ to the sheriff of Oxfordshire in favour of William son of Elias. This followed the usual form, but it was cancelled and the sheriff was instructed to restore a manor 'which had been adjudged to him' (*Rot. Litt. Claus.* I, 216b, 217).

[184] *Rot. Litt. Claus.* I, 216–216b.

[185] *Rot. Litt. Pat.* pp. 144, 144b; *Rot. Litt. Claus.* I, 216b, and below, p. 499.

[186] See below, pp. 360, 495.

such evidence to the king or the Twenty-Five or both. The king now wanted to know everything: through whom and when and in what words and where and on whose order had the inquest taken place. The sheriff was to hold a new inquisition which was to be sent to the king under the seals of the jurors.[187] John clearly considered that someone was pulling a fast one. The implication of his instruction, none the less, is that the case would turn on the evidence of a recognition in the county court.

The Twenty-Five probably played a large part in these cases. They were not conducting a revolution. The procedures followed were not new. All that happened is that routine processes governing seisin and right were introduced into the operations of the king's court. Almost certainly the court was tolerant of baronial claims: William de Mowbray's, for example, was bogus, based on alleged precedents in the reign of Stephen. Equally clearly they excluded the royal grace from the execution of judgement. But they staked out a claim which marked one of the great unnoticed victories of 1215, more important immediately than the broad assertions about judgement of peers and the law of the land. They established and extended routine process governing seisin and right in cases involving tenants-in-chief. As if in retribution for justice long delayed, many cases were now settled within a week.

Luck was with them. The minority of Henry III left the door wide open. Justices on eyre, the bench at Westminster, the *magna curia* comprising justices, officers of state and magnates, combined to set their seal on the work which the Twenty-Five had begun. For ten years after John's death actions of right, disseisin, *mort d'ancestor*, the final concord, became the standard currency of the court. The settlement of the land following the civil war of 1215–17 would have been much more difficult otherwise. By the time Henry III

---

[187] See below, pp. 247, 495–6.

achieved full majority in 1227 a boundary had been crossed. King John's system was beyond recall. Things would never be the same again.[188]

The new tone was sounded in a blaze of fury shared by the justices in eyre and the suitors of a county court. During the commotion and civil war of 1215–17 William count of Aumale deprived Gilbert de Gant of his demesne manor of Edenham, Lincs. In 1219 Gilbert sought and got restitution by an action of *novel disseisin* before the justices in eyre at Lincoln; the case was determined on the verdict of a jury. The count defaulted. Fulk d'Oyry, the count's steward, then took some kind of backstairs action which led the justices to protest to the regent, William Marshal and the Justiciar, Hubert de Burgh. They had received, so they said, letters in the name of the king which apparently aimed at overturning the judgement. They now laid down the law. With heavy irony and at some length they noted that they had been appointed to do justice reasonably and to the honour of the king. They were astonished that they were now to suffer public contradiction and to be rendered contemptible in the eyes of those to whom they were to do justice:

In the particular matter we have done nothing except with the counsel and judgement of the whole county court, and nothing contrary to law or the approved custom of the realm, as you can see from the record of the said assize which we send to you with the common assent and testimony of the whole county. Indeed the aforesaid Gilbert de Gant, after the receipt of the letter of the lord king, came to us with the support of the whole county clamouring for him and on his behalf and also for themselves and for the liberty sworn and conceded to the whole realm, as they said, seeking immediately and loyally that the state of his possession adjudged to him by the court of the lord king according to the

---

[188] This did not mean that kings and *curiales* were henceforth unable to override or suborn judicial process. It did mean, however, that when this occurred, as it did very markedly on occasion once Henry III had achieved his majority, the terms of the argument were changed. Cap. 3 of the baronial *gravamina* of January 1264, which uses cap. 40 of Magna Carta to pillory the king's supporters, provides a telling illustration (*Documents of the Baronial Movement of Reform and Rebellion 1258–67*, ed. R. F. Treharne and I. J. Sanders (Oxford, 1973), pp. 270–5).

due custom of the realm, should not be altered without judgement on account of a mandate based on false evidence.[189]

Gant remained in seisin. Now the county court of Lincoln was something of a radical hotbed.[190] It required some political imagination to drag Magna Carta into the issue, as the suitors of the court plainly did. But their instinct was true, for the case is a model of the changes which took place between 1215 and 1217. Under John, Aumale would have approached the king with a large proffer to gain his ends and in all probability that would have ended the matter. Under Henry III something similar took place. An approach was made to the highest authority. But what would earlier have been an exercise of royal *voluntas* now looked like a nasty little intrigue in which Fulk d'Oyry persuaded the Justiciar and the Marshal to exercise their influence on Aumale's behalf. Peter des Roches also took a hand in the game, and, as a result, the case spluttered on; but the decision for Gilbert de Gant was not overturned.[191]

One other tenant-in-chief brought an action of disseisin before the justice in the eyre which began in 1218.[192] One, John de Courcy, in the last year of his life, optimistically

---

[189] *Royal Letters*, I, 21–2. See Lady Stenton's discussion of the case in *Rolls of the Justices in Eyre for Lincolnshire 1218–9 and Worcestershire 1221*, pp. li–liv, and no. 151 for the record of the action. See also Carpenter (1990), pp. 102–3, 165–6.

[190] See below, pp. 390–2, and *Rolls of the Justices in Eyre for Lincolnshire 1218–9 and Worcestershire 1221*, no. 45, where Lady Stenton notes that the county court went its own way in restoring peace in the county after the battle of Lincoln but before the general peace of Lambeth.

[191] Aumale sought to reverse the judgement by action of attaint, in which he was backed by Peter des Roches as one of his pledges (*Pipe Roll 3 Henry III*, p. 129). Gilbert de Gant's attorney pleaded that Aumale was excommunicate – probably for participation in a tournament at Northampton – but Peter des Roches and the bishop of London allowed the plea to proceed. After several postponements Aumale lost by default again in Michaelmas 1220 (*Curia Regis Rolls*, VIII, 158; IX, 258).

[192] *Maurice de Gant* v. *the earl of Chester* concerning Leeds and Bingley, a ransom case arising from the civil war. Gant failed on the ground of prior judgement in the *magna curia*, but the action was not thought inappropriate (*Rolls of the Justices in Eyre for Yorkshire, 1218–9*, no. 1133). *William de Coleville* v. *the count of Aumale* was another *cause majeure* determined by *novel disseisin*, but Coleville was Aumale's tenant (*Rolls of the Justices in Eyre for Lincolnshire 1218–9 and Worcestershire 1221*, pp. liv–vi and nos. 439, 708, 712, 732; *Curia Regis Rolls*, VIII, 30–1, 163–4; *Patent Rolls, 1216–25*, p. 119; *Rotuli Hundredorum*, I, 260b).

launched an action of *mort d'ancestor* in the hope of recovering lands in Ulster which he had lost in 1204–5.[193] Many were involved in actions of right. In these, major disputes were brought to court and frequently to final concord: *Robert de Vieuxpont* v. *the countess of Eu*, concerning Tickhill;[194] *the earl of Hereford* v. *the earl of Salisbury*, concerning Trowbridge, an issue at the heart of the crisis of 1215;[195] *William de Percy* v. *Richard de Percy*, in which the court commented directly on the issue of the *casus regis*.[196] *Matilda de Say* v. *William de Mandeville earl of Essex* concerning the partition of the Mandeville honour, yet another action linked to the *casus regis*.[197] Many of these issues were of ancient origin;[198] it was as if families seized the opportunity to reach agreement at a time when it could be done effectively and cheaply.[199] But some originated in the conflicting grants of John's reign, especially from grants in bail made in the years of crisis and civil war. These cases, too, were largely resolved, sometimes with considerable political friction and prolonged difficulty in enforcing judgement.[200] The regency and the courts were

[193] *Excerpta e Rot. Fin.*, I, 11.

[194] *Curia Regis Rolls*, IX, 212–13; *Yorks. Fines 1218–31*, pp. 42–3. Plea of Michaelmas 1220; concord 9 February 1222.

[195] *Curia Regis Rolls*, XII, no. 2646; XIV, no. 751. Plea, 1226; concord 1230.

[196] *Yorks. Fines, 1218–31*, pp. 1–2; *Rolls of the Justices in Eyre for Yorkshire 1218–9* , no. 1115; concord 6 May 1218; subsequent action 1219.

[197] *Bracton's Note Book*, II, no. 8.

[198] The Tickhill dispute originated at the beginning of the twelfth century (Holt 1972, p. 51; Marjorie Chibnall, 'Robert of Bellême and the castle of Tickhill' in *Droit privé et institutions régionales, Etudes historiques offertes à Jean Yver*, Paris, 1976, pp. 151–6). The Trowbridge dispute concerned the inheritance of Edward of Salisbury, *d*. by 1130. The Say–Mandeville dispute originated in 1185 (Holt 1991b, pp. 24–5).

[199] See the final settlement, 1219, of Market Weighton among the heirs general of Trussebut (*Rolls of the Justices in Eyre for Yorkshire 1218–19*, no. 304; *Yorks. Fines 1218–31*, p. 33); the settlement, 1222, between Idonea Fossard and Peter de Maulay and Isabel his wife, concerning the Fossard barony (*ibid*, p. 37); and the resolution, 1224–5, of the descent of the Lucy estates in Cumbria between Aumale and Moulton (*Curia Regis Rolls*, XI, nos. 1223, 2710; XII, nos. 866, 1576).

[200] See for example *Hubert de Burgh* v. *Reginald de Briouze* concerning the three castles 1218–19 (*Bracton's Note Book*, no. 1330; *Rot. Litt. Claus.* I, 386b, 404). Concorded 1224–5 (*Curia Regis Rolls*, XI, nos. 1894, 2418, 2788; XII, nos. 59, 307), action renewed 1228 (*Curia Regis Rolls*, XIII, no. 592; *Cal. Charter Rolls*, I, 74, 83). See Painter (1949), pp. 45, 85 and Carpenter (1990), pp. 138–9, 247, n.16). Compare *William Marshal earl of Pembroke* v. *Faulkes de Bréauté*, 1219–20, concerning Luton, in which the Marshal

determined to prevent such grants from embedding conflicting titles as they had done in the past. On occasion 'justice' was brutal – or so it was alleged. Peter de Maulay, seeking Upavon against Gilbert Basset in 1229, claimed that he had been disseised unjustly and without judgement by Hubert de Burgh and his men who 'had threatened that he would be so placed that he would see neither his hands nor his feet' if he failed to surrender the manor.[201] But on the whole, there were marked differences from what had gone before. In many cases justice was quick. In 1219 the heirs general of Trussebut made their pleas and came to concord within the space of a single eyre.[202] The dispute over Tickhill was settled in under two years.[203] And justice was no longer sold. The vast proffers of King John's day were a thing of the past.[204] Cap. 40 of Magna Carta had done its work.

Litigants were now ready enough to emphasize the evil doings of King John's day. Humphrey earl of Hereford's claim to Trowbridge was based on the allegation that Ella countess of Salisbury had no entry other than through King John who had disseised the earl's father wilfully – per voluntatem suam – and without judgement.[205] Hubert de Burgh, of all people, made much the same allegation in his pursuit of the three castles.[206] Robert de Ros was more sophisticated and more original: in pursuing the advowson of Market Weighton against the prior of Finchale he argued

offered 1000 m. to be allowed a duel against Faulkes. The Marshal recovered the estate in 1228–9 after Faulkes's fall (Curia Regis Rolls, VIII, 77–8, 248–52; IX, 205; Rot. Litt. Claus. II, 27; Cal. Charter Rolls, I, 102; Annales Monastici, III, 92). See Carpenter (1990), pp. 165, 203, 367.

[201] Curia Regis Rolls, XV, no. 131.

[202] See above, p. 170, n. 199. A consequent case of advowson dragged on into 1220 (Curia Regis Rolls, VIII, 93, 193; IX, 185).

[203] See above, p. 170, n. 194.

[204] The proffer of 1000 m. by William Marshal, made apparently in a mood of angry bravado (above, p. 170, n. 200) and of £1000. by Eustace de Stuteville (below, p. 176) are exceptional. John de Courcy offered 10 m. for an action of mort d'ancestor (above, pp. 169–70), William of Lancaster a palfrey for a jury of the counties bordering on Westmorland (Curia Regis Rolls, XI, no. 2732). See also in general the nova oblata in the Pipe rolls of 3, 4 and 5 Henry III.

[205] Curia Regis Rolls, XII, no. 2646.   [206] Bracton's Note Book, no. 1330.

thus: 'touching King John's charter (confirming the advowson to Finchale) he says that it ought not to hurt him because the king confirms a gift reasonably made and the gift was not reasonable, and therefore the king's charter ought not to hurt him'.[207] But amidst this rhetoric, part political, part procedural, an important change was taking place. The tenant-in-chief was escaping from the immediate jurisdiction of the king. Two well-known cases highlight this process. In 1236 John earl of Chester was summoned to answer a writ *de rationabile parte* brought by the heirs general to the lands of the earldom. One of his arguments was that he ought not to answer before the lord king because it was a common plea and that it was manifestly contrary to the Great Charter that common pleas should follow the king and not be held in a certain place.[208] A year later, Gilbert Marshal earl of Pembroke used precisely the same argument when vouched to warrant his elder brother's charters to Fulk fitz Warin and John Marshal.[209] The one case concerned the succession to an earl, the other enfeoffments made by an earl of estates now claimed to be royal escheats. Each argument was countered. In the case of Chester one of the heirs general argued that the earl had already been before the king and council in the matter and that, although common pleas should not follow the king, *placita singularia* might. In the case of Pembroke the court ruled that it was not a common but a private plea which especially touched the person of the king and should therefore be terminated *coram eo*. No one said that as barons they were immediately justiciable. No one, on either side or in the judgement-seat, referred to tenure. The two earls,

[207] *Rolls of the Justices in Eyre for Yorkshire 1218–19*, no. 1151.
[208] *Curia Regis Rolls*, xv, no. 1958. The writ was most probably a *praecipe de rationabile parte* (*Early Registers of Writs*, pp. lxvii–lxviii). As noted there, the equivalent writ in Glanvill xii, 5 is confused. The suggested amendment of the address is a less likely solution of the difficulty than the simple amendment of 'tenent de domino rege' to 'tenent de vobis' (ed. Hall, p. 138; *Early Register of Writs*, p. lxviii, no.3), the error probably originating in a confusion of 'vobis' and 'nobis'.
[209] *Curia Regis Rolls*, xvi, no. 8.

indeed, were implicitly denying any special jurisdictional obligation based on their immediate dependence on the Crown.

The mechanism at the heart of these changes was the writ *praecipe*. Historians have been so concerned with the *praecipe* as an intrusion into private jurisdiction that the *praecipe in capite* of the thirteenth century appears as little more than a vestigial survival, all that was left after the prohibition of cap. 34 of Magna Carta.[210] This was not so. In the *praecipe in capite* the baron finally achieved a general writ of right, the first and the only one he ever had. It did for him what the writ of right had long done for the tenant. It laid claim in right and inheritance to a tenement held of the king in chief.[211] It was firmly established as a writ of right, categorized as such by Bracton, and it was classified as a writ *de cursu*, in the Bench and the next session of the general eyre, in the thirteenth-century registers of writs.[212] Its appearance in the eyre begun in 1218 set the seal on the victory of 1215.[213]

There is no similar writ surviving from the reign of King John. Yet there were signs of change. The surviving Justiciar's writs of 1199 included nine *praecipes* which are still essentially the writs of summons of Glanvill's day. The only modifications are that now they stipulated that the demandant should give surety for pursuing his claim.[214] Two of the nine also include a claim in right and inheritance: neither of

---

[210] Naomi D. Hurnard (1948); M. T. Clanchy (1964).

[211] 'quod clamat esse ius et hereditatem suam et tenere de nobis in capite' (Bracton, fo. 328b, ed. Thorne, IV, 49; Clanchy, 1964, 548).

[212] Bracton, fo. 328b, tr. Thorne, IV, 49; *Early Registers of Writs*, pp. xxvii–xxix; *Brevia Placita* p. xlix and more generally pp. xlviii–lix.

[213] *Curia Regis Rolls*, VII, 349, Easter term 1220, where the terms of the writ are clearly implied, noted by Hurnard, pp. 177–8 and Clanchy (1964), 544. There is another possible example from Michaelmas 1219 (*Berevill v. the abbot of Croxton, Curia Regis Rolls*, VIII, 135–6) and a clear reference to the writ in *Leviva daughter of Ailwin v. the prior of Westacre*, Michaelmas 1220 (*Curia Regis Rolls*, IX, 301). I owe these last two references to the kindness of Dr Paul Brand.

[214] *Pleas before the King and his Justices*, I, 10.

these concerned tenancies-in-chief.[215] How general this
became in subsequent years it is impossible to say without
any of the original writs. It is certain, however, that in the
case of tenants-in-chief men began to refer to the *praecipe* as a
writ of right.[216] In addition it is probable that for the
undertenant the *praecipe* was now issued as a writ *de cursu*.
Considerable numbers were purchased in the royal eyre of
1204 at a price low enough to suggest that the procedure was
intended as routine.[217] But for the tenant-in-chief it still
remained *de gracia*, as in Glanvill's day.[218] In this, as in other
matters, the undertenant enjoyed a regular procedure which
his lord only achieved after 1215.

The *praecipe in capite*, then, was a great unrecorded
baronial victory which gave backbone to cap. 40 of the
Charter. Two cases, thirty years apart, bring home the
point. The first, from 1204, concerns Sturminster Marshal,
Dorset.[219] Sturminster was the patrimony of the senior line
of the great house of Beaumont; it descended through the
counts of Meulan until it was surrendered into the king's
hand, along with the Meulan fee in Normandy, by Count
Robert in 1203, as a consequence of the treason of his son. In
1204 it was listed in the English records as *terra Normannorum*
among other similar escheats to the Crown.[220] But there
were in fact three claimants to it. The resulting action came
before the king and the record provides rare detail of the

[215] *Ibid.* nos. 3481, 3541. It is perhaps optimistic to classify this variant as a 'modification'. Compare Clanchy (1964), 543, n.1.
[216] See above, pp. 142–3.   [217] *Pipe Roll 6 John*, p. xxii–xxxiii.
[218] Glanvill treats the writ as *de gracia* but only by implication (I, 5, ed. Hall, p. 5). Compare Van Caenegem, *Royal Writs*, p. 250. It may be that there was some softening in this by John's reign. John's letter to the Justiciar of Ireland, discussed below (p. 186), allowed the Justiciar to issue writs in actions of right and *mort d'ancestor* concerning half a knight's fee or less. No distinction was drawn in this between tenants, or tenancies-in-chief and others. This was included in the Irish register of writs (*Early Registers of Writs*, pp. 1–2), and it may well be that this is to be dated as early as 1210. See Paul Brand, 'Ireland and the Literature of the early Common Law'. *The Irish Jurist*, XVI (1981), 95–113, especially 95–9. However, I have found no action between barons concerning a tenancy-in-chief defined in such terms.
[219] *Curia Regis Rolls*, III, 124.   [220] F. M. Powicke (1961), pp. 344–5.

king and his court in action in a case involving his barons. The first party was William Marshal: he claimed that the count of Meulan had enfeoffed him in Sturminster long before his surrender, and he proffered a charter in evidence. The second was William de Redvers, earl of Devon, claiming in right of his wife, Count Robert's daughter: he argued that he had already got homage and fealty from the men of Sturminster by precept of the count and his wife. The third was the countess of Meulan herself who claimed that she had been in seisin and had been disseised by precept of the king.[221] Not surprisingly, the parties could not be brought to agreement and they were given a day on the morrow before the king 'that they might have right in the matter by the counsel of his court'. In fact only William Marshal turned up and that before the justices. He was given his fourth day, they still failed to appear, and on the fifth he once more claimed his seisin. So,

the lord king took counsel with those who were present with him. But they were only few and, so they said, had not seen cases of this kind occur at all frequently before, so they advised that the whole case should be deferred to the morrow of the Assumption [15 August] when the archbishop and the other great and wise men of the land could be present. However, the Marshal was unwilling to accept delay and insisted (*semper voluit*) on having his seisin. So, because he would not accept a postponement, the king acted through the counsel of those present and placed the manor in the state in which it was before it was taken into his hand, namely in the custody of the countess [of Meulan] and her bailiffs. It would then please the king if earl William [Marshal] could obtain his seisin from them through his charters and through the letters of the count which he had, addressed to the aforesaid bailiffs.

So ends the record of the plea. The rest is quickly told. William Marshal obtained royal letters of 9 September 1204 putting him in seisin, and so he remained until his death. It

---

[221] Her plea was correct. While it is true, as Powicke notes, that Sturminster was listed among *terrae Normannorum* (*Rot. Norm.*, pp. 126, 140), it was noted that the countess of Meulan held the land by precept of the king. It was, in fact, her dower, or at least so she claimed.

remained for the countess to pursue her claim to dower after he had died.[222]

The second case comes from 1234 and concerns the manor of Cottingham, part of the Stuteville patrimony.[223] The contenders were Eustace de Stuteville, nephew of Nicholas (William de Stuteville's brother and heir), and Nicholas's two daughters represented by their husbands, Hugh Wake and William de Mustac. Each party claimed to have been seised, and each claimed to have been disseised by the will of King Henry III. The king apparently appeared in court in person. He told a complicated story, indeed a rigmarole which would have disgraced his father. He had found Eustace in seisin. While still in seisin Eustace had offered him £1000 not to be disseised except by judgement, or 500 m. if the king took the land into his hand pending judgement of the issue in his court – a proffer, indeed, which reverted to the practices of the time of John. But Henry admitted that he had disseised Eustace *per voluntatem*, without summons and without judgement (presumably accepting the lower proffer, although that is not stated or recorded). Later he gave seisin to Hugh and William, only to deprive them again by counsel of the magnates for waste and sale of woods, until such time as judgement and justice were done in his court. Amidst this tale of confusion Eustace renewed his proffer of £1000 that he should be treated by the judgement of the court. The proffer was admitted. Judgement was given. On the ground that the king had disseised Eustace first, *per voluntatem suam*, without summons and judgement, the court considered that this should first be amended. So Eustace was put in seisin. Nevertheless he was 'to answer the same Hugh and William and their wives by assize of *mort d'ancestor* or by writ of right'. Bracton copied

---

[222] *Rot. Litt. Pat.* p. 45b; *Rot. Litt. Claus.* I, 7b; *Curia Regis Rolls*, III, 124; VIII, 116–17; *Bracton's Note Book*, II, no. 71.
[223] *Curia Regis Rolls*, XV, no. 1026. For Cottingham see *Early Yorkshire Charters*, IX, 5.

this case into his *Note Book* and no wonder: it was in every way remarkable.[224]

At first sight these two cases are strikingly similar. Each was apparently initiated by plaint: no writ is mentioned. The issues were alike. Each case moved easily to and fro between the king and his justices sitting *coram rege*. In each the king acted with counsel. In each the interim judgement was to convey seisin to the party in possession before the action began. The case of 1234 provides a rare example of justice still being bought and sold at high cost as it had been under John.[225] But there the similarities end. In 1204 King John was plainly in control. He took counsel from his men, but the interim judgement was his. In 1234 King Henry, apparently as a witness in his own court, admitted that he had disseised a vassal *per voluntatem* without either summons or judgement. He wished and instructed that in his court judgement and justice should now be done. Father and son look very different. Moreover, the procedure of 1204 was much more fluid than that of 1234. In 1204 the only certain point of contact with the common law was with the law governing the summons. The judgement, that it would well please the king if William Marshal could get seisin from the countess of Meulan, was worthy of Pontius Pilate. In sharp contrast the court in 1234 put Eustace de Stuteville in seisin but directed that he was to answer the other parties if they pursued their case by either *mort d'ancestor* or writ of right (i.e. by a *praecipe in capite*). The record stated that that was *secundum legem terrae*. The common law had permeated the inner sanctum in which the king held jurisdiction over his immediate vassals. Magna Carta itself did not ensure that; it

---

[224] *Bracton's Note Book*, III, 123–5, no. 1106. See also *Select Cases of Procedure without Writ*, p.cli. For the writ of 24 June 1234 putting Eustace in seisin see *Excerpta e Rot. Fin.*, I, 259. See also Turner (1968), pp. 50, 250–1.

[225] No proffer was recorded in the action of 1204, but William earl of Devon proffered 500 m. for the succession to the lands of the count and countess of Meulan. This included a grand assize to determine whether he had the greater right to hold Rumbridge and Langley of the king or the king to hold it in demesne (*Rot. de Ob. et Fin.* pp. 235–6). There is no evidence that it ever took place.

was nowhere in black and white; but that is what it had brought about.

In some ways the Crown had itself to blame. The more the king's justice was delegated, the more frequently his judges went out on eyre, and the longer the Bench sat at Westminster; the more difficult it became to separate the king's immediate jurisdiction from the rest. The right to plead solely before the king or Chief Justiciar was a common enough ecclesiastical privilege, but already in 1201 a litigant was ready to argue that 'all pleas before the justices of the bench are understood to be held before the king or his chief justiciar'.[226] The closure of the Bench between 1209 and 1214, the abeyance of jurisdiction *coram rege* between 1216 and 1234, both had the effect of sustaining a single multi-purpose jurisdiction.[227] Within this the king's control of his immediate vassals was diffused and dissolved. Yet the Crown did not lose thereby. The judges of John's reign had a clear enough idea of matters which should be referred to the king – royal writs and charters, agreements concerning tenancies-in-chief or affecting service due to the Crown – and John himself had an interest in justice which led him to intervene.[228] During the minority of Henry III, too, important matters affecting the Crown were referred to the *magna curia* or held over pending the king's majority.[229] Gradually,

---

[226] *Curia Regis Rolls*, I, 462. Lady Stenton was surely right in not accepting this as a judicial view (*Pleas before the King and his Justices*, I, 102) as against Maitland (*Select Pleas of the Crown*, I, pp. xiv–xv), Powicke (*E.H.R.*, xxxix (1924), 265–6) and Sayles (*Select Cases in the Court of King's Bench*, I, p. xxiii). It may be, as she also suggests, that the words originated in the writ brought by the demandant, Henry of Rugby, but, if that was so, it is difficult to see why the judges, in proceeding with the case, sought the assent of the king. By the same token it cannot be accepted, as in Turner (1968), p. 82, that the justices of the Bench went ahead without reference to the king.

[227] Sayles, *Select Cases in the Court of King's Bench*, I, p. xxvi–xxxviii. Compare: 'Two central courts which largely duplicated each other's work did not therefore arise out of the logic of legal development. They were the offspring of politics: of absentee kings, the disputes with John, the stipulations of the Charter' (Sayles, IV, p. xxxi), to which might be added the minority of Henry III.

[228] Flower (1943), pp. 27–30; Doris M. Stenton (1963), pp. 92–7.

[229] Sayles, *Select Cases in the Court of King's Bench*, I, pp. xxxiii–xxxiv. See also Lady Stenton's analysis of the memoranda roll of the justices in Yorkshire 1219 (*Rolls of the Justices in Eyre for Yorkshire 1218–9*, pp. xxix–xxx, 413). For an example of reference to

the king's superiority was given a more precise definition. The pretensions of the earl of Pembroke in 1237 were resisted on the ground that the plea was a private one which especially touched the person of the king, and the court ruled that 'a plea which touched the person of the king should be terminated before him'.[230] What 'touched the king'? Bracton's list of royal pleas differed only a little from Glanvill's.[231] He saw no surrender. On the contrary he expatiated on the grounds on which pleas were so reserved. Moreover, by his day 'what touched the king' had come to include a mass of *quo warranto* proceedings, investigations into liberties and franchises, and royal estates or escheats allegedly lost to the Crown. All franchises in Bracton's view belonged to the Crown.[232] A generation from Magna Carta the superiority of the Crown was changed, not defunct. On the ruins of his feudal lordship the king's men were building a doctrine of royal prerogative.

The crisis of jurisdiction which occurred in the years either side of 1215 has been explained traditionally in personal terms: King John undid the good work of his father. In McKechnie's words:

Far from using the perfected machinery of Exchequer, Curia and local administration in the interests of good government, John valued them merely as instruments of extortion and outrage – as ministers to his lust and greed.[233]

---

the king's majority of a case based on royal charters concerning a tenancy-in-chief, see *Rolls of the Justices in Eyre for Gloucestershire, Warwickshire and Staffordshire 1221–2*, p. xlv, and no. 242.

[230] See above, p. 172, and for general comment on this development Ehrlich (1921), pp. 23–6, 49–50. There were precedents in John's reign, to go no further back. See the charter of 14 June 1204 to Fulk d'Oyry quitclaiming his men of Gedney from service on assizes and recognitions 'nisi assisa fuerit de aliquo speciali jure quod pertineat ad personam nostram disrationandum' (*Rot. Chartarum*, pp. 134b–135).

[231] Fos. 105b–106, tr. Thorne, II, 301–2. Compare Glanvill, I, 3, ed. Hall, p. 4. The *addicio de cartis* adds issues concerning royal charters and writs, which, in practice, had always been referred to the king (fo. 6, 34, ed. Thorne, II, 109–10).

[232] Donald W. Sutherland, *Quo Warranto Proceedings in the Reign of Edward I 1278–94* (Oxford, 1963), pp. 13–15.

[233] McKechnie (1914), p. 50.

This view went back to Stubbs.[234] It is still repeated, though usually in a form influenced by Lady Stenton's appraisal of John's judicial work.[235] Such an explanation, in which the supposed psyche of the king is derived from the very facts it is supposed to explain, will not do. The king's personality mattered. The inadequacy of jurisdictional structure and legal procedure mattered much more. In these a major reform was required and was achieved. Yet in one matter the traditional account comes close to the facts. Whatever his influence, malign or not, King John took a close personal interest in the supervision of justice. Whatever the inadequacies of the system, he certainly jolted it.

In his teens John Lackland had for his tutor Ranulf Glanville, Henry II's great Justiciar.[236] Well before he became king he showed an interest in judicial matters. As count of Mortain, lord of seven English counties, he had his own court, with its own justices headed by his chancellor, Stephen Ridel, sitting usually at Marlborough.[237] In 1199, while in Normandy, he apparently heard English pleas, including one which confirmed a case first held at Westminster.[238] His first extended visit to England from February to April 1200 is marked by the first surviving *coram*

[234] Compare Stubbs (1897), I, 575, commenting on the provisions concerning amercements in Magna Carta caps. 20–23: 'Such a clause (*sic*) proves that the careful provisions of the Exchequer on this point had been transgressed by the king who had, as we learn from the historians, imposed amercements of scandalous amount and with wanton tyranny, just as he compounded by fines for imaginary offences.'

[235] See, for example, Bryce Lyon – 'He respected neither custom nor procedure and seemed to settle each plea upon the basis of his own whim' (*A Constitutional and Legal History of Medieval England*, New York, 1980, p. 281), and Turner (1968, p. 44) – 'One reason for his close watch over the courts must have been the fear and suspicion that made him seek to concentrate all power in his hands.' The closest approximation to the old Stubbsian view is to be found, curiously enough, in Richardson and Sayles (1963), pp. 384–87.

[236] The evidence, which describes Ranulf as John's *magister*, is provided solely by Howden (*Gesta Henrici*, I, 304–5) and refers to the summer of 1183 when John was fifteen. Howden is unlikely to have been wrong in such a matter.

[237] For Lancashire and Somerset cases tried at Marlborough see *Curia Regis Rolls*, I, 262 (which lists the justices) and *Rot. de Ob. et Fin.* p. 8. Actions were tried by the count's court but were initiated by royal writ; they embrace the usual range of assizes. See *Devon and Cornwall Notes and Queries*, xx (1936–8), p. 400; *Rot. de Ob. et Fin.* p. 262.

[238] *Pipe Roll 1 John*, pp. 68–9.

rege roll. He took such charge of royal justice that the bench at Westminster was 'practically in abeyance'.[239] Thereafter the king's personal direction was marked by the royal eyres of 1201 and 1204, the dislocation of the general eyre after 1209, and the cessation of pleas in the bench in the same year. These were matters of concern in 1215. Yet, despite the signs that the fount of justice was drying up, the king's influence was not wholly malign. As Lady Stenton has shown, he was genuinely interested in justice even in the hard-pressed years of the Interdict and his own excommunication.[240] Indeed, more than that, he was inventive. As has long been recognized, the first action by writ of attaint, whereby a jury of twenty-four knights re-examined the verdict of a jury of twelve, was entered on the roll of the bench in Michaelmas 1202 as being 'on the authority of the writ of the lord king from overseas'.[241] The entry reads as if the king's writ *de ultra mare* merely initiated this particular action, and it is so interpreted by legal historians. But not so, for what came from overseas was a full-blown proforma of the writ of attaint, similar in form to the proformas of Glanvill or the later registers of writs. It is entered on the dorse of the Fine roll of the summer of 1201.[242] There is no real doubt that the writ was designed in the king's court in Normandy. What precise part John played we cannot determine. The Justiciar of England and the judges of the Bench apparently played none. It is noteworthy that the one novelty with which the king can reasonably be linked was designed to investigate, and if need be quash, the verdicts of local jurors. Its purpose was supervisory. And it is fitting that

---

[239] The words are Lady Stenton's. For her discussion of this visit see *Pleas before the King and his Justices*, I, 57–86. Compare the above (p. 57) with: 'the Justiciar and Judges alike found that they had a master' (p. 86).

[240] Doris Mary Stenton (1964), pp. 88–114.

[241] *Curia Regis Rolls*, II, 97–8. There is also an action of Michaelmas 1201 which looks similar, *ibid.*, II, 33. See also Richardson and Sayles, *Select Cases of Procedure without Writ*, pp. lxxxvii–lxxxviii.

[242] *Rot. de Ob. et Fin.* p. 193. The probable date is June–July 1201. The proforma is followed by a writ to Geoffrey fitz Peter dated 19 August.

it should appear on the Fine roll, for it is in this roll that the king's control of government is seen at its most immediate and unremitting.

The Fine roll was drawn up in Chancery. It travelled with the king; from time to time in the early years of the reign it recorded his passages to and fro across the Channel. A copy, the Originalia roll, was made at regular intervals for despatch to the Exchequer where the sums promised were put in charge. With few exceptions the Originalia roll was the source of all the major fines entered for account on the Pipe roll.[243] Throughout the reign there were only two variations to these arrangements, which are easily understood. In 1199 some fines were agreed by Geoffrey fitz Peter, as Chief Justiciar, before John arrived in England for his coronation. Then in 1214 Peter des Roches, the new Justiciar conducting affairs with the king absent in Poitou, kept a roll of offerings of his own concerned largely with payments for legal writs.[244] These instances apart, all *nova oblata* entered each year on the Pipe rolls were unspecified. There are no headings attributing the authority for the proffers to Geoffrey fitz Peter or Peter des Roches or, indeed, to any one else. The authority was the king's. How many proffers were agreed with him in person it is difficult to say. Administrative responsibility lay with the Keeper of the Seal; occasionally others, the Justiciar or a judge or a great official or curial magnate, intervened.[245] But the Chancery was now

[243] Exceptions to this were very few, a consequence of special arrangements or infringements of the system. There was of course a trickle of proffers agreed in the Bench or with justices in eyre for the purchase of writs and the like. This is clear from a comparison of the Fine rolls with the related Pipe rolls and from the Plea rolls. Hugh de Neville, as chief forester, had the king's general licence to accept proffers from the sale of forests etc. (*Rot. Litt. Pat.*, p. 31b); these appear from time to time under his name on the Pipe rolls.

[244] *Rot. de Ob. et Fin.* pp. 533–50; there is another hitherto unprinted fragment in P.R.O. c 60/7b.

[245] The system of authorization of both fine and entry on the roll is best seen in the roll of 15 John (*Rot. de Ob. et Fin.* pp. 464–526), where the annotations clearly reflect the transfer of the seal from Richard Marsh to Ralph de Neville, with an intervening period of authorization by Peter de Roches. The rolls of the earlier years have fewer annotations.

the controlling office[246] where communication with, and intervention by, the king was immediate.[247]

It had all been very different under King Richard. The great bulk of the entries on the Pipe rolls of his reign are for proffers authorized by the Chancellor, William de Longchamp, or by the two successive Justiciars, Walter, archbishop of Rouen and Hubert, archbishop of Canterbury. The sole surviving Originalia roll, a fragment of 1195–6, records proffers, which, with one exception, were agreed with Hubert Walter.[248] Richard intervened from time to time. His sale of privileges in 1189–90, before leaving for the crusade, was notorious: 'he would have sold London itself if he had found a buyer'.[249] He received proffers and levied amercements again in 1194 on his return from captivity in Germany,[250] and he acted jointly with Hubert Walter in assessing fines at Les Andelys and Pont de l'Arche in 1197.[251] In addition some important proffers concerning tenants-in-chief were agreed with him. Either he intervened or tenants-in-chief insisted on going to the top. In 1193, for example, Hervey Bagot offered 200 m. to Walter archbishop of Rouen, then Justiciar, for succession to the barony of Robert of Stafford. In the following year it was raised to

---

[246] See the heading of 1205 – 'Oblata recepta in cancellaria post mortem domini H. Cant. archiepiscopi cancellarii anno regni domini regis septem' (*Rot. de Ob. et Fin.* p. 298).

[247] For fines certainly agreed with the king, or where the king intervened, see Robert de Tregoz (*Memoranda Roll 1 John*, p. 90), Matthew fitz Herbert (*Rot. Norm.*, pp. 51, 96), the abbot of Peterborough (*Rot Lib.*, p. 59), Asceline de Waterville (*Rot. Lib.*, p. 59), Bartholomew of Moulton, where the king confirmed a fine agreed by Geoffrey fitz Peter – an unusual case (*Rot. de Ob. et Fin.* pp. 254–5; *Pipe Roll 7 John*, p. 212). See also the memorandum on the dorse of the Fine roll of 3 John – 'Dominus Rex concessit Rogero constabulario Cestrie custodiam terre et heredis Willelmi filii Roberti filii Rannulfi, per sic quod finem faciet cum domino Rege cum venerit in Angliam ad voluntatem suam' (*Rot. de Ob. et Fin.* p. 192).

[248] *Memoranda Roll 1 John*, pp. 85–8. The exception is a fine of 1000 m. by Simon of Kyme which was apparently made with the king. This item was brought from Normandy for entry on the roll by Geoffrey fitz Peter and William de St Mère Eglise (p. 88).

[249] William of Newburgh in *Chronicles of Stephen, Henry II and Richard I*, 304–6. Compare *Hoveden*, III, 13 and *Gesta Henrici*, II, 90–1.

[250] Holt (1985a), p. 74.

[251] *Pipe Roll 9 Richard, passim.* Hubert Walter probably held these matters over for consultation with the king.

300 m. and was now included among the fines agreed on the king's return from Germany.[252] An even clearer example of this staged approach is provided by a proffer of 100 m. from Roger Bigod earl of Norfolk that he should not be disseised except by judgement of a court of the lands to which his half-brother was laying claim. This proffer was recorded on the fragment of the Originalia roll of 1195–6 and was certainly agreed with the Chief Justiciar, Hubert Walter.[253] In the following year Roger Bigod served with King Richard in Normandy. He now proffered 700 m. to the king for identical protection. The Exchequer was informed *per breve Regis de ultra mare* and by the end of the account of 1196 Roger had paid in full.[254] The case is worth bearing in mind. No one could stop the king intervening, even over-riding his Justiciar. On the other hand, we cannot know where the impetus came from, whether in this case Richard imposed the new fine or Roger raised his bid. Moreover, it is perfectly clear that in the first instance Hubert Walter and Roger Bigod felt that it was quite in order to try to settle the matter without reference to the king. It is one of several such examples. The offerings authorized by Hubert during his last year as Justiciar included 100 m. from the earl of Arundel for the castle, town, mill and park of Arundel, 500 m. from Peter de Brus for the succession to his father, 500 m. from Osbert de Longchamps for the king's grace and restoration of land and office, 400 m. from Philip, bishop of Durham, for the wapentake of Sadberge, and several proffers ranging from £100 to 50 m. for wardship and marriage or, from widows, for freedom to marry with royal approval.[255]

---

[252] *Pipe Roll 5 Richard*, p. 85; *Pipe Roll 6 Richard*, p. 41. On the first occasion the account was not put in charge.

[253] *Memoranda Roll 1 John*, p. 86.

[254] *Ibid.* and *Chancellor Roll 8 Richard*, p. 138.

[255] *Pipe Roll 10 Richard*, pp. 42–3, 63, 93–4, 210 (cp. 227). See also the division of the lands of Ralph d'Aubigné (15 fees held of William d'Aubigné of Belvoir) among heirs general 15 April 1197 (*Pipe Roll 6 Richard*, p. 118 and *Feet of Fines 7 & 8 Richard I*, no. 134). The evidence of the Pipe rolls is far from easy to interpret. Fines of different authorization occasionally appear under the same heading. For example, in 1198 the proffer of £1000

Under Richard tenants-in-chief were making proffers and fines with the Justiciar in the Exchequer or Bench. This is the essential contrast to what happened under John.

Two cases point the contrast. They are not entirely comparable because one concerns simple free tenants and the other tenants-in-chief, but they well illustrate the change which came about in 1199. The first occurred just before Hubert Walter resigned the justiciarship in 1198. It began as a dispute over suit of court. The men of Thanet complained that the abbot of St Augustine was seeking undue services and customs; in particular he required them to 'follow' (i.e. perform suit at) his court, whereas they claimed that they only needed to plead and stand to right at Minster in Thanet. They attorned thirty men who subsequently withdrew and were amerced for false claim – except for two, Samuel and Norman of Thanet 'who were the ringleaders'; and they 'were put into prison because they crossed the sea and complained to the lord king before they had made their complaint to the justices of England, and thereby they had defaulted to them; they were not to be freed except by the chief justiciar'.[256] So much for the power of the Bench at the end of Hubert Walter's tenure. The second case is the dispute of 1207 between Eustace de Vescy and Richard de Umfraville for the custody of Henry Batail.[257] It came to

of Godfrey de Lucy, bishop of Winchester, appears under the heading *Nova oblata per H. Cant' archiepiscopum*. Nevertheless, it was probably agreed with the king, for the entry referred to a royal writ, which had already been executed, ordering payment of £500 to Stephen of Thornham. That it was different from the other entries under this heading is signalled simply by a single blank line (*Pipe Roll 10 Richard*, p. 26). This is part of a larger problem concerning the interpretation of *per* – 'on the authority of'. Did it mean that the person named was responsible for agreeing the fine in question or simply for passing it to the Treasurer's clerk for entry in the Pipe roll? Was he the authority or merely the source? My argument above, which is based on an examination of the headings from 1189 to 1214 and of the surviving Fine rolls, relies on *per* referring to the agreements themselves and not simply to their entry on the roll. But there are occasional difficulties and possible exceptions, and, in any case, the first and stronger sense of the word embraces the second.

[256] *Curia Regis Rolls*, VII, 343–4. The amercement of 200 m. on the men of Thanet was among the *nova oblata* of Hubert archbishop of Canterbury in 1198 (*Pipe Roll 10 Richard*, p. 210). For the analogy with cap. 17 of Magna Carta see above, p. 71.
[257] See above, pp. 146–7.

the notice of the king after the justices, Simon of Pattishall and James of Potterne, had allowed the two barons to reach a concord. The concord was quashed. Each justice was amerced 100 m. for granting licence to concord without the licence of the king.[258] The amercements were subsequently pardoned, in Potterne's case after he had begun payment, but the king's mastery had been asserted. Under Richard I such a matter might have reached the king, but it would have been perfectly in order for Hubert Walter to deal with it. He would not have been amerced for doing so.

At the margin John defined his authority very precisely. Ireland was a special problem. He saw the court of the Justiciar as *curia nostra*.[259] But distance meant that the Justiciar had to have some independence, and in letters of November 1204 John laid down what this was to be. The Justiciar's writ would run throughout Ireland in actions of right and *mort d'ancestor* covering half a knight's fee or less. He could also apparently initiate writs of *novel disseisin, de fugitivis et nativis*, and *de divisis faciendis* except between baronies.[260] Plainly the king intended that all more serious actions of right and *mort d'ancestor*, and all cases of division of baronies, should be initiated by his writ and hence subject to his immediate supervision. If that applied to Ireland, how much more rigorously to England, especially after 1204 when the king was largely resident. In the light of this the cessation of the Bench and the suspension of eyres in 1209 require little special explanation. John intended to change the administration of justice from the moment of his accession. He duly did so.

One result was to diminish the supply of justice; the

[258] *Rot. de Ob. et Fin.* pp. 386, 412, 447; *Pipe Roll 9 John*, p. 207.
[259] *Rot. Litt. Pat.*, pp. 45–45b, 46.
[260] *Rot. Litt. Pat.*, p. 47b; *Calendar of Documents relating to Ireland*, ed. H. S. Sweetman, (London, H.M.S.O.), 1875, I, no. 236. The letters determined the period of limitation for the possessory assizes and *de fugitivis* (*Early Registers of Writs*, p. xxxv). The restriction to a half knight's fee survives in the standard writ of right in the Irish register of writs of 1227 (pp. 1–2). See also Paul Brand, 'Ireland and the Literature of the Early Common Law', *The Irish Jurist*, XVI (1981), 95–113, especially 98–9.

demand was too great to be met by one court, still less by one man. Another was to confuse justice with patronage. Offers for writs were entered on the Fine roll alongside reliefs, fines made in widowhood, proffers for wardship, purchases of privileges and penalties to avoid the king's wrath. The Fine roll was also used to record the amercements of the royal eyre of 1204.[261] But it was much more than a mix-up in the record. Good lordship was inherently contradictory. The king had to do justice, certainly; but he also had to reward faithful service. The cry for justice was also a demand for reward. The king's response embodied both judgement and patronage. John's political acumen, his insistent search for financial supply, his finely tuned and wary personal assessments of his great vassals, at times his mere whim, therefore played a part. Justice was done, and also sold, denied and deferred. By his own mastery he deprived himself of institutional safeguards. If Hubert Walter had survived in office as Justiciar, the Exchequer and Bench might have become the offices of issue of all original writs, including those concerning baronies. But he did not survive, and John's choice of him as Chancellor only served to advance the shift of power from Exchequer and Bench to Chancery on which the king was determined.[262] As the reign advanced, the new Justiciar, Geoffrey fitz Peter, faded into the background. By 1212 John had thrust himself into a very exposed position. He now had to face the consequences.

---

[261] *Rot. de Ob. et Fin.* pp. 280–6. All the entries are on the dorse of the roll.
[262] See the illuminating passages on the emergence of the Chancery in Galbraith (1948), pp. 69–70. Compare Hardy's introduction to *Rot. de Ob. et Fin.* p. vii, where the shift from *curia regis* to Chancery is noted.

CHAPTER 6

CRISIS AND CIVIL WAR

Magna Carta reflects two distinct conditioning circumstances. On the one hand it emerged from the increasing
maturity of European political thought and practice, from
the concept of rule according to law, from the demand for
the preservation of the rights of subjects within a feudal and
ecclesiastical hierarchy and from routine patterns of government which went with more disciplined and sophisticated
forms of administration. On the other hand it was a product
of a political crisis. It sprang directly from the flexibility and
severity of Angevin methods of government under the
ruthless and capable direction of King John, from the urgent
requirements imposed by foreign wars for the defence and,
after 1204, the recovery of Normandy, and from the final
collapse of John's military and diplomatic schemes on the
field of Bouvines in July 1214.

Thus the Charter was not simply a statement of administrative practices, or desired regulations or principles of law.
These were no more than the terms of reference establishing
broad limits within which the opposing parties made their
demands, or compromised and hedged, or sought hidden
advantages, or skilfully provided escape routes from the
letter of the documents. The Charter and its associated
documents are complex records which bear the imprint of
nearly three years of political crisis and protracted, dis-
continuous negotiation. They cannot be properly understood apart from this crisis, for to separate them from the
detail of politics is to risk anachronism and to hinder our
understanding of the relative importance which men then
attached to particular issues and demands. By 1215 negotia-

tion had acquired a momentum of its own, and particular details had achieved a crucial significance out of all proportion to their ultimate effects, if any, on the course of English history. Thus the restoration of a castle, the claim to an inheritance, the dismissal of a royal official, and issues such as these, became nodal points, important both in themselves and as tests of the king's good faith, from which there grew suspicion, mistrust and civil war.

This crisis began in August 1212 with a baronial plot to murder or betray the king. It falls conveniently into two periods, divided by the defeat of John's allies at Bouvines on 27 July 1214. Up to then it is to be traced chiefly in royal concessions and promises; thereafter these were quickly overtaken by baronial demands for reform. In both periods the quarrel had some of the characteristics of a legal action, indeed of two legal actions, for in 1213 some of the barons challenged the king's demands for service overseas, thus in effect initiating a plea of service in the royal court, and in 1215 both parties made an appeal to the papal Curia, thus acknowledging the feudal superiority which King John had formally conceded to Rome. War followed the breakdown of these forms of legal action. It began on 5 May 1215 with the baronial withdrawal of homage and fealty and ended with the renewal of homage and fealty at Runnymede on 19 June.

King John's character left deep marks on this period for the crisis called forth all his genius for political manœuvre, through the whole range of moves from dictatorial bullying to bribery and shallow promises. Indeed, he refused to accept the inevitability of a major political crisis until his last gambler's throw for triumph abroad failed at Bouvines. Hence, while he began to make concessions of various kinds from the summer of 1212 onwards, he still persisted with his plans for a campaign on the continent and with many of the internal and financial demands which were essential to finance a war. Concession was only fragmentary and was as yet closely tied to his continental plans; where necessary he still pressed his internal demands as hard as ever. He levied the scutage for the Poitevin campaign of 1214 at 3 m. per fee, a rate heavier than in any previous known assessment, despite the obvious certainty that it would arouse opposition and resistance. Even in the summer of 1214 he was still prepared to provoke rather than propitiate.

Financial need, suspicion of treachery and the desirability of buying support combined to give John's policy towards his subjects a complex, almost contradictory, appearance. In earlier years the king's will had on the whole expressed consistent, explicable attitudes and policies towards individuals. Now it was operating under severe strain and in ignorance of where men stood or where they might soon come to stand. Hence, while he bullied and laid insupportable financial burdens on some, he wooed and conciliated others; his attitude even towards a single individual might suddenly pass from hostility and suspicion, with all their attendant financial burdens and guarantees of good behaviour, to apparent trust and generosity, with all their consequent possibilities of financial and political profit. John moved rapidly from a taking to a giving mood; his changes of front are frequently bewildering; in some cases his motives can now only be guessed.

Some of the heaviest financial demands which the king ever made on individual subjects come from the months immediately preceding or during the expedition to Poitou when the king's financial needs were at their most demanding. Within the space of a year William fitz Alan offered 10,000 m. for the succession to the fitz Alan barony, Thomas of Erdington 5000 m. for the custody of these same lands and for the marriage of one of the sons, John de Lacy 7000 m. for the succession to the honour of Pontefract and other estates of his father, Warin de Montchensy 2000 m. for the inheritance of his family estates and for quittance of debts owed to Jews, Margaret, widow of Robert fitz Roger of

Clavering, £1000 for the lands of her husband and her dower and that she should not be compelled to marry, Richard de Rivers £500 for the marriage of Matilda de Lucy, lady of Ongar, Thomas of Moulton 1000 m. for the custody of the Lucy heiresses of Egremont, Peter de Maulay 7000 m. for the hand of Isabella of Thornham, and Geoffrey de Mandeville the inordinate sum of 20,000 m. for the hand of Isabella of Gloucester, the erstwhile queen.

These sums reflect an increase rather than a diminution in John's financial appetite. So also do the methods now regularly adopted by the king and his Exchequer to ensure ready payment. John de Lacy was required to pay off his debt of 7000 m. at regular intervals over three years, Peter de Maulay his debt of 7000 m. at 2000 m. in 1214 and 1000 m. per annum thereafter, Richard de Rivers his debt of £500 in five instalments within the year, Geoffrey de Mandeville his debt of 20,000 m. in four instalments in nine months. Both these last made their offers in January 1214 and had to pay their first instalments before the king sailed to Poitou in February. Neither of them could meet this commitment; as a result in February Geoffrey was deprived of the estates of his newly wedded wife.[1] The king was ready to use extreme measures to ensure that such terms were kept. He insisted that debtors followed the well-tried method of providing guarantors by demanding hostages until they found them,[2] or by placing them in open custody while they sought them, or by threatening them with imprisonment if they failed to find them.[3] Debtors and their guarantors were required to provide charters which recorded the terms of payment[4] and they were driven to

---

[1] Richard paid half his first instalment. For further discussion see Dr Patricia M. Barnes in *Pipe Roll 16 John*, pp. xxiii–xxiv.
[2] See the cases of Mabel de Clere and Hugh and Basilia de Hodeng' (*Rot. de Ob. et Fin.* pp. 478, 507).
[3] See the case of Ralph of Greasley (*ibid.* p. 539).
[4] See the cases of Roger Bigod (*ibid.* p. 465), William Malet (*ibid.* p. 468), William of Bodiham (*ibid.* p. 472), Stephen Langton, on behalf of Morgan, provost of Beverley (*ibid.* p. 475), Simon of Kyme and Thomas of Moulton (*ibid.* pp. 482–3).

accept the most severe penalties for non-payment. Peter de Maulay put all his lands in pledge to guarantee the terms of payment of his debt of 7000 m., agreeing that if he defaulted he should lose all the first annual repayments he might have made.[5] Thomas of Langley, who offered 100 m. and a palfrey to have the custody of Wychwood, pledged the safe custody of this forest and the payment of the debt in all his lands and chattels.[6] Geoffrey de Mandeville submitted a charter stating that he would be liable in all his lands and tenements if he failed to keep the terms of payment of his debt of 20,000 m.[7] Warin de Montchensy guaranteed his good behaviour and the repayment of his debt of 2000 m. by oath, by charter and by pledging all his land.[8] These were threatening phrases. Dispossession was becoming a regular instrument of policy; it was the antithesis of all legal and orderly government and by using it, either as threat or actuality, the king was bringing civil war all the nearer.

John's increasing readiness to reveal the reality of force which lay behind the legal facade of government was matched by an open admission that this financial oppression was geared directly to his war plans on the continent. Hitherto this connexion had often been implied rather than openly stated. Now John emphasized the close interrelation of war and finance by pardoning debts or postponing repayment in return for a fixed amount of military service over and above the normal feudal commitments of his vassals. Robert of Berkeley, for example, agreed in June 1213 to provide the king with ten knights for a year at his own expense in return for a quittance of 500 m. of a debt which he owed to the king; at the end of the year he was to

---

[5] *Pipe Roll 16 John*, p. 94. The Pipe roll contains a list of potent pledges including Ranulf earl of Chester and William de Ferrers, earl of Derby. An unprinted fragment of the Fine roll indicates that Peter des Roches played a special part – '[super] omnibus aliis plegiis suis constituit se dominus Wint. Episcopus superiorem plegium'. P.R.O., c 60/5d, m.3.
[6] *Rot. de Ob. et Fin.* p. 485.   [7] *Ibid.* pp. 520–1.   [8] *Ibid.* p. 514.

repay the residue according to such terms as he could obtain.[9] Debtors sometimes agreed to provide as many as twenty knights in return for a pardon of part or all they owed, or for a temporary relaxation during the period of service, after which they might seek new terms. Nearly thirty such arrangements were made between June and November 1213, enough to have provided the king with a force of over 150 knights and twenty sergeants serving for a year, a considerable nucleus for a field army and a convenient source of reinforcements for castle duties. On 1 November, when the projected expedition to Poitou had been abandoned for the year, the arrangements made so far were put in abeyance,[10] and in December the king decided to soften the immediate effect of his demands by spreading the total service over two years instead of one in the expectation that the reduced number of knights would be better equipped and in order to give the debtors some relief.[11] They had to meet these reduced commitments when the expedition finally sailed in February, and all this was additional to their customary feudal service. Hence in 1214 many both served or sent their service and also paid scutage. They had to meet two obligations, not just one, and this may well have contributed to the rapidly increasing resistance to the scutage when the account was held in the autumn.

The need for money was not John's only motive. From the summer of 1212 he was sharply sensitive to signs of treachery and possible rebellion, and vengefully suspicious even of hitherto trusted agents and supporters. After the plot against his life he took steps to ensure loyalty in the future by exacting from suspects charters of fealty in which they pledged all their lands as proof of their loyalty, or more material guarantees in the form of castles: Fotheringhay from Earl David of Huntingdon, Barnard Castle from Hugh de Balliol, and Pontefract and Castle Donington from John de Lacy. Others surrendered hostages. In extreme cases all these methods were used simultaneously. Just after the plot against his life John informed the sheriffs of Northumberland that Richard de Umfraville had submitted a charter dealing with the surrender of his four sons and his castle of Prudhoe as hostages for his faithful service, 'so that if we can attaint him of being at the colloquy in which treachery was planned against us or was a party to such treachery, then his sons and his castle and all his lands shall come into our hands, and we shall deal with his person as we would a traitor'.[12] These disciplinary processes had much in common with the king's financial exploitation of his feudal rights. They shared the same methods in the exaction of guarantees in the form of charters, sureties or hostages. They shared the same objectives and penalties. Political misbehaviour, actual or threatened, frequently led to the imposition of a heavy amercement or fine for the king's good will. Conversely, heavy financial burdens forced a man into political subjection in which he bought remission with subservience. Imprisonment might be the fate equally of the debtor or the political suspect. Conversely, the prisoner rarely gained release without buying it. Hence it is impossible to distinguish the political from the financial elements in many of the agreements between the king and his subjects. Hugh de la Huse, for example, offered the king 500 m. that he should be freed from prison; he was to pay 100 m. before his release and find guarantees for the payment of the remainder and for his faithful service in the future.[13] Robert of Castle Carrock offered 200 m. for his freedom and the recovery of his lands of which he had been disseised by the king's order; this was to cover 70 m. still outstanding of a fine he had made for jurisdictional privileges.[14] Walter de Turberville

---

[12] *Rot. Litt. Claus.* I, 122*b*. For the discussion of other instances see Holt (1961), p. 83 and n.
[13] *Rot. de Ob. et Fin.* pp. 470–1.   [14] *Ibid.* pp. 481, 506–7.

offered the services of himself and two other knights in order to be quit of 150 m. he owed of a certain fine; if he did not serve the king faithfully 'all his land was to come into the King's hands and on this he gave the King his charter'.[15] When John de Lacy offered 7000 m. for the lands of his father, he took an oath and made out a charter confirming the terms of repayment and conceding that if he ever left the king's service and joined his enemies then all his lands should come into the king's hands; twenty of his tenants guaranteed de Lacy's terms of payment and his faithful service by their charters and agreed that they would side with the king if their lord turned against him.[16] These agreements were at once the product of the king's financial urgency, of his suspicions of treachery and of the increasingly disturbed state of the realm.

Such arrangements helped to create an uncertain and uneasy atmosphere which was darkened further by the capricious and erratic manner in which the king dealt with their enforcement. His stringent insistence on early and frequent terms of payment was matched by his willingness to forgo them, or perhaps even pardon debts completely, in return for political subservience. This underlay the arrangements whereby payment was replaced by military service in Poitou. It frequently affected the payments due from the king's own agents and officials. The chief forester Hugh de Neville, who in 1212 offered 6000 m. for the king's good will and for various other reasons, was pardoned 1000 m. in the same year and acquitted a further 1000 m. in 1213 in return for the service of twenty knights for a year.[17] Peter de Maulay, who was to give the king devoted service as castellan of Corfe during the civil war, was excused payment of his outstanding debts in April 1215 until further notice.[18]

---

[15] Ibid. p. 484.   [16] Ibid. pp. 494–5.
[17] Pipe Roll 14 John, pp. 157–8; Rot. de Ob. et Fin. p. 469.
[18] Rot. Litt. Claus., I, 197b.

In John de Lacy's case the king openly stated the principle of *quid pro quo* and applied it blatantly. As part of the initial agreement he agreed to pardon the last 1000 m. of the proffer, due in the fourth year of repayment, in return for the faithful service which he had had from de Lacy's father and hoped to have from de Lacy himself. Here events overtook him. John de Lacy went to Poitou in 1214 and made his service pay. In June he was given respite in the terms of payment. In July Castle Donington, which had remained in the king's hands as a guarantee, was restored to him. He was one of the very few English barons to take the Cross with the king on 4 March 1215. On 5 March he received a pardon on all his debts, including £2800 still outstanding from the arrangement of 1213.[19]

The three years which immediately preceded Magna Carta laid bare the weakness of the subject's defences against the feudal prerogative of the Crown. More than ever before King John was exploiting his customary rights as financial and political weapons. In one aspect he was doing nothing more than grant privileges, exercise justice, take reliefs for the succession to estates, arrange marriages; doing all those things which were attributes of feudal lordship. Yet, in another, he was financing war, enforcing obedience by the brazen exercise of power, disciplining his subjects by the threat or fact of imprisonment, by the exaction of hostages, the surrender of castles and the pledging of land, by financial pressure which subjected a man to burdens near or beyond his powers of repayment and threatened his estate and patrimony. These were simply two aspects of the same actions. One of the prime objectives of the Great Charter was to prevent such confusion of the routine exercise of justice and other rights of lordship with important matters of policy, whether these were derived from

[19] *Ibid.* I, 167, 169; *Gerv. Cant.* II, 109; *Rot. Litt. Pat.* p. 129b; *Pipe Roll 16 John,* p. 93.

long-term developments or from the transitory whim of the king.

However, the Charter was not a simple reaction against varied agreements and arrangements which the king was forcing on his men with increasing violence, suspicion and stringency. The fine for privileges embodies not only the power of the Crown but also the aspirations of the subject. The Charter was nothing but a vast communal privilege for which the king's subjects paid, not now by the offer of vast sums or the surrender or subjection of their lives and property, but by the restoration of their allegiance on agreed terms. The collapse of royal power which underlay this change was not unprepared. It was foreshadowed every time the king relaxed a financial demand in the hope of securing a subject's obedience, every time he tried to win allegiance and support by alienating the rights of the Crown, every time he acknowledged the legal and social aspirations of the men he ruled. He was whetting their appetites, accustoming them to what they wanted, creating a demand which could be kept under control only as long as royal power went unchallenged. Under pressure the exercise of feudal lordship and patronage became a dangerous game.

Hence there was a subtle and complex relationship between the Charter and John's treatment of his subjects in the last few years before the crisis. Some of the arrangements of these, as of earlier years, formed direct antecedents to particular sections of the Charter. For example, they yielded a fine crop of proffers by widows or their relatives designed to ensure that they enjoyed their rightful property and avoided a new marriage into which the king was ever ready to drive them. In 1214, Cecilia, widow of Lawrence Chamberlain, offered 40 m. 'in order to have her land which belonged to her by inheritance and for having her reasonable dower of the land which had belonged to her husband and for permission to marry whom she wished'. She was also to have a reasonable part of the chattels of her dead husband.[20] Similar arrangements were now popular with ladies great and small, from the thrice married countess of Aumale who in 1212 offered 5000 m. for her inheritance, dower and freedom to avoid or accept marriage as she wished,[21] down to Aline, widow of William son of Walkelin, who offered 30 m. and one palfrey in 1214 for her dower, for the chattels belonging to her on William's tenement and that she should not be compelled to marry.[22] These proffers, and similar ones concerned with the marriage of heirs and heiresses, embodied aspirations which the Crown had acknowledged as far back as the Charter of Liberties of Henry I.[23] But financial urgency was now compelling King John to accept them frequently. They are sometimes recorded in the Fine roll in words which approach common form.[24] And although the king often laid down that those who bought the right to marry should still seek his consent, or at least not contract a marriage with his enemies, there are signs that he was having difficulty in enforcing this restriction, even though it was one accepted in differing ways in the Charter of Henry I and later in the Great Charter itself. While he was away in Poitou in 1214 John learned that one of his Nottinghamshire tenants, Philip of Strelley, had married the widow of Walter of Strelley who was within his gift, without his assent, and he now ordered Peter des Roches to 'take such amends from Philip that he should stand as an example whereby others would dread to attempt such things against the lord king'.[25]

All these arrangements anticipated one or more of the

---

[20] *Rot. de Ob. et Fin.* p. 545.   [21] *Rot. Chartarum*, p. 189.
[22] *Pipe Roll 16 John*, p. 160.   [23] See above, pp. 36–7.
[24] Compare the proffers of Maurice de Gant on behalf of his sister, Eve, and of Isolde, widow of Walter de Baskerville, both of which contain the phrase 'non distringatur ad se maritandam sed si se maritare voluerit hoc de assensu domini Regis (fiat) faciat' (*Rot. de Ob. et Fin.* pp. 488, 500). Closely similar phrases are very common both in these and in earlier years.
[25] *Ibid.* p. 524.

provisions included in caps. 7, 8 and 26 of Magna Carta. Perhaps to contemporaries, even to the king himself, they represented no real alienation of, or threat to, royal power. The impression conveyed by the record evidence that John was now selling more readily, may have appeared to contemporaries simply as the result of financial urgency, on the one hand, accidentally combined with a temporary and fortuitously large number of bereavements, on the other.[26] Yet to let widows have their way was to encourage the acceptance of the principle that they should have their way. Moreover this particular type of concession was not isolated. To admit the justice of the claims of widows, even in return for payment, was to encourage the demand that justice should be done in other spheres. To such demands King John found it more and more politic to accede. He became ready to satisfy local interests, to acknowledge long re-membered claims to privilege and estate, to permit and even insist that title should be settled by lawful process in his court.

This frequently emphasized concern for right and justice is well illustrated by a proffer made in 1214 by Margaret de Chesney, widow of Robert fitz Roger of Clavering and Warkworth. She offered the king £1000 for the inheritance of her husband on condition that she should answer in court to any claim against it. The king laid down that he was to hold Norwich castle, which had been in Robert's custody, for as long as he pleased, but he also agreed that Margaret was to have such right as she could establish in his court to the inheritance of William de Chesney, her father, and to those parts of her inheritance which her husbands, Robert fitz Roger and Hugh de Cressy, had alienated. She was not to be distrained to marry, nor was she to be summoned for her father's debts to the Jews, and she was to have her dower

---

[26] It was nevertheless viewed as a reforming concession by at least one contemporary. See the comments of the Barnwell chronicler quoted below, p. 214.

according to the custom of England even if her son, John fitz Robert, was unwilling to give it to her.[27] This remarkable proffer demonstrates that the king was still very far from total surrender; he was asking for £1000 and retaining Norwich castle; but he was recognizing many points in the matter of inheritance, dower and marriage which were later to be established as principles in the Great Charter. More significantly still, he was insisting throughout on legal process in his court both for Margaret and her son and for anyone who might bring a claim against her. Sometimes this insistence on legal process clearly benefited the king. Amidst his barren initial triumphs in Poitou in May 1214 he still found time to consider the affairs of the family of Strelley, undertenants of the honour of Peverel of Nottingham. Another local landowner, Philip of Stanton, had informed the king that the recently dead Justiciar, Geoffrey fitz Peter, had fined for the custody of the land and heir of Walter of Strelley. Philip alleged that Geoffrey had not paid the fine, that he had given the custody to him and that, on his death, his son, Geoffrey de Mandeville, had disseised him. John now instructed Peter des Roches to seek out the truth of the matter; if Philip's case was correct, then he was to have seisin, 'since Geoffrey de Mandeville would then have no right in the matter save by force'; the heirs, however, were not to be disparaged.[28] Here the king was using legal process to curb the pretensions of a great magnate whose allegiance was suspect. It was in these same letters, too, that the king ordered the punishment of Philip of Strelley who had married Walter's widow without permission.[29] But he was concerned to see that Philip of Stanton's claim was settled properly and with care, for Peter des Roches was instructed to search the rolls of the Exchequer. Moreover, the instruction that there should be no disparagement of the heirs seems to have been added quite spontaneously by the king. This

---

[27] Pipe Roll 16 John, p. 175. Rot. Chartarum, p. 203.
[28] Rot. de Ob. et Fin. pp. 523–4, 533.   [29] See above, p. 198.

attention to detail is noteworthy. Yet this was a case where Geoffrey de Mandeville apparently alleged unlawful disseisin by the Crown under cap. 52 of the Charter. He recovered the custody at Runnymede in 1215 and granted it to Philip of Strelley.[30]

In other cases John was clearly concerned that the admission of a claimant's case should not infringe the rights of others. When Asceline de Waterville offered four palfreys that she should not be disseised without judgement of her land in Elsworth, Cambridgeshire, the king laid down that she was to stand to right if any claim to it was made against her.[31] Sometimes, in permitting such claims, he was ready to admit that there had been an unjust disseisin which now had to be reversed. Richard Gubiun and Roger the Forester were allowed to offer 500 m. and a palfrey for the lands of which they had been disseised without judgement on condition that they should stand to right against any claims against them.[32] Sometimes the king admitted that the unlawful disseisin had been his own work. In July 1213 Robert of Castle Carrock offered 200 m. for delivery from gaol and for the land of which he had been disseised by royal order. Robert was even to have a reasonable aid from his tenants to help him to pay the fine.[33] In December 1213 Isolde Biset, a widow, was also able to make good her claim that the king had disseised her of her vill of 'Maggurman', and the Justiciar of Ireland was ordered to see that she had such seisin of the vill as her husband, Henry Biset, had held at his death. She was able to bring influential pressure to bear to support her case, for her offer of 100 m. and a palfrey was guaranteed by Geoffrey de Longchamps, Walter of Dun-

---

[30] Rot. Litt. Claus. 1, 216b; Book of Fees, p. 287.
[31] Rot. de Ob. et Fin. p. 516, a fine of January 1214. Compare a similar entry for Geoffrey de Conyers, July 1213 (ibid. p. 476). See also above, pp. 161–3.
[32] Ibid. p. 513, a fine of December 1213.
[33] Ibid. p. 481. No reason is known for Robert's imprisonment, but compare a reference to an offer for his 'justiciary' (ibid. pp. 506–7). For a similar disseisin by the king see the case of Roger de la Mare (ibid. p. 544).

stanville, Fulk fitz Warin, and Ranulf, earl of Chester.[34] Her father-in-law had been steward of the household under Henry II and her daughters married into families of substance.[35] The king's departure to Poitou early in the new year prevented her from obtaining immediate seisin despite her payment of part of the offer, but the king continued to favour her. In March 1215 he instructed the sheriff of Nottinghamshire that she was not to be distrained for the debts of yet another dead husband, Walter de Baskerville, and in August he sent new letters to the Justiciar of Ireland ordering the restoration of the vill of Maggurman; further restorations in Fingal arising from the fine of 1213 were ordered in February 1217.[36] Isolde obtained justice, but slowly; her claims, like many others, were only settled after the surrender by the king at Runnymede and the civil war which followed.

It was sometimes easier to admit such royal disseisins than to correct the consequences, however genuine was the king's interest in repairing past acts of injustice. In June 1213, for example, he ordered the Justiciar to inquire whether Geoffrey de Lucy had been disseised of the manor of Newington 'by our will or by the judgement of our court'; if the former, then the land was to be restored, since Geoffrey was ready to answer any claims brought against him.[37] Geoffrey was the brother, presumably illegitimate, of the Lucy co-heiress, Roese of Dover. In 1223 a jury recorded that she had granted to him the manor of Newington,[38] and his possession had certainly been confirmed by her uncle, Godfrey de Lucy, bishop of Winchester, and by the king, on Godfrey's death, in 1204.[39] Geoffrey was a royal agent active in the administration of the Channel Isles, the fleet and the ports of Sussex. However, he suffered the king's anger for some reason and was deprived for a time of Newington and other

---

[34] *Ibid.* pp. 511–12.   [35] Rivers, Neville and Plessey.
[36] *Rot. Litt. Claus.* I, 191b, 224b, 298b.   [37] *Rot. Litt. Claus.* I, 136b.
[38] *Curia Regis Rolls,* XI, no. 416.   [39] *Rot. Chartarum,* p. 137.

estates, and during this interval, in November 1212, Roese recovered control of the manor, along with the rest of her inheritance from Richard de Lucy, which she then enfeoffed to William Briwerre.[40] The writ of June 1213, therefore, marks an attempt by Geoffrey to recover this estate from another and more powerful royal official. A year later another potent interest intruded when Roese's granddaughter, also called Roese, was married to Richard fitz Roy, one of the king's illegitimate sons. By the end of 1215 all three men were laying claim to Newington.[41] By this time Geoffrey had joined the rebellion, and although he recovered the estate after the end of the war, his title was still being challenged by legal action from the other two in 1223.[42] In this case, therefore, the writ of June 1213 marked little more than the interjection of fair words from the king into a battle between confused claims which were not easily reconciled.

Yet John was not a political simpleton, who imagined that all might be saved by a façade of verbal concession designed to camouflage inaction. Between 1213 and the outbreak of war he did much to provide himself with a following by acknowledging the lawful claims and reasonable expectations of those among the magnates whose support he wanted and might reasonably expect to enjoy. This cost more than words. In the Welsh Marches, for example, the king decided to re-admit to his favour two powerful lords, William Marshal and Walter de Lacy, both of whom had been too close to William de Briouze's insubordination in 1209–10, and who might well revive the Briouze cause in the Marches if left to themselves. Walter de Lacy was restored to his English possessions except Ludlow in July 1213; he recovered Ludlow town in October and the castle

[40] *Curia Regis Rolls*, XI, no. 416; Painter (1949), pp. 75–6; *Rot. Chartarum*, pp. 189–189b; *Rot. Litt. Claus.* I, 127–127b.
[41] *Rot. Litt. Claus.* I, 230, 239b, 242b, 268b.   [42] *Curia Regis Rolls*, XI, no. 416.

in April 1215.[43] William Marshal was permitted to offer
£1000 for the custody of Haverford castle in October 1213;
in the following January he was given custody of Cardigan,
Carmarthen and Gower and pardoned part of the Haverford proffer to cover his expenses.[44] In the civil war the
Marches scarcely faltered in their loyalty to the king. There
were other calculated concessions of this kind. In May 1214
the honour of Tickhill was granted to Ralph de Lusignan,
husband of the claimant, Alice, countess of Eu,[45] and in the
following October, after negotiations which had begun a
year earlier, William de Fors, titular count of Aumale, was
established in his English inheritance, which included the
honours of Cockermouth, Skipton and Holderness.[46] Some
concessions resulted not from royal calculation, but from
compulsion. The settlement which the king negotiated
with the Church in the winter of 1212–13 involved him
in the restoration of the two condemned conspirators
of the previous summer, Robert fitz Walter and Eustace
de Vescy. Letters for their re-instatement were ordered in
July.[47]

Such recognitions of right, title or expectancy could
scarcely be made without danger to the king. Within a
period of eighteen months, he had made enough concessions
to whet men's appetite. It must have become less and less
easy to argue or assume that such concessions should be
directed and limited by the personal and political convenience of the king. The claims of the counts of Eu to hold
Tickhill had been acknowledged hitherto only by King
Stephen.[48] If this claim was now to be recognized why not
other claims to tenure by grant of Stephen? What was there
to restrain William de Mowbray, for example, who was to
use the crisis of 1215 as an occasion for claiming the castle of

43 Rot. Litt. Claus. I, 147, 173b, 175; Rot. Litt. Pat. p. 132b.
44 Rot. Litt. Pat. pp. 105, 109b; Rot. de Ob. et Fin. pp. 499, 522.
45 Rot. Litt. Pat. p. 116.   46 Ibid. p. 112b; Rot. Chartarum, p. 201b.
47 Rot. Litt. Pat. p. 101.   48 Rot. Curiae Regis, II, 162.

York and the forest of Yorkshire, which his ancestor had held in the Anarchy?[49] Again why should the recognition of such claims depend on personal favour? William de Fors, for example, had a thoroughly reasonable claim in law to the estates which John granted to him; it depended on direct inheritance from his mother. Yet he only achieved recognition after one of the major tenants of the honour of Holderness, Robert de Ros, had urged the king repeatedly that William should be allowed to come to England to seek his rights. The king's attitude was clear enough; William was to come 'to do our grace and will';[50] by the time he acquired his land he had proved himself in the service of the king during the campaign in Poitou in 1214, and he finally received his estates on condition that he married Evelina, daughter of Richard de Munfichet.[51] More ominous still was the restoration of Eustace de Vescy and Robert fitz Walter. If they could obtain restoration after notorious treason and public condemnation as traitors in the shire courts, what might others achieve after a more general and better organized rebellion? Up to a point John was draining off the sources of opposition by these concessions. Thereafter he was opening the floodgates of rebellion. The culmination of these measures came at Runnymede in the many acts of restoration which were exacted from the king once the Charter had been sealed. William de Fors, at least, saw these implications. In June 1215 he was one of the Twenty-Five barons responsible for the enforcement of the Charter upon the king. By 11 August he had become a partisan of the king once more, and on 31 August the sheriff of Yorkshire was instructed that William should have his right in the manor of Driffield, which had once belonged to his grandfather, but had not apparently been included in the

---

49 See below, pp. 247, 431–2.   50 *Rot. Litt. Pat.* p. 104b.
51 *Rot. Chartarum*, p. 201b.

restoration of 1214.[52] What could not be gained by favour could be gained by rebellion or the threat of it.

Sometimes the increasingly urgent need for political security and the equally desirable requirement that right should seem to be done, or at least attempted, failed to blend, and the king's efforts simply added to the sense of injury or aggravated the competing claims of his subjects. Two cases in particular, concerning the families of Bohun and Mandeville, came to be involved in the settlement at Runnymede in 1215 and probably contributed to the outbreak of rebellion. They both originated on 29 April 1212 when the king accepted the nomination of attorneys from William Longespee, earl of Salisbury, and Geoffrey de Say, the former in a claim to the honour of Trowbridge, held by Henry de Bohun, and the latter in a claim to the whole of the Mandeville barony, held by the Justiciar, Geoffrey fitz Peter.[53] Both plaintiffs had an arguable legal case, but neither was clear-cut.[54] That between Longespee and Bohun dragged on interminably. It was complicated from the start by being linked to an investigation into the service due from the honour which was begun concurrently by the king. In June 1213 Henry de Bohun tried to plead sickness as an excuse for absence from the hearing, and since such an excuse was inadmissible in a plea of service, the honour of Trowbridge was taken into the king's hands.[55] The king retained it until 1215, and during the intervening period William of Salisbury gradually intruded into the

---

[52] *Rot. Litt. Pat.* pp. 152, 154.   [53] *Curia Regis Rolls*, VI, 270.

[54] Trowbridge had been granted by Edward of Salisbury, the great-great-grandfather of William's wife, to the Bohuns in frankmarriage. William therefore had a claim to homage due on such grants after three generations, but not to possession. Geoffrey de Say was the cousin of William de Mandeville, who died in 1189. Geoffrey fitz Peter had married the daughter of Geoffrey's elder brother, William de Say. Geoffrey de Say had seisin of the Mandeville fee for a time at the beginning of the reign of Richard I but lost it to Geoffrey fitz Peter on failing to pay the fine he had offered for it (see Painter, 1949, pp. 40, 262–3; *Complete Peerage*, XI, 465–6). The Says now alleged that they had been disseised by the will of King Richard (*Rot. Litt. Claus.* I, 168b). See Holt (1991b).

[55] *Curia Regis Rolls*, VI, 320.

estate.[56] By April 1215 William seems to have got control, and when the king visited Trowbridge on 12 May he confirmed this by granting to William the lands of all those tenants of the honour who had joined Henry de Bohun, who was now in rebellion.[57] By this time the possession of the honour had become an issue of war. Henry de Bohun laid claim to it at Runnymede, and letters ordering its restoration to him were among the first to be issued in execution of the Charter.[58]

The king's readiness to take sides against Henry de Bohun is readily explicable. The plea of service which accompanied William of Salisbury's opening claim was provoked by Henry's refusal to pay scutage on the 'new enfeoffment' of the honour.[59] There is no such obvious explanation for the action between Geoffrey de Say and Geoffrey fitz Peter. Within a decade or so a number of stories of personal jealousy between John and his Justiciar or members of his family were circulating in baronial households and monastic *scriptoria*, but there is no contemporary confirmation of any of them in the records or indeed any certain indication of a quarrel between the king and Geoffrey fitz Peter or his sons at this stage.[60] However, Geoffrey's dispute with the Says was a mirror-image of the king's dispute with Arthur of Brittany and this must have contributed to increasingly uneasy relations.[61] Geoffrey fitz Peter died at the end of October 1213, but the case was renewed against his son, Geoffrey de Mandeville, in the Hilary term of 1214.[62]

---

[56] *Pipe Roll 17 John*, p. 83.   [57] *Rot. Litt. Claus.* I, 194b, 200.
[58] *Rot. Litt. Claus.* I, 215. For the text see appendix 11, below, p. 495. For further discussion see below, p. 360. The history of the dispute during the civil war is obscure, although it is to be presumed that William of Salisbury intruded once more. Dr Sanders states that there was a compromise between William and Henry later in 1215 (*English Baronies*, Oxford 1960, p. 91). Henry died in 1220. His widow released her claim to dower in Trowbridge to William Longespee in 1222, and his son Humphrey sold further portions of the honour to him in 1229 (*V.C.H. Wiltshire*, VII, 128; cp. V, 47). In 1242–3 the honour was divided between the two families (*Book of Fees*, pp. 720–3, 737, 741–2). See also above pp. 170–1.
[59] *Pipe Roll 14 John*, pp. xxvi, 150   [60] See Painter (1949), pp. 259–62.
[61] See Holt (1991b).   [62] *Curia Regis Rolls* VII, 110–11.

Although it was then dismissed and although Geoffrey de Say himself died in May 1214 the action was revived by his son who accompanied the king to Poitou in 1214 and there offered him the enormous sum of 15,000 m. for seisin of the lands of William de Mandeville, of which he alleged his father had been disseised by the will of King Richard. At this stage John simply instructed the new Justiciar, Peter des Roches, to take advice and do what seemed best to him.[63] This was not a very constructive suggestion from a king in a matter of such importance, and, indeed, by this time John's attitude towards the Mandevilles alternated inconsequentially between suspicion and cajolery. In November 1213 he instated Geoffrey de Mandeville in the lands and wardships held by his father, Geoffrey fitz Peter.[64] The arrangement made no reference to fitz Peter's custodies and indeed his most important, the Tower of London, was transferred to a royal familiar, William, archdeacon of Huntingdon, on 3 November.[65] Nor was de Mandeville recognized as earl of Essex. At Runnymede in 1215 Geoffrey claimed custody of the Tower. The claim remained in dispute during the summer months and contributed to the renewal of war in the autumn.[66]

Geoffrey's claim to the Tower was somewhat tenuous; it can only have been based on the fact that his father had held it in custody or on the old Mandeville claim to hold it in inheritance which had been pressed under King Stephen. It was not the family's sole ground for complaint. After Geoffrey fitz Peter's death John withheld the manor of Aylesbury and the honour of Berkhamsted, which had been granted to Geoffrey and his heirs at fee farm in 1204 and 1205 respectively.[67] It was not until the restorations after Runnymede that these estates were restored to fitz Peter's younger son, William de Mandeville.[68] Finally, the mar-

[63] Rot. Litt. Claus. I, 168b, and above pp. 147–8.   [64] Rot. de Ob. et Fin. pp. 502–3.
[65] Rot. Litt. Pat. p. 105b.   [66] See below, pp. 361, 366.
[67] Rot. Chartarum, pp. 127–8, 151b.   [68] Rot. Litt. Claus. I, 217.

riage between Geoffrey de Mandeville and the king's ex-
wife, Isabella of Gloucester, in January 1214 had produced
endless complications. Geoffrey had made the enormous
offer of 20,000 m. for her. He had failed to keep the terms of
payments and had lost control of her estates for a time in
1214. In May 1215 the king's final offer of compromise
included the offer to submit the debt which Geoffrey owed
for his wife to the judgement of his court.[69] At Runnymede
Geoffrey was still trying to establish what he considered was
his rightful control of the honour of Gloucester. Hugh de
Neville was instructed to perambulate the chaces of the
honour in Keynsham, Cranbourne and Chetred; the sheriffs
of Somerset and Gloucester were instructed to see that he
was allowed the advowson of the abbeys and religious
houses which Earl William of Gloucester had founded, and
they and three other sheriffs were ordered to see that
Geoffrey had all the liberties which pertained to the honour
as Earl William had held them.[70] In the case of the
Mandeville family John's instinct for manipulating men by a
combination of bribery and coercion ended by contributing
directly to the crisis of 1215. Each step taken to win over
Geoffrey was accompanied by reservations which were
bound to cause a grievance. So evenly were the bribes and
the attendant penalties and reservations combined that it is
quite impossible to say which was uppermost in the king's
mind. Nobody gained from what the king had done. The
Say claim was abandoned at some stage, and Geoffrey de
Say, like Geoffrey de Mandeville, became a rebel. The
Mandevilles gained least of all. Geoffrey was killed in a
tournament at London in 1216 and the Gloucester inheritance passed to the Clares. When both Geoffrey and
William were dead their sister found that they had had debts
outstanding to Stephen Langton, archbishop of Canterbury,

---

[69] For a general review of the Mandeville case, see Painter (1949), pp. 282–4, 306–7, etc.,
and *Complete Peerage*, v, 126–30. For the letters of 10 May, see *Rot. Litt. Pat.* p. 141.
[70] *Rot. Litt. Claus.* I, 216, 216b.

amounting to 7000 m. This originated in 1214 in the transfer of part of Geoffrey de Mandeville's proffer for the marriage of Isabella of Gloucester to the church of Canterbury in part settlement of the losses suffered during the Interdict. Matilda de Mandeville now leased Debden and Saffron Walden to Archbishop Edmund in settlement.[71]

John's arrangements with the Mandevilles illustrate the easy manner in which the manipulation of justice and the imposition of financial agreements which were at once seductive and punitive passed into civil war. In many ways the arrangements of these later years were little different from those of the middle years of the reign or the period immediately following the accession when John was clearly in a selling mood. In these earlier periods, too, John's use of his powers had sometimes provoked rebellion. But this made the onrush into civil war all the easier, for previous rebellion had been notably unsuccessful. The fate of William de Briouze stood as an example to Geoffrey de Mandeville and neither the king nor Geoffrey knew at what point this would cease to stand as a warning and become an offence to be avenged. Similarly, neither they nor anyone else knew at what point privilege won by payment or subjection to the king would become a right to be asserted by force of arms against him. No one could predict where men who had been parties to such transactions would turn once the onset of war gave them some choice of allegiance in which they could give their support to the king in return for further gains, or rebel in order to gain release from earlier burdens or to win rights hitherto denied. John may have shown great skill in using the weapons of financial and political blackmail which his feudal prerogative could be made to allow him, but they were weapons which were uncontrollable. Their effects were unknown quantities depending ultimately on the political sense and judgement, even on the whims and

---

[71] *Cal. Charter Rolls*, I, 196; *Pipe Roll 9 Henry III*, rot. 8 m 2r.

prejudices, of his victims. That these were problems on the king's mind seems clear from the cat-and-mouse tactics he adopted in dealing with men like Geoffrey de Mandeville or John de Lacy. They are also reflected in John's increasing readiness to reinforce his varied methods of securing individual allegiance by more general concessions, actual or promised. From 1212 onwards he was obviously trying to convey an impression of reform, to create an atmosphere of concession which might blur the outlines of the harsh administration of earlier years.

This involved the reversal of government policies. It is most striking in the case of *debita Judeorum*, debts owed to Jews which had reverted to the Crown on the death of the creditors. Since 1210 especially these had become a major source of income to the king and one of the main instruments of financial persecution of the aristocracy. On 18 August 1212, two days after he had heard of the plot against his life, John announced that he proposed to relax such debts, and non-baronial debtors were summoned through the sheriffs to come to the king to make new arrangements.[72] Concessions were also made to some baronial debtors in the months which followed.[73] Other changes were less clear-cut. In 1212 a new forest eyre had been started by three groups of justices.[74] Such investigations were normally concerned among other things with the behaviour of the forest officials. However, this occasion was unusual in that the eyre was followed by closer inquiries into the actions of some of these officials, at least in the northern counties where opposition to the king was already far advanced. On 25 September commissions were appointed to investigate the custody of the forests of Leicestershire and all counties north of Trent and to inspect the pasturing of the

[72] *Rot. Litt. Claus.* I, 132.
[73] See the concessions to James de Caux, Robert de Ros, Saer de Quincy and Robert de Ferrers (*Rot. de Ob. et Fin.* pp. 490, 496–7, 499, 512).
[74] *Pipe Roll 14 John*, pp. xxiii–xxiv.

211

king's demesne woods and the profits due from pannage.[75] Another instruction of May 1213 seems to have arranged for reports from county juries on the actions of the verderers in the northern forests.[76] In the Staffordshire forests several local foresters were imprisoned.[77] The king seems to have allowed the eyre to develop in a manner which permitted and even encouraged local complaints. In other instances much could be achieved simply by dropping projects half completed. On 1 June 1212 John ordered a close inquiry into feudal tenures, which, in the words of J. H. Round, 'might not unworthily be compared with the Domesday Inquest itself'.[78] And yet it led to very little. There is some indication that the information was used to make a few annotations on the Pipe roll of Michaelmas 1212,[79] but thereafter so little use was made of this major administrative effort that its purpose is still debatable.[80] John was not given the time or scope to reveal what his intentions had been. It all remained wasted effort.

In February 1213, after a progress through the chief disaffected area in northern England, the king proceeded to make greater and more openly avowed concessions. He had already replaced the chief forester, Hugh de Neville, as sheriff of Cumberland by the future rebel, Robert de Ros, and now, on 25 February, he replaced the sheriffs of Yorkshire and Lincolnshire by local knights.[81] He also sent general letters to the men of these two counties stating that he had been greatly moved by the number of the complaints he had heard about the extortions of the sheriffs and their officers and of other royal bailiffs. He now announced that he was sending a commission of four to take depositions on such exactions which had occurred since the Irish expedition of 1210 so that he might correct them. The commission was

---

[75] Rot. Litt. Claus. I, 125.   [76] Ibid. I, 129b.   [77] Rot. de Ob. et Fin. p. 543.
[78] Round (1899), p. 261. For the returns see Book of Fees I, passim.
[79] Pipe Roll 14 John, p. xxv.
[80] Painter (1949), pp. 209–11; Holt (1961), p. 81.   [81] Rot. Litt. Pat. pp. 96b, 97.

CRISIS AND CIVIL WAR

also to take evidence of other matters: of the extent to which his bailiffs had usurped the pleas of the Crown and increased the revenues of hundreds, wapentakes and tithings in these two counties; of property surrendered to Jewish creditors as pledges of debt – what was the property? Who held it? By what title? And for how long?; and of the Jews' own property in houses and demesnes – of whom was it held? How much of it was held at fee and how much at a year's term? What was its revenue and by how much did its real value exceed this?[82] Local juries in short were being used to investigate four broad areas of royal administration: the conduct of sheriffs, the exaction of increased revenues from local offices, the administration of pleas of the Crown, and the administration of the Jews. This writ stands midway between the articles of the general eyre in which such matters were examined by the royal justices with the interests of the king uppermost in their minds, and the inquiries instituted under the terms of the Great Charter which were designed to protect the local inhabitant from the depredations of the king's men. The investigation seems to have had some effect for it was about this time that the king pardoned all the new shire increments which were being exacted regularly from sheriffs as additions to the annual farms for their office.[83] Here the king anticipated one of the concessions of 1215, which was extended in the Great Charter to hundreds, wapentakes and ridings, as well as shires.[84]

Just as the king's treatment of individual barons provoked the demand for the restoration of rights at Runnymede, so

[82] *Ibid.* p. 97.
[83] The old increments, as opposed to the new, were those assessed before the accession of Richard I, except in the case of Cambridgeshire and Huntingdonshire, where the old increment was imposed in 1194. The exact point at which the increments were pardoned is difficult to establish because no Pipe roll for 15 John survives. I have followed B.E. Harris, 'King John and the Sheriffs' Farms', *E.H.R.* LXXIX (1964), 540–1. Compare Dr Barnes, *Pipe Roll 16 John*, pp, xxi–xxiii.
[84] Cap. 25.

213

did these general concessions lead on to the more general concessions of 1215. The king's use of local men as the new sheriffs in Yorkshire and Lincolnshire, the fact that the investigating commission in these counties was made up of local knights all of whom later joined the rebellion, the use of local juries to produce the evidence against the bailiffs, foresters or verderers, the conciliatory language of the promise to relax Jewish debts and the sympathy paraded for the local population under the burden of shrieval government, all demonstrate that these moves were largely, if not solely, made as promises, indications or acts of reform. They were maintained only so long as they brought advantage to the king. In 1214, when it had become clear these measures had failed to pacify the north, two of the sheriffs introduced in February 1213 were dismissed.

Nevertheless, the new tone in royal policy which the threat of open opposition had engendered was clear enough to be recorded with varying accuracy by several monastic writers ten years or so after the event. One was even moved to judicious praise:

Amid so many hazards he did something which should be remembered to his honour. For the foresters were levying novel and burdensome exactions on almost all England, and the king showed pity for those affected and completely remitted them. There were others who by reason that they were keepers of the ports were molesting burgesses and travellers and merchants, and these too he restrained and had their exactions remitted. He is also said to have acted with more kindness towards widows and to have shown considerable energy in maintaining the peace, at least in temporal matters... He began to destroy evil customs and to restrain the violence and greed of the sheriffs and their agents, who were a sore affliction on the people, since they held their shrievalties and lesser offices at an annual charge and sought only this, namely how to exact money from the people in their charge. And he removed such men from office and substituted others who would treat the people justly and take the advice of prudent men and would seek the peace and quiet of their charges rather than the emptying of their purses. And he began a searching enquiry into these matters so that he should know who had received such extortions while in office. But it was not carried through to a conclusion because there intervened that time of terror and tumult when all were called to arms for fear of the French.

This surprisingly accurate and sympathetic account survives in the chronicle of Barnwell Priory.[85] Others remembered less, and with less accuracy and insight. The Dunstable annalist recalled that there had been inquiries into the behaviour of sheriffs and added a touch of dramatic invention by saying that some were imprisoned and that others fled.[86] At St Albans the memory of what had happened was clouded. Here there was a tradition that the king's ministers had called a council at St Albans where they had enjoined the maintenance of the laws of Henry I, forbidden evil customs and ordered the sheriffs to desist from their exactions.[87] In this a core of truth, the examination of official behaviour, was contained in a story which emphasized the position of St Albans and exaggerated the constitutional tradition popular at that house. At Bury St Edmunds on the other hand a completely different story survived. Here they remembered that the king had sworn to eject foreigners from his council and to trust in the advice of the magnates of the land.[88] The continuator of the chronicle of William of Newburgh had yet another story of a royal oath to restore ancient liberties performed some time during April or May when the king and his army were awaiting a French invasion in Kent.[89] There is no contemporary warrant for any of this.[90]

John's motives are easily discernible. He was buying time and support. From the summer of 1212 onwards his main objective was to launch a counter-attack against King Philip

---

[85] *Walt. Cov.* II, 214–15. The writer confused the chronology of the second of these passages. Its conclusion, which refers to the threatened French invasion of April 1213, demonstrates that these reforms cannot have been a consequence, as he suggests, of the arrival of the papal legate, Nicholas of Tusculum, in September 1213. There is nothing relevant in Nicholas's report to Rome of 21 October.

[86] *Annales Monastici*, III, 35.   [87] *Chron. Maj.* II, 551.

[88] *Memorials of St Edmund*, II, 24.

[89] *Chronicles of Stephen, Henry II and Richard I*, II, 518.

[90] Both stories may be derived ultimately from the oath which John took on 20 July, on the occasion of his absolution (see below, p. 219).

Augustus in France, and to this end all else could for a time be sacrificed. Just as he was providing palliatives for his subjects, so he was making arrangements to settle his quarrel with Pope Innocent.[91] Here, too, the baronial plot of August 1212 may have had an effect. John sent his agents to Rome to accept the pope's terms in November 1212. He surrendered the kingdom to the papal nuncio at Dover on 15 May 1213, and he was absolved from excommunication by Stephen Langton on 20 July. Hence the two streams of negotiation and concession ran on concurrently, and soon they flowed together. So far there had been little indication that the lay magnates were willing to give their support to the papacy and the exiled bishops. Langton had addressed a special exhortation to those who bore knightly arms in his letters of admonishment sent to the English people during the Interdict,[92] and indeed the king's opponents later claimed that their actions had compelled the king to seek terms from the pope.[93] But this was primarily designed to obtain a favourable hearing at the Curia. In fact the Justiciar and other lay magnates had negotiated on the king's behalf during the Interdict,[94] and both English and Irish magnates had issued letters in support of the king's resistance to papal pretensions.[95] Hence the union of lay and ecclesiastical opposition in 1212 was very much a *mariage de convenance*. It seems to have originated in the flight to France of Robert fitz Walter, who proceeded to justify his treason by alleging to Philip of France that King John had tried to ravish his daughter and by trying to convince the papal nuncio, Pandulf, that he had fled through distaste at serving an excommunicate king.[96] The nuncio and the pope may

---

[91] For a valuable account of Innocent III's handling of the crisis in England see Cheney (1976), pp. 360–86.
[92] *Gerv. Cant.* II, lxxxii–lxxxiii.   [93] *Diplomatic Documents*, p. 29.
[94] *Gerv. Cant.* II, c, ci, ciii, cxv.
[95] *Rot. Litt. Claus.* I, 132b; *Cal. Docs. Ireland*, I, 73–4. For further comment see S. Painter, *William Marshal* (Baltimore, 1933), pp. 173–4, and H. G. Richardson & G. O. Sayles, *The Irish Parliament in the Middle Ages* (Philadelphia, 1952), pp. 285–7.
[96] *Histoire des ducs de Normandie*, pp. 119–21, 124–5.

have been easier to convince than the king of France. At least Innocent's terms to John came to include the two traitors of 1212 and indeed implied that their cause and that of the Church had been identical.[97] This had serious and complex effects. The restoration of fitz Walter and de Vescy was included with that of the deprived churchmen. Stephen Langton was empowered to place the king under ecclesiastical penalties once more if this was not properly executed,[98] and hence the archbishop could intrude into John's treatment of these two ineradicable rebels. He may well have done so as early as July when his steward, Elias of Dereham, was one of those deputed to receive the compensation due to Eustace de Vescy.[99] Thereafter circumstances were likely to drive the archbishop and the erstwhile traitors together, for they all shared dissatisfaction at John's dilatory execution of the agreement. He made sure that the castles of the two barons were destroyed before they recovered their lands.[100] It was only in November that he agreed to make an accurate assessment of fitz Walter's damages and he did it then only in an attempt to buy his support.[101] De Vescy received no such concession. Similarly, as the summer wore on Langton and his colleagues found themselves driven into the unpopular measure of continuing the Interdict in an attempt to ensure that proper restitution was made to the Church for John's depredations.[102] The possibilities created by this common claim against the king were soon turned into realities by John's own actions. He had envisaged his surrender of his two kingdoms to the papacy as a diplomatic coup against his enemies at home and abroad. At home he assumed that it would bring him pontifical support in the settlement of the Interdict and in influencing appointments

[97] *Selected Letters of Innocent III*, pp. 132–3.
[98] *Rot. Litt. Pat.* p. 101b. Compare the pope's authority to Langton to pronounce excommunication in the case of John's relapse (*Selected Letters of Innocent III*, p. 141).
[99] *Rot. Litt. Claus.* 1, 146. [100] Holt (1961), pp. 94–5.
[101] For the political manœuvres of the autumn, see Holt (1961), pp. 94–6.
[102] Mercati (1927), pp. 274–89. See also Painter (1949), pp. 195–7.

to the many sees which had fallen vacant since the outbreak of the quarrel. In this he was quickly proved right. He also seems to have approached the pope for assistance against any possible rebellion. Innocent sent a letter of 31 October to his legate, Nicholas of Tusculum, ordering him to declare null and void all conspiracies and factions which might have been formed during the quarrel between the pope and king.[103] Meanwhile John had made his attitude very clear as soon as the legate arrived in England. He had the instrument of the surrender of his kingdoms read before the assembled clergy and barons in St Paul's and performed homage and fealty to the legate before the high altar. He then urged the legate in private that he should receive him, his heirs and all his goods within the protection of the Church, and that he should give him legatine letters of protection pending the arrival of papal letters from Rome. Nicholas granted this request and urged the dispatch of similar letters from the Curia.[104] He wrote on 21 October; the papal letters of 31 October must have been on their way when his letter reached Rome.

There were good reasons for John's precautions and for the urgency reflected in the letter of the legate. The concessions of the winter had failed to prevent overt resistance to the king's demands for military service in the summer of 1213. The danger was particularly great in the north where men were arguing that they were not bound to serve overseas by the terms on which they held their land.[105] This was a skilful move, for it avoided an open declaration of rebellion by defiance or act of war, and aimed to force the king to establish his title to his demands in a plea of service. Now Langton had some grounds to intervene in such a dispute. He had been admonished by the pope to do all he could to secure the safety and peace of the king and the

---

[103] *Selected Letters of Innocent III*, p. 165.   [104] Mercati (1927), pp. 278–9.
[105] For a more detailed discussion of these developments, see Holt (1961), pp. 88–92.

realm.[106] Furthermore, John had engaged himself by some kind of oath on the occasion of his absolution, most probably by a renewal of the coronation oath. His reasons for doing so are obscure. It may be that he intended this as an ultimate concession to the malcontents or as a sign that he reigned once more as a communicant king. But it is also possible that the renewal took place at Langton's urging, for the first solemn promise of the coronation oath was to maintain the Church in peace. However, the evidence does not establish this, still less does it show that Langton demanded the renewal because he already saw the rest of the oath, with its promises to prevent evil and injustice and exercise due equity and mercy in judgement, as an immediately essential constitutional check on the king.[107] Men quickly came to exaggerate the extent and significance of John's concessions on this occasion. In 1215 the baronial agents at Rome asserted that he had sworn to preserve ancient baronial liberties which had been confirmed by the charters of his predecessors.[108] Ten years later the Coggeshall chronicler implied that the oath had been something of a *quid pro quo*, a condition of absolution,[109] and at about the same time Roger Wendover gave a form of oath in which he expanded the usual coronation oath to include a promise to restore the good laws of Edward the Confessor.[110] For Roger this was the first step on the road to Runnymede.[111] He too treated the oath as an integral part of the settlement with the Church.

However, whoever had inspired the oath and for whatever motive, it had been given in a form which associated secular and ecclesiastical matters in a single royal promise of good behaviour. Secular opposition could now emerge from

---

[106] *Selected Letters of Innocent III*, p. 155.
[107] For further discussion of Langton's role see Roberts (1968), pp. 10–13.
[108] *Diplomatic Documents*, p. 29.   [109] *Coggeshall*, p. 167.
[110] *Chron. Maj.* II, 550, 552.
[111] As Sir Maurice Powicke, who accepts Wendover at this point, clearly saw (Powicke, 1928, pp. 111–13).

the dark arcana of conspiracy into the arena of legal altercation and it looked almost inevitably to the archbishop for support since the renewal of the oath had been associated with his return and absolution of the king. Pope Innocent himself later noted how the outbreak of opposition followed hard on Langton's return,[112] and indeed Langton was bound by his office, by the terms of settlement with the pope and by the events of 20 July; willy-nilly he had to intervene. Hence when John marched north in a punitive campaign against the recalcitrants in September 1213 Langton apparently insisted that he should only proceed against them by judgement. Moreover he seems to have referred specifically to the oath of 20 July and to have been ready to back his intervention by ecclesiastical censure. He was demanding judicial process as if the northerners' case was a simple plea of service devoid of political undertones and implications. Such at least was the tradition of Langton's intervention which survived at St Albans in the next reign.[113] But the story of ecclesiastical intervention was widely known,[114] and John certainly seems to have felt himself inhibited, for he avoided open or provocative action against the northerners. Instead, he isolated the northern opposition, by promising the restoration of their liberties, a promise which he failed to keep, and by attracting their potential allies, especially among the magnates of the eastern and home counties, by threat, concessions or bribe.[115] As a result he was able to launch his long-planned campaign in February 1214. He was also able to avoid any formal settlement of the northerners' case against overseas service; in 1214 he demanded service and scutage from them, just as he had begun to do in 1213. On the other hand he had to

---

[112] *Selected Letters of Innocent III*, p. 196.   [113] *Chron. Maj.* II, 551–2.
[114] *Walt. Cov.* II, 212; *Coggeshall*, p. 167.
[115] Holt (1961), pp. 92–8. It was at this point that Geoffrey de Mandeville was instated in his inheritance and that investigation was ordered into the losses suffered by Robert fitz Walter during his exile.

face the consequences of these methods. When he sailed in 1214 he left behind a small but powerful group of opponents in the northern counties who were just as determined as the king in standing by the case they had advanced and maintained in the previous year. Indeed, the settlement with the Church, the king's oath of 20 July, and the archbishop's readiness to intervene had all combined to permit their advance into a position from which retreat was impossible on honourable or even sufferable terms. So matters remained until the summer when the defeat of the king's allies at Bouvines and the failure of his campaign in Poitou made catastrophe as inevitable at home as it had proved abroad.

The campaign of 1214 and the battle of Bouvines played a pivotal role in the crisis which produced the Great Charter. Up to Bouvines John was prepared to promise and concede, to bully and to bribe, but he always seems to have been confident that opposition was not yet so extensive and demanding as to prevent his campaign on the continent. After Bouvines, on the other hand, he was clearly preparing for a civil war at home; he knew that widespread and insistent opposition was now certain.[116] This change in his attitude is certain and clear-cut. It provides unequivocal evidence of the varying extent of opposition, for John read the political signs accurately enough until Bouvines upset all calculations, and it suggests that the opposition was never so deep and extensive in 1213 as to force the king to anything more than the vaguest of promises, on the one hand, and to restricted reforms or concessions to individuals on the other. He ended the year with nothing irrevocably conceded. Only once apparently did he go beyond this. On 1 November he met the recalcitrant northerners at Wallingford and through the mediation of the legate, the archbishop and the magnates lay and ecclesiastical reached some kind of agreement

---

[116] *Ibid.* pp. 100 ff.

with them in which he promised to restore their ancient liberties.[117] The evidence takes us so far and no further. Nothing elucidates these ancient liberties.[118] The king abrogated the agreement as soon as he could and it was quickly forgotten. The baronial agents who were sent to the Curia in 1215 to seek papal support sought a precedent for royal concessions in John's oath of 20 July 1213 and not in any intervening agreement or promise.[119] From 20 July onwards John had skilfully avoided committing himself.

Royal concessions imply baronial demands. Even so, there is no certain indication that there had been a formal demand for concession and reform at any point in the year. The evidence suggests that there was individual grievance, ill-formed discontent, general weariness and anger at the king's government, but nothing co-ordinated until the northerners stood out against the king's demand for service, and even this was only a beginning. After Bouvines in contrast there was a sudden change. John returned to England on 15 October 1214. By Christmas he was faced with a co-ordinated demand for the confirmation of the laws of Edward the Confessor and the laws and Charter of Henry I.[120] On 6 January 1215 he was compelled to enter into formal negotiations with his opponents at London. By then they were an organized body, bound together by an oath in a covenant or *conjuratio*, a body which was coherent and strong enough to require and obtain general letters of safe conduct pending a settlement, and which was capable of representing its case at the Curia as something more than a mass of individual petitions and grievances. By this time an authentic challenge to the Crown had rung out, for a covenant to fight for liberties was being set against the fealty

[117] For the possible association of the 'unknown' charter with this meeting, see below, p. 420.
[118] *Coggeshall*, p. 167; the Dunstable annals in *Annales Monastici*, III, 40.
[119] *Diplomatic Documents*, p. 29.
[120] For a discussion of the significance of this demand, see above, pp. 93–5, 113–16.

due to the king. Wisely, in the circumstances, the king's opponents came to the meeting in arms.[121]

This change is clearly reflected in the documents which cover the meeting at London.[122] It is not so obvious in the narrative sources in which the story was recorded some ten or fifteen years later. Indeed only the most perceptive, the chronicler whose work survives in its earliest form at Barnwell, preserved a clear, comprehensible record. He states that the refusal of some of the northerners to pay scutage led to interchanges in which the barons came to demand the confirmation of the Charter of Henry I. Matters were delayed until the New Year when there was a formal meeting at London, and here, despite differences of opinion in the baronial party in the face of the king's request for delay, there was a clearly expressed demand, supported by some of the bishops, for a confirmation of Henry's charter. Indeed, the words of these annals seem to reflect the formal phrases of a *conjuratio*; 'this was the voice and opinion of all and every one of them, that they would pledge themselves to sustain the house of the Lord and stand fast for the liberty of the church and the realm'.[123] The author of the *Histoire des Ducs de Normandie*, who came to England with the Flemish troops a year later, tells of something similar. Soon after the king's return from Poitou there was a baronial *conseil* or *parlement* at which the barons, some of whom he names, demanded that the king should stand by the charter granted by Henry I and confirmed by King Stephen; swearing on holy relics to stand together in support of this they threatened defiance and war if he refused.[124]

Other chroniclers presented a more confused story less consistent with the record evidence. Ralf of Coggeshall

---

[121] *Selected Letters of Innocent III*, p. 194; *Chron. Maj.* II, 584. See also below, pp. 228–9.
[122] For the safe conduct, see *Rot. Litt. Pat.* p. 126b, and *Curia Regis Rolls*, VII, 315. For the embassy at Rome, see *Diplomatic Documents*, pp. 28–30.
[123] *Walt. Cov.* II, 217–18.
[124] *Histoire des Ducs de Normandie*, pp. 145–6. See also below, pp. 410–11.

probably drew on some source shared with the Barnwell annals. He wrote that the northerners came together as if of one voice to compel the king to reform the liberty of the church and the kingdom and to abolish the evil customs which the king and his two predecessors had introduced to the detriment of church and realm; he too knew of the demand for the Charter of Henry I.[125] However, unlike the Barnwell annalist, he carried the story back to the end of 1213, where he noted that almost all the barons of England had covenanted together to protect the liberty of the church and the whole realm.[126] Wendover plunged into much deeper confusion. Coggeshall and the Barnwell chronicler were clear that there was no demand for the confirmation of the Charter of Henry I until the winter of 1214–15, after the king's return from Poitou; indeed, both are quite precise on this point. Wendover, in contrast, retailed a story which has developed into one of the legendary episodes of English history. He had already shown anachronistic symptoms in associating the laws of Edward the Confessor with the oath of 20 July 1213 and the laws of Henry I with the administrative reforms of that year.[127] Now he reported a dramatic story which he knew to be rumour, but which had the attraction of linking the basis of the barons' demands, the Charter of Henry I, with the intervention of Stephen Langton. This told that on 25 August 1213, after holding a meeting at St Paul's concerned with the ending of the Interdict, Langton called the assembled barons on one side and revealed that he had discovered a charter of Henry I whereby they might achieve their liberties; overjoyed at the discovery, they swore in the presence of the archbishop that if necessary they would soon fight for these liberties until death, a covenant in which the archbishop shared by promising them his full support.[128]

---

[125] *Coggeshall*, p. 170   [126] *Ibid.* p. 167.   [127] See above, pp. 215, 219.
[128] *Chron. Maj.* II, 552–4.

Despite the increasing distrust of Wendover's work in recent years this story still survives in the text-book. Yet there is no supporting evidence for it. It was not the only current explanation of the appearance of the Charter of Henry I. The Winchcombe annals reported another story that 'it was discovered by certain English magnates who were exiled in foreign parts'.[129] A copy of the Charter of Henry I was probably available in the archiepiscopal archives, but not in the version given by Wendover nor in that associated with the 'unknown charter'.[130] Langton was at St Paul's on 25 August; the sermon he preached on that occasion was noted by the Waverley annalist,[131] and indeed the text of the sermon still survives.[132] It gives no indication at all that the archbishop was ready to partake in a baronial conspiracy. On the contrary it reveals a man urgently concerned with ecclesiastical business, with ending the Interdict and recovering what the Church had lost. Wendover's rumour is quite inconsistent with the evidence of the Barnwell chronicle in all its features, and with the Coggeshall chronicle in the details concerning the Charter of Henry I. It is even inconsistent with other features of his own story, for when he came to deal with the winter of 1214–15, when the opposition was really developing along the lines he had described, he could only bring forth the Charter of Henry I once again and have yet another baronial covenant. This is presented in a second dramatic story, almost as well known as the first, in which the barons swore on the high altar of the abbey of Bury St Edmunds to make war on the king and withdraw their fealty if he was unwilling to confirm King Henry's charter.[133] This again is unsupported. There is no mention of the incident in the Bury evidence, which is especially detailed for these

[129] B.M. Cottonian MS, Faustina B, I, fo. 25.   [130] See appendix 2, below, pp. 423–4.
[131] *Annales Monastici*, II, 277.
[132] Lacombe (1930), pp. 408–20; listed in Roberts (1968), p. 149.
[133] *Chron. Maj.* II, 582–3.

years.[134] Bury was an unlikely venue for potential rebels whose chief weight still lay in the northern counties.[135] The story may represent some local agreement among the East Anglian barons but only a few of them are known to have turned against the king by the New Year.[136] Wendover's account is best shelved. His successor Matthew Paris wrote a life of Stephen Langton, fragments of which still survive,[137] and there are indications that he had access to Canterbury sources,[138] but there is no evidence that Wendover was in any such special position. Matthew simply repeated these stories without addition or comment.

Wendover's taste for the dramatic is not the only point at issue here, for his narrative exaggerates the continuity and inevitability in the developing opposition to the king. Some continuity there was. Some kind of covenanted conspiracy must have been organized as early as 1212 for treason could scarcely be plotted on any other basis; moreover the plotters had planned to elect a new king.[139] One of the leading conspirators of 1212, Eustace de Vescy, was prominent among those northerners who refused scutage in 1214[140] and brought down on himself a special papal mandate that he was not to trouble the king.[141] The other leader, Robert fitz Walter, became the commander of the baronial forces in 1215 with the imposing title of 'Marshal of the Army of God and Holy Church'. Yet in other ways this continuity is less striking. The plotters of 1212 were quelled and dispersed,

---

[134] See the *Electio Hugonis*. The surviving annals of St Edmund, however, terminate in 1212.

[135] Two possible dates have been suggested for this gathering. Kate Norgate suggested 4 November, when the king himself was at Bury (Norgate, 1902, p. 221). His presence makes this most unlikely. A more likely possibility is 20 November, the feast of St Edmund, which is supported by Wendover's statement that the barons came together 'as if for prayer'. This might have provided some cover for a gathering of conspirators, but if so the absence of information in the Bury sources is all the more surprising. For further discussion see below, pp. 406–11.

[136] Holt (1961), pp. 102–3.

[137] F. Liebermann, *Ungedruckte Anglo-Normannische Geschichtsquellen*, pp. 318–29.

[138] Powicke (1928), pp. 102–3; Richard Vaughan, *Matthew Paris*. p. 16; Holt (1964). 67–88.

[139] Possibly Simon de Montfort (*Walt. Cov.* II, 207; *Annales Monastici*, III, 33).

[140] Holt (1961), p. 100.   [141] *Foedera*, I, part I, 126; *Letters of Innocent III*, no. 981.

and even though the two leading traitors returned to the country in 1213 the new baronial schemes for resistance to service overseas were much subtler than the old plans for regicide. But even this new level of opposition was not maintained. By 1214 many were serving in Poitou, and many more were paying scutage. It was not until after Bouvines that the baronage turned against the king in any numbers, and even then many waited for the spring and the baronial capture of London before committing themselves.

The negotiations at London at the beginning of January only produced deadlock. John sought delay and in return he gave the barons a safe conduct until Low Sunday (26 April), when he agreed to answer their demands. This gave both parties time for political manoeuvre. They both appealed to Rome, they both tried to curry favour at the Curia, and they both continued negotiations at home. Henceforward negotiations proceeded in two courts, at Rome and in England; the first was the superior of the two, but was less well informed both as to English law and the interplay of parties. Neither could be in immediate touch with the other. The time-lag was at least thirty days each way.[142] At Rome negotiations were conducted by royal agents who had left England before Christmas and by baronial agents who left after the negotiations at London in January; both were soon out of personal touch with affairs at home. When papal letters arrived in England they embodied papal instructions which were at least a month old and were based on information derived from England which was at least two months old, at the time of their arrival. They were sometimes grotesquely unrealistic, ineffective or even dangerous in a rapidly changing situation. It was with this primitive

---

[142] See L. Landon, *Itinerary of Richard I* (Pipe Roll Soc., new series, XIII), pp. 184–91. Richardson & Sayles suggest an increase to five weeks (Richardson & Sayles, 1963, pp. 450–5).

machinery that men of good will strove for a settlement. It was all the more difficult to achieve since the negotiations were quasi-legal in character both in England and at Rome. In England the king's opponents were submitting demands based on the Charter of Henry I, which had been confirmed in 1154 by Henry II, and on John's own oath to observe good law and exercise justice; and they were still maintaining the case against the service and scutage which the king had demanded in 1214.[143] At Rome both parties were appealing to the pope as a feudal superior. Hence any settlement would have to embody something more than political horse-trading. It would have to be embodied in a form which had legal validity and authority, a form which seemed to arise from action at law and not from the use of force or the threat of it, a form which would require the underwriting authority of the king and could not be challenged as unlawful if submitted to the papal Curia.[144] These requirements do much to explain the final form of the settlement and the long process of negotiation from January to June 1215 in which the king and his opponents manoeuvred for position in an attempt to drive each other outside the legal framework of the argument. In this the king was bound to win. Ultimately the liberties his opponents sought could only be achieved by rebellion.

Not all the men involved were men of good will, the king least of all. Throughout, even when he sealed Magna Carta, John had not the slightest intention of giving in or permanently abandoning the powers which the Angevin kings had come to enjoy. He would surrender to force if he had to and with the grim consolation that in so doing he was putting his opponents in the wrong. Otherwise he stood his ground on

[143] This seems certain from Innocent III's letters of 1 April 1215 admonishing the barons to pay the scutage for the Poitevin army (*Selected Letters of Innocent III*, p. 202). For the increasing resistance to the Poitevin scutage, see Holt (1961), pp. 98–102, and *Pipe Roll 16 John*, pp. xiv–xvi.
[144] For a more detailed account of the action at the Curia see Cheney (1976), pp. 367–75.

the traditional rights of the Crown and bided his time until the increasing recalcitrance of his vassals gave him an indefeasible case at the Curia. Hence he immediately challenged the newly founded covenant for the Charter of Henry I by demanding a renewal of fealty in which men were required to swear allegiance to him not only against all men, as in the usual form of oath, but also against the Charter.[145] This he was unable to exact. Meanwhile his agents at Rome were taking every advantage of the awkward legal situation into which the barons had already had to advance. The results of their efforts are revealed in letters of 19 March in which Pope Innocent attempted to solve the dispute. He addressed letters to John, asking him to hear the just petitions of the barons and to treat them kindly.[146] To the barons he addressed a brusque condemnation of the leagues and conspiracies which had pressed claims on the king by force of arms; such leagues were to be abandoned henceforth under the pain of excommunication; they were to make any requests they might have, not with insolence, but with reverence which conserved the king's honour.[147] Langton was sent a sharp rebuke for failing to mediate successfully between the king and his opponents; indeed Innocent had already received some hint of Langton's intervention on the baronial side in 1213 for he now pointed out that the demands made against the king had not been heard until after Langton's return. The archbishop was told to bring the two parties into agreement, and since the pope included a résumé of the letters he had sent to the king and the barons, Langton was left in no doubt on the kind of agreement Innocent envisaged.[148] By March therefore the pope had made up his mind. This was confirmed in letters of 1 April in which he directed the barons to pay the Poitevin

---

[145] *Walt. Cov.* II, 218.
[146] The letters addressed to the king do not survive, but are summarized in the letters to the barons (*Selected Letters of Innocent III*, p. 195).
[147] *Ibid.* pp. 194–5.   [148] *Ibid.*, pp. 196–7.

scutage.[149] He was already aware that John was about to take up the Cross; this is at least implied by the concern he showed in the letters of March and April that the quarrel might delay the king's 'good design'. His knowledge was well founded; indeed it was most probably derived from the king's agents at the Curia. John took the Cross on 4 March. The alliance between king and pope was consummated. John had won the battle at Rome. The one power which could compel him to make concessions had abandoned the task.

Innocent's actions were founded on law, not simply on a narrowly conceived view of the interests of the Church. The three letters of 19 March were intended as a formal settlement of the dispute. The pope later wrote that this had been reached after much deliberation and in the presence of the baronial agents at the Curia, and he clearly expected that his decision would settle the matter; if there was further disagreement then it was to be settled by judgement of peers in the king's court according to the laws and custom of the realm.[150] These three letters, with or without additional provisions, came to figure in the quarrel as 'the triple form of peace' (triplex forma pacis),[151] which the pope's agents in England later described as 'honest, reasonable and acceptable to all God-fearing men'.[152] It was so only in so far as the dispute could be settled within the framework of established judicial process. The pope's letters of 19 March and 1 April show that he would not abandon this in favour of the wider reconsideration of the customs of the realm which the barons were seeking. Hence he laid down that they were not to demand concessions until they had rendered the services they owed to the king;[153] in particular they must pay

---

[149] *Ibid.* p. 202.
[150] See Innocent's Letters of 18 June (*M.C.C.E.* pp. 43–4; *Letters of Innocent III*, no. 1013, pp. 272–3).
[151] For a discussion of the *Triplex forma pacis*, which some authorities have equated with Magna Carta, see appendix 3, pp. 413–17.
[152] *E.H.R.* XLIV (1929), 92.   [153] *Selected Letters of Innocent III*, p. 194.

scutage, which was a customary render from their baronies, which they themselves had paid until recently, which they were refusing arbitrarily and of which the king should not be deprived without judgement.[154] The implications of Innocent's arguments were brutally clear. The barons were not to begin their case by depriving the king of just those rights they were seeking for themselves; they could act only as supplicants. And thus, it might be added, if the king would not accede to their request, they could not act within the law at all. Innocent's strict sense of legality had made war and reform inseparable.

Meanwhile in England the two opposing parties were still trying to reach agreement on their own. Sporadic attempts at negotiation continued after January. Letters of safe conduct of 19 February were made out for the northerners who were to come to Oxford on the 22nd to speak with William Marshal, Stephen Langton, and his fellow bishops.[155] There was another gathering of some kind at Oxford on 13 April.[156] The Barnwell annals also record unsuccessful negotiations after which the barons proceeded to fortify their castles and arm themselves.[157] There may well have been other efforts and not all these exchanges can have been so unsuccessful, for the king sent letters of 13 March to the barons and bachelors of Poitou who were coming to England, thanking them for their eager support and ordering them to return home 'because the business for which they had been required had been settled'.[158] Apparently at this point John felt that civil war would be avoided. However, this marked only a very slight and temporary easing in his military preparations. Moreover nothing had been settled by Easter week, the term he had set both for his reply to the baronial requests of January and to the safe conducts he had given to the barons who had been at London then.

[154] *Ibid.* p. 202.   [155] *Rot. Litt. Pat.* p. 129
[156] *Memorials of St Edmund*, II, 124–5.   [157] *Walt. Cov.* II, 219.
[158] *Rot. Litt. Pat.* p. 130b.

In January it had been arranged that the parties should meet at Northampton on Low Sunday, 26 April.[159] The barons came in arms. The northerners mustered at Stamford in Easter week and then marched south, gathering strength as they went. Before they reached Northampton they were joined by Robert fitz Walter, Geoffrey de Mandeville, and presumably other men from East Anglia.[160] The king did not come; all he did was to issue a safe conduct of 23 April lasting up to 28 May to those who came to speak with him through the mediation of the archbishop.[161] Indeed he spent the second half of Easter week on a rapid progress of some of his usual haunts in the southern counties. Not until 30 April, when he reached Wallingford, was he within reasonable distance of the place appointed for negotiations. By then the barons had moved to Brackley, a manor of one of their party, Saer de Quincy, earl of Winchester,[162] and there they seem to have remained during the course of negotiations. The king meanwhile moved restlessly between Wallingford, Reading and London. Hence the principals never met; the argument was carried on through mediators, usually through the archbishop and William Marshal, earl of Pembroke.

Nothing has survived of the baronial demands.[163] The king's part is comparatively well recorded in a charter of 9 May, letters patent of 10 May and a letter of 29 May in which he informed the pope of the negotiations.[164] This last was concerned to show that the king had acted throughout in an unexceptionable and reasonable manner, and although it recounts his own offers accurately enough, it presents the baronial attitude as one of blind recalcitrance and blank refusal of the king's suggestions. It makes no mention at all of

[159] For the account of these negotiations I have relied heavily on Cheney (1956), 311–41.
[160] *Walt. Cov.* II, 219.   [161] *Rot. Litt. Pat.* p. 134.
[162] *Complete Peerage*, XII, part II, 750–1.
[163] For a discussion of this, see below, pp. 238–40.
[164] *Rot. Chartarum*, p. 209b; *Rot. Litt. Pat.* p. 141; *Foedera*, I, part I, 129. For the texts of the first two, see appendix 11, below, pp. 492–3.

the barons' demands or even of the fact that they had by then defied the king. Hence it is impossible to dovetail the actions of the barons into a letter which seems to present an accurate chronological account of events. Moreover although the letter makes it clear that all the king's proposals were made after the arrival of the *forma pacis* announced in the letters of 19 March, it fails to indicate whether the barons presented their demands and defied the king before or after the arrival of the papal letters. Events occurred so rapidly that contemporaries quickly became confused. Later papal letters of 19 June and 24 August state that the barons took up arms and renounced their fealty without waiting for the papal terms[165] – information which must have been derived from England. In contrast, letters of 5 September of the papal commissioners in England state that the barons had renounced their fealty in defiance of the triple form of peace[166] and the Barnwell annals also record that the letters arrived before the final breach.[167]

In the circumstances this did not matter except as a debating point on which the pope expressed his injured dignity. The barons seem to have been quite intransigent in pressing their demands, while the king was equally unwilling to surrender any point of principle. Indeed the papal letters of 19 March might have been tailored to fit his needs. First he stood on his legal rights, asserting that England was now part of the patrimony held of St Peter and the Roman Church, that he was a crusader entitled to the normal crusading privileges and freedom from attack, and finally appealing against all breakers of the peace through the persons of William Marshal and William, earl Warenne.[168] He was prepared to talk, but only on these terms, and when

---

[165] *M.C.C.E.* p. 43: *Letters of Innocent III*, no. 1013, pp. 272–3; *Selected Letters of Innocent III*, p. 214.
[166] *E.H.R.* XLIV (1929), 92.   [167] *Walt. Cov.* II, 219.
[168] *Foedera*, I, part I, 129. I am assuming that the king's letter follows the chronological order of events. Cf. Professor Cheney's view (1956), 318.

he promised concessions it was 'saving our appeal': his
enemies were to be responsible for any breaches of the
peace.[169] He then proceeded to meet the terms of the papal
settlement. As an answer to the baronial complaints he
offered to abolish the evil customs which had arisen in his
own reign and that of his brother, Richard I, and to submit
the customs which had arisen in the time of his father to the
advice of his faithful men.[170] When this was rejected by the
barons, the king tried to persuade the archbishop to excommunicate his opponents as disturbers of the peace. When this
failed he went on to offer the barons the kind of adjudication
which Innocent had envisaged in case of disagreement over
terms. In letters patent of 10 May, in words which at once
echoed the phrases of Innocent and foreshadowed those of
Magna Carta, he promised his opponents that 'he would not
arrest or disseise them or their men nor would he go against
them by force of arms except by the law of the land and by
judgement of their peers in his court'.[171] He also offered the
judgement of his court to Geoffrey de Mandeville for the
fine he had made for his wife and to Giles de Briouze, bishop
of Hereford, for the fine he had made for the lands of his
father, William.[172] Finally he added something apparently
all his own: he proposed to submit the dispute to the
arbitration of eight barons, four chosen by him and four by
his opponents, sitting under the direction of the pope as
supreme arbiter. He had already announced this scheme in a
charter of 9 May in which he stated that, pending such an
arbitration, he would not be bound by any previous discussion or offer and that the proposal was saving the acknowledgement in the interim of the debts and services which

---

[169] H. G. Richardson & G. O. Sayles took a different view of this phrase, relating it to the
king's appeal to Rome (Richardson & Sayles, 1963, p. 458). This is supported neither by
the context nor by the fact that the appeal to Rome had been answered. It is, however, a
possible interpretation.
[170] *Foedera*, I, part I, 129.   [171] See appendix 11, below, pp. 492–3.
[172] *Rot. Litt. Pat.* p. 141.

1 Runnymede, looking north, from above Cooper's Hill: 1973

2 The 'unknown' charter: actual size 210 mm long × 285 mm wide

3 Detail of the left-hand part of the 'unknown' charter

4 Charter of Henry I, Latin version: actual size 295 mm long × 180 mm wide

5 Charter of Henry I, Anglo–Norman version: actual size 295 mm long × 185 mm wide

7 Detail of the upper left-hand section of the Articles of the Barons

6 The Articles of the Barons: actual size 555 mm long × 265 mm wide

8 Magna Carta: the Charter sent to Lincoln: actual size 465 mm long × 450 mm wide

9 Detail of the upper left-hand part of the Charter

10 The treaty on the custody of London: actual size 125 mm long × 455 mm wide

11 Detail of the right-hand part of the treaty

were due to him before the dispute started.[173] John stood firmly on the principle that his opponents must first show themselves his vassals, a principle which now had the support of Innocent's letters. Furthermore, he now had such confidence in Innocent's attitude that he was ready to accept his arbitration. John was gambling on a certainty. He had won the diplomatic battle in the sense that he had had the better of the argument. But this can have been of little comfort immediately. The barons had already renounced their fealty on 5 May.[174] If John's offers of 9 and 10 May were designed to re-establish peace, they failed. On 12 May he ordered the seizure of the estates of the rebels.[175] The war had begun.

It was a war which only the king could win. He was fighting recalcitrant vassals whom he could dispossess, imprison or outlaw, if he was successful. His aim was simple and tangible. The barons, in contrast, were trying to compel their lord to agree to their demands, to limit his own sovereignty, to abandon what he would regard as the traditional rights of the Crown. Their aim was far more complex than his. Indeed the greater their success the further they drove themselves into this logical impasse: force alone would make John surrender, yet force was the least adequate authority for the kind of concession they had in mind. Worse still, they were now in the position of recalcitrant parties in a suit, indeed doubly so, for they had refused the king's offer of judgment in his court and they had also rejected Innocent's arbitration which they themselves had sought in January. Few parties have ever gone to war against such logical odds, and they were conscious enough of the difficulty. In the articles they drew up in June they did their best to evade further papal intervention in the dispute, and

---

[173] Appendix 11, below, p. 492.
[174] *Annals of Southwark and Merton*, ed. M. Tyson (Surrey Archaeological Collections, XXXVI, 1936), p. 49.
[175] *Rot. Litt. Claus.* I, 204.

in cap. 61 of the Great Charter they tried to place the king under such severe penalties that he would not attempt to fight, either with or without papal support. Yet they were wrong-footed from the start, and it was easy enough for John, Innocent and the papal agents in England to regard the Charter as an unlawful act of extortion. Hence all John had to do was to sit tight and wait for yet another fulmination from Rome to re-open the argument in his favour. In the end the barons tried to find a way out of the impasse by recognizing Prince Louis of France as king, but this too proved ineffective. There was no way out until a king was prepared to grant their demands of his own free will with papal approval, and they got this first from a ten-year-old king. Hence they were fighting not just an individual but a system of legal appeal the ready acceptance of which was part of the atmosphere they breathed. Their persistence in the face of royal and papal majesty is a measure of their discontent and depth of feeling. Yet they went to war not simply in a spirit of blind irritation. Innocent had asked that the quarrel should be settled according to the laws and custom of the realm. This was what they were now trying to define, and they were fighting to establish their right to do so.

CHAPTER 7

QUASI PAX

War was endemic in the medieval state. Self-help, distraint, the ordinary processes of administrative compulsion, the focusing of government on the castle, the use of outlawry and the frequent outbreaks of lawlessness, all imparted warlike features to peacetime rule. This was accentuated in times of crisis when urgent measures were taken for the munitioning, repair and replenishment of fortresses, and when the dispatch of mercenary crossbowmen to different parts of the country reflected closely and immediately the tactical and political concerns of the king. By May 1215 such a crisis had been experienced intermittently for nearly three years, especially in those areas which were to become the main centres of the rebellion, in the north above all, and in East Anglia and the home counties. Here men had become accustomed to preparations for war. By April 1215 the barons were negotiating in arms. By this time, too, the king had mustered large mercenary forces from Flanders, Poitou and Gascony. The crisis also had its political aspects. By 1215 all but the blindest of the English aristocracy must have been aware that loyalty was becoming a matter of negotiation with the king, that the ordinary ties which bound a feudal society together had become subject to political considerations which distorted them and which led the king to buy and his vassals to sell loyalty as if it were a commodity to be extracted and surrendered by extortion, or to be marketed in return for privilege and office. All this encouraged the drift towards war. Men had become accustomed to the possibility; they had prepared for it; they had been encouraged to think that it was an imminent danger. In the end the formal act of defiance which began it may well have seemed like a relief from the intolerable tedium of waiting for it and from the alternative but equal difficulties of continuing to negotiate in arms or abandoning warlike postures altogether.

Yet the step into war was deliberate enough. It could scarcely be anything else when Pope Innocent had placed most of the legal advantages in the hands of the king and when the rebels were risking, in the form of their lives, freedom and property, something more tangible than they stood to gain. Hence, more than most civil wars, the war of 1215 began with a conscious and open confrontation of competing attitudes and programmes embodied on the one hand in the king's offers of May and on the other in the petitions which the barons had been pressing since January. The rebels went to war because the king refused their demands and because they saw insufficient gains in the legal processes which John, at Innocent's urging, offered them. The king went to war because he could fight it with advantage as a war against recalcitrant vassals and because he had found the demands of the opposition intolerable. The discussions following Easter had not simply revealed irreconcilable enmities; they had also brought into focus what the war was to be about.

It is doubtful whether John would have been ready to accept even the first point in the baronial claim: the confirmation of the Charter of Henry I. This was of more than antiquarian relevance in 1215, since many of its provisions could be applied directly against John's methods of government. It promised concessions over a large range of feudal matters, on the exercise of justice and on the extent of the royal forest.[1] Moreover it opened the door to further restrictions, for Henry had agreed to abolish all evil customs with which the realm of England was oppressed; the rest of the Charter simply enumerated the most obvious of

---

[1] See above, pp. 36–8.

them.[2] This provision could well be developed in great detail and at great length in directions which had not been envisaged in 1100. A hint of this is to be found in the Barnwell annals. These state that when the king was faced with the demand for the confirmation of the Charter of Henry I at London in the first week of January, he sought delay on the grounds of 'the novelty of the business'.[3] This would have been a lame excuse if the only issue at stake had been the specific concessions of Henry I and nothing more, for these were scarcely novel. How much further the barons' demands went at this stage is uncertain. Some time in the early months of 1215, however, they had gone far enough to amount to a list of specific points appended to the Charter of Henry I. This seems to be the stage represented by the so-called 'unknown' charter to which J. H. Round first drew the attention of English scholars in 1893.[4] This consists of a copy of the charter of Henry I followed by promised or proposed concessions by King John which are crudely summarized as additions to Henry's grant. Some of these simply repeat points in Henry's charter, as for instance in the matter of reliefs and testamentary dispositions.[5] Some simply gloss sections in Henry's charter: widows are to be allowed to stay in their husband's house for forty days after his death; heiresses are not to be disparaged, and the forest bounds are to be restored, not now to the limits of 1087, but to the limits of 1154.[6] Some concern points of feudal practice not mentioned in Henry's charter: cap. 3 contains stringent provisions for the administration of lands in royal wardship, which are to be in the hands of four knights of the fee. Some are concerned with John's demands for military service overseas: they restrict such service to Normandy and Brittany and also lay down limits on the

---

[2] For the text, see appendix 4, below, pp. 424–6.
[3] 'Cumque ille inducias peteret pro rei novitate' (*Walt. Cov.* II, 218).
[4] See appendix 4, below, pp. 419–28.
[5] Caps. 2, 5; cp. Charter of Henry I, caps. 2, 7.   [6] Cap. 9.

king's demands for scutage.[7] Other sections are concerned
with alleviating the Crown's exploitation of the forest law
and indebtedness to the Jews: debts due to the Jews from
royal wards are not to carry usury;[8] owners of private
woods within the royal forest are protected; and it is laid
down that no one is to lose life or limb for a forest offence.[9]
These additions open with the provision that King
John will not take a man without judgement, or receive
anything for doing justice, or commit injustice.[10] This
section may have been inspired by the papal letters of 19
March and the king's subsequent concessions of 9 and 10
May. The document as a whole must be attributed to one or
more of the many negotiations which took place between
January and June 1215.[11] But by June these rough-and-
ready provisions had been by-passed by the much lengthier
and more sophisticated arrangements embodied in the
Articles of the Barons. Indeed the 'unknown' charter may
already have been outmoded by May. The king's charter of
9 May refers to the 'issues and articles' which he and the
barons were discussing.[12] According to Roger of Wendover
the barons sent a schedule to the king from Brackley, a
schedule which contained chapters or *capitula* which, when
read out, provoked the king to violent and furious refusal.[13]
They already seem to have known what sort of guarantee
they wanted. Wendover states that they asked the king to
seal their schedule to indicate his acceptance.[14] It was just
this that they obtained in June when the king put his seal to
the Articles of the Barons. Thus at least one striking feature
of the Articles of June seems to have been foreshadowed in
May. Everything indicates that the barons entered the war
with their demands as clearly stated as the counter-proposals
of the king.

[7] Caps. 7, 8. For a discussion of the obscure cap. 8, see below, pp. 318–19.
[8] Cap. 11.   [9] Cap. 12.   [10] Cap. 1.
[11] For a discussion of the dating see appendix 4, below, pp. 420–3.
[12] See appendix 11, below, p. 492.   [13] *Chron. Maj.* II, 586
[14] *Ibid.* and for further discussion see below, pp. 246–7.

However, neither side was burning its boats. The safe conducts which the king had authorized on 23 April still ran to 28 May.[15] The barons seem to have taken every opportunity to continue negotiation. The king, too, was curiously reluctant to admit that a war had broken out. He made no reference to the baronial defiance in the letter he sent to the pope at the end of May.[16] In the letters patent of 10 May and letters of 27 May concerned with a truce and safe conduct, the barons appear as 'our barons',[17] and in the public documents as a whole the seriousness of the situation is obscured. They refer to the 'barons who are against us'[18] or to the 'barons opposing us',[19] but never to the 'barons making war on us'. It is only in the more private correspondence between the king and his sheriffs, contained in letters close, that his opponents are bluntly and accurately described as 'our enemies'.[20] The reason for this reticence is obscure unless it was that the king thought that to acknowledge the rebellion might impede a settlement. Both parties were in delicate balance, competing for the allegiance of the undecided or the weakly committed. The king was using disseisin or the threat of it as a method of ensuring loyalty where he thought it dubious. He, too, was ready to negotiate. On 16 May he instructed some of his agents to accept a truce until the 21st, if the archbishop were to announce it.[21] A day later the balance was drastically disturbed. On Sunday 17 May the barons seized London by ruse and with the collusion of a party in the city, while many of the citizens were at mass. They replaced the mayor, Roger fitz Alan, by their own nominee, Serlo the mercer.[22] They now had a bargaining counter.

---

[15] See above, p. 232. [16] Ibid. [17] Rot. Litt. Pat. pp. 141, 142.
[18] Ibid. p. 141. [19] Rot. Chartarum, p. 209b. [20] Rot. Litt. Claus. I, 204.
[21] Rot. Litt. Pat. p. 136b
[22] Chronicles of Edward I and Edward II, 1, 17; Liber de Antiquis Legibus, p. 4. Both are in error in giving the feast of SS. Gordianus and Epimachus, 10 May, for the baronial seizure of London. The correct date of 17 May is established by royal letters of 16 and 18 May (Rot. Litt. Pat. p136b; Foedera, I, pt. I, 121).

The fall of London was decisive. If Bouvines brought on a political crisis and Innocent III's intervention a war, the baronial seizure of London led directly to Runnymede, for it forced the king to go much further in accepting the baronial demands than he had done hitherto. London was 'the capital of the Crown and realm';[23] its seizure was the first major charge which the papal agents, Peter des Roches and Pandulf, levelled against the king's opponents in September.[24] The barons apparently exploited their good fortune by bringing pressure to bear on the waverers,[25] and many only joined the cause against the king at this late stage.[26] Enough seem to have done so to persuade the king that further resistance was useless, at least for the moment. Exchanges between the two parties were soon renewed. Letters of 25 May provided for a safe conduct up to the 31st for Saer de Quincy, earl of Winchester, to come and speak with the king.[27] Letters of the 27th provided for a similar safe conduct for Stephen Langton and those who came with him to Staines, and in letters of the same day four royal agents were informed that a truce had been arranged.[28] Letters announcing the conditions and duration of the truce were not enrolled and have not survived, but it cannot have extended beyond 10 June, from which date it or a subsequent truce was extended to 15 June.[29] The letters of 27 May in fact marked the cessation of hostilities. In three weeks the barons had done very well for themselves.

John opened the new round of negotiations on 29 May by repeating his offer of papal arbitration in the presence of a papal messenger just arrived from Rome.[30] He can scarcely have expected to achieve more than a demonstration of baronial recalcitrance which could be duly reported at the

---

[23] 'Corone pariter et Regni sui caput'; thus the letters of 5 September of Peter des Roches and the other papal commissioners (E.H.R. XLIV, 92).
[24] Ibid.   [25] Chron. Maj. II, 587.   [26] Holt (1961), pp. 106–10.
[27] Rot. Litt. Pat. p. 138b.   [28] Ibid. p. 142.   [29] Ibid. p. 143.
[30] Foedera, I, part I, 129.

Curia. He then moved from Odiham to Windsor where he stayed from 31 May to 3 June. If the barons used the safe conduct to Staines which had been issued on the 27th, negotiations must have fallen already into the geographic setting they were to have on 15 June. How long and what form the discussions took is not clear. There may have been a temporary break on 5 June, for on that day John began a short and rapid journey which took him as far as Winchester and led him through an area thick with royalist troops.[31] This may perhaps indicate that he momentarily considered breaking off negotiations, but if so the numbers and condition of his troops can scarcely have been propitious for an immediate campaign, for the project was soon abandoned. New letters of safe conduct to those who came on behalf of the barons were dated at Merton on 8 June, covering the period from 9 June to midnight on the 11th.[32] On the 9th royal letters were dated at Odiham,[33] but by nightfall the king was probably back at Windsor,[34] where he stayed until the 26th.

At this point the story is illuminated by an account of the election of Abbot Hugh of Bury St Edmunds, derived from a man who was probably an eye-witness of many of the incidents described. The writer tells us that Hugh set out to seek royal approval of his election on 5 June. He found both John and Stephen Langton at Windsor on 9 June and the king told him to appear in the 'meadow of Staines' on the following day where he hoped to settle the matter. Hugh duly appeared there on the 10th. The chronicler tells us that he had to wait a long time, but after much discussion and exchange of views the abbot was given the royal kiss of

---

[31] See *Rot. Litt. Pat.* p. 138b. Savaric de Mauleon and his Poitevin followers were based on Winchester (*ibid.* pp. 136b, 137b). While at Winchester on 6 June John ordered Faulkes de Bréauté to send 400 Welsh troops to William Longespee, Earl of Salisbury, at Salisbury (*Rot. Litt. Claus.* I, 214).

[32] *Rot. Litt. Pat.* pp. 142b–3. [33] *Rot. Litt. Claus.* I, 214b.

[34] *Electio Hugonis*, pp. 168–70.

peace and was asked to dine at Windsor.[35] The chronology of this narrative is fully confirmed, for letters patent announcing Hugh's election and granting him the temporalities of the abbey were issued from the Chancery under the date of 11 June.[36] This story provides clear evidence that the king was at Runnymede on 10 June, for the words 'the meadow of Staines' can scarcely mean anything else. He would not have gone there simply to settle the case of Abbot Hugh. The safe conduct issued to the baronial representative on the 8th and the fact that Langton was with the king on the 9th make it almost certain that the main problem to be settled at Runnymede on the 10th was not Abbot Hugh's election, but the issues between the king and the rebel barons.

The phrases of the letters of safe conduct issued between 25 May and 8 June suggest that the negotiations were now producing something concrete. The letters of the 25th and the 27th issued in favour of Saer de Quincy, Langton and his companions, state that these men were coming 'to treat concerning peace'.[37] The letters of the 8th, in contrast, state that the baronial agents were now coming 'to make and secure peace'.[38] Thus something definite seems to have been expected from the negotiations of the 9th to the 11th. It seems probable, too, that something was achieved, for on the 10th the king's military agents throughout the southern and midland counties were informed that the truce had been extended to the early morning of the 15th.[39] Whereas earlier negotiations had been in the hands of envoys, now,

---

[35] Ibid.
[36] Rot. Litt. Pat. p. 142b. Letters of 2 June had previously ordered the transference of the abbey to the custody of Thomas of Barrow (ibid.).
[37] 'ad tractandum de pace' (ibid. pp. 138b, 142).
[38] 'ad pacem faciendam et firmandam' (ibid. p. 142b).
[39] Rot. Litt. Pat. p. 143. The addressees were William of Salisbury, Savaric de Mauleon, Richard fitz Roy, William Briwerre, William de Cantilupe, Waleran the German, John of Bassingbourn, William de Harcourt, Roger de Neville, Stephen Haringod and Geoffrey de Martigny.

apparently, arrangements were being made for a full assembly of the opposing parties.

It was 10 June, therefore, that marked the first important stage in the final negotiations, a stage which can only have been reached when the king and the baronial envoys were largely agreed on terms. This in turn must have meant that the king had accepted many of the baronial demands, that he had been forced to a far wider abandonment of his position than he had envisaged in the early days of May. The baronial envoys must have got enough of the terms they wanted, and they must have got them in a form which convinced them, and would convince the rest of the baronial party, of the king's good faith. In short there must have been a document stating terms, a document which committed the king and which the envoys could show to their friends in London. It is precisely such a document which survives as the Articles of the Barons.[40]

These Articles are a remarkable and chance survival from the negotiations of 1215, for they had no permanent importance. They have survived because Stephen Langton, the chief intermediary, apparently pocketed them in 1215, whence they found their way into the archiepiscopal archives where they remained until they passed into the hands of Gilbert Burnet in the seventeenth century.[41] They carry no date. Historians have assumed rather easily that they were not presented to the king until 15 June or even that they were not drawn up until then in the first plenary session at Runnymede. However, these views were developed very much faute de mieux and in ignorance of the events of 10 June. In fact the Articles fit the role of a preliminary agreement between the king and baronial envoys which we have envisaged on 10 June much more convincingly than that which has been allotted to them traditionally on 15 June.[42] It is highly

<hr />

[40] On the title, see appendix 5, below, p. 429.   [41] Collins (1948), 235–8.
[42] For a further discussion of these and other relevant points, see appendix 5, below, pp. 429–32.

implausible to imagine that a general meeting of the opposing parties could have been arranged without some such preliminary written agreement; the results would have been chaotic. Furthermore, it is clear that the Articles were not a baronial demand presented to the king for his assent. The document is headed, 'These are the clauses which the barons seek and which the lord king concedes,'[43] a simple statement which can only mean that the writer knew that the king was agreeing to the petitions he was about to draft. They were drawn up by both parties in conference and they were written, to judge from the hand, by one of the king's clerks.[44] They are a fair copy of points agreed in discussion, a fair copy which was amended here and there and which still left room for further insertions.[45] They carried the king's great seal. This indeed is their most striking feature, for the Articles had little of the characteristic form of a charter or letter patent. Legally, they did not convey or grant anything. There was nothing in them to be strengthened or made valid by the appending of the seal. The sealing of such a document was quite abnormal if not unique. Such an astonishing breach of diplomatic practice seems to be related directly to the circumstances of 10 June. The baronial envoys must have required something to warrant the fact to the rest of their party at London that they had reached a preparatory agreement with the king. A sealed draft gave them just that. Moreover it provided the barons with a form of agreement identical with what they had sought at Easter. Then, apparently, they had required

---

[43] The title is in the same hand as the rest of the document and is coeval with it.

[44] McKechnie (1914, p. 39) suggested that the document was the work of a Chancery clerk. The hands on the Chancery rolls of 1215 are in general more florid than that of the Articles; usually, too, the writing is larger. But some of the hands on the Patent rolls in particular can only be distinguished from that of the Articles after considerable study. Indeed, the difference between the hand of the Articles and that of a Patent roll entry is often no greater than that between one entry on the rolls and another.

[45] The most obvious addition is to caps. 45 and 46. There is a gap of some four lines between cap. 48 and the *forma securitatis*.

the king to seal their schedule of demands.[46] It was just such a schedule that the king had now sealed, and at least one of his opponents proceeded to exploit it at once. By 21 June William de Mowbray had told the king that a local inquiry had taken place into his title to certain Yorkshire properties. The claim cannot have been based on Magna Carta. If it had any legal basis at all, and de Mowbray seems to have implied that it had, it was that provided by the Articles and these in turn must have been in existence soon enough for this case to have been known at Runnymede by 21 June. 10 June is possible, 15 June scarcely likely.[47]

There may well have been a further consideration in the minds of the baronial envoys and the king on 10 June. To seal the Articles gave them the advantage of an official status in circumstances in which other more radical demands were in the air. Certain features of the Articles were probably fairly recent. Those sections of the *forma securitatis* and of cap. 25 which express baronial suspicions of papal intervention most probably originated after the arrival in England of the papal letters of 19 March, and the *forma securitatis* as a whole looks like a baronial reply to the offer of judgement by peers and papal arbitration which the king made on 9 and 10 May.[48] It may well be that a number of obvious omissions were equally recent. There is nothing in the Articles of the demands for the restriction of overseas service which had figured in the 'unknown' charter and nothing again of the radical restriction of the bounds of the forest which that document contained. This may well have left the negotiators of 10 June uneasy. They must also have been concerned with yet another disturbing circumstance. In 1215 the concept of delegates exercising full authority on behalf of

---

[46] *Chron. Maj.* II, 586.

[47] For a further discussion of William de Mowbray's claim, see above, pp. 166–7 and appendix 5 below, pp. 431–2.

[48] Cheney, in contrast, argued that the king's vigorous rejection of the Brackley schedule may be explained by the fact that it contained some provision similar to the *forma* (1956, 317). Cp. Painter (1949), pp. 315–16.

a group or community was still undeveloped. Despite the fact that the Articles enjoyed the prestige of the great seal, neither the king nor the envoys can have been certain that they would gain sufficient acceptance to permit the re-establishment of peace. In recounting events at Runnymede on and after the 15th the Barnwell annals state that some of the northerners left the meeting and, on the excuse that they had not been present, proceeded to make war.[49] If a contemporary could imagine a rejection of the Charter in these terms then the king and the baronial envoys could far more easily imagine that the Articles might meet a similar rejection. A small committee could produce terms and produce them in a far more businesslike manner than a larger gathering. But it could not guarantee that the terms would be accepted; for this a full assembly was essential.

These factors seem to underlie the events of the second stage in the negotiations, 15 June. At the time this was considered crucial for it was the date given to Magna Carta. However, its significance was quickly lost. The chroniclers gave various dates to the settlement ranging from 18 to 23 June; only one, Roger of Wendover, gave the 15th and he may well have derived this from the Charter itself.[50] Hence the events of the 15th are perhaps the most obscure of all. Indeed apart from the dating clause of the Charter there is only one certain piece of evidence: the fact that the 15th was the terminal date for the extension of the truce ordered on 10 June. It is scarcely likely that these two facts are unrelated. The letters of 10 June are very precise in that they extended the truce up to the early morning of the 15th.[51] They made no provision for lengthy discussion and it would seem that something was expected to happen, and happen quickly, which would make peace or war certain. That something

<hr />

[49] Walt. Cov. II, 222.   [50] Cheney (1956), 327–8.
[51] Rot. Litt. Pat. p. 143. Cp. the safe conduct of 8 June which ran to the end of the 11th ('ad diem completam': ibid.).

did happen is established by the dating clause of the Charter and it can only have been something which could be accepted as authorizing the Charter as a final settlement. The most likely explanation is that all parties present agreed to accept the Articles as a basis for a settlement. Such an act, carried out with due solemnity, would have had great significance. It would make it certain that a formal peace would now be concluded; it would raise the Articles from the status of a draft produced in committee to that of a preliminary settlement to which all who agreed at Runnymede were committed; and it would provide a point of authorization for the final terms of the Charter, for the Articles were the foundation on which the Charter was built. They were an interim arrangement in which a charter was already envisaged as the final form of settlement.[52]

This is hypothetical. Others have argued that the crucial event of the 15th was the drafting or the sealing of the Articles, others that the Charter itself was written and sealed on this day,[53] another again that a surviving 'draft' of the Charter was completed then and became the warrant for the final version.[54] All, however, have accepted that the meeting of the 15th occurred in an atmosphere of deep mutual suspicion between the two parties in which pledges and guarantees of some kind were essential to the achievement of a final settlement. This indeed left its mark on the choice of the place of meeting. Runnymede, as its name indicates, was a traditional site for assemblies. It was also conveniently placed between London and the king's base at Windsor, and it served the barons' purpose admirably. Staines, which became their base, lay on the north side of the river, Windsor on the south. The direct route between them lay over Staines bridge which carried the old Roman road from

---

[52] See below, pp. 250–1.
[53] For a further discussion of these views, see appendix 5, below, pp. 429–32.
[54] Galbraith (1967). For a discussion of 'drafts' see below, pp. 445–6.

London to Silchester. Hence they still had the river crossing as a defence, and their flank was protected on the north bank by the marshy valley of the Colne. Runnymede itself had similar admirable features. It was protected to the east and south by low-lying ground between Staines and Egham over which a causeway had to be constructed some years later.[55] A second line of defence was provided by a small stream which flowed down to the Thames in an easterly direction from a low range of hills culminating in Cooper's Hill to the west. Between Cooper's Hill itself and the meadow there was a series of ponds which marked an old river course.[56] Runnymede was almost an island.[57] When the barons entered this area from the east they could be sure that the king could only approach down the southern bank of the river from the west. There they negotiated in the open, at best under canvas, warily and in arms.

Some historians, including Stubbs himself, have held that the Great Charter was agreed on 15 June, that is before the first day of the plenary conference had ended.[58] Certainly, all parties must have felt some urgency, for, apart from the need to settle the quarrel and re-establish peace, Staines and Windsor must have been crowded with the baronial and royal parties. However, such an hypothesis is extremely unlikely, for 'firm' peace, as the contemporary records describe it, was not mentioned until the 18th and did not take effect until the 19th.[59] It seems, therefore, that the drafting of final terms took at least four days, and indeed monastic writers later recorded that there had been much discussion and negotiation to and fro.[60] There was a great deal to be done. The Articles only approached the formal

---

[55] *V.C.H. Surrey*, III, 420.   [56] Now known as Langham ponds.
[57] There is no evidence that the present so-called 'Magna Carta island' had anything to do with the ceremony or that it then existed as such.
[58] Stubbs states that the Articles were sealed on 15 June and the Charter 'issued' or 'executed' on the same day (Stubbs, 1897, I, 569; *Select Charters*, 6th ed., Oxford, 1888, p. 290). See also Bémont (1892), p. xxi; Norgate (1902), p. 234.
[59] See below, pp. 252–3.   [60] *Walt. Cov.* II, 221; *Chron. Maj.* II, 589.

language of a grant in the *forma securitatis*; they therefore had
to be redrafted appropriately almost throughout. Furthermore, those who had drafted the Articles had left certain
points on one side to be settled in the Charter. Cap. 1 stated
that heirs were to pay relief at the ancient rate to be laid
down in the Charter; the *forma securitatis* also left the interval
given the king for the correction of breaches of the agreement loosely defined as a 'reasonable period to be determined in the Charter'. Cap. 12 was even vaguer; it simply
demanded that weights and measures should be reformed.
All these points had to be settled and were settled in the
Charter. How it was done is not clear; the problem of
reliefs, at least, seems to have provoked an argument which
left its imprint on the phrasing of the Charter.[61] In other
cases the drafters of the Articles made more specific provision. In cap. 25 they deferred any decision on disseisins
committed by Henry II and Richard I to the consideration
of the archbishop and bishops. The effect of this was to refer
the king's claim to respite as a crusader to an ecclesiastical
committee.[62] This in turn affected the restitution of similar
disseisins to both the Welsh and the Scots which was
covered in caps. 45 and 46. By the time the Charter was
complete the archbishop and his suffragans had settled these
matters.[63] The Charter also included provisions which were
not in the Articles at all; the methods of summoning the
great council (cap. 14), the principle of amercement by peers
(cap. 21), and the afforestations made and custodies acquired
by Henry II and Richard I (cap. 53). At many points, too,
the Charter diverged in detail from the Articles, giving extra
legal precision here, covering the interests of the Crown
there, moving always towards greater length and complexity. All this must have required time, more if these matters
were decided in plenary sessions, which is unlikely, less if

---

[61] See below, p. 309.   [62] This included a stay of legal actions for three years.
[63] For a further discussion of these important clauses and of the ecclesiastical attitudes they
reveal, see below, pp. 286–8, 341–3, 359–66.

they were referred to committees, less again if the committee which had met on 10 June continued in session during the interval before the general assembly met at Runnymede. But, however the work was done, the time required cannot have been short. Many of these matters were among the most controversial in the Charter. The restitution of rights which cap. 25 of the Articles envisaged was to become one of the main causes of the renewal of the war in the autumn. The arguments which led from the Articles to the arrangements in the Charter must have been fought long and hard.

The Charter was not the only matter for discussion, for by itself it was only part of the settlement. It created work. Presumably the barons at Runnymede proceeded to elect the Twenty-Five barons. There must have been some discussion too of the methods whereby the Charter was to be put into effect, of how soon the Charter was to become effective, of when and how the barons were to lay down arms and restore London to the king.[64] Looming over all was the possibility of further intervention from Pope Innocent. This, too, was a point on which the Articles laid down stringent restrictions which were revised in the Charter.[65]

Hence the last stage of the settlement, the firm peace of 19 June, only came after a period of intensive negotiation and hard committee work. Peace was secured or made 'firm' by the renewal of the barons' homage, for by this and this alone was the state of war consequent on the baronial defiance brought to an end. It was a serious and formal act which must have been carried out by each erstwhile rebel individually, in an atmosphere of due solemnity. On 28 May John had received the regalia of the Empress Matilda at Reading from the custody of the Master of the Temple;[66] presuma-

---

[64] All these matters were later treated as integral parts of the peace agreement (see below, pp. 263–6, 481–3).
[65] For a further discussion of this, see below, pp. 288–9.   [66] *Rot. Litt. Pat.* p. 142.

bly it was now put to good use to re-emphasize the majesty of the Crown. That homage was renewed on 19 June is stated in writs to Stephen Haringod which John had authorized on the previous day.[67] And the object of these writs was not to announce or execute the Charter, but to restrain the king's agents from further acts of war after the deadline of the 19th. These two operations, the renewal of homage and the restraint of royal agents, were the essential features of peace. The king would not grant, nor would the barons accept, a concession of privileges while still at war, for it would offend the majesty of the one and deny legal title to the other. The point is clearly made in royal letters of 21 June addressed to Saer de Quincy, earl of Winchester: 'We order you to restore the castle of Fotheringhay, which we have committed to your custody, to Earl David as soon as he has done homage to us; and if by chance he dies before he has done homage then you shall restore the castle to us.'[68] Earl David of Huntingdon was not to enjoy the restoration of property due to him under the terms of the Charter until he was once more the king's man.

Neither of these acts was concerned with the terms of settlement; indeed, the letters to Stephen Haringod make no reference to the Charter. The terms were secured by a further oath, described in the Charter itself, in which all parties present, the barons as well as the king, swore to observe the terms it embodied in good faith and without evil intent.[69] The names of those in the king's party who swore the oath were listed, as if they were a counterpart to the

---

[67] For the text see appendix 11, p. 493. Kate Norgate has argued that the 'die Veneris' (19 June) of this writ is an error for 'die Lunae' (15 June) (Norgate, 1902, p. 234, n. 2). McKechnie, in contrast, followed Blackstone in arguing that the enrolling clerk erred in transcribing xxiii as xviii (McKechnie, 1914, p. 41; Blackstone, 1762, II, p. xxxvii). There is no sound reason for assuming that either mistake occurred. The writ is preceded on the rolls by writs of the 18th and followed by writs of the 19th. The situation is easily comprehensible if we imagine that John knew on the 18th that homage would be renewed on the following day and that he immediately authorized writs forbidding acts of war after the 19th with the intention of issuing them as soon as homage had been renewed. Cheney took a similar view (1956, 326, 331).

[68] *Rot. Litt. Pat.* p. 144.   [69] Cap. 63.

Twenty-Five.[70] These oaths were the crucial act whereby the Charter was put into effect; from now on it was law. As long as the oath remained neither the king nor his opponents could break the agreement without the taint of perjury.

It is a presumption, but a strong one, that this oath was also performed on 19 June. In later letters of 23 July it was stated that 'peace was made and sworn' as though they were inseparable acts.[71] The oath must have followed the renewal of homage,[72] and in all likelihood it must have preceded the authorization of writs concerned with the enforcement of particular clauses of the Charter both in individual cases and at large. Now several of these writs were dated 19 June. They included general letters providing for the election of juries in the counties for the investigation of evil customs under cap. 48 and for the enforcement of the oath of obedience to the Twenty-Five barons under cap. 61.[73] They also included the first of numerous letters concerned with the restoration of hostages under cap. 49 and with the restoration of property under cap. 52 to those who had been disseised by the Crown. These last dealt with problems which had not yet been settled when the Articles were drawn up.[74] By the 19th it seems clear that all uncertainty had now been removed, and that precisely those terms which are contained in the Charter were being enforced in the restoration of property.[75] If the Charter's

[70] See the 'obsecutores at observatores' in *Chron. Maj.* II, 605. The list includes all the lay advisers of M. C. proem except William, earl of Salisbury, Alan of Galloway, Peter fitz Herbert and John fitz Hugh. 'Hugo de Beneval' is probably Hugh de Neville.
[71] See appendix 11, below, p. 497.
[72] This is clearly established by cap. 62, which provides a pardon for all breaches of the peace arising from the quarrel between the two parties and covering the period from Easter 1215 'up to the establishment of peace' (*usque ad pacem reformatam*). This pardon, which clearly refers to the firm peace of 19 June, could not have been effective until after the renewal of homage had brought the war to an end.
[73] See below, appendix 11, pp. 493–5.   [74] See above, p. 251.
[75] The letters of restitution of 19 June and later sometimes dealt with castles, a point not mentioned in cap. 25 of the Articles, but inserted in cap. 52 of the Charter. The writ of 19 June ordering William of Salisbury to restore the honour of Trowbridge to Henry de Bohun is especially significant for while it makes a temporary exception in the case of Trowbridge castle, it clearly states that the terms of peace provided for the restoration of castles (see appendix 11, below, p. 495).

terms were now settled on these matters, which were among
the more debatable and controversial, it is likely that
the whole document had been agreed, that the terms
were known, and that, once homage had been renewed,
the oath to the terms of the Charter was also solemnly
performed.

Such seems the likeliest reconstruction of the events of 19
June. Some modern authorities have gone further and
suggested that the firm peace of the 19th was agreed with the
terms of the Charter still unsettled.[76] But whatever the
individual variants in recent reconstructions, most of them
have shared in a common effort to avoid anachronisms.
King John did not sign Magna Carta; there is no evidence
that he could write. He did not even seal it; sealing charters
was the task of the spigurnel, a member of the Chancery
staff.[77] Furthermore, there is no evidence at all that in the
ceremonies at Runnymede, either on 19 June or on any
other day, there was some kind of solemn and ceremonial
sealing of an 'original' Magna Carta. There is not even any
evidence that such a sealed 'original' ever existed; all that
survive are four charters, one, possibly two of which reside
in the counties to which they were sent in 1215;[78] and there
is no evidence that any sealed engrossment of the Charter
was available before 24 June when the first seven were
delivered for distribution.[79] All that was needed by 19 June
was an agreed draft, which stated the terms of settlement
fully and precisely and from which the sealed engrossments
could be copied. But there is no evidence of anything
equivalent to a modern exchange of contracts. Magna Carta
was not a treaty; we need not imagine that the barons carried
off a sealed charter in triumph.[80] The settlement of the 19th

---

[76] See Cheney (1956), 330–2.   [77] Crump (1928), 247–53.
[78] For further discussion, see appendix 6, below, pp. 441–2.
[79] See appendix 11, below, pp. 494–5.
[80] Some authorities have taken a different view (see Collins (1948), 245, 249). For a
criticism of this, see Cheney (1956), 334–5.

was made *viva voce*; it comprised verbal and formal acts –
the renewal of homage and the oath to observe the terms of
settlement. It was reinforced not by bonds of parchment,
but by the solemnity of an oath and the dread and political
disadvantages of perjury; and the terms of settlement provided for the immediate extension of this oath so that all
throughout the land should be bound in one great 'commune of the realm' devoted to its observance.[81]

Yet the oath is testimony to the existence of the document
with its terms fully stated. So also are the Letters Testimonial in which the archbishops, the bishops and the papal
nuncio inspected the Charter, attested its terms and guaranteed that nothing would be added or taken away.[82] These
are undated. Nevertheless, the oath, the document and the
Letters Testimonial were in a neat triangular relationship in
which each subsumed the others. The tie was close. The
names of the great churchmen in the Letters Testimonial are
exactly the same as those in cap. 1 of the Charter, arranged in
exactly the same order, with the same protocol. Of the
three, the document was prime; without it there could be no
oath and no *inspeximus*. But the form which it took,
whether it was a sealed charter – an 'original', or an agreed
and final draft – a warrant for the charter exemplifications,
is, on the face of it, a matter of pure guesswork. Another
conjecture is more probable and more important. It is
reasonable to suppose that, before the rebellious barons
made their peace by renewing homage, they would want to
know what they were getting in return, what, in short, the
king and his men were swearing to observe. If so, the terms
must have been proclaimed, and the Charter itself may well
bear the mark of such a proclamation; for, immediately after
the address and invocation, it opens with the names of those
who had given their counsel and advice, from the archbishops of Canterbury and Dublin, the bishops, the papal

---

[81] Cap. 61   [82] See below, pp. 491–2.

envoy to the great earls of the king's party and others of his barons, allies and supporters. Then in the penultimate sentence of the Charter, these same men attest the grant – 'Witness the above mentioned and many others.' Thus the commitment of the witnesses is stated, and their function as advisers enhanced, right at the beginning of the Charter. This unusual arrangement suggests that before the terms were announced they were given all the weight, both ecclesiastical and lay, which it was possible to muster in support at Runnymede by the simple measure of announcing the witnesses right at the beginning.[83] The same was done in the reissues of 1216 and, less emphatically in 1217, the one issued during, the other at the end of, the civil war. By 1225 normality had returned and red tape was reapplied; as in any other charter the witnesses are at the end.

So the terms were probably proclaimed. Indeed it is difficult to see how otherwise men could have been brought to the final peace of 19 June. If so, there is one important corollary. Not even our most optimistic estimate of the literacy of the Anglo-Norman baronage would allow us to assume that such a long and complex document was proclaimed in Latin. It must have been done in the vernacular of the aristocracy, in Anglo-Norman. Such a translation does indeed survive.[84]

Like the Articles of the Barons, the Charter would most probably be drafted by a Chancery clerk; three of the surviving exemplifications were certainly engrossed in Chancery. The king's clerks may have been ready, or been instructed, to break their usual practice in locating witness-lists in order to meet the special circumstances at Runnymede. But they turned always to Chancery practice. They were providing a legal instrument, not an historical record. Hence they referred to events in the past tense on the

[83] Perhaps even more than could be mustered, for it is possible that one of the attestors, William of Salisbury, was in fact absent. See below p. 444.
[84] See below, pp. 474–7.

assumption or in the knowledge that these events would occur as part of the settlement, not in the knowledge that they had already taken place at the time of drafting. Thus the *forma securitatis* of the Articles refers to the peace and liberties which 'the lord king has conceded and confirmed by his charter' at a time when the Charter could not even have been drafted, still less sealed and delivered. Similarly, the *inspeximus* of the Charter provided in the Letters Testimonial, in which the bishops attested the terms of the Charter,[85] cannot have existed when cap. 62 of the Charter was drafted with the words 'we have caused letters testimonial to be made for them'. Yet the Charter as a whole recorded an act of concession which had taken place in the past. 'Know ... that we have granted to God and have confirmed by this our present charter ... and we have granted to all free men of our realm' – these are the operative phrases typical of the English charter of this time, and they reflect the fact that a charter was not a dispositive but an evidentiary document. It was a record of a transaction agreed verbally by the parties concerned and executed by some kind of formal and public act; in the case of grant of land, by livery of seisin. In such a straightforward act a charter was not even essential to a grant, although a grantee expected and usually got one.[86] It is unlikely that Magna Carta departed from usual practice in these matters; indeed the king's opponents had every reason for insisting that it was followed. Hence the Charter became law, not when the first exemplification was sealed, but when the king and those present at Runnymede solemnly swore to observe its terms. This act gave immediate authority to the terms of settlement. Each exemplification of the Charter, in contrast, was a record which provided evidence for those not present at

[85] On these, see below, pp. 491–2.
[86] For a discussion of these problems see Plucknett (1948), pp. 577–9; F.M. Stenton, *Transcripts of Charters relating to Gilbertine Houses*, xviii (Lincoln Record Soc., 1922), pp. xvi ff.; V. H. Galbraith, 'Monastic Foundation Charters of the 11th and 12th centuries', *Cambridge Historical Journal*, iv (1934), 205–22.

Runnymede and for generations yet to come of what had been agreed. It is for this reason that the Charter, in the view of modern authorities, has come to be 'disengaged from the recorded ceremonial of 19 June'.[87] It was so also for monastic writers at the time. The Coggeshall chronicler describes events at Runnymede in the following manner:

A quasi peace was made between the king and the barons and all swore on holy relic to observe it inviolate, even the king. And then the form of peace was drawn up in a charter so that each county throughout England should have a charter of the same tenor certified with the royal seal.[88]

The Dunstable annalist gives roughly the same sequence of events:

At length they met at Runnymede and on 19 June peace was made between the king and the barons, which lasted only for a little time. And the king received homage, which the barons had withdrawn at the beginning of the civil war . . . And the king then restored to many of them their castles and other rights, and charters were completed there concerning the liberties of the realm of England which were deposited in safe keeping in each bishopric.[89]

The Barnwell writer gives a different sequence but he was equally clear that the essential features of the peace were formal and verbal, and that the Charter was simply confirmatory.

They agreed a place where the parties could meet conveniently, and after long discussions they were reconciled, for the king agreed to everything they wished and confirmed it by his charter. Thus those who were present were received into the kiss of peace and renewed their homage and fealty.[90]

The Charter, once sealed, should have settled matters, as indeed the barons and the archbishop hoped and intended. It was granted in perpetuity. It committed John and his successors publicly for all time. A sealed charter changed the game. Landowners at all social levels were well aware of the value of such documents. This is well illustrated by the

---

[87] The words are Cheney's (1956, 333).   [88] *Coggeshall*, p. 172.
[89] *Annales Monastici*, III, 43.   [90] *Walt. Cov.* II, 221.

arrangements made in 1224 between the men of Wycombe and Richard Terry, steward of Robert de Vieuxpont. Richard certified in writing that Alan Basset was surety that Robert would affix his seal to the deed concerning common of pasture in Wycombe to be executed between Robert and Alan on the one hand and the men of Wycombe on the other. The seal was to be affixed by Michaelmas 1224. If not, Richard agreed that Alan would seize his lands in Wycombe and surrender them to the men of Wycombe for them to hold until the deed had been sealed.[91] The preservation, loss or destruction of charters could determine the survival or disappearance of privileges. John was clearly very sensitive to their importance in his relations with his vassals. When he granted the lordship of Westmorland to Robert de Vieuxpont in 1203 Robert had to undertake that he would not use or show to anyone the charter recording the grant as long as the king lived, except with the king's consent.[92] It was characteristic of the age and essential to the situation that such arrangements, which enfeebled charters, were themselves recorded in charters.

Where high policy was involved men showed similar concern for the acquisition, preservation or destruction of documentary records. When Henry II made peace with his eldest son and his allies in 1174 he insisted on the surrender of the charters which the young king had made out in favour of the Count of Flanders.[93] In 1215 John himself demanded that the barons should confirm the renewal of their fealty in writing. They did not respond. This did not invalidate their renewal of fealty, but John clearly wanted documentary confirmation and made it known that he had not got it. In 1217 the Treaty of Lambeth apparently provided for the restoration of John's charter of liberties along with other

91 *Cal. Ancient Deeds*, I, no. A 388.
92 *H.M.C. Wells MSS*, II, 549: and see Holt (1961), pp. 221, 226. Compare the arrangements made with Henry de Bohun concerning the earldom of Hereford in 1200, above, pp. 160–1.
93 *Gesta Henrici*, I, 82–3.

government records in the possession of the French.[94] Two generations later Edward I used the occasion of his Scottish campaigns to recover the documents which embodied the agreements between the rebel barons of 1215 and Alexander II of Scotland.[95] The track of potentially damaging documents was still being followed, and they were being collected, perhaps for destruction, perhaps for future use. For the Crown the Great Charter was the most damaging of all. No doubt Edward would have liked to dispatch that too to some quiet shelf of oblivion, but by this time its position had been secured by repeated re-issue and confirmation. It was already well on its way to immortality.

Magna Carta owed some of its durability to its form and to the care with which it was drafted. It was not a treaty but a freely given grant in perpetuity, made 'in reverence for God and for the salvation of our soul and those of all our ancestors and heirs, to the honour of God and the exaltation of Holy Church'. Such an act, whether royal or private, was invalid if issued under duress. Now John was certainly acting under strong compulsion when he issued the Charter. Pope Innocent annulled it partly on the grounds that it had been granted under duress,[96] and one of the king's friends, William Briwerre, later used the same argument to oppose the confirmation of 1224.[97] But the fact of force mattered less than its appearance. The king would not have executed a solemn grant in perpetuity in favour of men who were not yet in his peace.[98] To his opponents also it must have

[94] Richardson (1944), 426 n.   [95] *Acts of Parliament of Scotland*, I, 108, 111–12.
[96] *Selected Letters of Innocent III*, p. 215.   [97] *Chron. Maj.* III, 76.
[98] It seems arguable at first sight that the king had already granted a charter to men technically his enemies, namely the charter of 9 May. To a large extent, however, this charter duplicated the letters patent of 10 May, and if any document was sent to the rebels at this stage it was the letters patent, accompanied by similar ones making individual concessions to Geoffrey de Mandeville and the Bishop of Hereford. The charter of the 9th, in contrast, seems to have been a public announcement of the conditions John was attaching to his offer. Finally, none of these documents were grants in perpetuity. They simply announced temporary concessions pending the arbitration of the committee of eight and the pope. John's attitude to his offer is clearly indicated in his letter to the pope of 29 May: '... in tantum nos humiliavimus quod haec praedicta eis optulimus' (*Foedera*, I, part I, 129).

seemed essential that the Charter should appear to have been granted freely and without duress, for anything less would deprive it of validity and ease the way for papal annulment, the possibility of which they clearly recognized. For different reasons both parties must have wanted to eliminate the impression that the Charter had been traded for a baronial renewal of homage, however much this impression represented the underlying situation.

From this point of view, the terms used in the Charter and related documents are interesting. The writs issued in execution of the Charter make it quite clear that a war had occurred. The letter patent to Stephen Haringod refers to the prisoners and hostages taken 'because of this war'[99] and several letters order the restitution of property 'as before the war'[100] or mention the seizure of land and chattels 'because of the war'.[101] More significantly still, in the agreement on London, Robert fitz Walter still styled himself 'Marshal of the Army of God and Holy Church'.[102] In these documents the writers showed no inhibitions. In the Charter, however, the atmosphere is quite different. Although it describes itself as a peace,[103] it mentions no war. The trouble has simply been a *discordia*,[104] a dispute, and the baronial acts of war simply *transgressiones*,[105] or breaches of the peace. The whole atmosphere of the Charter is one of legality. Thus, under cap. 61 a plaintiff was to seek redress of the king and, in the case of default, compulsion was to be achieved not by war but by 'distraining and molesting us'. The difference in tone between the Charter and associated documents may be partly explained by John's unwillingness hitherto to admit publicly that the situation had been

---

[99] *Rot. Litt. Pat.* p. 143*b*.   [100] *Ibid.*   [101] *Rot. Litt. Claus.* I, 215*b*–16*b*.
[102] See appendix II, below, pp. 490–1.   [103] Caps. 51, 52, 61.
[104] Caps. I, 61, 62. The term *discordia* was often used to mean a wider period than that of the war (see, for instance, Magna Carta, cap. I). This distinction, however, was not always clearly made (see Magna Carta, cap. 62, and the writ to Stephen Haringod (appendix II, below, p. 493)).
[105] Cap. 62.

one of war.[106] But the main factor must have been that while the writs were simply administrative instruments, the Charter was a solemn concession in perpetuity 'concerning the liberties and security of the kingdom'.[107] It must therefore contain no hint that force had gone into its making.[108]

In some ways therefore the Great Charter withdrew itself from the circumstances of conflict which had given it birth. One effect of this was that it was not in itself sufficient to re-establish peace or even secure its own execution. Some problems, like the election of county juries for the investigation of evil customs and the enforcement of the oath to the Twenty-Five, were simple enough and were covered by writs of 19 June directed to the sheriffs. Other problems were not so easy. Since the Charter would not admit its origin in force, it could scarcely call on force to secure its own execution. In fact it contained nothing to secure its own observance, except its reference to the king's oath to observe its terms. Force was applied in a completely separate document, an agreement concerning the custody of London. This, unlike the Charter, was a treaty; it described itself as such; it was made between the king on the one hand and Robert fitz Walter, 'Marshal of the Army of God', and other earls and barons on the other; it was drawn up as an indenture in sealed counterparts which were exchanged; the part which carried the barons' seals still survives in the Public Record Office.[109] It is this document which applied the screw. It laid down that the barons were to continue to hold London and that the archbishop was to have custody of the Tower until 15 August. By then the oaths to obey the Twenty-Five were to be exacted throughout the land as laid

[106] See above, pp. 232–3, 241.
[107] The phrase is taken from the Treaty on London (see appendix II, below, pp. 490–1).
[108] Compare Galbraith (1966), especially p. 309 – 'The whole thing is a sham: in form a free grant of a sovereign king to his subjects in perpetuity: in fact a baronial walk-over.'
[109] Chancery Miscellanea 34/1/1. It is described in the *Catalogue of the Museum of the Public Record Office* (H.M.S.O. 1948), p. 19 (see Pls. 10, 11).

down in the writs of 19 June, and the king was to meet all claims against him to the restoration of rights and property, whether admitted by himself or adjudicated by the Twenty-Five. If all this was done by 15 August, or if outstanding claims were delayed through no fault of the king, then the capital and the Tower were to be restored to him; otherwise they were to remain in the hands of the barons and the archbishop respectively. Hence the baronial possession of London, which had compelled the king to accept the rebels' demands in the first place, was now used to enforce the execution of the Charter, especially in those clauses which in providing for the restoration of rights brought the king the most immediate hurt and the barons the most tangible gain. If the Charter avoided force studiously, this exploited it brutally, and in a manner but barely cloaked by the fiction that the barons continued to hold the city as bailiffs of the king. These were not the bailiffs John would have chosen of his own accord.

The treaty is undated. It has been suggested, on no very compelling grounds, that it should be allocated to the third week in July, when a conference was held at Oxford.[110] But there is no real doubt that it belongs to 19 June or thereabouts. It is unlikely that the barons agreed to terms without imposing just such a time limit on their execution as the treaty imposed. Nor is it likely that the king would have accepted a firm peace without some agreement on the custody of London. The treaty is clearly closely linked to some of the documents of June. It refers to the letters patent of 19 June providing for the taking of oaths to the Twenty-Five.[111] Its arrangements about the custody of the Tower were made in the light of baronial claims apparently made in

---

[110] Richardson (1944), p. 424. Cheney (1968, pp. 292–301) supported Richardson's conclusion. Galbraith, in contrast, favoured the opinion put forward above (1967, pp. 354–5). The issue is discussed below, pp. 481–3.
[111] It does not refer to the letters to sheriffs and juries of the counties of 27 June as McKechnie stated (1914, p. 43, n. 4).

June.[112] The deadline of 15 August, if it was to be taken seriously, can scarcely have been arranged very much later than June.[113] Letters of 23 July addressed to the barons of Yorkshire put the matter beyond serious question.[114] These ordered the restoration of castles, goods, prisoners and ransoms, and they state that such restoration was part of the 'peace agreement' and was to be concluded by 15 August. Now the words used for the agreement (*reformacio pacis*) were used in 1215 for the agreement of 19 June and no other; the provision for the restoration of prisoners and ransoms clearly refers to the writ of 18 June to Stephen Haringod;[115] and the provision for the restoration of castles and the mention of the date of 15 August can only come, among surviving documents, from the treaty. These letters therefore establish that the treaty was an integral part of the settlement at Runnymede.

This treaty is of crucial importance in our understanding of the events of the summer of 1215. Far more than the Charter it dealt with the realities of power. Far more than the Charter it demonstrated the unease and suspicion which lay between the two opposing parties. Much more clearly than the Charter it emphasized that the restoration of right and the satisfaction of ancient claims lay at the very heart of the baronial demands. These were here made the test of the king's good faith and it was in this that the breakdown of the settlement of June occurred most rapidly and most obviously. This was not simply because King John failed to keep good faith, although he tried to evade both the letter

[112] The Barnwell annalist states that the Tower was placed in the archbishop's custody after Geoffrey de Mandeville had laid claim to it. He associated this with the general restoration of rights which followed 19 June (*Walt. Cov.* II, 221). The treaty implies that some judgement was pending in the phrase 'saving to whomsoever his right in the custody of the Tower of London' (appendix II, below, pp. 490–1).

[113] It is worth noting that the archbishop and bishops later chose 16 August as the day on which outstanding issues between the two parties should be settled with their mediation. The implication seems to be that they would adjudicate on matters still unsettled at the term of expiry of the treaty (*Walt. Cov.* II, 223).

[114] See appendix II, below, p. 497.

[115] See appendix II, below, p. 493, and above, p. 253, on the problem of the date.

and spirit of his promises quickly enough, but because he was required to accept the barons' decision on what he was to restore to his subjects. This was more than either he or the pope could stomach. Yet the chances of war had given the barons such advantages that they could scarcely ask for less. This was an irreconcilable conflict of attitudes and interests. The Charter passed over it. The treaty revealed it, but did nothing to solve it. It proved soluble only by war.

CHAPTER 8

THE QUALITY OF
THE GREAT CHARTER

Historians have debated long and hard about the quality of
Magna Carta. The debate has not been about that alone, but
also about the origins of the Charter and the character of the
men who produced it. This necessary attempt to carry the
argument outwards into broader fields has contributed to
some confusion in which assessments of the Charter and
assessments of the men who were involved have been used
to determine the problem of origin and responsibility. On
this Stubbs's attitude was certain, clear and consistent. For
him Magna Carta was the greatest single formative document in English history, and he was under no doubt that the
barons of the opposition were in the main responsible for it:
'Who were the barons that now impose limits on royal
tyranny, and place themselves in the vanguard of liberty?
How have they come to sit in the seats and wield the swords
of those whom so lately we saw arrayed in feudal might
against king and people?'[1] As to their character Stubbs was
in no doubt: 'The barons maintain and secure the right of the
whole people as against themselves as well as against their
master'; their demands 'were no selfish exaction of privilege
for themselves';[2] they had 'cut themselves loose from
Normandy and Norman principles and reconciled themselves to the nobler position of leaders of their brother
Englishmen'.[3]

These views were at first accepted by Tout, for whom
Robert fitz Walter was 'the first champion of English
liberty',[4] but most historians of Tout's generation showed

[1] Stubbs (1896), I, 579.   [2] *Ibid.* I, 570.   [3] *Ibid.* I, 571.
[4] *D.N.B.* VII, 222.

increasing doubt. Stubbs's approach lay open to a double attack, first against his attitude to the Charter and secondly against his attitude to the baronage. The earliest critics followed both lines of argument. As early as 1894 Petit-Dutaillis argued that the 'barons had no suspicion that they would one day be called the founders of English liberty' and that the Charter simply embodied the immediate practical interests which had driven them into rebellion.[5] In 1908 he went further and stated that the Charter marked 'an ecclesiastical and aristocratic reaction against the growth of the crown', and that 'its most salient characteristic' was 'the restoration of the old feudal law'.[6] Meanwhile in 1904 Edward Jenks had roundly denounced both the Charter and its authors. For him the Charter was not so much a landmark as a stumbling block in English constitutional development. It was the work of the class 'which cherished memories of the days when every baron was king in his own land', and hence it preserved class distinctions and embodied class interests. Determined to have a clean sweep, Jenks ended by including all concerned in his denunciation: 'John and William Marshall and even Stephen Langton, are not to be mentioned in the same breath with Edward I, and Robert Burnell, and Winchelsey.'[7]

These were the most striking but not the most serious attacks on Stubbs. Indeed, they shared in the historical method they were attacking, for neither Petit-Dutaillis's resuscitation of the 'feudal law' nor Jenks's assumption that class interests and constitutional progress are inconsistent was any more realistic than Stubbs's concept of national liberty. They have not been followed up wholeheartedly.[8]

---

5 Petit-Dutaillis (1894), pp. 57–8.
6 Petit-Dutaillis (1908), I, 129. The French edition of Stubbs, to which these studies were appended, was published in 1907. Tout arranged the English translation.
7 Jenks (1904), 260–73, esp. pp. 263, 272.
8 J. E. A. Joliffe continued this line of argument, although with much greater subtlety: 'While the rebels as a party turned a fraction of John's inventiveness against him, their secular leaders were, as individuals, deeply involved in the feudal past . . . In politics, in

Stubbs's defences were not so much stormed as infiltrated by a route which he himself had opened. He had clearly appreciated and carefully stated that the barons who won the Charter were subject to other influences. In his view, Stephen Langton 'sympathized with, and partly inspired and advised the confederates'; hence, in the Charter, 'it was probably by the bishops, Langton in particular, and the legal members of the confederacy, that the rights of the freeholder were so carefully fenced round with provisions'.[9] This now created an opportunity of retaining the Charter while casting out the baronage. It was soon taken. In 1902 Kate Norgate argued that the barons were

no more capable of rising to the lofty conception embodied in the Charter – the conception of a contract between king and people which should secure equal rights to every class and every individual in the nation – than they were capable of formulating it in the minute details and the carefully chosen phraseology of the Charter or even of the Articles . . . The terms were drawn up by Stephen Langton with the concurrence of the other bishops who were at hand, and of the few lay barons, on either side, who were statesmen enough to look at the crisis from a higher standpoint than that of personal interest.[10]

Kate Norgate's views have been followed frequently by later writers.[11] Not all have been ready to allow, with her, that even a few of the barons might have been statesman-like.[12] Others have rightly pointed to the influence which the king's advisers and administrators must have had.[13] But in the main Langton has been accepted as a preponderant influence.

These later views depended heavily on Sir Maurice

the wider sense of a constitution, the Great Charter is therefore nothing – worse, it is an arrest of progress towards a better co-ordinated community and a more strictly governed state' (1952, 88–103, esp. 90–1).
9   Stubbs (1896), I, 571, 582.
10   Norgate (1902), p. 234.
11   See, for example, McKechnie (1914) (1st ed., 1905), p. 62; McIlwain (1939), p. 103; Painter (1949), pp. 314–15, 347; *idem* (1947), 47–8.
12   See Painter's view that it was impossible for Langton to 'overcome John's intransigence and the all-consuming greed of the barons' (1949, p. 347).
13   Poole (1951), pp. 470–9.

Powicke's Ford Lectures on Stephen Langton delivered in 1927. Yet Powicke himself did not share them. Instead he was in the true line of descent from Stubbs. He had already pointed out in 1917 that 'Archbishop Langton and several of the barons on each side were not likely to overlook the growing significance of the freeman in English society'[14] and ten years later he went out of his way to reassert the essentials of Stubbs's attitude towards the baronage in general: 'Let us call the charter a baronial document as much as we please, but do not let us imply thereby that it was a piece of selfish and reactionary class legislation.' The barons in Powicke's view were men versed in the affairs of state, who were 'not mentally incapable of discussing general customs with a bishop, or too proud to speak to a prosperous burgess'; their party included hotheads, and some had wrongs to avenge, but their programme was 'the outcome of long deliberation, not solely concocted in haste or passion, but derived from saner counsels'. In these counsels Langton shared.[15] It is a pity that these cautious and balanced views have had less influence with later writers than the passages in which Powicke described Langton's dramatic interventions between the king and the baronage, for in essentials these were based directly on the chronicle of Roger of Wendover. It was Wendover rather than any modern writer who first produced Langton as a *deus ex machina*, and Wendover has remained the basis of the case for Langton ever since.[16] These are shifting sands on which to found an argument.[17] Few have been ready to abandon them.[18] Yet in the end it is

[14] *M.C.C.E.* p. 109.   [15] Powicke (1928), pp. 120–8, esp. pp. 122, 128.
[16] Compare Cheney's comments on Wendover's evidence on the alleged deposition of King John (1948a, pp. 107–8).
[17] See above, pp. 215, 219, 224–6.
[18] See, for example, Davis (1963), pp. 10–11, where, despite the author's warnings on the unreliability of Wendover, the main incidents of Wendover's narrative are still retained. Among later writers, Richardson & Sayles (1963, pp. 337–6) have gone furthest in questioning the influence of Langton. They have not, however, re-examined the evidence on Langton's activities in 1215 or the evidence of the Charter itself. Moreover their arguments on the responsibility of the baronage do much to revive

the documents rather than the chroniclers which provide the most reliable evidence.

However, the evidence of the documents is far from clear or easy to use. It is scarcely valid, for example, to select this or that clause or group of clauses as typifying the quality of the Charter without establishing that the contemporary importance of these sections justifies their selection. A failure to do this undoubtedly contributed, for example, to the anachronistic interpretations which have been inflicted on caps. 12 and 39. Indeed, one of the virtues of Petit-Dutaillis's approach was that he attempted, by using the contemporary authority of the *Histoire des ducs de Normandie*, to establish some kind of standard relevant to the circumstances of 1215:[19]

The king went to Staines [so the *Histoire* states] and there he had to accept such terms as the barons wished. He was forced to agree that a woman should never be married so that she would be disparaged; this was the best agreement which he made with them, had it been well kept. In addition he had to agree that he would never cause a man to lose life or limb for any wild beast that he took, but that he should be able to pay a fine. These two things could easily be borne. He had to fix reliefs for land, which had been excessive, at such a figure as they wished. They wished to have all powers of *haute justice* in their lands. And they demanded many other things, with good reason, of which I make no mention. Above all this they wanted Twenty-Five barons to be chosen so that the king should treat them in all matters by the judgement of these Twenty-Five. He would redress through these all the wrongs he did them and they likewise would redress through these all the wrongs they did him. And they also wished that the king would not appoint any bailiff anywhere in his land except through the Twenty-Five. The king agreed to all this by force, and for the observance of this peace gave his charter to the barons as one who could do no other.[20]

Compared with the documents, this is *ex parte* and single-minded evidence, in which the author viewed the Charter as

---

Stubbs's original thesis. As I have shown above, Stubbs was not, and did not need to be, an extravagant protagonist of Langton.

[19] Petit-Dutaillis (1894), pp. 57–8; (1908), pp. 131–4.

[20] *Histoire des ducs de Normandie*, pp. 149–50. I have relied to some extent on the translation in Petit-Dutaillis (1908), p. 132.

a document of exclusively baronial privilege. It is relevant, but inaccurate[21] and in no way decisive. In comparison the documents themselves are far less clear-cut. One confusing factor is the contrast between the form and content of the settlement. In form it was conventional and conservative. In the circumstances of 1215, when papal annulment was probable, it had to be.[22] The liberties were conveyed by a solemn grant in perpetuity embodied in a charter. The settlement was guaranteed by oaths and by the pledge of the capital. Its execution was to be enforced by distraint, the customary method which all understood and used. Some of the content of the Charter also fitted this traditional pattern. It was obviously concerned, among other things, with baronial privilege. In restoring rights, it concluded a suit in the king's court and provided for the conduct of further suits. It bore the imprint of the campaign which had achieved it. It followed the pattern set by the Charter of Henry I in devoting its first section to the liberties of the Church. The next sections, as in Henry's charter, were concerned with the king's feudal rights. Magna Carta, like Henry's charter, represented an attempt to state the detailed implications of the oath to destroy evil and maintain just customs which kings swore at their coronation.

However, not all the content of the Charter is consistent with such an interpretation, still less with the lurid light of class privilege which the *Histoire* throws upon it. In the first place the Charter was a grant to 'all free men of our realm'. It presupposed a wider market for its benefactions than is suggested by the *Histoire*. It was not unique in this. The ordinances of León of 1188 were issued in favour of 'all of my realm, clerical and lay'[23] and they were drawn up in a session of the king's court which included citizens and

---

[21] Magna Carta contained no provision about punishment for offences against the king's venison or the appointment of the king's bailiffs.
[22] See above, pp. 261–3.   [23] Muñoz y Romero (1847), pp. 102–3.

knights as well as magnates and bishops.[24] The Golden Bull of Hungary of 1222 was conceded to 'nobles and other men of the realm'.[25] In Aragon the *Privilegio General* of 1283 was granted to 'nobles, mesne tenants, knights, *infanciones*, citizens and all and every man in our realm'.[26] In Sicily one of the conditions which Urban IV laid down for Charles of Anjou was that he should maintain the privileges of 'counts, barons, knights and all men in his realm'.[27] Perhaps on the continent there was a more obvious tendency to enumerate the various social grades on which privileges were conferred, but this in itself is scarcely significant. The Magna Carta of 1225 was granted not to 'all free men of our realm' as in 1215 but to 'archbishops, bishops, abbots, priors, earls, barons, and all of our realm'. With this list few continental grants could compete.

Some of the continental liberties, however, were much more restricted than these. The concessions made at Constance in 1183 were concerned exclusively with the privileges of the towns of the Lombard League.[28] Frederick II's concessions of 1220 were addressed to the ecclesiastical princes of the Empire[29] as were those of 1231–2 to the secular princes and magnates.[30] A narrow base for privilege was again revealed in the Sicilian concessions of 1283 which were made to 'barons, counts and other holders of fiefs'.[31] It was illustrated finally, and perhaps most clearly of all, in the various petitions, ordinances, and charters produced in France during the crisis of 1314–15. These occasionally suggest that the demands made against the king were widely based. The resistance to the Crown in Picardy, Artois, Beauvaisis, Vermandois and Ponthieu came from a league of

---

[24] *Ibid.* pp. 102, 106. On the representative capacity of the citizens, see Post (1943), 211–32. See also, on the restricted sense of 'boni homines' in cap. 3 of the decrees, Evelyn S. Procter, 'The interpretation of clause 3 of the decrees of León (1188)', *E.H.R.*, LXXXV (1970), 45–53.
[25] Marczali (1901), p. 134.   [26] *Herrschaftsverträge, p. 23*.
[27] *Reg. Urban IV*, II, 122.   [28] *M.G.H., Const.* I, 411 ff.   [29] *Ibid.* II, 89.
[30] *Ibid.* II, 211.   [31] Trifone (1921), pp. 99–100.

the nobility and lesser men.[32] In Burgundy the league included the representatives from eleven towns.[33] In Normandy Louis X recorded that there had been complaints from 'prelates, churchmen, knights, other nobles and subjects and the commons'.[34] But such evidence is rare and meant very little. Most of the documents of these quarrels told a different story. In 1314 Philip the Fair's concessions were made 'at the instance of barons and nobles of the realm of France, leagued together to recover the privileges, liberties, franchises, customs and immunities enjoyed by churchmen, dukes, counts and other subjects of the King of the French in the time of St Louis'.[35] In Normandy Louis X negotiated with the 'barons, knights and other noble subjects and bishops',[36] in Burgundy with the 'nobles' or 'the clergy and nobles',[37] in Amiénois with the 'nobles'[38] and in Champagne with the 'nobles and other persons'.[39]

Throughout Europe the sharp aristocratic flavour of these documents fairly represented their real content. In the kingdom of Sicily the concessions of 1283 paid some attention to the great towns of southern Italy, but it was in the main concerned with aristocratic privilege. It laid down for example that 'no services were to be demanded from counts, barons and other noble and knightly men, which did not become their estate and condition'.[40] In Germany the concessions of 1220 and 1231 were aimed at securing princely privilege even to the damage of the towns which turned to seek imperial protection against aristocratic encroachment. In France the ordinance of 1314 and the

---

[32] Dufayard (1894a), 245–6.   [33] Ibid. 248.
[34] 'Gravem querimoniam prelatorum, ecclesiasticarum personarum, militum, aliorum nobilium, et subditorum, ac popularium, Ducatus nostri Normannie recepimus' (Ordonnances, 1, 587–8).
[35] Dufayard (1894b), 289   [36] Ordonnances, 1, 551.   [37] Ibid. 1, 558, 569.
[38] Ibid. 1, 562.   [39] Ibid. 1, 573–4 (cp. ibid, 1, 577).
[40] 'Item statuimus quod comitibus, baronibus et aliis nobilibus et militaribus viris, per justitiarios et alios officiales curie nulla servitiorum executio demandetur que statum et conditionem eorum non deceat' (Trifone, 1921, p. 100).

provincial charters of 1315 were almost exclusively concerned with the maintenance and revival of feudal jurisdiction, with the recovery of the right of private war, with the exclusion of royal officials from fiefs and with the exemption of the nobility from royal jurisdiction. These were the foundation charters of a *noblesse*. They promoted rather than healed class division. In 1316 Philip V was able to persuade the nobles of Champagne to abandon their conspiracy by arguing that aristocratic leagues excited the lower orders. The leagues did in fact provoke isolated attacks against seignorial jurisdiction.[41] The contemporary song, the *Dit des Alliés*, blamed the nobles for seeking their own selfish ends and argued that justice was to be sought not at the hands of the aristocracy but from the Crown.[42] In some areas such charges were justified. In Champagne the league was sustained by the personal ambition of Louis de Nevers, in Picardy by the intervention of Robert of Artois, who was pursuing a claim to that county, and by Robert, count of Flanders.[43] In Picardy the towns sided with the Crown.

Magna Carta provoked nothing like the *Dit des Alliés*.[44] This was a fair reflexion of its quality. It was not alone in taking non-baronial interests into account. Just as Magna Carta limited the amercement of villeins so as not to deprive them of their livelihood and restricted the king's bailiffs' exercise of purveyance, so the Golden Bull of Hungary provided that the king's ministers as they followed the court or moved about the country were not to oppress or despoil the poor, and that counts were to lose their offices if they

---

[41] Dufayard (1894*a*), 266–7. For a peasants' rising see *Rec. Hist. Franc.* XXI, 43. Discontent was increased by the bad harvests and plague of 1314–15.
[42] P. Paris (ed.), *Annuaire Historique* (1837), pp. 158–71. For comment, see Dufayard (1894*a*), 267–70.
[43] Dufayard (1894*b*), 267–71.
[44] Nor did the baronial movement of 1258. Here the Song of Lewes makes an interesting comparison with the *Dit des Alliés*.

'destroyed' the people in their charge.[45] But Magna Carta acknowledged non-baronial interests far more than most of the continental concessions and it covered a wider range of such interests more thoroughly than any other similar grant. This is partly revealed in the clauses concerned with municipal privilege, with trade, and with the interests of freeholders. It is demonstrated most convincingly of all in cap. 60 which laid down that all the liberties which the king had conferred on his men they in their turn would confer on their men. This was not simply laid down as an airy principle. It was enforced precisely in cap. 15 of the Charter, which provided that the king should not grant permission for anyone to take an aid from his vassals except on the three occasions on which the Crown itself might take a gracious aid. Similarly cap. 16, which laid down that nobody was to be compelled to do more service than he ought for his tenement, was equally applicable whether the lord was the king or a great baron. So also were the provisions on wardship, marriage and the rights of widows.[46] When the framers of the Charter set out to protect the interests of under-tenants, they meant business. Within ten years knights and freeholders in Westmorland and Lancashire appealed to the principles of cap. 60 against the magnates of these counties and the Crown proceeded to order its enforcement.[47]

This comprehensive quality of Magna Carta was revealed in many different ways. It was a grant to all free men throughout the realm.[48] The French charters of 1315, in

[45] 'Jobagiones ita sequantur curiam vel quocumque proficiscantur, ut pauperes per eos non opprimantur nec spolientur.'
'Si quis comes honorifice se iuxta comitatus sui qualitatem non habuerit vel destruxerit populos castri sui, convictus super hoc coram omni regno dignitate sua turpiter spolietur cum restitucione ablatorum' (Marczali, 1901, p. 138).
[46] This is more obvious in the Articles than in the Charter, where the specification of reliefs in cap. 2 and the long addition made to the provisions of the Articles in cap. 4 adjusted these sections more immediately to the policies of the Crown. On the other hand the general intent is revealed in cap. 8 where the widow is not to marry 'without our assent if she holds of us, or without the assent of her lord of whom she holds, if she holds of another'.
[47] See below, pp. 394-5.
[48] On the position of the palatinates of Chester and Durham, see below, pp. 379-80.

contrast, were provincial. Such inadequately consorted action as the French nobility managed to achieve was the result of treaties and alliance between one local league and another.[49] Then again Magna Carta used the term 'free man' in a characteristic and unique manner. The sense of these words varied. In cap. 15, which protected the free man from unreasonable demands for aids from his lord, the words clearly applied to under-tenants. This sense is also consistent with cap. 30, which protected the free man's horses and carts from seizure by the king's bailiffs. In cap. 34, in contrast, the Charter assumed that the 'free man' might hold a court, the jurisdiction of which could be infringed by the writ *praecipe*. Such a court would enjoy much more than petty manorial jurisdiction. The drafters of the Charter also used these words comprehensively to describe the whole spectrum of social grades which held land by free tenure. Hence in cap. 27 they provided that where a 'free man' died intestate his chattels were to be distributed by his nearest relatives and friends and by the view of the Church. Similarly the most famous of all the provisions of the Charter, cap. 39, erected defences against arbitrary imprisonment and disseisin by the king which it applied not to any one social grade or even to an enumeration of them, but to the free man. Most strikingly of all, cap. 9 of the Articles, which dealt with amercements, distinguished only three social grades – villeins, merchants and free men. These provisions were expanded in the Charter, which laid down that barons were to be amerced by their peers.[50] Until that exception was made it seems that they too were included in the general provision for free men. Even after they had been excepted the provision covering the amercement of free men still applied to all non-baronial tenants, and hence to military tenants holding their lands by knight service.

---

[49] Dufayard (1894a), 249, 252.   [50] Magna Carta, cap. 21.

This broad generic use of the term 'free man' is not matched in any other similar concession or statement of laws and liberties. It is most closely approached perhaps in cap. 28 of the Statute of Pamiers, which provided that 'no man is to be sent to prison or held captive as long as he can give sufficient pledges of standing to right'.[51] But there was no exact parallel even here, for the drafters of the statute clearly used the term 'man' in contra-distinction to the term 'lord'.[52] Their thinking was far removed from that laid bare in Magna Carta. Other continental grants showed similar differences. The section in the Golden Bull of Hungary which most closely approached cap. 39 of Magna Carta laid down that 'no noble was to be taken or destroyed for the favour of any powerful lord unless he had first been summoned and convicted by judicial process'.[53] Similarly the chapter of the Sicilian concessions of 1283 which provided for judgement by peers was restricted to 'counts, barons and holders of fiefs'.[54]

Magna Carta then assumed legal parity among all free men to an exceptional degree. This automatic acceptance of a cohesive society had important results. The documents of 1215 assumed that the liberties at issue were to be held by a community, not by a series of individuals of this or that status, but by the realm.[55] The Charter itself obscured this, perhaps deliberately. It admitted the corporate capacity of

---

[51] 'Item nullus homo mittatur in carcerem aut retineatur captus, quamdiu poterit sufficientes plegios dare quod stabit juri' (Vic & Vaissette, 1872–1904, VIII, 632; Timbal, 1949, pp. 181–2).

[52] Compare cap. 29: 'Item nullus dominus recipiat plegios aut aliam cautionem ab hominibus suis, ne recedant cum voluerint a dominio suo sub forma prescripta'; and cap. 33: 'Item nullus homo capiatur pro debito domini sui nisi plegius fuerit aut debitor' (ibid.). The sense of the terms here was tenurial, not social. Compare cap. 34: 'Item nullus baro sive miles sive burgensis sive ruralis audeat pignorare vel capere res alterius per violenciam' (ibid.).

[53] 'Volumus eciam, quod nec nos, nec posteri nostri aliquo tempore servientes capiant, vel destruant, favore alicuius potentis, nisi primo citati fuerint et ordine iudiciario convicti' (Marczali, 1901, p. 135). On the meaning of serviens, see Hantos (1904), pp. 68–72, 187.

[54] See above, p. 76.

[55] For what follows, see Holt (1960), pp. 63–7 and above, pp. 55–7.

the Church and the towns in confirming their liberties, but for the rest it conveyed its privileges severally to all free men of the realm. Many of its chapters permitted this interpretation. The concession on reliefs in cap. 2, for example, could be held by every baron as an individual; each free man could claim protection against arbitrary imprisonment and diseisin under cap. 39. But it could not be applied to cap. 40 which laid down that right and justice should not be sold, denied or delayed, or to cap. 45 which laid down that only those who knew the law of the land and were willing to observe it were to be employed as justices, constables, sheriffs and bailiffs, or to cap. 25 which conceded that shires, hundreds, wapentakes and ridings were to be held at the ancient farms. These were privileges which could only be held by a community, whether the community was hundred, shire or kingdom. Other documents accepted this readily. The Articles bluntly stated that the king was conceding customs and liberties to the kingdom.[56] The treaty concerning the custody of London referred to the 'charter concerning the liberties and security granted to the kingdom'.[57] Many of the documents revealed an infection of communal ideas.[58] In both the Articles and the Charter the Twenty-Five barons were to act 'with the commune of the whole land'. The baronial leaders themselves referred to the 'common charter of the realm'.[59] In receiving the surrender of rebel leaders at the end of 1215 even the king accepted that the Charter of Liberties had been granted 'in common to the barons of England'.[60] These were broad claims. They were nevertheless accepted and repeated by some of the best contemporary chroniclers. The Dunstable annalist referred to the 'Charters of liberties of the realm of

---

[56] Cap. 48.   [57] See appendix II, below, pp. 490–1.
[58] See above, pp. 55–7.   [59] See appendix II, below, p. 499.
[60] See the surrenders of Gilbert fitz Reinfrey and John de Lacy: 'Nec adhaerebo in aliquo cartae, quam idem Rex communiter fecit baronibus Angliae de libertatibus' (Foedera, I, part I, 136–7). In form these documents were no doubt the work of the Chancery clerks.

England'.[61] Ralph of Coggeshall stated that the northerners combined against the king to 'compel him to reform the liberty of church and realm' and to abolish evil customs with which they were afflicted.[62] The Barnwell chronicler likewise accepted that the barons were standing against the king 'for the liberty of Church and realm'.[63] Stubbs commented that 'the Great Charter is the first great public act of the nation, after it has realised its own identity'.[64] This enthusiastic statement has borne much criticism over the years. Behind it, however, there lies a real core of incontrovertible evidence. To impose the 'nation' on the thirteenth century was woefully anachronistic.[65] But Stubbs nevertheless grasped the essentials. Men then believed that liberties had been won, if not for the nation, then for the community or for the realm.

Whence came this quality? To explain it there is no need or reason to abandon Stubbs's cool appraisal, either in exaggerating or detracting from the role of Langton and his fellow churchmen. Even if the more dramatic features of the St Albans tradition of his activities are left on the shelf, there is still a great deal to substantiate his influence. First, it is certain that his absolution of King John in 1213 was associated with some formal promise of reform by the king; whether this was at Langton's instigation or not is less clear.[66] Secondly, it is very likely that he intervened to prevent John taking armed action against the northerners in the autumn of 1213; Wendover's story is sufficiently corroborated at this point to be acceptable at least in outline.[67] Thirdly, it is certain that from the autumn of 1213 onwards Langton was the chief mediator between the king and his opponents. He was present at all the discussions.[68]

[61] 'Chartae super libertatibus regni Angliae' (*Annales Monastici*, III, 43).
[62] *Coggeshall*, p. 170.   [63] *Walt. Cov.* II, 218.   [64] Stubbs (1896), I, 571.
[65] See Helen M. Cam, 'Stubbs, Seventy Years After', *Cambridge Historical Journal*, IX (1947), 134 ff.
[66] See above, pp. 218–19.   [67] See above, p. 220.
[68] See above, pp. 222–6, 229–32.

He was named as a go-between in most of the letters of safe conduct covering the negotiations.[69] He was present at Runnymede, where he acted as a mediator and an arbitrator, and he continued in this role until he left the country in the autumn.[70] All this is beyond serious question and was never in doubt at the time. Innocent III's letters of 19 March 1215 assumed without question that the archbishop would play a determining part in the negotiations.[71]

None of this, however, substantiates the argument that Langton was responsible for all that was best in the Great Charter. There is not even anything to support Stubbs's mild suggestion that Langton was responsible for the protection it afforded to the freeholder. Langton was steeped in the theology and political assumptions of his time. At Paris he had taught that human lordship was subject to the divine; accepting the usual distinction between will and law, he had argued that men might oppose the unjust actions of kings when they proceeded from will but not when they proceeded from judgement.[72] During his exile, in 1207, he reiterated these views in letters sent to England in which he reminded the knightly order and others in authority of the liege homage they owed to God.[73] There can be no doubt that Langton had the intellectual equipment to influence the course of events in 1215 and that he shared in the ideas from which the Great Charter drew its strength. Yet the evidence, as Powicke saw, presents him as a mediator and a moderator, rather than an originator. These implications were there even in his letters of 1207, for they were concerned with ecclesiastical matters and men's loyalty to the Church. They were not in themselves an indication that Langton was ready or eager to intervene in secular matters. On the contrary, he was determined to avoid any impression that what he had

---

[69] See above, pp. 231–2, 241–4.   [70] See below, pp. 366, 368, 371–3.
[71] See above, p. 229.   [72] Powicke (1928), pp. 94–5; Roberts (1968), pp. 123–30.
[73] Powicke pp. 96–7; *Gerv. Cant.* II, lxxxii–lxxxiii.

written should damage the king or the Crown.[74] The same spirit informed the sermon he preached at St Paul's in August 1213.[75] Hence to many men Langton's role, like that of many mediators, was ambiguous. On the one hand, the opposition clearly looked to him for support and relied extensively on his arbitration.[76] On the other, he felt compelled in the summer of 1215 to make two public statements on behalf of the king which implied that the barons had failed to keep their part of the bargain agreed at Runnymede.[77] Even at the time, men who must have known more than most were uncertain of the extent of Langton's implication in the baronial movement. Innocent III simply noted that Langton's return to England in 1213 had coincided with the demand for reform.[78] Even at the end, when Langton had gone into exile, the king had no precise evidence. He wrote to Hubert de Burgh:

Inquire with care from your prisoners and others whether they did what was done by the Archbishop's counsel. And cause diligent enquiry to be made whether you can find letters which he sent to the barons or others at the time of the rebellion against us; and send them, and also what the prisoners have told you, as speedily as you can to our lord the Pope and to us.[79]

The only precise charges John could rake up were that Stephen had refused to surrender Rochester castle and failed to perform the services due from the temporalities of his see.[80] These were not treasonable offences, whatever the king might say.

---

[74] 'Ne vero videamur haec in domini regis et coronae suae dixisse praejudicium, oremus omnes Deum pariter et Dominum nostrum Jesum Christum, ut omnes hostes domini regis et regni et eos qui humiliationem eorum desiderant, pie conterat aut convertat.' Compare 'nec alia intentione onus nobis impositum recepimus, quam ut salutem domini regis et regni fideliter procuremus' (*Gerv. Cant.* II, lxxxiii).

[75] Lacombe (1930), pp. 417–18.   [76] See below, pp. 286–9.

[77] See below, pp. 497–9.   [78] See above, pp. 220, 229.

[79] Galbraith (1948), p. 136. The reference to letters is based on a conjectural reading (*ibid.* p. 162).

[80] *Ibid.* p. 136. On the question of Rochester castle, see below, pp. 361–2.

Other churchmen besides Langton were involved. In 1212 William fitz Walter, archdeacon of Hereford, and Gervase of Howbridge, canon and later chancellor of St Paul's, went into exile with Robert fitz Walter.[81] Eustace de Vescy was likewise accompanied by John, parson of the Vescy living of North Ferriby.[82] John of Ferriby and Elias of Dereham, the archbishop's steward, later received the compensation due to Eustace.[83] Elias also did sterling service for the baronial cause in distributing copies of the charter and the accompanying writs. He, Gervase of Howbridge and the archbishop's brother, Simon Langton, defied the papal excommunication of the rebels in the autumn of 1215 and were excluded from the terms of the Treaty of Lambeth in 1217. Gervase was deprived of his dignities for his contumacy,[84] but Simon Langton went on to become dean of York and Elias had a distinguished career as a canon of Salisbury, as steward in turn of Stephen Langton and Edmund of Abingdon, and as a notable director of ecclesiastical building.[85] Gervase, Simon and Elias were the most determined clerical supporters of the baronial movement. They, if anybody, must have provided its intellectual *élite*. However, there were generally close relations between the baronage and the higher ranks of the clergy. Bishop Eustace of Ely was said to have played a great part in the negotiations before his death early in 1215.[86] Others were engaged in transactions which cannot

---

[81] *Rot. Litt. Claus.* I, 165b. There is some doubt whether Gervase derived his name from Heybridge or from Howbridge (in Witham). Marion Gibbs chose Heybridge (*Early Charters of the Cathedral Church of St Paul, London*, Camden ser., LVIII, 1939). Richardson followed Morant in choosing Howbridge (1933, p. 252). There is little to determine the matter: the bishops held a lordship in Howbridge; Heybridge was a manor of the canons (D.B., II, 12a, 13b). The place-name evidence indicates that Howbridge provides the better identification (*Place Names of Essex*, English Place-Name Society, XII, 1935. pp. 301, 303–4).

[82] *Rot. Litt. Pat.* p. 96b.   [83] See above, p. 217.

[84] *H.M.C. 9th Rep.* I, 28b.

[85] For the extensive literature on Elias see Holt (1964), p. 86, n. 2 (see also Powicke, 1928, pp. 136–8). For a careful and very useful re-examination of Elias's architectural and artistic work see Selby Whittingham, *A Thirteenth-Century Portrait Gallery at Salisbury Cathedral* (Salisbury, 1979), especially pp. 13–15, 29–30.

[86] *Walt. Cov.* II, 219.

now be fully disentangled. The two Mandeville brothers, Geoffrey and William, incurred debts of 7000 m. with Stephen Langton.[87] In Lincolnshire the Kymes borrowed money from the bishop, Hugh of Wells.[88] Maurice de Gant, another important rebel, sold land to Jocelin, bishop of Bath.[89] Perhaps the most revealing and intimate record of these ties is provided by a will drawn up for Hugh of Wells while he was in exile in 1212. The bequests included 20 m. for the soul of the relict of Geoffrey de Mandeville, 20 m. to Thomas de Mandeville, 40 m. to William de Mandeville, 300 m. to the daughters of William of Stratton for their dowry and 40 m. 'to a knight of Nottinghamshire whose daughter Gerard d'Athée would have for his son'. The maker of such a will would not be without influence with the lay nobility. One of the executors was Elias of Dereham. But bishops were not incendiaries. Even in exile Hugh set aside the sum of 608 m. 8s. 1d. for the payment of the debts which he owed the king.[90]

The extent and quality of ecclesiastical influence on the Charter is not easy to determine.[91] Churchmen were a powerful influence in some of the continental grants. The Statute of Pamiers, for example, was drawn up by a committee of twelve, of whom four were churchmen: two bishops, one Templar and one Hospitaller.[92] It was issued by the advice of an archbishop and seven bishops.[93] In Hungary all ten witnesses to the Golden Bull were bishops; of the seven copies produced, one went to the pope, one to the Hospitallers, one to the Templars and two to cathedral chapters.[94] Yet neither of these grants reflects the kind

[87] Cal. Charter Rolls, I, 196.   [88] Ibid. I, 62–3.   [89] H.M.C. Wells, I, 471.
[90] Ibid. I, 431–2.
[91] For a comment on the whole period 1215–25 see Cheney (1976).
[92] Catalogue des Actes de Simon et d'Amauri de Montfort, ed. A. Molinier (Paris, 1874), p. 73.
[93] Vic & Vaissette (1872–1904), VIII, 626; Timbal (1949), p. 177.
[94] Marczali (1901), p. 142.

of influence which Langton and his colleagues have been alleged to have had on Magna Carta. Preponderant ecclesiastical influence seems instead to have produced a concentration on the special interests of the Church. Ten of the first eleven chapters of the Statute of Pamiers were concerned with ecclesiastical topics ranging from the treatment of heretics to the recovery of the church's property and the maintenance of ecclesiastical privilege and jurisdiction. Similarly Urban IV's conditions for the Angevin acquisition of Sicily laid down precise boundaries between the kingdom and the papal patrimony in an attempt to settle some of the territorial quarrels which had existed hitherto between the Sicilian kings and the papacy.[95]

Magna Carta bore some imprint of this. Its first clause confirmed the general liberties of the Church and the recent concession of freedom of election. Granted *in perpetuum*, this now infected the whole of the Charter. All the liberties were to be held *in perpetuum* as if in free and perpetual alms; and this was repeated in 1216 and 1217, in the Charter of the Forest of 1217, and in all later reissues of both charters. Some clauses reveal an immediate canonical influence. Cap. 40, which stated that justice was not to be sold, denied or delayed, asserted the principle of free justice which was laid down in the metropolitan decrees of Stephen Langton of 1213–14, the decrees which Hubert Walter promulgated as legate at York in 1195 and the first synodal decree of Hugh of Lincoln of 1186.[96] Even here, however, the evidence is by no means certain. This provision occurred not only in the Charter, but also in the Articles and the 'unknown' charter.[97] It was widely known. Cap. 13

[95] *Reg. Urban IV*, II, 123–4.
[96] C. R. Cheney, *From Becket to Langton* (Manchester, 1956), p. 153; F. M. Powicke & C. R. Cheney, *Councils and Synods* (Oxford, 1964), I, 34.
[97] Articles, cap. 30: 'unknown' charter, cap. I.

of the Statute of Pamiers also laid down that justice was to be given freely,[98] and the matter had been discussed in England by no less an authority than Richard fitz Neal.[99] This enforces caution, although it does not necessarily exclude canonical influences, which certainly affected secular thinking and practice on the rights of the Crown[100] and, later in the thirteenth century, on representation and consent.[101]

However, canonical influence was sometimes narrower and ecclesiastical intervention more restricted than laymen would have liked. The clearest and most certain evidence on the attitude of Langton and his colleagues is not to be found in the chronicles, or even in contemporary canon law, but in the Articles and the Charter. In these they acted throughout with a proper regard for the distinctions between the spiritual and the temporal, refusing to permit secular interference in the former, and intruding themselves as little as possible into the latter. The Articles required the intervention of the archbishop and bishops at several points. In cap. 25 they were required to adjudicate on disseisins committed by Henry II and Richard I, if it was decided that King John was to be given the stay against legal action to which a crusader was entitled;[102] from their judgement there was to

---

[98] 'Item in justiciis exhibendis aut judiciis faciendis nulla exactio fiat a partibus sub pretextu alicujus consuetudinis aut occasione advocatorum sive assessorum, set gratis omnino exhibeatur justicia et pauperi non habenti advocatum detur a curia' (Vic & Vaissette, 1872–1904, VIII, 628; Timbal (1949), p. 179).
[99] See above, p. 107.
[100] Riesenberg (1956), esp. pp. 81–112; Richardson (1960), pp. 151–61; E. H. Kantorowicz, 'Inalienability: a note on canonical practice and the English coronation oath in the thirteenth century', *Speculum*, XXIX (1954), 488–502, and *The King's Two Bodies* (Princeton, 1957), pp. 347–58.
[101] Gaines Post, '*Plena Potestas* and Consent in Medieval Assemblies', *Traditio*, I (1943), 355–408, and *Speculum*, XVIII (1943), 211–32.
[102] This seems to be the obvious construction of the Latin. For a similar use of the word *inde* see Articles, cap. 37, and Magna Carta, cap. 55. However, the framers of the Articles may have meant that the archbishop and his colleagues were to decide whether the king was to have the crusader's term. If so they phrased this provision badly. Such a decision would be involved whichever reading was intended. Langton and his colleagues settled both this and the ensuing action to be taken on disseisins by Henry and Richard (see below, pp. 341–2).

be no appeal to a higher ecclesiastical court.[103] Cap. 37 referred unjust amercements and fines to the judgement of the Twenty-Five barons together with the archbishop and any whom he wished to summon with him. Finally, caps. 45 and 46 provided for the restoration of charters of fealty and hostages to the Welsh and of hostages, liberties and rights to the King of Scotland. The exception was then entered against these two clauses that the king might do otherwise, on the basis of the charters he had, 'by the judgement of the archbishop and others whom he wished to summon with him'.

The archbishop was apparently required to intervene in all these matters because they involved spiritual jurisdiction. This was clearly so in cap. 25 where the king's respite as a crusader was at stake. In the case of caps. 45 and 46 it is likely that the charters and agreements which John had exacted from the Welsh and Scots involved a pledge of faith, and the same probably applied in cap. 37. Langton and his colleagues settled these matters within the terms of their spiritual jurisdiction. They decided first that the king was to enjoy the crusader's privilege. They could do no other. Hence they applied the stay of action against all claimants who alleged unjust disseisin on the part of Henry and Richard.[104] They applied this principle to similar disseisins committed against the Welsh,[105] and they also extended it to cover other complaints against these two kings.[106] They could do nothing about the restoration of John's disseisins, even if they had wanted to do, since cap. 25 of the Articles had provided that these were to be restored as an act of grace.[107] Thereafter the line between spiritual jurisdiction and politi-

---

[103] 'appellatione remota'.　　[104] Magna Carta, cap. 52.
[105] Magna Carta, cap. 56. This was envisaged in Articles, cap. 44.
[106] Magna Carta, cap. 53.
[107] The intention of Articles, cap. 25, is illuminated by Articles, cap. 44, which provided that John's disseisins against the Welsh were to be restored 'sine placito'. Under cap. 25 such cases were only to go to judgement if they were disputed. In that case they were referred not to the archbishop, but to the Twenty-Five.

cal mediation became blurred. Cap. 58 of the Charter provided for the immediate restoration of the charters of fealty and hostages which Llywelyn of Wales and other Welshmen had surrendered. In the case of the Scots there was a different arrangement: in cap. 59 Alexander was to recover his sisters, hostages, liberties and rights like other barons of England, but there was to be judgement of peers in the king's court as to whether it ought to be otherwise because of the charters of King William the Lion. These included the Anglo-Scottish treaties of 1209 and 1212 under the second of which both William and Alexander had formally recognized King John and the infant Henry as lord.[108] Langton took a firm determining line in the case of the Welsh – indeed he and others later provided an exemplification of Llywelyn's charter;[109] in the case of the Scots he let the issue go to judgement of peers. So the archbishop passed this particular matter back to secular judgement. Whatever his role as a political mediator, in the Charter he would not readily intervene in a secular issue between lord and vassal.[110] In the matter of unjust fines and amercements the Charter provided him with a means of making a similar withdrawal. In cap. 37 of the Articles his adjudication, along with that of the Twenty-Five, was essential to the settlement of such cases. Cap. 55 of the Charter now laid down that if he could not be present then the Twenty-Five were to proceed with their judgement without him.

All this is consistent with the conventional division between the temporal and the spiritual, which seems to have been accepted by all concerned in the crisis. The king's opponents only over-stepped the mark at one point. The last sentences of the Articles laid down that John was to provide

[108] *Anglo-Scottish Relations 1174–1328: Some Selected Documents*, ed. E. L. G. Stones (London, 1965), pp. xlv–xlviii, 12–13.
[109] Beverley Smith (1984). I have revised this section somewhat in the light of Professor Smith's cogent argument. For Llywelyn's charter of 1211 see *ibid.* pp. 361–2, and for further discussion of the date of the exemplification see below pp. 486–7.
[110] Compare Innocent's letters of 19 March, above, pp. 229–30.

charters of security from the archbishop, the bishops and Master Pandulf guaranteeing that he would not attempt to seek anything from the pope which might revoke or detract from the agreement, and that any such papal response should be held null and void. In short, the leading churchmen were required to deny the right of appeal to the Curia in a matter which had already been referred to it, and which came within the spiritual sphere since it involved the performance of the most solemn oaths. It was all the more difficult to deny such an appeal since King John was now the pope's vassal. Hence they rejected this demand. All they would provide in the Charter were letters testimonial which simply attested the terms of the agreement. On this point they were not at one with the rebel barons.[111]

The Charter and its associated documents thus reveal varied ecclesiastical influences, some of a limited, almost guarded nature. They also drew on a broad current of thought derived from the common law and the precise thinking of legal and administrative minds. This is easily appreciated from a direct comparison of the Articles with the Charter of 1215, and of the 1215 Charter with the reissue of 1217. In each case there was a marked trend towards legal precision, towards noting exceptions, plugging holes, and covering foreseeable eventualities. Only thirteen chapters of the Charter restated the provisions of the Articles without a major amendment or a minor change in drafting.[112] Some of these alterations were important. All were an improvement in drafting. Caps. 8 and 13 of the Articles, for

---

[111] For this interpretation of the letters testimonial, see Cheney (1956), 335–6, and Holt (1957), 418 n. For a similar usage of the phrase 'litteras testimoniales', see Johnson & Jenkinson (1915), II, p. x (6). There is little to support Collins's argument (1948, 245, 249) that the letters testimonial were surrendered to the king as a counterpart to the Charter. Magna Carta, cap. 62, clearly states that the letters were made out for the barons, not the king. They later came into the Crown's hands (see below, p. 314, and for the text of the letters, appendix 11, below, pp. 491–2).

[112] Caps. 3, 8, 10, 17, 22, 28, 30, 31, 32, 34, 45, 47, 60. See Holt (1972).

example, attempted to limit the burden of suit of court by laying down that no one should be summoned except the juries and the two parties, and that the assizes should be 'shortened'.[113] This combination of the impracticable and the obscure was replaced in the Charter by the thoroughly reasonable proposal that if all the assizes could not be settled in one day then sufficient knights and freeholders should remain to complete the business. Someone had decided that the work of the courts had to be completed properly. Cap. 14 of the Articles, which asked that sheriffs should not intervene in pleas of the Crown without the coroners, was also unsatisfactory and obscure. Its intention was clarified in cap. 24 of the Charter which laid down that neither sheriff, constable, coroner nor any other royal bailiff was to hold pleas of the Crown. Cap. 32 of the Articles obscurely demanded that London and other cities should pay tallage and aids in the same manner as scutage and aids were assessed on the kingdom. Whether this meant that they were to be assessed by the common counsel of the realm, or assessed by the consent of the city and other towns,[114] or simply that they were to be reasonable, was not clear. Magna Carta left much of this obscure, perhaps deliberately, but it did at least remove the inappropriate association of tallage with consent. Cap. 31 of the Articles asked that merchants should be free to travel at the ancient custom without any *maletotes*. Magna Carta, cap. 41, imposed the reasonable exception of wartime, when merchants of enemy countries were to be held to guarantee the fair treatment of British merchants then in enemy lands. Cap. 33 of the Articles took the difficulty of wartime into account in asking that there should be freedom to enter and leave the country, but even then it had not covered all possible exceptions. Cap. 42 of the Charter

---

[113] For the translation of 'abbrevientur', see Powicke (1920), 401–2.
[114] Both these processes were suggested in the Londoners' petition to John of the spring of 1215 (see below, pp. 320–1). The most likely intention was that the consent was to be sought from London on occasions when it was sought from the whole realm.

also excepted those who had been imprisoned or outlawed according to the law of the realm. Cap. 23 of the
Articles demanded the destruction of fish-weirs throughout the realm. Cap. 33 of the Charter excepted those on
the sea-coast. On some matters the Articles were quite
inadequate. Cap. 9 dealt with the amercement of free men,
villeins, and merchants; it imposed limits on such penalties
and laid down that all these classes were to be assessed by
the oath of honest men of the neighbourhood.[115] Magna
Carta, cap. 20, made it clear that this method of assessment was to apply in all cases. The Charter also included
the provision that earls and barons were to be amerced
by their peers. This had not been included in the Articles
at all.

The rebel barons must have been aware of the need to
produce a legally watertight agreement. They were not
without administrative experience,[116] and they chose their
most experienced administrator, Saer de Quincy, earl of
Winchester, to conduct the final negotiations.[117] But they
had had their fling in the Articles. It therefore seems likely
that much of this amendment was the work of judges,
officials and clerks. But neither their intervention nor that of
Langton and his colleagues extended to those characteristic
features of the Charter which distinguished it from many
similar documents. The 'free man' was as prominent in the
Articles as in the Charter. The 'unknown' charter did not
use the term, but in passage after passage it conveyed
privileges not to particular classes, but to 'men'. It assumed,
on the one hand, that a 'man' might lose his life for an

---

[115] The punctuation of this clause in *Stubbs's Charters* and Bémont (1892) is not warranted
by the original.
[116] Among the Twenty-Five, Roger Bigod, Saer de Quincy, and William of Huntingfield
had acted as justices; John fitz Robert, Robert de Ros, William d'Aubigné and William
of Huntingfield as sheriffs. Robert de Ros was still in office as sheriff of Cumberland.
[117] See above, p. 242. Saer was a baron of the Exchequer, named first after the Justiciar,
Geoffrey fitz Peter, in 1212 (*Rot. Litt. Claus*, I, 132b). He was a member of the Bench at
Westminster, sitting with Simon of Pattishall and others, in Michaelmas, 1213 (Doris
M. Stenton, 1958, 125).

offence against the forest law,[118] and on the other that he might be required to perform military service overseas.[119] It even used the terms 'man' and 'baron' as loose alternatives.[120] Other documents of the reign tell the same story. Peter de Brus conferred his Langbargh charter on 'his knights and free tenants of Cleveland and their men'.[121] King John's Chancery likewise addressed general letters patent more and more, as the reign advanced, to the 'barons, knights, and free-tenants' of the shire,[122] or simply to the 'knights and honest men'[123] or to 'all men and free-tenants'.[124] English law in the late twelfth century recognized few distinctions within the class of free men. Early twelfth-century law-books set rather a different tone. 'The king's judges', ran the Laws of Henry I, 'are the barons of the shire who hold free land therein . . . villeins, cottars, farthing-men and base and worthless men of this kind are not to be counted among the judges of the laws.'[125] In the early years of Henry II, Richard de Lucy, the king's justiciar, remarked in court that it was not the custom in days of old for petty knights to have seals.[126] But here Richard was jesting at the expense of a litigant. By this time Henry II's measures were confirming not only that knights had access to the judicial processes of the king's court, but that freeholders had too. Tenurial diversity prevented tenurial distinctions from determining social boundaries. Barons held as knights; they also held burgage tenures. Burgesses were addressed as barons; some acquired military tenures and established themselves as landed families. Many military tenures were so sub-divided that the services due from them could only be expressed in monetary terms. By John's reign, Richard de Lucy would have been surprised to find not only that most knights had seals but that many freeholders, including sokemen, had them too. Where tenants did not as yet possess this mark of

[118] Cap. 12.   [119] Cap. 7.   [120] Caps. 2, 5.   [121] See above. p. 67.
[122] See, for example, *Rot. Litt. Pat.* p. 121.   [123] *Ibid.* p. 122b.   [124] *Ibid.* p. 124b.
[125] Leges Henrici Primi, 29, *Gesetze*, I, 563.   [126] *Chron. Battle*, p. 214.

tenurial and legal independence, they borrowed their lord's seal; the lord seems to have seen nothing unusual or demeaning in lending it.[127]

The Crown recognized this tenurial diversity and social cohesion in several ways. It gave barons, knights and freeholders equal access to judicial processes. It used barons, knights and free men to serve its administrative purposes.[128] It required free men with revenues of 16 m. to maintain the military equipment of a knight and prescribed a lesser scale of armament for the less wealthy.[129] In John's reign, indeed, a man might resist the imposition of villeinage by arguing that he was 'under the oath of the lord king to maintain arms as a free man'.[130] Twice in John's reign, in 1205 and 1213, preparations were made for mustering this body of free men in defence of the realm.[131] No doubt the king had little use for the motley army thus arrayed. But he was ready enough in earlier years to force drengs, thegns and cornage tenants to make contributions in cash in lieu of service overseas,[132] and in the army he summoned for the campaign in Poitou in 1214 service was imposed on men who claimed not to hold in chief, or who held by sergeanty, or in one case on a man who was a tenant of land held in free alms.[133] Tenurial distinctions did not stand in the way of the Crown's military requirements.

However, Magna Carta made more than a passing bow in the direction of the knight, the under-tenant and the free man. The knights and gentry were a real political power. England could not have been governed without them. They not only did the local hack-work as jurors and coroners. They were also called to act at times as sheriffs and under-

---

[127] For an example see 'The Glapwell Charters', ed. R. R. Darlington, *Journal of the Derbyshire Archaeological and Natural History Society*, LXXVI (1956), no. 1.
[128] See the Inquest of Sheriffs, *Stubbs's Charters*, p. 176.
[129] See the Assize of Arms, *ibid.* p. 183.
[130] 'in jurata domini regis ad arma habenda ut liber homo' (*Curia Regis Rolls*, I, 45).
[131] Michael Powicke, *Military Obligation in Medieval England* (Oxford, 1962), pp. 48–62.
[132] Holt (1961), p. 197.   [133] *Pipe Roll 17 John*, p. 102.

sheriffs or to serve as judges in eyre, where they might sit on
the bench alongside William Raleigh or Simon of Pattishall.[134] King John himself turned to seek their support in
November 1213 when he summoned four knights from
every shire to discuss the business of the realm.[135] In the
rebellion which began in 1215 the actions of knights, gentry
and under-tenants were often determined by the influence
of their lords. But circumstances sometimes permitted them
to show some independence and, where they could choose,
they frequently sided against the king.[136] Hence they were a
force to be reckoned with, won over, and encouraged.
Indeed their connexion with the rebellion may lie even
deeper. Sir Cyril Flower noticed that a very large proportion of the actions recorded on the rolls of the king's court
came from the eastern half of the kingdom.[137] Undoubtedly,
as Flower remarked, this partly reflected the factors of
distance and accessibility. But it is difficult to ignore other
correlations. First, the eastern half of the kingdom was also
peculiar in that it contained a greater proportion of small
freeholders.[138] Secondly, the rebellion of 1215 was centred
largely on the Home Counties, East Anglia, Lincolnshire,
Yorkshire and the North. Free men, litigation, and the cause
of Magna Carta went together.[139]

Enough has been said elsewhere of the gradual growth of
local liberties,[140] of the increasing demand for judgement,

[134] See Doris M. Stenton (1958). For an excellent and revealing examination of the role of
'unprofessional' judges in one county, see *Feet of Fines for the County of Lincoln, 1199–
1216*, ed. Margaret S. Walker (Pipe Roll Soc., new series, XXIX, 1953), pp. xxvi–xxxvi.
Mrs Walker comments that the numbers of the professional judges 'were so small that a
general eyre would have been quite impossible had they not been supplemented by
unprofessional judges' (p. xxxvi).

[135] *Stubbs's Charters*, p. 282.

[136] Holt (1961), pp. 35–60.

[137] Flower (1944), p. 11.

[138] For recent comment on this, see *Feet of Fines – Norfolk, 1198–1202*, ed. Barbara Dodwell
(Pipe Roll Soc., new series, XXVII, 1950), pp. xii–xiii, xxvii ff.

[139] This is not to detract, of course, from the reasons which drove the barons of these areas
into rebellion (see Powicke, 1928, pp. 126–8; Painter, 1949, pp. 285–99; Holt, 1961, pp.
194–6, 212–14). See also above, pp. 123–87.

[140] See above, ch. 3, pp. 50–74.

restoration of right and the maintenance of good and ancient custom,[141] and of the rôle played in these developments by knights and lesser tenantry.[142] Magna Carta was not a sudden intrusion into English society and politics. On the contrary, it grew out of them. There is no need to deny the influence of Langton, other churchmen, or the king's officials and clerks. There is equally no need to suggest that they simply conjured all that was best in Magna Carta out of their intellects and their canonical or theological training. The evidence will not stand this construction. Nor yet does it support the case that the Charter stood for something outside the scope of lay thinking and above the mundane interest and ambitions of the temporal world. It is a mistake to couch the argument in terms of selfishness or altruism. Laymen had been assuming, discussing and applying the principles of Magna Carta long before 1215. They could grasp it well enough. But they were not for that reason unselfish. The barons did not talk of free men out of loftiness of purpose, or make concessions to knights and burgesses out of generosity. They did so because the political situation required it and because the structure of English society and government allowed them to do no other.

The same factors imposed limits on their thinking. They had been accustomed to corporate action by local communities. John's methods of government now forced them to envisage corporate action by the community of the realm. But if this was their greatest single achievement, it also marked the limits of their thinking. When they came to apply compulsion on the king they chose a committee of Twenty-Five, all of them great magnates except for the Mayor of London. When they considered consent to aids and scutage they laid down that it was to be achieved by mustering all the tenants-in-chief of the Crown. When they chose a leader, the best title they could manage for him was

---

[141] See above, ch. 4, pp. 75–122.   [142] See above, pp. 61–74.

'Marshal of the Army of God and Holy Church'. The community of the realm which they envisaged was as yet ill-formed. It was dominated by the great baronial families. They, if anyone, represented it. Its law and custom were primarily concerned with their liberties and privileges. Their immediate action on achieving Magna Carta was to demand the restoration of property. The quality of Magna Carta derived not so much from their conscious determination, as from the way their minds had been conditioned. Beyond that they found it difficult to go. The Charter pulled together the work of the twelfth century. It was less adequate as a foundation on which the thirteenth century could build.

CHAPTER 9

THE ACHIEVEMENT OF 1215

Magna Carta was not a simple statement of law. That part of it which was confirmed in 1217 and 1225 did in fact become law. But it was not an accurate statement of law as it had been before 1215. Its supporters claimed that it was. Indeed, their arguments had been concentrated on reviving the 'good old laws' and confirming existing privileges and liberties.[1] But theirs was only one side of the case. The other side was equally convinced. The papal agents who excommunicated the king's opponents in the autumn denounced them for introducing new laws and depriving the king of his customary rights.[2] Maitland asserted that 'the charter contains little that is absolutely new. It is restorative. John in these last years has been breaking the law; therefore the law must be defined and set in writing.'[3] McKechnie likewise frequently assumed that John had been breaking principles which Magna Carta largely confirmed.[4] But this is to accept the opposition's case and to by-pass important problems. How far, for example, did Magna Carta state existing law? Where it did, had John been breaking it? Whether it was law or not, was John the only king to contravene its principles?

None of these questions permit simple answers applicable to every clause. For example, it was existing law to levy aids by consent as cap. 12 of the Charter confirmed, but there is

---

[1] See above, pp. 113–17. For general comment see Cam (1965).
[2] See below, pp. 370–4.   [3] Pollock & Maitland (1898), I, 172.
[4] For examples where McKechnie simply accepts that John had been doing the opposite of what Magna Carta lays down, see McKechnie (1914), pp. 300, 322, 334, 337, 368, 413, 434.

no certain evidence that John or any other king had habitually levied aids in any other manner. In contrast, it seems to have been generally accepted that knightly tenants of escheats in the king's hands should pay reliefs at the rate of £5 per fee. John had sometimes broken this rule, and so occasionally had Henry II.[5] In contrast yet again, there was nothing precise to establish the size of a baronial relief, and large sums had been exacted not only by John, but also by Richard, Henry II, Henry I and William Rufus. Where was the law in this? What was custom? Was it what these kings had done, or what their subjects thought they should have done?

To penetrate beyond the Charter in search of substantive law is to discover not so much a body of established custom, still less a set of statutes, as an argument. Even Glanvill and fitz Neal, the two prime authorities on late twelfth-century practice, did not always tell the same story.[6] They sometimes stated opinions rather than legal certainties.[7] Even so they presented a clear enough picture of many aspects of twelfth-century administration. If they were to be accepted as a statement of twelfth-century 'law', as a standard wherewith to measure the provisions of the Charter, then it is clear that much of the Charter would fall outside it. But they were approaching their task as royal administrators, and they concentrated on particular aspects of the king's government. A wider cast through the records of the twelfth century and the reign of John would bring in a much greater variety of rulings and claims which could be maintained as precedents for the Charter. If not precisely defined by law or generally accepted, £100 for a baron was thought to be a reasonable relief.[8] Municipal charters defined, and plaintiffs in the king's court sought to define, the occasions on

---

5 See below, p. 304.
6 See below, p. 307, for their views on wardship and relief.
7 R. W. Southern, 'A note on the text of "Glanville"', *E.H.R.* lxv (1950), 87–8.
8 See above, p. 52, and below, pp. 304–5.

which lords might take a gracious aid.[9] There were many precedents, including the charter of liberties of Henry I, for the limitation of pecuniary penalties.[10] Men were used to provisions that heirs should be married without disparagement.[11] Widows were frequently able to buy their freedom to marry again or to avoid marriage at the king's dictation.[12] The king's court heard complaints that estates of wards had been wasted,[13] or that men had been unlawfully disseised by earlier monarchs.[14] The Crown itself had recently granted the Church's freedom of election,[15] pardoned increments on the farms of the shires,[16] and granted to the Londoners that there should be no fish-weirs on the Thames and Medway.[17] It had regularly investigated the behaviour of its officials; the last occasion was as recent as 1213.[18] Hubert Walter had already anticipated the provision that sheriffs should not hold pleas of the Crown by laying down in 1194 that no sheriff was to act as justice in his own shire or in any shire he had held since Richard's first coronation.[19] King John himself had anticipated the provisions of cap. 41 for the safe conduct of foreign merchants in letters he had issued to the officials of southern and eastern England in 1200.[20]

There were precedents enough for Magna Carta. But they do not stand alone. For every baronial relief of £100 there were many more which far exceeded that sum. For every attempt to impose a limit on pecuniary penalties there were many more examples of the king's power and readiness to exact large sums as fines and amercements. There were

---

[9] See above, pp. 57–9, 121.   [10] See above, pp. 37, 58.
[11] See above, pp. 54–5.   [12] See above, pp. 53–4, 197–8.
[13] See above, p. 121.   [14] See above, pp. 90–2, 135–8, 154–8.
[15] *Stubbs's Charters*, pp. 283–4.   [16] See above, p. 213.   [17] See above, p. 57.
[18] See above, pp. 212–13.   [19] *Stubbs's Charters*, p. 282.
[20] 'Sciatis voluntatem [nostram] esse quod omnes mercatores de quacunque fuerint terra salvum habeant ire et redire cum mercibus (*sic*) suis in Angliam. Volumus etiam quod eandem habeant pacem in Anglia quam mercatores de Anglia habeant in terris illis unde fuerint egressi et ideo vobis precipimus quod hoc faciatis denunciari in ballia vestra et firmiter teneri permittentes eos ire et redire sine impedimento per debitas et rectas et solitas consuetudines in ballia vestra' (*Rot. Chartarum*, p. 60b).

notable examples of disseisin, of imprisonment for debt or disobedience, of widows and heiresses given in marriage to boost the influence of the king's friends and officials, of officials who used their office to line their pockets, and of sheriffs who were required to pay large increments or profits on their shires at the Exchequer. To select those precedents which foreshadowed the Charter and reject the rest is to resort to hindsight. To attribute the quality of law to such selected precedents is to distort what happened. Magna Carta became law not because it stated existing law, but because its re-issue and enforcement under Henry III made it so. This process is revealed at its clearest by comparing, for example, the provision of cap. 2 that barons should pay reliefs of £100 with the provisions of cap. 15 that the king would not give a lord permission to take an aid from his free men unless to ransom his body, knight his eldest son and marry his eldest daughter once. There were precedents for both these regulations before 1215.[21] It is equally true that both were frequently ignored. The first was repeated in the Charters of 1216, 1217 and 1225 and came to determine the amount of baronial reliefs and to define tenure by barony throughout the greater part of the thirteenth century.[22] The second was omitted in all these re-issues and failed to become part of the law of the land. As a result the Crown supported its tenants-in-chief in levying aids on a wide variety of occasions, just as it had done before 1215.[23] Thus by 1225 cap. 2 of the 1215 Charter had become law and cap. 15 had not. But before 1215, and even in the 1215 Charter itself, the one was no more 'lawful' than the other.

Sometimes Magna Carta stated law. Sometimes it stated what its supporters hoped would become law. Sometimes it stated what they pretended was law. As a party manifesto it made a party case with scant regard for fact or existing

---

[21] See above, pp. 52, 121.   [22] See below, pp. 304–6.
[23] See below, pp. 317–18.

practice. Cap. 1 of the Articles demanded that heirs should succeed to their inheritances at the ancient reliefs to be laid down in the Charter. Cap. 2 of the Charter claimed to state what these ancient reliefs were. This was reasonable in the case of the £5 relief on the knight's fee, but no one could seriously maintain that the £100 relief for the earl or baron was truly and properly 'ancient' in the sense that this sum had customarily been paid in the past. Cap. 12 of the Charter involved similar difficulties. That aids should be assessed by consent was well enough agreed by all concerned. But there was little if anything to justify a similar restriction in the case of scutage. Some aids, it is true, had been assessed as scutages in the past, and this practice continued in the reign of Henry III. But this terminological confusion can scarcely explain the blatant attempt to put aids levied by consent and the monetary compensation for military service on the same footing. Hitherto, once a campaign was agreed, the scutage had been assessed by royal decree at an amount determined by the Crown on those who did not serve or send their service.[24] Here the Charter stated not law but innovation. Worse still it used the accepted law on aids to cloak the innovation on scutage. The provision was dropped from the re-issue of 1216 and was not re-introduced in subsequent re-issues. Even so, the attempt to associate scutage with consent and to confuse scutage with aid continued under Henry III.[25]

The sections of the Charter which dealt with the royal forest tell a similar story to cap. 12. Hitherto the royal forest had been a matter for the king's will. Fitz Neal had drawn a sharp contrast between the forest law and the law of the land. In the twelfth century kings seem to have afforested land by will without any kind of consent, or consultative

---

[24] See above, p. 85. For the scutage of 1214 where the king announced 'Know that we have decided (*statuimus*)', see *Rot. Litt. Claus.* I, 166b.
[25] See below, pp. 398–9.

process.[26] Forest eyres were ordered by the king; their object was to preserve the king's rights; men were summoned before the justices of the forest to hear the king's precepts.[27] Occasionally there was some slight sign of weakening on the part of the Crown. In 1100 Henry I announced that he was retaining in his hand the forests of his father, 'by the counsel of my barons'.[28] The *Pseudo-Cnut de Foresta* of the reign of Henry I seems to have been an attempt by a forest official to pretend that the forest regulations had their origins in pre-Conquest England.[29] But in the main the Charter marked a sharp break.[30] Hitherto the forest law and the extent of the forest had largely been a matter for the king. Now the community was intervening to regulate its boundaries, investigate its officials and amend its regulations. The claim to do so represented a massive intrusion into the Crown's powers. This was secured and extended in the Charter of the Forest of 1217.

However, law was not a completely malleable material which would easily conform to any shape required by the drafters of the Charter. They could not invent entirely new forms which no one would recognize. If they were to be able to argue that they were stating ancient custom which

---

[26] 'R. episcopus Sar. forestariis regis de Ebor. salutem. Dimittite habere Thurstino archiepiscopo Eboracensi et hominibus suis omnia aisiamenta sua et necessaria sua in nemoribus archiepiscopatus que rex posuit in forestam suam' (*Early Yorkshire Charters*, I, 33–4).

[27] *Hoveden*, IV, 63.   [28] Charter of liberties, cap. 10.

[29] *Gesetze*, I, 620–6.

[30] The proem to the Assize of the Forest – 'per consilium et assensum archiepiscoporum, episcoporum, et baronum, comitum et nobilium Anglie' – which appears in *Stubbs's Charters*, p. 186, is clearly not authentic. Stubbs failed to remark, as he had noted elsewhere, that it is derived from a sixteenth-century version of the Assize (*Hoveden*, II, 245, n.; *Gesta Henrici*, II clxi). An earlier statement (*c.* 1400) that the Assize was made 'per concilium et assensum tocius regni sui' appears in the *Sherwood Forest Book*, ed. Helen E. Boulton, Thoroton Society, Record Ser., XXIII (1965), p. 59. This again, as it stands, cannot be authentic. Roger of Howden, on whom the great part of the evidence depends, and who was involved in the enforcement of the Assize as a justice, adopts a more authoritarian tone, describing it as 'precepta' of the king (*Gesta Henrici*, II, clxi–ii; *Hoveden*, II, 245; and compare *Gesta Henrici*, I, 323–4). On the complex problem of these texts see Richardson and Sayles (1963), pp. 444 ff; Holt (1971), pp. 97–9; and the important correction by Corner (1980), pp. 9–13.

the Angevins had broken, then the Charter had to bear some comprehensible relationship to the practice of the twelfth century. This imposed strict limits on what they could hope to achieve or visualize themselves achieving. They could devise easily enough regulations governing the feudal relationships between Crown and tenants-in-chief. On this they could select precedent from the promised concessions of Henry I and the Crown's practice since his reign. Government routine also enabled them to range with some confidence over matters of feudal service. They could cope with many judicial questions because of the judicial processes which had developed since the accession of Henry II. But they moved less easily on matters which involved the king's officials, or the management of his revenues, or the affairs of his household. The twelfth century yielded few adequate precedents for intervening in these matters. The one obvious occasion which could be exploited was the absence of Richard I on the crusade and in captivity, but then the magnates had acted with almost obsequious deference to the wishes of the king.[31] Thus, in basing their case on custom and precedent the barons of 1215 chose strictly limited ground. They could not move far from it without themselves risking the counter-charge of innovation. This imposed limits on their actions and conditioned their thinking. They could solve the familiar problem because it was necessarily one where precedent suggested a solution. But the less familiar was doubly difficult because it found them without either experience or precedent. Where they were required to think originally they were inhibited from doing so. As a result, their measures were often inadequate. It was not that they were unintelligent. They were blinkered.

Even so, the achievement of 1215 was considerable in fields which were familiar. For the first time the magnates

[31] See the treaty between Count John and William de Longchamps, above, pp. 120–1.

were able to introduce some law and order into the tenurial relationships between Crown and vassal. The most obvious victory, embodied in caps. 2 and 43, was on reliefs. The relief of £5 per knight's fee largely confirmed twelfth-century practice. Its origins can be traced in the *Leis Willelme*.[32] Glanvill stated it as a rule[33] and fitz Neal accepted it for tenants of escheats in the Crown's hands.[34] In the case of escheats it had been largely applied by the Crown, although Henry II, occasionally, and John, perhaps more frequently, had resorted to higher rates.[35] It was less usual in the case of the smaller tenants-in-chief who might be required to pay either at £5 per fee[36] or at a much higher and arbitrary rate.[37] Moreover on this there was a sharp division of opinion among the authorities, for while Glanvill applied the £5 rate to all non-baronial tenants by knight service, fitz Neal, by limiting it to tenants of escheats, certainly did not. Thus the effect of this provision was to extend the £5 rate as a regularly enforced rule to tenants by knight service whether they held by escheat or in chief.[38] It became the usual rate of payment for tenants-in-chief who held only one fee or for those who could produce charters of feoffment which specified the knight service without describing the tenure as baronial.[39]

The £100 relief for the earl or baron had fewer precedents. Both Glanvill and fitz Neal were in agreement that barons were accustomed to pay any arbitrary sum to which they could get the king to agree.[40] The only formal justification of the ruling in the Charter was that, if baronial reliefs were to be fixed at all, then £100 was regarded as a reasonable sum.[41] Even fitz Neal slipped unconsciously into

---

[32] Leis Willelme, 20, 2, *Gesetze*, I, 507.   [33] Glanvill, IX, 4, ed. Hall, p. 108.
[34] *Dialogus*, pp. 96, 121.   [35] Round (1917), pp. 57–8; Holt (1961), p. 190.
[36] Round (1917), pp. 64–70.   [37] Sanders (1956), p. 100.   [38] *Ibid.* p. 99.
[39] Round (1917), pp. 66 ff.   [40] Glanvill, IX, 4, ed. Hall, p. 108; *Dialogus*, p. 96.
[41] Pipe Roll 10 Richard I, p. 222.

naming this amount,[42] and indeed there are examples of it being charged in the late twelfth century.[43] The real justification for the provision, however, was political rather than legal. It lay in the enormous sums which the Crown had charged as reliefs under Henry II, Richard and John. The Crown could not deny succession to a loyal subject where the descent was clear.[44] But it could demand sums large enough to affect the successor's security of tenure. The Crown could not withhold the inheritance for failure to pay, but it could go through the usual processes of distraint, and by 1201 fines for land were included among those debts for which land might be distrained.[45] Such reliefs not only put the successor in the Crown's debt, but also tended to drive him into debt elsewhere. In extreme cases large reliefs might be accompanied by other conditions – by the surrender of charters of fealty or castles as a pledge of loyalty.[46] In one striking instance, inordinate relief was used to enforce the surrender of land to the Crown. In 1205 Nicholas de Stuteville promised 10,000 m. for the succession to the lands of his brother William and guaranteed payment by surrendering Knaresborough and Boroughbridge, which had been given to William by Henry II.[47] An agreement of such severity may have resulted in part from the fact that

---

[42] *Dialogus*, pp. 94–5.   [43] Round (1917), pp. 60–1; Sanders (1956), p. 98.

[44] *Dialogus*, p. 121. Compare Charter of Henry I, cap. 2, and the passage from the Norman custumal quoted below, p. 312. This evidence does not seem to have been taken into account in S. E. Thorne's thesis that heritability of land was not finally established and accepted until the age of Glanvill (1959, 193–209). For studies of the problem of inheritance and heritability see above, p. 105 n. 146.

[45] *Hoveden*, IV, 152. The word 'fine' was applied to voluntary proffers as well as to fines for inheritances. Hence the intention of the ordinances of 1201 is far from clear. Fitz Neal had assumed that land for which a voluntary proffer had been made was seised into the king's hands if the terms of payment were not met (*Dialogue*, p. 119). The Pipe rolls do not suggest any startling change of practice in 1201 or afterwards. In the case of a voluntary proffer distraint might follow immediately on failure to pay, in the case of a relief only after distraint on chattels and a special judgement in the Exchequer at the end of the session. But action never seems to have been carried so far in a case of a simple succession.

[46] See the case of John de Lacy, above, p. 195.

[47] *Rot. de Ob. et Fin.* p. 305.

Nicholas did not succeed directly to his brother, but to his nephew, Robert, who had survived his father for two years as a minor in the custody of Hubert Walter;[48] the case therefore bore some resemblance to the 'king's case'.[49] Nicholas also had to defeat the conditions under which Hubert Walter had acquired the custody for a minimum period of four years.[50] Indeed he made no attempt to recover these estates until Hubert Walter died. Whatever the explanation of the size of the proffer the king intended to use it as a means of recovering Knaresborough and its appurtenances into the royal demesne. No serious attempt was made to collect Nicholas's debt. Meanwhile the Crown continued in control of a strategically important castle and of revenues which varied between £220 and £540 per annum. This case came before the Twenty-Five barons. They attempted to recover Knaresborough for Nicholas, and this action contributed to the renewal of the civil war in the autumn.[51] In the end they failed. The manors were transferred to Hubert de Burgh along with Nicholas's debt in 1229,[52] but they returned to the Crown after his fall. Baldwin Wake, Nicholas's grandson, still owed 9998½ m. of the debts of Nicholas in the reign of Edward I, and the same sum was still outstanding against John Wake in 1333.[53] Knaresborough continued in the Crown's hands and subsequently formed part of the duchy of Lancaster, a permanent reminder of the arbitrary reliefs of the days before the Charter. It remained an exceptional case. The £100 relief was established.[54] This represented a major baronial victory.

The barons achieved similar successes in related fields.

---

[48] *Early Yorkshire Charters*, IX, 13.
[49] For the king's case, see above, p. 84 and Holt (1991b).
[50] See below, p. 314.   [51] See below, p. 364.
[52] *Cal. Charter Rolls*, I, 99–100, 131.
[53] P.R.O. Chancery Miscellanea, 87/6, no, 111; 86/713, no. 284. I am indebted to Dr E. B. Fryde for this information.
[54] Stacey (1987), pp. 217–8. For the later amendment of the baronial relief to 100 m., see below, p. 309.

Cap. 3 laid down that a minor should not be required to pay a relief on achieving his majority and succeeding to his inheritance. Glanvill had held this view,[55] but it had not been generally accepted in the twelfth century. Fitz Neal, like Glanvill, recognized that the revenues received during a minority weakened the lord's case to exact a relief and he went so far as to lay down that 'you cannot exact a relief when a ward comes of age, who has been an appreciable time in your wardship, and the issue of whose property you have received'.[56] But he also maintained that the minor only succeeded to his inheritance freely as an act of royal grace.[57] The practice of the Crown did not even go as far as fitz Neal. Eustace de Vescy was charged with a relief of 1300 m. in 1190 after his lands had been in the custody of the Crown since 1182–3.[58] During this interval they had yielded a gross income of £578. 3s. 4d. in the hands of royal custodians in 1184–5 and they were let out to farm at nearly £400 per annum between 1186 and 1188.[59] This scarcely conformed to the equitable principle which Glanvill and fitz Neal had supported. Yet even this demand was mild compared with that made on John de Lacy. In 1213 John was required to pay 7000 m. after his lands had been in the custody of the Crown for twenty-two months; in 1212 alone they had yielded over £1520.[60] Minors had sometimes escaped with much smaller charges on attaining their majority, but there can be no doubt that the matter had lain within the arbitrary operations of the will of the king.

The Crown's rights of wardship were also cut down in other directions.[61] Cap. 37 laid down that the king was not

---

[55] Glanvill, IX, 4, ed. Hall, p. 107.   [56] *Dialogus*, p. 97.
[57] *Dialogus*, pp. 94, 96.
[58] *Pipe Roll 2 Richard I*, p. 21; *Pipe Roll 29 Henry II*, p. 140.
[59] *Pipe Roll 31 Henry II*, pp. 8–9; *Pipe Roll 33 Henry II*, pp. 12–13; *Pipe Roll 34 Henry II*, p. 4.
[60] *Pipe Roll 14 John*, p. 3.
[61] There is now a fuller treatment of these matters in Waugh (1988), pp. 64–104, especially pp. 83–91.

to claim prerogative wardship of fees held of other lords by military service in virtue of lesser tenures held of him by fee-farm, socage, burgage or petty serjeanty. Here the Charter expanded a principle which had already been laid down by Glanvill in the case of burgage tenures.[62] It also followed earlier attempts to deal with competing claims to wardship which had been included in municipal charters.[63] The Charter also drew heavily on earlier precedent in caps. 6, 7 and 8. Cap. 6 laid down that heirs were not to be married in such a way that they were disparaged, and that the agreement of the nearest relatives was to be asked before the marriage was contracted. This came close to similar provisions in the Charter of Henry I and the 'unknown' charter.[64] Cap. 7 provided that widows were to have their marriage portion, dower and inheritance without any kind of payment and that their dower was to be assigned to them within forty days of their husband's death. Cap. 8 provided that widows were not to be compelled to marry if they did not wish to do so, on the condition that they were not to marry without the consent of their lords, whether the king or another. Both these clauses followed broadly similar rulings in the Charter of Henry I.[65] They established privileges for which widows had been striving over the past generation and which the Crown had been admitting more and more.[66] But they also gave legal substance to the licence to marry, whether from king or lord. The widow would no longer be sold so easily, but, if she wished to remarry, she would still have to seek and most probably buy permission.[67]

[62] 'Verumptamen ratione burgagii tantum non prefertur dominus rex aliis in custodiis' (Glanvill, VII, 10, ed. Hall, p. 84).
[63] See above, p. 59.   [64] Charter of Henry I, cap. 3; 'unknown' charter, cap. 4.
[65] Caps. 3 and 4. Compare 'unknown' charter, caps. 4 and 6.
[66] For examples, see above, pp. 53-4, 197-9.
[67] Walker (1979), pp. 101-10. There are nevertheless some examples of pressures brought to bear and of the strategic disposal of well-endowed aristocratic widows by the Crown. See ibid., p. 103 and R. R. Davies, Lordship and Society in the March of Wales 1282-1400 (Oxford, 1978), pp. 268, 281, 283.

In all these arrangements the drafters of the Charter kept close to precedent of some kind or other. Even so, their work revealed contention and uncertainty. The repetitive phrasing of cap. 2 suggests that they had originally intended to distinguish between the relief of an earl and a baron.[68] Neither Glanvill nor fitz Neal suggested any grounds for this, but the *Leis Willelme* of the early twelfth century mentions three rates of relief: the earl's, the baron's which was half the earl's, and the vavassor's.[69] There is no indication of why some such distinction was considered and then abandoned in 1215. It was not re-introduced until 1297 when the baronial relief was reduced to 100 m. in the Confirmation of the Charters. The Confirmation persisted in referring to the relief of 100 m. as 'ancient'; the reduction put an end to this confusion.[70] However, a tradition persisted throughout the thirteenth century that the baronial relief had been established at 100 m. in the original Charter. It was incorporated in Bracton,[71] and it was also given in versions of the 1217 Charter which survived in transcripts at St Albans, Guisborough[72] and in a collection of laws and annals compiled in London in the late thirteenth century which eventually formed part of the Black Book of Christ Church, Dublin.[73]

---

[68] 'The heir or heirs of an earl for the whole barony of an earl for £100; the heir or heirs of a baron for a whole barony for £100.'

[69] Leis Willelme, cap. 20, *Gesetze*, I, 507.

[70] See Bémont (1892), pp. 47–8 n and Reynolds (1989).

[71] Bracton fo. 84, tr. Thorne, II, 244.

[72] Holt (1964), 70; *The Chronicle of Walter of Guisborough*, ed. Harry Rothwell (Camden 3rd ser., LXXXIX, 1957), p. 162.

[73] H. J. Lawlor, 'An unnoticed charter of Henry III, 1217', *E.H.R.* XXII (1907), pp. 514–18. I had not been able to inspect this version when I discussed it on a previous occasion (1964, 77). The volume in which it occurs was described by Aubrey Gwynn, 'Some unpublished texts from the Black Book of Christ Church, Dublin', *Analecta Hibernica*, XVI (1946), 283–337. Gwynn also elucidated the history of the MS. I have now been able to inspect and collate the text of the Charters through the kindness of the Dean of Christ Church, the Very Rev. N. D. Emerson. The reading *marcas* occurs only in the 1217 version (fo. 165ᵛ). The 1215 version reads correctly *libras* (fo. 162ᵛ). For further comment see Reynolds (1989), 234–8 and for the appearance of the 100 m. relief in 'draft' versions of the 1215 Charter, below, pp. 445–6.

There seem to have been more serious discussions and doubts on the problem of disparagement. Some obviously wanted more stringent regulations than those in the Charter. The Articles and the 'unknown' charter followed the Charter of Henry I in providing for positive control over the king. He was to marry heirs as their nearest relatives advised. This would have tended to deprive the king of his right of marriage, and it may have been for this reason that the Charter contained the weaker regulation that he was simply to advise the relatives of his intentions. But there may well also have been even more serious divisions of opinion. To restrict the king's right of marriage was to restrict an exercise of patronage from which any one of his vassals might benefit and on which all of them relied in the government of their own fiefs. More-over, as things stood the law was clear. The Crown's right acted as a defence of the heiress or the widow[74] and even on occasion of the under-tenant against his lord.[75] To abandon these certainties for an entirely novel situation in which the relatives, rather than the lord, would appear as plaintiffs or defendants in such cases was to risk much.[76] It is hardly likely that the barons would have ventured this if they had not been driven into it by the manner in which the Crown had sometimes used its right of marriage to endow loyal supporters and agents, perhaps 'new' men, at worst foreigners, with landed estate far beyond their normal expectations. Under Richard and John, Robert de Vieuxpont, Robert of Thornham, and Peter de Maulay, who came from Poitou, owed some or all

---

[74] See above, pp. 54–5, 200.
[75] In 1211 Richard de Wyville offered 10 m. that his lord William de Mowbray should be required to show why he had married Richard's daughter Alice, while still under age, to someone other than Roger de Mowbray, without the king's licence (*Pipe Roll 13 John*, p. 29). Richard also held land of the archbishopric of York which was then in royal custody – hence the king's interest in the case.
[76] On disparagement see Walker (1982) and Holt (1985), pp. 20–8; compare Waugh (1988), pp. 81–2 n. D. M. Stenton (1957) pp. 48–56 is still essential reading.

their landed possessions to this.[77] John was in no way disturbed by the protest vented in the Charter. In 1216 he married off Margaret, widow of Baldwin de Redvers, and heiress to the barony of Stogursey, to his Norman captain and sheriff Faulkes de Bréauté.[78] Hence the barons must have been torn between opposite considerations. On the one hand it was unwise to interfere with a well-established right and with the associated legal procedures. On the other hand they were bent on excluding the parvenu. This provision was excluded from the re-issues of 1216, 1217 and 1225. John was now out of the way. His successor was a minor and could not exercise the prerogative. The government depended for the time being on the support of the dead king's foreign captains. The provision was not revived until 1258 when it was directed against a new wave of foreigners.[79] Meanwhile the Crown's rights were enforced at once. In 1218 Thomas of Moulton had to give sureties that he would appear before the council to answer the charge that he had married Ada de Morville, widow of Richard de Lucy of Egremont, without licence from the Crown.[80]

There were also difficulties in the matter of wardship.

---

[77] Robert de Vieuxpont owed his interests in the Tickhill fee to his marriage to Idonea, heiress of John de Bully. He also married his daughter to the heir of the Greystoke fee (Holt, 1961, pp. 233–4). Robert of Thornham married the heiress of the Fossard barony. These lands were worth over £400 per annum in 1212 (*Early Yorkshire Charters*, II, 328–9; *Pipe Roll 14 John*, pp. 5–6). Peter de Maulay married the daughter and heiress of Robert of Thornham (*Pipe Roll 16 John*, p. 94).

[78] Baldwin was son and heir of the earl of Devon but predeceased his father. His son, of whom Faulkes had custody as a result of his marriage, succeeded to the title. Margaret's father, Warin fitz Gerold, died in 1216 and she inherited half his lands (*Complete Peerage*, IV, 315–19). On this particular marriage see Holt (1985b), 27–8.

[79] The intent was then made explicit, as it had not been in 1215: 'Item petunt de maritagiis domino regi pertinentibus, quod non maritentur ubi disparagentur, videlicet hominibus qui non sunt de natione regni Angliae' (Petition of the Barons, *Stubbs's Charters*, p. 374).

[80] *Patent Rolls, 1216–25*, pp. 165–6. Thomas had bought the custody and marriage of Richard's daughters and heirs in 1213 (above, p. 191). He married them to his sons. His own marriage to the widow rounded off the operation. Some time between February 1213 and July 1215 Ada had fined to be allowed to remarry at her own will (P.R.O., K.R. Memoranda Roll, 2 Henry III, m. 1).

Cap. 4 of the Charter provided that custodians were to take no more than the reasonable issues, services and customs from the lands in their charge. If they wasted the estate then it was to be placed in the hands of two suitable men of the fee. Cap. 5 insisted that custodians were to maintain the land in proper condition and return it fully stocked to the heir when he came of age. These arrangements were very much a compromise. Cap. 3 of the 'unknown' charter suggests that some had advocated the much more radical solution of committing all custodies to four knights of the fee, who were to account for the revenues along with officials of the Crown. The Articles, in contrast, simply provided that a custodian who wasted an estate should lose the custody.[81] Once again the rights of all feudal lords were at stake, as well as those of the king. Twelfth-century opinion on the matter varied. The Charter of Henry I left wardships with the widow or nearest relative.[82] But the author of the Ancient Custumal of Normandy, who discussed the matter at some length, decided that the mother of a minor should not have custody because she might marry again and have sons by her second marriage. The nearest relative of the minor was, in his view, equally unreliable since he might covet the inheritance. But the lord had been connected with the minor's dead father by homage and fealty and could not in any case hold the inheritance in demesne; he therefore should have custody. The writer was equally convinced that vassals' children should be brought up in the lord's household, thus encouraging future good relations when they achieved manhood.[83] Some of this was distinctly hopeful. Nevertheless, the case for giving wardship to the lord was well rooted. Even the 'unknown' charter did not deny it to the king. It simply excluded his right to bestow the wardship on a

---

[81] Cap. 3.   [82] Cap. 4.
[83] Le très ancien Coutumier de Normandie, *Coutumiers de Normandie*, ed. E. J. Tardif (Rouen, 1881), I, 10–12.

person of his choosing. Such a restriction was difficult to apply or accept because wardships were treated as property which men could convey and for which they could sue or be sued in the courts. A plea of 1210, for example, between Eustace de Vescy and Geoffrey of Hickling concerning the fee of one knight in Hickling and Sutton, Norfolk, revealed that Geoffrey's father, Brian, had held the land of Eustace's father, William. Geoffrey admitted that he had been in the custody of William as a minor, but he argued that William had conveyed the wardship to Robert de Valoines, who had then taken his homage. Geoffrey had also performed homage to Theobald de Valoines, Robert's heir. Thomas de Valoines, Theobald's heir, was now claiming the homage due, and Geoffrey expressed his readiness to perform homage to whomsoever he should according to the instructions of the court. The court decided in favour of Thomas de Valoines on the grounds that his father had also received it.[84] An even longer chain of conveyance was revealed in 1220 on the death of Saer de Quincy, earl of Winchester. It was then reported to the Crown that Robert de Vieuxpont had disseised Saer's son and heir, Roger de Quincy, of Liddel and its appurtenances, which Nicholas de Stuteville had assigned to his nephew Eustace de Stuteville until he came of age. The custody of the land had come into the hands of William de Valoines. He bequeathed it on his death to Saer de Quincy and Saer subsequently gave it to Roger. Robert de Vieuxpont was now ordered to restore the custody to Roger.[85] There is nothing to suggest that such transactions were exceptional. When King John confirmed various custodies, including William Bertram and Henry Percy, to William Briwerre in 1200, he agreed that William's heirs and assigns might continue to hold them if he

---

[84] *Curia Regis Rolls*, VI, 136. Eustace then reopened the case as a plea of service (*ibid.* VI, 316–17).
[85] *Patent Rolls, 1216–25*, p. 243.

died.[86] Such transactions clearly assumed that wardships had a monetary value. Indeed this was openly acknowledged. In 1204 Hubert Walter, archbishop of Canterbury, accounted at the Exchequer for 400 m. he had offered for the custody of Robert, son of William de Stuteville, and all his lands, including castles, tenements, fee farms, wards and sureties. It had been agreed that he was to hold the land for four years beginning in June 1203 'or for a longer period until he had recovered his outlay or his reasonable costs'. This agreement was to stand whatever happened to Robert, and Hubert was to have all the ploughs which were found on these tenements. If Hubert died, as in fact he did in 1205, then the wardship was to go to his legatees.[87] A wardship was an investment. Men expected a reasonable profit from it. Hence to insist that all wardships should be in the hands of knights of the fee, as was envisaged in the 'unknown' charter, was to sacrifice all these opportunities in return for an uncertain guarantee against wasting.[88] The price was too much; hence the compromise solution of the Charter. The Charter was imperfect here in other ways. Cap. 5 gave some indication of what was understood by wasting. But if the custodian expected a profit, wasting was likely to be a matter of degree. No provision was made for the compensation of the ward where wasting had occurred. This was not envisaged until the Provisions of Westminster of 1259[89] and not introduced until the Statute of Gloucester of 1278.[90] Even then the law had not fully coped with the difficulties of providing proper protection for the ward.[91]

However, on all these matters of feudal incidents the Charter provided a reasonably clear set of regulations, most of which became permanent features of English law in the thirteenth century. Where it was vague or weak, it was

---

[86] *Rot. Chartarum*, p. 48b.　　[87] *Pipe Roll 6 John*, pp. 191–2.
[88] For a parallel attitude to wardship see Articles, cap. 43; Magna Carta, cap. 46.
[89] Cap. 20, *Stubbs's Charters*, p. 394.　　[90] Cap. 8 (see Plucknett, 1949, p. 83).
[91] McKechnie (1914), p. 209–11; Walker (1978).

because it was trying to avoid excessive intrusion into the property of the Crown and its great vassals, or because the problems themselves were intractable.[92] On other matters these difficulties increased. Even on the closely related topic of feudal service the Charter spoke far less clearly and with much less certainty. It came to be detached more and more from what was customary. Its provisions were less permanent, and where they were permanent they tended to be less adequate.

These qualities are well illustrated by cap. 16. This provided that no one was to be compelled to do greater service than he ought for a knight's fee or for any other free tenement. This was a worthy sentiment but far from precise in the circumstances. Ought a knight to be compelled to serve or send service to Poitou and for how long? These questions had provided one of the occasions for the rebellion against King John. The Charter did not answer them. Here at least, the 'unknown' charter had achieved some clarity in laying down that overseas service was to be limited to Normandy and Brittany; it had also provided for the alleviation of the amount of service demanded.[93] But neither the Articles nor the Charter specified the amount or duration of the service or the areas for which it might be demanded. Cap. 16 was all that survived from the demands and persistent resistance of 1213–14. The desire to prevent any kind of excessive demand for service may have contributed to its broad generalities.[94] But it looks very like a confession of failure. The abandonment of a precise demand was hidden behind a sweeping provision which the parties could interpret each in his own way. The Crown continued

---

[92] For further discussion see Walker (1978, 1979, 1982); Waugh (1988).
[93] See above, pp. 239–40.
[94] It is possible that it was partially provoked by the inquest into feudal service of June 1212 and was designed to guard against a possible increase in feudal service. But there is nothing to establish that such was the purpose of the inquest, or that cap. 16 was related to it. Cap. 16 was concerned with service due from the knight's fee, not from the tenancy-in-chief.

to demand and obtain service in Poitou and Gascony under Henry III and Edward I.

The Charter achieved precision only on the fringes of the main problem. Cap. 29 provided that military tenants should be excused castle guard for the appropriate length of time if they were also required to serve in the field. This laid down a principle occasionally claimed and allowed prior to 1215. It also provided that military tenants were not to be compelled to render castle guard in cash if they were willing to serve in person. This scarcely halted the general process towards commutation which had begun in the twelfth century and continued in the thirteenth.[95] In John's reign castle guard was still sometimes performed in person.[96] But there is no indication apart from the Charter of any serious attempt to maintain this. Most of the cases recorded in the rolls of the king's court concerned commuted service. Not one involved a plea by an under-tenant that he was entitled to perform the service in person. Indeed, in one action, William fitz Alan, an under-tenant of Simon of Kyme, went to the grand assize to maintain the existing rate of commutation against an attempt at re-assessment. He did not claim to perform the service in person.[97] Other sections of the Charter settled other relatively minor problems. Cap. 16 was at least clear when applied against King John's attempts to exact fines for overseas service from tenants in thegnage, drengage or cornage.[98] Cap. 43 also provided a clear prohibition against the exaction of excessive service from tenants of escheats. John's demands for military service had borne more heavily on tenants of escheats than on any other class of men. Tenants-in-chief had been

---

[95] Painter, 'Castle-Guard', *American Historical Review*, XL (1935), 450–9. See also Round, 'Castle Guard', *Archaeological Journal*, LIX (1902), 144–59; F. M. Stenton (1961), pp. 192–217; Poole (1946), pp. 48 ff.

[96] *Curia Regis Rolls*, IV, 13, 30.

[97] *Curia Regis Rolls*, IV, 137–8; V, 30.

[98] See above, p. 293.

allowed substantial reduction in service quotes, from which their tenants too must have benefited indirectly. But he had not allowed escheats to escape so lightly. The service due from them and from lands in temporary custody was carefully investigated.[99] Tenants of the honours of Peverel or Lancaster, for example, were required to perform or fine for service on occasions when others were presumably escaping with a simple payment of scutage to their lords.[100] One of the most striking features of the muster roll for 1214 was the contrast between the reduced quotas of the tenants-in-chief and the comparatively heavy burden placed on tenants of lands in royal custody.[101] Cap. 43 reflected the fact that the new quotas differed radically from the old service due and even more from the actual enfeoffment. When the tenant-in-chief was removed the under-tenants were no longer buffered against the king's demands.

Some aspects of cap. 12 have already been discussed.[102] In the matter of aids it simply reasserted the usual processes of consent.[103] Along with cap. 15, however, it introduced a new definition of gracious aids. Both the king and his vassals could now take them only for the ransoming of their bodies,

---

[99] *Book of Fees*, pp. 17–51.

[100] For the assessment of the knights, thegns and socage tenants (*firmarii*) of Lancashire see *Pipe Roll 3 John*, pp. 275–6. By 1214 the separate identity of the various Nottinghamshire and Derbyshire escheats had almost disappeared in the scutage accounts (see *Pipe Roll 16 John*, pp. 160–1).

[101] *Pipe Roll 17 John*, pp. 101–3. See also Mitchell (1914), pp. 104–5 and Keefe (1983).

[102] See above, p. 301.

[103] The discussion of caps 12 and 14 has been refined considerably by Gavin Langmuir (1972), especially in distinguishing between the *commune consilium regni* of caps. 12 and 14 and *commune assensum* (pp. 472–82). With some reservation, I have let my rather loose equation of *consilium* with conent, in this particular context, stand. Although the terms were clearly distinguished in certain legal contexts, such as a licence to marry, it is less easy to see a distinction in the context of general taxation. Despite the different formulae, there is no good ground for thinking that the procedure for the aid envisaged in caps. 12 and 14 was any different from that of the Thirteenth of 1207 which was granted *per commune consilium et assensum concilii nostri apud Oxoniam* (*Stubbs's Charters*, p. 278). If we followed these words literally, they would point to some form of common counsel, however obtained, which was distinct from 'our' council which gave its assent at Oxford. A constitutional history derived from linguistics alone would look very odd.

the knighting of their eldest sons and the first marriage of
their eldest daughters. Hitherto, opinion had not been so
certain. Glanvill accepted the gracious aid for the knighting
of the eldest son and the marriage of the eldest daughter, but
did not mention the aid for ransom. Instead, he questioned
whether a lord might not levy an aid to make war and
concluded that this was possible only if the tenants
wished.[104] The ancient Custumal of Normandy accepted the
same three occasions as Glanvill.[105] But there was no
consensus. Some earlier claims agreed with the Charter.[106]
On the other hand John permitted his tenants-in-chief to
levy aids to pay their reliefs,[107] even to clear off their
debts.[108] After 1217, when this clause was no longer in the
Charter, permission was given for lords to collect aids to
assist them on the crusade, or to pay a relief, or to support
them in the king's service in Poitou.[109] The aid for ransom
was, in the nature of things, exceptional. The other two
gracious aids as defined in 1215 did not become statutory
until the Statute of Westminster of 1275, when their amount
was also prescribed.[110]

The demand for the control of scutage was much less
straightforward. It had no legal basis, and it may well be that
cap. 12 simply put an unsatisfactory conclusion to a long and
unsatisfactory debate. Cap. 8 of the 'unknown' charter had
laid down that scutage should be fixed at 1 m. per fee. It had
also envisaged that 'more might be taken by the counsel of

[104] Glanvill, IX, 8, ed. Hall, p. 112.
[105] Coutumiers de Normandie, I, 36.
[106] See above, pp. 58, 121. Compare F. M. Stenton (1961), pp. 173, 276–7; also a charter (c. 1204) of Hugh of S. Aubin conveying the services of a quarter of a vavassoria 'salvis tamen tribus auxiliis consuetud[inariis] institutis per Normanniam' (Cartulary of S. Evroult, Paris, B. N., Ms lat. 11055, fos. 124v–125); and the charter of Thomas count of Perche to his knights of the castlery of Bellême, 1215, which allows four occasions for the feudal aid (below, p. 412).
[107] Rot. de Ob. et Fin. pp. 422, 494–5.
[108] Pipe Roll 11 John, pp. xxiv–xxv, 21, 126. This demand was challenged by the tenants. For other aids under John, see McKechnie (1914), p. 259, and Pollock & Maitland (1898), I, 350.
[109] Patent Rolls 1216–25, pp. 284, 361, 550.
[110] Statutes of the Realm, I, 35; cap. 36 (see Plucknett, 1949, p. 77).

the barons if the burden of an army occurred'. This wording is far too obscure to convey any precise intention. The most likely interpretation is that the barons were prepared to acknowledge that the Crown might require tenants to fine for personal service but that, if so, it was to be at a generally agreed figure. None of these proposals survived discussion. The fixed rate of scutage was abandoned and was not revived until 1217, and then only with a loose proviso that it was to be taken as it used to be under Henry II.[111] The distinction made in the 'unknown' charter between a general demand for scutage and the 'burden of an army' was lost. Instead the limited proposal for consent which it envisaged was extended to all scutages, and scutage was confused with aid. John himself had earlier contributed to this confusion. He had levied a total of eleven scutages during the reign. In two out of the eleven instances the levy had been made despite the fact that there was no full-scale campaign. In 1205 the magnates had resisted John's intention to fight in France and had agreed to a scutage as a consolation.[112] This levy had some of the features of an aid. The confusion went even deeper in 1204, for the scutage of $2\frac{1}{2}$ m. of that year was in fact an aid granted for the purpose of defending Normandy by the consent of a council held at Oxford.[113] John proceeded to collect despite the fact that there was no campaign in 1204, as indeed he was entitled to do. But he also used the levy as an occasion for demanding heavy fines for service, for which he had no sound case. The demand was resisted.[114] When the magnates confused scutage and aid in 1215 they were only paying the king back in his own coin. But they repaid him in an obtuse, ineffective manner. They missed dealing with the really significant development of the

---

[111] Magna Carta (1217), cap. 37. Under Henry scutage was assessed at rates varying from 1 m. to 2 m. per fee. The incidence varied considerably. See Keefe (1983), who commented on the proviso that it should be taken as under Henry II – 'If so, it was hardly to be taken at all' (p. 140).
[112] Coggeshall, pp. 152–4; Gerv. Cant, II, 98; Chron. Maj. II, 490.
[113] Chron. Maj. II, 484.   [114] Holt (1961), pp. 90, 205–6.

MAGNA CARTA

reigns of Richard and John: the association of the fine for
service with the demand for long-term service overseas at
reduced quotas. It may be that they did not regard the issue as
vitally important. The fact that the Poitevin scutage was used
as an occasion for rebellion led contemporaries to exaggerate
its importance.[115] The association of scutage with consent in
cap. 12 may well have encouraged historians to do likewise.[116] But scutage and fines for service were not major
financial burdens comparable to the penalties which men
might incur in other ways. They were not levied on those
who served. Even those who resisted the king's demands
in 1213–14 had served willingly in earlier years, in Normandy, Poitou, Wales, Scotland and Ireland.[117] Before then
scutage had only met with resistance in the exceptional levy
of 1204. It was raised to prominence by the inevitable
frequency of John's demands and by the actions of the
barons in 1214. It was in some ways inflated beyond its real
importance.

Cap. 12 included one further confusing and novel provision. It demanded that the processes of consent should be
applied to the taxation of London. Boroughs, whether royal
or private, were in fact tallaged at the will of their lord. It
seems, however, that men were beginning to confuse such
taxation with the aid. A charter granted by Maurice de Gant
to his men of Leeds in 1208 arranged that they should pay
the king a reasonable aid 'when he imposed his aid on the
cities of England'.[118] If this was confused in one direction
then the Londoners were confused in another. In the spring
of 1215 they demanded that 'all tallages should be abolished

[115] Hence Alexander Swereford stated that the civil war was caused by the scutage (*Red
Book of the Exchequer*, I, 12).
[116] See, for example, McKechnie (1914), p. 76. Neither Norgate (1902, p. 123) nor
McKechnie, who followed her (1914, pp. 69–76), is reliable on scutage. They wrote
before the publication of the relevant Pipe rolls. The best summary of individual levies
is in the introductions to these and in Mitchell (1914).
[117] Holt (1961), pp. 90–1. For more general comment see Keefe (1983), especially pp.
134–40.
[118] Ballard (1913), p. 92.

320

except those levied by the consent of the realm and the city'.[119] The confusion was perpetuated in the Articles[120] and it was only eliminated formally in the Charter. Cap. 12 now imposed the principle that London should pay aids. It did so despite the fact that John had not acceded to the Londoners' request in the charter he had conceded to the city on 9 May 1215.[121] Worse still it states a debatable principle in a confusing manner. By omitting all reference to tallage the Charter achieved formal consistency at the cost of its real intent. It failed to specify whether the Crown could still tallage London or not. The omission of this clause in 1217 left the Londoners still tallageable. They had to continue the fight to establish the privilege of compounding at a fixed sum, and later to revive the claim to pay aids.[122] Their position might not have been very different if cap. 12 had been retained. It was far from watertight.

In general cap. 12 was one of the least satisfactory or adequate in the whole Charter. It dragged in the novel demand for consent to scutage and the Londoners' demand to pay aids only to ignore the crucial developments in taxation of the last two reigns. It had nothing to say of the new forms of taxation: of the attempts to assess taxation on land accurately, or of the far more vigorous and successful efforts to tax revenues and chattels. These all fell within the category of aids. Hence the Thirteenth of 1207 would have come within its terms. The Thirteenth yielded nearly £60,000, and was by far the most severe tax of John's reign, indeed of the whole century. It provoked evasion and resistance. Yet it had been conceded 'by common counsel

---

[119] Bateson (1902), 726. See also Susan Reynolds, 'The Farm and Taxation of London 1154–1216', *Guildhall Studies in London History*, I, (1975), 211–17.
[120] Cap. 32.
[121] He did, however, grant them the privilege of an annually elected mayor which was included in the petition (*Rot. Chartarum*, p. 207; *E.H.R.* XVII, 726).
[122] Williams (1963), pp. 205–9.

and the assent of our council at Oxford'. It had been lawful; and such taxation remained lawful after 1215. The Charter made no provision to limit the assessment or to distinguish revenues from chattels or to determine methods of assessments or to restrict penalties for evasion. The effect of cap. 12 was to transfer these matters to debate in great councils. That, indeed, is where the argument usually took place under John's successors.

Originally the baronial proposals made a further obvious omission. The Articles included nothing on how consent to aids was to be sought and given. They simply referred to the common counsel of the realm.[123] Magna Carta, cap. 14, now laid down that all tenants-in-chief were to be summoned by general writs of summons issued to the sheriffs and royal bailiffs. The greater barons were to receive individual writs. The writs were to specify the reason for the summons and were to name the precise day and place of meeting; on the day arranged the business was to be settled by those who had come. Such a summons, fully answered, would have produced an impossibly large assembly of at least 800.[124] But the clause was not designed with this in mind. It sprang rather from the notion that all the land of England was held by the king or his tenants-in-chief. It is likely that both parties had a hand in such an arrangement. The provision that business was to proceed despite absentees was in the interests of the Crown, but it was also accepted by the barons for it was applied to the decisions of the Twenty-Five.[125] The Crown was one of the most potent forces behind the development of consent in the course of the thirteenth century. On the other hand there were some notable complaints against taxation levied without consent or with consent improperly obtained. In one of these instances, in 1255, the barons appealed to the terms of cap. 14, despite the fact that it was excluded, along with cap. 12, from the 1216 and subsequent

[123] Cap. 32.   [124] Painter (1943), p. 48.   [125] Magna Carta, caps. 55, 61.

re-issues.[126] Only the distinction in the method of summons seems to point to one side more than the other. The one precedent for the contrast implied in the Charter between the greater and the lesser barons is to be found in the Dialogue of the Exchequer.[127] Under cap. 14 the king was able to send individual writs to the greater barons and let the rest come, or, better still and more likely, stay away in answer to the general summons. Within limits he could decide who the greater barons were,[128] and it seems that those who came would bind the rest. If John was forced into this scheme, he nevertheless shaped it to his own convenience and in a manner which set the pattern for the future.

On questions of feudal service the Charter's achievement was varied. On minor matters it was precise and, on the whole, successful. On some major matters its provisions were vague or obscure; these usually survived in the re-issue of 1217. On other important topics it was radical and, to the Crown, objectionable. This part of it was ultimately rejected. Hence cap. 16 survived; cap. 12 did not.

The provisions concerned with justice are not so easily categorized. Here the Charter had a much more secure base in the judicial system which Henry and his sons had developed. Indeed one of its main achievements, in caps. 17, 18 and 19, was to perpetuate and modify this system in the interests of the litigant. Cap. 17 provided that common pleas should not follow the king as he moved about the country, but should be held in a definite place. This involved a return to the informal division of the court into two, one sitting

---

[126] See below, p. 400.

[127] *Dialogus*, p. 96. Fitz Neal distinguished between greater and lesser baronies, not barons. Magna Carta does not mention lesser barons, but implies their existence by mentioning the greater.

[128] It should be noted that cap. 14 did not distinguish between the greater barons and 'others', but simply distinguished the greater barons within the class of tenants-in-chief. The reading is *illos* not *alios*. The distinction was not related to the different scales of relief established in cap. 2 (Round, 1917, pp. 46–51). See also Reynolds (1984a), pp. 306–7.

with the king and the other, the Bench, usually holding its sessions at Westminster. In 1209 King John apparently ordered the cessation of pleas in the Bench.[129] It was becoming difficult, if not impossible, to run two courts effectively. Immediately the move was possibly occasioned by the effects of the Interdict on those judges who were clerks; a few certainly went into exile. John presumably acted in the matter with the advice of the Justiciar, and certainly the court with the king showed considerable concern in saving litigants inconvenience. But there were no sessions of the Bench until it was slowly and partially revived from 1212 onwards at a time when the king was increasingly involved in the deepening political crisis and the campaign in Poitou. John had not been inefficient. Some of his best judges had accompanied him on his travels. It was simply that the itinerant court was often less convenient geographically than the fixed Bench. The itinerant court moved on. The Bench, in contrast, sat in regular and lengthy sessions. It had the advantage of continuity. The Charter therefore provided for a return to the arrangements of the earlier years of the reign.[130]

Cap. 17 sought more justice. So also did cap. 18. Indeed it probably sought more than was possible. It laid down that possessory assizes were to be held in the county where the case arose. There were to be quarterly circuits of two justices who were to sit with four knights of the shire. The drafters of the Charter sought prompt litigation at the cost of increasing the burden on the justices. In 1217 the number of

---

[129] *Curia Regis Rolls*, v, 327.
[130] For the above paragraph, see Doris M. Stenton (1958), 116–26, and her introduction to *Pipe Roll 6 John*, pp. xxi–xx (see also Flower, 1944, pp. 19–20). Richardson & Sayles's conclusion that John's actions in these matters were 'gratuitous acts of folly' (1963, pp. 384–7) allows insufficient weight to Lady Stenton's careful review of the evidence. The problem has now been re-examined in great detail in Clanchy (1985), who proposes important revisions of the interpretation of *communia placita* and *in certo loco*. He also provides a valuable account of John's administration of justice from 1209 onwards, but, in so doing, may well underestimate the king's personal intervention in earlier years, which was very fully studied by Lady Stenton. See above, pp. 180–2.

circuits was reduced to one per year and the association of knights with the justices was made less definite.[131] The Charter also ranged over a wide variety of matters connected with the operations of the courts. It touched on appeals by women,[132] the Crown's retention of the lands of felons,[133] and the issue of the writ of life and limb.[134] It excluded sheriffs and other royal bailiffs from holding pleas of the Crown.[135] It laid down that justices and other officials were to be chosen from those who knew the law of the land.[136] It forbade the use of the writ *praecipe* in such a manner that a free man might be deprived of the jurisdiction of his court.[137] This clause, which some of the older authorities hailed as a demonstration of the 'feudal' outlook of the barons of 1215, was only of minor political importance.[138] Neither King John nor his father had deliberately intruded into the property rights of their tenants by denying their established rights of jurisdiction. In 1215 the barons likewise made no attempt to prevent appeals to royal jurisdiction through the lengthy processes initiated by the writ of right. The writ *praecipe* was a summary means of bringing a civil action about property into the royal court, but it did not exclude private jurisdiction. It compelled the holder of a private court to appear in the royal court to claim and prove his right to exercise it. If he did so he was allowed it. Cap. 34 was concerned less with an unreal conflict between 'feudal' and 'anti-feudal' principles than

---

[131] Magna Carta (1217), cap. 12.   [132] Cap. 54.   [133] Cap. 32.
[134] Cap. 36.
[135] Cap. 24. This had been foreshadowed in 1194 (see above, p. 299). There were twenty occasions between 1194 and 1209 when sheriffs or under-sheriffs acted as judges in their own shire. There were fourteen more cases in 1210 – their activity in this year was subsequently investigated by another eyre (see C. F. Slade in *Pipe Roll 12 John*, pp. xvi–xxii).
[136] Cap. 45 (see also *Pipe Roll 12 John*, p. xxii).
[137] Cap. 34. The writ in question was the *praecipe quod reddat*. This instructed a sheriff to order the tenant of a named piece of land to restore it to a plaintiff or to appear before the king or his justices to give reasons for not doing so (Glanvill, I, 6, ed. Hall, p. 5).
[138] Compare McKechnie (1914), p. 346: 'The grievance here dealt with lay at the heart of the quarrel of 1215.'

with an administrative nuisance. It limited the use of the *praecipe* to cases between tenants-in-chief of the Crown and led to the development of an effective writ of prohibition against its misuse in other actions.[139] Meanwhile litigants sought and lawyers provided other devices, like the writs of entry, as alternative methods of bringing actions into the royal courts. But the subsequent legal results of cap. 34, which were considerable, should not be permitted to exaggerate its contemporary importance.[140] Much more crucial for the tenant-in-chief was the securing in the next ten years or so of the *praecipe in capite* as the barons' writ of right.[141]

The Charter dealt with all these matters reasonably competently. It aimed at ensuring the exercise of even-handed justice in regular sessions of the courts and it laid down the administrative framework within which that might be achieved. However, it was much more difficult to relate these concepts to the government itself. The king's officials were relatively easy to deal with. Cap. 38 laid down that no one need answer unsupported charges originating from bailiffs.[142] But the king himself was a different matter. True, John had taken a serious and increasingly personal interest in the courts of justice. But justice was a source of revenue. Like his predecessors, John was ever ready to accept special proffers from vassals in search of their own

---

[139] The writ *de non intromittendo*.
[140] This interpretation of cap. 34 was securely established by Naomi D. Hurnard (1948), pp. 157–79 (see also Doris M. Stenton in *Pipe Roll 6 John*, pp. xxiii–xxxiii). Some important amendments to Miss Hurnard's views are suggested by Clanchy (1964), 542–8. These arguments are supported by more general studies of the interrelations of royal and private jurisdiction (see in particular Cam, 1957, 427–42).
[141] See above pp. 141–4, 173–4.
[142] McKechnie (1914, pp. 370–5) and others have taken a much narrower view of this clause, namely that it was aimed at preventing bailiffs from examining defendants without witnesses. The use of the word *loquela* rather than *visus* indicates that the bailiff was here considered as a party, not as an official of the court. It seems likely that the clause was aimed against unsupported allegations by officials. For a good example see the case of Baldwin Tyrel, where members of the royal household stated that they were required on oath to report words spoken against the king (*Curia Regis Rolls*, VII, 168–73) (see also the action against the sheriff of Devon, above, pp. 66–7).

particular view of justice. Furthermore, after 1204 he was almost continuously accessible in England. This encouraged a vigorous market.[143] Against this cap. 40 of the Charter now simply asserted the principle that justice should not be sold, denied or delayed.[144] This clause was repeated in all reissues of the Charter. During the next decade the king was a minor, with restricted patronage. Within that period the writ *praecipe in capite* became a writ *de cursu*. The charter and these surrounding circumstances changed matters fundamentally. No later king persistently sold justice as John had done. Justice was still sold; there were numerous public complaints against the practice in the fourteenth century, but these were directed against Chancery and conciliar jurisdictions, which were then emerging alongside the common law. Cap. 40 could only be applied to these new forms of jurisdiction by renewed political struggle and debate, by then largely centred in parliament.[145]

Cap. 39 encountered similar difficulties. Like cap. 40, it embodied traditional procedures and received notions which had been repeated most recently in the papal letters of 19 March and John's offer to the dissidents of 10 May.[146] It seems to have been aimed first against purely arbitrary action by the Crown: against arbitrary disseisin at the will of the king,[147] or the summary process which John apparently tried to inflict on the northerners in the autumn of 1213,[148] or against arrest and imprisonment on an administrative order.[149] An answer to such actions was not difficult to find, given the general acceptance of the equation of justice with judgement. It could be provided, as in the 'unknown' charter, by a simple proviso that there should be no arrest without judgement.[150] However, the Articles and the

---

[143] Flower (1943), pp. 480, 488–96.
[144] For the origins of this provision, see above, pp. 285–6.
[145] Stubbs (1896), II, 636–7.   [146] See above, pp. 230, 234.
[147] For examples, see above, pp. 81–3.   [148] See above, p. 220.
[149] Powicke (1917), pp. 114–21.   [150] Cap. 1.

Charter went further in laying down that the king should not proceed against any free man 'except by lawful judgement of his peers or by the law of the land'.[151] The meaning of these terms has been elucidated as far as possible by Powicke.[152] The word 'peers' was used in the general sense of social equals.[153] Judgement by peers or by the law of the land were advanced as loose, but not exclusive, alternatives.[154] The intention was that men should be judged by their peers or by some other method which was in accordance with the law of the land. This left room for indictment or appeal, which might involve the duel or end in outlawry if the accused failed to appear. It also included the civil actions which had emerged under Henry II, any one of which might lead to the dispossession of a litigant.

As Powicke showed, this interpretation of the clause seems to have been accepted in the actions of Hubert de Burgh and Gilbert Basset in 1233–4. Cap. 39, in fact, left the form of judgement no more precise than it had been hitherto. This is surprising since John's actions required explicit regulation at this point. In the main he had not acted

[151] The Articles do not include the word 'lawful'.
[152] Powicke (1917), pp. 98–107.
[153] See above, pp. 75 6, for the general usage of the word. See also information additional to that in Powicke in Poole (1951), p. 475 n. Nevertheless the case of William Marshal clearly implies that both he and the king acted on the basis that William's peers were his fellow barons. The involvement of peers in the promulgation of the process against William de Briouze suggests the same (see above, p. 109). Compare also the proffer of Roger Bigod, below, p. 331.
[154] Powicke (1917), p. 99. Cp. the argument for the conjunctive sense of the famous *vel*, see Vinogradoff, *M.C.C.E.* p. 80. It is worth noting that the clerk who transcribed the version of the Charter used in the confirmation of 1253 used the word *aut* here (see Holt, 1964, 81). The Anglo-Norman version of the Charter uses *o* (i.e. *ou*). See below, p. 474. Ullmann's interpretation of this clause is vitiated partly by his return to the conjunctive sense of *vel* and partly by his miscomprehension of the word *judicium* which means 'judgement' in the English legal records of the period. It may have meant 'court' to a canonist, but the terms of the two systems were not interchangeable. It is therefore quite unacceptable to read this clause as Ullmann seems to do: '. . . by a court of peers and according to the law of the land'. Ullmann also refines the words *lex terrae* so as to exclude the custom of the realm (1961, pp. 165–6). This is unjustified. Compare Powicke (1917), p. 101, which suggests that *lex terrae* rather than *lex regni* was used so as to include local custom.

arbitrarily in important political actions. He had used lawful process of one kind or another and in varying situations, against Geoffrey of York, John de Courcy, William Marshal, William de Briouze, Robert fitz Walter and Eustace de Vescy.[155] The condemnation of de Briouze especially was a frightening demonstration of the extent to which the formal processes of the law could be turned against men whom the king was determined to destroy. This, rather than straightforward arbitrary behaviour, was the real problem which faced the drafters of the Charter. Cap. 39 led not to agreed procedure but to wrangling. When Richard Marshal and Gilbert Basset appealed to judgement by peers in 1233 they were answered by Peter des Roches, 'There are no peers in England.'[156] When the decrees of outlawry against Gilbert Basset and Hubert de Burgh and other supporters of the earl marshal were annulled, it was not by proclaiming the primacy of the judgement by peers which they had demanded over other processes, but by declaring that there had been irregularities in the procedure of outlawry in the shire court and that some of the acts which had led to their sentence had been done in time of war after a formal defiance.[157] The law of the land still stood, including exactly the same processes which John had used against fitz Walter and de Vescy and, in the end, against William de Briouze.

John was primarily responsible for this. On 19 March Innocent III had written that the king's quarrel with the dissident barons should be determined in his court by their peers in accordance with the custom and law of the realm.[158] This in effect would have restricted the form of process, and when John followed up these instructions in his letters

---

[155] See above, pp. 107–9.
[156] 'dixit quod non sunt pares in Anglia, sicut in regno Francorum; unde licet regi Anglorum per justitiarios, quos constituerit, quoslibet de regno reos proscribere et mediante judicio condempnare' (*Chron. Maj*, III, 252).
[157] Powicke (1917), pp. 105–7 (see also Powicke, 1947, I, 125–40).
[158] *M.C.C.E.* p. 43: *Letters of Innocent III*, no. 1013.

patent of 10 May he made a vitally important amendment: 'We shall not go against them except by the law of our realm or by the judgement of their peers in our court.'[159] Now, as Powicke pointed out, judgement by peers *or* by the law of the realm is very different from judgement by peers *according to* the law of the realm.[160] Judgement by the law of the realm rather than the reference to the king's court, which was already mentioned in Innocent's letters, was the significant reinforcement of John's position. He had now made it unassailable. It may be that the barons tried to weaken it by amending the law of the realm to the law of the land, but they were committed to the phrase in one form or other. The law of the land was just what they were trying to establish and define. The royal initiative in choosing forms of action and influencing judicial process, which John had exploited so ingeniously, came under its protection. His son and grandson and their successors did not use these powers so skilfully or ruthlessly. But they used them. The Charter limited them to an increasing extent as time passed, not so much because cap. 39 stated anything explicit, as because it created conditions for argument. Who was the free man? What was judgement by peers? What was the law of the land? Cap. 39 owed its greatness to the assertion of the principle that judgement should precede execution. Inevitably, it stated it in imprecise generalities which were to be exploited by generation after generation.

That is to look forward in time. Looking backwards the terms are much more precise and stand in sharper contrast. For lawful judgement of peers was an antique remedy which might have been applied to all the legal actions between tenants-in-chief which had gone so awry in the years before 1215. In this light the two processes of cap. 39 stand as contrasting options determined by tenure and jurisdictional

[159] See appendix 11, below, pp. 492–3.   [160] Powicke (1917), p. 103 and n.

330

structure: lawful judgement of peers between barons for baronies before the king as lord; the law of the land for other men, sometimes for barons in other causes, and in other courts than *coram rege*. The intention could well have been to provide every baron with the privilege for which Roger Bigod paid 1000 m. in 1189–90. He sought the earldom of Norfolk and the assurance that his [half] brother, Hugh, should not be given seisin of any of the Bigod lands *nisi per judicium curie domini regis factum per pares suos*.[161] This supposed a royal court of barons precisely analogous to the demand of 1215; analogous not just to the lawful judgement of peers of cap. 39 but also to the court of Twenty-Five. In the event the dissolution of the king's feudal jurisdiction rendered such a sharp distinction unnecessary. In the fourteenth century judgement of peers for the baron came to mean a distinct process, narrowly defined, for major actions such as treason. Nevertheless, he got better day-to-day justice, not by establishing a court of privilege, but by embodying himself within the common law. In so doing, in a longer term, he set cap. 39 free to journey towards trial by jury and due process.

Over the whole field of law, feudal service and feudal incidents, the achievements of the Charter, for all its occasional vagueness and inadequacy, were considerable. The king's opponents had a sound case, both for intervening in general and for providing most of the particular solutions which they chose. If the subtlety of John's government found them wanting in powers of expression and definition, the general aim and principle of the Charter was clear enough. Some of the problems they faced were beyond solution at this stage. English kings still exercised powers of arbitrary arrest and imprisonment in the seventeenth century. The actions of the courts were not even then indepen-

---

[161] *Pipe Roll 2 Richard I*, p. 101.

dent of the royal will.[162] On the continent similar powers lasted as long as the *ancien régime*. Magna Carta did not and could not solve such matters overnight.

Where it concerned justice the Charter asserted broad principles which had their roots deep in the past. On the question of finance this was not so easy. Financial administration changed while the principles of justice remained unaltered. Yet they overlapped in the imposition of amercements. Here in caps. 20, 21 and 22, the Charter turned once again to precedent. Cap. 20 provided that amercements should fit the nature of the offence, that they should not be so heavy as to deprive a man, even a villein, of his means of livelihood,[163] and that they should be assessed by local juries. Cap. 22 applied the same principles to the clergy, but limited the assessment in their case to temporalities. Cap. 21 departed from precedent in laying down that barons should be amerced by their peers, but it also related amercements to the offence in question. The broad principles of these clauses had many precedents. Glanvill had stated that men were to be amerced by the men of the neighbourhood in such a manner that their livelihood was not affected.[164] The principle that amercements should fit the crime had been acknowledged in the Charter of Henry I.[165] Private charters both before and after 1215 included provisions similar to those in Magna Carta.[166] Some went further in laying down maxima for monetary penalties.[167] Becket himself had

---

[162] For much-needed emphasis on the constitutional continuity of the period between the later middle ages and the seventeenth century, see J. S. Roskell, 'Perspectives in English Parliamentary History', *B.J.R.L.* XLVI (1964), 448–75.

[163] For the meaning of *contenementum*, see Tait (1912), 720–8 (see also Poole, 1946, pp. 89–90).

[164] 'Est autem misericordia domini regis qua quis eatenus per iuramentum legalium hominum de visneto immerciandus est ne aliquid de suo honorabili tenemento amittat', Glanvill, IX, II ed. Hall, p. 114.

[165] Cap. 8.

[166] See above, pp. 58, 67–8.

[167] See above, p. 58. See also a grant of Adam fitz Alan Bouseier of Milburn, Westmorland, to William de Surays and Beatrice his wife in which Adam agreed that if the grantees were convicted of an offence without bloodshed they should fine six pence, if with

claimed that the law of Kent limited amercements to 40s.[168] How far the amercements of free men were assessed by local juries under John is difficult to establish. The justices certainly imposed amercements but this need not have excluded later assessment by juries. They also pardoned them, often because the debtor was poor.[169] But despite instances of alleviation, the number of heavy amercements increased as the reign advanced both in the king's court and before the justices in eyre.[170] Presumably these were the trends which produced cap. 20. The origins of cap. 21 were much clearer. Barons were amerced at the Exchequer.[171] They had frequently been amerced extremely heavily, especially for offences against the forest law. Sometimes an amercement on what was arguably a formal matter could develop into an enormous offer to recover the good will of the king. By the end of the thirteenth century, for example, a fixed scale had emerged for the amercement of non-baronial bailiffs for the escape of a criminal; in most counties

---

bloodshed a shilling 'saving my person and the person of my heirs' (c. 1190–1200) (H.M.C. Various, II, 338). Compare also a grant of John fitz Geoffrey of Willoughby to John son of Andrew of Willoughby which includes: 'volo autem et concedo quod si predictus Johannes filius Andrei vel heredes sui vel assignati sui in curia mea cadit, non debet amerciari ultra sex denarios argenti' (c. 1250) (University of Nottingham, Middleton Deeds, MiD. 1171).

[168] Materials for the History of Thomas Becket, ed. J. C. Robertson (Rolls Series, 1877), III, 62.

[169] See in general Vernon Harcourt (1907), 732–40. Harcourt produced one instance of an assessment by jury in 14 Henry II (734 n.). For other references to affeerment see Pipe Roll 22 Henry II, p. 129; Pipe Roll 24 Henry II, p. 63; Pipe Roll 26 Henry II, p. xxvii. Maitland assumed that the procedure described by Glanvill and in cap. 20 of the Charter was in operation (Pollock & Maitland (1898) II, 513), but produced no supporting evidence. The matter was not discussed by Flower or A. L. Poole. The records themselves are enigmatic on this point (see, for example, Lincs. Assize Rolls, 1202–9, pp. 168–94), but since amercements were so numerous and were usually uniformly assessed at ¼ or one mark, it seems likely that juries were used only when the debtor protested against the assessment. However, the many cases where amercements were pardoned on grounds of poverty provide no direct evidence of this.

[170] Flower (1944), pp. 463–72. For justices in eyre see the record of the 'autumnal' justices of 1210, Pipe Roll 12 John, pp. xv–xvi. This eyre was exceptional.

[171] 'Henricus (de Bolhay) est baro domini regis; amerciandus est ad scaccarium' (Curia Regis Rolls, II, 267). Compare Lincolnshire Assize Rolls 1202–9, case 173. For the affeerment of a baron (Eustace de Vescy), apparently to be made in the Exchequer for a penalty imposed by itinerant justices, see Rot. Lib., p. 58.

it cost the offender £5.[172] Under John a baron, Robert de Ros, was charged with 300 m. for the same offence.[173] In another case in 1196 Robert was imprisoned and had to carry the amercement of 1200 m. when a French prisoner escaped with the collusion of one of his sergeants.[174] Collusion was a serious crime and the loss of a ransom a weighty matter, but it is questionable whether the size of this amercement was justified by Robert's baronial status and the nature of the offence. The Charter's remedy for barons was perhaps naïve and cumbersome. Amercement by peers was put forward to avoid personal assessment by the king and to mitigate amercement in the Exchequer by introducing a baronial element more sympathetic to the transgressor and less concerned with the king's revenue. It failed. The chapter remained in the later re-issues of the Charter, but it was simply evaded by the Crown through a convenient interpretation of the word 'peers'. Bracton's gloss, 'that is by the barons of the exchequer or before the king himself', fairly represented thirteenth-century practice.[175] The Crown reasserted the *status quo*. In the long run the baron was protected not by any procedural innovation but by the expansion of the older idea of a maximum penalty.[176]

These clauses were restricted to amercements. The Charter laid down nothing for the future to regulate debts contracted willingly by the debtor. It seems to have assumed, as indeed fitz Neal had argued,[177] that these were in a different category where the debtor was much more

---

[172] Vernon Harcourt (1907), 738.
[173] *Rot. de Ob. et Fin.* p. 413. The amercement was later pardoned (*Rot. Litt. Claus.* I, 99).
[174] *Pipe Roll 9 Richard I*, p. 61.
[175] 'Et hoc per barones de scaccario vel coram ipso rege', Bracton, fo. 116b, tr. Thorne, II, 330. By *coram ipso rege*, as Vernon Harcourt points out, Bracton probably intended the *coram rege* court, or the king in council (1907, 737 and n.). For such amercements *coram rege* under John, see *Pipe Roll 2 John*, p. 18. A more personal process is suggested by the amercement for a forest offence imposed on the abbot of Furness *per os regis* in 1206 (*Rot. de Ob. et Fin.* p. 365).
[176] Vernon Harcourt (1907), 737–8; McKechnie (1914), pp. 297–8.
[177] *Dialogus*, pp. 119–21.

responsible for his own plight. It arranged for the remission of unjust fines and offerings contracted with King John,[178] but otherwise it only touched the fringes of the problem. Cap. 9 provided that distraint was to fall on the principal debtor before the pledges and on chattels before land, but it did not forbid distraint on land. Indeed it allowed it implicitly. Nor did it prohibit imprisonment for debt. Cap. 26 prescribed the procedure which the king's officers were to follow in collecting debts on the death of a tenant, but it still allowed them to intrude into his estates in pursuit of the king's debts.[179] Cap. 16 of the Articles demanded a regulation covering cases of intestacy. Cap. 27 of the Charter provided it but included a saving clause to protect the interests of creditors, among whom the Crown was likely to be foremost. Cap. 10 provided that debts owed to Jews were not to accrue interest during a minority, and cap. 11 protected widows and minors from excessive demands for the repayment of debts to both Jews and others, but the Charter had nothing to say about the acquisition of Jewish bonds by monasteries, or of the inordinate rates of interest which were charged. It allowed the reversion of the debts of dead Jews to the Crown. It said nothing of the manner in which the Crown had in the past distrained on land to collect the debts both of dead Jews and, on the occasion of the heavy Bristol tallage of 1210, of Jews who were alive. It simply left distraint of this kind to come under the general processes laid down in cap. 9. It even implicitly allowed the Crown to collect interest as well as capital on this kind of debt except during the minority of an heir.[180] In 1208 John took into his hand a debt of £1015. 7s. 11d. which Henry d'Oylly owed to Simon the Jew of Oxford. He laid down

---

[178] Cap. 55 (see below, pp. 362–5).

[179] The procedure outlined in this clause differed from that already in use in restricting distraint to the amount of the debt (cp. *Pipe Roll 5 John*, p. 103).

[180] This interpretation assumes that the *debitum illud* of the last section of this clause refers not to Jewish debts in general, but to those debts which lay against minors. This interpretation is confirmed by 20 Henry III, cap. 5 (*Statutes of the Realm*, I, 3).

that Henry was to pay it off at 200 m. per annum. If he did not keep these terms then the chancellor, Walter de Gray, who held Henry's bond, would restore the bond to Simon the Jew and Henry would lose all he had paid hitherto.[181] Caps. 9, 10 and 11 were no protection against this.

These clauses were superficial. It may well be that the drafters of the Charter hesitated to interfere permanently in the administration of the Crown at a point where amendments to royal procedure might come to have important and restricting effects on their own capacity to collect debts or distrain upon their tenants. These clauses reveal a healthy respect for existing usages and rights. To the Christian layman of this time, the Jews were an unfortunate financial necessity. Nothing could be done about them or their debts, or the Crown's established prerogative to collect the debts of dead Jews. Indeed it seems likely that caps. 10 and 11 were omitted from the re-issues of 1216 and 1217, not because they were damaging to the real interests of the Crown, but because they seemed to be an unjustifiable if trivial invasion of its rights; the principle of the two clauses was soon confirmed by the Crown itself in the Statute of Merton of 1236.[182]

A similar attitude was again revealed in cap. 25, which excepted the royal demesne from the ruling that shires, hundreds, wapentakes and ridings were to yield the ancient farms without any increment. The Crown could be left to manage itself in its own private sphere. Peter de Brus's charter of liberties for Cleveland shows how this was done and how a local community reacted.[183] Peter purchased the wapentake at the ancient farm of 10 m. *blanche* and an increment of £20. His charter ignored the assay of the old farm and treated farm and increment as an annual sum of 40 m. His tenants then agreed, in return for their liberties, to

---

[181] *Pipe Roll 10 John*, p. 139.   [182] 20 Henry III, cap. 5 (*Statutes of the Realm*, I, 3).
[183] See above, pp. 67–70.

make up any reasonable deficit in the farm, as presented by Peter's sergeant, and to meet the reasonable expenses of the sergeant as testified by Peter and his stewards. Similar arrangements probably underlay all bids in which local communities combined to secure the appointment of particular sheriffs or some such control over local government.[184] In short, men were ready to contribute to increments in return for a *quid pro quo* which involved arrangements for account. That could scarcely be achieved in every case: hence the prohibition of cap. 25; it countered an increase in ancient, established assessment on local communities except by agreement. But one matter was omitted: there was no mention of custodian-sheriffs and no prohibition of 'profits' in excess of the shire farm. The implication is that if the king wished to make arrangements of that kind, which involved a variable and unpredictable yield in addition to the farm and the payment of the sheriffs' expenses, that was his look out. Increments would lead to a revised assessment of the local community. Profits, which were variable and therefore incapable of assessment, would not.

This last clause also reveals another broad influence on the Charter. It had already been conceded by the king in the spring of 1213.[185] Indeed the Charter rarely intruded into any administrative matter except where it confirmed a selected precedent.[186] Only perhaps on the question of purveyance did it move away from this sure ground, and even here it largely confined itself to regulating the demands of the king's bailiffs.[187] It did not forbid such demands, nor

---

[184] See above, pp. 61–4.   [185] See above, p. 213.

[186] On caps, 1, 33 and 41, see above, pp. 298–9. Cap. 41 was probably occasioned by the fifteenth on merchants which John had imposed in 1203–5, by the increasingly tight control which his custodians of the ports came to exercise in the middle and later years of the reign, and by the restrictions which were imposed because of the war with France and the Interdict. Cap. 42 invaded the traditional position of the Crown as stated in the Constitutions of Clarendon, cap. 4, and was excluded from the 1216 and subsequent re-issues. It had a precedent, however, in the compromise of Avranches of 1172 (*Gesta Henrici*, I, 32).

[187] Caps. 28, 30, 31. Cap. 31, which laid down that the Crown was not to take wood for castle repair without the consent of the owner, applied to the king as well as his bailiffs.

did it touch on the use of purveyance for the maintenance of the royal court or for the supply of the royal armies. These were big issues, which were only just taking shape and were to be the source of later crises.

On administrative matters the Charter presented little more than patchwork derived from selected precedent and applied to the fringes of the fabric of government. Even so the permanent regulations which the Charter was intended to establish were, taken as a whole, a remarkable statement of the rights of the governed and of the principle that the king should be ruled by law. If the supporters of the Charter had ended their work with this it might well have stood without a civil war; the dangers would have come from attempted evasion not from direct contravention. But they did not. Instead they tackled matters which were infinitely more dubious and contentious. They were dubious because there was less legal justification for intervention. They were contentious not only because they led to a renewal of the war between the king and the barons, but also because they increased the factious dissidence within the baronial party.

The royal forest was the first of these to develop. The drafters of the Charter had no good precedent for intervening here.[188] On the other hand the enormous amercements for forest offences which the Crown had sometimes imposed, and the manner in which it had used its rights to exploit economic development carried out on private estates within the forest, took the issue beyond the confines of legal precedent.[189] Hence they were faced from the first with a powerful and radical demand for the partial destruction of the royal forest and the control of what remained. The

[188] See above, pp. 85, 301-2.
[189] For the general development of the forest in the twelfth century, see Poole (1951), pp. 29-35, Young (1979), pp. 1-73 and Turner (1899). See also the introductions to the printed Pipe rolls for the years 1175-7, 1198-9, 1207-9 and 1212.

'unknown' charter envisaged that the bounds should be restricted to the limits in force at the accession of Henry II.[190] It also provided for a reduction in the severity of forest penalties and for the maintenance of the rights of those who had private woods within the forest; they were to enjoy full rights of pasturage and fuel and were to have their own foresters.[191] The crucial demand here was for the reduction of the bounds, for Henry II had rivalled and probably outdone his grandfather and the earlier Norman kings in extending royal forests in almost every suitable shire in the land. If executed it would have involved a serious diminution in the rights and financial resources of the Crown.[192] The Charter met it with an inadequate and unsatisfactory compromise. First, cap. 47 confirmed cap. 47 of the Articles, which had demanded the disafforestation of all areas afforested by John. This admitted the principle of limiting the bounds, but made negligible material concessions since John had afforested next to nothing and disafforested extensive areas in all parts of the country.[193] It was therefore an extremely dangerous provision which whetted but did not satisfy the appetite. Perhaps this was realized. Further disafforestations were considered, but in the end John was given the crusader's respite on areas afforested by Henry II and Richard I.[194] At the same time little was done about the manner in which the forest law was enforced. The only concession here was to restrict the suit of court of men who lived outside the forest to those cases in which they were

---

[190] Cap. 9. [191] Caps. 10, 12.

[192] For the extent of the royal forest in the thirteenth century and some discussion of the earlier bounds, see Bazeley (1921), 140–72. For a more detailed map of the northern royal forests, see Holt (1961), map 2 and pp. 194–5. See also the appropriate sections of the Victoria County Histories and Turner (1899). There is further comment in Young (1979), pp. 18–21.

[193] A rare example of afforestation by King John in Lancashire is mentioned in *Close Rolls, 1227–31*, p. 101, where it is noted that he afforested Smethdown, but gave Thingwall to 'a certain poor man' in exchange. For John's disafforestations, see above, pp. 60–1 and Young (1979), pp. 20–1.

[194] Cap. 53.

personally concerned as either a principal or a pledge.[195] There was no repetition or expansion of the clauses in the 'unknown' charter which had envisaged the reform of the forest regulations. These were replaced by cap. 48, which arranged for a general inquiry by local juries into the evil customs of the forest and foresters, and into the behaviour of the sheriffs and other bailiffs of the king. The programme for reform had in fact been shelved, but at great cost to all parties. The radicals who had advanced the proposals of the 'unknown' charter had not got what they wanted. The king had made minimal concessions on the bounds and delayed any action on the customs of the forests, but had permitted local inquiries into all aspects of local administration. The moderates had achieved a compromise, but one which soon proved unworkable. The investigations into the forest provoked outbreaks of lawlessness which undermined the forest administration and gave the king just cause for complaint.[196] The forest clauses were an immediate and dangerous failure which settled nothing. On the contrary they provided grounds for the renewal of war.

The various measures taken in the Charter for the restitution of property and rights were potentially even more disastrous. On one issue the barons took a reasonable line. Cap. 46 of the Charter laid down that barons who had founded abbeys were to enjoy custody of them during vacancies if they could prove their right of advowson by ancient tenure or royal grant.[197] Here the claim was directed to rights which might accrue in the future. But in all the other similar clauses the barons turned their eyes upon the past. In effect, they attempted to apply their concept of

[195] Cap. 44. The object here was to escape amercements for default of court in answer to a general summons.
[196] See below, p. 352.
[197] This was provoked in part by the confused claims to patronage into which the Crown had steadily penetrated in the course of the twelfth century, partly by John's custody of certain abbeys during the Interdict and partly by John's confinement of such grants of patronage to his friends (see Susan M. Wood, *English Monasteries and their Patrons in the XIII Century*, Oxford, 1955, and Cheney, 1949, 134–6).

justice retrospectively. Procedure, judgement, amercement, were not only to be reasonable in the future. Restitution was also to be made for all the sins of commission or omission which could be charged against the Crown in the past. This created two grave problems. First, to what was this to be applied? Secondly, from what period was such restitution to be demanded?

The first question was answered more firmly than the second. Cap. 25 of the Articles provided for the restitution of lands, liberties and rights which had been seized unjustly by the Crown. Caps. 44 and 46 applied the same principle to the Welsh and the Scots. Cap. 37, even more dangerously, demanded that proffers or penalties which had been accepted or imposed unjustly and contrary to the law of the land should also be pardoned. The Charter confirmed all this with little apparent demur or difficulty.[198] It also revealed that there had been a demand for the restitution of abbeys in royal custody to which there were private claims and of land held by the Crown in prerogative wardship. However, on these matters, which were comparatively unimportant, the king was given the crusader's respite.[199]

The extent of retrospection was more difficult and much more toughly fought. The original cry of the baronial party for the restoration of the laws of Edward the Confessor and Henry I indicated that they regarded 1154 as a suitable dividing line for separating good from evil custom. This indeed was applied in the demand for disafforestation in the 'unknown' charter.[200] By June 1215, however, this radical approach had been countered by the king's offer of the spring in which he attempted to distinguish between evil customs which had arisen since 1189 and those of his father's reign 'if there were any that were evil'.[201] The Articles carried matters further, for caps. 25, 44 and 46 clearly

---

[198] Caps. 52, 55, 56, 59. On the attitude of the bishops to these clauses and the difficulty of the Scottish treaties, see above, pp. 286–8.
[199] Cap. 53.   [200] Cap. 9.   [201] See above, pp. 117, 234.

revealed some doubts whether John's acts of injustice and violence could be placed in the same category as those of his predecessors. John was responsible for his own acts and was there to answer claims. He was not responsible for what his brother and father had done. Hence cap. 25 demanded that claims against him were to be met immediately or submitted to the judgement of the Twenty-Five. Claims against them were to be submitted to judgement by peers or, if the king was given the crusader's respite, to the judgement of the archbishop and bishops. The Charter confirmed these doubts. Here a sharp line was drawn between John's acts of injustice and those of his predecessors. He was committed to immediate restitution, while their acts, like their afforestations, were covered by the crusader's privilege.[202] For the king this was only a temporary respite, but much could happen before it ended. Meanwhile he had won an important point. The dividing line between valid and less valid acts of government, which his opponents had first placed at 1154 and which he had earlier considered conceding at 1189, was now put at 1199. He had gained something from the passage of time and the intricacies of negotiation.

These retrospective clauses were among the most important and most bitterly fought in the whole Charter. The barons demanded their execution at once as soon as peace was agreed at Runnymede. But they were not easy to execute. The more important the case the more likely it was to lead to acrimonious discussion and division. Some of these contributed directly to the renewal of war in the autumn. Indeed the first acts of war were direct continuations of legal actions of this kind.[203] That John resisted the baronial demands was natural enough. He must also have reflected bitterly on cap. 62 of the Charter. This required him to proclaim an amnesty for all breaches of the peace committed since Easter 1215. It also required him to remit

---

[202] Caps. 47, 52, 53, 56, 57, 59.   [203] See below, pp. 361–5.

all ill will and rancour incurred since the beginning of his quarrel with the barons. The clauses of the Charter which demanded restitution scarcely encouraged the remission of such rancour. John might have responded to a *quid pro quo*, but he was not well cast in the rôle of a solitary penitent.

The establishment of the committee of Twenty-Five under the terms of cap. 61 was strictly related to these clauses of restitution.[204] Cap. 25 of the Articles required them to adjudicate on all cases of unjust disseisin which John disputed. Cap. 37 required them to intervene in a similar manner in all disputed cases of unjust fines and amercements. Both these functions were confirmed in the Charter.[205] The committee of Twenty-Five was not regarded as a council but as a court to which appeal might be made against breaches of the Charter. It had no power to act unless it received a complaint. The barons clearly expected that it would not have to remain in continuous plenary session. A small quorum of four was to be available to hear complaints and was empowered to require the king to satisfy those that were justified.[206] As a court it was given the power of distraint against the lands, castles and possessions of the Crown, saving the persons of the royal family. This was not a licence to make civil war.[207] The barons already had the capacity to levy war against the king and had already done so through the formal process of defiance and renunciation of fealty. The Charter now allowed them to distrain the king by acts which were in practice warlike, and yet still remain the king's men and retain title to land and liberties. Cap. 61 was not conceived as a primitive form of constitutional

---

[204] For a similar line of argument see Palmer (1985), pp. 390–5.
[205] Caps. 52, 55.
[206] Robert fitz Walter's letters to William d'Aubigné provide evidence that the Twenty-Five did not remain together after Runnymede (*Foedera*, I, part I, 134). Their surviving writs provide clear evidence for the operations of a quorum of four (see appendix 11, below, pp. 499–500).
[207] Plucknett (1949), pp. 75–6.

control over the king. If it had been it would justly merit the ponderous criticism which it has sometimes received.[208] It was a legal device, cunningly and precisely arranged to apply compulsion and at the same time enable the barons to remain within the limits of peaceful relationships. The establishment of the committee of Twenty-Five did not itself cause the civil war in the autumn. War arose rather from the task which the committee was required to perform. The retrospective clauses of restitution, not their method of enforcement, were the real cause of the breakdown.

Once again the Charter showed little sense of equity. While a machinery of compulsion was devised against the king, caps. 49 and 58 laid down that he was to surrender all hostages and charters of fealty which he had obtained from his men. The methods of compulsion which he had built up were now destroyed. Similarly, while the barons remained in arms, he was required to dismiss his foreign mercenaries,[209] and remove his Tourangeaux bailiffs from offices.[210] Justices, constables, sheriffs and bailiffs were to be chosen in future from those who knew the law of the land and were ready to observe it.[211] It may be granted that the foreigners were harsh and efficient administrators, who also exploited office in their own interests.[212] But this was true of many

[208] See, for example, McKechnie (1914), pp. 129, 473.
[209] Cap. 51.
[210] Cap. 50.
[211] Cap. 45. It may be that this clause was also directed against the employment of inefficient justices (see *Pipe Roll 12 John*, p. xxii). On this see R. V. Turner, 'The reputation of royal judges under the Angevin Kings', *Albion*, XI (1979), 301–16. For a legendary condemnation of a royal justice, possibly Osbert Fitz Hervey, see 'The vision of Thurkill' ed. H. L. D. Ward, *Journal of the British Archaeological Association*, XXXI (1875), 434, 452–3; and P. G. Schmidt, 'The vision of Thurkill', *Journal of the Warburg and Courtauld Institutes*, XLI (1978), 61–3.
[212] For the evidence against Gerard d'Athée and Engelard de Cigogné in Gloucestershire see *The Pleas of the Crown for the County of Gloucester, A.D. 1221*, ed. F. W. Maitland, pp. xiv, xxvii, and *The Rolls of the Justices in Eyre for the Counties of Gloucestershire, Warwickshire and Staffordshire, 1221-2* (Selden Soc.), pp. lxiii–lxv. For Philip Mark in Nottinghamshire see Holt (1952), 18 ff., and Patricia M. Barnes in *Pipe Roll 16 John*, pp. xi–xii.

sheriffs and bailiffs.[213] Their iniquities did not depend directly on their nationality. The object of these clauses was not so much to reform local administration as to strip John of the support the aliens gave him.[214] Some men wanted to go even further. Within a decade or so a version of the security clause was known at St Albans which provided for the exile of the king's alien officials, not simply for their dismissal from office. It also laid down that for the better distraining of the king the castellans of Northampton, Kenilworth, Nottingham and Scarborough should swear that they would do with their castles as the Twenty-Five commanded, and that such castellans should be chosen as were trustworthy and would execute this faithfully.[215] At least the authentic Charter avoided these extremes. Nevertheless, it went too far. It could only be justified perhaps by placing John's past conduct in the scales. It sprang from hate and suspicion which were themselves derived from the king's misdeeds. But not all had suffered from these. Some men were still loyal to the king. Some could recall, not bitter acts, but generosity and the share of power which the royal favour had given them. Much as they may have approved of the Charter's plea for justice, they can only have suspected its attempt to disarm, restrict and subject the king. Their greatness depended on his. They took the oath to the Charter, but they can scarcely have awaited its outcome with any confidence. The Charter described itself as a peace. It was not so much this as a pause and a source of fresh contention.

The prolonged session at Runnymede ended in profound unease. We are not in a position to measure the balance between optimism and realism in Langton's character. Him apart, no one could have expected that the agreed 'peace'

---

[213] See W. A. Morris. *The English Medieval Sheriff to 1300* (Manchester, 1927), pp. 143–66; Flower (1943), pp. 419–33; and Holt (1961), pp. 229 ff. (see also above, p. 121).
[214] A conclusion first advanced by Turner (1904), 250–4.
[215] For a discussion of this version, see Holt (1961), pp. 116–18, and Holt (1964), 76.

would be as firm as proclaimed. One document, discovered by Cheney in 1968, spelled out for the barons the consequences of what they had done.[216] This is a list of Twenty-Five barons entered in a Reading Abbey MS now in the library of Lambeth Palace. It is headed in a straightforward way. The barons named are those chosen to 'keep' everything contained in the charter of the king as the barons had demanded. But the concluding memoranda explain just what that meant. The London treaty released London in bail to the barons pending the execution of the Charter. This talked of the mayor surrendering London to the barons if the king contravened it. The security clause of Magna Carta envisaged that the Twenty-Five would 'distrain and distress' the king and return to his obedience once the fault was corrected. This stated that all these barons with so many knights and with the commune of all England would *rebel* (*insurgere*) against the king if by chance he contravened the Charter. The list spelled out the number of knights each of the Twenty-Five was to provide: Richard, earl of Clare, 140, Geoffrey de Mandeville, earl of Gloucester, 200, the young William Marshal, 200, William de Mowbray, 80, and so on; from all the Twenty-Five a total of nearly 1200 – something of a sledge-hammer to enforce distraint. This document laid bare what the distraint and distress of the king would amount to: civil war. The Twenty-Five would have been naive not to grasp that. Onwards into the summer Robert fitz Walter still boasted himself to be Marshal of the Army of God and Holy Church. This was the reality behind that vainglorious and seditious title.

[216] Cheney (1968).

CHAPTER 10

FROM DISTRAINT TO WAR

The optimism with which the Great Charter and the writs of 19 June referred to the newly agreed peace was soon put in question. By the middle of September the country was at war, and at war about the Charter. This was not a sudden or an accidental climax; it was the result of a lengthy development which can be traced back through the summer months to Runnymede itself. The Charter was made possible by its imprecisions and inexactness; these same qualities now meant that its application in practice was bound to become a matter of increasingly bitter debate and, in the end, open dispute. This was most obvious in those sections concerned with the restoration of rights arising from disseisin by the Crown or the exaction of unjust fines, and in the provisions of cap. 61 for the enforcement of these arrangements through judgement of the Twenty-Five barons. These clauses echoed with unanswered questions. What was an unjust disseisin or an unjust fine? What was understood by the words 'without lawful judgement' or 'contrary to the law of the land' in such cases? If the king had failed to meet all the demands against him by 15 August, the terms set in the treaty about London, what was to happen then? How long thereafter were the barons to continue to hold London? If the king failed to accept the judgement of the Twenty-Five and they proceeded to distrain and molest him as the Charter laid down, what was to happen if the king refused to be brought to heel? The baronial answers to these questions seemed deceptively simple. Unjust disseisins and fines were to be defined by the Twenty-Five; if outstanding issues had not been settled by 15 August then they were to continue to hold London; if the king refused to accept the arbitration of the Twenty-Five then he was to be distrained until he did. Hence they simply tried to enforce the letter of the Charter. They did not defy the king, as they had done in the spring. They did not need to, for they were now not making war but simply applying distraint, and they moved almost insensibly from the application of distraint under cap. 61 of the Charter into a new civil war by the process familiarly known in mid-twentieth century as escalation. For this process the Charter and the London Treaty were indeed an exact formula.[1]

Yet, although this was implicit in the settlement of June, it was not immediately obvious. Rather than admit that the settlement of June had been imprecise and inadequate, men on both sides argued that their opponents were guilty of ignoring and breaking it. Hence differences of interpretation were viewed and condemned as breaches of agreement, and much of the debate continued to be conducted in these terms throughout the summer, not least for their value as propaganda. But gradually men were brought to face the problems which had been unanswered in June. When they did so, they came to realize that these problems were quite intractable to negotiation, for they were not simply neat problems of law and justice, but also actions involving power and sovereignty which could only be resolved by war. On the baronial side this realization was marked by the decision to dispense with John and elect Prince Louis of France as king. This was reached some time in the autumn,

---

[1] I have differed markedly from the version of events given by Richardson (1944), 422–43; (1945), 184–200. Apart from his identification of the *triplex forma pacis* and dating of the London Treaty, which has been discussed already (above, pp. 230, 264–5, and appendix 9, below, pp. 481–3), I cannot accept Richardson's statement that there was a baronial defiance of the king in September, or his assumption that the bishops' letters on the barons' fealty belong to a council held at Oxford in the third week in July, of the general importance he attaches to this council, or his excessively severe criticism or the Barnwell annals. For a discussion of some aspects of the Oxford council see appendix 10, below, pp. 484–9. The other issues are discussed below, pp. 349, 358, 365–9, 371–3. Richardson's views are conveniently summarized in Richardson & Sayles (1963), pp. 460–1.

perhaps as early as September.[2] John, in contrast, realized it much earlier, perhaps as early as June when he submitted to the demands of the barons at Runnymede. At least he soon set himself to test one of the central ambiguities in the Charter. The barons had promised that they would give the king such security as he wished, except for castles and hostages, that they would observe the terms of peace. John now asked for a charter which would have spelt out the implications of their renewal of homage and fealty, by making clear that it bound them to serve him in life, limb and earthly honour and to protect and preserve his and his heirs' rights and his realm. This the barons refused, and the king went on to ask the bishops to testify to their refusal in writing.[3] John had made his point. He had shown that his view of the homage due to him and the baronial loyalty to the Charter were inconsistent and unreconciled. According to the Barnwell annals he suspected that the general oath of obedience to the Twenty-Five was 'taken against himself' since it involved his coercion to observe the Charter.[4] He had now gone some way to demonstrate this, for he had shown that the baronial leaders would not accept an elucidation of their homage which included the preservation of the king's rights and the realm. Against the new-fangled loyalty to the Charter John was setting up the traditional rights of his Crown. As the summer wore on this argument, reiterated, amplified and pressed home with exacting logic, became his major polemical resource. It was a sound one. By the autumn it had helped to provide him with a party sufficiently strong to fight a civil war.

Whether John ever intended to accept the Charter is

---

[2] See below, pp. 375–7.
[3] The bishops' letters are undated; they were enrolled on the dorse of the patent roll membrane covering 28 June to 3 July, but this is no guide to the date of the king's demand which he is likely to have pressed as soon as homage was renewed at Runnymede. Richardson (1944, 425 n.) argued that these letters should be allocated to the Oxford council of July. For further discussion of this see below, pp. 486–8. For the text of the letters, see appendix 11, below, pp. 497–8.
[4] *Walt. Cov.* II, 222.

uncertain. There is no convincing evidence that he ever proceeded to apply it beyond the limits to which he was compelled by immediate political circumstances. On the other hand it is quite possible that he would have been content to let the Charter age into a shibboleth, venerated in theory but largely ignored in practice, as had happened with the Charter of Henry I. The king's decision was probably not sudden or clear-cut. Henry I would have fought against his charter if the men of the time had tried to compel him to observe it. John would have been less likely to fight against his if it had been applied less stringently. Hence, as long as there was doubt about the definition of its terms, as long as there was doubt about how far the barons would try to force him into a wholesale restoration of rights, the king may have felt that the burden of the Charter was less weighty than the possible alternatives which might follow on an attempt to challenge it. This was all the more important since it was essential for him to present himself as entirely reasonable and innocent of any intention to revoke the settlement of June. If he were to attack, he would need the backing of the pope, both in general and in order to release him from his oath to the Charter. It was equally clear that he would have to manœuvre so that he seemed to go to war, not in order to attack the Charter, but in order to defend himself against the unreasonable manner in which it was being applied by his opponents. He achieved this through the political skill with which he exploited the intransigence of his opponents.

There was much to exploit. In many respects the Charter was a comparatively moderate settlement which said little or nothing about some baronial demands and made inadequate provision for the satisfaction of others. It was less radical than the Articles in that it applied the crusader's respite not only to the restitution of disseisins committed by Henry II and Richard I, which the Articles had envisaged as a possibility, but also to the disafforestation of the forests created by these two kings as well as several other problems.[5] It had also failed to maintain the provision of the Articles forbidding an appeal to Rome against its terms.[6] It was less radical than the 'unknown' charter in that it included nothing on overseas service; it imposed no immediate limitation on scutage;[7] and it not only abandoned the demand for the restoration of the bounds of the forest to the limits of 1154, but also replaced the specific recommendations for the reform of the forest law by a general provision for the investigation of forest administration.[8] It was less radical than some additional demands which were in the air.[9] It was even less radical in some respects than the concessions which John himself had envisaged in the spring of 1215.[10]

The Charter was not the only expression of this new moderation. It is also a striking feature of one of the most important acts of the barons at Runnymede, the choice of the Twenty-Five. Only four of these had openly resisted the Poitevin scutage of 1214 prior to the defeat at Bouvines.[11] Eleven had either served in Poitou or sent their service; two certainly, and possibly a further four, had only joined the opposition to the king in the last month prior to Runnymede; three had been guarantors of the safe conduct given to the barons who came to London in January; one rejoined the king before the renewal of war in the autumn; two more surrendered by the new year.[12] After Runnymede these men had still to show that they could control the recalcitrants, with their almost endemic hostility to the king, or even preserve any kind of discipline in the baronial ranks.

There are signs that the settlement was greeted with unruly discontent from its birth. In letters of 23 July the king

[5] See above, pp. 341–2.   [6] See above, pp. 288–9.
[7] See above, pp. 239–40, 318–20.   [8] See above, pp. 338–41.
[9] See above, p. 345.   [10] See above, p. 342.
[11] Eustace de Vescy, William de Mowbray, Roger de Montbegon and Richard de Percy.
[12] See Holt (1961), pp. 50, 109–11, 135.

ordered the barons of Yorkshire to restore all castles, lands, prisoners, hostages and chattels which had been seized during the war. The letters seem to have assumed that hostilities still continued, for they covered the period since as well as before the firm peace of 19 June.[13] By August John was clearly preparing for civil war in the north.[14] In part these disturbances may have sprung from discontent with the deficiencies of the settlement of June. Some ten years later the author of the Barnwell chronicle recalled that some of the northerners had left Runnymede and then proceeded to make war on the king on the grounds that they had not been present at the settlement.[15] But the causes of unrest lay not only in what the Charter had omitted or amended but also in the possibilities it had created. Here cap. 48, which provided for the investigation of evil customs in the administration of the shires and the royal forests, was a major error. It encouraged protest, and protest was but vaguely divided from action. The Barnwell chronicle also records that in the north the king's manors were raided and his forests harried with the destruction of timber and the slaughter of game.[16] The wild men were breaking loose and the king was quick to exploit it. Some time in July he persuaded the bishops to make out letters stating that when this section of the Charter had been discussed at Runnymede it had been understood by all parties that those forest regulations which were essential to the keeping of the forest were to remain unaffected.[17] This was a rather ill-defined summary of what had presumably been an ill-defined argument. Nevertheless, it lays bare once more the king's intention to confront the Charter with the traditional rights of the Crown.

All this was unavoidably and to some extent unintentionally encouraged by the methods adopted to distribute and

---

[13] See appendix 11, below, p. 497.
[15] *Walt. Cov.* II, 222.　[16] *Ibid.*
[14] Holt (1961), pp. 121–2.
[17] See appendix 11, below, pp. 498–9.

execute the Charter.[18] The king's supporters present at Runnymede seem to have taken the oath to obey the Twenty-Five there and then,[19] but this was only an elementary, easily arranged preliminary. Writs of 19 June, enrolled on the dorse of the Patent roll, provided for the enforcement of the oath to the Twenty-Five, for the election of the juries of twelve who were to inquire into evil customs and for the public reading of the Charter throughout the country.[20] It is by no means certain that the Chancery followed its usual practice in arranging for the dispatch of these writs. A distribution list enrolled immediately after the text seems to indicate that they had gone to twenty-one counties by 24 June; two more were ready for distribution on that day, and a further twelve either then or some time before 22 July.[21] Later writs of 27 June addressed to sheriffs and to the juries of twelve clearly assume that the earlier writs had all gone out and been executed,[22] but the distribution list, as it stands, does not establish this. There is also a much more serious difficulty. The writs of the 19th could scarcely have been executed properly without the Charter; yet it is almost certain that the writs went out alone. The first two charters mentioned in the distribution list were delivered to the Bishop of Lincoln, apparently for the counties of Oxford and Bedford, on 24 June. By then at least twenty-three writs had been made out. Only eleven more charters are mentioned as against a probable total of thirty-five writs; the last

---

[18] For discussions of this problem see Poole (1913), 448–50; Richardson (1944), 426–8; and especially Cheney (1956), 334–41, on which I have relied chiefly here. See also below, pp. 354–5, 442, 494–5.

[19] *Chron. Maj.* II, 605–6. Thus the text of the *Chronica Majora*. Compare the continuation of William of Newburgh (*Chronicles of Stephen, Henry II and Richard I*, II, 520). There is nothing to support Matthew Paris's improbable note in the *Liber Additamentorum* that these men swore that they would compel both the king and the barons to observe the settlement (*ibid*, II, 606). These lists are late additions, probably made by Paris in the 1250s.

[20] See appendix 11, below, pp. 493–5.

[21] See appendix 11, below, pp. 493–5, and for further discussion of the distribution see Holt (1982) and below, pp. 354–5.

[22] See appendix 11, below, pp. 496–7.

six charters were not delivered until 22 July. The distribution list also shows that even from the first the barons and the bishops took a hand in the distribution. The first writ, sent to Yorkshire, was delivered to the future rebel, Philip fitz John, who held fees of William de Mowbray, one of the Twenty-Five; Saer de Quincy, earl of Winchester, another member of the Twenty-Five, received the writs for Warwickshire and Leicestershire; Eustace de Vescy, yet another, that for Northumberland; twelve writs and ten of the thirteen charters mentioned in the list were delivered to the archbishop's steward, Elias of Dereham. The remaining charters went to bishops. Only the delivery of one writ to the Mayor of London, of one to Engelard de Cigogné, sheriff of Gloucester, and of twelve to Henry de Ver, one of the king's household clerks, seems to reflect the normal pattern of delivery to the local agent of the Crown either direct or through a royal messenger. The charters may well have been issued only to those who demanded them and were prepared to pay for copies; some may have made their own copies.[23] This may also apply to the writs, but, since the distribution of writs was a normal part of the work of government, it may be that they were delivered to baronial and episcopal agents either because this happened to be the most convenient method of delivery or because the parties who were to benefit by them, suspicious of the king's intentions, insisted on having them and delivering them for proper execution in the shires.[24]

However, whatever the underlying reasons for this procedure, it is clear that the Charter must have become known and been applied very unevenly. Monastic writers later preserved a variety of stories which probably reflect different stages in varying local procedures. The Barnwell chronicler either assumed or knew that the procedure

[23] See below, pp. 442, 493–5.
[24] Here I have largely followed the arguments first put forward by Professor Cheney (1956), 340–1. For further discussion of the despatch-list see Holt (1982), 149–50.

outlined in the writ of 19 June was carried out: he states that the Charter was carried round through towns and villages and that all swore to observe it on the king's instructions.[25] Ralph of Coggeshall knew of the writs of 19 June and assumed that charters were sent to every county;[26] this at least suggests that one was sent or brought to Essex, where the rebellion was strongly rooted. The Dunstable annalist in contrast states that the charters were sent to a safe place in each bishopric;[27] this may mean simply that he had seen or knew of a local copy which had been deposited in a cathedral. But accurate knowledge of the Charter itself and of the methods of distribution is rare in narrative sources. On the whole they knew very little of the contents of the Charter and this must have been equally true of those who were required to act on it in 1215. Those who took the oath to obey the Twenty-Five must often have been at a loss as to who these men were and what they were supposed to do, except for hearsay derived from a participant at Runnymede, or from one of the barons or from the archbishop's steward, who were seeing to the distribution of the writs. Those who were elected to serve on the juries investigating local administration must often have been ignorant of their terms of reference, except for some similar verbal, often hearsay, indication, perhaps from one who might well be a very interested party.[28] As the news of the settlement at Runnymede spread throughout the land, it can only have loosened the reins of government, encouraged attacks on local officials, tempted men into invading royal rights or resorting to self-help against both Crown and neighbour. The Charter must have started many a local war.

In part these circumstances arose from the normal pro-

---

[25] *Walt. Cov.* II, 222.   [26] *Coggeshall*, p. 172, and see above, p. 259.
[27] *Annales Monastici*, III, 43, and see above, p. 259.
[28] See the actions of William de Mowbray in using, and perhaps establishing, a local jury to satisfy his own territorial claims (appendix 11, below, pp. 495–6).

cedure whereby recipients of grants acquired documentary confirmation on their own initiative. In part they were the result of royal negligence, probably of deliberate dilatoriness. In part they arose from baronial suspicion of the king's intentions. This was real enough, even to the extent that the barons feared the loss of their one trump card, their retention of London. Early in July Robert fitz Walter wrote to William d'Aubigné of Belvoir informing him that a tournament arranged for Stamford on 6 July had been postponed to 13 July when it would be held on the heath between Staines and Hounslow. The change was necessary, Robert pointed out, because of the security of the capital: 'You well know', he wrote, 'what great benefit it is to you and all of us to keep the city of London, which is our refuge; and what shame and danger it would be to us, if by our own fault we lost it. Yet you should know that we have been warned that there are some who are waiting for us to leave the aforesaid city only in order to occupy it suddenly themselves.'[29] The suspicions were not all on one side. If the barons doubted the king's good intentions, he must have been just as concerned that the Charter should not be so enforced that his government was dismembered and deprived of its powers of local enforcement. Hence he complied with the relevant sections of the Charter with as much reluctance as the letter of the document permitted. He was required to dismiss his foreign mercenaries immediately on the completion of the peace agreement,[30] and this he proceeded to do; at least Hugh de Boves, one of the commanders of the Flemish mercenaries, was ordered by a letter of 23 June to send home those at Dover.[31] But no such

---

[29] *Chron. Maj*, II, 614–15. The attribution of this letter to the dorse of Close Roll 17 John at *Foedera*, I, part I, 134, is incorrect. The arrangements described in the letter are susceptible to a different construction, viz. that the tournament which *had* taken place was now being extended. The above seems to make better sense. The issue does not affect the argument at this point.

[30] Cap. 51.   [31] See appendix 11, below, p. 496.

time-limit was applied in cap. 50, which required the dismissal of the alien sheriffs and bailiffs, and hence the execution of this clause, like the rest of the Charter, came under the London Treaty which laid down 15 August as the date for completion. The king moved only slowly. Geoffrey de Martigny was ordered to surrender custody of North-ampton castle by letters patent of 2 July.[32] Gloucestershire, which had been in the hands of Engelard de Cigogné, was transferred to Ralph Musard on 8 July.[33] But it was not until 19 July that Andrew de Chanceaux was ordered to surrender Herefordshire and Hereford castle,[34] and it was only on 20 July that Peter de Chanceaux was ordered to surrender Bristol castle.[35] Philip Mark was never removed from his crucial post as sheriff of Nottinghamshire and constable of Nottingham castle, from which position he directed the fortunes of the royalist cause in the north and east midlands during the civil war.[36]

Perhaps it is surprising that John went as far as this in complying with the Charter.[37] That he went no further need not necessarily have resulted from bad faith. The Charter did not compel him to order a large number of immediate dismissals, and he was as wary of dismissing loyal and effective agents as the barons were of losing control of London. He had every reason to be. The renewal of hom-age implied that the king would now be able to resume the normal collection of the revenues due to him.[38] He apparently tried to do so, but the attempt as it was remem-bered later in the Barnwell chronicle was frequently disast-rous; where the barons were in control the king's agents were driven off or imprisoned.[39] The barons had already

[32] *Rot. Litt. Pat.* p. 146b.   [33] *Ibid.* p. 148b.   [34] *Ibid.* p. 149b.   [35] *Ibid.*
[36] Holt (1952), 18 ff.
[37] For further discussion of the new shrieval appointments at this time see appendix 10, below, pp. 484–6.
[38] This was not stated in the Charter, although the London Treaty reserved to the king the farms, revenues and manifest debts due to him during the baronial period of custody (see below, pp. 490–1).
[39] *Walt. Cov.* II, 222.

appointed their own sheriffs in the counties they controlled at the outbreak of the war in May;[40] the Barnwell writer records similar arrangements in August in the counties of Essex, Northampton, Norfolk and Suffolk, Cambridge and Huntingdon, Lincoln, Yorkshire, Nottinghamshire and Northumberland;[41] and in September the Twenty-Five were clearly relying on one of their number, Robert de Ros, whom they addressed as custodian of Yorkshire, for the execution of their mandates in that county.[42] Thus the rebels had created their own local administration, which was never properly dismantled after Runnymede. When the Exchequer ultimately came to hold accounts for this period it had to abandon any attempt to recover royal revenues for the 'time of war', which was taken to run from Easter 1215 onwards, without any interval of peace in the summer of 1215 for which account might be demanded. This was realistic. Hubert de Burgh was appointed sheriff of Norfolk and Suffolk by the king on 24 July 1215.[43] His deputy, Walter of Ellingham, managed to hold only one county court in Norfolk and two in Suffolk before the barons thrust in their agent once more by force of arms; it was recorded in 1218 that he had received no revenues during the summer of 1215.[44] Such was the restoration of royal government which was achieved after Runnymede.

It was amid these uncertainties that the issue of war or peace came to be settled. King and barons waited for each other to execute the terms of the agreement fully, and as a

---

[40] Roger de Cressy, at least, was operating as such in Norfolk and Suffolk (Richardson, 1944, 441–2).
[41] *Walt. Cov.* II, 224. Richardson queried the dating of this list since it names John de Lacy as sheriff of Yorkshire rather than Robert de Ros who was in charge of this county in September (1944, 431 n.). Yet other record evidence confirms the chronicle, for de Lacy's steward, Gilbert of Nocton, was collecting revenues in Yorkshire on the authority of the barons in the Michaelmas term of 1215 (P.R.O., L.T.R. Memoranda Roll, 2 Henry III, mm. 1 d, 6 r).
[42] See below, pp. 364–5, 499–500.
[43] *Rot. Litt. Pat.* p. 150.
[44] Richardson (1944), 441–2.

result neither did. The king waited for the proper restoration of his government and the collection of his revenues before he would complete the measures imposed on him by the Charter; the barons waited for the completion of these measures before they would disarm and abandon London. Both sides were holding back for something which only one could achieve: its own interpretation of the Charter, and especially of those clauses which provided for the restoration of property which had allegedly been seized by the king unjustly and without judgement. On this they soon proved irreconcilable. For the baronial party royal disseisin was a simple matter; it was neither more nor less than a denial of right and title established by law. In the king's eyes, in contrast, the title was often more arguable than established. Moreover the disseisin of one often meant the endowment of another; such cases frequently arose from competing claims where the king favoured one of the parties; and even where disseisin was more obvious and certain, land seized by the king was frequently transferred to some favourite or agent either in custody, or during royal pleasure, or perhaps even in inheritance. Hence for the barons the Charter underpinned title. For the king, in contrast, it undermined the customary exercise of patronage. On 5 July he informed the barons of the Exchequer that he had granted the manor of Laughton to Brian de Lisle to maintain him in the royal service. The grant was to last, not, as in the usual formula, 'as long as it shall please us', but 'for as long as we are able to warrant it to him'.[45] One of the fundamental powers of monarchy, the king's capacity to reward his faithful men, had been seriously weakened.

This was implicit in the bare terms of the Charter. By September it had become one of the principal charges against the barons.[46] Immediately, however, men were less concerned with the constitutional implications of these clauses

[45] *Rot. Litt. Claus.* I, 219. [46] See below, pp. 373–4.

than with their vigorous exploitation for immediate and material gain. Twelve members of the Twenty-Five obtained letters of restitution of one kind or another between 19 and 28 June. Altogether over fifty claims were met in these ten days.[47] A considerable proportion of them arose from acts committed during the crisis of the previous three years; some arose from disseisins ordered during the war since Easter. Many were unimportant. The scene was not unduly disturbed by the acknowledgement of Eustace de Vescy's right to have his dogs in the forest of Northumberland,[48] or by John of Sandford's claim to act as the Queen's chamberlain.[49] But some were much more serious. Richard de Clare claimed Buckingham, which had been the marriage portion of his daughter, who had been widowed when William de Briouze's son died in prison.[50] Robert fitz Walter claimed Hertford castle of which he had had custody earlier in the reign.[51] The barons pressed home the attack just as enthusiastically as the king had earlier used his powers. William de Mowbray made territorial demands in Yorkshire far beyond his entitlement within the strict terms of the Charter.[52] Henry de Bohun now demanded a settlement of his claims to the honour of Trowbridge. The king sought a postponement of the case, but had to order a restoration of the manors of the honour on 19 June. The most Henry would allow him was respite until 28 June on the claim to Trowbridge castle.[53] John tried to argue that such cases should be left open until the usual investigations by juries had taken place.[54] But this was often unavailing. When Geoffrey de Mandeville, for example, demanded rights of advowson in the abbeys and religious houses which his predecessors as earls of Gloucester had founded in the

---

[47] *Rot. Litt. Pat.* pp. 143b–145b; *Rot. Litt. Claus.* I, 215–17.   [48] *Ibid.* p. 216b.
[49] *Ibid.* p. 216.   [50] *Rot. Litt. Pat.* p. 143b.   [51] *Ibid.* p. 144b.
[52] See above, p. 247, and appendices 5 and 11, below, pp. 431–2, 495–6.
[53] See appendix 11, below, p. 495.
[54] A point clearly appreciated by Wendover (*Chron. Maj.* II, 606). See also John's intervention in the Mowbray claim.

counties of Gloucestershire and Somerset, John first ordered the sheriffs of the two counties to make inquiries into the earls' rights through local jurors whose names were to be sent to him.[55] On the same day, 23 June, these instructions were replaced by orders that the sheriffs were to give Geoffrey such seisin as his predecessors had enjoyed.[56] The king was losing control. The *Histoire des ducs de Normandie* tells of him stricken with gout, carried to do judgement in such cases into the presence of the Twenty-Five, who were unwilling either to excuse him or to sit in judgement in his chamber.[57] Within this highly coloured and dramatic picture there was a real kernel of truth.

However, the king's surrender was not total. When the meeting at Runnymede ended several important cases were still unresolved. The Bohun claim to Trowbridge castle was still open. William de Lanvallei had demanded custody of Colchester castle and this too was postponed.[58] So was the Mandeville claim to the custody of the Tower of London.[59] Meanwhile the archbishop and the king were engaged in confused negotiations about Rochester castle, the custody and constableship of which had been granted to the archbishops by Henry I. Archbishop Hubert Walter had had charge of it earlier in the reign, but Langton and King John apparently agreed that it should be in the hands of Reginald of Cornhill until Easter 1215, and this had later been extended until the Easter after the general council met at Rome (Easter 1216). On 25 May John had written to the archbishop urgently requesting that the castle should be transferred to Hubert de Burgh and Philip d'Aubigné until the agreed term, or earlier if peace was reached in England.[60] He was now faced with the fact that peace had been formally agreed; by the terms of his own arrangements the

---

55 *Rot. Litt. Claus.* I, 216.   56 *Ibid.* I, 216b.
57 *Histoire des ducs de Normandie*, p. 151.
58 See below, p. 366 (cp. *Walt. Cov.* II, 221, where Colchester is said to have been restored at Runnymede).
59 *Ibid.*   60 *Rot. Litt. Pat.* p. 138b.

castle was now completely within Langton's control. What followed is uncertain. According to Wendover the castle was restored to the archbishop at Runnymede;[61] the Barnwell writer on the other hand mentions Langton's failure to stick to the terms of the original amended agreement among the reasons for his breach with the king in the autumn.[62] At all events both sides considered that they had strong arguments in their favour. Rochester remained in the custody of Reginald of Cornhill, apparently as the archbishop's agent. On 9 August, in letters which clearly assume that the amended agreement was still in force, John ordered Langton to surrender it to Peter des Roches, bishop of Winchester.[63] Langton refused, according to Ralph of Coggeshall on the grounds that he could not be deprived of either Rochester or the Tower of London without judgement.[64] At the end of September Reginald of Cornhill handed over the castle to the barons. Their seizure of it and the king's attempt to prevent it are the first recorded actions of the second civil war.[65] By this time Langton had gone abroad, in the king's eyes 'a notorious and barefaced traitor to us, since he did not surrender Rochester to us in our so great need'.[66] He had deprived the king of control of the one vital fortress between London and the royal garrisons and ports in Kent through which mercenary reinforcements could come from the continent. John had to spend nearly two months in laying siege to it before it fell into his hands in December.[67]

Important as it was, the dispute over Rochester was a fairly simple one about right and title. So were most of those which arose under cap. 52 of the Charter as unlawful disseisins, for such disseisin could be reasonably defined in terms of a failure to recognize due procedure or arguable

[61] *Chron. Maj.* II, 606.   [62] *Walt. Cov.* II, 225.   [63] *Rot. Litt. Pat.* p. 181b.
[64] *Coggeshall*, p. 173.   [65] Painter (1949), pp. 361–2.
[66] Galbraith (1948), pp. 136, 161–2.
[67] For further comment on Rochester now see Reynolds (1989).

title; the king himself was accustomed enough to think and issue orders in these terms. Cap. 55, however, which provided for the pardoning of unjust fines and amercements, was very much more complex, for men had made fines for land and privileges to a greater or less extent of their own will, and where the king had amerced it had been for a reason, more or less respectable or capricious. Who was now to define an unjust proffer for privileges or an unjust amercement? There could be no objective standard, only one derived from political passions and long-nursed grievances, perhaps simply from the ability to bring pressure upon those who were now judging the matter. Undoubtedly, fines and amercements would have been best left alone, to be forgotten or revised in the quieter atmosphere of the Exchequer. But such a court was now no longer an acceptable tribunal and the barons proceeded to investigate at least two such fines: that of Giles de Briouze, bishop of Hereford, for the lands of his father, William, and that of Nicholas de Stuteville for the lands of his brother, William.

The process of the first case is obscure. John had strong arguments for denying succession to the Briouze family since William had fled the land as an outlaw whose lands were lawfully forfeit. However, the king had compromised in 1215 by accepting a fine from Giles de Briouze for the succession. This apparently amounted to 9000 m.[68] and the king took precautions to see that it was adequately backed by guarantors.[69] Giles felt that the amount or some other feature of the arrangement gave him good grounds for complaint, for this fine and that of Geoffrey de Mandeville were the two matters on which the king promised special individual concessions in May.[70] The case was not settled at Runnymede. The lands of William de Briouze were still in

[68] *Walt. Cov.* II, 225.   [69] *Rot. Litt. Claus.* I, 189b.
[70] The two cases were analogous to the *casus regis.* See Holt (1991b), pp. 35–7.

the king's hands on 22 July, but by then they seem to have
been under discussion, for the king ordered Roland Bloet,
custodian of Bramber and Knepp, to restrict his demands to
the reasonable issues; he was neither to waste the forests nor
to levy tallage.[71] Even then nothing seems to have been
settled, and it was only after he had joined the rebels in the
autumn that Giles recovered his inheritance by making
peace and arranging a new fine with the king on 20
October.[72] He had but brief enjoyment of his gains, for
within a month he was dead.[73]

There is no certain indication that the Briouze case was
brought before the Twenty-Five for a formal judgement.
That of Nicholas de Stuteville certainly was. His complaint
was a simple one. In 1205 he had offered the enormous sum
of 10,000 m. for the succession to the lands of his brother,
William, and had surrendered Knaresborough and
Boroughbridge as guarantees of payment. The king, happy
in the retention of these two manors along with Knaresborough castle, made no serious attempt to collect the debt,
which was far beyond Nicholas's capacity to pay.[74] In 1215
it still remained on the rolls, swollen by other accounts due
from the improvident Nicholas.[75] The Twenty-Five now
sat in judgement on it, and on 30 September four of them
boldly announced to the royal custodian, Brian de Lisle, that
they had judged Knaresborough castle to Nicholas de Stuteville as his right, and that he was to surrender it forthwith.
On the same day the same four barons ordered the baronial
custodian of Yorkshire, Robert de Ros, to muster forces to
help Nicholas de Stuteville in 'distraining and molesting' the
garrison of the castle.[76] The words are those of cap. 61 of the
Charter; the Twenty-Five were applying the legal powers of

---

[71] *Rot. Litt. Claus.* I, 222.
[72] *Rot. Litt. Pat.* p. 157*b*; *Rot. Litt. Claus.* I, 232*b*.
[73] *Rot. Litt. Pat.* pp. 159, 159*b*.   [74] See above, p. 306.
[75] For details of Nicholas's debts, see Holt (1961), pp. 27, 173.
[76] See appendix 11, below, pp. 499–500.

compulsion which it had given them. Yet this was in fact an act of war. It may indeed have been provoked by the onset of war, for the judgements of the Twenty-Five came to be influenced increasingly by political and strategic motives. Cap. 59 of the Charter gave scope to King Alexander of Scotland to renew the ancient claims of his house to the three border shires of Northumberland, Cumberland and Westmorland. He sent agents to discuss business with the king on 7 July.[77] Some time in the autumn the Twenty-Five formally adjudged the three counties to him, and the rebellious northern baronage later gave him their homage.[78] Alexander remained one of the rebels' staunchest allies.

John could scarcely do anything but resist the kind of judgement the Twenty-Five tried to impose in de Stuteville's case. There could be no complaint against the offer Nicholas had made except for its size, and size was a relative matter. If the king had given way on this then any proffer which a petitioner considered too burdensome might be called in question. The Twenty-Five were here equating the unjust fine with the expensive one, and it was an equation which the king could not accept. Furthermore they were threatening a serious extension of the scope of cap. 55 by laying down that property surrendered as a guarantee of such a fine should now be restored. This was perhaps a logical conclusion to be drawn from the original provision, but no more than that. Again the king was likely to resist. To press for judgement on such matters meant that the Twenty-Five would have to use the processes of distraint; to do so in important cases, where castles were at stake, was tantamount to war.

The dangers of this seem to have been clearly realized. When the meeting at Runnymede broke up both parties arranged that outstanding business should be referred to a

---

[77] *Rot. Litt. Pat.* p. 150. [78] Holt (1961), pp. 131–3.

new session arranged for 16 July at Oxford. John came a day late and remained there until the 23rd.[79] In the interval a few less important claims were settled: the abbot and monks of Malmesbury were given control of Malmesbury town and castle, and the rights of warren of the bishop of London and the chapter of St Paul's in Clacton and Walton were confirmed. During or after the meeting orders were issued transferring Colchester castle to William de Lanvallei.[80] It may be too that some kind of solution of Giles de Briouze's claims was under discussion,[81] and a number of administrative changes were ordered, some of which complied with the demand in the Charter for the dismissal of the foreigners.[82] But the major questions remained unresolved. There is no evidence that anything was done about Rochester, or the Mandeville claim to the Tower, and if the Briouze succession was discussed it was certainly not settled; nor apparently was the possession of Trowbridge castle, on which the records are silent at this point. Moreover, the king was now demanding as well as making concessions. He wrote to the archbishop and the barons at Oxford on 15 July saying that he was unable to attend on the following day and that he was sending the archbishop of Dublin, Pandulf, Earl William Marshal, the earls of Warenne and Arundel, and Hubert de Burgh to act for him. He was very clear on what they were to do. 'They are to do for you', he informed the barons, 'what we ought to do for you, and to receive from you what you ought to do for us.'[83] There is no certain indication of what the king had in mind, but it was probably at this conference that the archbishop and his suffragans felt obliged to give him the letters supporting the maintenance of

---

[79] Rot. Litt. Pat. p. 149b; Chron. Maj. ii, 606, where Wendover gives the correct date but, in naming Westminster, the wrong place.
[80] Rot. Litt. Claus. i, 221; Rot. Litt. Pat. pp. 149b, 151.   [81] See above, pp. 363–4.
[82] See appendix 10, below, pp. 484–6.
[83] 'Ad faciendum vobis id quod vobis facere debemus et recipiendum a vobis que nobis facere debetis' (Rot. Litt. Pat. p. 149).

his traditional rights in the royal forests.[84] On this at least John won a trick.

The Oxford council was a failure.[85] If it had any decisive effect it was in driving the two parties further apart. The baronial mood is reflected in the chronicle of Melrose – 'The king gathered his forces and came on the agreed date. But he contested the articles of peace and so they departed in great bitterness.'[86] Meanwhile John was already safeguarding himself against the renewal of war. On 2 July he arranged for the reinforcement of his household troops with the knights and sergeants of Geoffrey de Martigny, one of his Tourangeau captains who had hitherto been castellan of Northampton.[87] Geoffrey and others similar, Hugh de Boves, the commander of the Flemings, Faulkes de Bréauté and Theodoric the German, were in attendance on the king in the days preceding the Oxford council.[88] At the council itself and immediately afterwards the king moved even more consciously towards war. On 22 July he was arranging for the establishment of credits of 1100 m. with the Knights Templar in Poitou; by 13 August these were being earmarked to pay the wages of mercenary knights who were coming to England.[89] By this time John was in no doubt that war was certain. He had already, on 9 August, asked Stephen Langton to surrender Rochester.[90]

Hence later exchanges between the two parties should be regarded less as genuine attempts to settle the outstanding issues than as polemical justifications of their attitudes. The detail of these exchanges is not well covered by the sources. The fullest account is that in the Barnwell chronicle, which describes lengthy efforts by the archbishop and bishops to

---

[84] See above, p. 352.
[85] Richardson's view, which largely conflicts with this, is examined below, appendix 10, pp. 484–9.
[86] *Chron. Melrose*, p. 60.   [87] *Rot. Litt. Claus.* I, 218.
[88] *Rot. Chartarum*, p. 213.
[89] *Rot. Litt. Claus.* I, 221b; *Rot. Litt. Pat.* pp. 152b–153, 153b.
[90] See above, p. 362.

bring the opposing parties together, first at Oxford on 16 August, the day after the expiry of the London Treaty, and secondly at Staines on 28 August.[91] Other chroniclers give a similar but less detailed sequence of events.[92] All assert that the king did not attend, and in fact the king's only recorded action was to send agents to an assembly of the bishops and barons at Oxford on 19 August.[93] On the next day he moved to Wareham and from there by sea to Sandwich and Dover to await the arrival of his troops from the continent. He was now making a vigorous attack on the conduct of the baronial party. According to the Barnwell chronicle, the agents he sent to meet the barons at Oxford in August were authorized to say that he 'had surrendered many things as he had agreed, but that he had received nothing in return since the peace, except the grave injuries and tremendous damages which had been inflicted on him and which no one was ready to amend'. They added, moreover, 'that it would be neither safe nor wise for him to make himself available on the day when peace had been anticipated since they had gathered together in arms and in such numbers'.[94] John's final word, apparently, was that it was not his fault that the peace agreement was not going forward as they had originally agreed.[95]

This represented deadlock. The London Treaty had expired without the settlement of important claims and disputes, without a proper restoration of the king's government and revenues, without a proper execution, satisfactory

---

[91] *Walt. Cov.* II, 223–4 (cp. the *Annals of Southwark and Merton*, p. 50, which clearly drew on the same source as Barnwell at this point).

[92] *Coggeshall*, p. 173 (cp. the continuation of William of Malmesbury in *Liber de Antiquis Legibus*, p. 202).

[93] *Rot. Litt. Pat.* p. 153. These letters are dated 30 August in error.

I am unable to follow Richardson's argument that these writs are inconsistent with the story in the Barnwell chronicle or that this source is seriously confused at this point. They do not, as he suggested, state or imply that the conference was originally arranged for, or later postponed to, the 20th. In any case there is no certainty that these were the first letters which the king sent to this assembly (cp. *B.J.R.L.* XXVIII, 429: XXIX, 192).

[94] *Walt. Cov.* II, 223.   [95] *Ibid.* II, 224.

to the king as well as the barons, of the clauses providing for inquiries into local customs, and without the king's full compliance with the clauses providing for the dismissal of his foreign agents. War followed automatically without any formal declaration or defiance. The barons simply proceeded by judgements of the Twenty-Five and the ensuing process of distraint, as was ordered in the case of Knaresborough. The king, equally, in besieging Rochester was simply seeking what he considered to be his right under an existing agreement. These two instances epitomized the conflict. At its simplest, as John had seen, it was a conflict between the oath to the Charter and the Twenty-Five, on the one hand, and the fealty due to the king, on the other. When the four members of the Twenty-Five ordered Brian de Lisle to surrender Knaresborough they required him to obey the oath he had sworn accepting the common charter of the realm; if he refused he was to beware of them in his person, lands and possessions, 'since all who disobey this judgement and order are against the judgement and law of the realm'.[96] When the first of the northern rebels made peace with the king at Christmas they were required to make out charters in which they asserted that they would not hold to any oath they might have given to the enemies of the king or adhere in any way to the charter of liberties which the king had granted to the barons of the realm.[97] These charters were made out to a common form and were presumably drafted to a Chancery proforma; John was ensuring that the repentant rebels publicly abandoned the oaths and documents which had justified their participation in the use of force.

John's arguments during the interchanges of July and August were designed very much for public consumption

---

[96] See appendix 11, below, p. 499.
[97] See the charters of submission of Gilbert fitz Reinfrey and John de Lacy, *Foedera*, I, part I, 136–7. There is a facsimile of the second of these in Johnson & Jenkinson (1915), II, pl. IX (5).

and to attract support. In fact, when the king argued that the agreement was breaking down through no fault of his own, he was conveniently forgetting that he had never executed the terms of the Charter properly within the time limit provided by the London Treaty. He had not met all claims against him or dismissed all his foreign officials. Moreover while he argued in this way with his opponents, he was preparing for war and, in so doing, making war more likely. It must have been at Oxford in July, at the very latest, that he sent to Pope Innocent III asking for the papal annulment of the Charter. From this point onwards, therefore, he was trying to talk the barons into a trap, to lull their suspicions of his intentions and delay their own preparations for the approaching conflict.

Nevertheless, the terms in which the argument was conducted were very much to the point. The claim that the barons had not performed their part of the bargain or had exceeded the agreement in applying some of its terms was an essential preparatory step to declaring it null and void. Indeed this was the only way in which the king could escape from his commitment until Pope Innocent released him from his oath to the Charter. Furthermore, it led on to the charge that the excesses of the baronial party amounted to breaches of the peace and to an unlawful assault upon the rights of the Crown. One or both these points were made in different contexts, either implicitly or explicitly, in the letters which the king sent to the Oxford conference in July, in the bishops' letters on the royal forests and in the exchanges of August which are recorded in the Barnwell chronicle. They brought real advantages to the king as soon as Pope Innocent intervened once more in this faraway disturbance.

Until the end of August Innocent was acting in complete ignorance of what had happened at Runnymede. Hence his interventions were quite out of date and out of touch. The first came in a letter of 18 June written after Innocent had heard of the baronial declaration of war. This was apparently addressed to the archbishop and bishops, who were ordered to excommunicate the barons and lay an interdict on their lands unless they accepted the papal *forma* of 19 March within eight days of the receipt of the letter.[98] There is no indication when this letter arrived in England. It can scarcely have been much before the end of July, and by then it had been overtaken by events; there is no evidence that it was used. The second came in a letter of 7 July which was written after Innocent had received John's letter of 29 May. This missive soon became highly important, for it was addressed not to the archbishop and bishops but to three commissioners who had presumably been chosen at John's request: Peter des Roches, bishop of Winchester, Simon, abbot of Reading and Pandulf.[99] Thus the execution of the letter was in the hands of men prepared to do John's will within the limits of their instructions, and these were of much more serious import than the earlier letters. The pope now criticized the archbishop and the bishops for permitting delays in the execution of his earlier mandates. He himself now pronounced excommunication against all disturbers of the king and the realm and any who gave them support. The archbishop and bishops were charged to pronounce sentence forthwith and the commissioners were empowered to suspend any who failed to do so.[100]

These letters removed any last remaining hope of compromise. In the circumstances they were 'an inflammatory document'.[101] During the summer the archbishop and his suffragans had been steering an increasingly difficult course between the two opposing parties, withholding execution, on the one hand, of papal mandates against the barons which they considered had been by-passed by the

---

[98] *M.C.C.E.* pp. 43–5: *Letters of Innocent III*, no. 1013.
[99] For comment on the procedure see Richardson (1945), 190–1. See also Cheney (1976), 375–86.
[100] *Selected Letters of Innocent III*, pp. 207–9. [101] Cheney (1976), 379.

developing negotiations in England,[102] supporting the king,
on the other hand, where they felt that the barons had failed
to live up to the agreement of June.[103] The mandate of 7 July
now left them little room for manœuvre, for it was not an
adjudication on the issues between the king and the barons,
against which they might have entered exceptions; Innocent
had already given his judgement on 19 March and saw no
need to repeat himself; it was a straight order for the
excommunication of disturbers of the peace and specifically
excluded any appeal against it. The mandate had only one
loop-hole: those to be punished were but loosely defined as
the 'disturbers of the king and kingdom along with their
accomplices and supporters'; the commissioners were left to
arrange matters necessary for the execution of the order and
hence to name those who could be so defined. Here there
was more room for argument, as contemporaries immediately realized, for each could imagine that so general a
denunciation did not apply to him,[104] while the king himself
might be thought by some to be one of the disturbers of the
realm.[105] Several traditions survived of the archbishop's
reaction to the papal mandate. According to Wendover he
objected to its execution, alleging suppression of the truth,
and demanded delay until he had spoken with the pope;
according to Coggeshall he objected to the commissioners'
interpretation of their mandate and refused to pronounce
sentence against those whom they had named; according to
the Barnwell chronicle the excommunication was in fact
pronounced at the conference at Staines on 28 August,
but only in the general terms of the papal mandate.[106]

---

[102] The archbishop had already been instructed to excommunicate conspirators against the
king in the papal letters of 19 March. Even at that stage Innocent was showing some
impatience at Langton's dilatoriness in securing a settlement (ibid. pp. 196–7).
[103] See above, pp. 349, 352.
[104] Chron. Maj. II, 630.
[105] Walt. Cov. II, 224.
[106] Chron. Maj. II, 630; Coggeshall, p. 174; Walt. Cov. II, 224. Powicke followed the
Barnwell account (1929, 89–90). Richardson and Painter rejected this on the grounds
that Langton would not have resorted to the ambiguities of a general excommunication

Whichever of these happened it is clear that Langton refused to accept the commissioners' interpretation of the pope's instruction and was suspended by them as a result. The suspension was confirmed by Innocent on 4 November after Langton had presented his case in person at the Curia.[107]

The archbishop's attitude is understandable, for the letters of the commissioners of 5 September attacked the whole conduct of the baronial party. In this they included not only the baronial defiance of the king and the seizure of London in May, but also the settlement of June itself and the barons' subsequent efforts to procure its enforcement. They were deliberately wrecking work in which the archbishop and his suffragans had shared. They revealed the real intentions behind the king's fair words for they abandoned the argument that he was trying to apply an agreement which the other side had broken and turned instead to attack the agreement itself. 'The dignity of the king has been filched,' they asserted, 'since they grant out lands, a thing unheard of, and nullify the approved customs of the realm, and establish new laws, and destroy or alter all that has been prudently ordained by the king, their lord, with the advice of the magnates who were then his familiars ... they have gone as far as they could in despoiling the king of his royal dignity.'[108] And the commissioners did not stop here. They went on to quash all conjurations, conspiracies and confederations against the king, broad terms from which they can scarcely have excluded the general oath of obedience to

(Richardson, 1945, 195–6; Painter, 1949, p. 343). However, Barnwell recounts this general excommunication in precisely the same terms as those in the papal letters, and both he and Coggeshall are clear that Langton's objections were not so much to the papal letters as to the interpretation which the commissioners placed upon them in excommunicating named individuals. This is an important point which Wendover failed to appreciate since he was clearly unaware that any barons were named at this stage. Cheney seemed to side with Powicke (*Selected Letters of Innocent III*, p. 207 n.).

[107] *Selected Letters of Innocent III*, p. 220.
[108] *E.H.R.* XLIV, 92.

the Twenty-Five. They then declared null and void all constitutions, assizes, enfeoffments and gifts of land made by the barons, and all judgements which had been made by them, or might be made by them in the future, against the king. Those who appealed to such actions to provide authority for liberties, possessions or free customs were declared excommunicate.[109] The commissioners had not mentioned Magna Carta; they had not released the king from his oath, a request for which had already been sent to and accepted by the pope; but they had done their best, in their own way and without exceeding the limits of their instructions, to destroy the work of Runnymede. They damned it as a disturbance, wilfully engineered, contrary to law, and destructive of the interests and peace of the realm.

More than any other single action these letters brought on open war. On 13 September John sent agents to the Curia to report, among other things, on the political situation in England and to seek the pope's advice and assistance.[110] On 17 September he authorized the first of many instructions for the seizure of the lands of his opponents.[111] The letters of the 5th had clearly revealed a change in attitude which had begun, but had been hidden, when the king asked for the annulment of the Charter in July, and was completed with the arrival of the bull of annulment, *Etsi karissimus*, about the end of September. This condemned the Charter as an agreement exacted by force, which was shameful, demeaning, illegal, unjust and derogatory to the king's rights and dignity.[112] The commissioners who had executed the pope's letter of 7 July had read his intentions correctly. King John

---

[109] *E.H.R.* xliv, 93.
[110] *Rot. Litt. Pat.* pp. 182–182b. These letters have usually been taken as announcing that war had broken out anew. In fact they do not say so directly, but simply state that the barons had risen against the king since he made peace with the Church. As Adams pointed out, this seems to be derived from the papal letters of 18 June (*M.C.C.E.* p. 44).
[111] *Rot. Litt. Claus.* i, 228.   [112] *Selected Letters of Innocent III*, pp. 212–16.

now stood on this. The charters in which repentant rebels renounced their oath to the barons and the Charter also stated that the pope had annulled it.[113]

The king's case was watertight. Yet in abandoning the Charter he was not, in his own view, abandoning the traditional pattern of lawful government so much as re-establishing it. This is the implication of the commissioners' letters of 5 September, and at the outbreak of war it was acknowledged in a remarkable manner by the king himself. In the same letters in which John denounced the archbishop to Hubert de Burgh as a bare-faced traitor, he instructed Hubert, who was Justiciar, to deprive Langton of his temporalities if he could do so 'in our court according to the customs of our realm'. Even though Langton was abroad and there was no one on whom to pass judgement, de Burgh was to do his best to keep the temporalities if he could do so 'by any judicial process'.[114] It may be that the king was still trimming his sails to the storm which had produced the Charter.[115] It is certain, too, that he would not wish to do anything which, by infringing the rights of the clerical order, might alienate the pope. But the words of this letter do not come entirely falsely from his lips. He would have argued that he was giving Langton what his vassals had usually enjoyed. There could be no clearer indication of the manner in which even so wilful a mind as his was influenced by the concepts of law and legal process which dominated his age.

King John was not alone in shifting his ground as the summer months advanced. So also did the barons, for gradually they were brought by circumstances to face the question which the London Treaty had left unanswered; what was to happen if it expired with the terms of the Charter still inadequately fulfilled? To say simply, as the

[113] *Foedera*, I, part I, 136–7.   [114] Galbraith (1948), pp. 136–7, 161–2.
[115] *Ibid.* p. 136.

treaty did, that they would then continue to hold London was to ignore rather than to answer the question, for this by itself would not necessarily compel the king to accept the judgements of the Twenty-Five or the findings of the juries investigating local administrative malpractices. In the end there could be only one answer: deposition and the choice of a new king. This solution, which some of them had considered as long ago as 1212,[116] was the only alternative to complete surrender in the face of an intransigent king backed by the authority of Pope Innocent.[117] The barons apparently took action at the beginning of September after the king's final refusal to meet them and while the enforcement of the papal letter of 7 July was under discussion. But they were loath to abandon the authority which the Charter had given them. According to the Barnwell chronicler, they summoned a council to choose a new king under the oath of obedience due to the Twenty-Five.[118] The loyalist magnates replied appropriately that 'they were not bound by oath to depose or expel the king, particularly since he had asserted his readiness to observe the agreed peace'.[119] Even though the papal commissioners were making ready to attack the Charter, the arguments John had followed hitherto now reaped their harvest. The baronial party had been driven into exceeding the terms of the Charter; the picture John had been trying to paint during the summer was now realized; support for the king had been made respectable. Those loyalist barons who had sworn to observe the Charter's terms and obey the Twenty-Five could now fight at his side with a clear conscience. John had won the war of nerves and

[116] See above, p. 226.
[117] The pope's letter of 18 June shows that he would not abandon the solution suggested in his *forma* of 19 March (*M.C.C.E.* p. 44). Innocent sent further letters of 24 August to the barons which stated that he wished John to stop oppressing them, but still insisted that they should submit peacefully and accept what the king might graciously concede (*Selected Letters of Innocent III*, pp. 217–19).
[118] 'Sub protestatione praestiti juramenti' (*Walt. Cov.* II, 224).
[119] *Ibid.* II, 225.

propaganda. When the opposition barons sent invitations to Prince Louis of France some time during the autumn they had lost the capacity to act for the community. They were now a faction seeking shelter behind a concocted claim to the throne from an alien prince. Since June there had been a sad but perhaps inevitable decline.

CHAPTER 11

THE RE-ISSUES AND
THE BEGINNING OF THE MYTH

The charter of 1215 was the work of King John's enemies. The re-issues of 1216 and 1217 were the work of his friends and supporters. The men who fought and won the war for John's son had also given him their advice at Runnymede and taken the oath of obedience to the Twenty-Five. They had fought not so much to destroy the Charter as to preserve Angevin control of the throne, to protect all the benefits they had received hitherto as friends and suporters of the king and to preserve their control of office and their influence in local politics. None of this precluded them from acknowledging that many of the demands of the original Charter were just and reasonable. Of those who had advised the king at Runnymede, only one, William Briwerre, opposed any of the later confirmations. In 1224 he advised the young Henry against confirmation on the grounds that the original grant had been exacted by force. Despite the fact that his objection was similar to Innocent III's, he was now firmly instructed by Stephen Langton to hold his tongue lest he endanger the peace of the realm.[1] The rebellion of 1215 had failed but much of its programme succeeded.

[1] *Chron. Maj.* III, 76. With some hesitation I retain Kate Norgate's amendment of Wendover's date for this incident (Norgate, 1912, pp. 214–16). Dr Carpenter reverts to Wendover's date of 1223 (1990, 297n). Three matters should be considered. First, the writs of 30 January 1223 ordering an inquiry into royal liberties do not refer to any measure of approval, advice, or even consultation, which Dr Carpenter's argument seems to suppose (*Foedera*, I, part I, 168). Secondly, the writs of April 1223 did not cancel the inquiry but only the immediate promulgation and enforcement of the findings in the counties. The king indicated that he did not intend to impose evil customs, but he still required returns to be brought to him at Westminster by the octave of Trinity (*Rot. Litt. Claus.* I, 569). Hence the possible consequences of the investigation were still hanging fire in the summer of 1223. Thirdly, with characteristic carelessness, Wendover refers not to the liberties which King John had enjoyed at the outbreak of the civil war, as in the writs, but to the liberties enjoyed by Henry II.

The men chiefly responsible for this were the great loyalist barons of John's reign: William Marshal, earl of Pembroke, Ranulf, earl of Chester, William de Warenne, earl of Surrey, William, earl of Salisbury, backed by the old king's agents, foremost among whom was the Justiciar, Hubert de Burgh. They were reinforced by the curialist bishops and by the papal legate Guala. The charters of 1216 and 1217 were issued under the seals of the legate and of William Marshal, earl of Pembroke and *rector regis et regni*. This announced a change in papal policy, all the more effective because the pope was the young king's feudal lord as well as his spiritual guardian. The old figures in the dispute had departed. Innocent III was dead. Langton had been summoned to Rome. Pandulf had become bishop of Norwich. The legate Guala now sought stability and peace.[2] There is nothing to suggest that these men re-issued the Charter simply to accelerate the return of peace. It is more likely that with John now dead they could at last express their real views. John's death also removed the chief justification of those debatable sections of the Charter which had led to the renewal of war in the autumn of 1215. There are few direct indications of these men's attitude. William Marshal seems to have regarded the war as a tragedy which was best forgotten.[3] Ranulf of Chester responded to the situation in 1215 by issuing a charter of liberties to his men of Cheshire. Unfortunately this bears no date, although it must fall within the limits March 1215 – October 1216 and most probably in June to September 1215.[4] Some of its provis-

---

[2] See especially Cheney (1976), 396–400; Galbraith (1966), 316–17.

[3] Such at any rate was the attitude suggested by the marshal's biographer (see *Histoire de Guillaume le Maréchal*, II. 14842–59, 15031–6).

[4] The earlier limit is established by Ranulf's statement that he had taken the Cross, which he did along with King John in March 1215; the later by the death of one of the witnesses, Hugh de Pascy, between May and October 1216 (see Tait's notes, 1920, p. 107). Barraclough narrows Tait's date-limits, rightly emphasizing that the Cheshire charter must be subsequent to Magna Carta. He also adds information on the MSS of the text (*The Charter of the Anglo-Norman Earls of Chester c. 1071–1237*, ed. Geoffrey Barraclough, Record Society of Lancashire and Cheshire, CXXVI, 1988, no. 394).

ions are similar to those in Magna Carta;[5] it is particularly striking that this charter, like John's, laid down that the barons of the county should grant to their men the same privileges which the earl had granted to them.[6] It is probable that it was issued because Magna Carta did not run within the franchise of Cheshire.[7] On the other hand the wording of the two documents is nowhere close enough to establish that one was copied from the other. Moreover cap. 17 of the Cheshire Charter reveals that the earl's barons presented certain petitions, chiefly concerned with the rights of wreck and the problem of the forest, which Earl Ranulf refused and which they now abandoned. But he did meet some of their requests. Indeed the Charter is largely made up of local concessions not directly connected with Magna Carta. Like Peter de Brus's Langbargh charter,[8] the Cheshire Charter was a local charter dealing with local problems. Its author was not likely to oppose the re-issue of Magna Carta if there were a reasonable demand for it which did not impinge on his own power. It was probably in such a

---

[5] Caps. 10, 11, 12, on relief, widows, wardship, disparagement, and testaments. For the text, see *ibid*. no. 394.

[6] Cheshire, cap. 18; Magna Carta, cap. 60.

[7] Tait (1920), p. 108. See also Barraclough (1953), pp. 19–22, which follows Tait. The Cheshire Charter became the local Charter of Liberties, and was confirmed frequently in later years, sometimes on the same occasions as Magna Carta (Tait, 1920, pp. 108–9; Barraclough, 1953, p. 22). But Magna Carta made no exception in favour of Cheshire or any other franchise. On the contrary caps. 56 and 60 imply that no exceptions were intended. Furthermore, it does not seem that Durham was treated in this way. There is no evidence that Magna Carta 1215 was sent to Durham, but the Church of Durham certainly had its originals of the 1216 and 1225 Charters of Liberties and of the 1217 and 1225 Charters of the Forest in the middle years of the thirteenth century, for they are noted on an added quire in the *Cartuarium Vetus*. There is no clinching evidence that these were originally sent to Durham, but this seems very likely, both on general grounds and because two of them, the Charter of the Forest of 1217 and the Charter of Liberties of 1225, carry similar contemporary endorsements in what seems to be the same hand. There may have been good reasons for treating Durham and Chester differently in 1215. The see was then vacant, as it had been on occasion in the past. This linked it more closely to the Crown; indeed it is possible that the acquisition of the royal assizes by the tenants of the bishopric had created a precedent. Cheshire, in contrast, was an area of strongly rooted and independent local custom.

[8] See above, pp. 67–8.

mood that Ranulf, William Marshal and their supporters proceeded to re-examine the work of 1215.

The re-issue of 1216 probably represents fairly closely what the attitude of these men had been in 1215. They now accepted most of the Charter's provisions which were concerned with feudal incidents and the operations of the judicial system, but they rejected all the retrospective clauses which John had been forced to accept, and they reserved judgement on many of those sections which intruded into problems of feudal service, finance and administration. These sections, which were described as 'weighty and doubtful' and were reserved for further discussion, included the provisions on scutages and aids, on the collection of debts, on free entry into and exit from the country, and on the investigations into the behaviour of sheriffs, foresters and other officials.[9] Other provisions quietly vanished without any comment at all. Cap. 6 of the 1215 Charter was now cut down to the bare statement that there should be no disparagement; the provision that the king should consult the nearest relatives was simply dropped. Cap. 25, which forbade the assessment of increments on shire farms, disappeared; so also did the provisions on intestacy.[10] In the main the loyalist magnates seem to have been concerned to restrict the Charter's intrusion into the administrative powers of the Crown. But they also showed an appreciation of the practical needs of the moment. There was now no demand for the dismissal of the alien administrators or soldiers, and no provision that officials were to be chosen from those who knew the law of the land. For the moment the aliens were indispensable to the success of the Angevin cause.

The 1216 Charter was an interim assertion of policy made in the middle of a civil war within a month of John's death.[11] But it was more than a hasty political stratagem. It

---

[9] For the text, see appendix 12, below, p. 510 n. [10] Cap. 27.
[11] John died on the night of 18/19 October at Newark. The Charter was dated 12 November at Bristol.

was sealed not only by the marshal, but also by the papal legate, Guala. This tacit rejection of the papal annulment of 1215 cannot have been made lightly. Furthermore it is clear that the marshal took the Charter seriously because he arranged for it to be sent to Ireland and a copy was duly forwarded under letters of 6 February 1217.[12] This would have been quite unnecessary if in the marshal's view the Charter had been nothing more than a sop to encourage surrender, for the Normans in Ireland had been loyal throughout the rebellion in England. Even during a war the administrative and legal minds which had presumably been responsible for the original improvement of the Charter's drafting at Runnymede were still at work adding to and improving the text. Cap. 3 now included the statement that heirs reached their majority at the age of twenty-one; cap. 5 was extended to cover ecclesiastical estates in custody; cap. 7 was considerably expanded to define the size of a widow's dower and to provide for the contingency that her dead husband's house might be a castle in which it would be inconvenient for her to stay for the forty days she was allowed after his death. Caps. 19 and 21 laid down more careful arrangements for the purchase of corn and the hiring of horses and carts by royal officials; the needs of war were also met by excluding towns in which there were castles from the restrictions on purveyance. A considerable amount of thought and care went into this re-issue of the Charter. It was produced at a critical point in the civil war. These additions reflect a remarkable interest in the Charter among administrative and judicial officials of the court and a remarkable confidence in the outcome of the war. These men were already building for the future.

These influences were even stronger in the second re-issue of the Charter, which followed the Treaty of Lambeth

---

[12] *Foedera*, I, part I, 145; *Patent Rolls, 1216–25*, p. 31. For the text of the Irish charter see H. G. Richardson, 'Magna Carta Hiberniae', *Irish Historical Studies*, III (1942–3), 31–3.

ending the civil war in September 1217.[13] This made considerable adjustments in the original provisions concerning assizes. These were now to be held once, not four times a year; unfinished business was now to be postponed to a later date in the judges' circuit, and difficult cases and all cases of darrein presentment were to be referred to the justices of the Bench.[14] Men with legal experience clearly took a hand here to reduce the demands of the 1215 Charter to manageable dimensions. It was most likely they, too, who framed two entirely new provisions which limited a tenant's capacity to alienate his fee by stating that he must be able to perform the service due,[15] and forbade collusive alienation of land in free alms whereby the tenant escaped the performance of secular service to his lord.[16] Amidst these legal refinements the 'grave and doubtful' clauses of the 1216 Charter almost vanished from view. All that was left of the more radical demands of 1215 was cap. 37, which laid down that scutage was to be taken henceforth as it had been in the reign of Henry II.[17] This was safe and unadventurous. Nothing was said of increments on shire farms or the collection of debts, or the question of the Jews or the investigation of officials. All this was quietly abandoned. The re-issue had its eye very much on the practical. It

[13] The treaty, which was agreed on 12 September, included a promise by Henry that he would concede all the liberties which the barons had demanded. This version of the Charter of 1217 is undated, and, though sealed, is not entirely satisfactory on other grounds, as Blackstone noted (p.xl, n.u). There are three possible dates: 12 September, 23 September, when a council was held at Merton, and 6 November, which is the date of the Charter of the Forest. Of the three the last two are the more likely and 6 November much the most probable. Blackstone favoured 23 September (p.xxxix), and Bémont 6 November (1892, p.xxviii). Stubbs (1896, II, 26) supported 6 November, although he had left the issue open in the *Charters* (1888), p.344. Blackstone himself noted (p.xxxix) the large number of copies which end with 'Data per manum venerabilis patris domini R. Dunelmensis episcopi cancellarii nostri apud sanctum Paulum London' sexto die Novembris anno regni nostri secundo', and, as Dr Carpenter has pointed out (1990, p. 60n.), this cannot have been derived from the Charter of the Forest. This seems to settle the question, but the matter awaits a further study by Dr Carpenter and Mr Vincent.
[14] Caps, 12, 13 (1225). On the latter see Doris M. Stenton (1964), pp. 45–6.
[15] Caps. 32 (1225). See Milsom (1976), 113–14, 117–19.
[16] Cap. 36 (1225); Milsom (1976), p. 10.
[17] Cap. 37. The rate under Henry II had varied between 1 m. and 2 m.

ordered the destruction of adulterine castles raised during the civil war.[18] It also inserted a saving clause protecting the liberties and free customs enjoyed by the upper ranks of the ecclesiastical and secular hierarchy.[19] This was placed next to cap. 60 of the 1215 document, which laid down that the barons were to concede to their men what the king had conceded to them. Side by side, the one had a moderating effect on the other.

The Charter of 1217 may well reflect one further influence. Cap. 48 of the 1215 Charter, which provided for investigations into local administration, laid down that the king was to be informed of any proposed remedies before they were put into effect. In the summer of 1215 the king must have had some kind of information on which to base his protest against the activities of these commissions. The investigators were likely to record the evidence as they were accustomed to do in any such local inquiry. None of this evidence now survives, but the documents of 1217 suggest that a considerable amount survived then and was used by the men who drafted the Charter. Cap. 42 (1225, cap. 35) laid down that the shire court was not to meet more than once a month. The sheriff was not to make his tourn more than twice a year, at Easter and Michaelmas. At Michaelmas he was to hold view of frankpledge without seeking pretexts of infringing well-established private liberties, and he was to be content with such profits from his view as sheriffs had been able to take in the reign of Henry II. This looks like a composite clause built up from local complaints. It is closely similar in tone and detail to the privileges men had been buying and defending locally before 1215[20] and it was a provision which became highly prized by the knights of the shire in the years which followed.[21]

The work of the commissions of 1215 must have been

---

[18] See below, p. 510, n. 1.   [19] See below, pp. 509–10.
[20] See above, pp. 61–2.   [21] See below, pp. 390–6.

even more valuable in compiling the Charter of the Forest. Indeed this Charter is the best evidence there is that their work survived, for it is unlikely that such lengthy regulations could have been drawn up so soon after the civil war without some kind of documentary preparation. Only one of its clauses, cap. 2, was taken direct from the 1215 Magna Carta;[22] a fragment of another repeated the provision of the 'unknown' charter that no one was to lose life or limb for an offence against the forest law.[23] The rest were new and they carried the regulation of the forest law far beyond anything considered or even suggested in any of the earlier documents.[24] The Charter also aimed at settling the old argument about the extent of the forest. Cap. 1 now laid down that the forests created by Henry II were to be disafforested except where he had afforested his own demesne woods. Cap. 3 applied a similar ruling to the afforestations of Richard and John. The Charter did not seek radical solutions. Cap. 4 pardoned all purprestures and assarts made within private woods since the accession of Henry II, and laid down that those who made such invasions of the forest in the future without royal licence would have to answer for them. But it came to carry radical implications, for it chose the coronation of Henry II as the standard for determining both the extent and customs of the forest.[25] This again seems to have been inherited from the demands of 1215.[26] The drafters of the Charter would have been either naïve or obtuse to put forward such a date themselves because it could mean one of two things – either the forest which Henry actually had at his accession, or alternatively the forest to which he was entitled at his accession. Between the two lay all that the Crown had lost in the reign of Stephen. This was of such dimensions that the execution of the clauses

---

[22] Magna Carta, cap. 44.   [23] Cap. 10; 'unknown' charter, cap. 12.
[24] For an account of these, see Turner (1899), *passim*, and Petit-Dutaillis (1908), II, 187–98.
[25] Caps, 1, 4, 5, 6, 15.
[26] See the provision of the 'unknown' charter, cap. 9, and above, pp. 341–2.

of disafforestation remained unsettled throughout the thirteenth century. Indeed the repeated demand for disafforestation was one of the main reasons for the periodical confirmation of the Charters from 1225 on to the end of the reign of Edward I.[27] The Forest Charter and the particular issue of disafforestation helped to keep Magna Carta alive.[28]

In 1217 the loyalists borrowed the rebels' clothing, or at least that part of it which they cared to wear. The two Charters of 1217 were a solemn pledge of policy which was further honoured in the next few years by the ejection of the old king's alien administrators and the redistribution of honours and office. When the Charters were finally reissued in 1225, nine of the Twenty-Five barons of 1215 were dead. Of the remainder, nine witnessed the new grant along with great loyalist magnates, Ranulf of Chester, William of Salisbury, Hubert de Burgh and others, who had fought them in 1215. This was the final moment of reconciliation.

Despite this, the attitude of the loyalists is revealed as clearly by what they left out of the re-issues as by what they kept in. Their selection was deliberate and bore immediate fruit in policy. They had no hesitation at all in retaining as much of the Angevin systems of government as their own objectives required and the terms of the Charter permitted. Hence they exacted charters of fealty to secure the surrender of the rebels just as John had done.[29] They were unembarrassed by many of the complaints of 1215. They asked for hostages where they thought them necessary.[30] The government felt quite free to permit lords to levy aids on as wide a variety of occasions as before 1215.[31] In 1223-4 Hubert de

---

[27] For an account of this, see Turner (1899), pp. xciii–cix.
[28] See Maddicott (1984) pp. 37–40; Young (1974), pp. 69–73; and especially David Crook, 'The Struggle over Forest Boundaries in Nottinghamshire 1218–1227', *Transactions of the Thoroton Society* LXXXIII (1979), 35–45.
[29] See above, p. 101 n.   [30] See above, p. 101.   [31] See above, p. 318.

Burgh revived the old policies of King John by demanding profits over and above the farms ordinarily due from the sheriffs for their shires.[32] He was simply continuing a general effort of re-organization which started much earlier at the very end of the war. It is marked by the care with which the Exchequer investigated sums due to it from the period before the war, by its attempts to collect together on separate memoranda all the outstanding sums due from its major debtors,[33] and by the immediate investigations arranged into debts due to the Jews and due from both the Jews and their debtors to the Crown.[34] The government faced great difficulties, and success came only slowly.[35] Nevertheless the administration of the minority of Henry III was not kid-gloved. On 13 November 1218 letters were sent to the sheriffs of Yorkshire and Lincolnshire on the subject of the Jewish debts owed by Gilbert of Benniworth, Norman Darcy, William de Scotigny and several other substantial men in the two counties. These men had failed to keep the arrangements they had made with King John about the repayments of their debts. The council therefore decided to transfer the debts to Elias the Jew of Lincoln, who had made a suitable payment for them, and arranged that he could exact both capital and interest. The sheriffs were instructed to inform the debtors that they were now to pay specified sums with interest to Elias from St Martin's Day onwards.

If they do not do this [the letters ran] then you shall give the aforesaid Elias seisin of all the land and revenues which belonged to the aforesaid debtors in your bailiwicks in the tenth year of King John, the which lands and revenues are our pledge for the aforesaid debts, as is contained in our rolls in which the charters and chirographs of the above are enrolled . . . And you shall follow our instructions carefully lest, through

---

[32] Mills (1925), 167–8. He moved with circumspection in seeking profits rather than increments. See above, pp. 336–7.
[33] Mills (1925), pp. 161–5.
[34] H. Cole, *Documents Illustrative of English History in the Thirteenth and Fourteenth Centuries* (Record Commission, 1844), pp. 285 ff.
[35] See Carpenter (1990) especially pp. 70–127, 222–7, 268–89.

your default, our debts shall not be paid at the terms given to Elias and lest we shall be the losers in this matter.[36]

These letters were drawn up in the presence of Peter des Roches and William Briwerre. The old watchdogs of John's Exchequer had not forgotten their tricks. These arrangements bore all the worst features of John's administration.[37] Yet they apparently went out under the seal of William Marshal.[38] By the best contemporary standards defaulting debtors were still fair game.

The re-issues of the Charter did not suddenly alter the conduct of men whether rebel or loyalist, baron, judge or administrator. There was no sudden change in government policy except where the Charter fixed precise limits, as for example in the case of reliefs. The fact that the king was a minor was important because it committed the government into the hands of a small inner clique which had to discuss, correspond and reach agreement if the government was to move at all. This encouraged the growth of conciliar government, but it is important not to exaggerate its cohesion. Much of the correspondence which passed between William Marshal, Hubert de Burgh, Peter des Roches and the papal legate was not concerned with deep constitutional or legal questions, but with the settlement of claims, the exercise of patronage and the distribution of land and office, with the kind of business which must often have been settled by a brief word over John's gaming table in the previous reign. The fiction of an active king was still maintained. Men petitioned him for justice even though he was too young to answer their requests.[39] But the respect for government was not yet so inbred that men accepted its decisions with equanimity. The history of the minority was one of intrigue and incipient or actual rebellion. The risings of Robert de

---

[36] *Patent Rolls, 1216–25*, pp. 179–80.
[37] Compare the example of Simon the Jew of Oxford, above, pp. 335–6.
[38] The *Teste ut supra* here seems to refer to the previous letter but one.
[39] See the petition of Philip of Oldcoates of 1220, addressed to the king on being appointed Seneschal of Poitou (P.R.O., Ancient Petitions, file 340, no. 16038).

Gaugy at Newark, William of Aumale at Castle Bytham, and Faulkes de Bréauté at Bedford are well known. There were also many minor squabbles in which men jostled each other for power and wealth. William of Salisbury, for example, entered on an agreement with the untrustworthy William of Aumale in which his son was to marry Aumale's daughter. All this was embodied in a charter before the arrangement was broken off. William then informed the Justiciar that he was not a party to any attack Aumale might make on the king's lands.[40] He clearly knew more than he thought was healthy of Aumale's schemes. After abandoning his erstwhile ally he did not hesitate to stab him in the back. When Aumale was proposed as seneschal of Poitou, William of Salisbury wrote to the legate, Pandulf, to point out that his disobedience in executing the small responsibilities allotted to him in England scarcely fitted him for the far greater responsibility in Poitou.[41] William of Salisbury was well qualified to comment. He issued general letters some time in 1219 which announced that he had forbidden his deputy sheriff of Lincoln to render any account at the Exchequer for the revenues of the shire 'until such time as the council of the king satisfies us in the matter of the lands and other things promised to us by the lord king and his council'. The earl said he was taking the revenues into his own hands and would be answerable for them at the Exchequer.[42]

The minority made room not so much for a new sense of responsibility as for the open discussion and easy contradiction of government decisions. The re-issue of the Charter did not so much create a new pattern of behaviour by

[40] *Royal Letters of Henry III*, ed. W. W. Shirley (Rolls Series), I, 19–20.
[41] *Ibid.* 129.
[42] P.R.O., K.R. Memoranda Rolls, 3 Henry III, m. 5d. The earl had been trying to obtain control of Lincoln castle, despite the fact that the hereditary castellanship belonged to Nichola de la Haye, who had conducted a vigorous defence of it in the king's interest during the civil war (Norgate, 1912, pp. 148–9). He had also intruded into the manor of Mere (Wilts.), from which the government was trying to eject him (Holt, 1961, pp. 244–5). For these and other activities of William of Salisbury now see Carpenter (1990).

government and individuals, as reinforce the methods of thought and argument from which it had sprung. These now became political clichés. When Geoffrey de Neville, Sheriff of Yorkshire, was imprisoned by his enemies, the legate exhorted the Justiciar to see that he was released 'in accordance with justice and the law of the land'.[43] When in 1220 Richard de Umfraville, a Northumbrian baron who had been connected with the movement against King John as far back as 1212, defended his right to maintain the castle of Harbottle, he asked that the decision on whether it was adulterine or not should be made 'in the court of the lord king by the judgement of my peers'.[44] Some time after the death of Robert de Vieuxpont, one of John's most vigorous supporters, in 1228, his widow Idonea de Bully issued a charter to the men of Bawtry in which she confirmed the privileges they had obtained from her husband. She also conceded that pleas in the town were no longer to be held every fortnight as was customary, but every month. Burgesses were not to suffer if they stayed away from the court unless the bailiff could show that they had absented themselves in order to evade an action. If the bailiff could prove this then they were to make amends 'by consideration of their peers and by the judgement of the court'.[45] This expressed once more the familiar phrases of 1215.[46]

How much of this was due to the burgesses of Bawtry must remain in doubt. The phrases of this charter may simply be the result of casual repetition. Nevertheless, a famous case which occurred in Lincolnshire in 1226 shows that local feeling about the Charter might be very strong.[47]

---

[43] *Royal Letters of Henry III*, I, 130. For the circumstances see Norgate (1912), pp. 159–60.
[44] P.R.O., Ancient Correspondence, II, 16. I am obliged to Dr Patricia Barnes for bringing this to my notice.
[45] Bodleian Library, Dodsworth MS 70, fo. 2. The date of this charter is 1228–35, when Idonea died.
[46] It may also be that the concession of the monthly interval between courts was derived from cap. 42 of the 1217 re-issue.
[47] On this whole question, including this case and others discussed below, now see Maddicott (1984).

The sheriff and four knights were summoned before the king . to explain certain difficulties which had arisen in the administration of justice within the county. The knights reported that the sheriff had heard pleas in the county court from dawn to dusk and had then decided to postpone the remaining business to the following day. Then, however, the knights of the county refused to enter the court to assist the course of justice on the grounds that the shire court ought to be held for one day only. The sheriff then postponed the outstanding cases to the courts of the wapentakes, but when he attempted to do judgement on those which came up in the court of Kesteven[48] the knights once more resisted on the grounds that such matters ought to be dealt with in the county court and nowhere else. The conflict thus arose directly out of the interpretation of cap. 42/35 of the 1217/ 1225 Charter. The interest of this action lies not only in this, but also in the arguments of Theobald Hautein and Hugh of Humby, who argued the case for the knights in the court of the wapentakes of Kesteven. Theobald had no hesitation in claiming knowledge of the intentions of the mighty. He had just come from the king's court, he said, where he had talked with the archbishop, the earl of Chester and other magnates, and he felt sure that very soon the knights would receive a writ protecting them from this kind of demand. He also gave a broad hint that he would not forget the names of those who complied with the sheriff's request. The knights then conferred outside the court, and here Theobald and Hugh presented the real grounds of their objection. The sheriff's actions, they argued, were 'contrary to their liberty which they ought to have by the charter of the lord king' and they maintained that the matter ought to be referred to the earl of Chester and other magnates of the county. They then acted as spokesmen of the knights in repeating their refusal in the county court. One wayward knight, Thomas

---

48 The ten wapentakes of Ancaster.

fitz Simon, steward of John Marshal, accepted the sheriff's argument that his office warranted him to hear pleas and he pronounced judgement on the first case. He was silenced by Theobald: 'You pronounce your judgement now: soon we shall see your lord and we shall tell him how you behaved in this county court.'[49]

Theobald and Hugh excused themselves when this case first came up in the Bench in Hilary 1226. However, they appeared in the Easter term and were far from abashed. They stated that the sheriff was trying to hold the shire court at intervals of five weeks or even less. The customary interval, they argued, was forty days, and since the king had granted to all his free men their liberties and ancient customs they considered that the position of the shire court ought not to be changed without the consent of the king and the magnates of the realm. In the case of the wapentake court they seem to have exploited the imprecision of the Charter, which laid down that the sheriff was to hold his tourn twice a year, but made no reference to any other sessions of the courts of hundred and wapentake. They stated that since the liberties had been conceded,[50] the sheriff had only held the court twice a year 'in accordance with the Charter of Liberty', but that his attempt to hold the session at Ancaster had infringed this. The Bench recorded no decision. Bracton, who later included the case in his note book, noted that Hugh and Theobald were dismissed by the order of the king. They had won their case.[51] It was by no means exceptional. It was closely similar to the action which the men of Devon brought against their sheriff in 1214 on the basis of the local charter of liberties which they had bought in 1204.[52] Eight years after the Lincolnshire case the king and magnates found

[49] *Curia Regis Rolls*, XII, no. 2142.
[50] This could refer either to 1217 or 1225, more probably to the latter date.
[51] *Curia Regis Rolls*, XII, no. 2312. The case has often been discussed (see Pollock & Maitland, 1898, I, 549–50, and Helen M. Cam, *The Hundred and the Hundred Rolls*, London, 1930, pp. 15–16).
[52] See above, pp. 66–7.

392

it necessary to interpret the provisions of cap. 42 on the sessions of hundred and wapentake.[53] The Lincolnshire action was simply one chapter in a long story. So it must have been too for some of the men involved. Theobald Hautein was one of the many Lincolnshire knights who had joined the rebellion in 1215. So also was Norman Darcy, one of the jurors who first reported on the case in the Bench.[54]

The men involved in this case confidently assumed that the Charter was law. It certainly was so in that it could now be used to reinforce an argument in the courts and claimed as a defence of individual or local privilege. But there was still some uncertainty about its status. In both 1216 and 1217 it was issued under the seals of William Marshal and the legate. It would not be truly secure until it had been granted by an adult king of his own free will. The magnates clearly appreciated this. Their first demand for a confirmation came in January 1224, a month after the partial declaration of Henry's majority.[55] All they got from Henry was the reply that what had been sworn on oath should be observed. This was clearly inadequate and the nervousness increased. The re-issue of the Charter in 1225 emphasized that it was granted of the king's free will, in exchange for the grant of a fifteenth on movables, and that the king would neither do nor procure anything to infringe or weaken it. As in 1215 the magnates were trying to guard against the possibility of papal annulment. However, even this re-issue was not entirely secure, for Henry was still subject, as a minor, to the disability that he could not make grants in perpetuity under the great seal. The re-issue was an exception, but this did not increase its security. When he came of age in 1227 Henry took no immediate action except to adjust some of the

---

[53] See below, pp. 395–6.
[54] Compare also the reported reaction of the county court of Lincolnshire to the case of Gilbert de Gant, 1218 (above, pp. 168–9).
[55] *Chron. Maj.* III, 76 (see Norgate, 1912, pp. 214–16 and above, p. 378 n., on the dating of this passage).

perambulations of the forest which had been executed after 1225.[56] He still accepted both charters, for juries of four knights were summoned from the counties in the summer to report along with sheriffs and foresters on the difficulties which had arisen in their enforcement.[57] But some slight doubts remained,[58] and it was not until ten years later, in January 1237, that both charters were finally confirmed in a binding and unexceptionable form. Henry then issued a 'small' charter of confirmation which copied the opening phrases of Magna Carta and confirmed all the liberties which he had conveyed when under age both in Magna Carta and in the Charter of the Forest. He now granted these in perpetuity 'notwithstanding that these charters were completed when we were a minor'.[59] Nearly twenty-two years after Runnymede the liberties were at last formally secure. Among the witnesses to the 'small' charter were Peter des Roches, Hubert de Burgh and William de Warenne, who had advised King John at Runnymede in 1215, and John de Lacy, Richard de Percy and Richard de Munfichet, who had been members of the Twenty-Five. Magna Carta was secured within a single generation, but only just.[60]

The confirmation of 1237 gave formal recognition to a surrender which followed almost inevitably on Henry's long minority. The king never resisted effectively for long; indeed it may have been impossible. Moreover on two occasions before 1237 he made the clearest practical recognition of the validity of the Charters. The first arose from the perambulations of the forest which followed the re-issue of 1225. Henry issued letters which recited the terms of the disaffor-

---

[56] Bazeley (1921), 140 ff.   [57] *Rot. Litt. Claus.* II, 212*b*–213.
[58] Wendover thought that the king quashed the Charter of the Forest in the summer of 1227 (*Chron. Maj.* III, 122). Turner clearly showed that he was wrong (1899, pp. xcviii–ci), but Wendover's story seems to reflect a real fear that the king might exploit the fact that he had granted the Charters as a minor.
[59] *Statutes of the Realm*, I, 28.
[60] Stacey (1987, pp. 112–13) adopts another view of the 'small' charter. This appears to be based on a mistaken reading of the *non obstante* clause.

estation clauses of the Forest Charter and the section of cap. 17 which laid down that all those who received these liberties from him were to grant the same to their men. He then went on to say that he had received complaints from the knights and men of Westmorland that, despite this, William of Lancaster, lord of Kendal, had retained certain woods and moors afforested 'to the damage of the knights and other honest men of the neighbourhood'. William was now instructed to disafforest them. Similar letters were sent to Robert de Vieuxpont, William de Warenne, John de Lacy, Robert Grelley, and others in the interests of named petitioners.[61] Henry clearly took a serious view of the principle that the benefits of the Charters should be available to under-tenants. He returned to the same point in letters of August 1234. Here he emphasized that the Charters had been granted to both great and small, reviewed the provision that what he granted to his men they should also grant to theirs, and finally ordered that this should be observed by all, both by his own bailiffs and by the magnates and their bailiffs; they were to make especially sure that the hundred courts, whether royal or private, were not to meet more than twice a year.[62] Here Henry, like the Lincolnshire knights in 1226, was interpreting cap. 35 in a very narrow sense. In October he addressed further letters to the sheriff of Lincolnshire, who had apparently been in doubt on the function of the wapentake courts ever since the re-issue of the Charter in 1225. The king now explained that he had had this particular clause read before the archbishop, bishops, earls and barons and that he had decided with their advice that these courts should henceforth be held every three weeks. He also laid down that there should be no general summons except on the occasion of the sheriff's tourn. He clearly realized the burden of suit of court, for his letters were couched in conciliatory language in which he explained that frequent

---

[61] *Patent Rolls, 1216–25*, pp. 575–6.
[62] *Close Rolls, 1231–4*, pp. 592–3 (cp. also *ibid.* p. 551).

sessions were necessary for the maintenance of the peace, and that he desired as far as possible to reduce the burden on the poor. The three-weekly interval he now laid down was in fact longer than the customary fortnightly one at which most local courts had apparently met hitherto.[63] Here was a king seeking a genuine and reasonable application of a section of the Charter. Henry's rejection of the forest perambulations and his attempts to escape from some of the consequences of the re-issue of 1225 are only part of the story. On other matters he was as ready as the magnates to accept the Charters as part of the law of the land.

Between 1225 and 1237 the Charters became securely established. They had now been confirmed twice in return for taxation. The Church was closely committed to preserving them.[64] Stephen Langton in 1225 and Edmund of Abingdon in 1237 had solemnly pronounced sentence of excommunication against violators. Some problems of interpretation had been settled; others, like the forest perambulations, remained unresolved. The Charters had become more than a legal and administrative prescription. They were a test of good faith, from 1237 onwards the first requirement and concession in the periodic reconciliations between the Crown and its great vassals. But from this point onwards the Charter came to be less immediately connected with each succeeding political crisis. As early as 1244 the emphasis was shifting from the Charter itself to schemes for conciliar control of the king which would ensure that he executed what he promised,[65] and it was only by making

[63] 'De interpretatione clausule contente in libertatibus, qualiter debeat intellegi' (*Close Rolls, 1231–4,* pp. 588–9). Sir Maurice Powicke attached great importance to the conciliatory language of this letter: 'A feudal assembly which legislates for the community in this way is already a national assembly' (Powicke, 1947, I, 148). The letter established that the magnates were consulted, but does not in any way imply that the concern for the poor which it expressed originated with them. The roll does not record that it was sent to any county other than Lincolnshire.
[64] For an important study of the ecclesiastical interest see Gray (1968).
[65] *Chron. Maj.* IV, 366–8. I am following C. R. Cheney in accepting Matthew Paris's date for this scheme (*E.H.R.* LXV, 1950, 213–21; cp. Denholm-Young, *E.H.R.* LVIII, 1943, 401–23).

extensive additions that the Charter could be brought into closer touch with the political objectives of the moment. Hence from 1237 onwards the Charter came to have a double history. On the one hand it became a shibboleth in the constitutional and political struggles of the thirteenth century. On the other it was advanced in evidence more and more in individual actions in the courts or in petitions to the Crown.[66] The characteristic process of interpretation began before the end of the reign of Edward I. It was instanced in the constitutional sphere by the Confirmation of the Charters of 1297 and the *Articuli super cartas* of 1300. It was illustrated in private actions by the claim advanced in 1283 that cap. 16 was concerned with rights of fishing not rights of hawking[67] and by the oblique equation in the Year Book of 1302–3 of trial by jury with judgement by peers.[68] The myth was being formed.

But the myth was not simply a creation of the later thirteenth and succeeding centuries. Already in 1237 the Charter had acquired mythical qualities which help to account for its later history. The Charter of 1215 embodied a revolutionary programme, that of 1217 and 1225 was a statement of law. The first was quashed, the second confirmed. Yet from the start men emphasized the continuity between the two. When William Marshal sent copies of the 1216 re-issue to Ireland in February 1217, the official formula of the covering letters was that it contained the 'liberties granted by us and our father'.[69] In time some men became completely confused. In 1231, for example, an Oxfordshire jury assumed that the regulations on sheriffs' tourns, which had been included for the first time in the

---

[66] See Thompson (1925), pp. 37–67, esp. 66–7.
[67] McKechnie (1914), pp. 302–4; Thompson (1925), pp. 61–2.
[68] *Year Book 30–31 Edward I*, p. 531. The passage is noted and discussed in Pollock & Maitland (1898), II, 625 n.; McKechnie (1914), p. 393 n.; Thompson (1925), p. 62. The accused rejected trial by jury on the grounds that the jurors were his accusers. He also claimed that since he was a knight he ought to be judged by his peers. The judge accepted this claim and a jury of knights was nominated.
[69] *Patent Rolls, 1216–25*, p. 31.

1217 Charter, were part of the 'Charter of Runnymede'.[70] One factor in this was that some of the demands made in 1215 and dropped from subsequent re-issues were still very much in men's minds. An obvious instance was the association of scutage and aid and the proposal that scutage like aids should be subject to consent. Consent to scutage never became established under Henry III. Like his father, he levied it as of right on the occasion of a campaign on those who did not acquit their service in other ways,[71] and this was frequently done without any kind of consultation. Despite this, scutage and aids were repeatedly confused, and scutage and consent associated. In 1217 an aid was collected to help pay the indemnity due to Prince Louis under the terms of the Treaty of Lambeth. This was described in both the Chancery and the Exchequer rolls as a scutage 'assessed by the common counsel of our realm'.[72] The confusion here was merely semantic for the aid was in fact levied as a tax of two marks on the knight's fee. Nevertheless, it is disturbing to find government officials permitting a statement which might be subject to misconstruction. There was even great confusion in the case of a genuine scutage in 1229 which was occasioned by the campaign in Brittany. This was levied at the rate of 3 m., which exceeded the strict terms of the 1217/1225 Charter, and this may explain some of the unusual features of its assessment. Whatever the reason, the Pipe roll of 1229 recorded that the scutage was assessed by the counsel of earls and barons who had met at Northampton on 23 July. It also stated that the archbishop and his suffragans were summoned to Westminster at Michaelmas to consent to the same scutage. They met the king's request by agreeing to give him an aid equivalent to their scutage assessment. They refused to admit that they did this because of the military summons they had received

---

[70] *Curia Regis Rolls*, XIV, no. 1188.   [71] Mitchell (1914), pp. 338–40 and *passim*.
[72] *Rot. Litt. Claus.* I, 371; P.R.O., K.R. Memoranda Roll 2 Henry III, m. 7d.

398

from him and they provided that neither party to the bargain was to lose or acquire rights as a result of it.[73] It was perhaps inevitable that the ecclesiastical tenants of the Crown should take the lead in this particular issue for they were likely to accept demands for overseas service less readily. They repeated this action in 1230 when a scutage for the campaign in Poitou was assessed by the lay magnates who were with the army. Once more the king had to accept a protest that the clergy had not been consulted, followed by an offer of an aid at the same rate as the scutage.[74] But the confusion was not limited to ecclesiastical circles or restricted to debates in great assemblies. Between 1215 and 1232 Geoffrey Worslype and Margaret his wife sold a number of small parcels of land in Moulsoe, Bucks., to Robert fitz Peter of Stratton. The land was transferred in perpetuity and the one service demanded was 'one penny for scutage when scutage is given in the realm by the common counsel of the realm'.[75] The ideas of 1215 ran deep.

Scutage was not the only tax affected by the provisions of the 1215 Charter. In 1217 Peter des Roches refused to pay the aid of 2 m. on the knight's fee on the grounds that he had not consented to it; William Marshal, the king's council, and later the barons of the Exchequer accepted his case.[76] In 1220 there was widespread resistance to the assessment of a carucage. Peter des Roches was involved again, along with the young earl marshal, and the earls of Chester and Salisbury. The writs of assessment stated that the tax had been conceded by the magnates and the king's faithful

---

[73] *Pipe Roll 13 Henry III*, rot. 7, m. 1d. The entry was copied by Madox (*Exchequer*, London, 1769, I, 607 n.) and discussed by Mitchell (1914), p. 186.

[74] Mitchell (1914), p. 192.

[75] P.R.O. Duchy of Lancaster, Cartae Miscellaneae, no. 53. I am indebted to Dr Patricia Barnes for bringing this charter to my notice The relevant phrase runs as follows: 'Reddendo inde unum denarium ad scutagium scilicet quando scutagium datur in regno per commune consilium regni.'

[76] Madox, *Exchequer*, I, 675 n.

subjects.[77] Nevertheless, the knights of Yorkshire refused to execute the writ of assessment on the grounds that the magnates of the county had not been consulted and knew nothing of the levy. In words which seemed to echo the provision of cap. 14 they said that the magnates should be consulted either viva voce or by letter: some of them made it clear that their objection was not to the carucage as such but to the fact that consent had not been sought in what they considered was the proper manner.[78] Thirty-five years later, if Matthew Paris is to be trusted, the magnates repeated the same argument even more explicitly by refusing Henry's demands for an aid on the grounds that they had not been summoned according to the terms of the Great Charter.[79] The Charter had helped to start a long and diffuse debate on the processes of consultation, consent and forms of representation. It clearly made the government very sensitive. The writs for the assessment of the fortieth of 1232 stated that the tax had been conceded by earls, barons, knights, free men and villeins; those for the assessment of the thirtieth of 1237 that it had been conceded by earls, barons, knights and free men on their own behalf and for the villeins.[80] These were unrealistic and impracticable assertions which nevertheless reflect some attempt to wrestle with the problem.

There was little in the text or the method of publishing the documents to explain why the demands of 1215 should have survived in this way. The re-issues were distributed to each shire as the original had been in 1215.[81] The government assumed that a copy was available in every county.[82] Instructions were issued on the occasion of each re-issue that the Charters should be read in full county court,[83] and this

---

[77] *Rot. Litt. Claus.* I, 437.
[78] *Royal Letters*, I, 151–2. This incident is thoroughly discussed by Mitchell (1914), pp. 130–2, and Powicke (1947), I, 33–4.
[79] *Chron. Maj.* v, 520–1. [80] *Stubbs's Charters*, pp. 356, 358.
[81] See Poole (1913), 450 ff. and Thompson (1925), pp. 93 ff.
[82] *Close Rolls, 1231–4*, p. 592. [83] *Rot. Litt. Claus.* I, 336, 377; II, 70, 72b.

was repeated in the case of the 'small' charter in 1237.[84] The system was continued in subsequent confirmations until 1265, when the sheriffs were instructed to publish the Charters twice yearly. Thus every step was taken to make sure that the texts were known. How far the measures were effective must have depended to a large extent on local circumstances. In Wiltshire the original of 1225 was deposited in Lacock Abbey by the knights of the shire and had presumably been in their hands up to then.[85] In Nottinghamshire Magna Carta, the Charter of the Forest and the perambulation of Sherwood were still preserved in the early fifteenth century by the knights and magnates concerned in local administration.[86] In Essex in 1238 Richard de Munfichet was instructed to have the Forest Charter read in full county court.[87] He had been one of the Twenty-Five and it is difficult to imagine that he would fail to make the most of his opportunity. But zeal and confusion were not necessarily inconsistent. In 1237 the Chancery clerks were themselves uncertain whether it was the 'small' charter or the two larger charters which were to be read in the counties.[88] Moreover, the re-issues of 1217 and 1225 may themselves have caused some misunderstanding. The saving clause reserved to all men both clerk and lay the liberties they already held. This could easily be interpreted so as to include the Charter of 1215 if men ignored the annulment of Pope Innocent.[89] The

---

[84] *Close Rolls, 1234–7*, pp. 421, 426, 451, 499, 534.   [85] Bémont (1892), p. 45.
[86] Holt (1960), 69.   [87] *Close Rolls, 1237–42*, p. 22.
[88] *Close Rolls, 1234–7*, pp. 426, 541.
[89] There is little, however, to be said for Kate Norgate's view that this clause was so drafted that it might permit reconsideration of the clauses which had been dropped after 1215 (1912, p. 215). It also appears in the Charter of the Forest, which included all the forest privileges contained in the Great Charter of 1215. The main intent was to ensure that neither Charter invaded liberties already in existence. The papal legate who sealed the 1217 re-issue can scarcely have taken the view that the concessions of 1215 were still valid. Nor yet can Stephen Langton. It is therefore most unlikely that Langton sought anything more than a straightforward confirmation of the 1217 document in 1224 and 1225 (cp. Norgate, *ibid.*).

Charter was widely known. Innocent's bull could scarcely compete.

Despite the widespread knowledge of the Charter confusion was sometimes profound. It was illustrated at its deepest and most complex at St Albans.[90] Here, the first great chronicler of the house, Roger of Wendover, reproduced a text of the Charter which embodied elements from the 1215, 1217 and 1225 texts and, in the case of the security clause, from some other unknown source. He was quite convinced that there were no differences at all between the Charters of John and Henry III. He also attributed the Charter of the Forest to John and dated it 1215. His successor, Matthew Paris, did no better. He acquired a full text of the 1215 Charter, which Wendover had never apparently seen. Even so all he did was to insert the clauses dropped from the 1217 re-issue in the conglomerate text which he copied from Wendover. Late in life he obtained an authentic exemplification of the Charter of Henry III which was used in the ceremony of confirmation at Westminster in 1253. It made no difference. He headed it 'The Great Charter of King John which Henry III swore once again to observe in the great hall at Westminster', and then tucked it away in his volume of illustrative documents without any attempt to question the title he had given it or collate it with the version he had already entered in his chronicle. Against closed minds the documents were powerless except to reinforce preconceptions, and this is precisely what they did at St Albans. For Wendover the fight for the Charters was a continuous struggle from 1215 to 1225 and onwards. To Matthew Paris the claims of the baronage and the Church against Henry III were the same as those against John. Many of his additions to the chronicle of Wendover imposed anachronistic attitudes typical of the 1250's on the baronage and clergy of John's time. Paris used his interpretation of the reign of John to strengthen his criticism of the government of Henry III.

The St Albans chroniclers were not alone in interpreting events in this way. The rebellion of 1215 was more successful than many. Part of its programme survived; the rebel leaders remained largely undisturbed in land and estate; some lived on to enjoy long and influential careers. By 1217, and even more by 1225, much had been won. It is from this or later periods that most of the chronicle narratives come, and this does much to explain the widespread hostility to King John which deepened as the thirteenth century advanced so that he rapidly became the prototype of the 'bad' king.[91] The approach may be summarized in a series of syllogistic propositions: The 1225 Charter stated law. The 1225 Charter was the same as the 1215 Charter. Therefore, the 1215 Charter had stated law. Therefore, King John had been a tyrant who had ruled contrary to law and custom. Therefore, finally, any ruler who infringed the Charter was likewise guilty of tyrannous behaviour.

The argument had an underlying basis of fact. The 1225 Charter was founded on that of 1215; Henry's ministers had revived some of the policies for which John had been attacked in 1215; Henry, like his father, had introduced aliens into high office. But it already included a myth of vital importance. To transfer the legal status which Magna Carta acquired between 1217 and 1237 to the Charter of 1215 was to swallow the basic proposition advanced by the baronial party in 1215. It was to accept that the original Charter had been a statement of good and lawful custom which King John had ignored and infringed. This contention had not passed unchallenged at the time.[92] Yet there is every sign that men were now prepared to accept it. The great loyalist magnates acknowledged it when they re-issued the Charter,

---

[91] Holt (1963), pp. 16–25.   [92] See above, pp. 373–4.

and the chronicles asserted it almost without question.[93] And in accepting this men also accepted that the Charter in some way embodied the liberties of the realm. They owned that a list of liberties, conceived primarily in baronial interests, was an integral part of the law of the land, that the barons had, in fact, acted on behalf of the whole community. The St Albans chroniclers accepted this without question in recording the actions of the next generation. Wendover presented the rebellion of Richard Marshal in 1233 as one in which Richard was defending both his own rights and the rights of the realm; he appears as a paragon of constitutional virtue, prepared to stand by the judgement of his peers and denouncing the perjured counsellors of the king, 'the adversaries of the realm and the opponents of justice', as infringers of the Charter.[94] How far Richard saw himself as the country's deliverer from injustice must remain in doubt. But Wendover was not so very far from reality. The protest of the Yorkshire knights of 1220 and of Theobald Hautein and the Lincolnshire knights in 1226 both demonstrate that the gentry, at least, accepted the magnates' claim to act for the realm. Forty years later at the end of another baronial rebellion the villagers of Peatling Magna were to assert it also.[95] Such evidence is only one side of the coin. By 1265 there were issues enough which divided knights from magnates, and as the years passed other classes and interests were to claim to represent the community. But the assumption of 1215 is not dissolved by demonstrating that the Charter was conceived in baronial interests or that it reflected particular social conditions which changed with the passage of time. Later generations may have differed on what the community was and on who was entitled to represent it,

---

[93] See above, pp. 259, 279–80. Compare the attitude of the *Histoire des ducs de Normandie*, above, p. 271.

[94] *Chron. Maj.* III, 257–62.

[95] *Select Cases of Procedure without Writ* (Selden Soc., LX, 1941), no. 30. See the comments of Powicke (1947), II, 509–10, and Helen M. Cam, *Law-Finders and Law-Makers in Mediaeval England* (London, 1962), pp. 81–2.

but they were rarely in any doubt that authority should be subject to law which the community itself defined. Magna Carta could not ensure that this would always be so, but it endured as an example. It set no mean standard.

THE MEETING AT BURY ST EDMUNDS, 1214

Dr Antonia Gransden and Dr R. M. Thomson are more inclined than I am to accept the evidence of Roger of Wendover that a great baronial gathering occurred at Bury St Edmunds late in 1214 at which the barons swore on the high altar that they would fight, if necessary, in order to compel the king to confirm the charter of liberties of Henry I.[1] We are all agreed that the difficulty arises from the abrupt termination of the *Annales S. Edmundi* in 1212; but it seems to me to carry speculation too far to suppose that the story of the meeting appeared in the lost continuation of the *Annales* or its source.[2] Indeed Dr Thomson provides strong grounds for thinking that this was not the case, for the author of the later *Cronica Buriensis* used John of Wallingford, not the Bury annals, as the source for his account of the meeting.[3] In Bury histories the story first appears in a condensed form in a chronicle of Bury composed by Bury monks at St Benet of Hulme in or after 1327.[4]

The matter therefore depends on the evidence, or lack of it, in the *Electio Hugonis*. Now the *Electio* mentions no such meeting, and, given its subject-matter, it may reasonably be asked – why should it? Dr Gransden relies in some degree on this argument. However, both she and Dr Thomson go further by maintaining that the *Electio* does, in fact, contain veiled references to incipient rebellion which are consistent with Wendover's story.

[1] See above, pp. 224–6.
[2] Antonia Gransden, *Historical Writing in England c. 550–c. 1307* (London, 1974), p. 359n.; *The Customary of the Benedictine Abbey of Bury St Edmunds in Suffolk*, ed. Antonia Gransden, Henry Bradshaw Society, XCIX, 1973, p. xxv, n.5.
[3] *Electio Hugonis*, p. 190.   [4] *Memorials of St Edmund*, III, 10–11.

Before examining these it is well to bear some dates in mind. First, John was at La Rochelle on 2 October and at Dartmouth on 15 October. He probably arrived in England about 7 October.[5] Secondly, he visited Bury on 4 November, when he attempted to settle the disputed election. Thirdly, the most likely date for a baronial meeting would be 20 November, the feast of St Edmund, when there was a good excuse for an assembly at Bury; and indeed Wendover states that the barons gathered 'as if for prayer'.

The first statement in the *Electio* which is adduced in support of the argument is put in the mouth of the king at an encounter with Hugh on 29 October – 'I have to consider myself and my crown before you and your honour. You have stirred up rebellion against me from which you can expect no good result' – and, on Hugh's denial – 'I do not say this with reference to you in particular, but on account of certain others as well.'[6] The second statement is given to Hugh's opponent, the sacrist, and is made as the king departed from Bury on 5 November – 'And unless he [Hugh] is quickly persuaded by the royal provision to abandon this wicked idea, it is to be feared that within a short time he will accomplish what he has even now set in motion against the royal dignity.'[7]

Now it is immediately obvious that neither of these passages can be related in any way to a meeting allegedly held on 20 November. Indeed, we may well wonder what 'war' the king was supposed to be envisaging. On 29 October he had been in England for no more than three weeks. The most that can be said is that on 4 November (the very day of his visit to Bury) payment was ordered to Peter Saracen (along with many other payments to other

---

[5] The conjecture is based on the transfer of the Fine roll which had been compiled in Poitou to the treasury by Peter des Roches on 7 October (*Rot. de Ob. et Fin.*, p. 532). Some at least of the king's household must have returned by that date.
[6] *Electio Hugonis*, pp. 116–17. I have used Dr Thomson's translation, on which see below.
[7] *Ibid.*, p. 129.

recipients), who had been sent to the papal legate, Nicholas of Tusculum, for writs *contra conjuratos*.[8] This activated the letters of the pope of 31 October 1213 ordering the legate to denounce all conspiracies and factions arising from the quarrel between kingdom and priesthood as soon as the Interdict was relaxed.[9] The writs *contra conjuratos* therefore became available from 1 July 1214. The payment, it should be noted, was one of a batch all authorized by the Justiciar, Peter des Roches; it was not initiated by the king. So by 4 November a precautionary measure had been taken, but whether this was against anything other than the legate's imminent departure from England is open to question; and this *conjuratio* concerned the Interdict and its consequences, not some new rebellion. Certainly the king may have been uneasy and suspicious; the attempt to collect the Poitevin scutage was running into the sands at the Michaelmas account of the Exchequer. However, the evidence does not allow for a week-by-week account of this spreading disaster;[10] meanwhile it is worth noting that the future baronial leader, Robert fitz Walter, who is likely to have figured large in any East Anglian movement, attested a royal charter to St Paul's issued at the New Temple on 22 November.[11]

So there are considerable difficulties in the chronology. Quite apart from this, it is very questionable whether the passages on which Dr Gransden and Dr Thomson rely refer to the incipient baronial rebellion in any way at all. The *Electio* recounts an election in which Hugh's party, which was ultimately successful, stood out against the regalian power. The 'royal dignity' deployed in the second passage is nothing more than the usual rhetoric on which the Crown and its supporters called in such cases. The same is true of the king's reference to his crown in the first passage. Moreover it

[8] *Rot. Litt. Claus.*, I, 175b; Cheney (1976), p. 366.
[9] *Selected Letters of Innocent III*, no. 61.   [10] Holt (1961), pp. 101–2.
[11] *Cal. Charter Rolls*, I, 153–4.

is plain that the 'rebellion', if that is what it was, was concerned particularly with the fortunes of Hugh – nothing else. In short it was part of the same rhetoric of the conflict of *regnum* and *sacerdotium*. In that context 'provoke conflict' would be a better translation of *Excitasti* – *bellum* than 'stir up rebellion'.

Two passages provide a useful cross-bearing – 'Hostem enim mihi infestissimum, in meum et meorum (quod absit) exterminium tota sua possibilitate promptissimum, sedentem mihi semper in insidiis ut machinetur in me malum'; and again – 'Ipse vero in ingressu suo, non pacis laetitiam, sed ignem portavit et gladium, dum contra me de regno et corona proposuit quaestionem.' These fiery words come not from the report of a chronicler, however detailed and exact, but from the missives directed by Henry II against Thomas Becket, the first before and the second after the archbishop's martyrdom.[12] Now Becket was not raising a baronial rebellion; and by Henry's standards the passages in the *Electio* are distinctly mild and legalistic. Letters of the Irish magnates of 1213 come even closer to the issue at St Edmunds. Declaring their support for King John, they asserted – 'Constat siquidem nobis omne id quod actum est de facto illo Cantuariensi [ie. the Canterbury election] contra dignitatem et libertatem suam et corone Anglicane quam consuevit habere iniuriose ad exheredationem suam et heredum suorum attemptatum esse.'[13] It is to such rhetoric that these passages in the *Electio* belong.

One further point will clinch this. To those involved in the events of 1215, and indeed to contemporaries who wrote about them, the rebellion was not *bellum*, but *conjuratio*, *commotio*, *discordia*, and ultimately, *gwerra*. The author of the *Electio* provides his own confirmation of this, for, in describ-

---

[12] *Materials for the History of Thomas Becket*, VII (Rolls Series, 1885), ed. J. C. Robertson and J. B. Sheppard, nos. 729, 739.
[13] H. G. Richardson and G. O. Sayles, *The Irish Parliament in the Middle Ages* (Philadelphia, 1952, 1964), pp. 286–7.

ing events after 25 April 1215 he writes – 'Evolutis post-
modum paucis diebus facta est commotio inter dominum
regem et barones Anglie.' As usual his chronology is sound,
but what are we to make of what follows? – 'because the
king was at the time trying to annul by force the charter
of major liberties confirmed to them by his *father*, the
illustrious King Henry' (my italics).[14] Can we really accept
that someone who is supposed to have known of, perhaps
even seen, Wendover's alleged assembly could confuse
Henry I and Henry II and attribute the former's charter to
the latter?

The subsidiary points advanced by Dr Thomson now
require little comment. There is no evidence that the
Northerners came south to Bury in the autumn of 1214, no
evidence that the charter of Henry I was carried from one
centre (say St Paul's) to another (say Bury), no evidence of
who attended the festival of St Edmund in that year. Not
many will be ready to follow Dr Thomson's hazardous logic
– 'all political considerations aside, *it would be strange if*
Langton, Bigod (the saint's hereditary standard–bearer), Fitz
Walter, and other eminent east Anglians *did not* meet at Bury
on the feast of St Edmund' (my italics). Perhaps so (as indeed
I allow above, p. 226): perhaps not. But if Fitz Walter was
indeed present he must have had a hard ride in winter
conditions to be in London on the 22nd. Fewer still are
likely to accept the assertion that Wendover 'is not the only
contemporary writer to mention this meeting . . . the other
is the author of the . . . *Histoire des Ducs de Normandie*'.[15] The
evidence simply does not justify such certitude. The *Histoire*
describes a baronial council or *parlement* at which a demand
was made for the confirmation of the charter of Henry I.[16]
It is not located at Bury, or indeed anywhere else. It is not
dated. It is prefaced by the remark that the barons conferred

[14] *Electio*, p. 166. Once again, I have largely used Dr Thomson's translation.
[15] *Ibid.*, p. 191.   [16] See above, p. 223.

'soon after' the king's return from Poitou, but it goes on, still referring to the same *conseil* or *parlement*, to describe the exchanges between the barons and the king into the early months of 1215. There is no real doubt that it refers to the critical meetings at London in the first week in January.

Yet with all that said the real problem remains. The evidence for the Bury meeting is Wendover's, no one else's. Wendover had access to varied information from a variety of sources. Some he used regularly. Otherwise he picked up bits and pieces like a magpie. It is very unlikely that he invented the accounts of the meetings at St Paul's and Bury. By one route or another they simply came his way; and their veracity depends ultimately, not on him, but on his sources. We shall not be able to evaluate them properly until we have a much more exact account of his sources and *modus operandi* of the kind which Mr Corner, for example, has given us for Roger of Howden.[17] In Wendover's case only one such source is apparent at present, namely William d'Aubigné of Belvoir, but that link scarcely helps with the meeting at Bury St Edmunds. Such an examination of Wendover will be hampered by the fact that his chronicle survives only in later MSS of which the earliest is that of his successor, Matthew Paris, and perhaps even more by his proven carelessness and readiness to tamper with his material. It will not be an easy task.

---

[17] D. Corner, 'The earliest surviving manuscripts of Roger of Howden's *Chronica*', *E.H.R.*, XCVIII (1983), 297–310; 'The *Gesta Regis Henrici Secundi* and *Chronica* of Roger, parson of Howden', *B.I.H.R.*, LVI (1983), 126–44.

NOTIFICATION OF THOMAS COUNT OF PERCHE, FEBRUARY 1215

The letter printed below was issued by Thomas count of Perche on behalf of his knights of the castlery of Bellême. It specifies four occasions for the feudal aid: the count's first knighting, his first ransom, the knighting of his eldest son, and the marriage of his eldest daughter. It is also of great interest in its language. The aids are described as *tallia* (*tailles* or tallages) levied both on knights and their men; and it provides a rare instance of the adverb *feodaliter*, here used synonymously with 'lawfully'.

Thomas accompanied Prince Louis to England and was killed at the battle of Lincoln in 1217, the subject of a famous drawing by Matthew Paris.

Thomas comes Pertici omnibus ad quos presentes littere pervenerint salutem in domino. Ad universorum noticiam volumus pervenire quod milites nostri de castellario Beilim' talliam de feodis suis et hominibus suis nobis debent tantummodo feodaliter pro hiis quatuor rebus que sequuntur: pro prima milicia nostra; pro prima captione nostra de guerra; pro milicia filii nostri primogeniti viventis; et pro prima filia nostra maritanda. Preter has tallias nec a militum feodis nec ab eorum hominibus tallias possumus feodaliter extorquere, et ne hujusmodi libertas ab aliquo heredum nostrorum in posterum infringatur, eam sigilli nostri caractere fecimus conmuniri. Actum anno gracie M cc quartodecimo mense februario.

Notes: Archives de l'Orne, H 2164. 177 × 90mm. No witnesses. Fold and tag for seal. For the date, the beginning of the year was 25 March.

TRIPLEX FORMA PACIS

The basic passage for the discussion of the *triplex forma pacis* occurs in letters of 5 September, covering the papal mandate 'Mirari cogimur', in which the papal agents in England excommunicated the leading baronial rebels. These were printed for the first time from the original by Sir Maurice Powicke in 1929.[1] The passage is as follows: 'nobiles viri ... et multi alii complices et fautores ipsorum coniurationibus et conspirationibus illicitis contra dignitatem regiam colligati contra ipsum Regem et pacem regni, quod est patrimonium Beati Petri, arma movere nequiter presumpserant et contra triplicem formam pacis quarum quelibet honesta et rationabilis erat et a viris Dominum timentibus merito acceptanda ipsum dominum suum contemptibiliter diffidarunt, fidelitatis sibi prestite vinculo dissoluto.'[2] It is placed in an exact relationship to the chronology of the event of the spring of 1215. It is clear that the *triplex forma pacis* preceded the baronial defiance and it is equally clear that this was the defiance made at the beginning of May, since it is followed by a reference to the fall of London (17 May), which the barons seized 'contempta forma pacis quam dominus Papa presentibus et consentientibus eorum nuntiis providerat observandam'.[3] Taken together these two passages establish that the *triplex forma pacis* was in fact the settlement which the pope announced in the letters of 19 March, and this is confirmed by Innocent's letters of 18 June which refer to the 'formam descriptam superius a

---

[1] *E.H.R.* XLIV (1929), 86–93. There is a corrupt text, of the papal mandate only, in Wendover's chronicle (*Chron. Maj.* II, 627–8).
[2] *Loc. cit.* p. 92.   [3] *Ibid.*

413

(nobis) nuntiis eorum presentibus cum multa deliberatione provisam'.[4]

However, Powicke argued that the *triplex forma pacis* was Magna Carta. He overlooked the letters of 19 March and the reference to a *forma* in the letter of 18 June. He then thought that the participation of the pope's 'familiar' in the agreement at Runnymede made the settlement between the king and baronage 'triplex', and, finally, that Pandulf and the other papal agents would not have 'cynically' disregarded so striking and recent a settlement as Magna Carta.[5] These arguments were further developed in 1945 by H. G. Richardson, who argued that the letters of 5 September referred to a second baronial defiance which was an essential prefatory step, in his view, to the renewal of war in the autumn;[6] and in 1963 by Richardson and Sayles, who maintained that the letters of 18 June made no reference to a *concordia* at Rome.[7]

This case has not proved convincing. Powicke stretched the evidence in arguing that the Runnymede settlement was *triplex*. Both he and Richardson exaggerated the extent of Pandulf's consent to the Charter; they also overlooked the reference to a *forma* in the letters of 18 June. It was incorrect to argue that the letters of 5 September contain no other possible reference to the Charter; they do, in the form of *nova iura* which are roundly denounced. Moreover there is no reference to a second defiance in the letter of 5 September, unless it be to the chaplain of Robert fitz Walter 'qui sine superioris mandato ausus fuit Christum dominum pollutis labiis diffidare'.[8]

These views were corrected simultaneously and independently by Sidney Painter and C. R. Cheney in 1949–50, both of whom emphasized the importance of the letters of 19 March and the obvious chronological sequence in the

---

[4] *M.C.C.E.* p. 44.   [5] Powicke (1929), 87–8.   [6] Richardson (1945), 185.
[7] Richardson & Sayles (1963), p. 361 n.   [8] Powicke (1929), 93.

narrative given in the letters of 5 September.[9] The best account of the *triplex forma pacis* is now that given by Cheney in 1956.[10]

The evidence leaves certain issues obscure or unsettled.

(1) There is conflicting evidence on the date of arrival in England of the papal letters of 19 March. The pope's letters of 18 June and 24 August state that the barons took up arms and renounced their fealty without waiting for the papal terms. This information must have been derived ultimately from England.[11] The letters of 5 September, in contrast, state that the barons had renounced their fealty in defiance of the *triplex forma pacis*[12] and the Barnwell annals also record that the letters arrived before the final breach.[13] John's letter of 29 May shows that the arrival of the letters antedated his own suggested concessions.[14] Whether it antedated the baronial demands made after Low Sunday (26 April) cannot now be established.

(2) None of the rival theories incorporate a satisfactory explanation of the following passage from a letter of Gervase, abbot of Prémontré, to the legate, Cardinal Guala, written 1215–16: 'Triplex forma pacis quae (ut dicitur) a sede apostolica emanavit, quarum quaelibet (si fuisset ad effectum perducta) in totius ecclesiae et vestram nihilominus ignominiam redundasset.'[15]

This opinion conflicts directly with the views of the *forma* expressed by Pandulf and the other papal agents in the letters of 5 September. It is scarcely possible that there were two different settlements which merited this title, and at present this discrepancy can only be explained as a difference of opinion or in sources of information.

(3) The exact nature of the *triplex forma pacis* is far from clear. Painter seems to have equated it with the three letters

[9] Painter (1949), pp. 345–6; Cheney (1950–1), 35–6.   [10] Cheney (1956), 315–17.
[11] M.C.C.E. p. 43; *Selected Letters of Innocent III*, p. 214.   [12] See above, p. 413.
[13] *Walt. Cov.* II, 219.   [14] See above, p. 233.
[15] B.J.R.L. XXXIII, p. 35 n.

of 19 March directed to the king, the archbishop and the barons,[16] and indeed these are the only documents which meet the term *triplex* satisfactorily. Cheney in contrast concluded tentatively that the *forma* was additional to the three 'hortatory' letters,[17] and for this it must be said that the two surviving letters of the 19th addressed to the archbishop and the barons do not seem to amount to a formal statement of terms of agreement. Without the third letter which was sent to the king it is impossible to resolve this difficulty. However, the surviving evidence suggests that the *forma* simply consisted of the three letters. This at least is implied in the letters of 18 June in the phrase 'formam superius descriptam', where the contents of three letters were apparently all that was 'described above'.[18] These letters would also suggest that the *forma* was not a set of peace terms designed to resolve the issues between the king and his opponents, but simply a papal ruling on the spirit and the methods by which they were to be resolved; this is what the letters provide. It may be doubted whether Innocent would go much further than this on a secular matter with which he was not directly familiar and in the detail of which he was not immediately concerned. Hence he made the provision, recalled in the letters of 18 June and presumably included in the lost letters of 19 March to the king, that if the parties could not agree the matter was to be settled by judgement of peers according to the law of the land in the king's court.[19] It is also noteworthy that the king's letter of 29 May assumes that he could make a variety of concessions in execution of the *forma*; there is little indication here that he was executing any precisely delineated papal terms except those later summarized in the letters of 18 June. The proposal for papal arbitration seems to have been his own work. There is no

---

[16] Painter (1949), p. 346.　　[17] *B.J.R.L.* xxxviii, 316.　　[18] *M.C.C.E.* p. 44.
[19] *Ibid.* p. 43.

reference to this in the letter of 18 June and it is unlikely to have been excluded from a place alongside, or in preference to, the reference to judgement by peers, if in fact it had originated at the Curia.

THE 'UNKNOWN' CHARTER

The 'unknown' charter survives in the Archives Nationales in Paris where it is classified as J. 655 in the Archives du Royaume. It was printed by Teulet in his edition of the *Layettes* in 1863,[1] but was not known to English historians until it was discovered by J. H. Round in 1893:[2] hence its name. It has formed part of the French royal archives since the thirteenth century along with two copies of the Magna Carta of 1216.[3]

The document consists of a copy of the charter of liberties of Henry I to which certain concessions by John have been added. The provenance of the document and the form 'Edouardus' suggest that it was the work of a Frenchman. When he produced it is uncertain, but, whatever the date, it is clear that he was copying for he made errors of repetition in transcribing which he subsequently corrected. Whether he was copying from a document which already associated Henry I's charter with additional concessions by John, or whether the copyist himself associated the two for the first time in this document cannot be determined. His errors were not limited to repetition. His text of Henry I's charter contains several omissions and variants. This must be kept in mind in evaluating the second part of the document.

---

[1] *Layettes du Trésor des Chartes*, ed. A. Teulet (Paris, 1863), 1, 34, 423, where the texts of Henry I's and John's concessions are separated.
[2] Round (1893), 288–94. [3] Hall (1894), 326–7.

AUTHENTICITY

The main objection to accepting this document as an authentic grant or even as a memorandum of an authentic grant lies in the archaism of the language used in listing John's concessions. The use of the third person and even more the first person singular were totally foreign to John's Chancery; nor do the words *baiulare, decenter, pecudes* occur frequently in formal documents of the Crown in the sense used here.

On the other hand the text of the Charter of Henry I is independent of but similar to those of the twelfth-century law-book *Quadripartitus* and the Red Book of the Exchequer.[4] This suggests that the originator of the document drew ultimately on a Treasury version of Henry's grant. Moreover the concessions attributed to John cover common ground with the Articles and Magna Carta. Seven of its twelve clauses also appear in the other two documents, and to some extent in the same order.[5] Where the 'unknown' charter diverges from the other two, its peculiarities are relevant to the situation at the end of John's reign, most obviously in its provisions on overseas service and on the extent and administration of the royal forests. Despite its obvious anomalies, therefore, there are insufficient grounds for rejecting it as an irrelevant forgery, concocted for example during Prince Louis's invasion of England in 1216–17, as was suggested by Hubert Hall.[6] The document is genuine enough in the sense that it is not a deliberate falsification. But it is far from clear how far removed it is from the actions it recorded and equally uncertain whether those actions comprised royal concessions announced or

4 See Riess (1926), 321–31. The relationship of the 'unknown charter' version to the Red Book version was noticed by both Round and Hubert Hall (*E.H.R.* VIII, 1893, 288; IX, 1894, 329). For a classification of the various texts of Henry I's charter, see Liebermann (1894), 21–48.
5 Caps. 1, 2, 3, 4, 5, 6, 11. Caps. 2, 3, and the first sentence of cap 4, and cap. 6 of the 'unknown' charter become caps, 1, 2, 3, and 4 of the Articles.
6 Hall (1894), 330–5.

promised, or points discussed between the two parties, or simply petitions submitted by the barons. On the whole it seems best to assume that it is based on memoranda thrown off at some stage in the discussions which preceded Magna Carta rather than on any formal promise or agreement. This is of some importance in settling the equally difficult matter of the date of the document.

DATING

A large number of possibilities have been suggested.

(1) Round, followed by Powicke and Painter, argued that the charter recorded the terms agreed between the king and the northerners in November 1213.[7] This is the best recorded occasion of an agreement between the two parties prior to Runnymede, and if the 'unknown' charter is accepted as reflecting some kind of formal grant this is the most likely date on the present evidence.

Against this, however, must be set the informality of the language of the document and the association of John's concessions with the Charter of Henry I, which was not certainly in the forefront of the baronial demands until the winter of 1214–15.[8] Furthermore, when the barons made their appeal to Rome after the meeting with the king at London in January, they apparently turned to John's oath of July 1213 as a precedent for reform and not to any intervening concession.[9]

Together these difficulties make this hypothesis unlikely. They also tell against the much more fanciful reconstruction of Ludwig Riess, who argued that the charter was a composite document recording concessions begun in August 1213 and continued while the king was in Poitou in 1214.[10]

---

[7] Round (1893), 292–3; Powicke (1928), pp. 117 ff.; Painter (1949), pp. 314 ff.
[8] See above, pp. 222–6.
[9] *Diplomatic Documents*, p. 29; *Coggeshall*, p. 170; *Chron. Maj.* II, 584.
[10] *Historische Vierteljahrschrift* (1910), pp. 449–58, favourably discussed by McKechnie (1914), pp. 174–5.

(2) Hubert Hall argued that the charter was a forgery, based in part on the Great Charter of 1217 and the Charter of the Forest of 1217, drawn up during Prince Louis's invasion of England in this year and designed to exaggerate the engagements of John's coronation oath in an attempt to portray him as a tyrant ripe for deposition.[11]

There is no real basis for this case; its only apparent support comes from the close similarity between the 'unknown' charter, the Charter of the Forest and the Magna Carta of 1217. This does not necessarily mean it was derived from them. Moreover, as H. W. C. Davis pointed out, these documents were drawn up after the Treaty of Lambeth, which itself deprived Prince Louis and his supporters of any motive for forgery.[12]

(3) The great majority of scholars who have discussed the document have concluded that it records discussions or exchanges which took place some time between January and June 1215.[13] This circumvents the objections to the first hypothesis above and is altogether the most likely reconstruction.

There have been many individual variations on this theme. Prothero argued that the charter represented a royal proposal made and rejected in the January meeting at London.[14] This is scarcely likely. McKechnie suggested, in the first edition of Magna Carta, that it was based on the schedule of demands which the barons sent to the king from Brackley in April 1215;[15] Petit-Dutaillis thought that it was a report by a French spy of negotiations just prior to the Articles;[16] H. W. C. Davis contended that it represented discussions intervening between the Articles and Magna Carta.[17] Davis's paper is the most illuminating of all in its

[11] Hall (1894), 330–5.   [12] Davis (1905), 719–20.
[13] Galbraith (1948), pp. 133–4; Poole (1951), pp. 471–2.
[14] Prothero (1894), 117–21.
[15] First ed. (1905), pp. 202–5. McKechnie then fell to the fascination of Riess's argument (see the 2nd ed., 1914, pp. 174–5).
[16] Petit-Dutaillis (1908), I, 120–2.   [17] Davis (1905), 719–26.

comparison of the 'unknown' charter with the Articles and the Great Charter, and in its appreciation of the point that the 'unknown' charter provides evidence of demands which were not satisfied in either of the other documents.

There is little reason for preferring any one of these variants against any other. Most authorities have perhaps relied too heavily on the method of fitting the demands of the 'unknown' charter into a logical progression which is then used to establish a chronology; this was followed to different conclusions by Hall, McKechnie and Davis. Yet it may well be that the logical and chronological sequences were different. There is some evidence that some of the provisions peculiar to the 'unknown' charter were discussed at Runnymede. Unlike the Articles or Magna Carta it contained detailed regulations on the administration of the forest law. These have a parallel in the Charter of the Forest of 1217.[18] Now Roger of Wendover made the mistake of allocating the Charter of the Forest to 1215 and attributing it to King John. This seems less surprising if we assume that these sections of the 'unknown' charter were still a matter of debate at Runnymede. Moreover the author of the *Histoire des ducs de Normandie et des rois d'Angleterre* states that John promised in 1215 that a man should not lose life or limb for any wild beast that he took.[19] This promise is identical with cap. 12 of the 'unknown' charter and with cap. 10 of the Charter of the Forest.

However, if this means that some of the points in the 'unknown' charter were still live issues at Runnymede it does not follow that they were first propounded there. There are only two indications of a more precise dating within the period January to June 1215 and they are slight and uncertain. First, the similarity between the 'unknown' charter and the Articles would suggest that no great interval of time separated the two, although it does nothing to

---

[18] Compare caps. 10 and 12 with Charter of the Forest, caps. 4, 9 and 10.
[19] Ed. F. Michel (Paris, 1840), p. 150.

support Davis's contention that the Articles were the first of the two to be produced. Secondly, the variations in the informal language of the document are of some interest. Cap. 1 is cast in the third person singular, 'King John concedes'; the remainder of the document uses the archaic first person singular. Now cap. 1 broadly states the principles of caps. 29 and 30 of the Articles and caps. 39 and 40 of the Charter on the administration of justice, which were partly anticipated in the king's concessions of 10 May.[20] The position of this clause at the beginning of the document and the difference in formulae may mean that the concession of 10 May was already known when these notes or memoranda were made.

The detailed dating of the charter is scarcely likely to be established on the present evidence and, even if it is, it will do little to indicate how long the points had been in circulation prior to its compilation, or how long they remained live issues afterwards. Its chief importance lies in its variants; for it demonstrates that the Articles and the Charter were not seen as the only road to political salvation in 1215. From this point of view, caps. 7, 8 and 9 are of especial importance.[21]

TEXT

This version of the Charter of Henry I is a rather careless transcript of the text which also figures in the twelfth-century law-book *Quadripartitus* and the Red Book of the Exchequer and is one version of the Charter which we can be certain was in circulation in 1215. The version which Roger Wendover gives is probably based on the original sent to Hertfordshire in 1100.[22] A version was copied into the

---

[20] See appendix 11, below, pp. 492–3, for the text and p. 234, above.
[21] For a further discussion, see above, pp. 239–40, 351.
[22] Liebermann (1894), 21–48.

archiepiscopal register Lambeth MS 1212, *c.* 1250;[23] this was similar to the version in the London MS of the *Leges*; both included the Westminster additions confirming the abbey's privileges. This text may stem from Harleian MS 458 where it is associated with the charters of liberties of Stephen and Henry II and with Anglo-Norman translations of all three. In all likelihood this last version played a part in 1215.[24]

Several authorities have suggested amendments to the text of John's concessions, but without any real justification. Hall's amendment of *gravamen* to *allevamen* in cap. 8 is the only one which affects the sense, but it does not facilitate the reading of this difficult clause.[25] There seems to be little point in attempting to 'improve' the text of so informal a document.

In the following printed version deletions and cancellations have been put in brackets thus – (homines[d]) or (mei[c]); the conventional numbering of the clauses has been followed, and the punctuation and use of capitals has been modernized. No attempt has been made to collate the text of Henry's charter, but the more serious errors and omissions are noted. The charter is illustrated on pls. 2, 3.

Henricus Dei gratia rex Anglorum omnibus baronibus et fidelibus suis salutem.

1. Sciatis me Dei misericordia et communi consilio baronum regni (mei[c]) Anglie ejusdem regni regem coronatum esse. Et, quia regnum oppressum erat iniustis exactionibus, ego, respectu Dei et amore quam [*sic*] erga vos omnes habeo, sanctam Dei ecclesiam in primis liberam facio ita quod nec vendam nec ad firmam ponam nec mortuo archiepiscopo vel episcopo vel abbate aliquid accipiam de dominico ecclesie vel de hominibus ejus donec successor ejus ingrediatur, et omnes malas consuetudines quibus regnum Anglie

---

[23] Lambeth MS 1212, fos. 187–8. There is a fourteenth-century copy of the same version at fos. 17–18.
[24] See below, pp. 474–7.
[25] Hall (1894), 328–9. For further discussion, see above, pp. 318–9.

iniuste opprimebatur inde auffero, quas malas consuetudines ex parte suppono:

2. Si quis baronum meorum, comitum, sive aliorum qui de me tenent mortuus fuerit, heres ejus non redimet terram suam sicut faciebat tempore fratris mei, set legitima et iusta relevatione relevabit eam. Similiter et (homines[d]) homines baronum meorum legitima et iusta relevatione relevabunt terras suas de dominis suis.

3. Et si quis baronum meorum vel hominum filiam suam nuptus tradere voluerit, sive sororem sive neptem sive cognatam, mecum inde loquatur. Sed neque ego pro hac licentia de suo aliquid accipiam neque defendam ei quin eam det, excepto si eam dare velit inimico meo. Et si, mortuo barone vel alio homine meo, filia heres remanserit, eam non dabo marito nisi secundum consilium baronum meorum.[26]

Et si uxor absque liberis fuerit[27] dotem et maritagium suum habebit et eam non dabo nisi secundum velle suum.

4. Si vero cum liberis uxor remanserit, dotem et mariationem [*sic*] suam habebit dum corpus suum legitime servaverit, et eam non dabo marito nisi secundum velle suum, et terre et liberorum custos erit, sive aliquis propinquior qui iustius esse debebit. Et precipio ut barones mei similiter se contineant erga filios et filias et uxores hominum suorum.

5. Monetagium commune quod capiunt per civitates et comitatus, quod non fuit tempore Edouardi regis, hoc ne amodo fiat omnino deffendo. Si quis captus fuerit, sive monetarius sive alius cum falsa moneta, justum inde fiat.

6. Omnia placita et omnia debita que fratri meo debebantur con(ce[c])dono exceptis rectis firmis meis et exceptis illis que pacta erant pro aliorum hereditatibus vel pro aliis rebus que justius aliis contingebant. Et si aliquis pro hereditate aliquid pepigerat illud condono, et omnes relevationes que [pro] rectis hereditatibus pacte erant.

7. Et si quis baronum meorum vel hominum meorum

---

[26] MS omits 'pro terra sua'.

[27] Recte: 'Et si, mortuo marito, uxor ejus remanserit, et sine liberis fuerit.'

infirmatur sicut ipse dabit vel dare disposuit pecuniam suam ita datam esse concedo; quod si ipse preventus vel armis vel infirmitate pecuniam suam non dederit nec dare disposuerit, uxor sua sive liberi aut parentes aut legitimi[28] ejus pro anima ejus dividant sicut melius eis visum fuerit.

8. Si quis baronum vel hominum meorum forisfecerit non dabit vadium in misericordia tocius pecunie sue sicut faciebat tempore patris mei et fratris mei, set secundum modum forisfacti ita emendabit sicut emendasset retro a tempore patris mei et fratris mei in tempore aliorum antecessorum meorum; quod si perfidie vel celeris [sic] convictus fuerit, sicut justum erit sic emendet.

9. Murdra etiam retro que [sic] ab illa die qua in regem coronatus fui, omnino condono, et ea que amodo facta fuerint juste emendentur secundum lagam regis Edouardi.

10. Forestas communi concessu baronum meorum in ꜹ manu mea sic retinui sicut pater meus eas habuit.

11. Militibus qui per loricas terras suas deserviunt terram dominicorum [sic] carrucarum suarum quietam ab omnibus geldis et ab omni opere proprio dono meo concedo ut, sicut benignitas mea propensior est in eis, ita mihi fideles sint. Et sicut a tam magno gravamine alienati [sic] sunt, ita equis et armis bene se instruant ut apti et parati sint ad servicium meum et ad deffensionem regni mei.

13.[29] Lagam regis Edouardi vobis concedo cum illis emendationibus quibus eam pater meus emendavit consilio baronum suorum.

14. Si aliquis aliquid de meo vel de rebus alicuius post obitum fratris mei Willelmi ceperit totum cito reddat absque emendatione. Et si quis aliquid inde retinuerit ille super quem inventum fuerit graviter mihi emendabit.

Testibus archiepiscopis, episcopis, baronibus, vicecomitibus et optimatibus totius regni Anglie apud Westmonasterium, quando coronatus fui.

---

[28] MS omits *homines*.
[29] Cap. 12 is omitted, as in the *Quadripartitus* and Red Book versions.

Hec est carta regis Henrici per quam barones querunt libertates, et hec consequentia concedit rex Johannes:

1. Concedit rex Johannes quod non capiet hominem absque judicio nec aliquid accipiet pro justicia nec injusticiam faciet. [Articles, cc. 29, 30; M.C., cc. 39, 40.][30]

2. Et si contingat quod meus baro vel homo meus moriatur et heres suus sit in etate, terram suam debeo ei reddere per rectum releveium absque magis capiendi [sic]. [Articles, c. 1; M.C., c.2]

3. Et si ita sit quod heres sit infra etatem, debeo quatuor militibus de legacioribus [sic] feodi terram bajulare in custodia, et illi cum meo famulo debent mihi reddere exitus terre sine vendicione nemorum et tunc [sic] sine redemptione hominum et sine destructione parci et vivarii; (et tunc^c),[31] quando ille heres erit in etate, terram ei reddam quietam. [Articles, cc. 2, 3; M.C., cc. 3,4.]

4. Si femina sit heres terre debeo eam maritare (set non inimicis meis. Si contingat quod meus baro aut homo meus^c) consilio generis sui ita quod non sit disparagiata; et si una vice eam dedero amplius eam dare non possum, set se maritabit ad libitum suum, set non inimicis meis. [Articles, cc. 3, 17; M.C., cc. 6, 8.]

5. Si contingat quod baro aut homo meus moriatur concedo ut pecunia sua dividatur sicut ipse diviserit, et si preoccupatus fuerit aut armis aut infirmitate improvisa uxor ejus aut liberi aut parentes et amici propinquiores pro ejus anima dividant. [Articles, cc. 15, 16; M.C., cc. 26, 27.]

6. Et uxor ejus non abibit de hospicio infra xl dies et donec dotem suam decenter habuerit et maritagium habebit. [Articles, c. 4; M.C., c. 7.]

7. Adhuc hominibus meis concedo ne eant in exercitu extra Angliam nisi in Normanniam et in Britanniam et hoc decenter, quia si aliquis debet mihi servicium decem militum consilio baronum meorum alleviabitur.

---

[30] From here on M.C. = Magna Carta, 1215.
[31] The scribe should clearly have cancelled the earlier, not the later *et tunc*.

8. Et si scutagium evenerit in terra una marca argenti capietur de feodo militis, et si gravamen exercitus contigerit amplius caperetur consilio baronum regni.

9. Adhuc concedo ut omnes forestas quas pater meus et frater meus et ego afforestaveramus, desafforesto. [Articles, c. 47; M.C., cc. 47, 53.]

10. Adhuc concedo ut milites qui in antiquis forestis meis habent[32] suum suum [sic] nemus, habeant nemus amodo ad herbgagia sua et ad ardendum; et habeant foresterium suum et ego tantum modo unum qui servet pecudes meas.

11. Et si aliquis hominum meorum morum [sic] moriatur qui Judeis debeat, debitum non usurabit quamdiu heres ejus sit infra etatem. [Articles, c. 34; M.C., c. 10]

12. Et concedo ne homo perdat pro pecude vitam neque membrum. [Cart. For., c. 10.]

---

[32] The word seems to have been blotted rather than deliberately expunged.

THE ARTICLES OF THE BARONS

This title seems to be derived from a combination of the head of the document 'Ista sunt capitula quae Barones petunt . . .', and the later endorsement 'Articuli magne carte libertatum sub sigillo regis Johannis'. It is not used by Spelman, who heads the document 'capitula super quibus facta est Magna Charta Regis Johannis'[1] or by Blackstone, who refers to the 'articles or heads of agreement'.[2] Richard Thompson refers to the 'Articles of Magna Carta'.[3] 'The Articles of the Barons' appears as a title in Stubbs's *Select Charters*[4] and has become customary since.

Two hypotheses have usually been advanced in explanation of the Articles; first, that they were presented by the barons on 15 June and conceded by the king forthwith,[5] and secondly that they were not drawn up until the 15th itself in the first general discussions between the two parties at Runnymede.[6] Neither hypothesis is satisfactory. The first is inconsistent with the wording of the heading and of caps. 48 and 49, where the king's consent to the baronial demands is clearly stated, and with the probability that the

---

[1] David Wilkins, *Leges Anglo-Saxonicae* (London, 1721), p. 356.
[2] (1762), II, xxiv.   [3] (1829), pp. 49 ff.   [4] 6th ed. (1888), p. 289.
[5] This argument is followed by Bémont (1892), p. xxi; by Stubbs in *Select Charters*, 6th ed. (1888), p. 290; by H. W. C. Davis in *Select Charters*, 9th ed. (1921), p. 285, and in *England under the Norman and Angevin Kings* (London, 1921), p. 376; by C. Petit-Dutaillis in *The Feudal Monarchy in France and England* (London, 1936), p. 332; by McIlwain (1939), p. 102; and by Painter (1949), p. 315.
[6] Blackstone (1762), II, xxiv, xxvii; McKechnie (1914), pp. 37 ff., where it is also suggested that the barons brought a list of demands to the Runnymede meeting; Crump (1928), 250–1; and Collins (1948), 234, where the views of Blackstone and McKechnie are followed. Kate Norgate also seems to adopt this approach, but her account is rather confused (Norgate, 1902, pp. 233–4).

document was drafted by a Chancery clerk.[7] The second encounters the obvious difficulty of time. On this matter there was some inconsistency in McKechnie's arguments, for while he maintained that the amendment of the Articles into the form of the Charter and the engrossment of the latter formed the principal business of 16, 17, and 18 June, he also considered that the Articles were produced in the course of one single day, 15 June. That the process of amendment took several days is highly probable,[8] but if this was so it is unconvincing to argue that the preliminary agreement of the Articles could have been produced on the first day of the discussions, for it was in the Articles that most of the major problems were first settled.

An obvious apparent escape from this difficulty might be found in the argument that discussions between representatives of the two parties had settled so much before 15 June that the production of the Articles was a largely formal matter. Behind the Articles, it might be argued, there were earlier drafts of a settlement which have not survived and on which the Articles themselves were based. This is a possible hypothesis, but one incapable of detailed proof.[9] Moreover if so much had been agreed before 15 June, we might wonder why the two parties drew up a document of such peculiar form as the Articles on the 15th itself, and why they did not proceed straight from these hypothetical earlier agreements to the Great Charter. The Articles, in this view, if cast in their traditional role, soon seem redundant, and in the end these arguments, far from confirming 15 June as their date, suggest an earlier one. There is no need to predicate lost

---

[7] See above, p. 246. [8] See above, pp. 250–2.
[9] It might be argued that the 'unknown' charter filled this role. This document by itself, however, would have helped little in the rapid production of the Articles on the first day of the assembly. It might equally have hindered it, for it was far more stringent in some of its provisions than the Articles (see above, pp. 239–40). The Brackley schedule may well have coincided at many points with the Articles but in the absence of a version of the former this cannot be proved. Further, the schedule, like the king's offer on 10 May, was rejected (on this, see above, pp. 232–5, 240).

documents of the period prior to the 15th, if the Articles themselves fit this rôle better than that which has usually been given to them.

These considerations led the present writer to advance the hypothesis in 1957 that the Articles were drawn up at Runnymede on 10 June and sealed in order to vouchsafe to the barons at London what their agents at Runnymede had agreed.[10] Professor C. R. Cheney concurrently and independently advanced a closely similar argument in which he suggested that the Articles were discussed and prepared before 15 June and were then drawn up in a fair copy and sealed on the 15th itself.[11] This circumvents most of the difficulties of the earlier theories on the subject but still leaves the sealing of such a peculiar document inadequately explained. The issue depends on a reconstruction of the circumstances which led to the sealing of the document; there is no direct evidence to determine it either way.

However, the similarities between Professor Cheney's views and mine are more important than the differences, which are largely on conjectural detail. We share the common ground that the Articles must have been prepared in some form before the first plenary meeting of 15 June, and for this there is some direct evidence. On 19 June the Chancery began to produce letters of restitution in execution of cap. 52 of the Charter. One of these ordered the surrender of York castle to William de Mowbray until his hereditary claim to it had been investigated.[12] Two days later the sheriff of Yorkshire was ordered to inquire into the authority and personnel of an inquest which, according to de Mowbray, had investigated his claim to the custody of the castle of York and the forest of Yorkshire along with the manor of Pocklington.[13] The sheriff was now told to repeat

---

[10] Holt (1957), 401 ff. These views are followed in Warren (1961), pp. 236 ff.
[11] Cheney (1956), 311 ff. Professor Cheney's views are followed by Davis (1963), p. 12.
[12] *Rot. Litt. Pat.* p. 143b.   [13] *Rot. Litt. Claus.* I, 215.

the inquiry. This case was a very remarkable one. First, the Mowbray claim went back to Stephen's reign and William had presumably argued that his ancestors had been disseised by Henry II.[14] Secondly, such a claim was valid under cap. 52 of the Charter only if proceedings had begun before the king took the Cross (4 March). In view of de Mowbray's strained relations with the Crown throughout the reign and his open hostility since 1214, this is most unlikely. Thus he had probably taken action on the authority of cap. 25 of the Articles which still left disseisins by Henry II open to question. Finally, de Mowbray had informed the king by 21 June that an inquest into his claim had been held. This inquest had not been authorized by the king; de Mowbray must have acted himself, perhaps through the offices of a baronial sheriff of Yorkshire; but, whatever the machinery used, the whole process must have started before 15 June. Even the eleven-day interval between 10 June and 21 June, which is the maximum the date I have suggested for the Articles would permit between the initiation of the action and de Mowbray's knowledge that it was complete, can only be considered adequate if it is assumed that he was acting in unseemly haste in exploiting the document in his family interests.

In the following the conventional numbering of the clauses has been followed. In the original (B.L. Add. MS 4838, from which this text is taken) they are unnumbered (see pls. 6, 7).

TEXT

Ista sunt Capitula que Barones petunt et dominus Rex concedit.

1. Post decessum antecessorum heredes plene etatis habebunt hereditatem suam per antiquum relevium exprimendum in carta. [U.C., c. 2; M.C., c. 2.][15]

---

[14] *The Complete Peerage*, IX, 370.   [15] U.C. = 'unknown' charter.

2. Heredes qui infra etatem sunt et fuerint in custodia, cum ad etatem pervenerint, habebunt hereditatem suam sine relevio et fine. [U.C., c. 3; M.C., c. 3.]

3. Custos terre heredis capiet rationabiles exitus, consuetudines, et servitia, sine destructione et vasto hominum et rerum suarum, et si custos terre fecerit destructionem et vastum, amittat custodiam; et custos sustentabit domos, parcos, vivaria, stagna, molendina et cetera ad terram illam pertinentia, de exitibus terre ejusdem; et ut heredes ita maritentur ne disparagentur et per consilium propinquorum de consanguinitate sua. [U.C., cc. 3, 4; M.C., cc. 4, 5, 6.]

4. Ne vidua det aliquid pro dote sua, vel maritagio, post decessum mariti sui, sed maneat in domo sua per xl dies post mortem ipsius, et infra terminum illum assignetur ei dos; et maritagium statim habeat et hereditatem suam. [U.C., c. 6; M.C., c. 7.]

5. Rex vel ballivus non saisiet terram aliquam pro debito dum catalla debitoris sufficiunt, nec plegii debitoris distringantur, dum capitalis debitor sufficit ad solutionem. Si vero capitalis debitor defecerit in solutione, si plegii voluerint, habeant terras debitoris donec debitum illud persolvatur plene, nisi capitalis debitor monstrare poterit se esse inde quietum erga plegios. [M.C., c. 9.]

6. Rex non concedet alicui baroni quod capiat auxilium de liberis hominibus suis, nisi ad corpus suum redimendum, et ad faciendum primogenitum filium suum militem, et ad primogenitam filiam suam semel maritandam, et hoc faciet per rationabile auxilium. [M.C., c. 15.]

7. Ne aliquis majus servitium faciat de feodo militis quam inde debetur. [M.C., c. 16.]

8. Ut communia placita non sequantur curiam domini regis, sed assignentur in aliquo certo loco; et ut recognitiones capiantur in eisdem comitatibus in hunc modum: ut rex mittat duos justiciarios per quatuor vices in anno, qui cum quatuor militibus ejusdem comitatus electis per comitatum,

433

capiant assisas de nova dissaisina, morte antecessoris, et ultima presentatione, nec aliquis ob hoc sit summonitus nisi juratores et due partes. [M.C., cc. 17, 18.]

9. Ut liber homo amercietur pro parvo delicto secundum modum delicti, et pro magno delicto secundum magnitudinem delicti, salvo continemento suo; villanus etiam eodem modo amercietur, salvo waynagio suo, et mercator eodem modo, salva marcandisa, per sacramentum proborum hominum de visneto. [M.C., c. 20.]

10. Ut clericus amercietur de laico feodo suo secundum modum aliorum predictorum, et non secundum beneficium ecclesiasticum. [M.C., c. 22.]

11. Ne aliqua villa amercietur pro pontibus faciendis ad riparias, nisi ubi de jure antiquitus esse solebant. [M.C., c. 23.]

12. Ut mensura vini, bladi, et latitudines pannorum et rerum aliarum, emendetur; et ita de ponderibus. [M.C., c. 35.]

13. Ut assise de nova dissaisina et de morte antecessoris abbrevientur; et similiter de aliis assisis. [M.C., c. 19.]

14. Ut nullus vicecomes intromittat se de placitis ad coronam pertinentibus sine coronatoribus; et ut comitatus et hundredi sint ad antiquas firmas absque nullo incremento, exceptis dominicis maneriis regis. [M.C., cc. 24, 25.]

15. Si aliquis tenens de rege moriatur, licebit vicecomiti vel alii ballivo regis seisire et imbreviare catallum ipsius per visum legalium hominum, ita tamen quod nichil inde amoveatur donec plenius sciatur si debeat aliquod liquidum debitum domino regi, et tunc debitum regis persolvatur; residuum vero relinquatur executoribus ad faciendum testamentum defuncti; et si nichil regi debetur, omnia catalla cedant defuncto. [U.C., c. 5; M.C., c. 26.]

16. Si aliquis liber homo intestatus decesserit, bona sua per manum proximorum parentum suorum et amicorum et per visum ecclesie distribuantur. [U.C., c. 5; M.C., c. 27.]

17. Ne vidue distringantur ad se maritandum dum voluerint

sine marito vivere; ita tamen quod securitatem facient quod non maritabunt se sine assensu regis, si de rege teneant, vel dominorum suorum de quibus tenent. [U.C., c. 4; M.C., c. 8.]

18. Ne constabularius vel alius ballivus capiat blada vel alia catalla, nisi statim denarios inde reddat, nisi respectum habere possit de voluntate venditoris. [M.C., c. 28.]

19. Ne constabularius possit distringere aliquem militem ad dandum denarios pro custodia castri, si voluerit facere custodiam illam in propria persona vel per alium probum hominem, si ipse eam facere non possit per rationabilem causam; et si rex eum duxerit in exercitum, sit quietus de custodia secundum quantitatem temporis. [M.C., c. 29.]

20. Ne vicecomes, vel ballivus regis, vel aliquis alius, capiat equos vel carettas alicujus liberi hominis pro cariagio faciendo, nisi ex voluntate ipsius. [M.C., c. 30.]

21. Ne rex vel ballivus suus capiat alienum boscum ad castra vel ad alia agenda sua, nisi per voluntatem ipsius cujus boscus ille fuerit. [M.C., c. 31.]

22. Ne rex teneat terram eorum qui fuerint convicti de felonia nisi per unum annum et unum diem, sed tunc reddatur domino feodi. [M.C., c. 32.]

23. Ut omnes kidelli de cetero penitus deponantur de Tamisia et Medeweye et per totam Angliam. [M.C., c. 33.]

24. Ne breve quod vocatur 'Precipe' de cetero fiat alicui de aliquo tenemento unde liber homo amittat curiam suam. [M.C., c. 34.]

25. Si quis fuerit disseisitus vel prolongatus per regem sine juditio de terris, libertatibus, et jure suo, statim ei restituatur; et si contentio super hoc orta fuerit, tunc inde disponatur per judicium xxv baronum; et ut illi qui fuerint dissaisiti per patrem vel fratrem regis, rectum habeant sine dilatione per judicium parium suorum in curia regis, et si rex debeat habere terminum aliorum cruce signatorum, tunc archiepiscopus et episcopi faciant inde judicium ad certum diem, appellatione remota. [M.C., cc. 52, 53.]

26. Ne aliquid detur pro brevi inquisitionis de vita vel membris, sed libere concedatur sine pretio et non negetur. [M.C., c. 36.]

27. Si aliquis tenet de rege per feodi firmam, per sokagium, vel per burgagium, et de alio per servitium militis, dominus rex non habebit custodiam militum de feodo alterius, occasione burgagii vel sokagii, nec debet habere custodiam burgagii, sokagii, vel feodi firme; et quod liber homo non amittat militiam suam occasione parvarum sergantisarum, sicuti de illis qui tenent aliquod tenementum reddendo inde cuttellos vel sagittas vel hujusmodi. [M.C., c. 37.]

28. Ne aliquis ballivus possit ponere aliquem ad legem simplici loquela sua sine testibus fidelibus. [M.C., c. 38.]

29. Ne corpus liberi hominis capiatur, nec imprisonetur, nec dissaisietur, nec utlagetur, nec exuletur, nec aliquo modo destruatur, nec rex eat vel mittat super eum vi, nisi per judicium parium suorum vel per legem terre. [U.C., c. 1; M.C., c. 39.]

30. Ne jus vendatur vel differratur [sic] vel vetitum sit. [U.C., c. 1; M.C., c. 40.]

31. Quod mercatores habeant salvum ire et venire ad emendum vel vendendum, sine omnibus malis toltis, per antiquas et rectas consuetudines. [M.C., c. 41.]

32. Ne scutagium vel auxilium ponatur in regno, nisi per commune consilium regni, nisi ad corpus regis redimendum, et primogenitum filium suum militem faciendum, et filiam suam primogenitam semel maritandam; et ad hoc fiat rationabile auxilium. Simili modo fiat de taillagiis et auxiliis de civitate Londoniarum, et de aliis civitatibus que inde habent libertates, et ut civitas Londoniarum plene habeat antiquas libertates et liberas consuetudines suas, tam per aquas, quam per terras. [M.C., cc. 12, 13.]

33. Ut liceat unicuique exire de regno et redire, salva fide domini regis, nisi tempore werre per aliquod breve tempus propter communem utilitatem regni. [M.C., c. 42.]

34. Si quis mutuo aliquid acceperit a Judeis plus vel minus,

et moriatur antequam debitum illud solvatur, debitum non usurabit quamdiu heres fuerit infra etatem, de quocumque teneat; et si debitum illud inciderit in manum regis, rex non capiet nisi catallum quod continetur in carta. [U.C., c. 11; M.C., c. 10.]

35. Si quis moriatur et debitum debeat Judeis, uxor ejus habeat dotem suam; et si liberi remanserint, provideantur eis necessaria secundum tenementum; et de residuo solvatur debitum salvo servitio dominorum; simili modo fiat de aliis debitis; et ut custos terre reddat heredi, cum ad plenam etatem pervenerit, terram suam instauratam secundum quod rationabiliter poterit sustinere de exitibus terre ejusdem de carucis et wainnagiis. [M.C., cc. 11, 5.]

36. Si quis tenuerit de aliqua eskaeta, sicut de honore Walingeford, Notingeham, Bononie, et Lankastrie, et de aliis eskaetis que sunt in manu regis et sunt baronie, et obierit, heres ejus non dabit aliud relevium, vel faciet regi aliud servitium quam faceret baroni; et ut rex eodem modo eam teneat quo baro eam tenuit. [M.C., c. 43.]

37. Ut fines qui facti sunt pro dotibus, maritagiis, hereditatibus, et americiamentis, injuste et contra legem terre, omnino condonentur; vel fiat inde per judicium xxv baronum, vel per judicium majoris partis eorumdem, una cum archiepiscopo et aliis quos secum vocare voluerit, ita quod, si aliquis vel aliqui de xxv fuerint in simili querela, amoveantur et alii loco illorum per residuos de xxv substituantur. [M.C., c. 55.]

38. Quod obsides et carte reddantur, que liberate fuerunt regi in securitatem. [M.C., c. 49.]

39. Ut illi qui fuerint extra forestam non veniant coram justiciariis de foresta per communes summonitiones, nisi sint in placito vel plegii fuerint; et ut prave consuetudines de forestis et de forestariis, et warenniis, et vicecomitibus, et rivariis, emendentur per xii milites de quolibet comitatu, qui debent eligi per probos homines ejusdem comitatus. [M.C., cc. 44, 48.]

40. Ut rex amoveat penitus de balliva parentes et totam sequelam Gerardi de Atyes, quod de cetero balliam non habeant, scilicet Engelardum, Andream, Petrum, et Gyonem de Cancellis, Gyonem de Cygony, Matheum de Martiny, et fratres ejus, et Galfridum nepotem ejus et Philippum Mark. [M.C., c. 50.]

41. Et ut rex amoveat alienigenas, milites, stipendiarios, balistarios, et ruttarios, et servientes qui veniunt cum equis et armis ad nocumentum regni. [M.C., c. 51.]

42. Ut rex faciat justiciarios, constabularios, vicecomites, et ballivos, de talibus qui sciant legem terre et eam bene velint observare. [M.C., c. 45.]

43. Ut barones qui fundaverunt abbatias, unde habent cartas regum vel antiquam tenuram, habeant custodiam earum cum vacaverint. [M.C., c. 46.]

44. Si rex Walenses dissaisierit vel elongaverit de terris vel libertatibus, vel de rebus aliis in Anglia vel in Wallia, eis statim sine placito reddantur; et si fuerint dissaisiti vel elongati de tenementis suis Anglie per patrem vel fratrem regis sine judicio parium suorum, rex eis sine dilatione justiciam exhibebit eo modo quo exhibet Anglicis justiciam, de tenementis suis Anglie secundum legem Anglie, et de tenementis Wallie secundum legem Wallie, et de tenementis Marchie secundum legem Marchie; idem facient Walenses regi et suis. [M.C., cc. 56, 57.]

45. Ut rex reddat filium Lewelini et preterea omnes obsides de Wallia, et cartas que ei liberate fuerunt in securitatem pacis.

46. Ut rex faciat regi Scottorum de obsidibus reddendis, et de libertatibus suis, et jure suo, secundum formam quam facit baronibus Anglie. } nisi aliter esse debeat per cartas quas rex habet per judicium archiepiscopi et aliorum quos secum vocare voluerit. [M.C., cc. 58, 59.]

47. Et omnes foreste que sunt aforestate per regem tempore suo deafforestentur, et ita fiat de ripariis que per ipsum regem sunt in defenso. [U.C., c. 9; M.C., c. 47.]

48. Omnes autem istas consuetudines et libertates quas rex concessit regno tenendas quantum ad se pertinet erga suos, omnes de regno tam clerici quam laici observabunt quantum ad se pertinet erga suos. [M.C., c. 60.]

49. Hec est forma securitatis ad observandum pacem et libertates inter regem et regnum. Barones eligent xxv barones de regno quos voluerint, qui debent pro totis viribus suis observare, tenere et facere observari, pacem et libertates quas dominus rex eis concessit et carta sua confirmavit; ita videlicet quod si rex, vel justiciarius, vel ballivi regis, vel aliquis de ministris suis, in aliquo erga aliquem deliquerit, vel aliquem articulorum pacis aut securitatis transgressus fuerit, et delictum ostensum fuerit quatuor baronibus de predictis xxv baronibus, illi quatuor barones accedent ad dominum regem, vel ad justiciarium suum, si rex fuerit extra regnum; proponentes ei excessum, petent ut excessum illum sine dilatione faciat emendari; et si rex vel justiciarius ejus illud non emendaverit, si rex fuerit extra regnum, infra rationabile tempus determinandum in carta, predicti quatuor referent causam illam ad residuos de illis xxv baronibus, et illi xxv cum communa totius terre distringent et gravabunt regem modis omnibus quibus poterunt, scilicet per captionem castrorum, terrarum, possessionum, et aliis modis quibus poterunt, donec fuerit emendatum secundum arbitrium eorum, salva persona domini regis et regine et liberorum suorum; et cum fuerit emendatum, intendant domino regi sicut prius. Et quicumque voluerit de terra jurabit se ad predicta exequenda pariturum mandatis predictorum xxv baronum, et gravaturum regem pro posse suo cum ipsis; et rex pubblice et libere dabit licentiam jurandi cuilibet qui jurare voluerit, et nulli umquam jurare prohibebit. Omnes autem illos de terra qui sponte sua et per se noluerint jurare xxv baronibus de distringendo et gravando regem cum eis, rex faciet jurare eosdem de mandato suo sicut predictum est. Item si aliquis de predictis xxv baronibus decesserit, vel a

terra recesserit, vel aliquo modo alio impeditus fuerit quominus ista predicta possint exequi, qui residui fuerint de xxv eligent alium loco ipsius pro arbitrio suo, qui simili modo erit juratus quo et ceteri. In omnibus autem que istis xxv baronibus committuntur exequenda, si forte ipsi xxv presentes fuerint et inter se super re aliqua discordaverint, vel aliqui ex eis vocati nolint vel nequeant interesse, ratum habebitur et firmum quod major pars ex eis providerit vel preceperit, ac si omnes xxv in hoc consensissent; et predicti xxv jurabunt quod omnia antedicta fideliter observabunt et pro toto posse suo facient observari. Preterea rex faciet eos securos per cartas archiepiscopi et episcoporum et magistri Pandulfi, quod nichil impetrabit a domino papa per quod aliqua istarum conventionum revocetur vel minuatur, et, si aliquid tale impetraverit, reputetur irritum et inane et numquam eo utatur. [M.C., cc. 61, 62.]

MAGNA CARTA, 1215

There are four surviving originals of the Great Charter, two at the British Library, one at Lincoln Cathedral and one at Salisbury Cathedral. These are conventionally designated Ci, Cii, L and S. Ci was badly damaged in the fire of the Cottonian library in 1731; an engraved copy of it was published by John Pine in 1733. The others are in good condition, although none now carry the king's seal. Yet another possible original, inspected and noted by Matthew Hale, was 'sent to the abbey of Tewkesbury'. As far as is known, this no longer survives.[1]

L, certainly, and S, probably, reside in the counties which obtained them in 1215; Ci possibly went to the Cinque Ports. Ci and Cii share a small number of amendments which are noted below in the text. These have been used to argue that they were drafted either (a) earlier or (b) later than L and S,[2] but they may well have been nothing more serious than copyists' omissions.[3] The debate is not of great moment. It derived essentially from the assumption that there was a single authoritative original which figured in the ceremonies at Runnymede and from which all other versions were copied. This assumption was first questioned

---

[1] Matthew Hale, *The History of the Common Law*, 4th edn (Dublin, 1797), p. 7. Hale died in 1676. He does not say where he saw it: if not at Tewkesbury, it must have been an original endorsed to Tewkesbury.

[2] L was treated as the most authentic and earliest version in the *Statutes of the Realm* (I, xxix); Richard Thompson, in contrast, gave priority to Ci, the most amended version (1829, p. 422). The discussion still continues; compare Fox (1924), 332–3, and Collins (1948), 262–3.

[3] If so, they must have been copied side by side or based on a common source which contained the shared errors.

among later authorities by Professor V. H. Galbraith,[4] and has now been rejected.[5] There is no sound reason for giving any one of the surviving texts priority over the others, nor is there any need to do so. With the possible exception of S, they are all exemplifications of equal weight and value.

S presents its own special problems.[6] The other three are plainly in a Chancery hand; S not so – not, at least, until the scribe of S is discovered at work in other Chancery documents. His hand is too 'bookish'. Yet this may not render S any the less authentic. In the circumstances at Runnymede and Windsor the Chancery could have impressed extra scribes to help with the lengthy exemplifications which the settlement required (although, if so, none of their work is apparent otherwise): more probably S could have been the work of one of the recipients, a messenger or agent of one of the counties, presented for authorization by the great seal – an acceptable though by now unusual procedure. It no longer bears either seal or attachment, but the remains of the tear at the foot of the document are consistent with one of the official methods of attaching the silken cord for the great seal. That it was a less usual method, which would be an unlikely model for imitators, confirms that S once carried the great seal. The fact that it may have been the work of a recipient does not destroy its standing as an authentic text. It is not spurious, still less a forgery.

The four versions were described by Sir John Fox in 1924,[7] by A. J. Collins in 1948[8] and by G. R. C. Davis in 1963.[9] Sir John Fox's manuscript collation of them is now British Library, Additional MS 41178; the variants are all of detail.

4 Galbraith (1948), pp. 123–4.
5 At least by Cheney (1956), 311–41, and by the present writer. This work has been followed by Warren (1961) and by Davis (1963).
6 For the following paragraph see Stroud (1981) and Holt (1982).
7 Fox (1924), 321–36.   8 Collins (1948), 233–79.   9 Davis (1963).

Magna Carta was not enrolled on the Charter roll, and there is no direct evidence that a copy was retained in the Treasury. One of the versions of the Treaty of Lambeth of 1217 lays down that Prince Louis was to restore the rolls of the Exchequer, the charters of Jews, and the charters of liberties made in the time of King John at Runnymede and all other writings of the Exchequer in his possession.[10] This implies not only that Louis possessed versions of the 1215 Charter but also that they formed part of the government archives. However, the only version which is known to have been in the government's possession is the Letters Testimonial, which were in the Treasury of Receipt in or about 1323 when they were copied into the Red Book of the Exchequer.[11] There is no evidence, however, that these were kept by the Chancery as an authenticated copy and counterpart to the Charter in 1215, as A. J. Collins has argued.[12] The Letters Testimonial were clearly made out for the barons, not for the king,[13] and it may be that they remained in baronial hands after Runnymede and were surrendered under the terms of the Treaty of Lambeth. It is not certain therefore that they were used by the Crown from the start as an authenticated original, although it is possible that the king had a second copy made for himself. This is not inherently unlikely; the execution of the provisions for investigations into the royal forests clearly became a matter of dispute on which the king called in the bishops as referees in support of his complaint;[14] he may equally well have acquired a copy of the Letters as an insurance against falsification.

I have attempted elsewhere to explain some of the differences in the order of clauses between the Articles of the

[10] E. Martène & U. Durand, *Thesaurus Novus Anecdotorum* (1717), I, coll. 857–9.
[11] Collins (1948), 248–51.
[12] *Ibid.* pp. 245, 258. For a discussion of the function of the Letters Testimonial, see above, p. 289.
[13] 'Et insuper fecimus *eis* fieri litteras testimoniales' (Magna Carta, cap. 62).
[14] See above, p. 352.

Barons and the Charter.[15] By and large a better, more logical order was achieved in the Charter than in the preparatory document. The unusual position of the witnesses at the beginning of the Charter, where they appear as advisers, is discussed above.[16] The list itself includes a problem to which Cheney drew attention.[17] It includes the name of William, earl of Salisbury. Now the *Histoire des ducs de Normandie* clearly states that the king made peace at Staines without consulting Earl William, who was then conducting a campaign against the rebels around Exeter, from which he can scarcely have had time to reach Runnymede by 19 June.[18] It may be that the king put the terms of settlement to the earl at Winchester, where they probably met between 5 and 8 June. The function of a witness was to attest the genuineness of the grant; he need not have been present when the Charter was made.[19] But such an explanation does not account for the story in the *Histoire*. Nor does the suggestion that William witnessed the terms of the Charter later than the 19th explain why he should be included among those who witnessed the authorization of the document on the 15th.[20] It may simply be, as I have hinted above,[21] that the name of the king's half-brother who, though absent, had played and was still playing a considerable role in the crisis, was included in order to boost the settlement and as an indication that he too would come into line. Given his quarrel over Trowbridge,[22] which was settled immediately in favour of his rival Henry de Bohun,

---

[15] Holt (1972), pp. 494–5.   [16] See above, pp. 256–7.   [17] Cheney (1956), 328–9.
[18] Ed. F. Michel (Paris, 1840), pp. 147–9. The evidence of the *Histoire* is somewhat strengthened by letters of 6 June ordering the despatch of troops to him at Salisbury (above, p. 243, n. 31).
[19] Flower (1944), p. 281.
[20] *Histoire des ducs de Normandie*, pp. 150–1. The *Histoire* may be confused at this point; it is also possible that William denied his complicity in the surrender at Runnymede in order to avoid losing face with his Flemish mercenaries who regarded it as a shameful surrender; the author's account of the 'vilaine pais' is linked to the disgust of the Flemish mercenaries at their ensuing dismissal.
[21] See above, p. 257, n. 83.   [22] See above, pp. 206–7, 360, 495.

William's agreement would be an essential component of the settlement.

Draft versions of the Charter constitute the most intriguing problem of all. At St Albans Roger of Wendover had access to a unique version of the security clause, different from and more radical than the version in the Articles or the Charter. This was probably rejected before the Articles were drafted, although the possibility that it was still in being as an alternative programme cannot be excluded.[23] So it is difficult to fit it into the events at Runnymede. This is easier in the case of a 'draft' discovered by Galbraith in the MSS of the Huntington Library (MS HM 25782) on which he commented in 1967.[24] Among the variant readings in this version (H) Galbraith pinpointed six which he suggested were drafting matters rather than the scribal errors and idiosyncrasies common enough in any document of such length. These are:

a. cap. 2: H has 100 m., not £100 for the baronial relief.
b. cap. 55: H reads 'Omnes fines qui facti sunt nobiscum pro dotibus, maritagiis, hereditatibus et amerciamentis et aliis injuste et contra legem...' The specification is omitted in M.C., but is almost identical to Articles cap. 37.
c. cap. 61: H reads 'dabimus licenciam' for M.C. 'damus licenciam'.
d. cap. 61: H reads 'Et nos nihil impetrabimus per nos nec per alium a domino papa...'. This comes close to Articles cap. 49 − 'Preterea rex faciet eos securos per cartas archiepiscopi et episcoporum et magistri Pandulfi quod nichil impetrabit a domino papa...'. M.C. reads − 'Et nos nichil impetrabimus ab aliquo...', thereby omitting all reference to the pope.
e. cap. 62: H reads 'faciemus eis habere litteras testimoniales' for M.C. 'fecimus eis fieri litteras testimoniales'.

---

[23] See above p. 345.   [24] Galbraith (1967).

f. cap. 63: H is dated 'Data per manum nostram apud Windesor' quinto decimo die Junii anno regni nostri septimodecimo'.

As Galbraith concluded, this is in all probability a copy of a draft intervening between the Articles and Magna Carta. In two clauses (c, e) it speaks in the future of matters which M.C. records in the present. In cap. 2 it makes sense of the wording concerning reliefs. In two clauses (55, 61) it approximates to the Articles rather than the Charter, and in one of these cases the difference is crucial, for it still includes the denial of appeal to the pope who was replaced in M.C. by the anodyne 'anyone'. Finally, it is dated at Windsor, where the hard work of drafting was most probably done rather than in the meadow of Staines. This could well have been a draft presented to the company at Runnymede; if so, after discussion and amendment, it could have become the warrant for the final version, and its date could well explain why 15 June is the date of all the exemplifications.

That would be a neat solution; and it may indeed be right. If there is a difficulty it is in the date and the warranty. There is yet another version (R) in the well known legal collection Bodleian, Rawlinson MS 641. This also has the 100 m. relief in cap. 2 but none of the other variants of H. R, however, is dated as M.C. except for the day, which in this version is 'sextodecimo die iunii'. It is possible that there was more than one 'draft'.

TEXT

The following is the text of Cii (Bémont 1892, pp. 26–39, collated with the original). The originals are written continuously. See pl. 8. Here the conventional numbering of the clauses has been followed.

Johannes dei gracia rex Anglie, dominus Hibernie, dux Normannie, Aquitannie et comes Andegavie, archiepiscopis, episcopis, abbatibus, comitibus, baronibus, justiciariis, forestariis, vicecomitibus, prepositis, ministris et omnibus ballivis et fidelibus suis salutem. Sciatis nos intuitu Dei et pro salute anime nostre et omnium antecessorum et heredum nostrorum ad honorem Dei et exaltacionem sancte Ecclesie, et emendacionem regni nostri, per consilium venerabilium patrum nostrorum, Stephani Cantuariensis archiepiscopi, tocius Anglie primatis et sancte Romane ecclesie cardinalis, Henrici Dublinensis archiepiscopi, Willelmi Londoniensis, Petri Wintoniensis, Joscelini Bathoniensis et Glastoniensis, Hugonis Lincolniensis, Walteri Wygorniensis, Willelmi Coventrensis, et Benedicti Roffensis, episcoporum; magistri Pandulfi domini pape subdiaconi et familiaris, fratris Aymerici magistri milicie Templi in Anglia; et nobilium virorum Willelmi Mariscalli comitis Penbrocie, Willelmi comitis Sarrisberie, Willelmi comitis Warennie, Willelmi comitis Arundellie, Alani de Galeweya constabularii Scocie, Warini filii Geroldi, Petri filii Hereberti, Huberti de Burgo senescalli Pictavie, Hugonis de Nevilla, Mathei filii Hereberti, Thome Basset, Alani Basset, Philippi de Albiniaco, Roberti de Roppel', Johannis Mariscalli, Johannis filii Hugonis et aliorum fidelium nostrorum:

1. In primis concessisse Deo et hac presenti carta nostra confirmasse, pro nobis et heredibus nostris in perpetuum, quod Anglicana ecclesie libera sit, et habeat jura sua integra, et libertates suas illesas; et ita volumus observari; quod apparet ex eo quod libertatem electionum, que maxima et magis necessaria reputatur ecclesie Anglicane, mera et spontanea voluntate, ante discordiam inter nos et barones nostros motam, concessimus et carta nostra confirmavimus, et eam

John, by the grace of God, King of England, Lord of Ireland, Duke of Normandy and Aquitaine, Count of Anjou, to the archbishops, bishops, abbots, earls, barons, justiciars, foresters, sheriffs, stewards, servants and all his officials and faithful subjects greeting. Know that we, from reverence for God and for the salvation of our soul and those of all our ancestors and heirs, for the honour of God and the exaltation of Holy Church and the reform of our realm, on the advice of our reverend fathers, Stephen, Archbishop of Canterbury, Primate of all England and Cardinal of the Holy Roman Church, Henry, Archbishop of Dublin, William of London, Peter of Winchester, Jocelin of Bath and Glastonbury, Hugh of Lincoln, Walter of Worcester, William of Coventry and Benedict of Rochester, bishops, Master Pandulf, subdeacon and member of the household of the lord pope, brother Aimeric, master of the knighthood of the Temple in England, and the noble men, William Marshal, Earl of Pembroke, William, Earl of Salisbury, William, Earl of Warenne, William, Earl of Arundel, Alan of Galloway, Constable of Scotland, Warin fitz Gerold, Peter fitz Herbert, Hubert de Burgh, seneschal of Poitou, Hugh de Neville, Matthew fitz Herbert, Thomas Basset, Alan Basset, Philip d'Aubigné, Robert of Ropsley, John Marshal, John fitz Hugh and others, our faithful subjects:

1. In the first place have granted to God and by this our present Charter have confirmed, for us and our heirs in perpetuity, that the English church shall be free, and shall have its rights undiminished and its liberties unimpaired: and we wish it thus observed, which is evident from the fact that of our own free will before the quarrel between us and our barons began, we conceded and confirmed by our charter freedom of elections, which is thought to be of the greatest necessity and importance to the English church, and obtained confirmation of this from the lord pope Innocent

obtinuimus a domino papa Innocentio tercio confirmari; quam et nos observabimus et ab heredibus nostris in perpetuum bona fide volumus observari. Concessimus eciam omnibus liberis hominibus regni nostri, pro nobis et heredibus nostris in perpetuum, omnes libertates subscriptas, habendas et tenendas eis et heredibus suis, de nobis et heredibus nostris.

2. Si quis comitum vel baronum nostrorum, sive aliorum tenencium de nobis in capite per servicium militare, mortuus fuerit, et cum decesserit heres suus plene etatis fuerit et relevium debeat, habeat hereditatem suam per antiquum relevium; scilicet heres vel heredes comitis de baronia comitis integra per centum libras; heres vel heredes baronis de baronia integra per centum libras; heres vel heredes militis de feodo militis integro per centum solidos ad plus; et qui minus debuerit minus det secundum antiquam consuetudinem feodorum. [Articles, c. 1; 1225, c. 2.]

3. Si autem heres alicujus talium fuerit infra etatem et fuerit in custodia, cum ad etatem pervenerit, habeat hereditatem suam sine relevio et sine fine. [Articles, c. 2; 1225, c. 3.]

4. Custos terre hujusmodi heredis qui infra etatem fuerit, non capiat de terra heredis nisi racionabiles exitus, et racionabiles consuetudines, et racionabilia servicia, et hoc sine destructione et vasto hominum vel rerum; et si nos commiserimus custodiam alicujus talis terre vicecomiti vel alicui alii qui de exitibus illius nobis respondere debeat, et ille destructionem de custodia fecerit vel vastum, nos ab illo capiemus emendam, et terra committatur duobus legalibus et discretis hominibus de feodo illo, qui de exitibus respondeant nobis vel ei cui eos assignaverimus; et si dederimus vel vendiderimus alicui custodiam alicujus talis terre, et ille destructionem inde fecerit vel vastum, amittat ipsam custodiam, et tradatur duobus legalibus et discretis hominibus de feodo illo qui similiter nobis respondeant sicut predictum est. [Articles, c. 3; 1225, c. 4.]

5. Custos autem, quamdiu custodiam terre habuerit, sustentet domos, parcos, vivaria, stagna, molendina, et cetera ad terram illam pertinencia, de exitibus terre ejusdem; et

III, which we shall observe and wish our heirs to observe in good faith in perpetuity. We have also granted to all the free men of our realm for ourselves and our heirs for ever, all the liberties written below, to have and hold, them and their heirs from us and our heirs.

2. If any of our earls or barons, or others holding of us in chief by knight service shall die, and at his death his heir be of full age and owe relief, he shall have his inheritance on payment of the ancient relief, namely the heir or heirs of an earl £100 for a whole earl's barony, the heir or heirs of a baron £100 for a whole barony, the heir or heirs of a knight 100s. at most for a whole knight's fee; and anyone who owes less shall give less according to the ancient usage of fiefs.

3. If, however, the heir of any such person has been under age and in wardship, when he comes of age he shall have his inheritance without relief or fine.

4. The guardian of the land of such an heir who is under age shall not take from the land more than the reasonable revenues, customary dues and services, and that without destruction and waste of men or goods. And if we entrust the wardship of the land of such a one to a sheriff, or to any other who is answerable to us for its revenues, and he destroys or wastes the land in his charge, we will take amends of him, and the land shall be entrusted to two lawful and prudent men of that fief who will be answerable to us for the revenues or to him to whom we have assigned them. And if we give or sell to anyone the wardship of any such land and he causes destruction or waste, he shall lose the wardship and it shall be transferred to two lawful and prudent men of the fief who shall be answerable to us as is aforesaid.

5. Moreover so long as the guardian has the wardship of the land, he shall maintain the houses, parks, preserves, fishponds, mills and the other things pertaining to the land from its revenues; and he shall restore to the heir when he

reddat heredi cum ad plenam etatem pervenerit, terram suam totam instauratam de carucis et waynagiis, secundum quod tempus waynagii exiget et exitus terre racionabiliter poterunt sustinere. [Articles, cc. 3, 35; 1225, c. 5]

6. Heredes maritentur absque disparagacione, ita tamen quod, antequam contrahatur matrimonium, ostendatur propinquis de consanguinitate ipsius heredis. [Articles, c. 3; 1225, c. 6.]

7. Vidua post mortem mariti sui statim et sine difficultate habeat maritagium et hereditatem suam, nec aliquid det pro dote sua, vel pro maritagio suo, vel hereditate sua, quam hereditatem maritus suus et ipsa tenuerint die obitus ipsius mariti, et maneat in domo mariti sui per quadraginta dies post mortem ipsius, infra quos assignetur ei dos sua. [Articles, c. 4; 1225, c. 7.]

8. Nulla vidua distringatur ad se maritandum, dum voluerit vivere sine marito, ita tamen quod securitatem faciat quod se non maritabit sine assensu nostro, si de nobis tenuerit, vel sine assensu domini sui de quo tenuerit, si de alio tenuerit. [Articles, c. 17; 1225, c. 7.]

9. Nec nos nec ballivi nostri seisiemus terram aliquam nec redditum pro debito aliquo, quamdiu catalla debitoris sufficiunt ad debitum reddendum; nec plegii ipsius debitoris distringantur quamdiu ipse capitalis debitor sufficit ad solucionem debiti; et si capitalis debitor defecerit in solucione debiti, non habens unde solvat, plegii respondeant de debito; et si voluerint, habeant terras et redditus debitoris, donec sit eis satisfactum de debito quod ante pro eo solverint, nisi capitalis debitor monstraverit se esse quietum inde versus eosdem plegios. [Articles, c. 5; 1225, c. 8.]

10. Si quis mutuo ceperit aliquid a Judeis, plus vel minus, et moriatur antequam debitum illud solvatur, debitum non usuret quamdiu heres fuerit infra etatem, de quocumque teneat; et si debitum illud inciderit in manus nostras, nos non capiemus nisi catallum contentum in carta. [Articles, c. 34.]

11. Et si quis moriatur, et debitum debeat Judeis, uxor ejus habeat dotem suam, et nichil reddat de debito illo, et si liberi ipsius defuncti qui fuerint infra etatem remanserint, provi-

comes of age all his land stocked with ploughs and wainage such as the agricultural season demands and the revenues of the estate can reasonably bear.

6. Heirs shall be given in marriage without disparagement, yet so that before a marriage is contracted it shall be made known to the heir's next of kin.

7. After her husband's death, a widow shall have her marriage portion and her inheritance at once and without any hindrance; nor shall she pay anything for her dower, her marriage portion, or her inheritance which she and her husband held on the day of her husband's death; and she may stay in her husband's house for forty days after his death, within which period her dower shall be assigned to her.

8. No widow shall be compelled to marry so long as she wishes to live without a husband, provided that she gives security that she will not marry without our consent if she holds of us, or without the consent of the lord of whom she holds, if she holds of another.

9. Neither we nor our bailiffs will seize any land or rent in payment of a debt so long as the chattels of the debtor are sufficient to repay the debt; nor shall the sureties of the debtor be distrained so long as the debtor himself is capable of paying the debt; and if the principal debtor defaults in the payment of the debt, having nothing wherewith to pay it, the sureties shall be answerable for the debt; and, if they wish, they may have the lands and revenues of the debtor until they have received satisfaction for the debt they paid on his behalf, unless the principal debtor shows that he has discharged his obligations to the sureties.

10. If anyone who has borrowed from the Jews any amount, great or small, dies before the debt is repaid, it shall not carry interest as long as the heir is under age, of whomsoever he holds; and if that debt fall into our hands, we will take nothing except the principal sum specified in the bond.

11. And if a man dies owing a debt to the Jews, his wife may have her dower and pay nothing of that debt; and if he

deantur eis necessaria secundum tenementum quod fuerit defuncti et de residuo solvatur debitum, salvo servicio dominorum; simili modo fiat de debitis que debentur aliis quam Judeis. [Articles, c. 35.]

12. Nullum scutagium vel auxilium ponatur in regno nostro, nisi per commune consilium regni nostri, nisi ad corpus nostrum redimendum, et primogenitum filium nostrum militem faciendum, et ad filiam nostram primogenitam semel maritandam, et ad hec non fiat nisi racionabile auxilium; simili modo fiat de auxiliis de civitate Londoniarum. [Articles, c. 32.]

13. Et civitas Londoniarum habeat omnes antiquas libertates et liberas consuetudines suas, tam per terras quam per aquas. Preterea volumus et concedimus quod omnes alie civitates, et burgi, et ville, et portus, habeant omnes libertates et liberas consuetudines suas. [Articles, c. 32; 1225, c. 9.]

14. Et ad habendum commune consilium regni de auxilio assidendo aliter quam in tribus casibus predictis, vel de scutagio assidendo, summoneri faciemus archiepiscopos, episcopos, abbates, comites, et majores barones sigillatim per litteras nostras; et preterea faciemus summoneri in generali per vicecomites et ballivos nostros omnes illos qui de nobis tenent in capite ad certum diem, scilicet ad terminum quadraginta dierum ad minus, et ad certum locum; et in omnibus litteris illius summonicionis causam summonicionis exprimemus; et sic facta summonicione negocium ad diem assignatum procedat secundum consilium illorum qui presentes fuerint, quamvis non omnes summoniti venerint.

15. Nos non concedemus de cetero alicui quod capiat auxilium de liberis hominibus suis, nisi ad corpus suum redimendum, et ad faciendum primogenitum filium suum militem, et ad primogenitam filiam suam semel maritandam, et ad hec non fiat nisi racionabile auxilium. [Articles, c. 6.]

16. Nullus distringatur ad faciendum majus servicium de feodo militis, nec de alio libero tenemento, quam inde debetur. [Articles, c. 7; 1225, c. 10.]

17. Communia placita non sequantur curiam nostram, set teneantur in aliquo loco certo. [Articles, c. 8; 1225, c. 11.]

leaves children under age, their needs shall be met in a manner in keeping with the holding of the deceased; and the debt shall be paid out of the residue, saving the service due to the lords. Debts owing to others than Jews shall be dealt with likewise.

12. No scutage or aid is to be levied in our realm except by the common counsel of our realm, unless it is for the ransom of our person, the knighting of our eldest son or the first marriage of our eldest daughter; and for these only a reasonable aid is to be levied. Aids from the city of London are to be treated likewise.

13. And the city of London is to have all its ancient liberties and free customs both by land and water. Furthermore, we will and grant that all other cities, boroughs, towns and ports shall have all their liberties and free customs.

14. And to obtain the common counsel of the realm for the assessment of an aid (except in the three cases aforesaid) or a scutage, we will have archbishops, bishops, abbots, earls and greater barons summoned individually by our letters, and we shall also have summoned generally through our sheriffs and bailiffs all those who hold of us in chief, for a fixed date, with at least forty days' notice, and at a fixed place; and in all letters of summons we will state the reason for the summons. And when the summons has thus been made, the business shall go forward on the day arranged according to the counsel of those present, even if not all those summoned have come.

15. Henceforth we will not grant anyone that he may take an aid from his free men except to ransom his person, to make his eldest son a knight and to marry his eldest daughter once; and for these purposes only a reasonable aid is to be levied.

16. No man shall be compelled to perform more service for a knight's fee or for any other free tenement than is due therefrom.

17. Common pleas shall not follow our court but shall be held in some fixed place.

18. Recogniciones de nova disseisina, de morte antecessoris, et de ultima presentacione, non capiantur nisi in suis comitatibus et hoc modo; nos, vel si extra regnum fuerimus capitalis justiciarius noster, mittemus duos justiciarios per unumquemque comitatum per quatuor vices in anno, qui, cum quatuor militibus cujuslibet comitatus electis per comitatum, capiant in comitatu et in die et loco comitatus assisas predictas. [Articles, c. 8; 1225, c. 12.]

19. Et si in die comitatus assise predicte capi non possint, tot milites et libere tenentes remaneant de illis qui interfuerint comitatui die illo, per quos possint judicia sufficienter fieri, secundum quod negocium fuerit majus vel minus. [Articles, c. 13.]

20. Liber homo non amercietur pro parvo delicto, nisi secundum modum delicti; et pro magno delicto amercietur secundum magnitudinem delicti, salvo contenemento suo; et mercator eodem modo, salva mercandisa sua; et villanus eodem modo amercietur salvo waynagio suo; si inciderint in misericordiam nostram; et nulla predictarum misericordiarum ponatur, nisi per sacramentum proborum hominum de visneto. [Articles, c. 9; 1225, c. 14.]

21. Comites et barones non amercientur nisi per pares suos, et non nisi secundum modum delicti. [1225, c. 14.]

22. Nullus clericus amercietur de laico tenemento suo, nisi secundum modum aliorum predictorum, et non secundum quantitatem beneficii sui ecclesiastici. [Articles, c. 10; 1225, c. 14.]

23. Nec villa nec homo distringatur facere pontes ad riparias, nisi qui ab antiquo et de jure facere debent. [Articles, c. 11; 1225, c. 15.]

24. Nullus vicecomes, constabularius, coronatores, vel alii ballivi nostri, teneant placita corone nostre. [Articles, c. 14; 1225, c. 17.]

25. Omnes comitatus, hundredi, wapentakii, et trethingi sint ad antiquas firmas absque ullo incremento, exceptis dominicis maneriis nostris. [Articles, c. 14.]

26. Si aliquis tenens de nobis laicum feodum moriatur, et vicecomes vel ballivus noster ostendat litteras nostras patentes

18. Recognizances of novel disseisin, mort d'ancestor, and darrein presentment shall not be held elsewhere than in the court of the county in which they occur, and in this manner: we, or if we are out of the realm our chief justiciar, shall send two justices through each country four times a year who, with four knights of each county chosen by the county, shall hold the said assizes in the county court on the day and in the place of meeting of the county court.

19. And if the said assizes cannot all be held on the day of the county court, so many knights and freeholders of those present in the county court on that day shall remain behind as will suffice to make judgements, according to the amount of business to be done.

20. A free man shall not be amerced for a trivial offence, except in accordance with the degree of the offence; and for a serious offence he shall be amerced according to its gravity, saving his livelihood; and a merchant likewise, saving his merchandise; in the same way a villein shall be amerced saving his wainage; if they fall into our mercy. And none of the aforesaid amercements shall be imposed except by the testimony of reputable men of the neighbourhood.

21. Earls and barons shall not be amerced except by their peers and only in accordance with the nature of the offence.

22. No clerk shall be amerced on his lay tenement except in the manner of the others aforesaid and without reference to the size of his ecclesiastical benefice.

23. No vill or man shall be forced to build bridges at river banks, except those who ought to do so by custom and law.

24. No sheriff, constable, coroners or other of our bailiffs may hold pleas of our Crown.

25. All shires, hundreds, wapentakes and ridings shall be at the ancient farm without any increment, except our demesne manors.

26. If anyone holding a lay fief of us dies and our sheriff or bailiff shows our letters patent of summons for a debt which

de summonicione nostra de debito quod defunctus nobis debuit, liceat vicecomiti vel ballivo nostro attachiare et inbreviare catalla defuncti inventa in laico feodo, ad valenciam illius debiti, per visum legalium hominum, ita tamen quod nichil inde amoveatur, donec persolvatur nobis debitum quod clarum fuerit, et residuum relinquatur executoribus ad faciendum testamentum defuncti; et si nichil nobis debeatur ab ipso, omnia catalla cedant defuncto, salvis uxori ipsius et pueris racionabilibus partibus suis. [Articles, c. 15; 1225, c. 18.]

27. Si aliquis liber homo intestatus decesserit, catalla sua per manus propinquorum parentum et amicorum suorum, per visum ecclesie, distribuantur, salvis unicuique debitis que defunctus ei debebat. [Articles, c. 16.]

28. Nullus constabularius, vel alius ballivus noster, capiat blada vel alia catalla alicujus, nisi statim inde reddat denarios, aut respectum inde habere possit de voluntate venditoris. [Articles, c. 18; 1225, c. 19.]

29. Nullus constabularius distringat aliquem militem ad dandum denarios pro custodia castri, si facere voluerit custodiam illam in propria persona sua, vel per alium probum hominem, si ipse eam facere non possit propter racionabilem causam; et si nos duxerimus vel miserimus eum in exercitum, erit quietus de custodia, secundum quantitatem temporis quo per nos fuerit in exercitu. [Articles, c. 19; 1225, c. 20.]

30. Nullus vicecomes, vel ballivus noster, vel aliquis alius, capiat equos vel carettas alicujus liberi hominis pro cariagio faciendo, nisi de voluntate ipsius liberi hominis. [Articles, c. 20; 1225, c. 21.]

31. Nec nos nec ballivi nostri capiemus alienum boscum ad castra vel alia agenda nostra, nisi per voluntatem ipsius cujus boscus ille fuerit. [Articles, c. 21; 1225, c. 21.]

32. Nos non tenebimus terras illorum qui convicti fuerint de felonia, nisi per unum annum et unum diem, et tunc reddantur terre dominis feodorum. [Articles, c. 22; 1225, c. 22.]

33. Omnes kidelli de cetero deponantur penitus de

the deceased owed us, it shall be lawful for the sheriff or our bailiff to attach and list the chattels of the deceased found in lay fee to the value of that debt, by the view of lawful men, so that nothing is removed until the evident debt is paid to us, and the residue shall be relinquished to the executors to carry out the will of the deceased. And if he owes us nothing, all the chattels shall be accounted as the deceased's saving their reasonable shares to his wife and children.

27. If any free man dies intestate, his chattels are to be distributed by his nearest relations and friends, under the supervision of the Church, saving to everyone the debts which the deceased owed him.

28. No constable or any other of our bailiffs shall take any man's corn or other chattels unless he pays cash for them at once or can delay payment with the agreement of the seller.

29. No constable is to compel any knight to give money for castle guard, if he is willing to perform that guard in his own person or by another reliable man, if for some good reason he is unable to do it himself; and if we take or send him on military service, he shall be excused the guard in proportion to the period of his service.

30. No sheriff or bailiff of ours or anyone else is to take horses or carts of any free man for carting without his agreement.

31. Neither we nor our bailiffs shall take other men's timber for castles or other work of ours, without the agreement of the owner.

32. We will not hold the lands of convicted felons for more than a year and a day, when the lands shall be returned to the lords of the fiefs.

33. Henceforth all fish-weirs shall be completely removed

Tamisia, et de Medewaye, et per totam Angliam, nisi per costeram maris. [Articles, c. 23; 1225, c. 23.]

34. Breve quod vocatur 'Precipe' de cetero non fiat alicui de aliquo tenemento unde liber homo amittere possit curiam suam. [Articles, c. 24; 1225, c. 24.]

35. Una mensura vini sit per totum regnum nostrum, et una mensura cervisie, et una mensura bladi, scilicet quarterium Londoniense, et una latitudo pannorum tinctorum et russetorum et halbergettorum, scilicet due ulne infra listas; de ponderibus autem sit ut de mensuris. [Articles, c. 12; 1225, c. 25.]

36. Nichil detur vel capiatur de cetero pro brevi inquisicionis de vita vel membris, set gratis concedatur et non negetur. [Articles, c. 26; 1225, c. 26.]

37. Si aliquis teneat de nobis per feodifirmam, vel per sokagium, vel per burgagium, et de alio terram teneat per servicium militare, nos non habebimus custodiam heredis nec terre sue que est de feodo alterius occasione illius feodifirme, vel sokagii, vel burgagii; nec habebimus custodiam illius feodifirme, vel sokagii, vel burgagii, nisi ipsa feodifirma debeat servicium militare. Nos non habebimus custodiam heredis vel terre alicujus, quam tenet de alio per servicium militare, occasione alicujus parve serjanterie quam tenet de nobis per servicium reddendi nobis cultellos, vel sagittas, vel hujusmodi. [Articles, c. 27; 1225, c. 27.]

38. Nullus ballivus ponat decetero aliquem ad legem simplici loquela sua, sine testibus fidelibus ad hoc inductis. [Articles, c. 28; 1225, c. 28.]

39. Nullus liber homo capiatur, vel imprisonetur, aut disseisiatur, aut utlagetur, aut exuletur, aut aliquo modo destruatur, nec super eum ibimus, nec super eum mittemus, nisi per legale judicium parium suorum vel per legem terre. [Articles, c. 29; 1225, c. 29.]

40. Nulli vendemus, nulli negabimus aut differemus rectum aut justiciam. [Articles, c. 30; 1225, c. 29.]

41. Omnes mercatores habeant salvum et securum exire de Anglia, et venire in Angliam, et morari, et ire per Angliam, tam per terram quam per aquam, ad emendum et venden-

from the Thames and the Medway and throughout all England, except on the sea coast.

34. The writ called *praecipe* shall not, in future, be issued to anyone in respect of any holding whereby a free man may lose his court.

35. Let there be one measure of wine throughout our kingdom and one measure of ale and one measure of corn, namely the London quarter, and one width of cloth whether dyed, russet or halberjet, namely two ells within the selvedges. Let it be the same with weights as with measures.

36. Henceforth nothing shall be given or taken for the writ of inquisition of life or limb, but it shall be given freely and not refused.

37. If anyone holds of us by fee-farm, by socage or by burgage, and holds land of someone else by knight service, we will not, by virtue of that fee-farm, socage or burgage, have wardship of his heir or of land of his that belongs to the fief of another; nor will we have custody of that fee-farm or socage or burgage unless such fee-farm owes knight service. We will not have custody of the heir or land of anyone who holds of another by knight service, by virtue of any petty sergeanty which he holds of us by the service of rendering to us knives or arrows or the like.

38. Henceforth no bailiff shall put anyone on trial by his own unsupported allegation, without bringing credible witnesses to the charge.

39. No free man shall be taken or imprisoned or disseised or outlawed or exiled or in any way ruined, nor will we go or send against him, except by the lawful judgement of his peers or by the law of the land.

40. To no one will we sell, to no one will we deny or delay right or justice.

41. All merchants are to be safe and secure in leaving and entering England, and in staying and travelling in England, both by land and by water, to buy and sell free from all

dum, sine omnibus malis toltis, per antiquas et rectas consuetudines, preterquam in tempore gwerre, et si sint de terra contra nos gwerrina; et si tales inveniantur in terra nostra in principio gwerre, attachientur sine dampno corporum et rerum, donec sciatur a nobis vel capitali justiciario nostro quomodo mercatores terre nostre tractentur, qui tunc invenientur in terra contra nos gwerrina; et si nostri salvi sint ibi, alii salvi sint in terra nostra. [Articles, c. 31; 1225, c. 30.]

42. Liceat unicuique decetero exire de regno nostro, et redire, salvo et secure, per terram et per aquam, salva fide nostra, nisi tempore gwerre per aliquod breve tempus, propter communem utilitatem regni, exceptis imprisonatis et utlagatis secundum legem regni, et gente de terra contra nos gwerrina, et mercatoribus, de quibus fiat sicut predictum est. [Articles, c. 33.]

43. Si quis tenuerit de aliqua eskaeta, sicut de honore Wallingefordie, Notingeham, Bolonie, Lancastrie, vel de aliis eskaetis que sunt in manu nostra et sunt baronie, et obierit, heres ejus non det aliud relevium, nec faciat nobis aliud servicium quam faceret baroni si baronia illa esset in manu baronis; et nos eodem modo eam tenebimus quo baro eam tenuit. [Articles, c. 36; 1225, c. 31.]

44. Homines qui manent extra forestam non veniant decetero coram justiciariis nostris de foresta per communes summoniciones, nisi sint in placito, vel plegii alicujus vel aliquorum, qui attachiati sint pro foresta. [Articles, c. 39; Cart. For., c. 2.]

45. Nos non faciemus justiciarios, constabularios, vicecomites, vel ballivos, nisi de talibus qui sciant legem regni et eam bene velint observare. [Articles, c. 42.]

46. Omnes barones qui fundaverunt abbacias, unde habent cartas regum Anglie, vel antiquam tenuram, habeant earum custodiam cum vacaverint, sicut habere debent. [Articles, c. 43; 1225, c. 33.]

47. Omnes foreste que afforestate sunt tempore nostro, statim deafforestentur; et ita fiat de ripariis que per nos tempore nostro posite sunt in defenso. [Articles, c. 47; 1225, c. 16; Cart. For., c. 3.]

maletotes by the ancient and rightful customs, except, in time of war, such as come from an enemy country. And if such are found in our land at the outbreak of war they shall be detained without damage to their persons or goods, until we or our chief justiciar know how the merchants of our land are treated in the enemy country; and if ours are safe there, the others shall be safe in our land.

42. Henceforth anyone, saving his allegiance due to us, may leave our realm and return safe and secure by land and water, save for a short period in time of war on account of the general interest of the realm and excepting those imprisoned and outlawed according to the law of the land, and natives of an enemy country, and merchants, who shall be treated as aforesaid.

43. If anyone dies who holds of some escheat such as the honours of Wallingford, Nottingham, Boulogne or Lancaster, or of other escheats which are in our hands and are baronies, his heir shall not give any relief or do any service to us other than what he would have done to the baron if that barony had been in a baron's hands; and we shall hold it in the same manner as the baron held it.

44. Henceforth men who live outside the forest shall not come before our justices of the forest upon a general summons, unless they are impleaded or are sureties for any person or persons who are attached for forest offences.

45. We will not make justices, constables, sheriffs or bailiffs who do not know the law of the land and mean to observe it well.

46. All barons who have founded abbeys of which they have charters of the kings of England, or ancient tenure, shall have custody thereof during vacancies, as they ought to have.

47. All forests which have been afforested in our time shall be disafforested at once; and river banks which we have enclosed in our time shall be treated similarly.

48. Omnes male consuetudines de forestis et warennis, et de forestariis et warennariis, vicecomitibus et eorum ministris, ripariis et earum custodibus, statim inquirantur in quolibet comitatu per duodecim milites juratos de eodem comitatu, qui debent eligi per probos homines ejusdem comitatus, et infra quadraginta dies post inquisicionem factam, penitus, ita quod numquam revocentur, deleantur (per eosdem, ita quod nos hoc sciamus prius, vel justiciarius noster, si in Anglia non fuerimus).[1] [Articles, c. 39.]

49. Omnes obsides et cartas statim reddemus que liberate fuerunt nobis ab Anglicis in securitatem pacis vel fidelis servicii. [Articles, c. 38.]

50. Nos amovebimus penitus de balliis parentes Gerardi de Athyes, quod decetero nullam habeant balliam in Anglia, Engelardum de Cygony, Petrum et Gionem et Andream de Cancellis, Gionem de Cygony, Galfridum de Martinny et fratres ejus, Philippum Marc et fratres ejus, et Galfridum nepotem ejus, et totam sequelam eorundem. [Articles, c. 40.]

51. Et statim post pacis reformacionem amovebimus de regno omnes alienigenas milites, balistarios, servientes, stipendiarios, qui venerint cum equis et armis ad nocumentum regni. [Articles, c. 41.]

52. Si quis fuerit disseisitus vel elongatus per nos sine legali judicio parium suorum de terris, castellis, libertatibus, vel jure suo, statim ea ei restituemus; et si contencio super hoc orta fuerit, tunc inde fiat per judicium viginti quinque baronum, de quibus fit mencio inferius in securitate pacis. De omnibus autem illis de quibus aliquis disseisitus fuerit vel elongatus sine legali judicio parium suorum, per Henricum regem patrem nostrum vel per Ricardum regem fratrem nostrum, que in manu nostra habemus, vel que alii tenent, que nos oporteat warantizare, respectum habebimus usque ad communem terminum crucesignatorum, exceptis illis de quibus placitum motum fuit vel inquisicio facta per preceptum nostrum ante suscepcionem crucis nostre; cum autem

---

[1] At foot of MS in Ci and Cii.

48. All evil customs of forests and warrens, foresters and warreners, sheriffs and their servants, river banks and their wardens are to be investigated at once in every county by twelve sworn knights of the same county who are to be chosen by worthy men of the county, and within forty days of the inquiry they are to be abolished by them beyond recall, provided that we, or our justiciar, if we are not in England, first know of it.

49. We will restore at once all hostages and charters delivered to us by Englishmen as securities for peace or faithful service.

50. We will dismiss completely from their offices the relations of Gerard d'Athée that henceforth they shall have no office in England, Engelard de Cigogné, Peter and Guy and Andrew de Chanceaux, Guy de Cigogné, Geoffrey de Martigny with his brothers, Philip Mark with his brothers and his nephew, Geoffrey, and all their followers.

51. Immediately after concluding peace, we will remove from the kingdom all alien knights, crossbowmen, sergeants and mercenary soldiers who have come with horses and arms to the hurt of the realm.

52. If anyone has been disseised or deprived by us without lawful judgement of his peers of lands, castles, liberties or his rights we will restore them to him at once; and if any disagreement arises on this, then let it be settled by the judgement of the Twenty-Five barons referred to below in the security clause. But for all those things of which anyone was disseised or deprived without lawful judgement of his peers by King Henry our father, or by King Richard our brother, which we hold in our hand or which are held by others under our warranty, we shall have respite for the usual crusader's term; excepting those cases in which a plea was begun or inquest made on our order before we took the cross; when, however, we return from our pilgrimage, or if

redierimus de peregrinacione nostra, vel si forte remanserimus a peregrinacione nostra, statim inde plenam justiciam exhibebimus. [Articles, c. 25.]

53. Eundem autem respectum habebimus (et eodem modo de justicia exhibenda),[2] de forestis deafforestandis (vel remansuris forestis)[3] quas Henricus pater noster vel Ricardus frater noster afforestaverunt, et de custodiis terrarum que sunt de alieno feodo, cujusmodi custodias hucusque habuimus occasione feodi quod aliquis de nobis tenuit per servicium militare, et de abbaciis que fundate fuerint in feodo alterius quam nostro, in quibus dominus feodi dixerit se jus habere; et cum redierimus, vel si remanserimus a peregrinacione nostra, super hiis conquerentibus plenam justiciam statim exhibebimus.

54. Nullus capiatur nec imprisonetur propter appellum femine de morte alterius quam viri sui. [1225, c. 34.]

55. Omnes fines qui injuste et contra legem terre facti sunt nobiscum, et omnia amerciamenta facta injuste et contra legem terre, omnino condonentur, vel fiat inde per judicium viginti quinque baronum de quibus fit mencio inferius in securitate pacis, vel per judicium majoris partis eorundem, una cum predicto Stephano Cantuariensi archiepiscopo si interesse poterit et aliis quos secum ad hoc vocare voluerit. Et si interesse non poterit, nichilominus procedat negocium sine eo, ita quod, si aliquis vel aliqui de predictis viginti quinque baronibus fuerint in simili querela, amoveantur quantum ad hoc judicium et alii loco eorum per residuos de eisdem viginti quinque tantum ad hoc faciendum electi et jurati substituantur. [Articles, c. 37.]

56. Si nos disseisivimus vel elongavimus Walenses de terris vel libertatibus vel rebus aliis, sine legali judicio parium suorum (in Anglia vel in Wallia),[4] eis statim reddantur; et si contencio super hoc orta fuerit, tunc inde fiat in Marchia per judicium parium suorum de tenementis Anglie secundum legem Anglie; de tenementis Wallie secundum legem Wallie;

² At foot of MS in Ci and Cii.   ³ At foot of MS in Ci and Cii.
⁴ At foot of MS in Ci.

perhaps we do not undertake it, we will at once do full justice in these matters.

53. We shall have the same respite, and in the same manner, in doing justice on disafforesting or retaining those forests which Henry our father or Richard our brother afforested, and concerning custody of lands which are of the fee of another, the which wardships we have had hitherto by virtue of a fee held of us by knight's service, and concerning abbeys founded on fees other than our own, in which the lord of the fee claims to have a right. And as soon as we return, or if we do not undertake our pilgrimage, we will at once do full justice to complainants in these matters.

54. No one shall be taken or imprisoned upon the appeal of a woman for the death of anyone except her husband.

55. All fines which were made with us unjustly and contrary to the law of the land, and all amercements imposed unjustly and contrary to the law of the land, shall be completely remitted or else they shall be settled by the judgement of the Twenty-Five barons mentioned below in the security clause, or by the judgement of the majority of the same, along with the aforesaid Stephen, Archbishop of Canterbury, if he can be present, and others whom he wishes to summon with him for this purpose. And if he cannot be present the business shall nevertheless proceed without him, provided that if any one or more of the aforesaid Twenty-Five barons are in such a suit they shall stand down in this particular judgement, and shall be replaced by others chosen and sworn in by the rest of the same Twenty-Five, for this case only.

56. If we have disseised or deprived Welshmen of lands, liberties or other things without lawful judgement of their peers, in England or in Wales, they are to be returned to them at once; and if a dispute arises over this it shall be settled in the March by judgement of their peers; for tenements in England according to the law of England, for tenements in Wales according to the law of Wales, for

de tenementis Marchie secundum legem Marchie. Idem facient Walenses nobis et nostris. [Articles, c. 44.]

57. De omnibus autem illis de quibus aliquis Walensium disseisitus fuerit vel elongatus, sine legali judicio parium suorum, per Henricum regem patrem nostrum vel Ricardum regem fratrem nostrum, que nos in manu nostra habemus, vel que alii tenent que nos oporteat warantizare, respectum habebimus usque ad communem terminum crucesignatorum, illis exceptis de quibus placitum motum fuit vel inquisicio facta per preceptum nostrum ante suscepcionem crucis nostre; cum autem redierimus, vel si forte remanserimus a peregrinatione nostra, statim eis inde plenam justitiam exhibebimus, secundum leges Walensium et partes predictas. [Articles, c. 44.]

58. Nos reddemus filium Lewelini statim, et omnes obsides de Wallia, et cartas que nobis liberate fuerunt in securitatem pacis. [Articles, c. 45.]

59. Nos faciemus Alexandro regi Scottorum de sororibus suis et obsidibus reddendis, et libertatibus suis, et jure suo, secundum formam in qua faciemus aliis baronibus nostris Anglie, nisi aliter esse debeat per cartas quas habemus de Willelmo patre ipsius, quondam rege Scottorum; et hoc erit per judicium parium suorum in curia nostra. [Articles, c. 46.]

60. Omnes autem istas consuetudines predictas et libertates quas nos concessimus in regno nostro tenendas quantum ad nos pertinet erga nostros, omnes de regno nostro, tam clerici quam laici, observent quantum ad se pertinet erga suos. [Articles, c. 48; 1225, c. 37; Cart. For., 17.]

61. Cum autem pro Deo, et ad emendacionem regni nostri, et ad melius sopiendum discordiam inter nos et barones nostros ortam, hec omnia predicta concesserimus, volentes ea integra et firma stabilitate (in perpetuum)[5] gaudere, facimus et concedimus eis securitatem subscriptam; videlicet quod barones eligant viginti quinque barones de regno quos voluerint, qui debeant pro totis viribus suis observare, tenere, et facere observari, pacem et libertates quas eis concessimus,

[5] At foot of MS in Ci.

tenements in the March according to the law of the March. The Welsh are to do the same to us and ours.

57. For all those things, however, of which any Welshman has been disseised or deprived without lawful judgement of his peers by King Henry our father, or King Richard our brother, which we have in our possession or which others hold under our legal warranty, we shall have respite for the usual crusader's term; excepting those cases in which a plea was begun or inquest made on our order before we took the cross. However, when we return, or if perhaps we do not go on our pilgrimage, we will at once give them full justice in accordance with the laws of the Welsh and the aforesaid regions.

58. We will restore at once the son of Llywelyn and all the hostages from Wales and the charters delivered to us as security for peace.

59. We will treat Alexander, King of the Scots, concerning the return of his sisters and hostages and his liberties and rights in the same manner in which we will act towards our other barons of England, unless it ought to be otherwise because of the charters which we have from William his father, formerly King of the Scots; and this shall be determined by the judgement of his peers in our court.

60. All these aforesaid customs and liberties which we have granted to be held in our realm as far as it pertains to us towards our men, shall be observed by all men of our realm, both clerk and lay, as far as it pertains to them, towards their own men.

61. Since, moreover, we have granted all the aforesaid things for God, for the reform of our realm and the better settling of the quarrel which has arisen between us and our barons, wishing these things to be enjoyed fully and undisturbed in perpetuity, we give and grant them the following security: namely, that the barons shall choose any twenty-five barons of the realm they wish, who with all their might are to observe, maintain and cause to be observed the peace

et hac presenti carta nostra confirmavimus; ita scilicet quod, si nos, vel justiciarius noster, vel ballivi nostri, vel aliquis de ministris nostris, in aliquo erga aliquem deliquerimus, vel aliquem articulorum pacis aut securitatis transgressi fuerimus, et delictum ostensum fuerit quatuor baronibus de predictis viginti quinque baronibus, illi quatuor barones accedant ad nos vel ad justiciarium nostrum, si fuerimus extra regnum, proponentes nobis excessum, petent ut excessum illum sine dilacione faciamus emendari. Et si nos excessum non emendaverimus, vel, si fuerimus extra regnum, justiciarius noster non emendaverit infra tempus quadraginta dierum computandum a tempore quo monstratum fuerit nobis vel justiciario nostro, si extra regnum fuerimus, predicti quatuor barones referant causam illam ad residuos de illis viginti quinque baronibus, et illi viginti quinque barones cum communa tocius terre distringent et gravabunt nos modis omnibus quibus poterunt, scilicet per capcionem castrorum, terrarum, possessionum et aliis modis quibus poterunt, donec fuerit emendatum secundum arbitrium eorum, salva persona nostra et regine nostre et liberorum nostrorum; et cum fuerit emendatum intendent nobis sicut prius fecerunt. Et quicumque voluerit de terra juret quod ad predicta omnia exequenda parebit mandatis predictorum viginti quinque baronum, et quod gravabit nos pro posse suo cum ipsis, et nos publice et libere damus licenciam jurandi cuilibet qui jurare voluerit, et nulli umquam jurare prohibebimus. Omnes autem illos de terra qui per se et sponte sua noluerint jurare viginti quinque baronibus de distringendo et gravando nos cum eis, faciemus jurare eosdem de mandato nostro sicut predictum est. Et si aliquis de viginti quinque baronibus decesserit, vel a terra recesserit, vel aliquo alio modo impeditus fuerit, quominus ista predicta possent exequi, qui residui fuerint de predictis viginti quinque baronibus eligant alium loco ipsius, pro arbitrio suo, qui simili modo erit juratus quo et ceteri. In omnibus autem que istis viginti quinque baronibus committuntur exequenda, si forte ipsi viginti quinque presentes fuerint, et inter se super re aliqua discordaverint, vel aliqui ex eis and liberties which we have granted and confirmed to them by this our present charter; so that if we or our justiciar or our bailiffs or any of our servants offend against anyone in any way, or transgress any of the articles of peace or security, and the offence is indicated to four of the aforesaid twenty-five barons, those four barons shall come to us or our justiciar, if we are out of the kingdom, and shall bring it to our notice and ask that we have it redressed without delay. And if we, or our justiciar, should we be out of the kingdom, do not redress the offence within forty days from the time when it was brought to the notice of us or our justiciar, should we be out of the kingdom, the aforesaid four barons shall refer the case to the rest of the twenty-five barons and those twenty-five barons with the commune of all the land shall distrain and distress us in every way they can, namely by seizing castles, lands and possessions, and in such other ways as they can, saving our person and those of our queen and of our children, until, in their judgement, amends have been made; and when it has been redressed they are to obey us as they did before. And anyone in the land who wishes may take an oath to obey the orders of the said twenty-five barons in the execution of all the aforesaid matters, and to join with them in distressing us to the best of his ability, and we publicly and freely permit anyone who wishes to take the oath, and we will never forbid anyone to take it. Moreover we shall compel and order all those in the land who of themselves and of their own free will are unwilling to take an oath to the twenty-five barons to distrain and distress us with them, to take the oath as aforesaid. And if any of the twenty-five barons dies or leaves the country or is otherwise prevented from discharging these aforesaid duties, the rest of the aforesaid barons shall on their own decision choose another in his place, who shall take the oath in the same way as the others. In all matters the execution of which is committed to those twenty-five barons, if it should happen that the twenty-five are present summoniti nolint vel nequeant interesse, ratum habeatur et firmum quod major pars eorum qui presentes fuerint providerit vel preceperit ac si omnes viginti quinque in hoc consensissent; et predicti viginti quinque jurent quod omnia antedicta fideliter observabunt, et pro toto posse suo facient observari. Et nos nichil impetrabimus ab aliquo, per nos nec per alium, per quod aliqua istarum concessionum et libertatum revocetur vel minuatur; et, si aliquid tale impetratum fuerit, irritum sit et inane et numquam eo utemur per nos nec per alium. [Articles, c. 49.]

62. Et omnes malas voluntates, indignaciones, et rancores, ortos inter nos et homines nostros, clericos et laicos, a tempore discordie, plene omnibus remisimus et condonavimus. Preterea omnes transgressiones factas occasione ejusdem discordie, a Pascha anno regni nostri sextodecimo usque ad pacem reformatam, plene remisimus omnibus, clericis et laicis, et quantum ad nos pertinet plene condonavimus. Et insuper fecimus eis fieri litteras testimoniales patentes domini Stephani Cantuariensis archiepiscopi, domini Henrici Dublinensis archiepiscopi, et episcoporum predictorum et magistri Pandulfi, super securitate ista et concessionibus prefatis.

63. Quare volumus et firmiter precipimus quod Anglicana ecclesia libera sit et quod homines in regno nostro habeant et teneant omnes prefatas libertates, jura, et concessiones, bene et in pace, libere et quiete, plene et integre, sibi et heredibus suis, de nobis et heredibus nostris, in omnibus rebus et locis, in perpetuum, sicut predictum est. Juratum est autem tam ex parte nostra quam ex parte baronum, quod hec omnia supradicta bona fide et sine malo ingenio observabuntur. Testibus supradictis et multis aliis. Data per manum nostram in prato quod vocatur Ronimed inter Windlesoram et Stanes, quinto decimo die Junii, anno regni nostri decimo septimo.

and disagree among themselves on anything, or if any of them who has been summoned will not or cannot come, whatever the majority of those present shall provide or order is to be taken as fixed and settled as if the whole twenty-five had agreed to it; and the aforesaid twenty-five are to swear that they will faithfully observe all the aforesaid and will do all they can to secure its observance. And we will procure nothing from anyone, either personally or through another, by which any of these concessions and liberties shall be revoked or diminished; and if any such thing is procured, it shall be null and void, and we will never use it either ourselves or through another.

62. And we have completely remitted and pardoned to all any ill will, grudge and rancour that have arisen between us and our subjects, clerk and lay, from the time of the quarrel. Moreover we have fully forgiven and completely condoned to all, clerk and lay, as far as pertains to us, all offences occasioned by the said quarrel from Easter in the sixteenth year of our reign to the conclusion of peace. And moreover we have caused letters patent of the Lord Stephen, Archbishop of Canterbury, the Lord Henry, Archbishop of Dublin, the aforesaid bishops and Master Pandulf to be made for them on this security and the aforesaid concessions.

63. Wherefore we wish and firmly command that the English church shall be free, and the men in our realm shall have and hold all the aforesaid liberties, rights and concessions well and peacefully, freely and quietly, fully and completely for them and their heirs of us and our heirs in all things and places for ever, as is aforesaid. Moreover an oath has been sworn, both on our part and on the part of the barons, that all these things aforesaid shall be observed in good faith and without evil intent. Witness the above-mentioned and many others. Given under our hand in the meadow which is called Runnymede between Windsor and Staines on the fifteenth day of June in the seventeenth year of our reign.

TRANSLATIONS OF THE CHARTERS

A surprising number of the documents of 1215 survive in Anglo-Norman translations. These include the Charter itself, the writ of 27 June directed to the sheriffs and twelve elected knights of each county authorizing them to distrain on those who refused the oath to the Twenty-Five, and versions of the charters of liberties of Henry I, Stephen and Henry II. The first two are included in the cartulary of the leper Hospital of S. Giles at Pont-Audemer, Normandy (Rouen, Bibliothèque Municipale, MS Y 200). The charters of liberties constitute Harleian MS 458 in the British Library.

The first two were published under the title of 'A vernacular-French text of Magna Carta, 1215'.[1] It is now clear that they are in fact in Anglo-Norman.[2] The writ, unlike the enrolled version on the Patent roll, was addressed to the sheriff of Hampshire. It is therefore reasonable to suppose that this vernacular version of the charter was intended for proclamation in the county court of Hampshire in 1215. If so, it lies at or near the origin of the public proclamation of the charters and other documents in both French and English, which was certainly being practised by the 1250s.[3] That leaves some obvious questions – were there other translations? Where and how were they

---

[1] Holt (1974).
[2] See Ian Short, 'The Vernacular-French Magna Carta: Some Linguistic Evidence', *Semasia*, IV (1977), 53–63. I recall that the original edition of the translation went into proof under the title of 'An Anglo-Norman text of Magna Carta' which was amended at a late stage because of conflicting advice from linguistic experts. It is satisfying that the issue is now resolved.
[3] Holt (1974), 349–50.

made? To these the Harleian MS suggests some possible answers.

Harleian MS 458 is only a bifolium. Liebermann used it in his work on the text of the charter of Henry I, but he did not appreciate its importance and misdated the translations on the second folio.[4] It has escaped attention since.[5] It is written in a careful, indeed handsome, business hand, or probably more than one.[6] These are not scrappy notes or hasty transcripts but texts clearly and spaciously arranged. Nothing is known of its history except that it passed through the hands of the antiquary Peter Le Neve in the late seventeenth, or early eighteenth, century. It may be significant that Le Neve did much work on the records in the Rolls Chapel.

It is undated. There are two grounds for relating it to the crisis of 1215. The first is that the script belongs to the first quarter of the thirteenth century and indeed would not look out of place in the more formal documents of John's Chancery. The second is the subject-matter. The recto of the first folio contains a version of the charter of liberties of Henry I. This is followed on the dorse by the coronation charters of Stephen and Henry II. Anglo-Norman translations of the charters of Stephen and Henry II then appear on the recto of the second folio which are followed on the dorse by a translation of the charter of Henry I. The text of the charter of Henry I is closely similar to that in Lambeth MS 1212 and includes the addition confirming the privileges of Westminster.[7] The scribe may have had an original charter of King Stephen on the desk before him, for he reproduced the distinctive capital 'S' characteristic of Stephen's charters.[8]

---

[4] Liebermann (1894), 37. See plates 4, 5.
[5] I first drew attention to it in Holt (1985a), pp. 14–15, where I acknowledge my thanks to Dr Martin Brett who rediscovered it and brought it to my notice.
[6] I tend to the view that it is the work of two and possibly three scribes. Dr Chaplais has suggested that there was one scribe only who varied his script somewhat. It does not matter for my present purposes.
[7] Liebermann (1894), 26–7, 37.　　[8] I owe this suggestion to Dr Chaplais.

The text of the charter of Henry II is better than the only other surviving version.[9]

It is therefore a deliberate collection of the charters of liberties of the kings of twelfth-century England. It is unique evidence that someone at some stage brought together the 'constitutional documents' relevant to the genesis of the Great Charter, and for the first time we have clear evidence that the charters of Stephen and Henry II were examined as well as that of Henry I.[10] It looks like preparatory work for 1215.

If that is so it is easier to understand the need for translation. We must imagine some sort of committee sitting without the modern convenience of circulated documents. The proceedings will be oral. There is a limit to passing documents round the table. There may be too many present; some will read Latin better than others; some may not read at all. Moreover, there are many, then as now, who can read well enough but cannot follow spoken Latin. So it will be best to provide a translation in the appropriate vernacular. But the business is important, indeed critical in the politics of the time; an 'off-the-cuff' translation will not do; it must be exact, it must be recoverable. It must therefore be written before it can be read. Hence the translations. Harleian MS 458 is too formal to be a working paper or minute of such a session; but it could well be a preparatory document laid before it. If all that is so it takes us into the inner workings of the *conjuratio* of 1215, into a piece of planning in which from its very nature clerks and laymen must have shared.

It has long been recognized that there is a difficulty in imagining that a lengthy document like Magna Carta could be read out in a county court with any hope of it being

---

9 It lacks the inappropriate *dei gratia* of Cotton MS, Claudius D. II, fo. 79. Like the Cottonian text it has Richard de Lucy as sole witness.

10 It should be noted that the *Histoire des Ducs de Normandie* refers to the charters of both Henry I and Stephen – 'les chartres que li rois Henris qui fu ayous son pere avoit données à lor ancissours et que li rois Estievenes lor avoit confremées' (p. 146).

generally understood.[11] The Pont-Audemer translation disposes of that. But the same problem arises with the assembly at Runnymede. Saer de Quincy could have followed the Charter in Latin perhaps, whether written or spoken, for he had been a baron of the Exchequer: likewise, on the king's side, Hubert de Burgh, the new Justiciar. But how many others? If those who participated in the planning stage required a translation, then the gathering at Runnymede required one so much more. If Magna Carta was proclaimed at Runnymede, as it was in the shire courts and as the terms of the *forma pacis* seem to require, then it must in all probability have been done in Anglo-Norman.[12]

This is not the place to enter into the more general debate about aristocratic and lay literacy on which Dr Clanchy, Dr Orme and Professor Turner and many others have done such valuable work.[13] But one comment is worthwhile. The above translations seem to come from a distinct stage in the story. The men involved in Magna Carta, from the planners and the Twenty-Five down to the local men who swore their oaths to the Charter in the county courts, were not literate in the sense that they had an adequate command of Latin. But they were literate in that they wanted precisely written documentary evidence and reinforcement in a language which, when read out or proclaimed, they could understand. And this they did.

[11] Holt (1974), 346–7.
[12] Clanchy (1979), pp. 170–1 and Maddicott (1984), p. 30, suggest that the vernacular may have been English, but I have found no evidence for this except for a Latin and 'Saxon' version of the charter of Henry I which no longer survives. This was probably a bilingual text of the early twelfth century (Holt, 1985a, p. 15, n.40). Whether Robert fitz Walter and Eustace de Vescy spoke to each other in English or Anglo-Norman is a matter for speculation. My own guess, a firm one, is Anglo-Norman. I also doubt whether English, as it was *c.* 1215, would seem a sufficiently precise tool, for the task of translating Magna Carta.
[13] Clanchy (1979); Nicholas Orme, *From Childhood to Chivalry* (London, 1984), especially pp. 147–50; R. V. Turner, 'The *Miles Literatus* in Twelfth- and Thirteenth-Century England; How Rare a Phenomenon?' *American Historical Review*, LXXXIII (1978), 928–45.

THE TWENTY-FIVE BARONS OF MAGNA CARTA, 1215

Three lists of the Twenty-Five barons have been known since Blackstone's day[1]: one in the *Chronica Majora* of Matthew Paris,[2] one in his *Liber Additamentorum*,[3] and one in a marginal annotation in a late thirteenth-century collection of law tracts and statutes.[4] The first two are identical and are based on the same source. The third is the best of the three. It has *Rogerus de Mumbezon* correctly where Matthew Paris erred into the form *Rogerus de Munbrai*.

The Twenty-Five were Richard, earl of Clare, William de Fors, count of Aumale, Geoffrey de Mandeville, earl of Gloucester, Saer de Quincy, earl of Winchester, Henry de Bohun, earl of Hereford, Roger Bigod, earl of Norfolk, Robert de Vere, earl of Oxford, William Marshal junior, Robert fitz Walter, Gilbert de Clare, Eustace de Vescy, Hugh Bigod, William de Mowbray, the Mayor of London, William de Lanvallei, Robert de Ros, John de Lacy, constable of Chester, Richard de Percy, John fitz Robert, William Malet, Geoffrey de Say, Roger de Montbegon, William of Huntingfield, Richard de Munfichet and William d'Aubigné of Belvoir.

A fourth list which was discovered by Cheney (1968) in a Reading Abbey MS in Lambeth Palace Library can now be added. This is printed below. Like the St Albans versions this list names Roger de Mowbray in error for Roger de Montbegon. It also names the earl of Arundel mistakenly for the count of Aumale.

---

[1] See *Law Tracts*, II, xxxii.   [2] *Chron. Maj.* II, 605.
[3] B. M., Cotton, Nero D I, fo. 123.   [4] B. M., Harleian MS 746, fo. 64.

The list is unique evidence in that it includes quotas of knights against all Twenty-Five except the mayor of London. These are not feudal quotas, although in a few cases they approximate to them or to the number of knights enfeoffed. It is more likely that they are estimates of the numbers each could bring to bear, if necessary, to enforce the Charter; and it should be borne in mind that in 1215 many knights of uncertain feudal dependence or loyalty are likely to have attached themselves to particular baronial leaders.

The memoranda at the head and foot of the list are discussed above, pp. 346 and below, pp. 482–3.

Yet another list of the Twenty-Five 'qui sunt iudices in terra Anglia' was copied by Robert Glover.[5] This has *Rogerus de Montegomerico* for Roger de Montbegon.

TEXT

Lambeth Palace Library, MS. 371, fol. 56ᵛ

Hec sunt nomina baronum qui electi sunt ad observandum omnia que continentur in carta regis secundum demandam baronum.

[column 1] Comes de Clara cum septem[6] viginti militibus.
Comes de Arundell' cum XL militibus.
Comes Gloucestrie cum CC militibus.
Comes Wintonie cum XL militibus.
Comes Herefordie cum XL militibus.
Comes Rogerus cum quaterviginti militibus.
[column 2] Comes Robertus cum XXX militibus.
Willelmus Marescallus cum CC militibus.
Robertus filius Walteri cum L militibus.
Gilbertus de Clara cum IIIIˣˣ militibus.
Eustachius de Vescy cum XXX militibus.

---

[5] B. L., Lansdowne MS 229, fo. 96.   [6] septem MS,? for septies.

Willelmus de Albeny cum X mlitibus.
Hugo Bigot cum XX militibus.

[fo. 57r column 1] Willelmus de Munbray cum IIII^{xx} militibus.
Galfridus de Say cum XV militibus.
Rogerus de Munbray cum X militibus.
Willelmus de Huntingfeld' cum VII militibus.
Ricardus de Monte Fichetto cum XXX militibus.
Willelmus Malet cum X militibus.
[column 2] Robertus de Ros cum XX militibus.
Willelmus de Lanvallay cum XV militibus.
Constabularius Cestrie cum XX militibus.
Ricardus de Percy cum X militibus.
Iohannes filius Roberti cum X militibus.
Maior[7] Londonie tradet civitatem Londonie baronibus si forte rex contra cartam suam venire voluerit. Omnes isti comites cum tot militibus et cum communa totius Anglie debent insurgere in regem si forte rex contra cartam suam venire voluerit. Summa militum M C IIII^{xx} et III.

Printed: *B.J.R.L.*, L, 1968, 307

---

[7] The remainder is written across the page.

THE DATE OF THE LONDON TREATY

The case for including the treaty concerning London in the final peace agreed at Runnymede on 19 June is simple and straightforward. It depends on three arguments fully developed above.[1] These are:

a. the strong probability that the firm peace would necessarily include some agreement about London;
b. the clear reference in the treaty to the execution of certain provisions of the Charter;
c. the fact that royal letters of 23 July relating to the 'peace agreement' refer to the restoration of castles, which can only come, among surviving documents, from the London treaty.

To these Galbraith has added a fourth argument viz.

d. The improbability that King John would accept an agreement with someone entitled 'Marshal of the Army of God and Holy Church' once peace had been restored.[2]

In 1944 Richardson argued that the treaty should be dated to the third week in July.[3] The ground for this is that the treaty is entered on the dorse of the membrane of the Close roll which covered the period 11–19 July.[4] Cheney also took this view, although more tentatively.[5] This is discussed in appendix 10 below, pp. 486–8.

---

[1] Above, pp. 263–6.
[2] Galbraith (1967), 354–5. The argument is not weakened by the fact that Robert continued to use the title (*Chron. Maj.* II, 614–15). The official view of it is revealed in the letters of the papal commissioners of 8 September – 'Robertum filium Walteri ... qui exercitus Dei se nominat mareschallum' (Powicke, 1929, 92).
[3] Richardson (1944), 424.   [4] *Rot. Litt. Claus.* I, 268b.
[5] Cheney (1968), 297–8.

Cheney also felt that the memorandum attached to the list of the Twenty-Five in Lambeth MS 371 had some bearing on the matter.[6] This includes the proviso that the 'mayor will hand over the city of London to the barons if the king happens to decide to contravene his charter'. Cheney took this to be part of a sequence of arrangements concerning London, in which case, he considered, the memorandum must antedate the treaty, which must accordingly record a situation subsequent to Runnymede, rendering a date of the third week in July the most likely. But there are difficulties. The treaty is an official record: the list an informal memorandum. They are not on a par or of equal weight; and there is no compelling need to read them sequentially on the presumption that the state of London was determined exclusively by the one or the other. If they are taken at their face value it is apparent that they are concerned with different if overlapping situations: the treaty with the execution of the whole agreement, including the performance of the oath to the Twenty-Five and the restoration of rights, within the time limit of 15 August; the memorandum with the operations of the Twenty-Five within the terms of cap. 61, to which it clearly refers, if the king contravened the Charter; this carried no time limit. There is no difficulty in viewing the two concurrently. The arrangements in the treaty took effect and would have ended, if all had gone well, on 15 August. The arrangements envisaged in the memorandum, on the other hand, were entirely conditional on the king's behaviour. Both arrangements depended in some degree on the fact which neither mention: the barons had thrust in their own candidate as mayor when they captured the city in May.[7]

Galbraith dated the treaty to 18 June and the memorandum to 'little if any later than 19 June'. He took a rather different line from that which I have advanced above – 'The

---

[6] Appendix 8, above, pp. 478–80.   [7] See above, p. 241.

explanation [of the differences between the two documents] is that in the king's eyes the barons had seized London from its lawful governor, the mayor, while the barons were careful to respect the mayor's position, regarding him as an ally.'[8]

[8] Galbraith (1967), 354–6, especially 356n.

THE OXFORD COUNCIL, 16–23 JULY 1215

One of the most important features of Mr Richardson's original paper on 'The Morrow of the Great Charter' was the emphasis he gave to the assembly held at Oxford in the third week of July. 'This July meeting,' he wrote, 'for which the evidence is exceptionally abundant, has been ignored or implicitly denied by historians. But it is vitally important if the sequence of events is to be understood. The broad result of the meeting was to carry a stage further the *concordia* of Runnymede.'[1]

This view differs radically from the one advanced above. The main points of difference are as follows.

(1) Richardson equated the *triplex forma pacis* with Magna Carta and not, as has been argued above, with the papal *forma* of March. This meant that he could interpret the approval which the papal commissioners expressed for the *forma* in September as approval of Magna Carta, and this in turn supported his hypothesis that the agreement was still being amplified in July. On the correct dating of the *triplex forma pacis* see appendix 3, above, pp. 413–17.

(2) He made the avowed presumption that the administrative changes and other measures taken at or about this time were taken by conciliar decision. For this there is no direct evidence. He rightly drew attention to an entry on the K. R. Memoranda roll of 2 Henry III, which states that William fitz Roscelin held the counties of Norfolk and Suffolk as the deputy of the baronial sheriff, Roger de Cressy, until 1 August, when a council was held at Oxford,

---

[1] Richardson (1944), 429.

and then the king committed the counties to Hubert de Burgh.[2] Letters patent notifying Hubert's appointment were in fact dated 24 July at Woodstock,[3] the day after John left Oxford. Now this entry on the Memoranda roll obviously associates this particular administrative change with the Oxford council, but it gets the date of the council wrong, it does not state directly that Hubert's appointment was made at Oxford and it certainly does not permit us to assume that the change was made 'by common agreement' at the council.[4] These *caveats* apply with even greater force to the other administrative changes at this time. Two involved the dismissal of Tourangeaux from their offices; Andrew de Chanceaux from the shrievalty of Herefordshire and the castellanship of Hereford on 19 July, and Peter de Chanceaux from the constableship of Bristol castle on the 20 July.[5] But the one was replaced by Hubert de Burgh and the other by Philip d'Aubigny, both of whom were among the most loyal and committed of the king's supporters. Moreover writs of 18 July ordered one of the Twenty-Five, William d'Aubigné, to hand over Sauvey castle to Hugh de Neville, the chief forester,[6] and writs of 24 July provided for the replacement of another, Robert de Ros, in the shrievalty of Cumberland.[7] Thus the administrative changes of this time were not all in the baronial interest. In some instances it is difficult to see any political motive. Letters of 25 July provided for the replacement of John Marshal as sheriff of Lincolnshire by Walter of Coventry, a steward of the earl of Chester.[8] Both were loyal agents of the king and it is doubtful if such a change had any other

---

[2] 'Post Pascha, incipiente guerra, Rogerus de Cressy per barones fuit vicecomes, et Willelmus filius Roscelini pro eo tenuit comitatus usque ad festum sancti Petri ad Vincula quando concilium fuit apud Oxoniam. Et tunc commisit dominus rex comitatus cum castellis Huberto de Burgo iusticiario...' (Richardson, 1944, 441–2).
[3] *Rot. Litt. Pat.* p. 150: not, as Mr Richardson (1944, 423) states, at Oxford.
[4] *Ibid.*   [5] *Rot. Litt. Pat.* pp. 149*b*–150.   [6] *Ibid.* p. 149.
[7] *Ibid.* p. 150. This order was not apparently obeyed (Holt, 1961, p. 122).
[8] *Rot. Litt. Pat.* p. 150*b*.

485

motive than administrative convenience. The best that can be said for Mr Richardson's view is that the council coincided with the dismissal of two foreigners, but it is relevant to note that two Tourangeaux, Engelard de Cigogné and Geoffrey de Martigny, had already been replaced, and that another, Philip Mark, never was.[9]

(3) He attributed most of the important and undated documents of the summer of 1215 to this meeting; these were:

a. the London treaty (below, pp. 490–1);

b. letters of the archbishop and his suffragans concerning the failure of the barons to provide charters of fealty (below, pp. 497–8);

c. letters of the archbishop and his suffragans concerning the royal forest (below, pp. 498–9).

To these we may now add:

d. a notification of the charter of submission to King John of Llywelyn of Wales of 11 August 1211.[10] This is in the names of Stephen archbishop of Canterbury, Henry archbishop of Dublin, William bishop of Coventry, Ranulf earl of Chester, William earl of Salisbury, William earl of Ferrers [Derby], and Hubert de Burgh, Justiciar. Hubert's designation imposes a *terminus post quem* of 15–19 June when he was made Justiciar. This document was not copied onto any of the surviving enrolments.

Of these the last two can be allotted to the session at Oxford with varying degrees of probability. The last is beyond serious doubt. All the signatories except the arch-

---

[9] Orders for the replacement of Engelard as sheriff of Gloucestershire were dated 8 July (*ibid*. p. 148*b*) and for the replacement of Geoffrey de Martigny as castellan of Northampton 2 July (*ibid*. p. 146*b*). Geoffrey had also been sheriff of Northamptonshire. Orders for his replacement by William of Duston were dated 25 June and further orders of 2 July instructed him to hand over the shire to Roger de Neville (*ibid*. pp. 145, 146*b*). However, Geoffrey later accounted for the custody of the shire up to 20 July (*Pipe Roll 17 John*, pp. 49–54). I am indebted for this and other references to B. E. Harris, 'The English sheriffs in the reign of King John' (M.A. thesis, Nottingham University, 1961).

[10] Beverley Smith (1984), 344–62.

bishop of Dublin and the bishop of Coventry were certainly present at Oxford on 23 July, the very same day for which a number of Welsh princes were given safe-conducts to meet the king there; and John indeed was in Oxford on that day.[11] The letters concerning the forest probably belong to approximately the same date and occasion. There must have been an interval after Runnymede to allow for the accumulation of some experience of how cap. 48 of the Charter was being applied; the letters were presumably made out at the request of the king, and it is reasonable to suppose that this was made when the king and the churchmen met; the third week in July at Oxford is the likely occasion.

There are no similar grounds for allotting the first two documents, a. and b., to the same meeting. As has been shown above, the London treaty was an essential part of the settlement at Runnymede.[12] The letters concerning fealty could have been requested by the king and supplied by the bishops any time after the renewal of homage on 19 June.

The names of the bishops in b. and c. scarcely help to carry the argument further, except to suggest that they were not coeval. The names of Richard bishop of Chichester and the legate Pandulf appear in the letters concerning fealty but not in those concerning the forest. Neither include Benedict of Rochester who appears in both the Charter and the Letters Testimonial; and these in turn do not include Richard of Chichester. Only the Charter and the Letters Testimonial maintain exact identity.

There remains the matter of enrolment. The letters concerning fealty were entered on the dorse of the membrane of the Patent roll dealing with 28 June to 2 July.[13] The London treaty and the letters concerning the forest were entered on the dorse of the membrane of the Close roll

---

[11] *Rot. Litt. Pat.*, p. 180; Beverley Smith (1984), 345–6, 350–1.
[12] See above, pp. 263–6, 481–3.　　[13] *Rot. Litt. Pat.*, p. 191.

covering 11–19 July.[14] (John, it should be noted, arrived in Oxford on 17 July and stayed until the 23rd.) The enrolment of the treaty was probably derived from the part carrying the baronial seals which still survives. In the case of both it is likely that officers of the Chancery wanted to have to hand a record of documents which would be stored in the Treasury. Now little is known of the treatment of incoming documents at this date.[15] It is likely that a clerk would enter incoming letters on receipt on the dorse of the current or immediately preceding membrane of the Close or Patent roll.[16] The difficulty in this case is that these two documents were not copied by any of the clerks who were working on the roll at the time. They are entered in a distinct intrusive hand which does not appear in any of the other entries on the dorse or recto of this or neighbouring membranes. So someone decided or was directed to enter them on a chancery roll. We cannot even be certain that he located them by deliberate choice on the dorse of m. 27 as the clerk working on the recto might well do. But he entered them together, the treaty first; and this association of the two is unlikely to be casual. But if they were entered together it does not follow that they were originated at one and the same time. The letters concerning the forest demonstrated that the agreement reached at Runnymede was breaking down. It is not too difficult to imagine circumstances in which this evidence of failure was discussed and recorded alongside the one document which imposed a deadline on the execution of the agreement. This, of course, is hypothetical, and the matter should not be judged on this alone. There are strong positive arguments for dating the treaty to Runnymede. The main argument for dating it to the Oxford meeting has been the position of the enrolment. It is a frail one.

In effect there are only four clear references to the Oxford

---

[14] *Rot. Litt. Claus.*, I, 220b–221; 268b.
[15] See Pierre Chaplais, *Diplomatic Documents*, p. 5. [16] Cheney (1968), 298–9.

council: in the chronicle of Wendover, where the date is given as 16 July and the place incorrectly as Westminster;[17] in the entry on the Memoranda roll quoted above; in the king's letters of 15 July in which he announced that he would be unable to attend on the morrow;[18] and in a verse narrative included in the chronicle of Melrose. This describes the origins of baronial discontent and then proceeds through the negotiations of the spring to a settlement, a *forma pacis*, to which the king finally agreed. However, on being asked to seal a *scriptum* embodying the concession he procrastinated and asked the barons to come to Oxford. There on the appointed day, he 'denounced the articles of peace'.[19] The poem was written very soon after 1215 and was annotated in a contemporary hand with three dates of the Roman calendar: 11 May at Northampton for the breakdown of negotiations in the spring, 18 June 'in the meadow of Staines' for the *forma pacis*, and 20 July for the meeting at Oxford.

This is a somewhat confused narrative. The poet does not mention the Charter and indeed implies that the king never set his seal to the terms of settlement. But he is very clear on one point: the Oxford meeting ended in breakdown. The rest, as Mr Richardson agrees, is conjecture.[20] One further item may be added with reasonable certainty and by common agreement of all authorities. It was at Oxford, at the very latest, that the king decided to seek the annulment of the Charter. John at least had failed to find any substantial achievement or measure of agreement in this enigmatic meeting.

---

[17] *Chron. Maj.* II, 606. [18] *Rot. Litt. Pat.* p. 149.
[19] 'articulis pacis contradixit' (*Chronicle of Melrose*, ed. A. O. and M. O. Anderson, London, 1936, p. 60).
[20] Professor Painter, however, embarks on a much more imaginative reconstruction of the discussions of the council (Painter, 1949, pp. 337–8). It should be noted here that the instructions for the restoration of Colchester to William de Lanvallei are in fact undated and are sandwiched between entries of 27–28 July (*Rot. Litt. Pat.* p. 151).

SELECT DOCUMENTS ILLUSTRATIVE
OF THE HISTORY OF
MAGNA CARTA, 1215

(1) *Agreement between King John and Robert fitz Walter, Marshal of the Army of God, and others concerning the custody of London* (P.R.O. Chancery Miscellanea, 34/1/1) (see pl. 10).

Hec est conventio facta inter dominum Johannem regem Anglie, ex una parte, et Robertum filium Walteri, marescallum exercitus Dei et sancte ecclesie in Anglia, et Ricardum comitem de Clara, Gaufridum comitem Essex' [et] Glouc', Rogerum Bigot comitem Northfolc' et Suthfolc', Saherum comitem Wint', Robertum comitem Oxon', Henricum comitem Hereford', et barones subscriptos, scilicet Willielmum Mariscallum juniorem, Eustachium de Vescy, Willielmum de Mobray, Johannem filium Roberti, Rogerum de Monte Begonis, Willielmum de Lanvalai, et alios comites et barones et liberos homines totius regni, ex altera parte, videlicet quod ipsi comites et barones et alii prescripti tenebunt civitatem London' de ballio domini regis, salvis interim domino regi firmis, redditibus et claris debitis suis, usque ad assumptionem beate Marie anno regni ipsius regis xvii^{mo}, et dominus Cantuar' tenebit similiter de ballio domini regis turrim London' usque ad predictum terminum, salvis civitati London' libertatibus suis et liberis consuetudinibus suis, et salvo cuilibet jure suo in custodia turris London', et ita quod interim non ponat dominus rex munitionem vel vires alias in civitate predicta vel in turri London'. Fiant etiam infra predictum terminum sacramenta per totam Angliam viginti quinque baronibus sicut continetur in carta de libertatibus et securitate regno concessis vel attornatis viginti quinque baronum sicut continetur in literis de duodecim militibus eligendis ad delendum malas consuetudines de forestis et aliis. Et preterea infra eundem terminum omnia que comites et barones et alii liberi homines petunt a domino rege que ipse dixerit esse reddenda vel que per xxv barones aut per majorem partem eorum judicata fuerint esse reddenda reddantur secundum formam predicte carte. Et si hec facta fuerint vel per dominum regem non steterit quo minus ista facta fuerint infra predictum terminum tunc civitas et turris London' ad eundem terminum statim reddantur domino regi salvis predicte civitati libertatibus suis et liberis consuetudinibus suis sicut prescriptum est. Et si hec facta non fuerint et per dominum regem steterit quod ista non fiant infra predictum terminum barones tenebunt civitatem predictam et dominus archiepiscopus turrim London' donec predicta compleantur. Et interim omnes ex utraque parte recuperabunt castra, terras et villas quas habuerunt in initio guerre orte inter dominum regem et barones.

(2) *Letters Testimonial of Magna Carta of Stephen Langton, archbishop of Canterbury, and others* (Collins, 1948, pl. 13, from *The Red Book of the Exchequer*).

Omnibus Christi fidelibus ad quos presens scriptum pervenerit, Stephanus Dei gracia Cantuariensis archiepiscopus, tocius Anglie primas et sancte Romane ecclesie cardinalis, Henricus, eadem gracia Dublinensis archiepiscopus, Willelmus Londoniensis, Petrus Wintoniensis, Joscelinus Bathoniensis et Glastoniensis, Hugo Lincolniensis, Walterus Wigorniensis, Willelmus Coventriensis et Benedictus Roffensis, divina miseracione episcopi, et magister Pandulfus domini pape subdiaconus et familiaris, salutem in Domino. Sciatis nos inspexisse cartam quam dominus noster Johannes illustris rex Anglie fecit comitibus, baronibus et liberis hominibus suis Anglie de libertate sancte ecclesie et libertatibus et liberis consuetudinibus suis eisdem ab eo concessis sub hac forma.

[The text of Magna Carta then follows.]

Et ne huic forme predicte aliquid possit addi vel ab eadem aliquid possit subtrahi vel minui, huic scripto sigilla nostra apposuimus.

(3) *Charter of 9 May 1215 announcing the conditions under which the king was giving terms to the barons (Rot. Chartarum, p. 209b).*

Johannes Dei gratia Rex Angliae etc. omnibus Christi fidelibus presentem cartam inspecturis salutem. Sciatis quod concessimus quod ponemus nos super quatuor barones nostros Anglie ex parte nostra quos elegemus, et barones nobis adversantes ponant se super quatuor alios quos eligent ex parte sua, ita quod dominus Papa sit supra illos de omnibus questionibus et articulis que petunt a nobis et que ipsi proponent, et ad que nos respondebimus quod nos stabimus per eorum consideracionem et faciemus id quod ipsi consi-derabunt inter nos super predictis, ita quod non teneamur ante consideracionem factam ad aliqua de hiis que prolocuta sunt inter nos et a nobis oblata, salvis nobis interim finibus, debitis, serviciis et omnibus sicut habuimus ante discordiam inter nos motam. Et interim in hujus rei testimonium hanc cartam nostram inde fieri fecimus. Teste me ipso apud Wyndesoram, ix die Maii anno regni nostri sextodecimo.

(4) *Letters patent of 10 May 1215 announcing the king's terms to the barons (Rot. Litt. Pat. p. 141).*

Rex omnibus ad quos littere presentes pervenerint salu-tem. Sciatis nos concessisse baronibus nostris qui contra nos sunt quod nec eos nec homines suos capiemus nec dissaisie-mus nec super eos per vim vel per arma ibimus nisi per legem regni nostri vel per judicium parium suorum in curia nostra, donec consideracio facta fuerit per quatuor quos eligemus ex parte nostra et per quatuor quos eligent ex parte sua et dominum Papam qui superior erit super eos, et de hoc securitatem eis faciemus quam poterimus et quam debebi-mus per barones nostros. Et interim volumus quod episcopi

Londoniensis, Wygorniensis, Cestrensis, Roffensis et W. Comes Warenne interim eos securos faciant de predictis. Et si forte contra aliquod interceptum fuerit, infra competens tempus per predictos octo emendetur. Et in hujus rei testimonium has litteras nostras patentes eis fieri fecimus. Apud Windesoram x die Maii anno regni nostri sextodecimo.

(5) *Letters patent from the king to Stephen Haringod of 18 June 1215 (Rot. Litt. Pat. p. 143b).*

Rex Stephano Harengod etc. Sciatis quod firma pax facta est per Dei gratiam inter nos et barones nostros die Veneris proximo post festum Sancte Trinitatis apud Runemed', prope Stanes; ita quod eorum homagia eodem die ibidem cepimus. Unde vobis mandamus firmiter precipientes quod sicut nos et honorem nostrum diligitis et pacem regni nostri, ne ulterius turbetur, quod nullum malum de cetero faciatis baronibus nostris vel aliis, vel fieri permittatis, occasione discordie prius orte inter nos et eos. Mandamus etiam vobis quod de finibus et tenseriis nobis factis occasione illius discordie, si quid superest reddendum ultra predictam diem Veneris, nichil capiatis. Et si quid post illum diem Veneris cepistis, illud statim reddatis. Et corpora prisonum et obsidum captorum et detentorum occasione hujus guerre, vel finium vel tenseriarum predictarum, sine dilatione deliberetis. Hec omnia predicta, sicut corpus vestrum diligitis, faciatis. Et in hujus rei testimonium has litteras nostras patentes vobis mittimus. Teste meipso apud Runemed', xviij die Junii anno regni nostri xvij.

(6) *General letters patent from the king to his bailiffs of 19 June 1215 (Rot. Litt. Pat. p. 180b).*

Rex vicecomiti, forestariis, warennariis, custodibus ripariarum et omnibus baillivis suis in comitatu (   ) salutem. Sciatis pacem firmam esse reformatam per Dei gratiam inter nos et barones et liberos homines regni nostri, sicut audire poteritis et videre per cartam nostram quam inde fieri fecimus, quam etiam legi publice precepimus per totam bailliam vestram et firmiter teneri; volentes et districte precipientes quod tu, vicecomes, omnes de baillia tua secundum formam carte predicte jurare facias xxv baronibus de quibus mentio fit in carta predicta, ad mandatum eorundem vel majoris partis eorum, coram ipsis vel illis quos ad hoc atornaverint per litteras suas patentes, et ad diem et locum quos ad hoc faciendum prefixerint predicti barones vel atornati ab eis ad hoc. Volumus etiam et precipimus quod xii milites de comitatu tuo, qui eligentur de ipso comitatu in primo comitatu qui tenebitur post susceptionem litterarum istarum in partibus tuis, jurent de inquirendis pravis consuetudinibus tam de vicecomitibus quam eorum ministris, forestis, forestariis, warennis et warennariis, ripariis et earum custodibus, et eis delendis, sicut in ipsa carta continetur. Vos igitur omnes, sicut nos et honorem nostrum diligitis, et pacem regni nostri, omnia in carta contenta inviolabiliter observetis et ab omnibus observari faciatis, ne pro defectu vestri, aut per excessum vestrum, pacem regni nostri, quod Deus avertat, iterum turbari contingat. Et tu, vicecomes, pacem nostram per totam bailliam tuam clamari facias et firmiter teneri precipias. Et in hujus rei testimonium has litteras nostras patentes vobis mittimus. Teste me ipso apud Runimede, xix die Junii, anno regni nostri xvij^{mo}.

Memorandum quod unum par literarum patencium de predicta forma de Ebor' liberatum fuit Philippo filio Johannis de Ebor'. Aliud par de Wigorn' W. Wigorn' episcopo. Item Willelmo de Lesnes clerico domini Bathon' duo paria literarum scilicet Dors' et Sumerset'. Item unum par majori et vicecomitibus London'. Item unum par Engelardo de Cygoin'. Item Comiti Winton' duo paria Leic' Warewic'. Eustachio de Vescy Northumberland. Henrico de Ver Linc', Norf', Suff', Notingham, Dereby, Lanc', Cumberland, Cantebr', Hunted', Essex', Cornub', Kanc'. Item domino Linc' episcopo die Sancti Johannis Baptiste [24 June] unum par in comitatu Oxon' et unum par de Bedeford'. Item eidem due carte. Item domino Wigorn' Episcopo unam cartam. Item Magistro Elye de Derham quatuor cartas et eidem duodecim brevia scilicet de Roteland', baronibus de Quinque portubus, Berkesir', Stafford', Sussex', Devon', Norhamt', Surreya, Suhamt', Salop', Westmeriland', Bukingeh'. Item apud Oxon' die Mercurie in festo Sancte Marie Magdalene [22 July] liberatum Magistro Elye de Derham sex carte.

(7) *Letters close from the king to William, earl of Salisbury, of* 19 *June* 1215 (*Rot. Litt. Claus.* I, 215).

Rex Willelmo Comiti Sarr' salutem. Sciatis quod pax hoc modo reformata est inter nos et barones nostros quod nos statim reddemus omnes terras et castra et jura unde nos dissaisiri fecimus aliquem injuste et sine judicio. Nos autem respectum petentes a Comite Hereford' de terris suis reddendis unde fecimus ipsum dissaisiri, non potuimus inpetrare respectum de planis terris, sed tantum de castro de Trobrigg' respectum habemus usque ad diem Dominicam proximam post festum Sancti Johannis Baptiste [28 June]. Et ideo vobis mandamus quod de omnibus planis terris suis quarum saisinam habetis per preceptum nostrum eidem comiti vel nuncio suo presencium latori plenam saisinam sine dilatione habere faciatis. Teste me ipso apud Windlesor' xix die Junii.

(8) *Letters patent to the custodians of the castle of York,* 19 *June* 1215 (*Rot. Litt. Pat.* p. 143b).

Rex custodibus castri Ebor' salutem. Mandamus vobis quod sine dilacione liberetis dilecto et fideli nostro Willelmo de Moubray vel certo nuncio suo castrum de Ebor' custodiendum donec inquisierimus utrum custodia ipsius castri eum hereditarie contingat necne. Et in hujus rei testimonium has litteras nostras patentes vobis mittimus. Teste ut supra [19 June at Runnymede].

(9) *Letters close of 21 June 1215 to the sheriff of Yorkshire* (*Rot. Litt. Claus.* I, 215).

Rex vicecomiti Ebor' salutem. Precipimus tibi quod statim visis literis istis inquiras per bonos homines de comitatu tuo et nobis scire facias si inquisicio facta fuit in comitatu Ebor' de custodia castri Ebor' et de custodia foresterie comitatus ejusdem et de manerio de Pokelinton, unde Willelmus de Munbray clamat habere custodias predicti castri et foresterie predicte jure hereditario et predictum manerium in dominico unde dicit inquisicionem factam fuisse. Inquiras etiam diligenter et sine dilatione per quos inquisicio illa facta fuit et quando et per que verba et ubi et per cujus preceptum et inquisicionem istam quam de novo facturus es nobis mittas sub sigillis eorum per quos inquisicio illa facta fuit. Teste ut supra [21 June at Windsor].

(10) *Letters patent from the king to Hugh de Boves of 23 June 1215* (*Rot. Litt. Pat.* p. 144).

Rex Hugoni de Bova, salutem. Mandamus vobis quod in fide qua nobis tenemini non retineatis aliquem de militibus vel servientibus qui fuerunt apud Dovr', sed in patriam suam in pace sine dilatione ire faciatis. Et in hujus rei testimonium has litteras nostras patentes vobis mittimus. Teste meipso apud Runimed' xxiij die Junii anno regni nostri xvij^{mo}.

(11) *Letters patent from the king to all sheriffs of 27 June 1215* (*Rot. Litt. Pat.* p. 145*b*).

Rex vicecomiti Warewic' et duodecim militibus electis in eodem comitatu ad inquirendum et delendum pravas consuetudines de vicecomitibus et eorum ministris, forestis et forestariis, warennis et warennariis, ripariis et earum custodibus, salutem. Mandamus vobis quod statim et sine dilatione saisietis in manum nostram terras et tenementa et catalla omnium illorum de comitatu Warewic' qui jurare contradixerint viginti quinque baronibus secundum formam contentam in carta nostra de libertatibus vel eis quos ad hoc atornaverint. Et si jurare noluerint statim post quindecim dies completos postquam terre et tenementa et catalla eorum in manu nostra saisita fuerint, omnia catalla sua vendi faciatis et denarios inde perceptos salvo custodiatis, deputandos subsidio terre sancte. Terras autem et tenementa eorum in manu nostra teneatis, quousque juraverint. Et hoc provisum est per judicium domini Cantuar' archiepiscopi et baronum regni nostri. Et in hujus rei testimonium has litteras nostras patentes vobis mittimus. Teste meipso, apud Winton' xxvij die Junii anno regni nostri xvij^{mo}.

Idem mandatum est omnibus vicecomitibus Anglie.

(12) *Letters patent from the king to the barons and others of Yorkshire of 23 July* 1215 (*Rot. Litt. Pat.* p. 150).

Rex comitibus, baronibus, vicecomitibus, militibus, libere tenentibus et omnibus aliis de comitatu Ebor' salutem. Mandamus vobis quod sicut diligitis vos et omnia vestra statim visis literis istis terras et tenementa, castra et municiones que abstulistis tempore guerre vel post, illis quibus ea abstulistis reddatis infra festum Assumpcionis Beate Marie proximo instans [15 August] sicut in reformacione pacis continetur. De catallis autem ablatis tempore quo scivistis treugas fuisse captas inter nos et barones nostros vel postquam pax fuit inter nos reformata et jurata, eis quibus ablata fuerint plene satisfaciatis. Et reddatis prisones qui tempore pacis facte capti tenebantur et quod de redempcionibus vel tenseriis tunc restabat solvendum penitus condonetis. Et si quid de redempcionibus vel tenseriis post pacem factam cepistis, illis inde satisfaciatis quibus est satisfaciendum. Quia in reformacione pacis ita convenit. Quod nisi feceritis, nos ita ad vos et tenementa vestra nos capiemus quod gravatos vos sencietis. Quia nolumus quod occasione detencionis aliquorum predictorum contra formam predictam pax in aliquo turbetur vel violetur. Teste me ipso apud Oxoniam, xxiii die Julii anno regni nostri septimo decimo.

(13) *Letters of Stephen Langton, archbishop of Canterbury, and others concerning the barons' fealty to King John* [no date] (*Rot. Litt. Pat.* p. 181).

Omnibus Christi fidelibus etc., Stephanus, Dei gracia Cantuar' archiepiscopus, totius Anglie primas et sancte Romane ecclesie cardinalis, Henricus Dublin' archiepiscopus, Willelmus London', Petrus Winton', Joscelinus Bathon' et Glaston', Hugo Lincoln', Walterus Wigorn', Willielmus Coventr', Ricardus Cicestr', episcopi et magister Pandulfus domini Pape subdiaconus et familiaris, salutem. Noverit universitas vestra, quod quando facta fuit pax inter dominum regem Johannem et barones Anglie de discordia inter eos orta, idem barones, nobis presentibus et audientibus, promiserunt domino regi, quod quamcumque securitatem habere vellet ab eis de pace illa observanda, ipsi ei habere facerent, preter castella et obsides. Postea vero quando dominus rex petiit ab eis, ut talem cartam ei facerent:

Omnibus etc. Sciatis nos astrictos esse per sacramenta et homagia domino nostro Johanni regi Anglie, de fide ei servanda de vita et membris et terreno honore suo, contra omnes homines qui vivere possint et mori; et ad jura sua et heredum suorum, et ad regnum suum custodiendum et defendendum—

ipsi id facere noluerunt. Et in hujus rei testimonium id ipsum per hoc scriptum protestamur.

(14) *Letters of Stephen Langton, archbishop of Canterbury, and others concerning the execution of cap. 48 of Magna Carta* [no date] (*Foedera*, I, part I, 134).

Omnibus Christi fidelibus ad quos presentes littere pervenerint, Stephanus, Dei gracia Cantuar' archiepiscopus, tocius Anglie primas et sancte Romane ecclesie cardinalis et H. eadem gracia archiepiscopus Dublin', W. quoque London', P. Winton', J. Bathon' et Glaston', H. Lincoln', W. Wygorn', et W. Coventr', ejusdem gracie dono episcopi, salutem in Domino. Cum dominus rex concesserit et per

cartam suam confirmaverit, quod omnes male consuetudines de forestis, et forestariis et eorum ministris, statim
inquirantur in quolibet comitatu, per duodecim milites
juratos de eodem comitatu, qui debent eligi per probos
homines ejusdem comitatus, et infra xl dies post inquisitionem factam penitus, ita quod nunquam revocentur, deleantur per eosdem; dum tamen dominus rex hoc prius sciat;
universitati vestre notum fieri volumus, quod articulus iste
ita intellectus fuit ex utraque parte, quando de eo tractaba-
tur, et expressus, quod omnes consuetudines ille remanere
debent, sine quibus foreste servari non possint, et hoc
presentibus litteris protestamur.

(15) *Letters of Geoffrey de Mandeville, earl of Essex and
Gloucester, and others to Brian de Lisle of 30 September 1215
(B.J.R.L., xxviii, 443).*

Galfridus de Mandevill', comes Essex' et Glovern', et
Saherus, comes Wynton', et Ricardus de Clara, comes de
Hertford', Briano de Insula salutem. Mandamus tibi quod,
visis litteris istis, teneatis iuramentum quod fecistis ad sectam
commune carte regni, ita quod reddatis Nicholao de Stotevill' castellum de Knaresburgh' quod ei adiudicatum est ut
ius suum per viginti quinque barones. Et, nisi feceritis, non
habeatis amodo in nobis fiduciam, nec de corpore vestro nec
de terris nec de catallis, quoniam omnes qui contradicunt
huic iudicio et huic mandato contra iudicium et ius regni
sunt. Teste Roberto de Verr', comite Oxon', apud Londonias tricesimo die Septembris anno Incarnacionis Domini
MCCXV.

(16) *Letters of Geoffrey de Mandeville, earl of Essex and
Gloucester, and others to Robert de Ros of 30 September 1215
(B.J.R.L. xxviii, 443).*

Galfridus de Mandevill' comes Essex' et Glovern', et
Saherus, comes Wynton', et Ricardus de Clara, comes
Hertford', Roberto de Roos custodi Everwykeschir' salu-

tem. Mandamus vobis quatinus illos in bailliva vestra, exceptis illis quos mandavimus venire nobis pro negocio regni, faciatis cum toto conamine adiuvare Nicholao de Stotevill' ad distringendum et ad gravandum illos de castello de Knaresburgh', sicut visum vobis erit utilius ei et patrie. Teste Roberto de Verr', comite Oxon', apud Londonias tricesimo die Septembris anno Incarnacionis Domini MCCXV.

MAGNA CARTA, 1225

The conventional numbering of the clauses in the 1225 text has been followed. The main variants of the 1216 and 1217 versions have been noted, but no attempt has been made to collate minor variations (Bémont, 1892, pp. 45–60, *Statutes of the Realm*, 1, 14–19, 22–5).

Henricus Dei gratia rex Anglie, dominus Hybernie, dux Normannie, Aquitanie et comes Andegavie, archiepiscopis, episcopis, abbatibus, prioribus, comitibus, baronibus, vicecomitibus, prepositis, ministris et omnibus ballivis et fidelibus suis presentem cartam inspecturis salutem. Sciatis[1]

---

[1] The 1216 version here reads: 'Sciatis nos, intuitu Dei et pro salute anime nostre et omnium antecessorum et successorum nostrorum, ad honorem Dei et exaltationem sancte ecclesie et emendationem regni nostri, per consilium venerabilium patrum nostrorum domini Gualonis tituli sancti Martini presbiteri cardinalis, apostolice sedis legati, Petri Wintoniensis, Reineri de Sancto Asapho, Jocelini Batthoniensis et Glastoniensis, Simonis Exoniensis, Ricardi Cicestrensis, Willelmi Coventrensis, Benedicti Roffensis, Henrici Landavensis, Menevensis, Bangorensis et Sylvestri Wygorniensis episcoporum, et nobilium virorum Willelmi Mariscalli, comitis Penbrocie, Ranulfi comitis Cestrie, Willelmi de Ferrariis comitis Derebie, Willelmi comitis Albemarle, Huberti de Burgo justiciarii nostri, Savarici de Maloleone, Willelmi Brigwerre patris, Willelmi Brigwerre filii, Roberti de Curtenay, Falkesii de Breaute, Reginaldi de Vautort, Walteri de Lascy, Rogeri de Clifford, Hugonis de Mortuomari, Johannis de Monemute, Walteri de Bellocampo, Walteri de Clifford, Roberti de Mortuomari, Willelmi de Cantilupo, Mathei filii Hereberti, Johannis Mariscalli, Alani Basset, Philippi de Albiniaco, Johannis Extranei et aliorum fidelium nostrorum, inprimis concessisse Deo et hac presenti carta confirmasse . . . .'
The 1217 version reads: 'Sciatis quod, intuitu Dei et pro salute anime nostre et animarum antecessorum et successorum nostrorum, ad exaltationem sancte ecclesie et emendationem regni nostri, concessimus et hac presenti carta confirmavimus pro nobis et heredibus nostris in perpetuum, de consilio venerabilis patris nostri domini Gualonis tituli Sancti Martini presbiteri cardinalis et apostolice sedis legati, domini Walteri Eboracensis archiepiscopi, Willelmi Londoniensis episcopi et aliorum episcoporum Anglie, et Willelmi Mariscalli comitis Pembrocie, rectoris nostri et regni nostri, et aliorum fidelium, comitum et baronum nostrorum Anglie, has libertates subscriptas tenendas in regno nostro Anglie in perpetuum.'

quod nos, intuitu Dei et pro salute anime nostre et animarum antecessorum et successorum nostrorum, ad exaltationem sancte ecclesie et emendationem regni nostri, spontanea et bona voluntate nostra, dedimus et concessimus archiepiscopis, episcopis, abbatibus, prioribus, comitibus, baronibus et omnibus de regno nostro has libertates subscriptas tenendas in regno nostro Anglie in perpetuum.

1. In primis concessimus Deo et hac presenti carta nostra confirmavimus pro nobis et heredibus nostris in perpetuum quod Anglicana ecclesia libera sit, et habeat omnia jura sua integra et libertates suas illesas. Concessimus etiam omnibus liberis hominibus regni nostri pro nobis et heredibus nostris in perpetuum omnes libertates subscriptas, habendas et tenendas eis et heredibus suis de nobis et heredibus nostris in perpetuum. [1215, c. 1.]

2. Si quis comitum vel baronum nostrorum sive aliorum tenencium de nobis in capite per servicium militare mortuus fuerit, et, cum decesserit, heres ejus plene etatis fuerit et relevium debeat, habeat hereditatem suam per antiquum relevium, scilicet heres vel heredes comitis de baronia comitis integra per centum libras, heres vel heredes baronis de baronia integra per centum libras, heres vel heredes militis de feodo militis integro per centum solidos ad plus; et qui minus debuerit minus det secundum antiquam consuetudinem feodorum. [1215, c. 2.]

3. Si autem heres alicujus talium fuerit infra etatem, dominus ejus non habeat custodiam ejus nec terre sue antequam homagium ejus ceperit; et, postquam talis heres fuerit in custodia, cum ad etatem pervenerit, scilicet viginti et unius anni, habeat hereditatem suam sine relevio et sine fine, ita tamen quod, si ipse, dum infra etatem fuerit, fiat miles, nichilominus terra remaneat in custodia dominorum suorum usque ad terminum predictum. [1215, c. 3.]

4. Custos terre hujusmodi heredis qui infra etatem fuerit non capiat de terra heredis nisi rationabiles exitus et rationabiles consuetudines et rationabilia servicia, et hoc sine des-

tructione et vasto hominum vel rerum; et si nos commiserimus custodiam alicujus talis terre vicecomiti vel alicui alii qui de exitibus terre illius nobis debeat respondere, et ille destructionem de custodia fecerit vel vastum, nos ab illo capiemus emendam, et terra committetur duobus legalibus et discretis hominibus de feodo illo qui de exitibus nobis respondeant vel ei cui eos assignaverimus; et si dederimus vel vendiderimus alicui custodiam alicujus talis terre, et ille destructionem inde fecerit vel vastum, amittat ipsam custodiam et tradatur duobus legalibus et discretis hominibus de feodo illo qui similiter nobis respondeant, sicut predictum est. [1215, c. 4.]

5. Custos autem, quamdiu custodiam terre habuerit, sustentet domos, parcos, vivaria, stagna, molendina et cetera ad terram illam pertinencia de exitibus terre ejusdem, et reddat heredi, cum ad plenam etatem pervenerit, terram suam totam instauratam de carucis et omnibus aliis rebus, ad minus secundum quod illam recepit. Hec omnia observentur de custodiis archiepiscopatuum, episcopatuum, abbatiarum, prioratuum, ecclesiarum et dignitatum vacancium que ad nos pertinent, excepto quod hujusmodi custodie vendi non debent. [1215, c. 5.]

6. Heredes maritentur absque disparagatione. [1215, c. 6.]

7. Vidua post mortem mariti sui statim et sine difficultate aliqua habeat maritagium suum et hereditatem suam, nec aliquid det pro dote sua vel pro maritagio suo vel pro hereditate sua, quam hereditatem maritus suus et ipsa tenuerunt die obitus ipsius mariti, et maneat in capitali mesagio ipsius mariti sui per quadraginta dies post obitum ipsius mariti sui, infra quos assignetur ei dos sua, nisi prius ei fuerit assignata, vel nisi domus illa sit castrum; et si de castro recesserit, statim provideatur ei domus competens in qua possit honeste morari, quousque dos sua ei assignetur secundum quod predictum est; et habeat rationabile estoverium suum interim de communi. Assignetur autem ei pro dote sua tercia pars tocius terre mariti sui que sua fuit in vita sua, nisi

de minori dotata fuerit ad hostium ecclesie.² Nulla vidua
distringatur ad se maritandam, dum vivere voluerit sine
marito, ita tamen quod securitatem faciet quod se non
maritabit sine assensu nostro, si de nobis tenuerit, vel sine
assensu domini sui, si de alio tenuerit. [1215, cc. 7, 8.]

8. Nos vero vel ballivi nostri non seisiemus terram
aliquam nec redditum pro debito aliquo quamdiu catalla
debitoris presencia sufficiant ad debitum reddendum et ipse
debitor paratus sit inde satisfacere; nec plegii ipsius debitoris
distringantur quamdiu ipse capitalis debitor sufficiat ad
solutionem debiti; et, si capitalis debitor defecerit in solutione debiti, non habens unde reddat, aut reddere nolit cum
possit, plegii respondeant pro debito; et, si voluerint,
habeant terras et redditus debitoris quousque sit eis satisfactum de debito quod ante pro eo solverunt, nisi capitalis
debitor monstraverit se inde esse quietum versus eosdem
plegios. [1215, c. 9.]

9. Civitas London' habeat omnes antiquas libertates et
liberas consuetudines suas. Preterea volumus et concedimus
quod omnes alie civitates, et burgi, et ville, et barones de
Quinque Portubus, et omnes portus, habeant omnes libertates et liberas consuetudines suas. [1215, c. 13.]

10. Nullus distringatur ad faciendum majus servicium de
feodo militis nec de alio libero tenemento quam inde
debetur. [1215, c. 16.]

11. Communia placita non sequantur curiam nostram,
set teneantur in aliquo loco certo. [1215, c. 17.]

12. Recognitiones de nova disseisina et de morte antecessoris non capiantur nisi in suis comitatibus, et hoc modo:
nos, vel si extra regnum fuerimus, capitalis justiciarius
noster, mittemus justiciarios per unumquemque comitatum
semel in anno, qui cum militibus comitatuum capiant in
comitatibus assisas predictas. Et ea que in illo adventu suo in
comitatu per justiciarios predictos ad dictas assisas capiendas

---

² 1216 omits 'et habeat . . . hostium ecclesie'.

missos terminari non possunt, per eosdem terminentur alibi in itinere suo; et ea que per eosdem propter difficultatem aliquorum articulorum terminari non possunt, referantur ad justiciarios nostros de banco et ibi terminentur.[3] [1215, c. 18.]

13. Assise de ultima presentatione semper capiantur coram justiciariis nostris de banco et ibi terminentur.

14. Liber homo non amercietur pro parvo delicto nisi secundum modum ipsius delicti, et pro magno delicto, secundum magnitudinem delicti, salvo contenemento suo; et mercator eodem modo salva mercandisa sua; et villanus alterius quam noster[4] eodem modo amercietur salvo wainagio suo, si inciderit in misericordiam nostram; et nulla predictarum misericordiarum ponatur nisi per sacramentum proborum et legalium hominum de visneto. Comites et barones non amercientur nisi per pares suos, et non nisi secundum modum delicti. Nulla ecclesiastica persona amercietur secundum quantitatem beneficii sui ecclesiastici, set secundum laicum tenementum suum, et secundum quantitatem delicti.[5] [1215, cc. 20–2.]

15. Nec villa, nec homo, distringatur facere pontes ad riparias nisi qui ex antiquo et de jure facere debet. [1215, c. 23.]

16. Nulla riparia decetero defendatur, nisi ille que fuerunt in defenso tempore regis Henrici avi nostri, per eadem loca et eosdem terminos sicut esse consueverunt tempore suo.[6] [1215, c. 47.]

17. Nullus vicecomes, constabularius, coronatores vel alii ballivi nostri teneant placita corone nostre. [1215, c. 24.]

18. Si aliquis tenens de nobis laicum feodum moriatur, et vicecomes vel ballivus noster ostendat litteras nostras patentes de summonitione nostra de debito quod defunctus

---

[3] 1217 has the same reading. 1216 follows 1215.
[4] 1217 has the same reading. 1216 follows 1215.
[5] 1217 has the same reading. 1216 follows 1215 with some slight omissions.
[6] 1216 omits c. 16.

nobis debuit, liceat vicecomiti vel ballivo nostro attachiare et inbreviare catalla defuncti inventa in laico feodo ad valenciam illius debiti per visum legalium hominum, ita tamen quod nichil inde amoveatur donec persolvatur nobis debitum quod clarum fuerit, et residuum relinquatur executoribus ad faciendum testamentum defuncti; et si nichil nobis debeatur ab ipso, omnia catalla cedant defuncto, salvis uxori ipsius et pueris suis rationabilibus partibus suis. [1215, c. 26.]

19. Nullus constabularius vel ejus ballivus capiat blada vel alia catalla alicujus qui non sit de villa ubi castrum situm est, nisi statim inde reddat denarios aut respectum inde habere possit de voluntate venditoris; si autem de villa ipsa fuerit, infra quadraginta dies precium reddat.[7] [1215, c. 28.]

20. Nullus constabularius distringat aliquem militem ad dandum denarios pro custodia castri, si ipse eam facere voluerit in propria persona sua, vel per alium probum hominem, si ipse eam facere non possit propter rationabilem causam, et, si nos duxerimus eum vel miserimus in exercitum, erit quietus de custodia secundum quantitatem temporis quo per nos fuerit in exercitu de feodo pro quo fecit servicium in exercitu.[8] [1215, c. 29.]

21. Nullus vicecomes, vel ballivus noster, vel alius capiat equos vel carettas alicujus pro cariagio faciendo, nisi reddat liberationem antiquitus statutam, scilicet pro caretta ad duos equos decem denarios per diem, et pro caretta ad tres equos quatuordecim denarios per diem. Nulla caretta dominica alicujus ecclesiastice persone vel militis vel alicujus domine capiatur per ballivos predictos.[9]

Nec nos nec ballivi nostri nec alii[10] capiemus alienum boscum ad castra vel alia agenda nostra, nisi per voluntatem illius cujus boscus ille fuerit. [1215, cc. 30, 31.]

22. Nos non tenebimus terras eorum qui convicti fuerint

---

[7] 1216 reads: 'si autem de villa fuerit, teneatur infra tres septimanas precium reddere'.
[8] 1216 omits 'de feodo . . . in exercitu'.
[9] 1216 omits 'Nulla caretta . . . ballivos predictos'.   [10] 1216 here follows 1215.

de felonia, nisi per unum annum et unum diem; et tunc reddantur terre dominis feodorum. [1215, c. 32.]

23. Omnes kidelli decetero deponantur penitus per Tamisiam et Medeweiam et per totam Angliam, nisi per costeram maris. [1215, c. 33.]

24. Breve quod vocatur 'Precipe' decetero non fiat alicui de aliquo tenemento, unde liber homo perdat[11] curiam suam. [1215, c. 34.]

25. Una mensura vini sit per totum regnum nostrum, et una mensura cervisie, et una mensura bladi, scilicet quarterium London', et una latitudo pannorum tinctorum et russettorum et haubergettorum, scilicet due ulne infra listas; de ponderibus vero sit ut de mensuris. [1215, c. 35.]

26. Nichil detur decetero pro brevi inquisitionis ab eo qui inquisitionem petit de vita vel membris, set gratis concedatur et non negetur.[12] [1215, c. 36.]

27. Si aliquis teneat de nobis per feodifirmam vel soccagium, vel per burgagium, et de alio terram teneat per servicium militare, nos non habebimus custodiam heredis nec terre sue que est de feodo alterius, occasione illius feodifirme, vel soccagii, vel burgagii, nec habebimus custodiam illius feodifirme vel soccagii vel burgagii, nisi ipsa feodifirma debeat servicium militare. Nos non habebimus custodiam heredis nec terre alicujus quam tenet de alio per servicium militare, occasione alicujus parve serjanterie quam tenet de nobis per servicium reddendi nobis cultellos, vel sagittas, vel hujusmodi. [1215, c. 37.]

28. Nullus ballivus ponat decetero aliquem ad legem manifestam vel ad juramentum[13] simplici loquela sua, sine testibus fidelibus ad hoc inductis. [1215, c. 38.]

29. Nullus liber homo decetero capiatur vel inprisonetur aut disseisiatur de aliquo libero tenemento suo vel libertatibus vel liberis consuetudinibus suis,[14] aut utlagetur, aut

---

[11] 1216 reads 'amittere possit' as in 1215.
[12] 1217 has the same. 1216 follows 1215.   [13] 1216 here follows 1215.
[14] 1216 here follows 1215.

exulet, aut aliquo alio modo destruatur, nec super eum ibimus, nec super eum mittemus, nisi per legale judicium parium suorum, vel per legem terre. Nulli vendemus, nulli negabimus aut differemus rectum vel justiciam. [1215, cc. 39, 40.]

30. Omnes mercatores, nisi publice antea prohibiti fuerint, habeant salvum et securum exire de Anglia, et venire in Angliam, et morari, et ire per Angliam tam per terram quam per aquam ad emendum vel vendendum sine omnibus toltis malis per antiquas et rectas consuetudines, preterquam in tempore gwerre, et si sint de terra contra nos gwerrina; et si tales inveniantur in terra nostra in principio gwerre, attachientur sine dampno corporum vel rerum, donec sciatur a nobis vel a capitali justiciario nostro quomodo mercatores terre nostre tractentur, qui tunc invenientur in terra contra nos gwerrina; et si nostri salvi sint ibi, alii salvi sint in terra nostra. [1215, c. 41.]

31. Si quis tenuerit de aliqua escaeta, sicut de honore Wallingefordie, Bolonie, Notingeham', Lancastrie, vel de aliis que sunt in manu nostra, et sint baronie, et obierit, heres ejus non det aliud relevium nec faciat nobis aliud servicium quam faceret baroni, si ipsa esset in manu baronis; et nos eodem modo eam tenebimus quo baro eam tenuit; nec nos, occasione talis baronie vel escaete, habebimus aliquam escaetam vel custodiam aliquorum hominum nostrorum, nisi alibi tenuerit de nobis in capite ille qui tenuit baroniam vel escaetam.[15] [1215, c. 43.]

32. Nullus liber homo decetero det amplius alicui vel vendat de terra sua quam ut de residuo terre sue possit sufficienter fieri domino feodi servicium ei debitum quod pertinet ad feodum illud.[16]

33. Omnes patroni abbatiarum qui habent cartas regum Anglie de advocatione, vel antiquam tenuram vel possessio-

---

[15] 1216 here follows 1215 and omits 'nec nos ... escaetam'.
[16] 1216 omits and inserts 1215, c. 44.

nem, habeant earum custodiam cum vacaverint, sicut habere debent, et sicut supra declaratum est.[17] [1215, c. 46.]

34. Nullus capiatur vel imprisonetur propter appellum femine de morte alterius quam viri sui. [1215, c. 54.]

35. Nullus comitatus decetero teneatur, nisi de mense in mensem; et, ubi major terminus esse solebat, major sit. Nec aliquis vicecomes vel ballivus faciat turnum suum per hundredum nisi bis in anno et non nisi in loco debito et consueto, videlicet semel post Pascha et iterum post festum sancti Michaelis. Et visus de franco plegio tunc fiat ad illum terminum sancti Michaelis sine occasione, ita scilicet quod quilibet habeat libertates suas quas habuit et habere consuevit tempore regis Henrici avi nostri, vel quas postea perquisivit. Fiat autem visus de franco plegio sic, videlicet quod pax nostra teneatur, et quod tethinga integra sit sicut esse consuevit, et quod vicecomes non querat occasiones, et quod contentus sit eo quod vicecomes habere consuevit de visu suo faciendo tempore regis Henrici avi nostri.[18]

36. Non liceat alicui decetero dare terram suam alicui domui religiose, ita quod eam resumat tenendam de eadem domo, nec liceat alicui domui religiose terram alicujus sic accipere quod tradat illam ei a quo ipsam recepit tenendam. Si quis autem decetero terram suam alicui domui religiose sic dederit, et super hoc convincatur, donum suum penitus cassetur, et terra illa domino suo illius feodi incurratur.[18]

37. Scutagium decetero capiatur sicut capi solebat tempore regis Henrici avi nostri.[18]

Et salve sint archiepiscopis, episcopis, abbatibus, prioribus, templariis, hospitalariis, comitibus, baronibus, et omnibus aliis tam ecclesiasticis quam secularibus personis libertates et libere consuetudines quas prius habuerunt.[19]

Omnes autem istas consuetudines predictas et libertates quas concessimus in regno nostro tenendas quantum ad nos

---

[17] 1216 here follows 1215, but adds 'et sicut . . . est'.
[18] 1216 here omits cc. 35. 36, 37 and inserts 1215, c. 56.
[19] 1216 and 1217 omit 'Et salve . . . habuerunt'.

pertinet erga nostros, omnes de regno nostro tam clerici quam laici observent quantum ad se pertinet erga suos. [1215, c. 60.]

Pro[20] hac autem concessione et donatione libertatum istarum et aliarum libertatum contentarum in carta nostra de libertatibus foreste, archiepiscopi, episcopi, abbates, priores, comites, barones, milites, libere tenentes, et omnes de regno nostro dederunt nobis quintam decimam partem omnium mobilium suorum. Concessimus etiam eisdem pro nobis et heredibus nostris quod nec nos nec heredes nostri aliquid perquiremus per quod libertates in hac carta contente infringantur vel infirmentur; et, si de aliquo aliquid contra hoc perquisitum fuerit, nichil valeat et pro nullo habeatur.

Hiis testibus domino Stephano Cantuariensi archiepiscopo, Eustachio Londoniensi, Jocelino Bathoniensi, Petro Wintoniensi, Hugoni Lincolniensi, Ricardo Sarrisberiensi, Benedicto Roffensi, Willelmo Wigorniensi, Johanne Eliensi, Hugone Herefordiensi, Radulpho Cicestrensi, Willelmo Exoniensi episcopis, abbate sancti Albani, abbate sancti Edmundi, abbate de Bello, abbate sancti Augustini Cantuar-

---

[20] '1216 and 1217 both exclude this final passage.

1216 here reads: 'Quia vero quedam capitula in priori carta continebantur que gravia et dubitabilia videbantur, scilicet de scutagiis et auxiliis assidendis, de debitis Judeorum et aliorum, et de libertate exeundi de regno, vel redeundi in regnum, et de forestis et forestariis, warennis et warennariis, et de consuetudinibus comitatuum, et de ripariis et earum custodibus, placuit supradictis prelatis et magnatibus ea esse in respectu quousque plenius consilium habuerimus; et tunc faciemus plenissime tam de hiis quam de aliis que occurrerint emendanda, que ad communem omnium utilitatem pertinuerint et pacem et statum nostrum et regni nostri. Quia vero sigillum nondum habuimus, presentem cartam sigillis venerabilis patris nostri domini Gualonis tituli sancti Martini presbiteri cardinalis, apostolice sedis legati, et Willelmi Mariscalli comitis Penbrocie, rectoris nostri et regni nostri, fecimus sigillari. Testibus omnibus prenominatis et aliis multis. Datum per manus predictorum domini legati et Willelmi Mariscalli comitis Penbrocie apud Bristollum duodecimo die novembris anno regni nostri primo.'

1217 reads: 'Salvis archiepiscopis, episcopis, abbatibus, prioribus, templariis, hospitalariis, comitibus, baronibus et omnibus aliis tam ecclesiasticis personis quam secularibus, libertatibus et liberis consuetudinibus quas prius habuerunt.

Statuimus etiam, de communi consilio tocius regni nostri, quod omnia castra adulterina, videlicet ea que a principio guerre mote inter dominum Johannem patrem nostrum et barones suos Anglie constructa fuerint vel reedificata, statim diruantur. Quia vero nondum habuimus sigillum, hanc [cartam] sigillis domini legati predicti et comitis Willelmi Mariscalli rectoris [nostri] et regni nostri fecimus sigillari.'

iensis, abbate de Eveshamia, abbate de Westmonasterio, abbate de Burgo sancti Petri, abbate Radingensi, abbate Abbendoniensi, abbate de Maumeburia, abbate de Winchecumba, abbate de Hida, abbate de Certeseia, abbate de Sireburnia, abbate de Cerne, abbate de Abotebiria, abbate de Middletonia, abbate de Seleby, abbate de Wyteby, abbate de Cirencestria, Huberto de Burgo justiciario, Ranulfo comite Cestrie et Lincolnie, Willelmo comite Sarrisberie, Willelmo comite Warennie, Gilberto de Clara comite Gloucestrie et Hertfordie, Willelmo de Ferrariis comite Derbeie, Willelmo de Mandevilla comite Essexie, Hugone le Bigod comite Norfolcie, Willelmo comite Aubemarle, Hunfrido comite Herefordie, Johanne constabulario Cestrie, Roberto de Ros, Roberto filio Walteri, Roberto de Veteri ponte, Willielmo Brigwerre, Ricardo de Munfichet, Petro filio Herberti, Matheo filio Herberti, Willielmo de Albiniaco, Roberto Gresley, Reginaldo de Brahus, Johanne de Munemutha, Johanne filio Alani, Hugone de Mortuomari, Waltero de Bellocampo, Willielmo de sancto Johanne, Petro de Malalacu, Briano de Insula, Thoma de Muletonia, Ricardo de Argentein', Gaufrido de Nevilla, Willielmo Mauduit, Johanne de Baalun.

Datum apud Westmonasterium undecimo die februarii anno regni nostri nono.

CHARTER OF THE FOREST, 1225

The main variants of the 1217 text have been noted but not minor variations (*Statutes of the Realm*, 1, Charters of Liberties, nos. 10, 12).

Henricus Dei gratia rex Anglie, dominus Hibernie, dux Normannie, Aquitanie et comes Andegavie, archiepiscopis, episcopis, abbatibus, prioribus, comitibus, baronibus, justiciariis, forestariis, vicecomitibus, prepositis, ministris, et omnibus ballivis et fidelibus suis presentem cartam inspecturis, salutem. Sciatis quod nos, intuitu Dei et pro salute anime nostre et animarum antecessorum et successorum nostrorum, ad exaltacionem Sancte Ecclesie et emendacionem regni nostri, spontanea et bona voluntate nostra dedimus et concessimus archiepiscopis, episcopis, comitibus, baronibus et omnibus de regno nostro has libertates subscriptas tenendas in regno nostro Anglie in perpetuum.[1]

1. In primis omnes foreste quas Henricus rex avus noster afforestavit videantur per bonos et legales homines; et, si boscum aliquem alium quam suum dominicum afforestaverit ad dampnum illius cujus boscus ille fuerit, deafforestetur. Et si boscum suum proprium afforestaverit, remaneat foresta, salva communa de herbagio et aliis in eadem foresta illis qui eam prius habere consueverunt. [U.C., c. 9; 1215, c. 53.]

---

[1] 1217 here reads: 'concessimus et hac presenti carta confirmavimus pro nobis et heredibus nostris in perpetuum, de consilio venerabilis patris nostri domini Gualonis tituli sancti Martini presbiteri cardinalis et apostolice sedis legati, domini Walteri Eboracensis archiepiscopi, Willelmi Londoniensis episcopi, et aliorum episcoporum Anglie, et Willelmi Marescalli comitis Penbrocie, rectoris nostri et regni nostri, et aliorum fidelium comitum et baronum nostrorum Anglie, has libertates subscriptas tenendas in regno nostro Anglie.'

2. Homines vero qui manent extra forestam non veniant decetero coram justiciariis nostris de foresta per communes summoniciones, nisi sint in placito, vel plegii alicujus vel aliquorum qui attachiati sunt propter forestam. [1215, c. 44.]

3. Omnes autem bosci qui fuerint afforestati per regem Ricardum avunculum nostrum, vel per regem Johannem patrem nostrum usque ad primam coronacionem nostram, statim deafforestentur, nisi sit dominicus boscus noster. [U.C., c. 9; 1215, cc. 47, 53.]

4. Archiepiscopi, episcopi, abbates, priores, comites, barones, milites, libere tenentes, qui habent boscos suos in forestis, habeant boscos suos sicut eos habuerunt tempore prime coronacionis regis Henrici avi nostri, ita quod quieti sint in perpetuum de omnibus purpresturis, vastis et assartis factis in illis boscis, post illud tempus usque ad principium secundi anni coronacionis nostre. Et qui decetero vastum vel purpresturam sine licencia nostra in illis fecerit, vel essartum, de vastis, purpresturis et essartis respondeant. [U.C., c. 10]

5. Reguardores nostri eant per forestas ad faciendum reguardum sicut fieri consuevit tempore prime coronacionis predicti regis Henrici avi nostri, et non aliter.

6. Inquisicio, vel visus de expeditacione canum existencium in foresta, decetero fiat quando debet fieri reguardum, scilicet de tercio anno in tercium annum; et tunc fiat per visum et testimonium legalium hominum et non aliter. Et ille, cujus canis inventus fuerit tunc non expeditatus, det pro misericordia tres solidos; et decetero nullus bos capiatur pro expeditacione. Talis autem sit expeditacio per assisam communiter quod tres ortilli abscidantur sine pelota de pede anteriori; nec expeditentur canes decetero, nisi in locis ubi consueverunt expeditari tempore prime coronacionis predicti regis Henrici avi nostri.

7. Nullus forestarius vel bedellus decetero faciat scotallas, vel colligat garbas, vel avenam, vel bladum aliquid, vel agnos, vel porcellos, nec aliquam collectam faciat; et per visum et sacramentum duodecim reguardorum quando

facient reguardum, tot forestarii ponantur ad forestas custodiendas, quot ad illas custodiendas rationabiliter viderint sufficere.

8. Nullum swanimotum decetero teneatur in regno nostro nisi ter in anno; videlicet in principio quindecim dierum ante festum Sancti Michaelis, quando agistatores nostri conveniunt ad agistandum dominicos boscos nostros; et circa festum Sancti Martini quando agistatores nostri debent recipere pannagium nostrum; et ad ista duo swanimota conveniant forestarii, viridarii, et agistatores, et nulli alii per districtionem; et tercium swanimotum teneatur in inicio quindecim dierum ante festum Sancti Johannis Baptiste, pro feonacione bestiarum nostrarum; et ad illud swanimotum tenendum conveniant forestarii et viridarii et non alii per districtionem. Preterea singulis quadraginta diebus per totum annum conveniant forestarii et viridarii ad faciendum attachiamenta de foresta, tam de viridi, quam de venacione, per presentacionem forestariorum ipsorum, et coram ipsis attachiatis. Predicta autem swanimota non teneantur nisi in comitatibus in quibus teneri consueverunt.

9. Unusquisque liber homo agistet boscum suum quem habet in foresta pro voluntate sua et habeat pannagium suum. Concedimus eciam quod unusquisque liber homo possit ducere porcos suos per dominicum boscum nostrum, libere et sine inpedimento, ad agistandum eos in boscis suis propriis, vel alibi ubi voluerit. Et si porci alicujus liberi hominis una nocte pernoctaverint in foresta nostra, non inde occasionetur ita unde aliquid de suo perdat.

10. Nullus decetero amittat vitam vel membra pro venacione nostra; set, si aliquis captus fuerit et convictus de capcione venacionis, graviter redimatur, si habeat unde redimi possit; si autem non habeat unde redimi possit, jaceat in prisona nostra per unum annum et unum diem; et, si post unum annum et unum diem plegios invenire possit, exeat de prisona; sin autem, abjuret regnum Anglie. [U.C., c. 12.]

11. Quicunque archiepiscopus, episcopus, comes vel baro, veniens ad nos ad mandatum nostrum,[2] transierit per forestam nostram, liceat ei capere unam bestiam vel duas per visum forestarii, si presens fuerit; sin autem, faciat cornari, ne videatur furtive hoc facere. Idem liceat eis in redeundo facere sicut predictum est.[3]

12. Unusquisque liber homo decetero sine occasione faciat in bosco suo, vel in terra sua quam habet in foresta, molendinum, vivarium, stagnum, marleram, fossatum, vel terram arabilem extra coopertum in terra arabili, ita quod non sit ad nocumentum alicujus vicini.

13. Unusquisque liber homo habeat in boscis suis aerias ancipitrum espervariorum, falconum, aquilarum, et de heyrinis, et habeat similiter mel quod inventum fuerit in boscis suis.

14. Nullus forestarius decetero, qui non sit forestarius de feudo firmam nobis reddens pro balliva sua, capiat cheminagium aliquod in balliva sua; forestarius autem de feudo firmam nobis reddens pro balliva sua capiat cheminagium, videlicet pro caretta per dimidium annum duos denarios, et per alium dimidium annum duos denarios, et pro equo qui portat summagium per dimidium annum unum obolum, et per alium dimidium annum obolum, et non nisi de illis qui de extra ballivam suam, tanquam mercatores, veniunt per licenciam suam in ballivam suam ad buscam, meremium, corticem vel carbonem emendum, et alias ducendum ad vendendum ubi voluerint; et de nulla alia caretta vel summagio aliquod cheminagium capiatur: et non capiatur cheminagium nisi in locis in quibus antiquitus capi solebat et debuit. Illi autem qui portant super dorsum suum buscam, corticem, vel carbonem, ad vendendum, quamvis inde vivant, nullum decetero dent cheminagium.[4]

---

[2] 1217 omits 'veniens . . . nostrum'.   [3] 1217 omits 'Idem . . . predictum est'.
[4] 1217 here adds: 'De boscis autem aliorum nullum detur chiminagium foristariis nostris, preterquam de dominicis boscis nostris.'

15. Omnes utlagati pro foresta tantum a tempore regis Henrici avi nostri usque ad primam coronacionem nostram, veniant ad pacem nostram sine inpedimento, et salvos plegios inveniant quod decetero non forisfacient nobis de foresta nostra.

16. Nullus castellanus[5] teneat placita de foresta sive de viridi sive de venacione, set quilibet forestarius de feudo attachiet placita de foresta tam de viridi quam de venacione, et ea presentet viridariis provinciarum; et, cum irrotulata fuerint et sub sigillis viridariorum inclusa, presententur capitali forestario nostro cum in partes illas venerit ad tenendum placita foreste, et coram eo terminentur.

17. Has autem libertates de forestis concessimus omnibus, salvis archiepiscopis, episcopis, abbatibus, prioribus, comitibus, baronibus, militibus et aliis tam personis ecclesiasticis quam secularibus, Templariis et Hospitalariis, libertatibus et liberis consuetudinibus in forestis et extra, in warennis et aliis, quas prius habuerunt. Omnes autem istas consuetudines predictas et libertates, quas concessimus in regno nostro tenendas quantum ad nos pertinet erga nostros, omnes de regno nostro[6] observent quantum ad se pertinet erga suos.

Pro[7] hac igitur concessione et donacione libertatum istarum et aliarum libertatum contentarum in majori carta nostra de aliis libertatibus, archiepiscopi, episcopi, abbates, priores, comites, barones, milites, libere tenentes, et omnes de regno nostro, dederunt nobis quintamdecimam partem omnium mobilium suorum. Concessimus eciam eisdem pro nobis et heredibus nostris quod nec nos nec heredes nostri

---

[5] 1217 inserts 'vel alius'.   [6] 1217 inserts 'tam clerici quam laici'.
[7] 1217 here reads: 'Quia vero sigillum nondum habuimus, presentem cartam sigillis venerabilis patris nostri domini Gualonis tituli Sancti Martini presbiteri cardinalis, apostolice sedis legati, et Willelmi Marescalli comitis Penbrok, rectoris nostri et regni nostri, fecimus sigillari. Testibus prenominatis et aliis multis. Datum per manus predictorum domini legati et Willelmi Marescalli apud Sanctum Paulum London., sexto die Novembris, anno regni nostri secundo.'

aliquid perquiremus per quod libertates in hac carta contente infringantur vel infirmentur; et, si ab aliquo aliquid contra hoc perquisitum fuerit, nichil valeat et pro nullo habeatur. Hiis testibus.[8]

---

[8] The witnesses follow as in M.C.

LIBERTIES AND PERPETUITY

'We have also granted to all the free men of our realm for ourselves and our heirs for ever (*in perpetuum*) all the liberties written below.' Thus cap. 1 of Magna Carta. The words are repeated in cap. 63 in corroboration – 'the men in our realm shall have and hold all the aforesaid liberties . . . for ever (*in perpetuum*), as is aforesaid'. The immediate precedent is contained in the Charter itself. Cap. 1 opens – 'In the first place [we have] granted to God and by this our present charter have confirmed, for us and our heirs in perpetuity, that the English church shall be free . . .', and also – 'we conceded and confirmed by our charter, freedom of elections . . . which we shall observe and wish our heirs to observe in good faith in perpetuity'. Here the Charter repeated John's grant of freedom of election to the church of 21 November 1214 – 'libere sint in perpetuum electiones'.[1] So cap. 1 of the Charter elides very easily from the liberties of the church to the liberties of the realm. It is as if ecclesiastical liberties infected all the rest, the whole placed within the broader notion of free and perpetual alms, the community of freemen viewed as if it were as permanent and undying as the church itself with all its component institutions. If so, the infection was a strong one; all subsequent reissues of the Charter and the Charter of the Forest are grants made in perpetuity.

Similar language was used for individuals – in ordinary grants occasionally, in quitclaims more frequently, in warranty clauses commonly. That apart, the norm was a simple

---

[1] *Stubbs's Charters*, pp. 283–4.

concession from the grantor and his heirs to the recipient and his heirs. Earlier in the Anglo-Norman world hereditary tenure by laymen and perpetual tenure by the church had grown up side by side, the one reinforcing the other in the act of benefaction; indeed the earliest grants to the reformed Norman church were expressed in the language of perpetual inheritance.[2] In time, free and perpetual alms came to express tenure in perpetuity in a sharply defined form. But tenure by the church was not a precondition. Any group or community, ecclesiastical or lay, could hold in perpetuity. Once it did so, it was defined all the clearer. Later, indeed much later, the capacity to do so would become essential to its definition; it would then be a corporation.

These notions were widespread in Europe. Many of the liberties conceded by kings and emperors from the twelfth to the early fourteenth centuries were granted *in perpetuum* or in equivalent terms: the Treaty of Constance of 1183, the *Privilegio General* of Aragon of 1282–3, many of the French provincial charters of 1314–5. In Hungary, the Golden Bull of 1222 provided for the perpetual right of resistance to the Crown.[3] In Italy, in 1263, Pope Urban IV laid down that the oath which the subjects of Charles of Anjou were to take on his accession was to be repeated every ten years in perpetuity.[4] The inclusion or exclusion of the phrase sometimes has an obvious enough explanation: in Germany, for example, the *Confoederatio cum principibus ecclesiasticis* of 1220 was granted for all time; the *Constitutio in favorem principum* of 1231 was not, and included a powerful savings clause for the emperor and his heirs.[5] It also occurs more predictably in fully executed concessions than in drafts or proposals. But it was common.

In England this can be observed in splendid detail in the Charter rolls of the reign of John. It is not always predictable

---

[2] Holt (1983), especially 199–201.
[3] Marczali (1901), pp. 142–3. The clause was dropped in the reissue of 1231.
[4] See above, pp. 79–80.   [5] *M.G.H., Const.* II, 90, 419–20.

or consistent. Grants of markets and fairs, for example, might be made in perpetuity or not. It did not matter whether the recipient was a layman, or a church, or a borough; it did not matter whether the concession were a new grant or a confirmation of an existing one; it did not matter whether it concerned a market, or fair, or both; the inclusion of the phrase or otherwise was unaffected by changes in the standard form of such charters. The only reasonable certainty is that the proportion of grants made in perpetuity increased markedly as the reign progressed from 25 per cent (11 out of 46) in the period up to the end of 1203, to 75 per cent (9 out of 12) for the years between 1212 and 1215. Even then some of the detail seems inexplicable: Maurice de Gant's grant of a market at Bingley of 19 May 1212 was given in perpetuity; his grant of a market at Irnham of 24 August 1212 was not.[6] We may simply be faced with the different conventions of particular Chancery clerks.

Borough charters provide firmer ground. Nearly fifty charters to townships and boroughs were issued in the first two years of the reign up to the spring of 1201. Only three were made in perpetuity; two of these concerned the annual farm and increment.[7] Now not all grants of farms, with or without increments, were made in perpetuity; some were made during pleasure or during good behaviour. But the grant of a farm with increment was one of the cases which might call the language of perpetuity into play. Grants of the status of a free borough constituted a second category; these were rare but were always made in perpetuity.[8] Together these two categories include almost all the examples on the charter rolls up to the summer of

6 Rot. Chartarum, pp. 186b, 200b.
7 Kingston, grant of township at farm and increment, 26 April 1200 (ibid., p. 52b); Gloucester, confirmation of 21 April 1200, including grant of farm and increment, where perpetuity seems to be accorded to the farm and increment only (ibid., pp. 56b–57); Les Andelys, confirmation of 30 May 1200 (p. 65b).
8 Lynn (ibid., p. 118); Yarmouth (ibid., pp. 175b–6).

1215. The exceptions seem explicable and were certainly unusual: Ilchester lost its charter in a fire; its confirmation of 10 May 1204 was made *in perpetuum*.[9] Les Andelys, crucial for the defence of the Seine valley, received a confirmation of the privileges of Rouen *in perpetuum*; and Bordeaux was also specially privileged when it received a quittance from *maletote* with a similar proviso.[10] Otherwise government practice was consistent and logical. In this light it is quite remarkable that *all* the borough charters recorded after June 1215, whatever their provisions and whatever the borough, Irish as well as English, a total of eight in all, were granted in perpetuity. Six of these were issued in July. For the time being, the pattern was changed.

There were other concessions which were always made in perpetuity or nearly so, and these bring us closer to Magna Carta. All the charters of disafforestation of 1204–5 were granted in perpetuity: Cornwall, Devon, Essex, the new forest of Staffordshire, Brewood, Hertfordlythe, Ryedale, Wharfedale, and the Fenland townships of Lincolnshire.[11] Closer still, grants of judicial liberties to communities were always perpetual, if we may judge by the very few examples. The extension of common law procedures to the knights and free tenants of the bishopric of Durham in August 1208 was embodied in a charter in which the liberties were granted *in perpetuum*.[12] Not very far away and in the same year the men of the wapentake of Langbargh received their liberties from Peter de Brus; also *in perpetuum*.[13]

All these grants, whether for markets and fairs, borough status or farms, disafforestation or judicial and administrative privileges, contributed to the preliminaries, the intellectual preconditions, of the *in perpetuum* of Magna Carta. All

---

9 *Ibid.*, p. 130b.   10 *Ibid.*, pp. 65b, 145b.
11 See above pp. 60–1 for the various charters. Ainsty is an exception which proves the rule. The disafforestation of 1200, which was a confirmation of one of Richard I, was not made in perpetuity. The men of the wapentake made further fine in 1207–8 and it was then disafforested in perpetuity (*Rot. Chartarum*, pp. 40b, 176b).
12 *Ibid.*, p. 182.   13 See above, pp. 67–8.

were in favour of communities, even the grants of markets which were conceded to manorial lords. And these communities were still ill-defined, at least in comparison with the corporations of the later middle ages.[14] Many of them seem inchoate even in comparison with contemporary ecclesiastical institutions, for as yet only the boroughs, and probably few of them, had a common seal.[15] Yet they all had courts whether of shire, wapentake, borough or manor. There was a focus, an institution governing the affairs of the community, a means of negotiation with the forces outside. Without it, perpetual liberties could scarcely be conceived and would be unlikely to survive. The difference between these liberties and Magna Carta is one of scale, certainly; it was a large leap from a manor to the *regnum Anglie*; but the main difference of principle was that the 'kingdom' in 1215 had to invent its representative mechanism or court – first the *conjuratio* and the Army of God and Holy Church, then the Twenty-Five, calling all the while on the 'commune of the whole land'. In the long run perpetual liberties required less frenzy, a calmer and more settled base of operation. It was to be found in the community of the realm and its representative institutions.

---

[14] See Susan Reynolds, 'The Idea of the Corporation in Western Christendom before 1300', in *Law and Social Change in British History*. ed. J. A. Guy and H. G. Beale (London, Royal Historical Society, 1984), pp. 27–33.

[15] James Tait, *The Medieval English Borough* (Manchester, 1936), pp. 234–40.

REFERENCES

Adams, G. B. (1917). 'Innocent III and the Great Charter', *M.C.C.E.*, pp. 26–45

Album Mályusz (1976). *Album Elemér Mályusz* (Studies presented to the International Commission for the history of representative and parliamentary institutions, LVI)

Ballard, A. (1913). *British Borough Charters 1042–1216* (Cambridge).

Barnes, Patricia M. (1954, 1959). Introductions to *Pipe Roll 14 John* and *Pipe Roll 16 John* (Pipe Roll Society, new series, XXX, XXXV)

Barraclough, G. (1953). *The Earldom and Palatinate of Chester* (Oxford)

Bateson, Mary (1902). 'A London Municipal Collection of the Reign of John', *E.H.R.*, XVII, 480–511, 707–30

Bazeley, Margaret L. (1921). 'The Extent of the English Forest in the Thirteenth Century', *T.R.H.S.*, 4th ser., IV, 140–72

Bémont, C. (1892). *Chartes des libertés anglaises* (Paris)

Beverley Smith, J. (1979). 'The Treaty of Lambeth, 1217', *E.H.R.*, XCIV, 562–79

    (1984), 'Magna Carta and the charters of the Welsh princes', *E.H.R.*, XCIX, 344–62

Blackstone, W. (1762). *The Great Charter and the Charter of the Forest* (Oxford, 1759); reprinted *Law Tracts*, vol. II (Oxford, 1762).[1]

Brooke, C. N. L. (1975). (Assisted by Gillian Keir), *London 800–1216: the Shaping of a City* (London)

Butterfield, H. (1944). *The Englishman and his History* (Cambridge)

Cam, Helen M. (1957). 'The Evolution of the Medieval English Franchise', *Speculum*, XXXII, 427–42.

    (1965). *Magna Carta – Event or Document?* (Selden Society)

Carpenter, D. A. (1976). 'The decline of the curial sheriff in England 1194–1258', *E.H.R.*, XCI, 1–32

    (1990). *The Minority of Henry III* (London)

Cheney, C. R. (1948a). 'The Alleged Deposition of King John', *Studies in Medieval History presented to F. M. Powicke* (Oxford), pp. 100–16

    (1948b) 'King John and the Papal Interdict', *B.J.R.L.*, XXXI, 295–317

    (1949). 'King John's reaction to the Interdict on England', *T.R.H.S.*, 4th ser., XXXI, 129–50

---

[1] All references are to this edition.

REFERENCES

(1950–1). 'Gervase, Abbot of Prémontré', *B.J.R.L.*, XXXIII, 25–56
(1956). 'The Eve of Magna Carta', *B.J.R.L.*, XXXVIII, 311–41.
(1967). *Hubert Walter* (London)
(1968). 'The Twenty Five barons of Magna Carta', *B.J.R.L.*, L, 280–307
(1976). *Pope Innocent III and England* (Päpste and Papsttum, IX, Stuttgart)
Clanchy, M. T. (1964). 'Magna Carta, Clause 34', *E.H.R.*, LXXIX, 542–8
(1979). *From Memory to Written Record* (London)
(1985). 'Magna Carta and the Common Pleas' in *Studies in Medieval History presented to R. H. C. Davis*, ed. H. Mayr-Harting and R. I. Moore (London), pp. 219–32
Collins, A. J. (1948). 'The Documents of the Great Charter', *Proceedings of the British Academy*, XXXIV, 233–79
Corner, D. (1980). 'The texts of the Assizes of Henry II' in *Law-Making and Law-Makers in British History*, ed. Alan Harding (Royal Historical Society), pp. 7–20
Crump, G. C. (1928). 'The Execution of the Great Charter', *History*, XIII, 247–53
Davis, G. R. C. (1963). *Magna Carta* (British Museum)
Davis, H. W. C. (1905). 'An Unknown Charter of Liberties', *E.H.R.*, XX, 719–26
Dickinson, J. C. (1955). *The Great Charter* (Historical Association)
Dufayard, C. (1894). 'La Réaction Féodale sous les Fils de Philippe le Bel', a, *Revue Historique*, LIV, 241–72; b, *Revue Historique*, LV, 241–90
Ehrlich, L. (1921). *Proceedings against the Crown (1216–1377)* (Oxford Studies in Social and Legal History, VI)
Farmer, D. L. (1956). 'Some price fluctuations in Angevin England', *Econ. H.R.*, 2nd ser., IX, 34–43
Flower, C. T. (1943). *Introduction to the Curia Regis Rolls, 1199–1230* (Selden Society, XLII)
Fox, J. C. (1924). 'The Originals of the Great Charter', *E.H.R.*, XXXIX, 321–36
Galbraith, V. H. (1944). *Roger Wendover and Matthew Paris* (Glasgow)
(1948). *Studies in the Public Records* (London)
(1966). 'Runnymede Revisited', *Proceedings of the American Philosophical Society*, 110, 307–17
(1967). 'A draft of Magna Carta (1215)', *Proceedings of the British Academy*, LIII, 345–60
Gillingham, J. (1984). *The Angevin Empire* (London)
Gillingham, J. and Holt, J. C. (1984). *War and Government in the Middle Ages: Essays in honour of J. O. Prestwich* (Woodbridge)
Gray, J. W. (1968). 'The Church and Magna Charta in the century after Runnymede', *Historical Studies*, VI, 23–38

REFERENCES

Green, Judith A. (1979). 'William Rufus, Henry I and the royal demesne', *History*, LXIV, 337–52

(1982). ' "Praeclarum et magnificum antiquitatis monumentum": the earliest surviving pipe roll', *B.I.H.R.*, LV, 1–17

(1986). *The Government of England under Henry I* (Cambridge)

Hall, H. (1894). 'An Unknown Charter of Liberties', *E.H.R.*, IX, 326–35

Hantos, E. (1904). *The Magna Carta of the English and the Hungarian Constitution* (London)

Harris, B. E. (1964). 'King John and the Sheriffs' Farms', *E.H.R.*, LXXIX, 532–42

Harvey, P. D. A. (1973). 'The English Inflation of 1180–1220', *Past and Present*, 61, 3–30

(1974). 'The Pipe Rolls and the Adoption of Demesne Farming in England', *Econ. H. R.*, 2nd ser., XXVII, 345–59

Hill, C. (1962). *Puritanism and Revolution* (London)

Holt, J. C. (1952). 'Philip Mark and the Shrievalty of Nottinghamshire and Derbyshire', *Transactions of the Thoroton Society*, LVI, 18ff

(1955). 'The Barons and the Great Charter', *E.H.R.*, LXX, 1–24

(1957). 'The Making of Magna Carta', *E.H.R.*, LXXII, 401–22

(1960). 'Rights and Liberties in Magna Carta', *Album Helen Maud Cam* (Louvain), I, 57–69

(1961). *The Northerners* (Oxford)

(1963). *King John* (Historical Association)

(1964). 'The St Albans Chroniclers and Magna Carta', *T.R.H.S.*, 5th ser., XIV, 67–88

(1971). 'The Assizes of Henry II: the Texts' in *The Study of Medieval Records: Essays in honour of Kathleen Major*, ed. D. A. Bullough and R. L. Storey (Oxford), pp. 85–106

(1972). 'Magna Carta and the Origins of Statute Law', *Studia Gratiana*, XV, 487–58

(1974). 'A Vernacular-French Text of Magna Carta 1215', *E.H.R.*, LXXXIX, 346–64, repr. and rev. in Holt (1985a), pp. 239–57

(1975). 'The End of the Anglo-Norman Realm', *Proceedings of the British Academy*, LXI, 3–45, repr. and rev. in Holt (1985a), pp. 23–65

(1981). 'The Pre-history of Parliament' in *The English Parliament in the Middle Ages: a Tribute to J. S. Roskell*, ed. R. G. Davies and J. H. Denton (Manchester), pp. 1–28

(1982). 'The Salisbury Magna Carta', *Hatcher Review*, 2, 147–52

(1984). 'The Loss of Normandy and Royal Finance', in Gillingham and Holt (1984), pp. 92–105

(1985a). *Magna Carta and Medieval Government* (London)

(1985b). 'Feudal Society and the Family in Early Medieval England: IV: the Heiress and the Alien' *T.R.H.S.*, 5th. ser., XXXV, 1–28

REFERENCES

(1987). '1086', in *Domesday Studies*, ed. J. C. Holt (Woodbridge), pp. 41–64

(1991a). 'Magna Carta 1215–17: the legal and social context', *Sewanee Mediaeval Colloquium*, V, 1–19

(1991b). 'The *casus regis:* the law and politics of succession in the Plantagenet dominions 1185–1247', *Sewanee Mediaeval Colloquium*, V, 21–42

Hoyt, R. W. (1950). *The Royal Demesne in English Constitutional History* (Ithaca)

Hurnard, Naomi D. (1941). 'The jury of presentment and the Assize of Clarendon', *E.H.R.*, LVI, 374–410

(1948). 'Magna Carta, Clause 34', *Studies in Medieval History presented to F. M. Powicke*, pp. 157–79

Jenks, E. (1904). 'The Myth of Magna Carta', *Independent Review*, IV, 260–73

Johnson, C. and Jenkinson, H. (1915). *English Court Hand* (Oxford)

Jolliffe, J. E. A. (1952). 'Magna Carta', *Schweizer Beiträge zur Allgemeinen Geschichte*, X, 88–103

(1963). *Angevin Kingship* (London)

Keefe, T. K. (1983). *Feudal Assessments and the Political Community under Henry II and his Sons* (Berkeley and Los Angeles)

Keeney, B. C. (1952). *Judgement by Peers* (Cambridge, Mass.)

Kirkus, A. Mary (1944). Introduction to *Pipe Roll 9 John* (Pipe Roll Society, new series, XXII)

Lacombe, G. (1930). 'An unpublished document of the Great Interdict', *The Catholic History Review*, XV (new series, IX), 408–20

La Monte, J. L. (1932). *Feudal Monarchy in the Latin Kingdom of Jerusalem* (Cambridge, Mass.)

Langmuir, G. L. (1972). '*Per Commune Consilium Regni* in Magna Carta', *Studia Gratiana*, XV, 467–85

Le Patourel, J. (1965). 'The Plantagenet Dominions', *History*, L, 289–308

(1984). 'Angevin Successions and the Angevin Empire', in his *Feudal Empires Norman and Plantagenet* (London), no. IX.

Liebermann, F. (1894). 'The Text of Henry I's Coronation Charter', *T.R.H.S.*, new series, VIII, 21–48

(1913). 'A Contemporary Manuscript of the "Leges Anglorum Londiniis Collectae"', *E.H.R.*, XXVIII, 732–45

McIlwain, C. H. (1939). *Constitutionalism and the Changing World* (Cambridge)

McKechnie, W. S. (1914). *Magna Carta* (Glasgow, 1905; 2nd edn 1914).[2]

(1917). 'Magna Carta, 1215–1915', *M.C.C.E.*, pp. 1–25

---

[2] All references are to the 2nd edition, unless otherwise stated.

Madicott, J. R. (1984). 'Magna Carta and the Local community 1215–1259', *Past and Present*, 102, 25–65

Marczali, H. (1901). *Enchiridion Fontium Historiae Hungarorum* (Budapest)

Mercati, A. (1927). 'La Prima Relazione del Cardinale Nicolo de Romanis sulla sua legazione in Inghilterra', in *Essays in History Presented to R. L. Poole* (Oxford), pp. 274–89

Mills, Mabel M. (1925). 'Experiments in Exchequer Procedure', *T.R.H.S.*, 4th ser., VIII, 151–70

Milsom, S. F. C. (1976). *The Legal Framework of English Feudalism* (Cambridge)

Mitchell, S. K. (1914). *Studies in Taxation under John and Henry III* (New Haven)

Muñoz y Romero (1847). *Colección de Fueros municipales y cartas de los reinos de Castilla, Leon*, vol. I (Madrid)

Norgate, Kate (1902). *John Lackland* (London)

(1912). *The Minority of Henry III* (London)

Painter, S. (1943). *Studies in the History of the English Feudal Barony* (Baltimore)

(1947). 'Magna Carta', *American Historical Review*, LIII, 42–9

(1949). *The Reign of King John* (Baltimore)

Pallister, Anne (1971). *The Heritage of Liberty* (Oxford)

Palmer, R. C. (1985). 'The Economic and Cultural Impact of the Origins of Property 1180–1220', *Law and History Review*, 3, 375–96

Petit-Dutaillis, C. (1894). *Étude sur la vie et le règne de Louis VIII* (Paris)

(1908). *Studies Supplementary to Stubbs' Constitutional History of England*, 3 vols. (Manchester)

Plucknett, T. F. T. (1948). *Concise History of the Common Law* (London)

(1949). *Legislation of Edward I* (Oxford)

Pocock, J. G. A. (1957). *The Ancient Constitution and the Feudal Law* (Cambridge)

Pollard, A. F. (1913). 'Contenementum in Magna Carta', *E.H.R.*, XXVIII, 117–18

Pollock, F. and Maitland, F. W. (1898). *History of English Law*, 2 vols. (Cambridge)

Poole, A. L. (1946). *Obligations of Society in the Twelfth and Thirteenth Centuries* (Oxford)

(1951). *From Domesday Book to Magna Carta* (Oxford)

Poole, R. L. (1913). 'The Publication of Great Charters by the English Kings', *E.H.R.*, XXVIII, 444–53

Post, G. (1943). 'Roman Law and Early Representation in Spain and Italy', *Speculum*, XVIII, 211–32

Powicke, F. M. (1908). 'The Chancery during the Minority of Henry III', *E.H.R.*, XXIII, 220–35

(1913). *The Loss of Normandy* (Manchester; 2nd edn, 1961)

(1917). 'Per judicium parium vel per legem terrae', *M.C.C.E.*, pp. 96–121

(1920). 'Article 13 of the Articles of the Barons', *E.H.R.*, xxxv, 401–2

(1928). *Stephen Langton* (Oxford)

(1929). 'The Bull "Miramur plurimum" and a Letter to Archbishop Stephen Langton, 5 September 1215', *E.H.R.*, xliv, 86–93

(1947). *King Henry III and the Lord Edward*, 2 vols. (Oxford)

Prestwich, J. O. (1954). 'War and Finance in the Anglo-Norman State', *T.R.H.S.*, 5th ser., IV, 19–43

Prothero, G. W. (1894). 'An Unknown Charter of Liberties', *E.H.R.*, IX, 117–21

Ramsay, Sir James (1925). *Revenues of the Kings of England* (Oxford)

Reynolds, Susan (1984a). *Kingdoms and Communities in Western Europe 900–1300* (Oxford)

(1984b). 'The Idea of Corporation in Western Christendom before 1300', in *Law and Social change in British History*, ed. J. A. Guy and H. G. Beale (Royal Historical Society), pp. 27–33

(1989). 'Magna Carta 1297 and the legal use of Literacy', *B.I.H.R.*, LXII, 233–44

Richardson, H. G. (1933). 'Letters of the Legate Guala', *E.H.R.*, xlviii, 250–9

(1941). 'The English Coronation Oath', *T.R.H.S.*, 4th ser., xxiii, 129–58

(1944). 'The Morrow of the Great Charter', *B.J.R.L.*, xxviii, 422–43

(1945). 'The Morrow of the Great Charter, an Addendum', *B.J.R.L.*, xxix, 184–200

(1948). 'Studies in Bracton', *Traditio*, vi, 61–104

(1949). 'The English Coronation Oath', *Speculum*, xxiv, 44–75

(1960). 'The Coronation in Medieval England', *Traditio*, xvi, 111–202

Richardson, H. G. and Sayles, G. O. (1963). *The Governance of Medieval England* (Edinburgh)

(1966). *Law and Legislation from Aethelbert to Magna Carta* (Edinburgh)

Riesenberg, P. (1956). *Inalienability of Sovereignty in Medieval Political Thought* (New York)

Riess, L. (1926). 'The Reissue of Henry I's Coronation Charter', *E.H.R.*, xli, 321–31

Roberts, Phyllis B. (1968). *Studies in the Sermons of Stephen Langton* (Toronto)

Round, J. H. (1917). 'Barons and Knights in the Great Charter', *M.C.C.E.*, pp. 46–77

(1893). 'An Unknown Charter of Liberties', *E.H.R.*, viii, 288–94

(1899). *The Commune of London and Other Essays* (London)

Sanders, I. J. (1956). *Feudal Military Service in England* (Oxford)

REFERENCES

(1960). *English Baronies: a study of their origin and descent 1086–1327* (Oxford)

Slade, C. F. (1949). Introduction to *Pipe Roll 12 John* (Pipe Roll Society, new series, XXVI)

Smith, S. (1941). Introduction to *Pipe Roll 7 John* (Pipe Roll Society, new series, XIX)

Southern, R. W. (1962). 'The place of Henry I in English History', *Proceedings of the British Academy*, XLVIII, 127–69

Stacey, R. S. (1987). *Politics, Policy and Finance under Henry III 1216–1245* (Oxford)

Stenton, Doris M. (1925–53). Introductions to *Pipe Rolls 2–10 Richard I* and *Pipe Rolls 1–6 John, 8, 10, 11, 13 John* (Pipe Roll Society, new series, *passim*).

(1926). Introduction to *The Earliest Lincolnshire Assize Rolls 1202–9* (Lincoln Record Society, XXII)

(1948). Introduction to *Pleas before the King or his Justices* (Selden Society, LXVII)

(1951). *English Society in the Early Middle Ages* (London, 3rd edn, 1962)

(1957). *The English Woman in History* (London)

(1958). 'King John and the Courts of Justice', *Proceedings of the British Academy*, XLIV, 103–28

(1964). *English Justice between the Norman Conquest and the Great Charter* (Philadelphia)

(1965). *After Runnymede: Magna Carta in the Middle Ages* (Charlottesville)

Stenton, F. M. (1961). *The First Century of English Feudalism* (Oxford)

Stroud, Daphne (1981). 'Salisbury's Magna Carta: was it issued by the Chancery?', *Hatcher Review*, II, no. 12, 51–8

Stubbs, W. (1897). *Constitutional History of England*, 3 vols. (Oxford)

Sutherland, D. W. (1973). *The Assize of Novel Disseisin* (Oxford)

Tait, J. (1912). 'Studies in Magna Carta: Waynagium and Contenementum', *E.H.R.*, XXVII, 720–8

(1920). *Chartulary of the Abbey of St Werburgh, Chester* (Chetham Society, LXXIX)

Thompson, Faith (1925). *The First Century of Magna Carta: Why it persisted as a Document* (Minneapolis)

(1948). *Magna Carta, its Role in the Making of the English Constitution, 1300–1629* (Minneapolis)

Thomson, R. (1829). *An Historical Essay on the Magna Carta of King John* (London)

Thorne, S. E. (1959). 'English Feudalism and Estates in Land', *Cambridge Law Journal*, pp. 193–209

Timbal, P. (1949). *Un Conflit d'Annexion au Moyen Age: l'Application de la Coutume de Paris au Pays d'Albigeois* (Paris, Toulouse)

REFERENCES

Trifone, R. (1921). *La Legislazione Angioina* (*Documenti per la Storia dell'Italia Meridionale*, vol. 1)

Turner, G. J. (1899). Introduction to *Select Pleas of the Forest* (Selden Society, XIII)

(1904, 1907). 'The Minority of Henry III', *T.R.H.S.*, new series, XVIII (1904), 245–95; 3rd ser., 1 (1907), 205–62

Turner, R. V. (1968). *The King and his Courts: The role of John and Henry III in the Administration of Justice 1199–1240* (Ithaca)

(1978). 'The *Miles Literatus* in Twelfth- and Thirteenth-Century England: How Rare a Phenomenon?', *American Historical Review*, 83, 928–45

(1988). *Men Raised from the Dust* (Philadelphia)

(1989). 'The Mandeville Inheritance, 1189–1236: Its Legal, Political and Social Context', *Haskins Society Journal*, 1

Ullmann, W. (1961). *Principles of Government and Politics in the Middle Ages* (London)

Van Caenegem, R. C. (1973). *The Birth of the English Common Law* (Cambridge)

Vernon Harcourt, L. W. (1907). 'The Amercement of Barons by their Peers', *E.H.R.*, XXII, 732–40

Vic, C. de and Vaissette, J. J. (1872–1904). *Histoire générale de Languedoc*, ed. E. Dulaurier, 16 vols. (Toulouse)

Walker, Sue S. (1978). 'The Action of Waste in the Early Common Law', in *Legal Records and the Historian*, ed. J. H. Baker (Royal Historical Society), pp. 185–206

(1979). 'Feudal Constraint and Free Consent in the making of Marriages in Medieval England' (Canadian Historical Association, Historical Papers, Saskatoon), pp. 97–110

(1982). 'Free Consent and the Marriage of Feudal Wards in Medieval England', *Journal of Medieval History*, VII, 123–34

Warren, W. L. (1961). *King John* (London)

(1973). *Henry II* (London)

Waugh, S. L. (1988). *The Lordship of England: Royal Wardships and Marriages in English Society and Politics 1217–1327* (Princeton)

White, A. B. (1915, 1917). 'The Name Magna Carta', *E.H.R.*, XXX (1915), 472–5; XXXII (1917), 554–5

Williams, G. A. (1963). *Medieval London* (London)

Young, C. R. (1979). *The Royal Forests of Medieval England* (Leicester)

INDEX

Aaron, Jew of Lincoln, 42, 72
Abingdon, abbot of, 511; Edmund
of, archbishop of Canterbury, 210,
283, 396; monastery of, 93
Abbotsbury, abbot of, 511
Actions, legal: attaint, 126, 181–2;
entry, 139; entry *sur disseisin*, 139
& n.; grand assize, 107, 124–5, 140,
146, 151, 155; *mort d'ancestor*, 124,
127, 129–32, 137, 163, 166–7, 169–
70, 177 (in Ireland), 186; *novel
disseisin*, 127, 132, 137, 163, 165,
167, 168–9 (in Ireland), 186,
limitation of, 133; right, 143–50,
166; warranty of charter, 138; *see
also* Writs
Aids, 42, 58, 381, 386; consent to,
121, 301, 317–22, 396, 398–400
Aigle, l', Gilbert de, 144–5, 159;
Isabella de, 144
Aimeric, master of the Temple in
England, 449
Ainsty, wapentake (Yorks.), 60, 64,
71, 521 n.
Alexander the Mason, 88, 89
Alexander II, king of Scotland, 261,
287, 365, 469
Alfonso III, king of Aragon, 79, 80
Alfonso IX, king of León, 25, 77
Aliens, 215, 367; Flemings, 31, 47;
Poitevins, 31, 47; Tourangeaux,
31, 47, 63, 344, 367, 485–6; in
Magna Carta, 344–5, 356–7, 464–
5, 484–6
Allerdale (Cumb.), barony of, 133 n.
Amercements, 43, 338; assessment
(affeerment) of, 58; of barons,
333–4; limitation of, 58–9, 67–8,

291, 332–4, 363; in Magna Carta,
332–4
Amiénois, men of, 114, 274
America, the United States of, 17;
Magna Carta in, 17–19
American Bar Association, 2
Ancaster (Lincs.), 391 n., 392
Ancient Constitution, the, 11–16
Andelys, Les, 183, 521
Andrew II, king of Hungary, 25, 79,
80, 114
Angevins, Angevin kings, 27, 30, 41–
5, 47, 73, 75, 82, 95, 102–3, 107,
114–17, 120, 123, 188, 228, 303,
378
Angoulême, Isabella of, queen of
England, 161 n.
Anjou: *see* Charles, count of
Appletreewick (Yorks.), 163 n.
Aragon, kingdom of, 25–6, 77, 79–
80; Aragonese crusade, 26; *see also
Privilegio General, Privilegio de la
Union*
Arches, Alan de, 164 n.
Argentan, Richard d', 511
Arley, 101 n.
Arsic, Manasser, 132 n.
Articles of the Barons, 52, 257, 276
n., 277, 279, 285–91, 301, 310,
312, 314–15, 321–2, 327, 339, 341,
343, 350–1, 419, 422, 443, 445–6;
date and function of, 245–52, 429–
32; title of, 429; text, 432–40
Artois, 273; Robert of, 275
Arundel, 184; earl of, *see* Aubigny
Assize, Assizes, 51–2, 289–90, 324–5,
383; of Henry II, 41; of the realm,
121; *see also* Actions legal; Money;

531

Printed in the United States
51498LVS00002B/172-198